Pro SQL Server 2005

Thomas Rizzo, Adam Machanic,
Julian Skinner, Louis Davidson,
Robin Dewson, Jan Narkiewicz,
Joseph Sack, Rob Walters

Apress®

Pro SQL Server 2005

Copyright © 2006 by Thomas Rizzo, Adam Machanic, Julian Skinner, Louis Davidson, Robin Dewson, Jan Narkiewicz, Joseph Sack, Rob Walters

ISBN (pbk): 1-59059-477-0

Printed and bound in the United States of America 9 8 7 6 5 4 3 2 1

Trademarked names may appear in this book. Rather than use a trademark symbol with every occurrence of a trademarked name, we use the names only in an editorial fashion and to the benefit of the trademark owner, with no intention of infringement of the trademark.

Lead Editor: Tony Davis
Technical Reviewers: Sajal Dam, Cristian Lefter, Alejandro Leguizamo, Alexzander Nepomnjashiy, Andrew Watt, Richard Waymire, Joe Webb, Roger Wolter
Editorial Board: Steve Anglin, Dan Appleman, Ewan Buckingham, Gary Cornell, Tony Davis, Jason Gilmore, Jonathan Hassell, Chris Mills, Dominic Shakeshaft, Jim Sumser
Project Manager: Kylie Johnston
Copy Edit Manager: Nicole LeClerc
Copy Editors: Ami Knox, Nicole LeClerc
Assistant Production Director: Kari Brooks-Copony
Production Editor: Kelly Winquist
Compositor: Susan Glinert
Proofreaders: Kim Burton, Linda Marousek, Linda Seifert, Liz Welch
Indexer: Broccoli Information Management
Artist: Kinetic Publishing Services, LLC
Cover Designer: Kurt Krames
Manufacturing Director: Tom Debolski

Distributed to the book trade worldwide by Springer-Verlag New York, Inc., 233 Spring Street, 6th Floor, New York, NY 10013. Phone 1-800-SPRINGER, fax 201-348-4505, e-mail orders-ny@springer-sbm.com, or visit http://www.springeronline.com.

For information on translations, please contact Apress directly at 2560 Ninth Street, Suite 219, Berkeley, CA 94710. Phone 510-549-5930, fax 510-549-5939, e-mail info@apress.com, or visit http://www.apress.com.

The source code for this book is available to readers at http://www.apress.com in the Source Code section.

This book is dedicated to my loving wife, Stacy, who provided the support, love, and encouragement that made this endeavor possible.

—Thomas Rizzo

Contents

About the Authors

TOM RIZZO is a director in the SQL Server group at Microsoft. Being an 11-year veteran at Microsoft, Tom has worked on a number of the different Microsoft server technologies such as BizTalk, SharePoint, and Exchange Server before joining the SQL Server group. Tom is a published author on topics ranging from SQL Server to developing collaborative applications using Microsoft's collaboration servers.

Tom authored Chapters 2, 7, 8, 9, 15, and 16.

ADAM MACHANIC is a database-focused software engineer, writer, and speaker based in Boston, Massachusetts. He has implemented SQL Server for a variety of high-availability OLTP and large-scale data warehouse applications, and he also specializes in .NET data access layer performance optimization. He is a Microsoft Most Valuable Professional (MVP) for SQL Server and a Microsoft Certified Professional (MCP).

Adam authored Chapters 4, 5, and 6.

JULIAN SKINNER studied Germanic etymology to PhD level before joining Wrox Press as an indexer in 1998 in order to get a real job. He became a technical editor shortly after that, later working as a technical architect and commissioning editor, before moving to Apress in 2003. He has consequently spent most of the last six years reading books about programming, focusing in particular on Microsoft technologies and, since 2000, on C# and the .NET Framework. He recently left Apress to concentrate on writing code.

Julian contributed many sections and code samples—and often whole chapters—to the books he worked on at Wrox, mostly hiding behind the relative anonymity of an "additional material" credit, but he is credited as a coauthor of *Professional ADO.NET*, *Professional ASP Data Access*, and *Beginning SQL*. He is also a coauthor of *The Programmer's Guide to SQL*, published by Apress.

Julian authored Chapters 11 and 12.

LOUIS DAVIDSON has been in the information technology industry for ten years, as a corporate database developer and architect. Currently, he is serving as a database administrator for Compass Technology Management in their Nashville data center, supporting the Christian Broadcasting Network and NorthStar Studios.

Davidson has a bachelor's degree from the University of Tennessee at Chattanooga in computer science with a minor in mathematics (though the minor in math is more of an indication of the amount of math required at UTC to get a computer science degree, rather than any great love or skill in the subject).

The majority of his experience, with slight deviations into Visual Basic, has been spent with Microsoft SQL Server from version 1.0 to whatever the latest version is in beta. Louis's primary areas of expertise are in database architecture and coding in Transact-SQL, and he has written thousands of numerous stored procedures and triggers throughout the years.

Louis was the sole author of *Professional SQL Server 2000 Database Design*, and he was a contributor to *SQL Server 2000 Stored Procedure Handbook*. It is said that in his ridiculously small amount of spare time he tends to play a lot of Nintendo (what is it with that silly princess—she's been captured by the freaking dragon again!) as well as watching a great deal of television that was popular in a

different era, most notably old English programs such as *The Avengers*, *The Saint*, *Monty Python's Flying Circus*, and *Black Adder*, to name a few. Quite often this spare time is also spent with his notebook computer writing something pertaining to SQL.
Louis authored Chapter 3.

◼**ROBIN DEWSON** has been hooked on programming ever since he bought his first computer, a Sinclair ZX80, in 1980. His first main application of his own was a Visual FoxPro application that could be used to run a fantasy league system.

From there, realizing that the market place for Visual FoxPro in the United Kingdom was limited, he decided to learn Visual Basic and SQL Server. Starting out with SQL Server 6.5, he soon moved to SQL Server 7 and Visual Basic 5, where he became involved in developing several applications for clients in both the UK and the United States. He then moved on to SQL Server 2000 and Visual Basic 6, through to SQL Server Yukon and Visual Basic .NET.

Robin is a consultant mainly in the city of London, where he has been for nearly eight years. He also has been developing a rugby-related website as well as maintaining his own site at http://www.fat-belly.com.
Robin authored Chapter 1.

◼**JAN D. NARKIEWICZ** (jann@softwarepronto.com) is chief technical officer of Software Pronto, Inc. His areas of expertise include Microsoft technologies, Oracle, and DB2. Jan also write books for Apress and serves as academic coordinator for U.C. Berkeley Extension's .NET/Windows program. His clients include E*Trade, Visa, eBay, and Oracle. Jan also acts as an expert witness in patent, copyright, and licensing-related litigation.
Jan authored Chapter 10.

◼**JOSEPH SACK** is a database administration and developer based in Minneapolis, Minnesota. Since 1997, he has been developing and supporting SQL Server environments for clients in financial services, IT consulting, manufacturing, and the real estate industry. Joseph received his bachelor's degree in psychology from the University of Minnesota. He is the author of *SQL Server 2000 Fast Answers for DBAs and Developers*, the coauthor of *Beginning SQL Server 2000 DBA: From Novice to Professional*, and is a Microsoft Certified Database Administrator (MCDBA).
Joe authored Chapter 14.

◼**ROB WALTERS** is a program manager in the SQL Server group of Microsoft. He has seven years of experience in software development and relational databases. When not talking about databases, Rob enjoys spending time with his wife, Tammie, their son, Bryan, and two overfed St. Bernard dogs.
Rob authored Chapter 13.

About the Technical Reviewers

SAJAL DAM works as an IT strategist at Dell, managing one of the largest SQL Server environments. The challenges of database performance tuning excite him the most. He has written a couple of books on SQL Server query performance tuning and is in the process of starting his next book on SQL Server 2005 performance tuning.

Besides his technical acumen, Sajal is passionate to learn how business decisions are made in successful corporations. To fulfill his passion, he has started his executive MBA from Duke alongside his other works.

In his free time, Sajal reviews other technical books and plays in the stock market. He can be reached at sajaldam1@hotmail.com.

CRISTIAN LEFTER is a SQL Server MVP, former developer, database administrator, and trainer. He is currently CEO of MicroTraining, a consulting and training company.

In his spare time, Cristian is a tech reviewer, author, and leader of two user groups (ITBoard and Romanian SQL Server User Group).

ALEJANDRO LEGUIZAMO has been working with SQL Server since 6.5, and with Microsoft Access since Office 97. He is certified in SQL Server 2000, mainly focused in data warehousing and business intelligence, plus ETL. He is certified in SQL Server 2000, and he has wide experience in training and consulting.

Alejandro earned a degree in business management focused on executive information systems. He is based in Bogotá, Colombia, and has been invited to participate as speaker and expert in the United States, Puerto Rico, Peru, Ecuador, Spain, Venezuela, and other countries, at events like internal trainings for Microsoft, the launch of SQL Server Reporting Services, Developer Days, TechEd 2005, among others. Alejandro was awarded the Microsoft Most Valuable Professional (MVP) award first in 2004, and again in 2005. Currently, he is a mentor to the well-known group of experts in SQL Server, Solid Quality Learning (http://www.solidqualitylearning.com), for the Iberoamerican operations and the BI division.

Currently, **ALEXZANDER NEPOMNJASHIY** is working as Microsoft SQL Server DBA with NeoSystems North-West Inc., an ISO 9001:2000 certified software company. As a DBA, he is responsible for drafting design specifications for solutions and building database-related projects based on these specs. As an IT professional, Alexzander has more than 11 years of overall experience in DBMS planning, designing, securing, troubleshooting, and performance optimizing. He can be reached at alexnep@onego.ru.

RICHARD WAYMIRE is a lead program manager with Microsoft and has worked on the development of Microsoft SQL Server 7.0, 2000, and 2005. He is the author of several books on SQL Server, including most recently *Teach Yourself SQL Server 2000 in 21 Days*, and he is also a contributing editor to *SQL Server Magazine*.

■**JOE WEBB** is the founder and chief operating manager of WebbTech Solutions. He has over 11 years of industry experience and has consulted extensively with companies in the areas of software development, database design, and technical training. Joe also serves on the board of directors for PASS, the Professional Association for SQL Server.

As a Microsoft MVP, Joe regularly speaks at technical conferences in the United States and in Europe. He is also the author of *The Rational Guide To: SQL Server Notification Services* and *The Rational Guide To: IT Consulting* (http://www.rationalpress.com).

When he's not working, Joe enjoys the farm life on his small farm in the middle of Tennessee, where he raises vegetables and livestock. He's been blessed with a wonderful wife and family.

■**ROGER WOLTER** has 27 years of experience in various aspects of the computer industry, including jobs at Unisys, Infospan, and Fourth Shift. He has spent the last seven years as a program manager at Microsoft. His projects at Microsoft include SQLXML, the Soap Toolkit, SQL Server Service Broker, and SQL Server Express. His interest in the Service Broker was sparked by a messaging-based manufacturing system he worked on in a previous life. He's currently splitting his time between the Service Broker and the SQL Server Express projects in SQL Server 2005.

Acknowledgments

While there are too many people to acknowledge, I will give it my best shot. First, I'd like to acknowledge the great team at Apress, including Tony Davis, the editor of this book, for his dedication and hard work getting this off the ground. At some points during the early days of SQL Server 2005, we thought this book would never make it due to shifting contributing authors and the shifting product. This book is a testament to Tony's dedication to providing the highest quality educational materials to his readers. I also would like to thank Kylie Johnston, who worked hard to keep us all on track. She had to herd cats—and sometimes very, very reluctant cats—but in the end she pushed us hard and made this book better than we would have made it ourselves.

I'd like to also thank my technical reviewers, Sajal Dam, Cristian Lefter, Alejandro Leguizamo, Alexzander Nepomnjashiy, Andrew Watt, Richard Waymire, Joe Webb, and Roger Wolter. They kept me honest and pointed out where I could improve my explanations to the benefit of all readers.

Finally, there are a number of people that work with me on SQL Server that I have to thank for their tireless explanations of the nitty-gritty technical details at all hours of the day. These include Jason Carlson and Brian Welcker from the Reporting Services team, Shyam Panther from the NS team, Michael Rys and Shankar Pal from the XML team, Srik Raghavan and Brian Deen from the WebData team, Mark Wistrom and Christian Kleinerman from the SQL Server engine team, Mahesh Prakriya from the Management Studio team, and Euan Garden, who used to be on the Management Studio team but now heads up our product planning efforts for SQL Server.

Thomas Rizzo

Introduction

This book provides a critical examination of all of the major new functionality in SQL Server 2005, covering such diverse topics as CLR integration, the new management tools, SQL Server Integration Services, Service Broker, Transact-SQL (T-SQL) programming, and database mirroring.

The book does not profess or even try to be a comprehensive reference on any one of these areas—as you are probably aware, this would often require a sizable book in itself. Instead, it provides practical, in-depth coverage of the core topics in each area, illustrated with realistic examples. Hopefully, we've done this in such a way that you will immediately be able to translate what you learn here into your business environment and have a firm foundation for exploring a particular topic further, should it be necessary.

SQL Server 2005 is a vast new release. This book provides you with a starting point, a road map, and a strong foundation on which to build. Its practical nature and careful guidelines and advice will mean that the book continues to be useful long after your initial assessment of SQL Server 2005 is complete.

Who This Book Is For

This book is for anyone who wants to learn about SQL Server 2005. The topics are diverse and deep, and there is something in here for everyone, whether you are a DBA, developer, or business intelligence (BI) practitioner. As long as you have a sound base knowledge of SQL and relational database in general, then this book will teach you about the extensive new feature set of SQL Server 2005 and about how best to put these features to work in your environment.

How This Book Is Structured

This book is written is such a way that you can read through the book cover to cover or dip in and out for specific topics. It is structured as follows.

Chapter 1: SQL Server Overview and Installation

This chapter details a brief history on the evolution of SQL Server from a "desktop database" to a full-fledged enterprise-class relational database management system (RDBMS). It provides a quick reference guide to the new SQL Server 2005 feature set for each of the SQL Server editions, and then steps through the whole installation process. Many readers will already have SQL Server installed, but if you're downloading it for the first time from MSDN (we recommend using SQL Server Developer Edition), then this chapter will get you set up and ready to work through all of the examples in the book.

Chapter 2: SQL Server Management Technologies

SQL Server Management Studio (SSMS) is the major new management tool for SQL Server 2005. It combines most of the tools that you previously used separately (Enterprise Manager, Query Analyzer, and so on), and adds additional capabilities. This chapter details the functional and interface enhancements that have been made and how they might affect you. It also takes a look at the new Server Management Objects (SMO) technology, the successor to SQL-DMO.

Chapter 3: T-SQL Enhancements for Developers

Reports of the imminent demise of T-SQL have been greatly exaggerated. This chapter explores the feature and performance enhancements from a developer's perspective, covering such topics as common table expressions (CTEs), new join types, improved error handling, and more.

Chapter 4: T-SQL Enhancements for DBAs

This chapter switches focus to the numerous administration enhancements such as DDL triggers, table and index partitioning, snapshots, and the new SNAPSHOT isolation level.

Chapter 5: .NET Integration

Although T-SQL is alive and well, there are some things that it just isn't meant to do. Previously, when T-SQL ran out of steam, developers were plunged into the complex world of extended stored procedures. No longer. In many people's eyes, the biggest advancement in 2005 is the inclusion of the common language runtime, or CLR, within the database. As a result, developers can now create objects (stored procedures, user-defined functions, and so on) using any of the .NET languages (VB .NET, C#, C++, etc.) and compile them into .NET assemblies. These assemblies are deployed inside the database and run by the CLR, which is hosted inside the SQL Server memory space. This chapter introduces programming with CLR objects via a step-by-step tour through development of a CLR stored procedure. It describes the .NET object model provided for SQL Server CLR development, along with best practices for developing CLR objects and various deployment issues.

Chapter 6: Programming Assemblies

This chapter continues the exploration of CLR integration with some in-depth examples on the use of CLR user-defined types, functions, aggregates, and triggers.

Chapter 7: SQL Server and XML

This chapter provides an overview of the XML technology as it relates to SQL Server. It takes a broad look at XPath and XML Schema support in SQL Server 2005, and then drills down into how to get XML into and out of the database. It covers how to get XML into your relational data columns using OPENXML, updategrams, and SQLXML's XML Bulkload provider. It then shows how to query the relational columns and return the results as XML, using FOR XML.

Chapter 8: SQL Server 2005 XML and XQuery Support

This chapter investigates native XML support in SQL Server 2005, via the new XML datatype. It shows how to create XML columns, insert data into those columns, and then retrieve that XML data using XQuery.

Chapter 9: SQL Server 2005 Reporting Services

SSRS 2005 is the latest and most powerful reporting technology from Microsoft. An integral part of the SQL Server 2005 database, it allows you to design, author, render, and deploy reports via the Web or a company intranet. This chapter starts out by showing you how to create a report using SQL Server 2000 Reporting Services and then how to migrate that report to SSRS 2005. Next, it describes, and shows how to take advantage of, the numerous SSRS 2005 feature enhancements, such as multi-valued parameters, interactive sorting, and the use of the new ad-hoc Report Builder.

Chapter 10: Analysis Services

Databases store data, but they become truly profitable when that data can used and interpreted to provide business intelligence (BI). Powered by the new Business Intelligence Development Studio (BIDS), SQL Server Analysis Services (SSAS) is the major new suite of technologies designed to support the development and administration of BI applications. Described in this chapter are the SSAS mechanisms for exploiting Online Analytical Processing (OLAP) and data mining.

Chapter 11: Security

As with most areas of SQL Server, the security features built into SQL Server 2005 have undergone a fairly radical overhaul. This chapter takes a look at the new features for granting and denying permissions to access resources in the database, and the new system of schemas, which now resemble ANSI SQL schemas far more closely. It addresses new security functionality, such as the Surface Area Configurator (SAC) feature and the new encryption functions.

Chapter 12: Service Broker

One of the most important new features of SQL Server 2005 is Service Broker. Service Broker is a message queuing technology that is native to SQL Server and allows developers to integrate SQL Server fully into distributed applications. Service Broker provides an asynchronous system for database-to-database communication; it allows a database to send a message to another without waiting for the response, so the application will continue to function if the remote database is temporarily unavailable. All of this is demonstrated in this chapter with in-depth working examples.

Chapter 13: Automation and Monitoring

SQL Server 2005 brings with it advancements in many areas that will make the daily administration and maintenance of SQL Server much easier. The first half of this chapter takes an in-depth look at SQL Server Agent 2005, the task scheduling service used by SQL Server to execute a variety of jobs, including T-SQL, replication, and maintenance tasks. The chapter then moves on to examine tools such as Maintenance Plans, SQLCMD, and database mail, and demonstrates how they can make a SQL Server DBA's life easier.

Chapter 14: Integration Services

SQL Server Integration Services (SSIS), formerly known as Data Transformation Services (DTS), is Microsoft's extraction, transformation, and loading tool that comes bundled with SQL Server 2005. It has been massively overhauled and expanded, and this chapter will lead you through all of the significant changes. It guides you through all of the data flow, control flow, and transformation tasks, using plenty of hands-on examples along the way to really demonstrate the power of this new tool.

Chapter 15: Database Mirroring

Although disabled in the first SQL Server 2005 release, database mirroring is a very significant new feature. Microsoft is committed to re-enabling it after a period of extra testing, so many DBAs will want to find out what it can do and prepare for its adoption. This chapter investigates the new database mirroring capability and gives detailed instructions on how to set up and use it. It relates database mirroring to existing technologies, such as failover clustering, replication, and log shipping, and provides advice on which technology is best to solve a particular problem.

Chapter 16: Notification Services

SQL Server 2005 now comes with a built-in dynamic subscription and publication mechanism— namely, Notification Services (NS). This chapter fully describes the NS architecture, walks you through how to create a NS application, and then covers how to program with NS: creating and modifying your subscribers, devices, and subscriptions; submitting events to NS; working with custom components; and so on.

Prerequisites

Ideally, you will be running the examples in this book on the final release version of SQL Server 2005 and Visual Studio 2005. However, at a minimum, you need at least the September CTP of SQL Server 2005 and the release candidate of Visual Studio 2005.

While some chapters do not require Visual Studio, having Visual Studio will give you the best overall experience with this book. Of course, you should follow the software prerequisites and system requirements suggested by both the SQL Server 2005 and Visual Studio 2005 documentation.

Source Code and Updates

As you work through the examples in this book, you may decide that you want to type in all the code by hand. Many readers prefer this because it is a good way to get familiar with the coding techniques that are being used.

Whether you want to type the code in or not, all the source code for this book is available in the Source Code area of the Apress website (http://www.apress.com). If you like to type in the code, you can use the source code files to check the results you should be getting—they should be your first stop if you think you might have typed in an error. If you don't like typing, then downloading the source code from Apress website is a must! Either way, the code files will help you with updates and debugging.

Errata

Apress makes every effort to make sure that there are no errors in the text or the code. However, to err is human, and as such we recognize the need to keep you informed of any mistakes as they're discovered and corrected. An errata sheet will be made available on this book's main page at http://www.apress.com. If you find an error that hasn't already been reported, please let us know.

The Apress website acts as a focus for other information and support, including the code from all Apress books, sample chapters, previews of forthcoming titles, and articles on related topics.

Contacting the Authors

You can contact this book's lead author, Tom Rizzo, either via his e-mail address at thomriz@microsoft.com or via his blog at http://www.sqljunkies.com/WebLog/tom_rizzo/default.aspx.

CHAPTER 1

SQL Server Overview and Installation

SQL Server 2005 is a major advancement over SQL Server 2000. Right from the very beginning of your SQL Server 2005 experience, you will notice great changes in the installation process. You'll see as you progress through this book that these changes continue throughout the product.

In this chapter, we'll briefly overview how SQL Server has evolved in recent years, and then we'll look at the current editions of SQL Server 2005 and the features offered with each.

We'll then examine the compatibility of different editions (32-bit and 64-bit) of SQL Server with the various available operating systems flavors and take a look at the minimum system requirements for SQL Server 2005 installation.

Having done that, we'll walk through the installation process itself step by step, discussing the major considerations you'll need to take into account along the way. If you've performed or seen an installation of Visual Studio .NET, then the SQL Server 2005 installation process will be familiar to you—it's very similar in its methodology. No longer do you have to run several installations to ensure all the components you want are there. A treeview structure now lists all the possible components and combinations, thereby allowing you to install everything you need in one pass. There are also two new example databases you can install and use for testing new functionality provided with SQL Server 2005.

Evolution of SQL Server

Table 1-1 briefly charts the evolution of SQL Server, up to SQL Server 2000.

The very first version of SQL Server emerged in 1989/1990. It was available for OS/2, and its code base was essentially the same as Sybase SQL Server 4.0. The first edition of SQL Server for Windows NT emerged in 1993 and was a basic port of Sybase SQL Server 4.0 from OS/2 to NT.

The emergence of SQL Server 6.5 marked the split from Sybase; the database engine was completely rewritten specifically for NT. From that point on, SQL Server has evolved rapidly into a powerful enterprise-level database. SQL Server started life as a small, inexpensive desktop database, with some GUI management tools, and has been progressively expanding its enterprise feature set,

Table 1-1. *History of SQL Server*

Year	Version	Description
1993	SQL Server 4.2 (a desktop database)	A low-functionality *desktop* database, capable of meeting the data storage and handling needs of a small department. However, the concept of a database that was integrated with Windows and had an easy-to-use interface proved popular.
1995	SQL Server 6.5 (a small business database)	A major rewrite of the core database engine. This was SQL Server's first "significant" release, and it included improved performance and important feature enhancements. It still had a long way to go in terms of its performance and feature set, but it was now capable of handling *small e-commerce and intranet* applications, at a fraction of the cost of competitors' offerings.
1998	SQL Server 7.0 (a web database)	Another significant rewrite to the core database engine. Version 7.0 was a defining release, providing a reasonably powerful and feature-rich database that was a truly viable (and still cheap) alternative for *small-to-medium businesses,* between a true desktop database such as Microsoft Access and the high-end enterprise capabilities (and price) of Oracle and DB2. It gained a good reputation for ease of use and for providing crucial business tools (e.g., analysis services and data transformation services) out of the box, which were expensive add-ons with competing databases.
2000	SQL Server 2000 (an enterprise database)	Vastly improved performance scalability and reliability sees SQL Server become a major player in the *enterprise database* market (now supporting the online operations of businesses such as NASDAQ, Dell, and Barnes & Noble). A stiff price increase slowed initial uptake, but 2000's excellent range of management, development, and analysis tools won new customers.

scalability, and performance to the point where it is a serious competitor—most significantly to Oracle—in the medium-sized enterprise market (although, of course, SQL Server competes only on the Windows platform).

It is interesting to contrast SQL Server's journey from small business to enterprise with that of Oracle's, which in some ways has been pushing in the opposite direction. From the very start, Oracle was designed to handle large databases, and high numbers of transactions and users. In terms of "out-of-the-box" performance and scalability (i.e., the numbers of transactions and users per single instance), many consider Oracle to still be the superior database. However, some perceive that this superiority comes at the expense of high costs and complexity—but that the performance numbers are getting closer.

Whatever the truth might be, it is certain that the competition between Oracle and SQL Server is set to intensify with the release of SQL Server 2005. Certainly part of the drive behind the release of Oracle 10*g* appears to be to reduce the total cost of ownership (TCO) of the database and to make it easier to mange, introducing, as it does, a whole swath of "automated" management tools.[1]

In the meantime, SQL Server 2005 marks a significant advance in Microsoft's march into the enterprise database arena.

---

1. Of course, this is not the whole story. Oracle has also invested heavily in technologies such as Real Application Clusters (RAC), which ultimately is designed to reduce the cost of implementing highly scaleable enterprise systems—although at the moment it is still a very expensive technology!

SQL Server 2005 Overview

SQL Server 2005 brings with it a vast array of new features, graphical user interfaces (GUIs), and management tools, many of which are covered in this book. The following list should give you a brief taste of these:

- The ability to host the .NET Framework common language runtime (CLR) in the database so that you can now program assemblies in Visual Basic 2005 and C# *in the database*. This may have interesting consequences for the SQL Server database programmer, who previously was limited to SQL and T-SQL, and it will have dramatic implications for the way applications may be architected.

- Deep support for XML, via a full-fledged XML datatype that carries all the capabilities of relational datatypes. You can enter an XML document into your database, have it validated, and extract just part of the document. This means that you can marry semistructured data with relational data, storing them in the same place and treating them in the same way. Additionally, server-side support is provided for XML Query (XQuery) and XML Schema Definition language (XSD) standards.

- A completely revamped GUI management tool called SQL Server Management Studio (SSMS), which provides a single, integrated environment for most management/administration requirements.

- A reporting framework (SQL Server Reporting Services, or SSRS) as an integral part of the database.

- A new application framework, the Service Broker, for asynchronous message delivery.

- Vastly improved and expanded SQL Server Integration Services (SSIS; formerly Data Transformation Services), a tool for extracting, transforming, and loading data (again, a feature that is a costly add-on with other relational database management systems).

The latter three are excellent examples of features that SQL Server provides as an integral part of the product, rather than as (extra-cost) add-ons.

Editions

SQL Server 2005 is available in the following distinct editions:

- *Enterprise*: This is the most powerful, scalable, and expensive SQL Server 2005 edition. It is targeted, as its name suggests, at enterprise businesses where performance availability and scalability are of paramount importance. It supports all available features.

- *Developer*: This is the same as the Enterprise Edition, but with restrictions on CPUs and licenses.

- *Standard*: This edition is a cheaper option than Enterprise and Developer, and it is targeted at small- and medium-sized businesses. It removes support for such features as partitioning and online indexing, but it does support many of the "high-end" features, such as Analysis Services, Integration Services, database mirroring, and so on.

- *Workgroup*: This edition is designed for small- and medium-sized businesses and departmental solutions. It supports many of the core SQL Server features, but it doesn't include high-availability features, and it also has limited analysis functionality.

- *Express*: This edition replaces Microsoft SQL Server Desktop Engine (MSDE). However, it inherits many (nonenterprise) features from SQL Server 2005 and comes complete with its own dedicated (albeit limited) development and administration tools. It is freely available and is an ideal database for departmental solutions, prototype or evaluation projects, and hobbyists.

Table 1-2 outlines the CPU, memory, and size limitations for each edition.

Table 1-2. *Hardware Limitations for Each SQL Server Edition*

Feature	Enterprise/Developer	Standard	Workgroup	Express
Maximum number of CPUs	No limit	4	2	1
Maximum amount of RAM	No limit	No limit	3GB	2GB
64-bit processor supported	Yes	Yes	Windows on Windows	Windows on Windows
Maximum size for a database	No limit	No limit	No limit	4GB

Features

Table 1-3 provides an overview of the "core" new features of SQL Server 2005, with a brief description of each and an indication of the edition(s) in which it is supported.

Table 1-3. *Core SQL Server 2005 Features*

Feature	Description	Supported In
Advanced performance tuning	Mining models can receive advanced performing tuning.	Enterprise
Advanced transforms such as data mining, text mining, and data cleansing	The Enterprise Edition allows the inclusion of Analysis Services–based transforms and mining capabilities within the SSIS packages.	Enterprise
Database available for use while transaction undo operations in progress	Databases can be available for use during the undo phase while a restore is in progress.	Enterprise
Data flow integration	SSIS can be used to improve the mining model for creating prediction queries.	Enterprise
Indexes on a view	SQL Server allows creation of indexes on a view.	Enterprise
Parallel indexing operations	Indexing can run in parallel on multiprocessor computers.	Enterprise
Online database restore	A database can be restored without taking it offline.	Enterprise
Online indexing of tables and views	Tables and views can be indexed while users are still working with the system.	Enterprise
Oracle replication	SQL Server databases can now replicate to an Oracle database.	Enterprise

Table 1-3. *Core SQL Server 2005 Features (Continued)*

Feature	Description	Supported In
Partitioning	Tables can be split up (physically or logically) into smaller units to speed processing of data and indexing.	Enterprise
Text mining	Structured text can be created for SQL Server Analysis Services (SSAS) from unstructured text.	Enterprise
Database mirroring	Changes completed in one database are mirrored in another.	Enterprise Standard
Database Tuning Advisor (DTA)	The DTA tool provides tuning advice for the whole database and replaces the Index Tuning Wizard.	Enterprise Standard
Failover clustering	A database can failover to another database on a point of failure.	Enterprise Standard
Integration Services, including graphical Extract, Transform, and Load (ETL)	Integration Services is a tool for extracting, transforming, and loading data. This used to be known as DTS.	Enterprise Standard
Notification Services, for sending out notifications to subscribers	Notification Services is used for applications that generate and send notifications of events that happen within SQL Server to any subscriber, whether it is a PDA, mobile phone, etc.	Enterprise Standard
Web services	Support for native web services allows you to expose specific SQL Server objects such as stored procedures, user-defined functions, and queries via HTTP(S).	Enterprise Standard
Full-text searching	Words or phrases can be searched in any column defined for full-text searching.	Enterprise Standard Workgroup
Log shipping	Transaction logs can be moved from one database to another to allow the transactions.	Enterprise Standard Workgroup
SQL Server job scheduling	Jobs can be created and processed using specific scheduling requirements. Failures can also trigger notification by e-mail, pager, etc.	Enterprise Standard Workgroup
.NET integration	The .NET Framework CLR is hosted in the database, so assemblies can now be programmed in Visual Basic 2005 and C#, in the database.	All
Advanced auditing, authentication, and authorization	Windows authentication and authorization can be used for user logins.	All
Auto database tune	Databases can be tuned automatically.	All
Data import and export	Data can be imported and exported from external data sources, such as Excel.	All
Error handling, datatypes, and recursive queries	TRY...CATCH error handling, recursive queries, and new data types such as XML can be used.	All

Table 1-3. *Core SQL Server 2005 Features (Continued)*

Feature	Description	Supported In
Express Manager tool	This stand-alone tool for managing and working with SQL Server is available as a separate download.	All
Hot Add Memory, dedicated admin connection	New memory can be added without bringing down the server, and there is a permanent admin connection for connecting to SQL Server when the GUI won't allow it.	All
Built-in data encryption	Data is encrypted on the physical computer.	All
Management Studio development GUI	This new GUI for working with SQL Server replaces SQL Server Enterprise Manager and resembles Visual Studio .NET's layout and method of working.	All
Management views and reporting enhancements	Reporting Services has new reporting management and views to allow secure deployment of reports.	All
Microsoft Baseline Security Analyzer (MBSA) integration	This tool, used to ensure that a system remains secure, now has integration for SQL Server. Information about MBSA can be found at http://www.microsoft.com/technet/security/tools/mbsahome.mspx.	All
Microsoft Update integration for automatic software updates	Any patches or service packs for download can be applied automatically.	All
Replication (merge and transactional)	Replication allows data from one database to be copied to another database, either transactionally from publisher to subscriber, or via merge, where every database publishes changes as well as subscribes to changes.	All
Service Broker	This tool offers asynchronous processing and reliable messaging between servers.	All
Stored procedures, triggers, and views	These are basic database programming units for working with the data.	All
Best Practices Analyzer	This separate, downloadable tool can be used to test that best practices within a database are being adhered to (see http://www.microsoft.com/downloads/details.aspx?familyid=b352eb1f-d3ca-44ee-893e-9e07339c1f22&displaylang=en).	All
UDTs	User-defined datatypes can be created from base data types.	All
Native XML indexing and full-text search	XML data can be indexed and full-text searched, just like other data types.	All
XQuery for XML datatypes	This is a method for working with XML data types where XQuery is based on the XPath query language, but enhanced (not yet W3C ratified).	All

Table 1-4 summarizes the business intelligence (BI) features of SQL Server 2005 and the editions in which they are supported:

Table 1-4. *Business Intelligence Features for Each Edition*

BI Feature	Description	Support
Account Intelligence, metadata translation analytics	Business analytics have improved to include these analytics.	Enterprise
Autocaching	Data can be automatically cached to improve performance.	Enterprise
Data-driven subscriptions	Reports can be provided that have a data-driven subscription. The report server gets the subscription settings prior to publishing the report.	Enterprise
Dimension and cell writebacks	Dimension and cell writebacks allow client applications to write to the partition's data.	Enterprise
Infinite click-through	Where the data allows, it's possible to click through groups to refine output.	Enterprise
Partitioned cubes, parallel processing, and server synchronization	Advanced data management creates partitions that allow the management and storage of data that allows parallel processing of the data.	Enterprise
Scale out report servers	Report server instances can be scaled such that they are not on the same report server.	Enterprise
Analysis Services	SQL Server 2005 Analysis Services (SSAS) is Microsoft's suite of technologies designed to support the development and administration of business intelligence applications (e.g., market segmentation analysis, product profitability, etc.).	Enterprise Standard
Data mining	Improved data mining uses the new key performance indicator (KPI) and Unified Dimensional Model (UMD) functionality, as well as data mining capabilities for extracting and mining data from databases.	Enterprise Standard
Data warehousing	A data warehouse–based database can be built for SSAS.	Enterprise Standard
Multidimensional Expressions (MDX) scripts, debugger, .NET sprocs, and KPI Framework	MDX scripts can be debugged, written in .NET, and have the ability to create key performance indicators (KPIs).	Enterprise Standard
Unified Dimensional Model (UDM)	Enterprise-based data modeling can be performed via the UDM within SSAS.	Enterprise Standard
Integration with Management Studio, Profiler, etc. for business intelligence	SSAS is integrated with Management Studio and other features.	Enterprise Standard Workgroup

Table 1-4. *Business Intelligence Features for Each Edition (Continued)*

BI Feature	Description	Support
Report builder for end users	Users can build their own reports rather than have developer-based reports deployed to them.	Enterprise Standard Workgroup
Business Intelligence Development Studio (BIDS)	SSMS is the GUI for SQL Server database solutions. For SSAS solutions, BIDS is a separate GUI built for the specifics of SSAS-based work.	All
BI native support for web services	SSAS can use data from different data sources.	All
Reporting Services	This tool is used for producing SQL Server reports.	All
Reporting data sources	The data used in reports can come from any SQL Server data source.	All
SQL analytical functions	Analytical functions for SSAS-based databases deal with areas such as dimensions, hierarchy, and levels.	All
Star query optimization	Star queries found in SSAS can be optimized.	All

Installation

Microsoft has gone all the way back to the beginning of your experience of SQL Server with its installation procedure to conform the interface to the Microsoft standard. Let's start with the system requirements for installation.

Minimum System Requirements

The minimum requirements of SQL Server 2005 for the basic SQL Server installation have not changed greatly from SQL Server 2000. You should have at a minimum a 500 MHz processor, but 1 GHz or higher is recommended with at least 512MB of RAM (1GB or more is advisable), unless you are running the Express Edition, which requires only 128MB of RAM.

You will need Internet Explorer 6 SP1 or above to run the help files, and you will need to have IIS installed and configured for XML functionality and Reporting Services. Depending on your operating system, there are also minimum service pack (SP) requirements. Tables 1-5 and 1-6 list the SQL Server editions and which operating systems each can run on. Table 1-5 details SQL Server 2005 32-bit editions, and Table 1-6 details SQL Server 2005 64-bit editions.

Table 1-5. *32-bit Operating Systems Each Edition Can Be Installed On*

	Enterprise	Developer	Standard	Evaluation	Workgroup	Express
Windows 2003 Datacenter SP1	X	X	X	X	X	X
Windows 2003 Enterprise SP1	X	X	X	X	X	X

Table 1-5. *32-bit Operating Systems Each Edition Can Be Installed On*

	Enterprise	Developer	Standard	Evaluation	Workgroup	Express
Windows 2003 Standard SP1	X	X	X	X	X	X
Windows SBS 2003 Premium	X	X	X	X	X	X
Windows SBS 2003 Standard	X	X	X	X	X	X
Windows 2000 Datacenter SP4	X	X	X	X	X	X
Windows 2000 Advanced SP4	X	X	X	X	X	X
Windows 2000 Server SP4	X	X	X	X	X	X
Windows XP Professional SP2		X		X	X	X
Windows XP Media SP2		X		X	X	X
Windows XP Tablet SP2		X		X	X	X
Windows 2000 Professional SP4		X		X	X	X
Windows XP Home		X				X
Windows 2003 Server Web Edition		X				X

Table 1-6. *64-bit Operating Systems Each Edition Can Be Installed On*

	Enterprise IA64	Developer IA64	Standard IA64	Express
Windows 2003 Server SP1 64-bit Itanium Datacenter	X	X	X	X
Windows 2003 Server SP1 64-bit Itanium Enterprise	X	X	X	X
Windows 2003 Server SP1 64-bit X64 Datacenter	X	X	X	X
Windows 2003 Server SP1 64-bit X64 Enterprise	X	X	X	X
Windows 2003 Server SP1 64-bit X64 Standard	X	X	X	X
Windows XP X64 Professional				X

■**Note** Not all operating systems install IIS automatically, so you may need to install it manually.

Installation Process

The installation process for SQL Server 2005 is now in line with other Microsoft products' installation procedures. SQL Server 2005 has a two-stage process, with the first stage performing checks and installing SQL Server 2005 prerequisites, and the second stage installing SQL Server itself. Both stages run whether you're installing SQL Server from scratch or performing further installations/upgrades.

Installation Prerequisites

SQL Server 2005 requires a number of prerequisites to be successfully installed before you can actually install SQL Server itself. These prerequisites differ depending on your operating system and on the functionality you require.

The main prerequisites are as follows:

- Application of the correct service pack
- Internet Explorer 6 with SP1
- .NET Framework 2.0

■**Tip** A log file is produced that lists every action performed during the installation. It is recommended that you store this log file, whether or not your installation was a success.

Installing SQL Server

Once you've installed all the prerequisites (see Figure 1-1), you can then proceed to run the SQL Server Installation Setup Process. The setup process in SQL Server 2005 has been improved to reflect the Microsoft standard of having all options available for installation in one pass.

Once the prerequisites have been taken care of, the installation wizard starts up. In the first main screen, the setup checks your system configuration to ensure that previous steps have been completed successfully and the required software is installed.

Checks performed at this stage include verifying that the operating system can cope with the edition of SQL Server 2005 you want to install and confirming that the minimum service pack has been installed. At the end of the process, a log file is created with the installation details. It is possible to save and store this file as a record of what succeeded and failed during the installation.

Figure 1-1. *SQL Server prerequisites*

Figure 1-2. *System Configuration Check dialog box*

Click Next to move to the Registration Information dialog box, and then click Next again. This takes you to perhaps the most productive enhancement to the installation process: the Components to Install dialog box (see Figure 1-3). Here, you can install all services in one pass. SQL Server and Analysis Server can also be installed on the new virtual server technology.

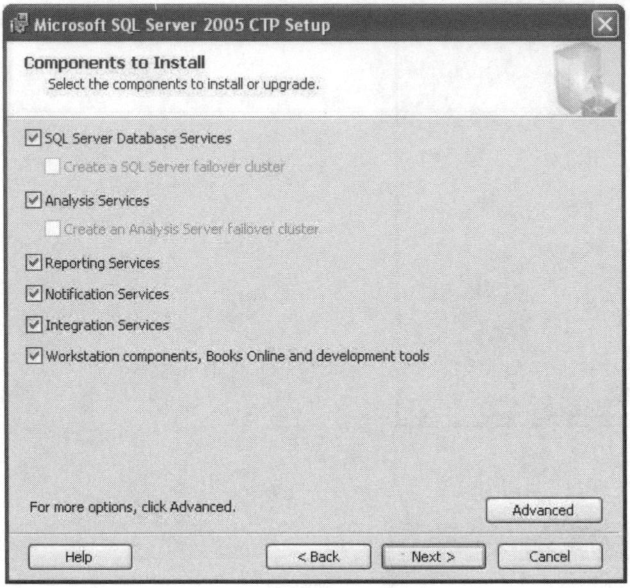

Figure 1-3. *Components to Install dialog box*

Click Advanced to go to the installation tree, which we describe in the next section.

Installation Tree

The installation tree is part of the Feature Selection dialog box shown in Figure 1-4. This feature is standard in virtually all Microsoft products, so chances are you have seen it before. This feature removes the burden of the two or three installation passes you had to perform in SQL Server 2000 to install SQL Server, Analysis Services, and Full Text Editing. It also allows you to add or remove components in one simple procedure.

The only main component that is not automatically selected in the tree is the Data Transformation Services (DTS) runtime for SQL Server 2000 DTS packages. If you are planning to migrate your SQL Server 2000 packages to SQL Server 2005, then you will need to select this option. Also, some of the samples and databases are not selected by default. There is now a specific example database for data warehousing called AdventureWorksDW, which is linked to the SQL Server example database. Finally, an example database for Analysis Services called AdventureWorksAS is also available.

After you click Next on the Feature Selection dialog box, you move to the Instance Name dialog box shown in Figure 1-5. As with SQL Server 2000, you can specify a named instance or a default instance.

Clicking Next moves you to the next area where the installation process has improved: security.

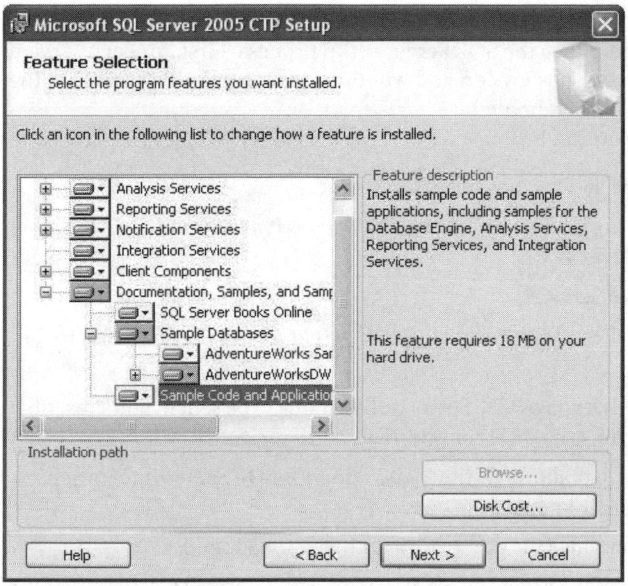

Figure 1-4. *Installation tree*

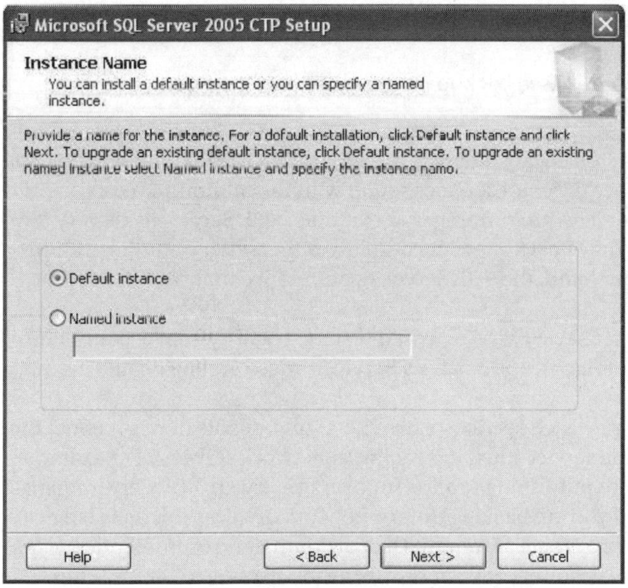

Figure 1-5. *Instance Name dialog box*

Improved Security

There are two major security enhancements to the SQL Server setup process. First, for each service that is installed, you can define how the service logs on and whether it automatically starts with the operating system (e.g., when the machine is rebooted).

SQL Server 2005 has ten services you can install:

- *SQL Server relational engine*: The service that runs SQL Server.

- *SQL Server Agent*: Used for running jobs set up within SQL Server. It also monitors SQL Server and sends out alerts and SQL Server WMIs.

- *Analysis Server*: Used for Analysis Services.

- *Report Server*: When running SQL Server reports, the service that allows these reports to be built and execute.

- *Notification Services*: The service that allows SQL Server notifications to be sent to any subscriber to that subject, whether via e-mail, Web, PDA, or phone.

- *Integration Services*: The service that allows the new and superior SQL Server Integration Services packages to run. Previously known as DTS.

- *Full-text search*: A service that provides the ability to search text for a literal.

- *SQL Browser*: A process that provides a list of SQL Server instances with the TCP/IP port or the named pipe for each instance for client connections.

- *SQL Server Active Directory Helper*: A client uniquely identifies an instance of SQL Server via a service principal name (SPN). If this name changes, this service will inform Microsoft Active Directory.

- *SQL Writer*: Used to allow Windows-based backup programs to back up SQL Server data, rather than SQL Server itself.

For each service, you can either use the Local System account or set up a Domain User account. This allows system administrators to have different services set up with the minimum required privileges on the computer on which the services are running. For example, SQL Server needs very few Windows system privileges, and using the Local System account gives this service administration rights that it does not need. On the other hand, the SQL Server Agent service that runs batch jobs does need administration rights.

With the settings shown in Figure 1-6, every service would use the Local System account and would auto-start SQL Server, SQL Server Agent, and Analysis Services; these are the default settings in the Autostart services area.

However, it is preferable that you give each service its own Domain User account to reflect the necessary privileges, especially when the service must interact with network services. For example, Reporting Services needs to interact with publishing reports for users via a web. SQL Server Agent will also need a Domain User account if you are backing up to a network drive, as this will also need to interact with network services. If you do create a Domain User account, it is recommended, especially for production systems, that these accounts have nonexpiring passwords; otherwise, you might find that a crucial service is unable to run.

The second enhancement is that it is now obligatory to place a strong password on the sa login when setting up the authentication mode, as shown in Figure 1-7. In SQL Server 2000, it was possible to proceed with the installation process without entering a valid and strong password—this was perhaps the largest security hole that existed in SQL Server 2000. In SQL Server 2005, this hole has been plugged.

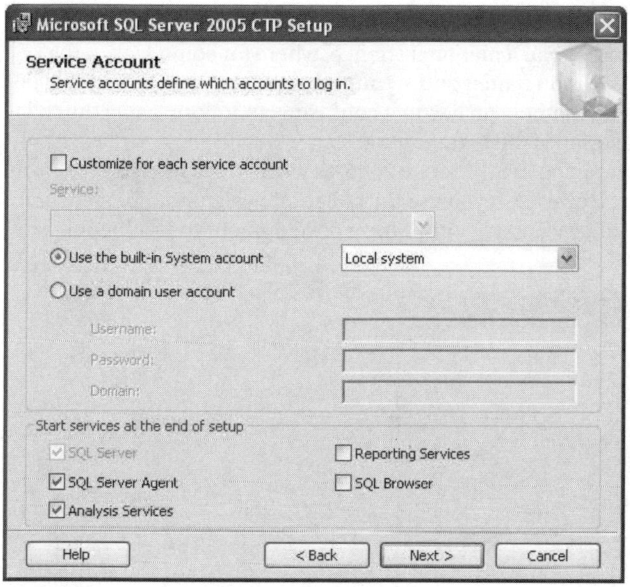

Figure 1-6. *Service Account dialog box*

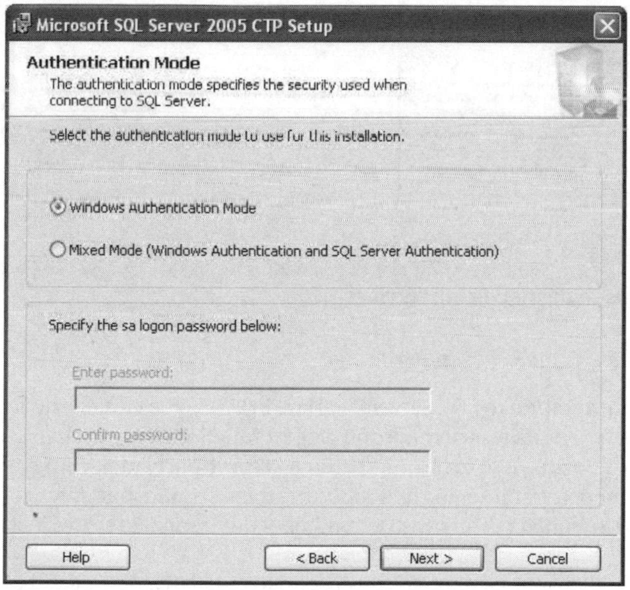

Figure 1-7. *Authentication Mode dialog box*

Click Next to move on to select collation settings.

Collation Settings

The Collation Settings dialog box has undergone a marginal change, where for some reason the default setup, SQL collations, uses the collation names and settings that existed in SQL Server 2000 and previous versions. These SQL collation names can become confusing; therefore, using the collation designator to create a Windows collation is the better option.

The collation settings have been simplified in SQL Server 2005, as you can see in Figure 1-8. You now have a clearer collation designator. However, if you use the collation designator, then ensure that you double-check the collation settings when you move from development to production.

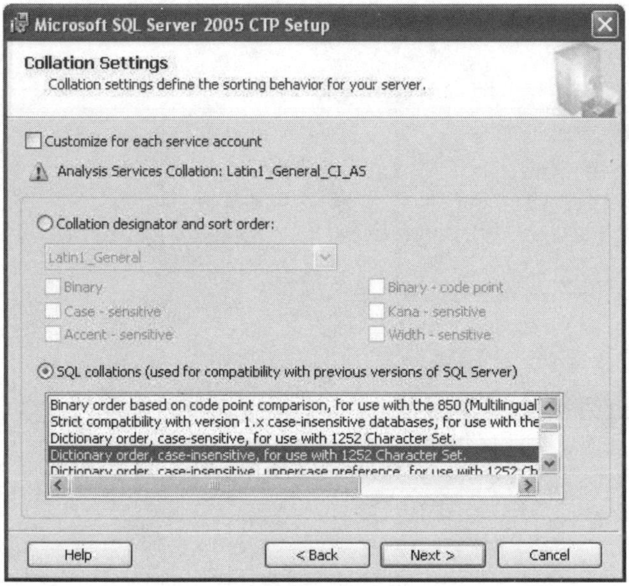

Figure 1-8. *Collation Settings dialog box*

The final action in the process is installing Reporting Services.

Reporting Services

Reporting Services were introduced as an addition to SQL Server 2000 late in 2003. The lack of a dedicated tool with which to build and deploy reports was perhaps the biggest functionality gap that existed in SQL Server. Up until then, all reporting had to be done through a third-party tool, with the most prevalent being Crystal Reports. There are still some great reporting tools around, but they can be complicated to use, because they are intended to work with a number of different data stores, not just SQL Server.

Reporting Services runs through an IIS instance, therefore you need to create two virtual directories for the web server to use. The necessity for two virtual directories relates to how Reporting Services works. There are two servers for producing reports: Report Server and Report Manager. Report Server is used to hold report definitions and cached report data; it is the location from which reports are produced. Report Manager is used to manage the reports defined in Report Server.

Another requirement is a database for Reporting Services to hold the reports and the details of running the reports within a separate database. From a performance perspective, the most efficient place to install the reporting database is on the same server as the data that will populate the reports.

However, if you have a heavily used instance, or reports that are intensive in their production, it may be desirable to move the reporting database to a separate, dedicated instance. Another reason to have the database in a different instance relates to the benefits in having a SQL Server instance built just for reporting. It removes Reporting Services from the normal, day-to-day maintenance tasks of the database and allows specific maintenance tasks to be built. Finally, having Reporting Services away from the main SQL Server instance reduces complexity when it is necessary to scale up any installation or apply any Reporting Services service packs, without your having to worry about your production data repository. If you can afford the reduction in performance, a separate SQL Server instance for reporting purposes is probably desirable.

■**Note** Delivery of reports can be through the Web or by e-mail.

There are two ways to install Reporting Services: you can either take the default values or set up the values yourself. Figure 1-9 shows that we are happy with the default values, which include the account to use for logging into the service, the name of the virtual directories for the web reports, and the name of the databases. We've also indicated that we want to create a connection for the Web Services account.

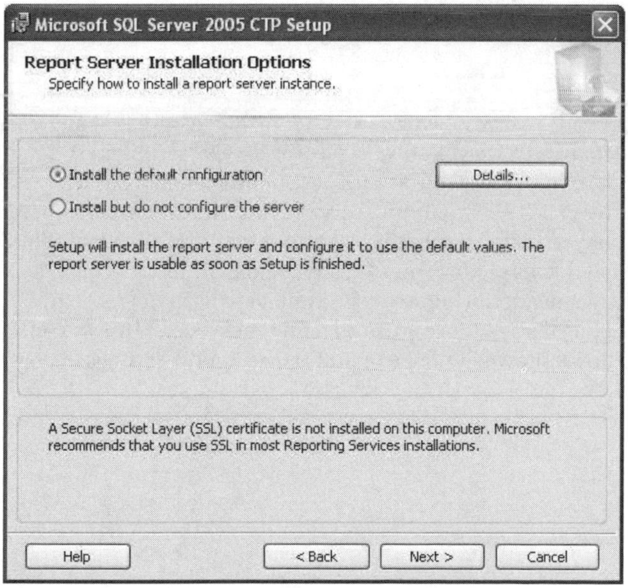

Figure 1-9. *Report Server default values dialog box*

Clicking Next will show a list of the values that SQL Server will apply (see Figure 1-10).

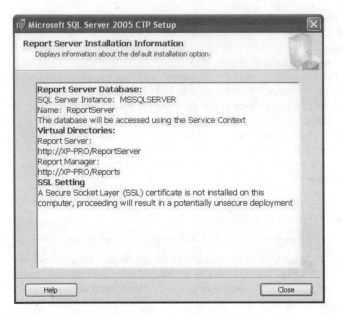

Figure 1-10. *Report Server default values settings*

We'll examine Reporting Services in more detail in Chapter 9.

Error Reporting

The final step prior to the installation starting involves the new error-reporting feature that allows fatal errors to be automatically sent to Microsoft or to your own reporting server (see Figure 1-11). Sending error reports to Microsoft will not compromise the security of your installation, and it increases the likelihood that the problem will be fixed in a future service pack. At the moment, there is no way of defining your own internal server, but no doubt this capability will come in later builds.

It is also possible to send to Microsoft details of how you are using your SQL Server. This is a great development, as Microsoft can then concentrate better on areas that are used the most and give priority for future development and bug fixes to those areas affecting most users. Unless you have a good reason to uncheck the two boxes shown in the Error and Usage Report Settings dialog box, leave them selected.

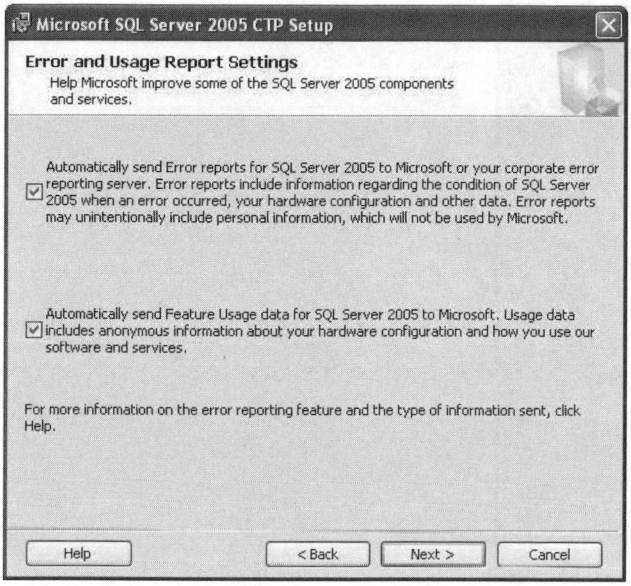

Figure 1-11. *Error and Usage Report Settings dialog box*

The errors to be sent are not just blue screens, but any error that is fatal, such as your server crashing.

Server Registration

Once you have installed SQL Server 2005, two workbenches will install, provided you chose all the defaults: SQL Server Management Studio (SSMS) and Business Intelligence Development Studio (BIDS).

SSMS, covered in detail in Chapter 2, is the tool that you will probably use most frequently. SSMS is an integrated management tool for developers and database administrators, whereas BIDS is a replacement for SQL Server 2000's Analysis Manager and is used for analysis services and building cubes, dimensions, and so on.

Registering a server as well as a database in SSMS is almost exactly the same as in SQL Server 2000, except for the look of the interface, as shown in Figure 1-12. The server instance is the physical name of the server on which SQL Server is installed.

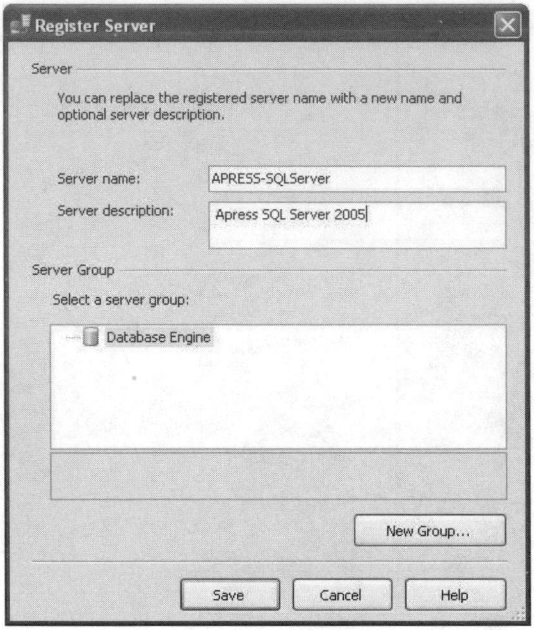

Figure 1-12. *Register Server dialog box*

Once the server is registered, it is possible to view the properties of that server from within Object Explorer. The first page of interest, shown in Figure 1-13, concerns memory and provides the option to enable the Address Windowing Extensions (AWE) API, via the "Use AWE to allocate memory" check box. This feature provides a number of options for dealing with memory management. For example, if the physical memory is greater than the virtual memory and you want SQL Server (when required) to use this physical memory when the virtual memory is low, then AWE can alter the amount of memory SQL Server is using dynamically.

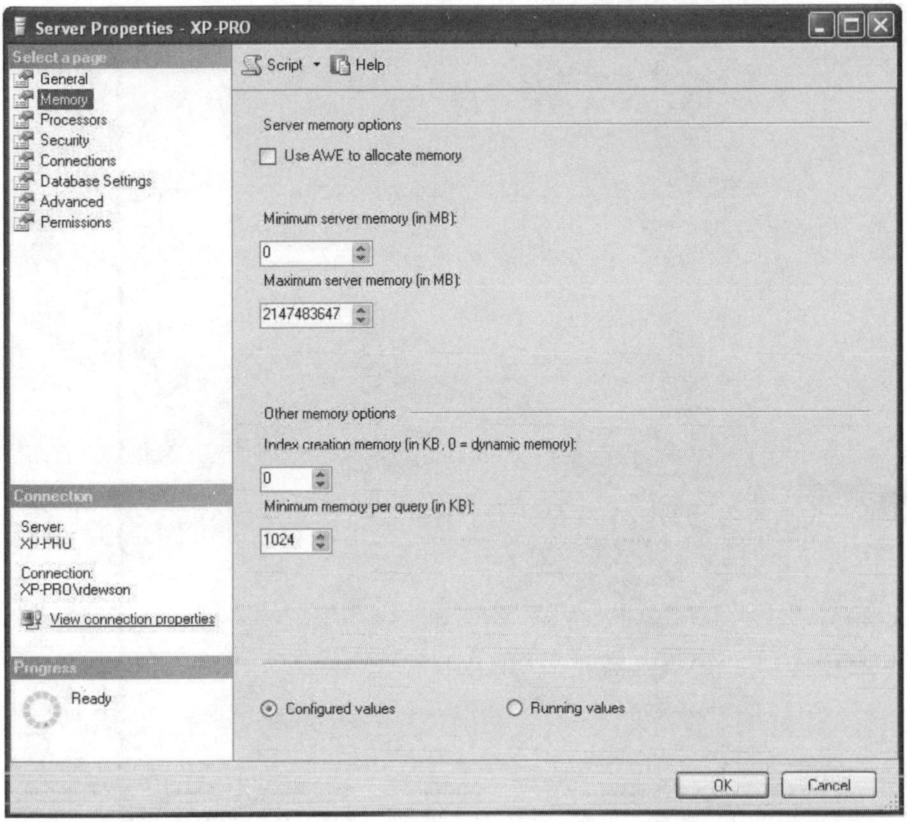

Figure 1-13. *Server Properties: Memory*

Next, take a look at the Processors screen in Figure 1-14. Here you can specify which CPUs SQL Server can use on a multiprocessor machine, or you can choose to allow SQL Server to automatically select the processor. Unless you have a specific need for a processor to not be used, then it is best to let SQL Server automatically choose the processor. If you do select specific processors, you have to keep in mind what other process threads might also use those processors.

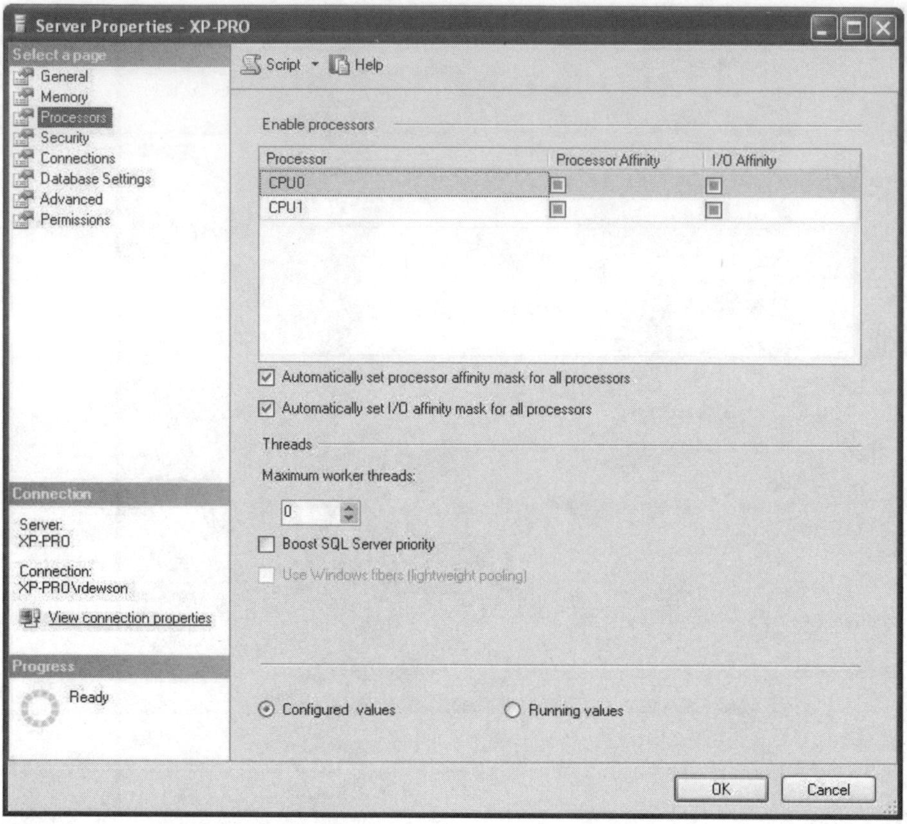

Figure 1-14. *Server Properties: Processors*

Sample Databases

SQL Server has expanded to include a new sample database called Adventure Works, with the sad loss of two stalwart but now outdated example databases, Northwind and Pubs. No sample databases are installed by default—you need to explicitly request them as part of the feature selection or install them during any future installation procedure.

Adventure Works is, in fact, three databases:

- *AdventureWorks*: This is the base, general-purpose relational schema for all standard examples.

- *AdventureWorksDW*: This is a relational schema for data warehousing examples.

- *AdventureWorksAS*: This database is available for use as an example of Analysis Services.

The following excerpt from SQL Server Books Online provides a concise overview of what the Adventure Works databases are about:

> *Adventure Works Cycles is a large, multinational manufacturing company that produces and distributes metal and composite bicycles to North American, European, and Asian commercial markets. While its base operation is located in Bothell, Washington, in the United States, with 500 employees, several regional sales teams are located throughout their market base.*

In the year 2002, Adventure Works Cycles bought a small manufacturing plant, Importadores Neptuno, located in Mexico. Importadores Neptuno manufactures several critical subcomponents for the Adventure Works Cycles product line. These subcomponents are shipped to the Bothell location for final product assembly. In 2003, Importadores Neptuno became the sole manufacturer and distributor of the Touring 1000 models.

Coming off a successful fiscal year, Adventure Works Cycles is looking to broaden its market share by targeting their sales to their best customers, extending their product availability through an external website, and reducing their cost of sales through lower production costs.

Side-by-Side Installation

It is possible to have SQL Server 2005 and SQL Server 2000 (or earlier) running on the same physical machine, although it is recommended that you keep the installations separate if possible.

You can also have SQL Server 2005 set up so that the databases work as if they were within a SQL Server 2000 environment. However, once you migrate any existing databases to SQL Server 2005, the only way to move them back to a previous SQL Server version is to extract the database objects, table objects, data, and so on, and reload them. You cannot restore a SQL Server 2005 backup to a previous version.

Upgrading from SQL Server 2000 and 7.0

You can upgrade databases from SQL Server 7.0 or SQL Server 2000 to SQL Server 2005, or version 9.0. It is not possible to move back any upgraded databases set to SQL Server 2005 to any previous SQL Server version, including their original version, once you do this upgrade, though.

It is possible to upgrade the database, any DTS, to SSIS packages as well as upgrade any replicated databases.

The upgrade process in some instances is simple and straightforward. However, Microsoft does provide an analysis tool called Upgrade Advisor that can help inform you of any code, objects, and so forth that may exist in the database you wish to upgrade. You can find the Upgrade Advisor tool at http://www.microsoft.com/downloads/details.aspx?familyid=cf28daf9-182e-4ac2-8e88-f2e936558bf2&displaylang=en.

Once a server is registered, it is possible to attach and upgrade a database through SSMS. A more common method is to restore a SQL Server 2000 or SQL Server 7.0 database from a backup. All databases can be restored with the exception of the system databases. System databases can't be restored because they have been drastically modified for security purposes and the capability to work with .NET assemblies, therefore the ability to restore any system databases prior to SQL Server 2005 is restricted to those that were user defined.

Summary

Installing SQL Server is no longer an awkward chore that requires several passes through the process to complete. The SQL Server 2005 installation process now follows the Microsoft standard installation format. With all the components available to install in one pass, there should be less confusion about the process and fewer installation problems.

SQL Server 2005 presents only a few new considerations to take into account during installation, with these mainly relating to Reporting Services and the installation tree. Updating the installed instance with new functionality, or even removing installed components, is much easier to decipher than in previous versions, so you can be confident you'll get it right the first time.

CHAPTER 2

SQL Server Management Technologies

With SQL Server 2005, it is a brave new world for DBAs when it comes to server management. In SQL Server 2000, you had scenarios where you would have to open four different tools to get your work done: Enterprise Manager, Query Analyzer, Profiler, and Analysis Manager. Never mind that the addition of new technologies such as Reporting Services and SQL Server 2005 Mobile Edition (the renamed SQL Server CE Edition) present their own management tools separate from the ones already pointed out. While each tool did its job well enough, the need to switch between tools and to master different user interfaces and command syntax each time lessened users' experiences with SQL Server. As a direct result of this sort of feedback, SQL Server Management Studio was born.

SQL Server Management Studio (often referred to as simply Management Studio or SSMS) combines most of the tools that you previously used separately and adds additional capabilities.

Furthermore, Management Studio is a completely rewritten application that uses the latest in Microsoft technologies, namely Windows Forms and the .NET Framework. No longer, except when using Computer Manager, do you have to deal with the idiosyncrasies of the Microsoft Management Console (upon which Enterprise Manager was built), such as modal dialog boxes, when performing your administrative tasks. This chapter will guide you through the new features and enhancements in Management Studio as well as other new management technologies in SQL Server 2005. For Management Studio, we'll cover the following topics:

- How to connect to and manage multiple components of SQL Server from the unified Management Studio console

- New user interface enhancements, including asynchronous treeview and filtering capabilities, nonmodal dialog boxes, dialog boxes that can output scripts of their actions, robust code authoring capabilities, and summary views

- New capabilities such as the dedicated admin connection, deadlock visualization, Performance Monitor correlation, Maintenance Plan Designer, Database Mail, dynamic management views, and enhanced help

- New command-line tools, such as SQLCMD

- A new API called Server Management Objects (SMO), which replaces Distributed Management Objects (DMO)

Connecting to and Managing Your SQL Servers

The very first thing you will notice in SQL Server 2005 is that you no longer have to fire up multiple tools to manage different SQL Server services, from the relational engine to Analysis Services.

Management Studio integrates all the essential management capabilities in one interface. You can connect to multiple SQL Server components in Management Studio, as shown in Figure 2-1.

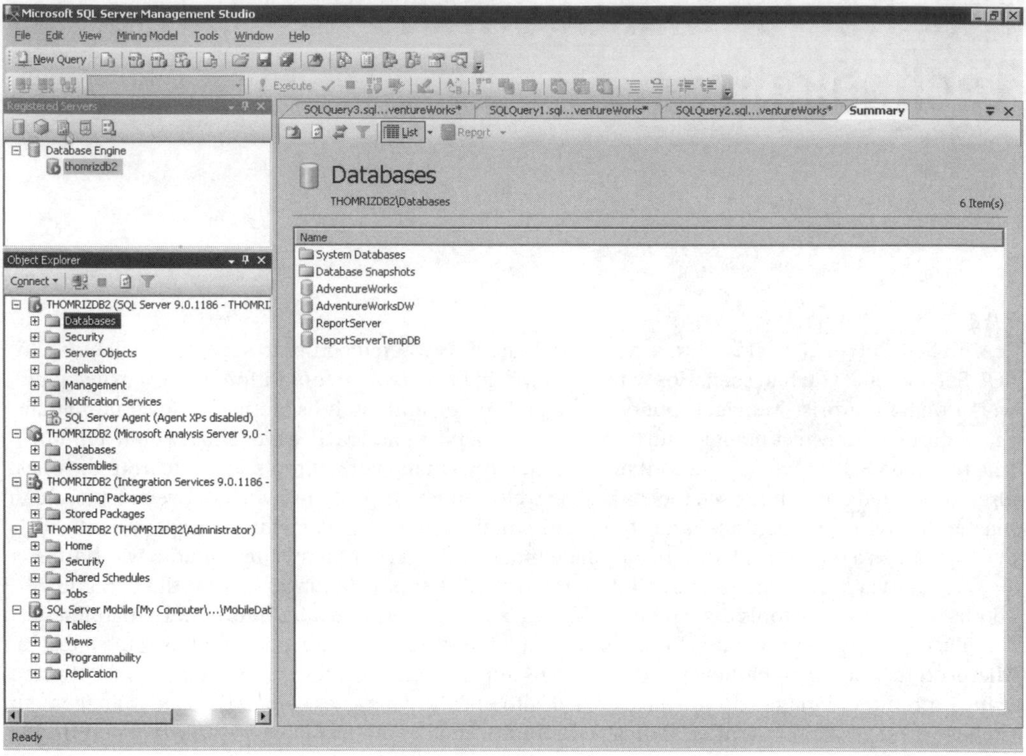

Figure 2-1. *Connecting to multiple SQL Server components*

Context-Sensitive Menus for Each Object Type

The components that you can manage with Management Studio are the relational engine, Analysis Services, Reporting Services, Integration Services, Notification Services, and even SQL Server Mobile Edition. Management Studio is smart enough to recognize when you click a particular type of object to display the correct context menu for that type of object. For example, when you right-click an Analysis Services cube, Management Studio lets you process the cube as one of the menu options, as shown in Figure 2-2.

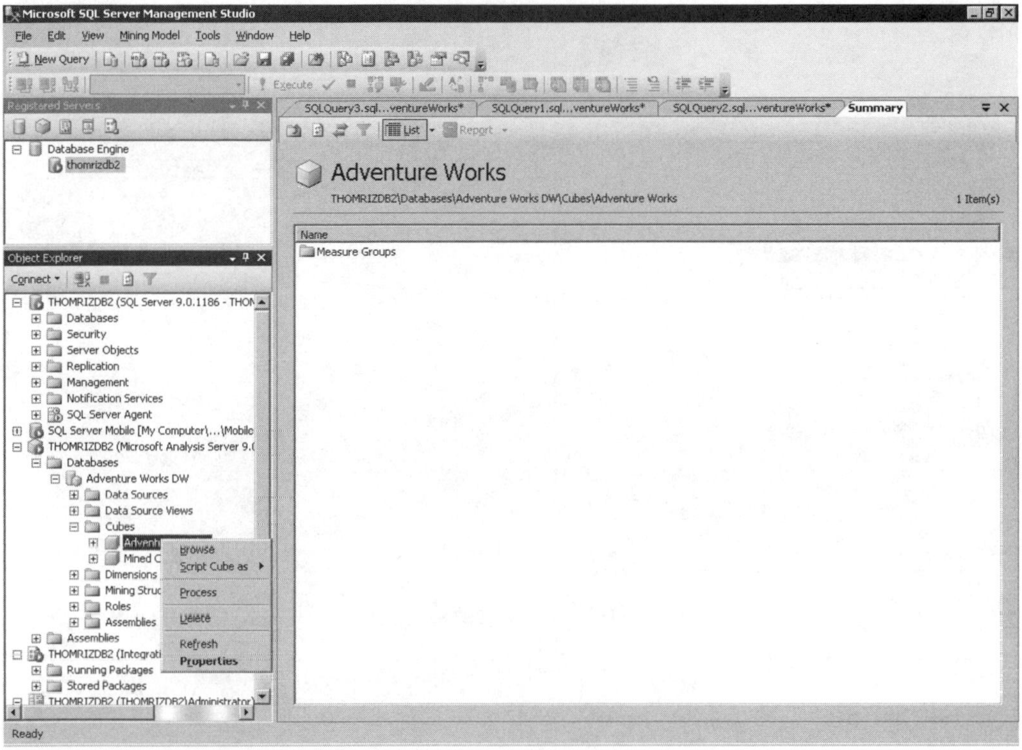

Figure 2-2. *Custom context-sensitive menus for different SQL components*

Mobile Database Support

If you're using SQL technologies such as SQL Server Mobile Edition, you'll be able to manage your mobile databases right from Management Studio. One caveat here is that you do need ActiveSync installed on the machine running Management Studio, and the mobile device must be connected to the physical machine as well.

■**Note** SQL Server Mobile Edition will also run on the Tablet PC operating system, so you can build applications that leverage Microsoft's two mobile operating systems, Windows Mobile Edition (formerly known as Windows CE) and Tablet PC, with one database.

Figure 2-3 shows how to connect to and browse mobile SQL Server databases from the Management Studio console.

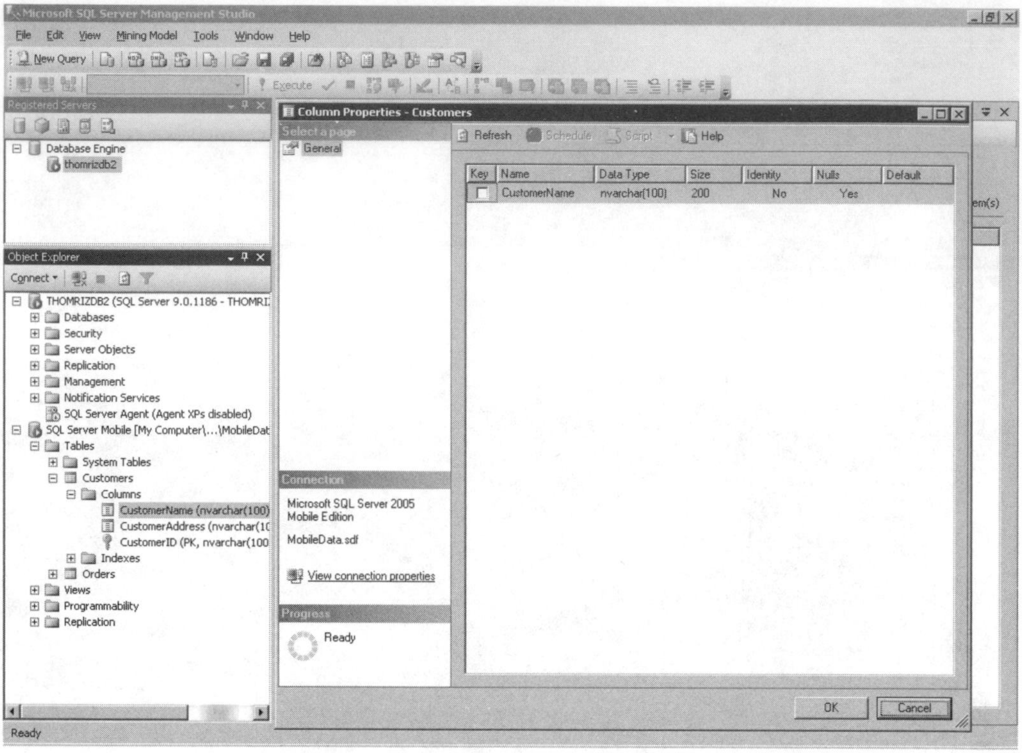

Figure 2-3. *SQL Server Mobile Edition support*

SQL Server 2000 Support

Management Studio supports administering both SQL Server 2005 and SQL Server 2000 servers. Features that are not supported by SQL Server 2000 such as database mirroring will, of course, not appear in Management Studio. This allows you to use one tool to manage a mixed environment that contains both versions of the database servers.

User Interface Enhancements

Beyond connecting to multiple components, Management Studio introduces a number of new user interface features. Hopefully, these user interface enhancements fix some of the pet peeves of DBAs. For example, have you ever wanted to open more than one dialog box in Enterprise Manager (EM)? Unfortunately you can't in EM, but you can in SSMS. In this section, we'll step through some of these SSMS user interface enhancements.

Asynchronous Treeview and Object Filtering

If you've worked with a large number of objects in Enterprise Manager, you know that when you expand the treeview on the left-hand side, you can step away for a cup of coffee, have a quick game of Ping-Pong with your fellow DBAs, and check the SQL Server newsgroups, all in the time it takes for EM to return the information. With Management Studio, loading objects is done asynchronously, so you can start opening an object that has many children while simultaneously performing other activities in the user interface.

Another enhancement is the ability to do *rich filtering* in many of the views in Management Studio. To filter, you just right-click the object container you are interested in filtering and select Filter. Filters do not persist between shutdowns of SSMS. For example, you can filter tables based on characters contained in the name of the table or the schema name, or based on the creation date of the table, as shown in Figure 2-4.

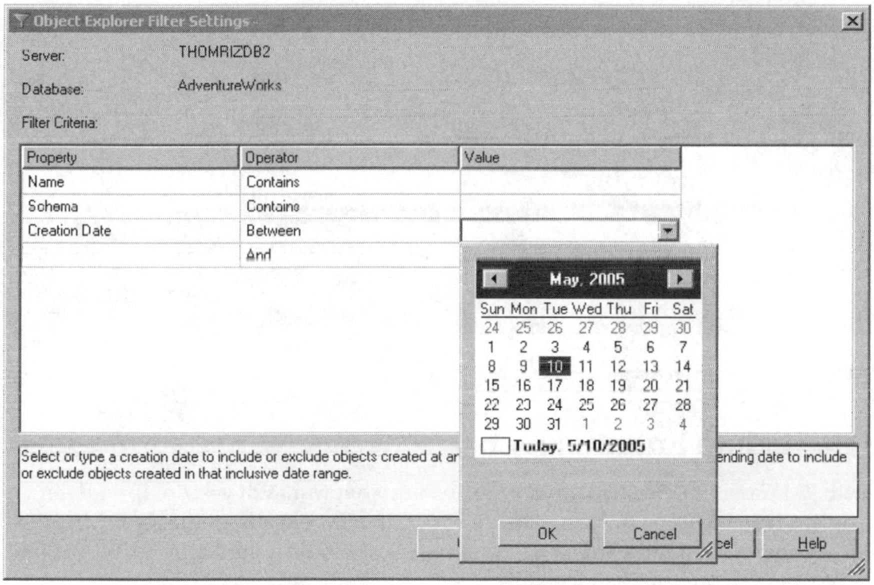

Figure 2-4. *Filtering objects*

Nonmodal and Resizable Dialog Boxes

I've lost count of the number of times I've heard a DBA curse EM for its modal mode of operation. One of the most requested features for EM was the ability to have multiple dialog boxes open at once. Among other things, this would allow the DBA to compare settings side-by-side for two objects. Management Studio includes this capability and also allows resizing of the dialog boxes. Figure 2-5 shows the new dialog box user interface in Management Studio with multiple dialog boxes open.

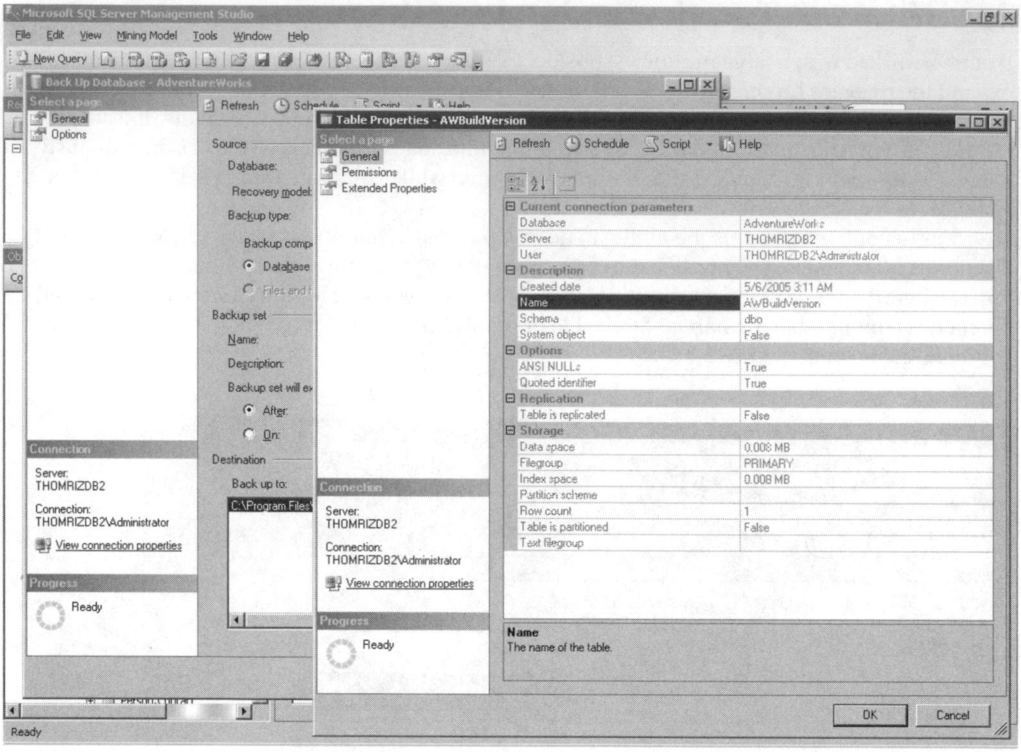

Figure 2-5. *The new dialog box interface*

Script and Schedule Enhancements

Another issue with EM was that DBAs had no way of knowing what work EM was doing on their behalf. For example, a DBA might be interested in knowing what EM did automatically behind the scenes as a result of certain user interface dialog box settings, so he could write scripts to do the same thing that could be executed on a defined schedule.

With Management Studio, you no longer have to fire up Profiler and start a trace, and then run EM to see what commands are sent to the server. Instead, right from the user interface, you can tell Management Studio to take what it would send to the server, based on your settings in the user interface, and instead script out the commands to the file system, to the clipboard, or to a new query window, or schedule them to execute at a later time.

Beyond scripting enhancements, you can now schedule the commands the server would run based on your dialog box settings. Management Studio creates an agent job to run at whatever time you schedule. This is useful if the server is busy and you want to have the actions run at another time when the server is less busy, or you want to have the script that the dialog box creates run on a recurring basis. In addition, multiple jobs can share the same schedule in the new SQL Server Agent, which minimizes the management of scheduling for you. Figure 2-6 shows how to create a scheduled job, based on the settings of a dialog box.

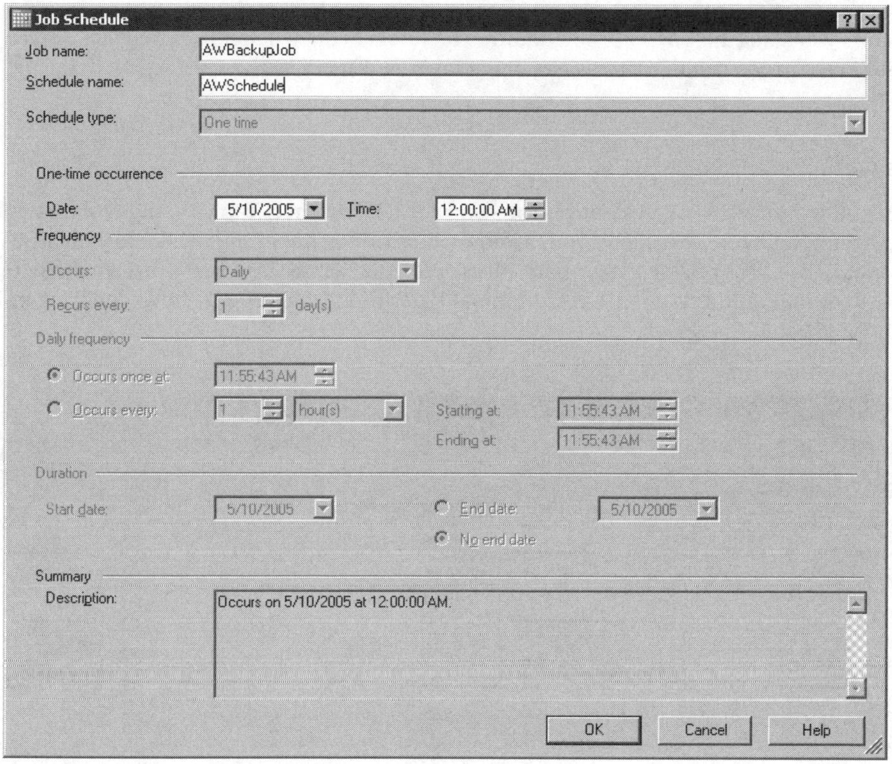

Figure 2-6. *Scheduling a backup job*

The first step to create your scheduled backup is to right-click the database you want to back up, select Tasks, and then select Back Up. From there, fill out the properties in the dialog box, such as the type of backup (full or differential) and the destination to which you want to back up. Scheduling the backup is as easy as clicking the Schedule button at the top of the form.

If you take a look at the code generated by Management Studio to back up your database, you can see the commands that Management Studio will send to the server. You can take the following T-SQL that Management Studio generates and use it in your own applications, or just look through it to see T-SQL best practices or learn how Management Studio performs its functionality against the server.

```
BACKUP DATABASE [AdventureWorks] TO  DISK =
N'c:\AdventureWorks.bak' WITH NOFORMAT, NOINIT,  NAME =
N'AdventureWorks-Full Database Backup', SKIP, NOREWIND,
NOUNLOAD,  STATS = 10
GO
```

Code Authoring

If you spend most of your time writing SQL Server code—whether you use T-SQL, Multidimensional Expressions (MDX), XML for Analysis (XML/A), or Data Mining Extensions (DMX)—you will be happy to know that all these languages are supported in Management Studio. SSMS also supports dynamic help, so as you write your code, the relevant topics from SQL Server Books Online are displayed to help you along the way. One new addition to the set of query languages that SQL Server supports, both in the product and in the management tools, is XQuery, which we cover in detail in Chapter 5.

Source Control

SSMS is tightly integrated with source control. You can check in and check out virtually everything inside of Management Studio. This allows you to know who made a change and when they made it, and to roll back to a previous version if necessary. Please note that SSMS supports Visual SourceSafe (VSS) and other source control systems that are compatible with VSS. Figure 2-7 shows checking in a script file in SSMS.

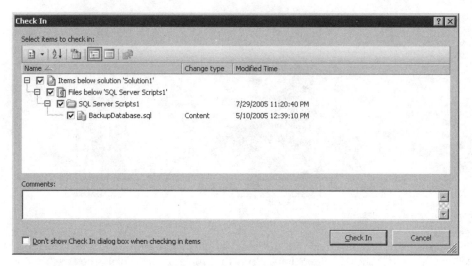

Figure 2-7. *Using the check-in functionality in SSMS*

Template Explorer

SSMS brings with it a greatly enhanced Template Explorer. SQL Server 2005 ships with templates for the database engine, Analysis Services, and SQL Server Mobile Edition. These templates cover the most common operations that you will want to perform from a code perspective, such as creating databases, stored procedures, triggers, and so forth. As you can see in Figure 2-8, SSMS supports many different templates to help you manage your server. Plus, Template Explorer is customizable in that you can add your own folders and templates. Therefore, you can take your best templates and put them in Template Explorer so they are always available to you. To do this, just right-click the folder in Template Explorer where you want to create your template, select New, and then select Template. From there, just write your code like you would any other script and save it. Now you have a template.

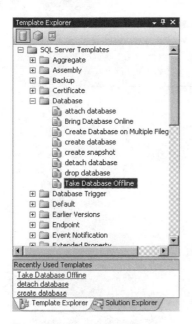

Figure 2-8. *Template Explorer*

When writing queries, Management Studio supports both an *offline* mode and a *SQLCMD* mode. In offline mode, you can be disconnected from the server to write your queries. SQLCMD will be covered in more detail later in the chapter, but for now you should know that in SQLCMD mode, you can write SQLCMD commands directly in SSMS, giving you the editor experience of SSMS and the ability to debug your SQLCMD code without having to run SQLCMD at the command line.

Autosave

The final enhancement is autosave. Since SSMS leverages the VS shell, you get recoverability built in. Therefore, if SSMS crashes, you will be prompted on the next startup to recover any work from your previous SSMS session.

Results Pane

You'll continue to see your familiar grid results window with SSMS, but there are a couple of useful additions. First, you can now print directly from the results pane. Second, XML results are now hyperlinked and can be opened in a separate window. This separate window is actually an XML editor, so you can modify your XML in a richer way. The only downside is that even if you modify the XML, there is no automatic save back to the database. You will have to save the XML to a file and import it, or write T-SQL code to insert it back into the database. Figure 2-9 shows the new linked XML result in SSMS.

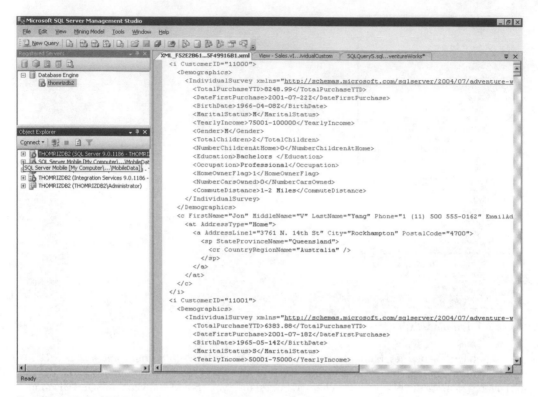

Figure 2-9. *Linked XML results open in an XML editor in SSMS*

Activity Monitor

To see activity in the system such as processes and locks, you normally use the Activity Monitor, which is located in Object Explorer under the Management node. With SQL Server 2005, the Activity Monitor has been enhanced to support both filtering and automatic refresh, both of which are useful when you are running large, complex SQL Server systems that may have many processes running on a single server.

Summary Views

For those of you who have used the Taskpad feature in EM, Summary Views will not look much different to you. The main difference is that Summary Views leverage a new user interface that can display information using either a listview or the new SQL Server 2005 Reporting Services report controls. Some of the most interesting reports are associated with the dynamic management view features, which you will learn about later in this chapter. Figure 2-10 shows the new Summary Views technology.

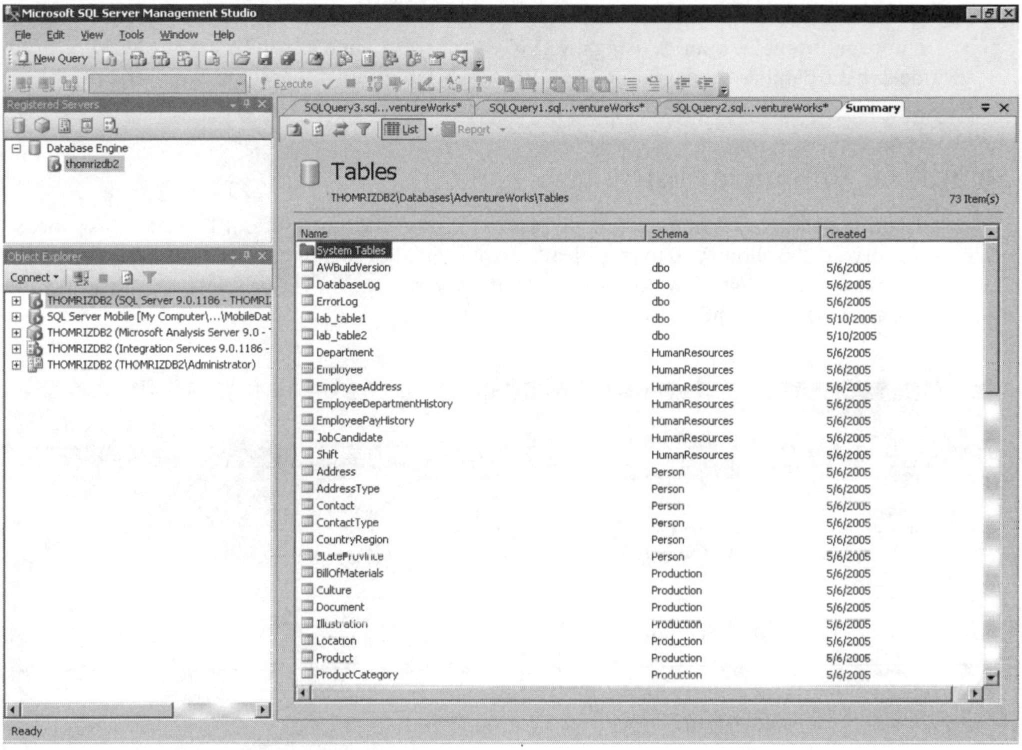

Figure 2-10. *Summary Views show vital information about database objects.*

Functional Enhancements

Management Studio is about a lot more than a few interface enhancements. It brings functional enhancements and new, often timesaving, capabilities. We'll look at some of these in this section.

Dedicated Administrator Connection

Have you ever had a server where the CPU was maxed out and you could not connect to the server to kill off the query that was consuming all the resources? If so, the dedicated administrator connection (DAC) may well become your favorite feature of SQL Server 2005. Whenever the server starts up, SQL reserves some resources for administrators to connect to the server.

Using the DAC, you can connect to the server or SQLCMD through SSMS. You can have only one DAC open at a time to a server. Therefore, you cannot use tools that open other connections in SSMS, such as the Activity Monitor or multiple explorers, such as Object Explorer and the Query Editor. The DAC uses a special prefix when you pass your instance name: `ADMIN:`. For example, if your instance is `SERVER\INSTANCE`, then to use the DAC you would use `ADMIN:SERVER\INSTANCE`.

A couple other things you should be aware of with the DAC as follows:

- Only members of the sysadmin role can use it.

- Out of the box, you can run the DAC only on the server. To enable network connections using the DAC, you can use `sp_configure` and set the remote admin connections option to true or 1.

- You can query dynamic management views, catalog views, or system processes.

- Do not run intensive queries using the DAC connection, such as running complex joins or re-indexing the database. It has limited resources associated with it that should be used only for debugging and killing off spids (using the KILL command) that may be bogging down the server.

Deadlock Visualization

Troubleshooting deadlocks is often a difficult process in any database system. To make this process easier, SQL Server 2005 allows you to graphically display deadlocks in the system, as shown in Figure 2-11. You can use this graphical representation to quickly track down why the system is deadlocking and take steps to minimize the deadlocks in the system.

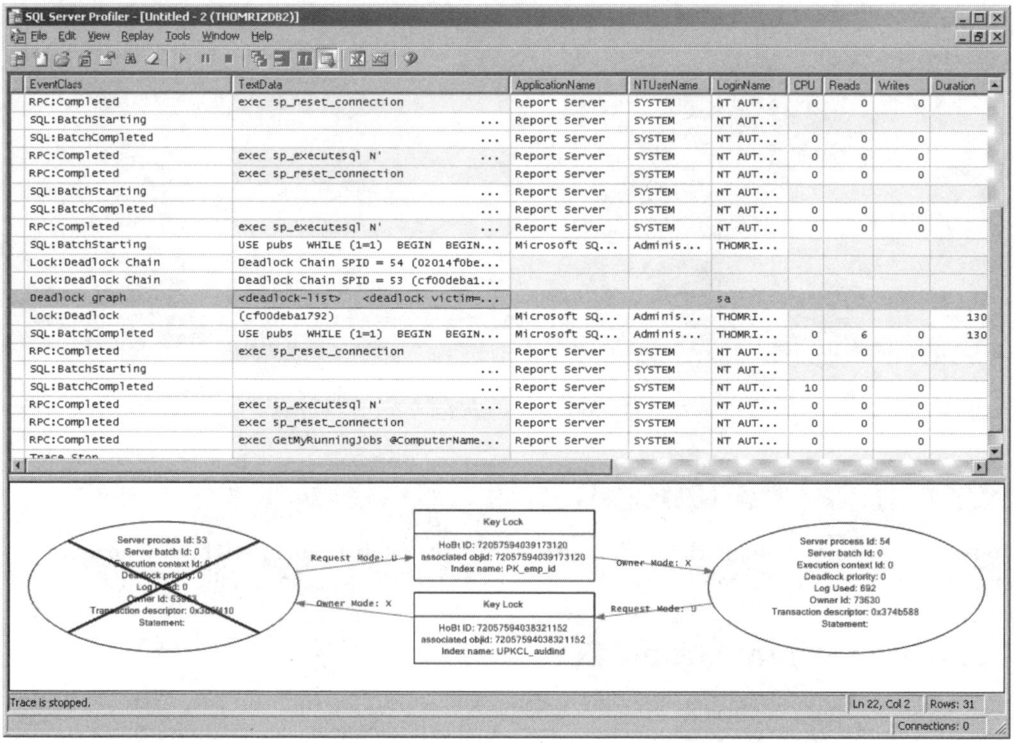

Figure 2-11. *Deadlock visualization*

As you can see in Figure 2-11, the deadlock graph includes the process ID, which will be important since you will use that ID to kill off one of the processes caught in the deadlock. Normally, SQL Server handles deadlocking automatically. The server will pick a victim if it needs to and end the process. However, if you find the system is not ending the deadlock, you can kill the deadlocked process yourself through the Activity Monitor. The important thing about deadlocks is not to get them after they happen—you should write your code to avoid having them happen at all, if possible. Follow good practices like keeping your transactions short and single batched, accessing objects in the same order every time, and using the new SNAPSHOT isolation level to try to prevent locking.

Performance Monitor Correlation

There may be times when you see spikes in Performance Monitor on your SQL Server machine, such as a high CPU usage, a large amount of memory consumption, or overall slower performance. You might be scratching your head, wondering what happened in SQL Server to cause this performance anomaly. Before SQL Server 2005, you would have to use Profiler to capture a trace; use sysprocesses that you looked at in Enterprise Manager; and capture your Performance Monitor logs, which required you to fire up Performance Monitor. After doing all this across all these different tools, you would need to manually reconcile what happened between them to figure out why performance was suffering in the system, which meant slogging second-by-second through each of the logs returned. Not a very fun experience, but it was useful if you wanted to get to the bottom of your performance problems.

With SQL Server 2005, you still need to capture a trace and examine your Performance Monitor logs. However, Profiler now lets you attach Performance Monitor logs. It will then scroll through your T-SQL statements and automatically show you, graphically, what happened in your Performance Monitor logs. The scrolling also works if you click in the Performance Monitor user interface in Profiler, which jumps you to the statement that correlates to that timestamp. This capability will save you time in troubleshooting your SQL Server environment. Figure 2-12 shows an example of Performance Monitor correlation in Profiler, where the vertical line in the chart is the point where the highlighted event occurred.

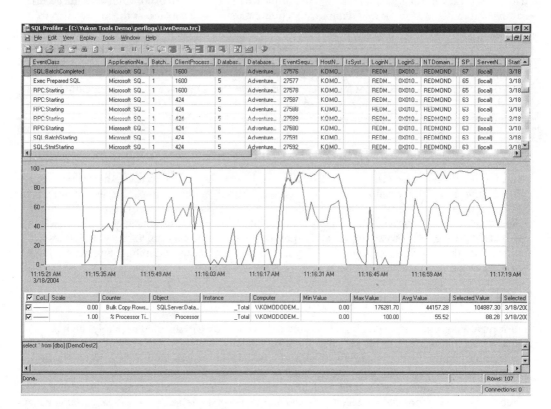

Figure 2-12. *Performance Monitor correlation*

Let's now see how to do a Performance Monitor correlation in SQL Server 2005:

1. Start Performance Monitor and begin capturing some information from the database server. The fastest way to start Performance Monitor is to go to the Start menu, click Run, type **perfmon**, and press Enter.

2. From there, you'll want to create a new counter log under Performance Logs and Alerts by right-clicking the Counter Logs node and selecting New Log Settings. Enter the name for your new log.

3. Click the Add Counters button and add new counters, such as **% Processor Time**. You'll also want to schedule your logging to start either manually or on a scheduled basis using the Schedule tab.

4. Once you're done, click OK and make sure to start your logging if you select to use the manual start option.

Next, you'll want to set up a trace on your SQL Server through Profiler. You can do this by clicking New Trace under the File menu in Profiler. Make sure to include the StartTime and EndTime in your trace. Name your trace, and make sure to set it to save the trace to a file.

Finally, you can blast your server to simulate some SQL activity. The easiest thing to do is to use the SQL Server Integration Services (SSIS) import/export wizard to export the AdventureWorks sample database and import that database to a new database. You can access the import/export wizard by right-clicking the AdventureWorks database in Management Studio and then selecting Export Data. Once this is done, you can stop capturing in both Performance Monitor and Profiler. Close the trace file as well.

In Profiler, select Import Performance Data from the File menu. Select the location where you stored your Performance Monitor log. Then, select File ➤ Open ➤ Trace. Select the location where you stored your Profiler trace. Now, you can use Performance Monitor correlation between the two to figure out what effect on the processor a certain SQL statement had.

Server Registration Import/Export

Another pet peeve of many SQL Server 2000 DBAs is the inability to import and export server registration information. For example, imagine you get all your server registrations just right in EM. Then you bring up another machine that you want to use to manage your servers, or you rebuild your client machine. Well, guess what—you have to re-create all your registrations on your new machine. With SQL Server 2005, you can import and export server registrations from SSMS. Plus, it does not matter what the type of server registration—you can import and export database engine, Analysis Services, or Reporting Services registrations.

Maintenance Plan Designer

DBAs have a common set of database operations that need to be performed regularly, such as backups, shrinking, integrity checks, and updating statistics. With SQL Server 2000, you could use the Database Maintenance Wizard to create and schedule these tasks. With SQL Server 2005, the Database Maintenance Wizard still exists, but it is now called *Maintenance Plans*.

The Maintenance Plan Designer, which you can launch from the Maintenance Plans node under the Management node in SSMS, is based on the new SSIS designer. This means that you can draw out your administrative tasks in a graphical workflow and define different courses of action based on whether the tasks succeed or fail. Within the Maintenance Plan Designer, you can perform several different tasks, such as running agent jobs or T-SQL scripts. With this level of flexibility, you can use the Maintenance Plan Designer to draw out most of the workflow used for database maintenance. Figure 2-13 shows the Maintenance Plan Designer.

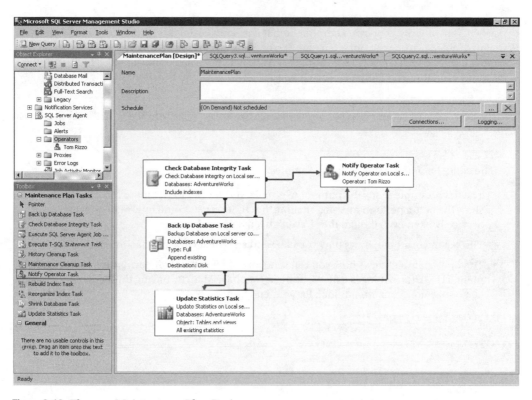

Figure 2-13. *The new Maintenance Plan Designer*

SQL Server Agent Changes

SQL Server Agent, which is a Windows service that executes scheduled administrative tasks, has been vastly improved in SQL Server 2005. First, scalability has been improved so that Agent can run more jobs while consuming fewer resources in the system. Second, it now supports Analysis Services commands and SSIS packaged execution in addition to its previous support of T-SQL commands. Finally, Agent now supports Windows Management Instrumentation (WMI) alerts beyond just SQL Server alerts and SQL Server performance condition alerts. You can pass in any WMI query that you want SQL Server to listen on. For example, you could use WMI to query server information outside of SQL Server, such as CPU or memory information. This topic is covered extensively in Chapter 13.

Database Mail

No more MAPI. Yes, you read that right: no more MAPI. If you've ever set up SQLMail, you know that you need to get MAPI onto your server and that MAPI can sometimes be fickle. SQL Server 2005 introduces Database Mail, which is SMTP based, not MAPI based. Beyond removing the MAPI requirement, Database Mail has been integrated with the new Service Broker technology so that mail is queued and handled asynchronously and applications do not have to wait for the mail to be sent before continuing. This will allow you to scale your applications that use Database Mail. Finally, Database Mail is 64-bit enabled, cluster aware, supports HTML mail, and allows you to specify more than one SMTP server as a failover account.

There is a caveat, though, regarding Database Mail that will require you to keep SQLMail around even in SQL Server 2005: Database Mail cannot read mail. This means that if you have applications that need to read mail from a SQL Server stored procedure or other server-side code, you will need to use SQLMail or write your own component that reads mail using Collaboration Data Objects (CDO) or WebDAV to access your Exchange Server. Let's take a look at how you would write some code that uses Database Mail. This code does not show all the features of Database Mail, so if you want to see even more functionality you can use, we'll point you to SQL Books Online.

Note Before running the following code, you need to run the Configure Database Mail Wizard in the SQL Server Surface Area Configurator.

The code that follows shows three examples.

- The first example sends the number of e-mails you specify to Database Mail. This is just to show the better performance of e-mailing in SQL Server 2005 and how mails are queued using Service Broker, even though they haven't been delivered yet.

- The second example shows how you can send an e-mail with an attachment.

- The final example shows how you can send an e-mail with HTML formatting and an attachment. HTML formatting is a new feature in Database Mail. By having this capability, you can customize how your e-mails look for your end users.

```
/**********************************/
/* Send @lots of emails           */
/**********************************/

DECLARE @i         INT
       ,@lots      INT
       ,@subject   NVARCHAR(100)
       ,@start_time DATETIME

SET @lots = 5
SET @start_time = GETDATE()

SET @i = 1
WHILE(@i <= @lots)
BEGIN
      SET @subject = 'Demo Message ' + CAST(@i AS VARCHAR)
      EXECUTE sendimail_sp @profile_name  = 'TestProfile'
         ,@recipients     = 'user1@thomrizdomain.com'
         ,@body           = 'My Test Message'
         ,@subject        = @subject
      SET @i = @i + 1
END

PRINT 'Sent ' + CAST(@i-1 AS VARCHAR) + ' e-mails in ' +
CAST(DATEDIFF(ms, @start_time, GETDATE())/1000.0 AS VARCHAR) +
' seconds'
GO
```

```
/************************************/
/* Send an email with an attachment  */
/************************************/

EXECUTE sendimail_sp
        @profile_name  = 'TestProfile'
        ,@recipients    = 'user1@thomrizdomain.com'
        ,@body          = 'Attached is the result of sysprocesses.
           Danger! Will Robinson!  Danger!'
        ,@subject       = 'Result of sysprocesses'
        ,@query         = 'SELECT spid, status, loginame FROM sysprocesses'
        ,@attach_query_result_as_file = 1
GO


/*****************************************/
/* Send an HTML email with an attachment  */
/*****************************************/

EXECUTE sendimail_sp
      @profile_name        = 'TestProfile'
      ,@recipients          = 'user1@thomrizdomain.com'
      ,@body                =     '<BODY><H1><CENTER>Sunshine!</CENTER></H1></BODY>'
         ,@subject           = 'To brighten your day'
         ,@file_attachments  = 'C:\sunshine.jpg'
         ,@body_format       = 'HTML'
GO
```

Catalog Views and Dynamic Management Views

Users of SQL Server 2000 were accustomed to querying system tables such as sysprocesses, sysobjects, syslocks, and syslockinfo to investigate what processes, objects, and locks existed in the database server. In SQL Server 2005, these become *system catalog views*. Several views have been added that have no equivalent in the old SQL Server 2000 system tables, for example:

- sys.modules: This view is used to find details of the modules loaded into SQL Server.

- sys.assemblies: This view is used to find out what .NET assemblies are loaded into the server.

- sys.sysprocesses: Information contained in this view can be used to build customized views for waits, connections, and other information about processes running on an instance of the database server.

Catalog views expose the metadata that the server uses. Many DBAs have hacked their way around the system tables in SQL Server 2000 to get at metadata information. This is a bad practice since the tables can change in future versions, as they have in SQL Server 2005. With catalog views, rather than going directly to the tables, you use the views. Therefore, when the tables change underneath, your queries do not break, since compatibility is maintained with the view.

Dynamic management views, on the other hand, allow you to peek into the server as it's running. The way you can tell the difference between a catalog view and a dynamic management view is that a dynamic management view is prefixed with sys.dm_. Think of dynamic management views as runtime information about your database server that is not persisted to disk, such as locks, threads, and tasks. System views, on the other hand, are the persisted information about your tables, sprocs, and constraints. Before using dynamic management views, you need to have the right permissions to view them. For server-wide dynamic management views, you need the VIEW SERVER STATE permission. For database-scoped dynamic management views, you need the VIEW DATABASE STATE permission. You can grant or deny these permissions using the GRANT or REVOKE keywords.

One of the interesting new SSMS features that takes advantage of dynamic management views is Summary Views. Using the Report drop-down in SSMS, you can see the built-in reports that use dynamic management views to diagnose long-running queries, queries that are taking a lot of memory, and other system diagnostic information. Unfortunately, these reports are not customizable in SSMS, but Microsoft is considering pulling these reports out of SSMS and letting you run them in Reporting Services, which would make them customizable. Figure 2-14 shows dynamic management view reports in SSMS.

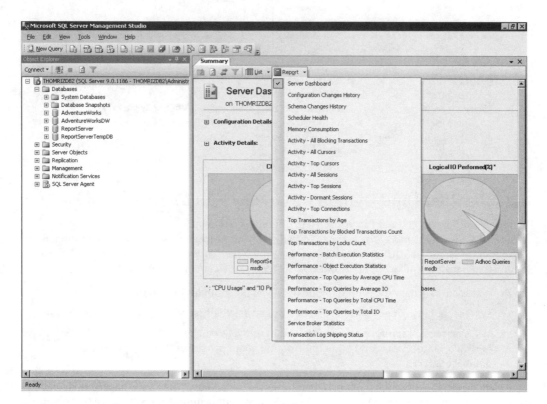

Figure 2-14. *Dynamic management view reports in SSMS*

You can also schedule an agent job to run to query the dynamic management views on a regular basis to collect performance information and place this information into a data warehouse. Off the data warehouse, you can use Reporting Services to figure out chart trending information for your systems (see Chapter 7 for more information on Reporting Services). Figure 2-15 shows using the new dynamic management views.

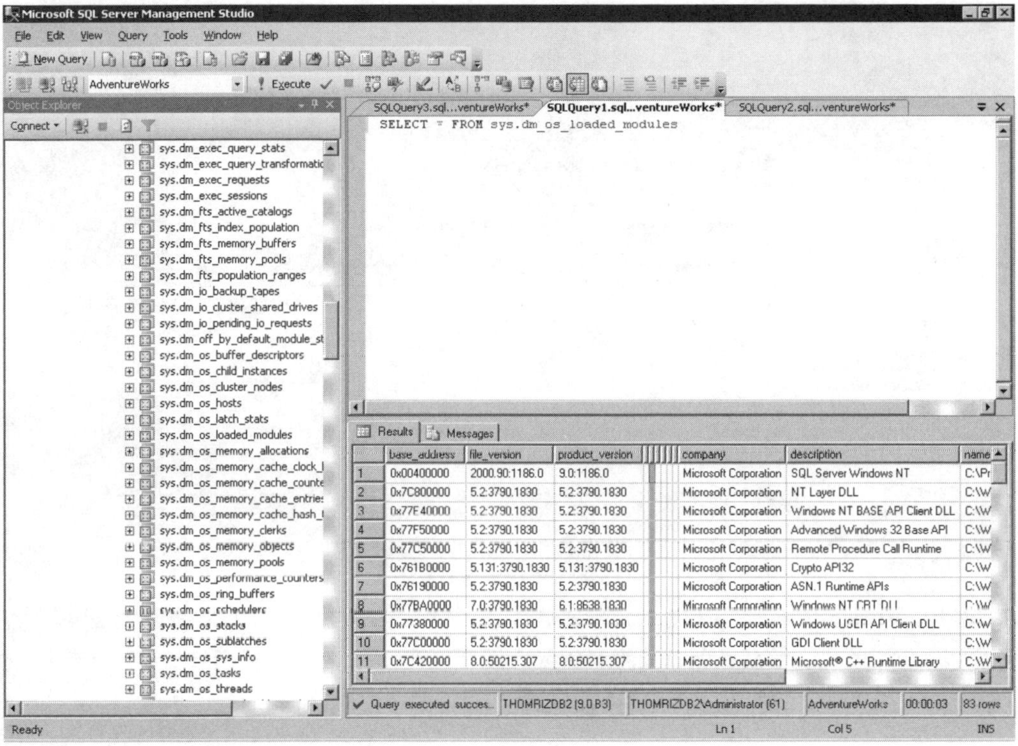

Figure 2-15. *Dynamic management views*

Default Server Trace

To enable tracking of server configuration changes over time, SQL Server 2005 allows you to turn on a default server trace. Some of the reports in SSMS that you saw in the previous section use this default trace to display these changes in a graphical way. You can open the trace file using Profiler or by running the following T-SQL command:

```
SELECT *
FROM fn_trace_gettable
('C:\Program Files\Microsoft SQL Server\MSSQL.1\MSSQL\LOG\log.trc', default)
GO
```

As its name implies, default trace is on by default. You can turn off default trace using sp_configure. Since default trace is located under the advanced options, you do need to first enable showing advanced options in sp_configure. The following script does this for you and disables the default trace:

```
sp_configure 'show advanced options', 1
reconfigure
GO

sp_configure 'default trace enabled',0
reconfigure
GO
```

Figure 2-16 shows the SSMS report that uses the default trace capabilities.

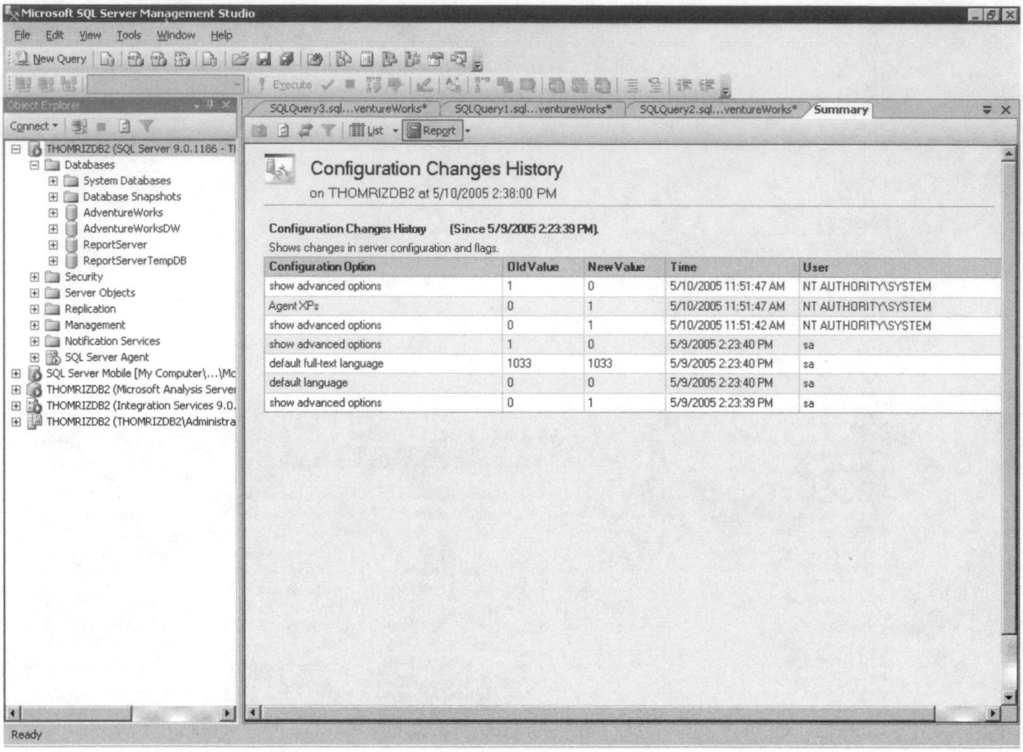

Figure 2-16. *Default trace report in SSMS*

Profiler Enhancements

With SQL Server 2005, Profiler gets an overhaul as well. The new Profiler supports the ability to trace both SSIS and Analysis Services commands. SQL Server 2000 was limited to tracing relational database calls only. With these capabilities, you can use traces to debug any problems you have in these additional components of SQL Server. Also, Performance Monitor correlation works with these new trace types.

Profiler allows you to save the trace file as XML. Furthermore, a traced ShowPlan result can be saved as XML and then loaded into Management Studio for analysis.

Finally, Profiler also integrates with the new Database Tuning Advisor (DTA), which replaces the Index Tuning Wizard. The DTA has a rich, new interface and works with the newer features in SQL Server 2005, such as recommending partitioning your tables using the new table partitioning features in the database engine. This topic is covered in detail in Chapter 13.

SQL Configuration Manager

Say good-bye to the Client Network Utility, Server Network Utility, and SQL Service Manager, and say hello to SQL Configuration Manager. The SQL Configuration Manager supports a number of different versions of SQL Server, including SQL Server 2000 and SQL Server 7.0, and components other than just the relational engine, such as Analysis Services and Reporting Services. The SQL Configuration Manager is a single interface where you can see whether your services are running and how the connectivity is configured to your SQL components.

SQL Configuration Manager is MMC based and can be launched stand-alone or as part of the Configuration Manager interface. Yes, MMC still is used in some parts of SQL Server management, but for the most part you will be using the new Management Studio interface. By integrating with the Configuration Manager, you can see your SQL information, such as protocol settings and service status, as part of your overall system information. Plus, SQL Configuration Manager uses WMI to talk to SQL Server, so it does not have to make queries to databases to get its information.

Figure 2-17 shows the new SQL Configuration Manager and its integration into the overall Computer Manager. You can also use the SQL Configuration Manager in its own console window rather than through Computer Manager.

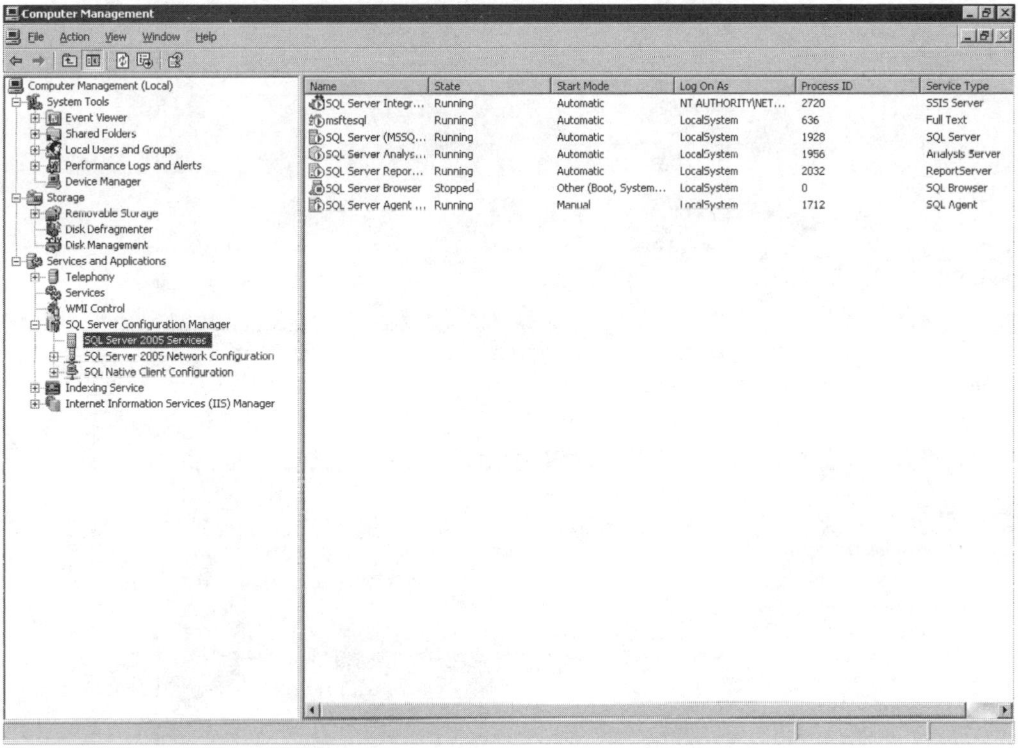

Figure 2-17. *The new SQL Configuration Manager*

Surface Area Configurator

A new tool in your SQL Server arsenal is the Surface Area Configurator (SAC). By default, SQL Server installs with the least amount of services and features enabled. For example, SQL Agent, SQLCLR, and web services support are all off by default. Using SAC, you can go in and turn on these disabled features and services. Everything you can do in SAC, you can also do via SQL commands. SAC runs in two modes, with the first being configuration for services and connections, as shown in Figure 2-18. The second is configuration for features, as shown in Figure 2-19.

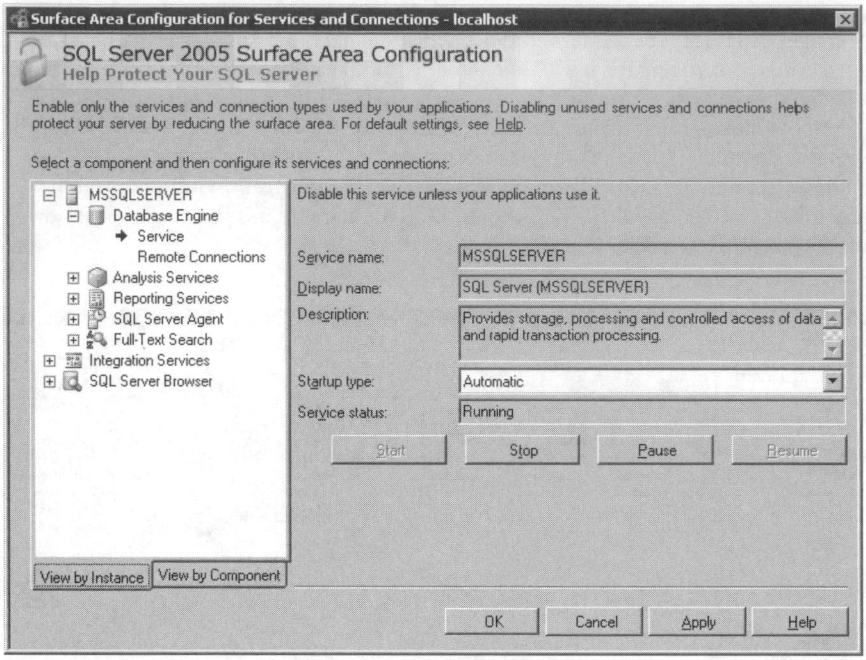

Figure 2-18. *SAC configuring services and connections*

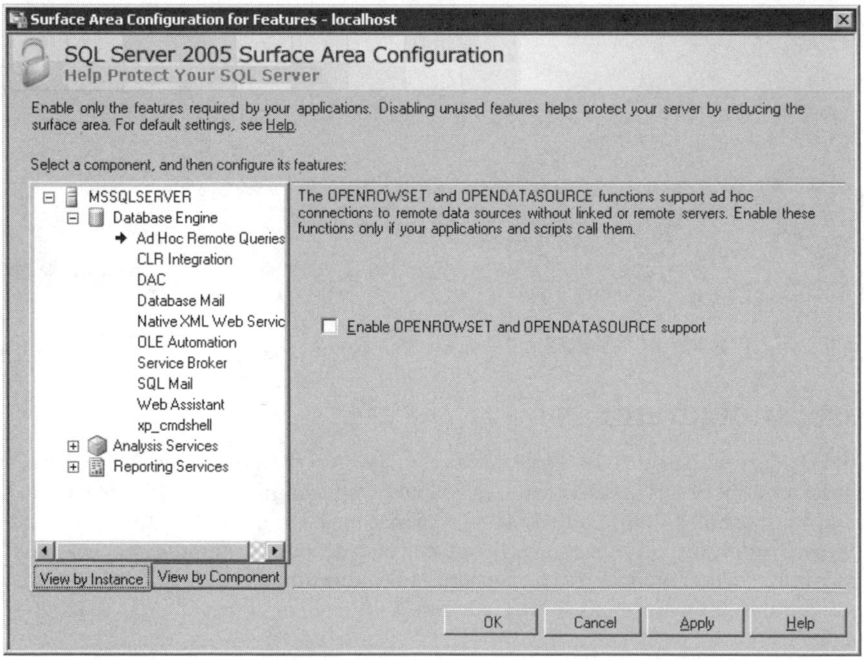

Figure 2-19. *SAC configuring features*

Enhanced Help and Community Integration

One of our favorite features is the new dynamic help that is tightly integrated with the SQL community as part of Management Studio. If you've used Visual Studio, you already know about dynamic help. SQL Server 2005 can watch what you're doing in Management Studio and, as you perform tasks, the dynamic help window changes to offer topics that may interest you for your current task. For example, as you are clicking through the treeview to manage your server, dynamic help displays a link to the help on managing your server.

Ask any technologist what his or her favorite tools are when working with Microsoft technologies, and Books Online, a web search engine, MSDN or TechNet, third-party SQL Server websites, and the Microsoft newsgroups will almost always be mentioned. The reason for all these different resources is that they each contain a wealth of information or at least access to a wealth of information. Through the new help system, SQL Server 2005 combines all of these tools into a single location. From the help, you can search not only Books Online locally, but also MSDN online and SQL community sites. Also, if you have a question, you can post it to the newsgroups to try and get it answered. You can determine whether you want Books Online results to appear in the main user interface as shown in Figure 2-20, or you can make the other results, such as community search results, the primary results, as shown in Figure 2-21.

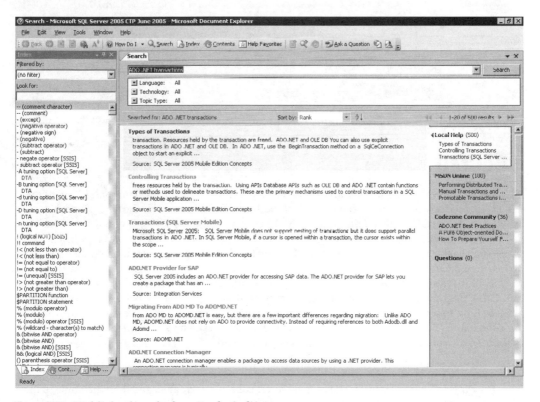

Figure 2-20. *Highlighted results from Books Online*

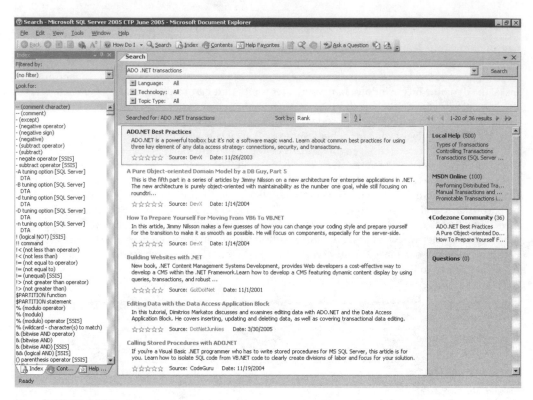

Figure 2-21. *Highlighted results from third-party community sites*

SQLCMD

Replacing osql, which still ships with SQL Server 2005, is the new SQLCMD command-line utility. Unlike its predecessors, SQLCMD uses the SQL Native Client, in particular the OLE DB provider when used from the command line and the .NET SQL provider from SSMS, to connect and run the T-SQL batches that you type into the tool. Plus, SQLCMD supports newer features in SQL Server 2005, such as the ability to connect to a server using the dedicated administration connection that we discussed earlier.

SQLCMD also allows you to place parameters in your scripts and then pass those parameters to SQLCMD programmatically. For example, you may want to script database backup, but you may not want to have to write a script for every database or every backup device. Instead, you may want to pass the name of the database and the name of the device to which to back up the database. With SQLCMD, the script would contain the following line of code:

```
BACKUP DATABASE $(db) TO DISK = "$(path)\$(db).bak"
```

The dollar sign ($) tells SQLCMD that the script contains a variable, and then the name of the variable is contained in parentheses. When you call SQLCMD, you can use the new -v parameter to pass in the appropriate values for your script variables. For example, from the SQLCMD command line, you could run backup.sql to back up the AdventureWorks database to a local folder, as follows:

```
SQLCMD /E /i backup.sql /v db="AdventureWorks" path="c:\backups"
```

Upon execution of this command, SQLCMD will return the following response:

```
Processed 17112 pages for database 'AdventureWorks',
file 'AdventureWorks_Data' on file 1. Processed 2 pages for
database 'AdventureWorks', file 'AdventureWorks_Log' on file 1.
BACKUP DATABASE successfully processed 17114 pages
in 50.374 seconds (2.783 MB/sec).
```

You can also set variables in your scripts, whereby one script loads another script, possibly to dynamically set variables from the second script. For example, you may want to take the backup example and connect to 50 servers with 100 databases. You could use variables to quickly write a SQLCMD script to perform this functionality. This topic is covered in much more detail in Chapter 13.

Server Management Objects

The final piece of new technology that we will look at for managing SQL Server 2005 is the new administration object model called Server Management Objects (SMO). This section will introduce you to SMO, and Chapter 11 will provide more details on SMO. SMO is the successor to SQL-DMO. SMO supports all versions of SQL Server back to SQL Server 7.0, so you can use SMO as your primary API across multiple versions of SQL Server. SMO also allows you to automate the administration of new features in SQL Server 2005, including XML, web services, and snapshot isolation, as well as many of the other enhancements. The easiest way to learn about SMO is to look at a sample application.

The application you learn how to create is a simple object browser that will look at your databases, the tables contained in those databases, and then the scripts used to create the databases. The application is a Windows-based application written in C#.

To get started using SMO in Visual Studio, you need to first add a reference to the object model. You can do this using the Add Reference option off the Project menu. You will find SMO under the namespace Microsoft.SqlServer.SMO, as shown in Figure 2-22.

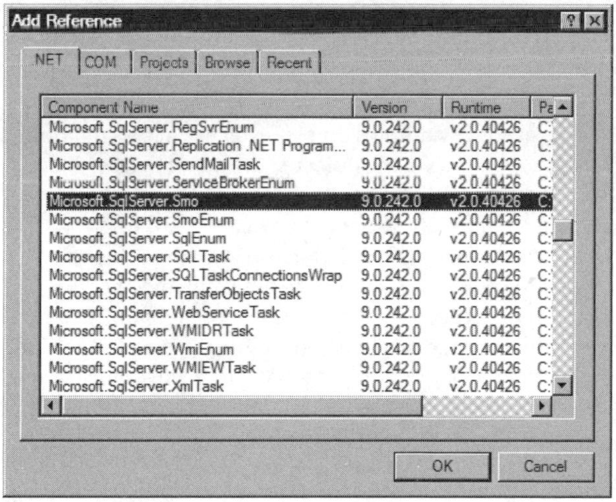

Figure 2-22. *Adding a reference to SMO in Visual Studio*

Now that you have your reference, you can start building the application. The application is a couple of simple buttons, list boxes, and text boxes, so you can skip over the user interface creation and instead jump to the code that implements the user interface functionality. Figure 2-23 shows the completed user interface in Visual Studio.

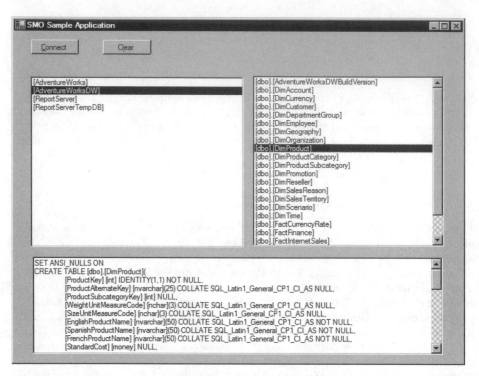

Figure 2-23. *The user interface for the SMO application*

To make it easier, you'll add a few using directives in your code for SMO, as well as other .NET Framework classes you will use. The code that follows does this:

```
using Microsoft.SqlServer.Management.Smo;
using System.Collections.Specialized;
using System.Text;
```

After setting your directives, the code declares some variables that you will use across methods. The first one declares a new Server object from SMO. The Server object is the factory class object from which other objects are created in SMO. For example, you can retrieve databases, tables, logins, and other database information from the children of the Server object.

Second, the code declares for arrays of different types such as Database and Table objects. We use fixed-length arrays here for simplicity, but you could use dynamic arrays using the ArrayList class. These arrays will hold the objects that the application uses for fast access to these object types. You can specify the server name if you have more than one server when calling the constructor for the Server object, or you can create a ServerConnection object and pass that along. Plus, you can use SQL authentication rather than Windows-based authentication.

```
Server srvSQLServer = new Server();
//You could also use dynamic arrays here
//with ArrayList
Database[] arrDBs = new Database[100];
Table[] arrTables = new Table[1000];
```

Now to the meat of the code. Let's take a look at what happens when you click the Connect button in the user interface. The first thing that occurs is the user interface and arrays are cleared of any existing information. Next, the code steps through all the Database objects in the Databases collection under the Server object. If the database is not a system database, which is checked by using the IsSystemObject property, the database is added to the array of Database objects:

```
private void btnConnect_Click(object sender, EventArgs e)
{
    listDatabases.Items.Clear();
    listTables.Items.Clear();
    txtSQLScript.Clear();
    ClearArray();
    listDatabases.DisplayMember = "Name";


    int i = 0;
    foreach(Database tmpdb in srvSQLServer.Databases){
        if (!tmpdb.IsSystemObject){
            listDatabases.Items.Add(tmpdb.ToString());
            arrDBs[i] = tmpdb;
            i++;
        }
    }

}
```

Next, when the user clicks a database in the user interface, the code walks through the tables in that database using the Tables collection and Table object under the Database object.

```
private void listDatabases_SelectedIndexChanged(object sender, EventArgs e)
{
    listTables.Items.Clear();
    txtSQLScript.Clear();
    listTables.DisplayMember = "ToString()";

    Database tmpdb = new Database();
    tmpdb = arrDBs[listDatabases.SelectedIndex];

    int i = 0;
    foreach (Table tmptable in tmpdb.Tables){
        if (tmptable.IsSystemObject != true){
            listTables.Items.Add(tmptable.ToString());
            arrTables[i] = tmptable;
            i++;
        }
    }
}
```

Finally, when the user selects a table in the user interface, the code uses the `Script` method to have SMO generate the T-SQL script to re-create the table.

```
private void listTables_SelectedIndexChanged(object sender, EventArgs e)
    {
        StringCollection sc = new StringCollection();

        //Get the table's script
        sc = arrTables[listTables.SelectedIndex].Script();

        StringBuilder sb = new StringBuilder();

        for (int i = 0; i < sc.Count; i++)
        {
            sb.AppendLine(sc[i]);
        }

        txtSQLScript.Text = sb.ToString();

    }
```

There you go—your first SMO application! Of course, this is a simple example of what you can do with SMO. As a developer, you will find that SMO is very functional and very approachable. One thing to note is that even though SMO is 100 percent written in .NET, SMO supports COM interoperability so that you can call SMO through your COM code (e.g., Visual Basic or VBScript).

Summary

In this chapter, we've taken a whirlwind tour of the new management technologies in SQL Server 2005. You've seen how SQL Server 2005 takes SQL Server management to the next level with new management tools, new APIs, and even new command-line tools. It's important that you get familiar with all of these technologies, since you will be using one or more of them to manage and monitor your servers.

■ ■ ■

CHAPTER 3

T-SQL Enhancements for Developers

With all of the excitement around the new .NET programming extensions to SQL Server 2005, it would be easy to overlook the new changes to Transact-SQL (T-SQL). As a matter of fact, Microsoft has made quite a few changes to T-SQL, and several of the changes are quite impressive (error handling and common table expressions are two of the most exciting) and take T-SQL to a whole new level of programming power and ease of use.

In this chapter, we have grouped the changes into four major categories:

- *Data Manipulation Language (DML)*: Changes to the base SQL statements used to manipulate data

- *General development*: Changes to programming extensions, like procedures and functions

- *Data Definition Language (DDL)*: Changes to commands used to define databases, tables, indexes, and so on

The examples in this chapter, and subsequent chapters, will be applicable to the new AdventureWorks database, the much improved test database that is shipped with SQL Server 2005. It has far more realistic data and is far more normalized than previous efforts.

Note One thing you should note about the AdventureWorks database: unlike previous versions of SQL Server demo databases, not every table is "owned" by dbo (database owner) any longer. Instead, all tables have been segmented into schemas such as HumanResources, Sales, Person, and Production. We discuss schemas in detail, but the key thing is that the schema is a container for objects in a database. Schemas and tables are owned by users in the database, but they are not part of the syntax as they were in previous versions. A schema of dbo does still exist and is the default, but best practices for future development will include the use of schemas.

Enhancements Affecting DML

Several really exciting changes have been made to the DML functionality in SQL Server 2005:

- *Old-style outer joins deprecated*: "=*" in a WHERE clause will now raise an error.

- TOP: This operator now allows you to do parameterized row counts, and works with more DML than just SELECT.

- *Common table expressions*: This ANSI 99 feature allows for recursion and code simplification.

- FROM *clause extensions*: New join types improve usability of derived tables and table-based functions.

- OUTPUT *clause*: Use this clause to get information on data that has changed.

- *Ranking functions*: Find positional information within a resultset through these functions.

- EXCEPT *and* INTERSECT: These set operators that provide the ability to compare sets of like data.

- *Synonyms*: These give you the ability to provide alternate names for database objects.

Each of these changes (especially the common table expressions) will make the base DML statements (INSERT, UPDATE, DELETE, SELECT) far more powerful and functional.

Old-Style Outer Joins Deprecated

This one should probably be in the title of the book, as it is going to be the most painful of all changes. Microsoft has said over and over, and book authors and experts (not always the same group, mind you) have said over and over: stop using non-ANSI-style joins, they will not be supported in a future version. Well, the future is now. For example:

```
USE AdventureWorks  --this is the default unless otherwise mentioned
GO
SELECT *
FROM   sales.salesPerson as salesPerson,
       sales.salesTerritory as salesTerritory
WHERE  salesperson.territoryId *= salesTerritory.territoryId
```

Trying this query will give you the following (really long and very descriptive) error message that says it as good as we could:

```
Msg 4147, Level 15, State 1, Line 5
The query uses non-ANSI outer join operators ("*=" or "=*"). To run this query
without modification, please set the compatibility level for current database to 80
or lower, using stored procedure sp_dbcmptlevel. It is strongly recommended to
rewrite the query using ANSI outer join operators (LEFT OUTER JOIN, RIGHT OUTER
JOIN). In the future versions of SQL Server, non-ANSI join operators will not be
supported even in backward-compatibility modes.
```

So what does this mean? It means that you need to rewrite your queries using ANSI join operators:

```
SELECT *
FROM   sales.salesPerson as salesPerson
          LEFT OUTER JOIN sales.salesTerritory as salesTerritory
               on salesperson.territoryId = salesTerritory.territoryId
```

Note that this restriction is only for outer joins, not for inner joins. For example:

```
SELECT  *
FROM    sales.salesPerson as salesPerson,
        sales.salesTerritory as salesTerritory
WHERE   salesperson.territoryId = salesTerritory.territoryId
```

works just fine and likely always will. Clearly you should code this using an INNER JOIN, but the preceding will work because this syntax is required for correlated subqueries.

■Note This may be an issue for many people who have not heeded the warnings over the years about the new join syntax. However, the old-style joins will still work if you change back into 80 Compatibility Mode (2000) or earlier using the sp_dbcmptlevel system stored procedure.

Common Table Expressions

The primary purpose of common table expressions (CTEs) is code simplification. They are loosely analogous to views in that they are defined as a single SELECT statement.

Once defined, they are used exactly like views. To illustrate, we'll take a look at a very simple example. The following query defines a CTE named simpleExample that contains a single column and row. Then a simple SELECT statement is issued to return the data defined by the CTE.

```
WITH simpleExample as
(
     SELECT 'hi' AS columnName
)

SELECT  columnName
FROM    simpleExample
```

which returns the following:

```
columnName
----------
hi
```

What makes the CTE significantly different from a view is that the CTE is not created as an object in the database and therefore is only available for this single statement. So in this sense, it will be treated by the compiler more or less as if you had coded a derived table (a named table expression that exists only for the duration of a query) as follows:

```
SELECT  columnName
FROM    (SELECT 'hi' AS columnName) AS simpleExample
```

This is an obviously simple example, but it serves to illustrate the basics of CTEs. If you needed to reference a given derived table in your query multiple times, this method would be of great help, since instead of recoding the query over and over, you would simply reference the CTE name. If the derived table was very large, it would *greatly* simplify the final query, so debugging the final result will be much easier.

The performance of the CTE should be on par with using derived tables. If you have queries where you use multiple derived queries, such queries will be evaluated multiple times. The same would be true for CTEs. In some cases, it will be better to use a temporary table to store the results of the query that you will use in the CTE, especially for complex CTEs that are used multiple times in a query.

There are two common uses for CTEs:

- *Simplify complex queries*: To encapsulate complex code in a way to make code cleaner

- *Create recursive queries*: To implement hierarchies traversing code in a single query (something not possible previously)

Simplifying Complex Queries

Consider the following scenario: the client has a need for a query that has queries to calculate salesperson totals year to date, compare that value to entire sales for the company, and then compare their sales to their quota for the year.

First, consider how this would be done using the SQL Server 2000 syntax. Each subset could be implemented as a derived table in a single query.

```
WITH YTDSalesPerson
AS
(
    SELECT  soh.SalesPersonID, sum(sod.LineTotal) as amount
    FROM    sales.SalesOrderHeader soh
              JOIN sales.SalesOrderDetail sod
                ON sod.SalesOrderID = soh.SalesOrderID
    WHERE   soh.Status = 5 -- complete
      and   soh.OrderDate >= '20040101'
    GROUP   by soh.SalesPersonID
)
SELECT  *
FROM    YTDSalesPerson
```

instead of having to deal with pulling out large sections of code from your original query. And say you make a correction or change to the calculation. It changes once and all usages change. All this without having to persist any data or objects. SQL Server does the real work! Consider also that the "black boxed" CTE works independently of the main query, so after testing it we won't have to worry if this part of the query works as we debug the larger query.

Using CTEs for Recursive Queries

The second use of CTEs allows for recursive hierarchies to be navigated without the need for complex recursion logic done manually. Hierarchies are common in real-world situations, such as employees and managers (managers are employees), or in manufacturing with parts within other parts (a automobile engine is a part, but it also consists of lots of other parts inside). However, using T-SQL, it was previously complicated to build queries that dealt with hierarchies. If the number of levels in a hierarchy was known beforehand, it was possible to use self-joins, but even this was very cumbersome. If you had unlimited numbers of levels, it was practically impossible.

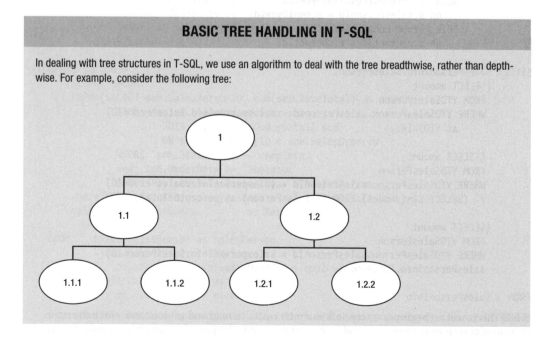

BASIC TREE HANDLING IN T-SQL

In dealing with tree structures in T-SQL, we use an algorithm to deal with the tree breadthwise, rather than depthwise. For example, consider the following tree:

In functional programming languages, it would have been common to recursively traverse a tree one node at a time, touching one node at a time. So you would go from node 1, to 1.1, to 1.1.1, back to 1.1, to 1.1.2, back to 1.1, back to 1, on to 1.2, etc. This works great for pointer-based languages, but in relational languages like T-SQL, a much better algorithm is to access all the children of a node in one query, then all the children of these nodes, and so on. So we would get node 1, then 1.1 and 1.2, and finally 1.1.1, 1.1.2, 1.2.1, and 1.2.2. It is a fantastic algorithm for dealing with sets, but in the following code sample, you will see that it was not very clean to implement in SQL Server 2000.

Take a look at an example that uses the employee table in the AdventureWorks database. This is a classic example of a single-parent hierarchy with the managerId column identifying all employees who report to a specified manager. Let's look at a typical breadthwise hierarchical query used in SQL Server 2000 to retrieve all employees who reported to the manager whose managerId was 140.

```
-- SQL Server 2000 example

DECLARE @managerId int
SET @managerId = 140

--holds the output treelevel, which lets us isolate a level in the looped query
DECLARE @outTable table (employeeId int, managerId int, treeLevel int)

--used to hold the level of the tree we are currently at in the loop
DECLARE @treeLevel as int
SET     @treelevel = 1

--get the top level
INSERT INTO @outTable
SELECT employeeId, managerId, @treelevel as treelevel
FROM   HumanResources.employee as employee
WHERE  (employee.managerId = @managerId)

WHILE (1 = 1) --imitates do...until construct
  BEGIN

    INSERT INTO @outTable
    SELECT employee.employeeId, employee.managerId,
           treelevel + 1 as treelevel
    FROM   HumanResources.employee as employee
             JOIN @outTable as ht
               ON employee.managerId = ht.employeeId
    --this where isolates a given level of the tree
    WHERE  EXISTS(    SELECT  *
                      FROM    @outTable AS holdTree
                      WHERE   treelevel = @treelevel
                         AND  employee.managerId = holdtree.employeeId)

    IF @@rowcount = 0
      BEGIN
          BREAK
      END
```

```
       SET @treelevel = @treelevel + 1
    END


SELECT    Employee.EmployeeID,Contact.LastName,Contact.FirstName
FROM      HumanResources.Employee as Employee
              INNER JOIN @outTable ot
                  ON Employee.EmployeeID = ot.EmployeeID
              INNER JOIN Person.Contact as Contact
                  ON Contact.contactId = Employee.contactId
```

Using CTEs, however, we get a much cleaner implementation:

```
-- SQL Server 2005 syntax
DECLARE @managerId int
SET @managerId = 140;

WITH EmployeeHierarchy (EmployeeId, ManagerId)
AS
(
    SELECT EmployeeID, ManagerID
    FROM   HumanResources.Employee as Employee
    WHERE  ManagerID=@managerId

    UNION ALL

    SELECT Employee.EmployeeID, Employee.ManagerID
    FROM   HumanResources.Employee as Employee
              INNER JOIN EmployeeHierarchy
                on Employee.ManagerID= EmployeeHierarchy.EmployeeID)

SELECT    Employee.EmployeeID,Contact.LastName,Contact.FirstName
FROM      HumanResources.Employee as Employee
            INNER JOIN EmployeeHierarchy
                ON Employee.EmployeeID = EmployeeHierarchy.EmployeeID
              INNER JOIN Person.Contact as Contact
                  ON Contact.contactId = Employee.contactId
```

So let's take this query apart and look at how it works. First, we define the name of the CTE and define the names of the columns that will be output:

```
WITH EmployeeHierarchy (EmployeeID, ManagerID)
AS
(
```

■**Tip** You may have noticed that we did not declare the names in previous examples. The column names being returned are optional, just like with views.

The first query gets the top level in the hierarchy. It is not required that it only return a single row, but in our case we are getting all rows where the managerId= 140, that is, all people who work for managerId = 140. We are using a variable here to keep it equivalent to the SQL Server 2000 example.

```
    SELECT EmployeeID, ManagerID
    FROM   HumanResources.Employee as Employee
    WHERE  ManagerID=@managerId
```

■**Tip** Recursive CTEs require a top-level statement and a UNION ALL, or you will get a syntax error from the compiler.

Then use UNION ALL to connect these rows to the next specified set:

```
UNION ALL
```

UNION ALL does not specify duplicates to be removed, so you will have to be careful to avoid cyclical relationships in your data. The problem comes when you might have a child row that may also be a predecessor to itself.

For example, consider the following table of data:

EmployeeID	ManagerID
1	3
3	5
5	1

The manager of employee 1 is employee 3. Then when you get the manager for employee 3, it is employee 5, and then employee 5's manager is 1. So when you get to the next row, you would end up in an infinite loop because you would find that the manager of 1 is 3, and we would just keep going until we hit the nesting limit of SQL Server code (32).

So now we get to the cool part. We get the children of the rows we got in the first part of the query by the name of the CTE, in our case EmployeeHierarchy. This is how the recursion works. It joins to itself, but again contains itself (hence the recursive nature of a query calling itself). It continues on until no EmployeeId is a manager of anyone else (down to where the real work gets done!).

```
SELECT Employee.EmployeeID, Employee.ManagerID
FROM   HumanResources.Employee as Employee
         INNER JOIN EmployeeHierarchy
             on Employee.ManagerID= EmployeeHierarchy.EmployeeID
)
```

Finally, we use the CTE. The loop happens without us even noticing from the outside by materializing the set of rows, then joining that to the full Employee table. The result is all persons who report to a given manager.

```
SELECT   Employee.EmployeeID,Contact.LastName,Contact.FirstName
FROM     HumanResources.Employee as Employee
         INNER JOIN EmployeeHierarchy
             ON Employee.EmployeeID = EmployeeHierarchy.EmployeeID
           INNER JOIN Person.Contact as Contact
               ON Contact.contactId = Employee.contactId
```

Before we leave CTEs altogether, there is one more really neat thing that we can do with them. In the query that gets the top level of the hierarchy, you can introduce values into the CTE that you can manipulate throughout the iterations of the query. The following query extends the query to include a level indicator and a hierarchy of the employee's managers, up to the top manager for the employee. In the recursive part of the CTE, we put code to add one for each level. In our case, we increment the tree level by one, and then we add the EmployeeId from the level to the hierarchy. We use varchar(max) since we don't know just how big the hierarchy will be (varchar(max) is one of the very cool new datatypes added to SQL Server 2005).

```
DECLARE @managerId int
SET @managerId = 140;

WITH EmployeeHierarchy(EmployeeID, ManagerID, treelevel, heirarchy)
AS
(
    SELECT EmployeeID, ManagerID,
           1 as treeevel, CAST(EmployeeId as varchar(max)) as heirarchy
    FROM   HumanResources.Employee as Employee
    WHERE ManagerID=@managerId

    UNION ALL

    SELECT Employee.EmployeeID, Employee.ManagerID,
           treelevel + 1 as treelevel,
           heirarchy + '\' +cast(Employee.EmployeeId as varchar(20)) as heirarchy
    FROM   HumanResources.Employee as Employee
           INNER JOIN EmployeeHierarchy
             on Employee.ManagerID= EmployeeHierarchy.EmployeeID
)

SELECT   Employee.EmployeeID,Contact.LastName,Contact.FirstName,
         EmployeeHierarchy.treelevel, EmployeeHierarchy.heirarchy
FROM     HumanResources.Employee as Employee
         INNER JOIN EmployeeHierarchy
             ON Employee.EmployeeID = EmployeeHierarchy.EmployeeID
           INNER JOIN Person.Contact as Contact
               ON Contact.contactId = employee.contactId
ORDER BY heirarchy
```

Running this returns the following:

EmployeeID	LastName	FirstName	level	heirarchy
103	Barber	David	1	103
139	Liu	David	1	139
130	Walton	Bryan	2	139\130
166	Tomic	Dragan	2	139\166
178	Moreland	Barbara	2	139\178
201	Sheperdigian	Janet	2	139\201
216	Seamans	Mike	2	139\216
59	Poe	Deborah	2	139\59
94	Spoon	Candy	2	139\94
30	Barreto de Mattos	Paula	1	30
154	Chen	Hao	2	30\154
191	Culbertson	Grant	2	30\191
47	Johnson	Willis	2	30\47
70	Martin	Mindy	2	30\70
82	Luthra	Vidur	2	30\82
71	Kahn	Wendy	1	71
274	Word	Sheela	2	71\274
164	Sandberg	Mikael	3	71\274\164
198	Rao	Arvind	3	71\274\198

223	Meisner	Linda	3	71\274\223
231	Ogisu	Fukiko	3	71\274\231
233	Hee	Gordon	3	71\274\233
238	Pellow	Frank	3	71\274\238
241	Kurjan	Eric	3	71\274\241
244	Hagens	Erin	3	71\274\244
261	Miller	Ben	3	71\274\261
264	Hill	Annette	3	71\274\264
266	Hillmann	Reinout	3	71\274\266

So now we have our hierarchy, it is sorted by manager, and we know how far away an employee is from the manager we passed in as a parameter.

CTEs are one of the cooler new T-SQL features in SQL Server 2005. They will be helpful in cleaning up code for sure, but more importantly, recursive queries will be far easier to deal with than ever before.

TOP

The TOP operator is used to specify the number of rows returned by a query. In previous versions of SQL Server, TOP required a literal. So if you needed to parameterize the number of values to return when a statement was coded, the alternative was to use SET ROWCOUNT @<variableName> to restrict the rows returned. This, however, affected ALL following T-SQL statements. It was also an issue that you needed to reset ROWCOUNT to 0 after every statement you used it on or big problems would occur when you started only affecting a couple of rows in subsequent statements.

TOP only affects a single statement and now it allows a variable to set the number of rows affected. For example, we can return a variable set of rows based on a variable from the AdventureWorks Person.Contact table.

```
DECLARE @rowsToReturn int

SELECT  @rowsToReturn = 10

SELECT  TOP(@rowsToReturn) * --note that TOP requires parentheses to accept
                            --parameters but not for constant
FROM    HumanResources.Employee
```

If the value of the TOP parameter is invalid, such as a NULL value or a negative value, SQL Server will return an error. In SQL Server 2005, you may update views that are defined using the TOP operator. However, after you update the values that show up in the view, the rows may vanish from the view.

Beyond parameterization, another change to the TOP operator is that it will work with INSERT, UPDATE, and DELETE (again with parameters if desired).

Tip When using TOP on INSERT, UPDATE, or DELETE statements, you must put parentheses around the expression, even if it is a literal.

For example, say we have a table and you want to insert the top five rows from a resultset (in this case, one that just has seven values from a UNION statement). We can do this with INSERT TOP (N):

```
CREATE TABLE testTop
(
        value   int primary Key
)
```

```
INSERT TOP (5) into testTop
SELECT  *  --this derived table returns seven rows
FROM    (SELECT 1  as value  union SELECT 2  union SELECT 3 union SELECT 4
            union SELECT 5 union SELECT 6 union SELECT 7) as sevenRows
go
SELECT  *
FROM    testTop
go
```

Our derived table contains seven rows, but the TOP operator on the INSERT statement means that this will return only five of them:

```
value
-----------
1
2
3
4
5
```

Now, we can use TOP on an UPDATE to change two rows only:

```
UPDATE TOP (2) testTop
SET     value = value * 100

SELECT  *
FROM    testTop
```

which returns the following:

```
value
-----------
3
4
5
100
200
```

Finally, using DELETE, we can remove three rows from the table:

```
DELETE TOP(3) testTop
go

select * from testTop
```

which leaves us with this output:

```
value
-----------
100
200
```

Each of these techniques is basically only good when you are trying to batch-modify a set. So you can do something like this:

```
INSERT TOP (10) otherTable (batchTableId, value)
FROM   batchTable
WHERE  not exists ( SELECT *
                    FROM    otherTable
                    WHERE   otherTable.batchTableId = batchTable.batchTableId)
```

It is not a technique that will be extremely useful, but it is a much more elegant solution than using SET ROWCOUNT because it is clear to the query processor what statement you intend to limit the number of rows from. Any other statements in any subordinate objects like triggers needn't be subject to the limitation, as was the case with ROWCOUNT.

This example has a pretty big gotcha that may not be completely obvious to you. Notice there was no mention of which rows would be modified or deleted. As cannot be stated too many times, tables are unordered sets, and modification statements have no ORDER BY clause to order the set they deal with. It will literally just INSERT, UPDATE, or DELETE whatever number of rows you state, purely at the will of the optimizer (the SQL Server 2005 Books Online goes so far as to state that the rows affected when TOP is used will be "random," which, while technically true, is perhaps pushing it). It stands to reason that whichever rows are easiest to modify, these rows will be the ones chosen. This is unlike how the SELECT statement returned the rows based on an ORDER BY clause if one was present, and it can be a bit confusing.

For example:

```
create table top10sales
(
 salesOrderId int,
 totalDue   money
)
```

```
insert  TOP (10) top10sales
SELECT salesOrderId, totalDue
FROM sales.salesOrderHeader
ORDER BY totalDue desc
```

Ten rows from the sales.salesOrderHeader table will be returned and inserted, but it will not be the top ten highest values. For this, you can use

```
INSERT top10sales
SELECT TOP (10) salesOrderId, totalDue
FROM   sales.salesOrderHeader
ORDER     BY totalDue desc
```

Now the values in the top10sales table are the top ten values in sales.salesOrderHeader. totalDue.

The value of adding TOP to the INSERT, UPDATE, and DELETE statements is to facilitate batching operations. For example, you might want to delete a large number of rows from a table, a few at a time, to keep the transaction small, thereby assisting in maintaining concurrent use of the table, with a small number of locks. So you could execute

```
BEGIN TRANSACTION
DECLARE @rowcount int
SET @rowcount = 100
WHILE (@rowcount = 100)  --if it is less than 100, we are done, greater than 100
  BEGIN                         --cannot happen
          DELETE TOP(100) sales.salesOrderHeader
          SET @rowcount = @@rowcount
  END
ROLLBACK TRANSACTION --we don't want to actually delete the rows
```

Note that using TOP is the preferred way of acting on only a fixed number of rows, rather than using SET ROWCOUNT <N>. SET ROWCOUNT will be deprecated in a near-term release of SQL Server.

Change The TOP operator accepts variables as well as literal values and can be used with INSERT, UPDATE, and DELETE statements.

This is a good addition, but bear in mind that TOP is merely a filter that tells SQL Server that once it starts processing rows it only needs to return a portion of the rows that the query would return. If the number is hard coded, it can help in optimization of the query, but using a variable means that the optimizer will have to assume you want all rows. This could have performance implications.

Extensions to the FROM Clause

SQL Server 2005 includes a couple of really nice changes that allow the FROM clause to extend the way you can manipulate data with the SELECT, INSERT, UPDATE, and DELETE SQL statements. The FROM clause now supports the following:

- *New join types*: CROSS APPLY and OUTER APPLY aid with use of user-defined functions.
- *Random data sampling*: This enables you to return random sets of rows from a table.

New Join Types

One particular annoyance in previous versions of SQL Server was that derived tables could not be correlated to other sets in the FROM clause. For example, the following type of query would not have been allowed:

```
SELECT Product.productNumber, SalesOrderAverage.averageTotal
FROM   Production.Product as Product
          JOIN      (    SELECT AVG(lineTotal) as averageTotal
                         FROM Sales.SalesOrderDetail as SalesOrderDetail
                         WHERE product.ProductID=SalesOrderDetail.ProductID
                         HAVING COUNT(*) > 1
                         ) as SalesOrderAverage
```

Of course, for the most part, a normal query like this was not a great problem because this query could easily be rewritten as an inner join. However, in SQL Server 2000, Microsoft added table-valued user-defined functions, for which rewriting as a join was not possible. The following example seems natural:

```
SELECT Product.productNumber, SalesOrderAverage.averageTotal
FROM   Production.Product as Product
          JOIN dbo.getAverageTotalPerProduct(product.productId)
                                                  as SalesOrderAverage
```

but this is also illegal. Instead, the function would have to be coded to return all rows for all products, which is probably not going to perform well at all, especially if you have a great many products.

This was one of the most frustrating problems with using table-based functions in SQL Server 2000. The APPLY operator allows queries of this style to make optimal use of derived tables and scalar functions. What it does is inject column data from the left-hand table source into the right-hand source (valued function or derived table). There are two forms of APPLY:

- CROSS APPLY: Only returns a rowset if the right table source returns data for the parameter values from the left table source columns.

- OUTER APPLY: Just like an outer join returns at least one row from the left table source, even if no rowset is returned from the right.

Tip The names of the join types will likely be confusing. OUTER APPLY seems very much like an OUTER JOIN, since a row is returned for each left table source regardless of what is returned in the right table source (note that LEFT and RIGHT are not allowed). However, CROSS APPLY seems quite wrong. A CROSS JOIN would return all rows in the left table source and all rows in the right table source. CROSS APPLY seems more like it should be called an inner apply, but this is not the case.

In the next block of code, we use the CROSS APPLY operator to execute the derived table once per row in the Production.Product table. The subquery gets only one row, which is the average amount for a sale of that product. If it hasn't been sold yet, an empty resultset would be the result of the CROSS APPLY operation and the Production.Product row would not be returned:

```
SELECT Product.productNumber, SalesOrderAverage.averageTotal
FROM    Production.Product as Product
          CROSS APPLY (    SELECT AVG(lineTotal) as averageTotal
                           FROM Sales.SalesOrderDetail as SalesOrderDetail
                           WHERE product.ProductID=SalesOrderDetail.ProductID
                           HAVING COUNT(*) > 0
                           ) as SalesOrderAverage
```

This returns the following results (truncated for readability):

```
productNumber                 averageTotal
--------------------          -------------------------------------
BB-7421                       81.650630
BB-9108                       183.775014
BC-M005                       9.990000
BC-R205                       8.990000
BK-M18B-40                    679.055917
BK-M18B-42                    693.944595
BK-M18B-44                    647.416582
BK-M18B-48                    678.707431
BK-M18B-52                    644.185253
BK-M18S-40                    641.530154
BK-M18S-42                    626.030041
BK-M18S-44                    619.874742
BK-M18S-48                    627.573507
BK-M18S-52                    683.637900
BK-M38S-38                    945.020248
>> resultset truncated <<
```

The real power of CROSS APPLY is with user-defined functions. Instead of a derived table, we'll create a function that returns the value of the largest sale of a given product from the Sales.SalesOrderDetail table.

```
CREATE FUNCTION production.getAverageTotalPerProduct
(
     @productId int
)
RETURNS @output TABLE (unitPrice decimal(10,4))
AS
     BEGIN
          INSERT  INTO @output (unitPrice)
          SELECT AVG(lineTotal) as averageTotal
          FROM Sales.SalesOrderDetail as SalesOrderDetail
          WHERE SalesOrderDetail.ProductID = @productId
          HAVING COUNT(*) > 0

          RETURN
     END
```

Now the statement can be rewritten as follows:

```
SELECT Product.ProductNumber, AverageSale.UnitPrice
FROM   Production.Product as Product
            CROSS APPLY
                    production.getAverageTotalPerProduct(product.productId)
                                                             as AverageSale
```

This returns the same results as previously. Obviously, your multistatement table-valued functions would usually be a lot more complex than this (otherwise, why bother to make it a function?), but for the purposes of this example, this allows us to make use of the function in a very nice format that is usable, and should have good performance. (Clearly what performs well enough varies on a case-by-case basis. Don't take anyone's word for it—test, test, and test some more.)

In the previous example, any product rows where there were no matching unit sales were not included in the output. We change this to an OUTER APPLY to get back all rows in the product table, and NULLs for the unit price column where there have been no sales:

```
SELECT Product.ProductNumber, AverageSale.UnitPrice
FROM   Production.Product as Product
            OUTER APPLY
                    production.getAverageTotalPerProduct(product.productId)
                                                             as AverageSale
```

Products that don't have any associated sales will return no rows, but you still get a row for each product:

ProductNumber	UnitPrice
AR-5381	NULL
BA-8327	NULL
BB-7421	81.6506
BB-8107	NULL
BB-9108	183.7750
BC-M005	9.9900
BC-R205	8.9900
BE-2349	NULL
BE-2908	NULL
BK-M18B-40	679.0559

```
BK-M18B-42              693.9446
BK-M18B-44              647.4166
BK-M18B-48              678.7074
BK-M18B-52              644.1853
BK-M18S-40              641.5302
>> resultset truncated <<
```

New Feature Using CROSS APPLY or OUTER APPLY allows a derived table or a table-valued function to have parameters applied for each row, making table-valued functions tremendously more useful.

Random Data Sampling

Sometimes it is desirable to get an idea about the distribution of data in a table, but it is impractical because there is just too much data. Obviously, it is seldom necessary to look at every piece of data to get an idea of how the data looks in the table. Take elections, for an example. An exit poll only needs to sample a small proportion of the population in order to predict the outcome with a high degree of accuracy.

TABLESAMPLE lets you get a random set of rows. You can specify either a percentage of the table or a given number of rows to return. However, what you will likely find weird about this operator is that it seldom returns exactly the same number of rows.

In the next example, the query returns a different selection of rows each time it is executed. What seems odd is just how large the variance in the rowcount will be. For this query, it typically will be between 1800 and 3000, which is approximately 2 percent of the number of rows in the sales.salesOrderDetail table, as there are 118,990 in the version of the table we are using and 2 percent is 2379).

```
SELECT  *
FROM    sales.salesOrderDetail TABLESAMPLE SYSTEM (2 PERCENT)
```

There is also an option to get a more exact count of rows:

```
SELECT  *
FROM    sales.salesOrderDetail TABLESAMPLE SYSTEM (500 rows)
```

Again, however, it will not actually return only 500 rows, and in testing, the count has been between 200 and 800, where 500 rows was specified. If you want to get back the same results each time you run one of these queries, you can specify the REPEATABLE option and a fixed seed for the randomizer.

```
SELECT  *
FROM    sales.salesOrderDetail TABLESAMPLE SYSTEM (500 rows) REPEATABLE (123456)
```

Given the same seed, you will get the same rows back. One thing to note here: this is not like the repeatable read isolation level. If another user makes changes to the data in the table, you will not get back the exact same rows. It is only true for a given "version" of the table.

We must note that these commands really seem weird to us, since they will not return the exact same number of rows each time, even when you specify a certain number of rows! It has to do with the random nature of the TABLESAMPLE operator, and that they do the sample in a single pass through the table. It should not hurt your queries, but if you need an exact number of rows for a test, you could INTERSECT two table samples (INTERSECT is new and covered later in this chapter in the section "EXCEPT and INTERSECT") and use TOP to get your set.

Pivoting Data

Excel has had pivot tables for quite some time, allowing users to rotate a table in such a way as to turn rows into columns, and back again. In SQL Server 2005, two new relational operators are being added to give some of the same functionality to T-SQL. These operators are PIVOT and UNPIVOT. In the following two sections, we will look at how these commands work.

PIVOT

One thing that was almost impossible to do in T-SQL was to take a set of rows and pivot them to columns. The PIVOT operator allows you to rotate the columns in a table to rows.

As a very simple example (as simple as it can be anyhow), consider the following table of data, which we will call SalesByMonth. (We put it in the Sales schema; if you are not building this in the AdventureWorks database, you may need to create the schema using the command CREATE SCHEMA sales.)

```
CREATE TABLE sales.salesByMonth
(
    year char(4),
    month char(3),
    amount money,
    PRIMARY KEY (year, month)
)
INSERT INTO sales.salesByMonth (year, month, amount)
VALUES('2004','Jan',   789.0000)
INSERT INTO sales.salesByMonth (year, month, amount)
VALUES('2004','Feb',   389.0000)
INSERT INTO sales.salesByMonth (year, month, amount)
VALUES('2004','Mar',  8867.0000)
INSERT INTO sales.salesByMonth (year, month, amount)
VALUES('2004','Apr',   778.0000)
INSERT INTO sales.salesByMonth (year, month, amount)
VALUES('2004','May',    78.0000)
INSERT INTO sales.salesByMonth (year, month, amount)
VALUES('2004','Jun',     9.0000)
INSERT INTO sales.salesByMonth (year, month, amount)
VALUES('2004','Jul',   987.0000)
INSERT INTO sales.salesByMonth (year, month, amount)
VALUES('2004','Aug',   866.0000)
INSERT INTO sales.salesByMonth (year, month, amount)
VALUES('2004','Sep',  7787.0000)
INSERT INTO sales.salesByMonth (year, month, amount)
VALUES('2004','Oct', 85576.0000)
INSERT INTO sales.salesByMonth (year, month, amount)
VALUES('2004','Nov',   855.0000)
INSERT INTO sales.salesByMonth (year, month, amount)
VALUES('2004','Dec',  5878.0000)

INSERT INTO sales.salesByMonth (year, month, amount)
VALUES('2005','Jan',     7.0000)
INSERT INTO sales.salesByMonth (year, month, amount)
VALUES('2005','Feb',  6868.0000)
```

```
INSERT INTO sales.salesByMonth (year, month, amount)
VALUES('2005','Mar',   688.0000)
INSERT INTO sales.salesByMonth (year, month, amount)
VALUES('2005','Apr',   9897.0000)
```

Most likely this would not be representative of a table in your database, but more likely the final output of a query that summarized the data by month. While this is the natural format for a set-based query, it is not likely that the user will want to look at the data this way; for starters, it is ordered funny (alphabetic order because of the clustered index on the key!), but even if it was ordered by month, it would still be pretty ugly. It is likely the desired output of this data might be

Year	Jan	Feb	Mar	...
2004	789.0000	389.0000	8867.0000	...
2005	7.0000	6868.0000	688.0000	...

Using SQL Server 2000 coding techniques, the query would look something along the lines of the following:

```
SELECT year,
       SUM(case when month = 'Jan' then amount else 0 end) AS 'Jan',
       SUM(case when month = 'Feb' then amount else 0 end) AS 'Feb',
       SUM(case when month = 'Mar' then amount else 0 end) AS 'Mar',
       SUM(case when month = 'Apr' then amount else 0 end) AS 'Apr',
       SUM(case when month = 'May' then amount else 0 end) AS 'May',
       SUM(case when month = 'Jun' then amount else 0 end) AS 'Jun',
       SUM(case when month = 'Jul' then amount else 0 end) AS 'Jul',
       SUM(case when month = 'Aug' then amount else 0 end) AS 'Aug',
       SUM(case when month = 'Sep' then amount else 0 end) AS 'Sep',
       SUM(case when month = 'Oct' then amount else 0 end) AS 'Oct',
       SUM(case when month = 'Nov' then amount else 0 end) AS 'Nov',
       SUM(case when month = 'Dec' then amount else 0 end) AS 'Dec'
FROM    sales.salesByMonth
GROUP  by year
```

Not terribly hard to follow, but pretty messy if you start to need more information. Using the new PIVOT operator, the code is changed to

```
SELECT Year,[Jan],[Feb],[Mar],[Apr],[May],[Jun],
          [Jul],[Aug],[Sep],[Oct],[Nov],[Dec]
FROM (
    SELECT year, amount, month
    FROM      sales.salesByMonth ) AS salesByMonth
    PIVOT ( SUM(amount) FOR month IN
            ([Jan],[Feb],[Mar],[Apr],[May],[Jun],
             [Jul],[Aug],[Sep],[Oct],[Nov],[Dec])
    ) AS ourPivot
ORDER BY Year
```

The most important part of this query is this:

```
    PIVOT ( SUM(amount) FOR month IN
            ([Jan],[Feb],[Mar],[Apr],[May],[Jun],
             [Jul],[Aug],[Sep],[Oct],[Nov],[Dec])
```

It produces a value for each of the columns in the IN clause that match values in the month column. This is done via the SUM (amount) FOR month section. The moderately confusing part is that it groups on the columns that are not a part of the PIVOT statement. Since year was not in an aggregate, it grouped the pivot on year. If we remove year from the query as follows:

```
SELECT [Jan],[Feb],[Mar],[Apr],[May],[Jun],
       [Jul],[Aug],[Sep],[Oct],[Nov],[Dec]
FROM (      SELECT amount, month
            FROM   sales.salesByMonth ) AS salesByMonth
     PIVOT  ( SUM(amount) FOR month IN
               ([Jan],[Feb],[Mar],[Apr],[May],[Jun],
                [Jul],[Aug],[Sep],[Oct],[Nov],[Dec])
     ) AS ourPivot
```

it groups on all rows:

Jan	Feb	Mar	...
796.0000	7257.0000	9555.0000	...

When you need to store variable attributes in your schema and you cannot determine all of the data requirements at design time, PIVOT is excellent. For example, a store that has many products may have very different attributes for each product. Instead of having different tables with different attributes for each type of product (a management nightmare), you implement a table that allows for varying properties to be created and a value associated with them. Building these "property" or "attribute" tables is an easy technique for associating values with a product, but writing queries to deliver to the client can be very cumbersome. Using PIVOT, we'll walk you through extending the Person.Contact table by creating a Person.ContactProperty table that contains properties that we did not know when the schema was designed. We will store the person's dog name, hair color, and even their car style:

Tip This kind of schema is generally only a good idea in extreme circumstances when the data is very variable. If the schema can at all be predicted, it is important to go ahead and do a full design. A good example of where we have used this sort of schema is storing the operating data from networking routers. They have tons of properties and each model has slightly different ones.

```
CREATE TABLE Person.ContactProperty
(
    ContactPropertyId int identity(1,1) PRIMARY KEY,
    ContactId      int REFERENCES Person.Contact(ContactId),
    PropertyName  varchar(20),
    PropertyValue sql_variant,
    UNIQUE (ContactID, PropertyName)
)

INSERT Person.ContactProperty (ContactId, PropertyName, PropertyValue)
VALUES(1,'dog name','Fido')
INSERT Person.ContactProperty (ContactId, PropertyName, PropertyValue)
VALUES(1,'hair color','brown')
INSERT Person.ContactProperty (ContactId, PropertyName, PropertyValue)
VALUES(1,'car style','sedan')
```

```
INSERT Person.ContactProperty (ContactId, PropertyName, PropertyValue)
VALUES(2,'dog name','Rufus')
INSERT Person.ContactProperty (ContactId, PropertyName, PropertyValue)
VALUES(2,'hair color','blonde')

INSERT Person.ContactProperty (ContactId, PropertyName, PropertyValue)
VALUES(3,'dog name','Einstein')
INSERT Person.ContactProperty (ContactId, PropertyName, PropertyValue)
VALUES(3,'car style','coupe')
```

If we look at the data in a basic T-SQL statement:

```
SELECT   cast(Contact.FirstName + ' ' + Contact.LastName as varchar(30)) as Name,
         ContactProperty.PropertyName, ContactProperty.PropertyValue
FROM     Person.Contact as Contact
           INNER JOIN Person.ContactProperty as ContactProperty
             ON  ContactProperty.ContactId = Contact.ContactID
```

then we get the typical resultset of a row per attribute:

Name	PropertyName	PropertyValue
Gustavo Achong	dog name	Fido
Gustavo Achong	hair color	brown
Gustavo Achong	car style	sedan
Catherine Abel	dog name	Rufus
Catherine Abel	hair color	blonde
Kim Abercrombie	dog name	Einstein
Kim Abercrombie	car style	coupe

It will usually be more desirable to display this data as a single row in the user interface or report. To do this currently, you would need to navigate the results and pivot the rows themselves. Not that this is always the wrong way to go. Data formatting is usually best done using the presentation layer, but in some cases doing this in the data layer will be best; depending on what kinds of clients are being used, or if you need to use the data in a different SQL query, data in this format may be troublesome to deal with.

Instead, we can use the PIVOT operator to take the propertyName values and rotate the data to provide a single row per contact. We use a derived table, selecting all of the columns required in the PIVOT from our ContactProperty table. We then pivot this, getting the attribute values by PropertyName for each ContactId.

```
SELECT   cast(Contact.FirstName + ' ' + Contact.LastName as varchar(30)) as Name,
         pivotColumns.* --demonstrating that * works, it should not
                        --be done this way in production code
FROM     Person.Contact as Contact
           INNER JOIN (SELECT ContactId, PropertyName,PropertyValue
                       FROM   Person.ContactProperty as property)
                                                             as PivotTable
             PIVOT( MAX(PropertyValue)
                    FOR PropertyName IN ([dog name],[hair color],[car style]))
                                                             AS PivotColumns
               ON Contact.ContactId = PivotColumns.ContactId
```

We are getting the maximum value of the PropertyValue column for the rotated value, since only one value can be nonnull. We are not restricted to only one unique value for the rotation, and this allows all sorts of aggregation to take place, making the PIVOT operator incredibly powerful. Then we specify the column that contains the values that we will pivot around. In our example, we are using the PropertyName column, specifying the values that will become the columns in our output. The query output is as follows (noting that there is a NULL value where there was no value for a given property):

```
Name                            ContactId    dog name                hair color
------------------------------  -----------  ----------------------  --------------------
Gustavo Achong                  1            Fido                    brown
Catherine Abel                  2            Rufus                   blonde
Kim Abercrombie                 3            Einstein                NULL

car style
--------------------
sedan
NULL
coupe
```

Note, we just used the first three ContactId values from the Person.Contact table for this example.

■**New Feature** The PIVOT takes a vertical set and converts it to a horizontal schema, allowing you to flatten a resultset to make it easier to consume by a client.

UNPIVOT

The (almost) opposite effect of PIVOT is, not surprisingly, UNPIVOT. Less useful on a day-to-day-basis, this is a fantastic tool to have when doing data conversions or dealing with poorly designed databases. Going back to the set of data we created with our salesByMonth query, using the INTO clause we create a table of data called dbo.salesByYear:

```
SELECT Year,[Jan],[Feb],[Mar],[Apr],[May],[Jun],
          [Jul],[Aug],[Sep],[Oct],[Nov],[Dec]
INTO  sales.salesByYear
FROM (
    SELECT year, amount, month
    FROM   sales.salesByMonth ) AS salesByMonth
    PIVOT  ( SUM(amount) FOR month IN
             ([Jan],[Feb],[Mar],[Apr],[May],[Jun],
              [Jul],[Aug],[Sep],[Oct],[Nov],[Dec])
    ) AS ourPivot
ORDER BY Year
```

which contains the following output:

```
Year   Jan         Feb          Mar          ...
2004   789.0000    389.0000     8867.0000    ...
2005   7.0000      6868.0000     688.0000    ...
```

Now, to get this back to the original format, we can use a query like the following:

```
SELECT  Year, cast(Month as char(3)) as Month, Amount
FROM    sales.salesByYear
            UNPIVOT (Amount FOR Month IN
              ([Jan],[Feb],[Mar],[Apr],[May],[Jun],
               [Jul],[Aug],[Sep],[Oct],[Nov],[Dec])) as unPivoted
```

which returns

Year	Month	Amount
2004	Jan	789.0000
2004	Feb	389.0000
2004	Mar	8867.0000
2004	Apr	778.0000
2004	May	78.0000
2004	Jun	9.0000
2004	Jul	987.0000
2004	Aug	866.0000
2004	Sep	7787.0000
2004	Oct	85576.0000
2004	Nov	855.0000
2004	Dec	5878.0000
2005	Jan	7.0000
2005	Feb	6868.0000
2005	Mar	688.0000
2005	Apr	9897.0000

This is another really nice addition to what T-SQL can do natively and will come in handy in quite a few cases. One thing you should note, however: UNPIVOT is not exactly the opposite of PIVOT. Null values in the table will not be returned as rows in the UNPIVOTed output. So, if we had the following table:

Year	Jan	Feb	Mar	...
2004	NULL	NULL	8867.0000	...
2005	7.0000	6868.0000	688.0000	...

we would not get rows in our output like the following:

Year	Month	Amount
2004	Jan	NULL
2004	Feb	NULL
2004	Mar	8867.0000
...		

The first two rows would not exist in the output.

OUTPUT

In SQL Server 2005, there is now an OUTPUT clause as part of DML statements to assist in auditing changes made during the statement. The OUTPUT clause specifies a statement to output a resultset of changes to a table variable.

Just like triggers, you use the inserted and deleted tables to access the rows that have been modified in a statement and the data that is being deleted.

For example, change FirstName in the Person.Contact table to the reverse of the original value. Note begin transaction and rollback transaction to avoid corrupting the data in the Person.Contact table.

```
BEGIN TRANSACTION

DECLARE @changes table (change varchar(2000))

UPDATE TOP (10) Person.Contact
SET     FirstName = Reverse(FirstName)
OUTPUT 'Was: ''' + DELETED.FirstName +
                ''' Is: ''' + INSERTED.FirstName + ''''
INTO    @changes

SELECT *
FROM    @changes

ROLLBACK TRANSACTION
--note that local variable tables are not affected by transactions!
```

This returns the following (assuming you haven't already made changes to the data in the Person.Contact.FirstName column):

```
change
----------------------------------------------------------------
Was: 'Gustavo' Is: 'ovatsuG'
Was: 'Catherine' Is: 'enirehtaC'
Was: 'Kim' Is: 'miK'
Was: 'Humberto' Is: 'otrebmuH'
Was: 'Pilar' Is: 'raliP'
Was: 'Frances' Is: 'secnarF'
Was: 'Margaret' Is: 'teragraM'
Was: 'Carla' Is: 'alraC'
Was: 'Jay' Is: 'yaJ'
Was: 'Ronald' Is: 'dlanoR'
```

■ New Feature The OUTPUT clause gives you the ability to access the changes from a DML statement without building triggers or any other method.

This is a very interesting new feature, and you can see some interesting potential uses, such as scanning the outputted table to see if certain changes were made, although audit trails will still be easier to implement using triggers.

Ranking Functions

Ranking functions are used to assist you in adding positional information to your resultset—for example, the position of a row within a set that we are returning.

■Tip We have also seen them referred to as *windowed functions*. Either terminology is fine.

Briefly, let's demonstrate this sort of operation using SQL Server 2000 code. Let's consider finding the position of a row within our set. This can easily be done using a subquery. Using the AdventureWorks database, consider the Person.Contact table. To demonstrate, we will rank the order of the contact names, using first name first, so there are duplicates. (Obviously, in a production system, you would likely never do this sort of thing, but the point of doing this here is to get a small set of data that we can work with to demonstrate how the ranking functions work. We will be using the following view to limit our sets for each query.)

```
CREATE VIEW contactSubset
as
    Select  TOP 20 *
    FROM    Person.Contact
    WHERE   FirstName like 'b%'
```

So we execute the following:

```
SELECT  FirstName,
            (   SELECT count(*)
                FROM    contactSubset as c
                WHERE   c.FirstName < contactSubset.FirstName) + 1 as RANK
FROM    contactSubset
ORDER   BY FirstName
```

which returns the following:

FirstName	RANK
Barbara	1
Barbara	1
Barbara	1
Baris	4
Bart	5
Benjamin	6
Bernard	7
Betty	8
Bev	9
Blaine	10
Bob	11
Bradley	12
Brenda	13
Brenda	13
Brian	15
Brian	15
Bridget	17
Brigid	18
Bruno	19
Bruno	19

The subquery gives us position or rank by counting the number of employees in a copy of employee that has names that are less than the current name in alphabetic ordering. Works great, not too messy, but what if we need two criteria? For the purposes of our example, say we want to use the last name of our contacts. The query gets more and more complex:

```
SELECT   FirstName, LastName,
         (   SELECT count(*)
             FROM    contactSubset as c
             WHERE   c.LastName < contactSubset.LastName
                OR   (c.LastName = contactSubset.LastName
                      AND c.FirstName< contactSubset.FirstName)
                 ) + 1 as orderNumber
FROM     contactSubset
ORDER    BY LastName, FirstName
```

In SQL Server 2005, we get these four new functions:

- ROW_NUMBER: Returns the row number of a row in a resultset.

- RANK: Based on some chosen order of a given set of columns, gives the position of the row. It will leave gaps if there are any ties for values. For example, there might be two values in first place, and then the next value would be third place.

- DENSE_RANK: Same as RANK but does not leave gaps in the sequence. Whereas RANK might order values 1,2,2,4,4,6,6, DENSE_RANK would order them 1,2,2,3,3,4,4.

- NTILE: Used to partition the ranks into a number of sections; for example, if you have a table with 100 values, you might use NTILE(2) to number the first 50 as "1", and the last 50 as "2".

For each of these functions, you have to specify an OVER clause, which basically specifies a sorting criterion that the functions will assign their ranking values. It does not have to be the same ordering as the ORDER BY clause, and when it is not, the results will be interesting. There is also an optional PARTITION BY criterion that you can apply to the OVER clause that allows you to break up the sections into different groups. This will be demonstrated at the end of this section.

As an example, look again at our contact subset:

```
SELECT   FirstName,
         ROW_NUMBER() over (order by FirstName) as 'ROW_NUMBER',
         RANK() over (order by FirstName) as 'RANK',
         DENSE_RANK() over (order by FirstName) as 'DENSE_RANK',
         NTILE(4) over (order by FirstName) as 'NTILE(4)'
FROM     contactSubSet
ORDER    BY FirstName
```

This returns the following:

FirstName	ROW_NUMBER	RANK	DENSE_RANK	NTILE(4)
Barbara	1	1	1	1
Barbara	2	1	1	1
Barbara	3	1	1	1
Baris	4	4	2	1
Bart	5	5	3	1
Benjamin	6	6	4	2
Bernard	7	7	5	2
Betty	8	8	6	2
Bev	9	9	7	2
Blaine	10	10	8	2

Bob	11	11	9	3
Bradley	12	12	10	3
Brenda	13	13	11	3
Brenda	14	13	11	3
Brian	15	15	12	3
Brian	16	15	12	4
Bridget	17	17	13	4
Brigid	18	18	14	4
Bruno	19	19	15	4
Bruno	20	19	15	4

You can see that we now have a ROW_NUMBER column that gives a unique ranking for each row, based on the ordering criteria specified. The RANK function assigns a ranking value to each row. It simply counts the number of rows with a lower value than the current one according to the ordering criteria—so when ordering by first name, there are four values "lower" than Bart (three instances of Barbara and a Baris), so Bart gets a rank of 5. This will inevitably leave "gaps" in the ranking numbers. DENSE_RANK only counts distinct values, so Bart gets a DENSE_RANK of 3 since only two distinct groups precede it.

Finally, have NTILE, which breaks up the set into a number of different groups, based on a parameter (we show it set to 4 in this example). NTILE groups will have exactly the same number of values in a group if it is possible to split them evenly (for example, two groups of 10 for 20 rows, three groups of 3 for 9 rows, and so on). This is true even if all the values in the table are the same. Otherwise, some groups may have fewer members.

We can specify multiple ordering criteria in the ORDER BY clause, as follows:

```
SELECT     FirstName, LastName,
           ROW_NUMBER() over (order by FirstName, LastName) as 'ROW_NUMBER',
           RANK() over (order by FirstName,LastName) as 'RANK',
           DENSE_RANK() over (order by FirstName,LastName) as 'DENSE_RANK',
           NTILE(4) over (order by FirstName,LastName) as 'NTILE(4)'
FROM       contactSubSet
ORDER      BY FirstName
```

Executing this, we get the following:

FirstName	LastName	ROW_NUMBER	RANK	DENSE_RANK	NTILE(4)
Barbara	Calone	1	1	1	1
Barbara	Decker	2	2	2	1
Barbara	German	3	3	3	1
Baris	Cetinok	4	4	4	1
Bart	Duncan	5	5	5	1
Benjamin	Becker	6	6	6	2
Bernard	Duerr	7	7	7	2
Betty	Haines	8	8	8	2
Bev	Desalvo	9	9	9	2
Blaine	Dockter	10	10	10	2
Bob	Gage	11	11	11	3
Bradley	Beck	12	12	12	3
Brenda	Barlow	13	13	13	3
Brenda	Diaz	14	14	14	3
Brian	Goldstein	15	15	15	3
Brian	Groth	16	16	16	4
Bridget	Browqett	17	17	17	4
Brigid	Cavendish	18	18	18	4

| Bruno | Costa Da Silva | 19 | 19 | 19 | 4 |
| Bruno | Deniut | 20 | 20 | 20 | 4 |

This gives us pretty much the same results, but now since there are no duplicates, the values for RANK and DENSE_RANK are the same as the ROW_NUMBER values.

What makes these functions so incredibly useful is that all of the ORDER BY clauses need not be the exact same. You can even have the same criteria ascending and descending in the same query:

```
SELECT    firstName,
          ROW_NUMBER() over (order by FirstName) as ascending,
          ROW_NUMBER() over (order by FirstName desc) as descending
FROM      contactSubSet
ORDER     BY FirstName
```

The preceding code returns the following:

FirstName	ascending	descending
Barbara	1	18
Barbara	2	19
Barbara	3	20
Baris	4	17
Bart	5	16
Benjamin	6	15
Bernard	7	14
Betty	8	13
Bev	9	12
Blaine	10	11
Bob	11	10
Bradley	12	9
Brenda	13	7
Brenda	14	8
Brian	15	5
Brian	16	6
Bridget	17	4
Brigid	18	3
Bruno	19	1
Bruno	20	2

Note Note that while the descending rows seem out of order, they are actually not, since the three values for Barbara (and the other duplicates) can be ordered in either direction. It could make using the rows interesting, so if it was important for 1 to correspond to 20 in the other column, using unique columns for ordering would be required.

As we mentioned earlier, there is also a PARTITION clause you can apply to your OVER clause that will let you apply the ranking functions to individual groups in the data. In our example data, we have several persons who have the same first name (for example, there are three persons named Barbara, and two name Brenda, Brian, and Bruno). If we wanted to include rankings of names in the subsets, in our case first name, we can change our query from earlier to be as follows:

```
SELECT     FirstName, LastName,
           ROW_NUMBER()over ( partition by FirstName order by lastName) as
                                                          'ROW_NUMBER',
           RANK()over ( partition by FirstName order by LastName) as 'RANK',
           DENSE_RANK()over ( partition by FirstName order by LastName) as
                                                          'DENSE_RANK',
           NTILE(2) over ( partition by FirstName order by LastName) as
                                                          'NTILE(2)'
FROM       contactSubSet
ORDER      BY FirstName
```

which returns the following:

FirstName	LastName	ROW_NUMBER	RANK	DENSE_RANK	NTILE(2)
Barbara	Calone	1	1	1	1
Barbara	Decker	2	2	2	1
Barbara	German	3	3	3	2
Baris	Cetinok	1	1	1	1
Bart	Duncan	1	1	1	1
Benjamin	Becker	1	1	1	1
Bernard	Duerr	1	1	1	1
Betty	Haines	1	1	1	1
Bev	Desalvo	1	1	1	1
Blaine	Dockter	1	1	1	1
Bob	Gage	1	1	1	1
Bradley	Beck	1	1	1	1
Brenda	Barlow	1	1	1	1
Brenda	Diaz	2	2	2	2
Brian	Goldstein	1	1	1	1
Brian	Groth	2	2	2	2
Bridget	Browqett	1	1	1	1
Brigid	Cavendish	1	1	1	1
Bruno	Costa Da Silva	1	1	1	1
Bruno	Deniut	2	2	2	2

Now you can see that the row numbers and rankings are based on the firstName groups, not the entire set. It isn't hard to see that by combining various OVER clauses, you can build very complex queries very easily.

The ranking functions are going to be incredibly valuable assets when writing many types of queries. They will take the place of many of the tricks that have been used for adding sequence numbers to sets, especially when dealing with partitioned sets. Understand, however, that there is no order to SQL sets. The data may be in the table in any order, and unless you specify an ORDER BY clause, the data that is returned to your client may be ordered by ROW_NUMBER, and it may not. For starters, you can include more than one ROW_NUMBER call in your query that has different ordering.

For example, say you want to see the top ten products for raw sales last year (assuming the year is 2005 right now!) and you want to see them grouped into quartiles. This is very easy to write using the RANK() and NTILE() functions.

```
WITH salesSubset AS
(
    SELECT  product.name as product,  sum(salesOrderDetail.lineTotal) as total
    FROM    sales.salesOrderDetail  as salesOrderDetail
                JOIN sales.salesOrderHeader as salesOrderHeader
                    ON salesOrderHeader.salesOrderId = salesOrderDetail.salesOrderId
                        JOIN production.product as product
                            ON product.productId = salesOrderDetail.productId
        WHERE   orderDate >= '1/1/2004' and orderDate < '1/1/2005'
        GROUP   BY product.name
)
SELECT  product, total,
        RANK() over (order by total desc) as 'RANK',
        NTILE(4) over (order by total desc) as 'NTILE(4)'
FROM    salesSubset
```

which returns the following:

product	total	RANK	NTILE(4)
Mountain-200 Black, 38	1327957.407668	1	1
Mountain-200 Black, 42	1139429.487144	2	1
Mountain-200 Silver, 38	1136622.492744	3	1
Mountain-200 Silver, 46	1029170.763900	4	1
Mountain-200 Silver, 42	1011486.176127	5	1
Mountain-200 Black, 46	1011074.368428	6	1
Road-350-W Yellow, 48	897217.963419	7	1
Road-350-W Yellow, 40	840970.646693	8	1
Touring-1000 Blue, 60	835290.155817	9	1
Touring-1000 Yellow, 60	826141.287192	10	1
Touring-1000 Blue, 46	810708.725268	11	1
<results truncated>			

This is probably a more efficient thing to do using Analysis Services, but you often need this kind of ad hoc query against the OLTP database. These functions really add tremendous power to the SQL language. Be careful with them, however, since they do not actually have to do with the order of the table itself, rather they calculate a position within a set, which is specified in the OVER clause.

You cannot use the ranking functions in a WHERE clause, so you will have to use a derived table, or a CTE to preprocess the query: for example, say we wanted to only look at the bottom 10 percent of sales, we can change our query to use NTILE with a parameter of 10 (10 equal groups) and get only those in group 10:

```
WITH salesSubset AS
(
    SELECT  product.name as product,  sum(salesOrderDetail.lineTotal) as total
    FROM    sales.salesOrderDetail  as salesOrderDetail
                JOIN sales.salesOrderHeader as salesOrderHeader
                ON salesOrderHeader.salesOrderId = salesOrderDetail.salesOrderId
                JOIN production.product as product
                ON product.productId = salesOrderDetail.productId
        WHERE   orderDate >= '1/1/2004' and orderDate < '1/1/2005'
         GROUP   BY product.name
)
```

```
SELECT   *
FROM     (SELECT  product, total,
                       RANK() over (order by total desc) as 'RANK',
                       NTILE(10) over (order by total desc) as 'NTILE(10)'
         FROM    salesSubset) as productOrders
WHERE    [NTILE(10)] = 10
```

With NTILE, if you put a tiling number greater than the number of values in the set, you will get a sequential number for all of the rows, in the proper order for the data, but you will not get all groups in the data. It can be confusing.

New Feature T-SQL has added the standard SQL functions ROW_NUMBER, RANK, DENSE_RANK, and NTILE. They make coding statements that require ordering far easier, as well as bring T-SQL a bit closer to standard SQL in addition to PL/SQL and DB2 SQL, which already have them.

EXCEPT and INTERSECT

EXCEPT and INTERSECT are new clauses that are in the same family as UNION in that they are used to combine multiple disparate query results into a single resultset. They give us the ability to do a few more interesting sorts of things with the data. As you know, UNION takes two sets of data that are shaped the same (same columns, same data types, or types that can be coerced into the same type) and lets you combine them. EXCEPT and INTERSECT have the same requirements to have the sets be alike, but they do different operations on them.

- EXCEPT: Takes the first set of data and compares it with the second set. Only values that exist in the first set, but not in the second, are returned.

- INTERSECT: Compares the two sets and returns only rows that each set has in common.

As an example, consider that we have a table that has a list of users and the projects that they have worked on (the actual table may be less readable, but the concept is the same):

```
CREATE TABLE projectPerson
(
        personId     VARCHAR(10),
        projectId    VARCHAR(10),
        PRIMARY KEY (personId, projectId)
)
go

INSERT INTO projectPerson VALUES ('joeb','projBig')
INSERT INTO projectPerson VALUES ('joeb','projLittle')
INSERT INTO projectPerson VALUES ('fredf','projBig')
INSERT INTO projectPerson VALUES ('homerr','projLittle')
INSERT INTO projectPerson VALUES ('stevegr','projBig')
INSERT INTO projectPerson VALUES ('stevegr','projLittle')
go
```

So we can see that joeb worked on projBig and projLittle. Now we can write the following queries. Using UNION, we could see who worked on one project or both projects:

```
SELECT  personId
FROM    projectPerson
WHERE   projectId = 'projBig'
UNION
SELECT  personId
FROM    projectPerson
WHERE   projectId = 'projLittle'
```

which returns the following:

```
personId
----------
fredf
homerr
joeb
stevegr
```

Next, if you want to see who worked only on projLittle, but not projBig, this was pretty ugly in SQL Server 2000.

```
SELECT  personId
FROM  projectPerson as projLittle
WHERE  projectId = 'projLittle'
  AND NOT EXISTS (    SELECT *
                      FROM    projectPerson as projBig
                      WHERE   projBig.projectId = 'projBig'
                        and   projBig.personId = projLittle.personId)
```

In 2005, you can run the following:

```
--worked on projBig but not projLittle
SELECT  personId
FROM    projectPerson
WHERE   projectId = 'projLittle'
EXCEPT
SELECT  personId
FROM    projectPerson
WHERE   projectId = 'projBig'
```

This returns the following:

```
personId
----------
homerr
```

Finally, say we want to see who worked only on both projects. In 2000, we need to run the query we did for INTERSECT, and UNION the result with the opposite, which is just too messy to be of value here. In 2005, the query is very straightforward:

```
SELECT  personId
FROM    projectPerson
WHERE   projectId = 'projBig'
INTERSECT
SELECT  personId
FROM    projectPerson
WHERE   projectId = 'projLittle'
```

This returns

```
personId
----------
joeb
stevegr
```

New Feature T-SQL has added the relational operators INTERSECT and EXCEPT to make determining characteristics about like sets easier to perform.

Synonyms

Another feature that is being added to SQL Server 2005 is synonyms. Synonyms give you the ability to assign different names to objects, for a couple of reasons:

- *Ability to alias object names*: For example, using the employee table as EMP
- *Ability to shorten names*: Especially when dealing with three and four part names—for example, server.database.owner.object to object

Synonyms can be created for the following objects:

- Tables (including temporary tables)
- Views
- Stored procedures (CLR and T-SQL)
- Replication filter procedures
- Extended stored procedures
- Table-valued functions (CLR and T-SQL)
- SQL scalar functions (CLR and T-SQL)
- User-defined aggregate functions (CLR)

The commands for creating synonyms are quite simple:

- CREATE SYNONYM <synonym name> FOR <object name>
- DROP SYNONYM

For example, in the AdventureWorksDW database, say we wanted access to the AdventureWorks.HumanResources.Employee table. We might create an Emp synonym, like this:

```
CREATE SYNONYM Emp FOR AdventureWorks.HumanResources.Employee
```

Now to see all of the Employees, we use the following:

```
SELECT * from Emp
```

Finally, we drop the synonym:

```
DROP SYNONYM Emp
```

Security is much like stored procedure security is in previous versions. If the object used is owned by the same owner, and the user has rights to the synonym, then it is the same as giving this user rights to the object (only via use of the synonym, not the base object). If the object and synonym have different owners, then the security chain is broken, and rights to the base object must be checked.

For example, let's create a new login and user in the AdventureWorks database:

```
CREATE LOGIN ANDREW WITH PASSWORD = 'ANDREW1'
CREATE USER ANDREW FOR LOGIN ANDREW
```

Now, we will create a synonym and a view on the sales.customer table.

```
CREATE SYNONYM synSecure FOR sales.customer
GO
CREATE VIEW viewSecure --as a contrasting example
AS
SELECT *
FROM sales.customer
GO
```

Then we will grant all rights on each to user ANDREW on these two objects:

```
GRANT SELECT,INSERT,UPDATE,DELETE ON synSecure to ANDREW
GRANT SELECT,INSERT,UPDATE,DELETE ON viewSecure to ANDREW
```

Now, change security context to user ANDREW and try to select from the base table:

```
EXECUTE AS LOGIN='ANDREW'
SELECT * from sales.customer
```

This returns the expected error:

```
Msg 229, Level 14, State 5, Line 1
SELECT permission denied on object 'Customer', database 'AdventureWorks',
schema 'Sales'.
```

while both of these will return the entire table:

```
SELECT * from viewSecure
SELECT * from synSecure
```

This works because both the synonym and the object are owned by the same user, in our case dbo. If you want to change the owner of an object or schema, use the ALTER AUTHORIZATION command.

■**New Feature** Synonyms give you the capability to reference objects using different names for simplification or encapsulation.

General Development

In addition to the commands you use to define your DDL and DML, T-SQL supports commands to implement functional code in stored procedures, functions, triggers, and batches. There have been several changes and new features for T-SQL commands, and we will discuss these in this section:

- *Error handling*: Some ability to deal with errors in T-SQL code

- .WRITE *extension to the* UPDATE *statement*: Easy mechanism to support chunked updates to (max) datatypes

- EXECUTE: Extensions to EXECUTE to specify a server at which to execute the code

- *Code security context*: Extensions to procedure and function declarations to specify security context

- *.NET declarations statements*: Extensions to declare .NET assemblies for use in T-SQL

Error Handling

For as long as any T-SQL programmer can remember, error handling has been the weakest part of writing T-SQL. The story in SQL Server 2005 is getting far better, as it will now support the use of TRY...CATCH constructs for providing rich error handling.

Before we show you the TRY...CATCH construct, we'll establish how this would need to be done in SQL Server 2000. We'll create the following two tables (again, if you're following along, create these tables in your own database, or simply in tempdb):

```
CREATE SCHEMA Entertainment
    CREATE TABLE TV
(
    TVid int primary key,
    location varchar(20),
    diagonalWidth int
            CONSTRAINT CKEntertainment_tv_checkWidth CHECK (diagonalWidth >= 30)
)

go

CREATE TABLE dbo.error_log
(
    tableName sysname,
    userName sysname,
    errorNumber int,
    errorSeverity int,
    errorState int,
    errorMessage varchar(4000)
)
GO
```

In previous versions of SQL Server, logging and handling errors was ugly, and required querying the @@error system variable to see if a runtime error had occurred, and then you could do what you wanted. Generally speaking, we like to include a facility for logging that an error occurs. For example:

```
CREATE PROCEDURE entertainment.tv$insert
(
        @TVid           int,
        @location       varchar(30),
        @diagonalWidth  int
)
AS
declare @Error int

    BEGIN TRANSACTION

    --Insert a row
    INSERT entertainment.TV (TVid, location, diagonalWidth)
    VALUES(@TVid, @location, @diagonalWidth)
```

```
    --save @@ERROR so we don't lose it.
    SET @Error=@@ERROR
    IF @Error<>0
      BEGIN
        -- an error has occurred
        GOTO ErrorHandler
      END

    COMMIT TRANSACTION

GOTO ExitProc

ErrorHandler:
    -- Rollback the transaction
    ROLLBACK TRANSACTION
    -- log the error into the error_log table
    INSERT dbo.error_log (tableName, userName,
                          errorNumber, errorSeverity ,errorState ,
                          errorMessage)
      VALUES('TV',suser_sname(),@Error,0,0,'We do not know the message!')
ExitProc:
GO
```

If we execute the procedure with an invalid parameter value disallowed by our CHECK constraint:

```
exec entertainment.tv$insert @TVid = 1, @location = 'Bed Room', @diagonalWidth = 29
```

since our table has a CHECK constraint making sure that the diagonalWidth column is 30 or greater, this returns the following:

```
Msg 547, Level 16, State 0, Procedure tv$insert, Line 13
The INSERT statement conflicted with the CHECK constraint
"CKEntertainment_tv_checkWidth". The conflict occurred in database "AdventureWorks"
,table "TV", column 'diagonalWidth'.
The statement has been terminated.
```

Checking the error log table, the error was logged, though somewhat useless:

```
SELECT * FROM dbo.error_log
```

This produces

tableName	userName	errorID	errorNumber	errorSeverity	errorState
TV	DOMAINNAME\LBDAVI	1	547	0	0

errorMessage
We do not know the message!

Error handling quickly becomes a rather large percentage of the code with repetitive blocks of code used to check for an error. Even worse, we could not stop this message from being sent to the client. So the burden of deciding what went wrong was placed on the client, based on using these error messages. Needless to say, error handling in SQL Server 2000 and earlier was a real pain, and this often lead to applications NOT using CHECK constraints.

TRY...CATCH lets us build error handling at the level we need, in the way we need to, by setting a region where if any error occurs, it will break out of the region and head to an error handler. The basic structure is

```
BEGIN TRY
    <code>
END TRY
BEGIN CATCH
    <code>
END CATCH
```

So if any error occurs in the TRY block, execution is diverted to the CATCH block and the error can be dealt with. For example, take a look at the following simple code sample:

```
BEGIN TRY
    RAISERROR ('Something is amiss',16,1)
END TRY
BEGIN CATCH
    select ERROR_NUMBER() as ERROR_NUMBER,
           ERROR_SEVERITY() as ERROR_SEVERITY,
           ERROR_STATE() as ERROR_STATE,
           ERROR_MESSAGE() as ERROR_MESSAGE
END CATCH
```

In the TRY block, all we are going to do is raise an error. Running this we get the following:

ERROR_NUMBER	ERROR_SEVERITY	ERROR_STATE	ERROR_MESSAGE
50000	16	1	Something is amiss

Notice when you execute this, you never see

```
Msg 50000, Level 16, State 1, Line 1
Something is amiss
```

Now let's look at a more detailed, more interesting example. First, we clear the tables we have built for our examples:

```
DELETE FROM entertainment.TV --in case you have added rows
DELETE FROM dbo.error_log
```

Next, we recode the procedure to employ TRY and CATCH blocks. Far less code is required, and it is much clearer what is going on.

```
ALTER PROCEDURE entertainment.tv$insert
(
    @TVid         int,
    @location     varchar(30),
    @diagonalWidth int
)
```

```
AS
    SET NOCOUNT ON
     BEGIN TRY
         BEGIN TRANSACTION
         INSERT TV (TVid, location, diagonalWidth)
                 VALUES(@TVid, @location, @diagonalWidth)
         COMMIT TRANSACTION
     END TRY
     BEGIN CATCH
         ROLLBACK TRANSACTION
         INSERT dbo.error_log (tableName, userName,
                              errorNumber, errorSeverity ,errorState ,
                              errorMessage)
         VALUES('TV',suser_sname(),ERROR_NUMBER(),
               ERROR_SEVERITY(), ERROR_STATE(), ERROR_MESSAGE())
         RAISERROR ('Error creating new TV row',16,1)
     END CATCH
```

Execution goes into the TRY block, starts a transaction, and then creates rows in our table. If it fails, we fall into the CATCH block where the error is sent to the log procedure as it was in the previous example, only we get access to the error information so we can insert meaningful information, rather than only the error number.

Now execute the procedure and check the error log table.

```
exec entertainment.tv$insert @TVid = 1, @location = 'Bed Room',
                             @diagonalWidth = 29
GO
SELECT * FROM dbo.error_log
GO
```

This returns the error message we created:

```
Msg 50000, Level 16, State 1, Procedure tv$insert, Line 18
Error creating new TV row
```

And from the SELECT from the error log:

tableName	userName	errorID	errorNumber	errorSeverity	errorState
TV	COMPASS.NET\LBDAVI	4	547	16	0

```
errorMessage
-------------------------------------------------------------------------------
 The INSERT statement conflicted with the CHECK constraint
"CKEntertainment_tv_checkWidth". The conflict occurred in database "AdventureWorks"
, table "TV", column 'diagonalWidth'.
```

we get the full error message. So we can save off the "ugly" error message and try to give a better message. It is not perfect, but it is leaps and bounds above what we had. The main limitation is that we will have to do some messy work to translate that constraint to a usable message. But at least this message was not sent to the user.

But this is not all. TRY...CATCH blocks can be nested to give you powerful error handling capabilities when nesting calls. For example, say we create the following procedure:

```
CREATE PROCEDURE dbo.raise_an_error
AS
 BEGIN
        BEGIN TRY
                raiserror ('Boom, boom, boom, boom',16,1)
        END TRY
        BEGIN CATCH  --just catch it, return it as a select,
                     --and raise another error
           SELECT ERROR_NUMBER() AS ErrorNumber,
                  ERROR_SEVERITY() AS ErrorSeverity,
                  ERROR_STATE() as ErrorState, ERROR_LINE() as ErrorLine,
                  ERROR_PROCEDURE() as ErrorProcedure,
                  ERROR_MESSAGE() as ErrorMessage
                  RAISERROR ('Error in procedure raise_an_error',16,1)
        END CATCH
 END
go
```

So all this procedure will do is raise an error, causing our CATCH block to start, select out the error as a resultset, and then reraise the error. This reraising of the error causes there to be a single point of impact for error handling. You can decide what to do with it when you call the procedure. For example, consider the following batch that we will use to call this procedure:

```
SET NOCOUNT ON
BEGIN TRY
    exec raise_an_error --@no_parm = 1 (we will uncomment this for a test
    select 'I am never getting here'
END TRY
BEGIN CATCH
    SELECT ERROR_NUMBER() AS ErrorNumber, ERROR_SEVERITY() AS ErrorSeverity,
           ERROR_STATE() as ErrorState, ERROR_LINE() as ErrorLine,
           Ecast(ERROR_PROCEDURE() as varchar(30)) as ErrorProcedure,
             cast(ERROR_MESSAGE() as varchar(40))as ErrorMessage
END CATCH
```

Running this, which simply causes an error to be raised by the subordinate procedure, we get two result sets:

First:

ErrorNumber	ErrorSeverity	ErrorState	ErrorLine	ErrorProcedure
50000	16	1	5	raise_an_error

ErrorMessage
Boom, boom, boom, boom

Then:

ErrorNumber	ErrorSeverity	ErrorState	ErrorLine	ErrorProcedure
50000	16	1	12	raise_an_error

ErrorMessage
Error in procedure raise_an_error

Uncomment the @no_parm = 1 bit from the statement, and you will see that that error is trapped and the message "Procedure raise_an_error has no parameters and arguments were supplied." is returned as a resultset.

If you want to ignore errors altogether, you can include an empty CATCH block:

```
SET NOCOUNT ON
BEGIN TRY
    exec raise_an_error @no_parm = 1
    select 'hi'
END TRY
BEGIN CATCH
END CATCH
```

You can also see that in all cases the code never executes the select 'hi' statement. There is no RESUME type of action in the TRY...CATCH way of handling errors.

While there is an error raised because of the invalid parameter, it is not visible to the caller. So it is incredibly important that you make certain that a CATCH handler is included unless you really don't want the error raised.

Warning Obviously, this is one of those places where you really need to be careful. In all probability, you will want to send up a flag of some kind to the client for *most* errors, though there are times when this is not the case.

The one type of error that will not be handled by the TRY...CATCH mechanism is a syntax error. For example:

```
SET NOCOUNT ON
BEGIN TRY
    exeec procedure --error here is on purpose!

END TRY
BEGIN CATCH
END CATCH
```

This returns the following:

```
Msg 102, Level 15, State 1, Line 3
Incorrect syntax near 'exeec'.
```

The only case where TRY...CATCH captures syntax errors is when used in an EXECUTE ('<SQL CODE>') situation. Here if you execute the following:

```
SET NOCOUNT ON
BEGIN TRY
    exec ('seeelect *')

END TRY
BEGIN CATCH
      SELECT  ERROR_NUMBER() AS ErrorNumber, ERROR_SEVERITY() AS ErrorSeverity,
              ERROR_STATE() as ErrorState, ERROR_LINE() as ErrorLine,
              cast(ERROR_PROCEDURE() as varchar(60)) as ErrorProcedure,
              cast(ERROR_MESSAGE() as varchar(550))as ErrorMessage
END CATCH
```

an error will be returned via the SELECT statement in the CATCH block. One of the limitations that you will have to deal with is when you are doing several operations in the same batch. For example, consider our tv$insert procedure. Instead of inserting a single row, let's say we are going to insert two rows:

```
...
BEGIN TRANSACTION
INSERT TV (TVid, location, diagonalWidth)
VALUES(@TVid, @location, @diagonalWidth)
--second insert:
INSERT TV (TVid, location, diagonalWidth)
VALUES(@TVid, @location, @diagonalWidth / 2 )

COMMIT TRANSACTION
...
```

How would we tell the two inserts apart if one of them had an error? It would not be possible, as either statement could break the rules of the TV table's CHECK constraint. In this case, one possible way to deal with this would be a custom error message value. So you might do something like this:

```
ALTER PROCEDURE entertainment.tv$insert
(
        @TVid                int,
        @location            varchar(30),
        @diagonalWidth       int
)
AS
    SET NOCOUNT ON
    DECLARE @errorMessage varchar(2000)
    BEGIN TRY
                BEGIN TRANSACTION
                SET @errorMessage = 'Error inserting TV with diagonalWidth / 1'
                INSERT TV (TVid, location, diagonalWidth)
                VALUES(@TVid, @location, @diagonalWidth)

                --second insert:
                SET @errorMessage = 'Error inserting TV with diagonalWidth / 2'
                INSERT TV (TVid, location, diagonalWidth)
                VALUES(@TVid, @location, @diagonalWidth / 2 )

                COMMIT TRANSACTION
    END TRY
```

```
        BEGIN CATCH
                ROLLBACK TRANSACTION
                INSERT dbo.error_log VALUES('TV',suser_sname(),
                        ERROR_NUMBER(),ERROR_SEVERITY(),
                        ERROR_STATE(), ERROR_MESSAGE())
                RAISERROR (@errorMessage,16,1)
        END CATCH
GO
```

Now we can execute it:

```
exec entertainment.tv$insert @TVid = 10, @location = 'Bed Room',
                        @diagonalWidth = 30
```

This returns

```
Msg 50000, Level 16, State 1, Procedure tv$insert, Line 28
Error inserting TV with diagonalWidth / 1
```

And then again with a number big enough to satisfy it, but not when it is divided by two:

```
exec entertainment.tv$insert @TVid = 11, @location = 'Bed Room',
                        @diagonalWidth = 60
```

which returns

```
Msg 50000, Level 16, State 1, Procedure tv$insert, Line 28
Error inserting TV with diagonalWidth / 2
```

The key here (other than we really like TV and don't like small ones) is to make sure to give your CATCH block enough information to raise a useful error, or the error messages you may produce using the new error handling will not be all that much better than what we had before.

Error handling in SQL Server 2005 is *vastly* improved over previous versions, but it is going to take a big mindshift to get us there. Once you start blocking errors from the client that has expected errors in the past, you may break code by trying to fix it. So careful study and some re-engineering will likely be in order to really start using the new error handling capabilities.

■**Change** The new TRY and CATCH blocks make safe coding easier for handling errors, including stopping error messages from ever making it to the client.

.WRITE Extension to the UPDATE Statement

In previous versions of SQL Server, modifying the data in text and image columns was a real beast using T-SQL code. There were arcane commands READTEXT and WRITETEXT to do "chunked" reads and writes (just reading and writing part of a value to save the resources of fetching huge amounts of data). In SQL Server 2005, the use of the text and image types is being deprecated for the new (max) datatypes: varchar(max), nvarchar(max), and varrbinary(max). Text and image are still available, but their use should be phased out in favor of the far better (max) types.

For the most part, you can treat the max datatypes just like their regular 8000 byte or less counterparts, but if you are dealing with very large values, this may not be desired. Each of the (max) types can store up to 2GB in a single column. Imagine having to fetch this value to the client, make some changes, and then issue an UPDATE statement for a two-character change? RAM is cheap, but not cheap enough to put 4GB on all of your machines. So we can do a "chunked" update of the data in the row using a new extension to the UPDATE statement. (Note that you can do chunked reads simply by using the substring function.)

As an example, consider the following simple table with a varchar(max) column:

```
create table testBIGtext
(
    testBIGtextId  int PRIMARY KEY,
    value          varchar(max)
)
```

Now we create a new value simply as an empty string:

```
insert into testBIGtext
values(1,'')
```

Next, we just build a loop and, using .WRITE, we put some text into the value at an offset for some length. Note that the offset must be less than or equal to the current length of the value in the column. The syntax is shown here:

```
UPDATE <tableName>
SET    <(max)columnName>.WRITE(<scalar value>, <offset in column>,<# of bytes>
WHERE ...
```

Then we just start a loop and write 1000 of each letter of the alphabet into the value column:

```
DECLARE @offset int
SET @offset = 0
WHILE @offset < 26
 BEGIN
       UPDATE testBIGtext
           --the text I am writing is just starting at the letter A --> char(97)
           --and increasing by adding the value of offset to 97 char(97) = a
           --char (98) = b. It is also used as the offset in the varchar(max) column.
           --It is multiplied by the length of the data being written to fill a
           --pattern of aaabbbccc...zzz only with a 1000 of each
       SET value.write(replicate(char(97 + @offset),1000),@offset*1000, 1000)
       WHERE  testBIGTextId = 1

       SET @offset = @offset + 1
 END
```

Everything else is just plain SQL. To check to make sure our data is in there:

```
select testBIGtextId, len(value) as CharLength
from  testBIGtext
```

This returns the following:

testBIGtextId	CharLength
1	26000

This is a tremendous win for SQL programmers. Long datatypes can easily be worked with using normal functions, *plus* there's a chunking mechanism so that when we have a column holding a couple hundred megabytes of information, we don't have to replace the whole thing in one operation.

■**New Feature** .WRITE allows for writing "chunks" of data into a large varchar(max), nvarchar(max), or varbinary(max) column.

EXECUTE

The EXECUTE command in previous versions of SQL Server could only be used to execute SQL on the same server. In SQL Server 2005, EXECUTE has added an AT parameter to specify that the command be executed on a linked server.

To see this in action, let's set up our local server as a remote linked server. So we will create a linked server using sp_addlinkedserver, call it LocalLinkedServer, and point this to our instance of SQL Server:

```
--note, if you are not running SQL Server as the default instance, you may
--have to change where I have specified localhost to point to your server instance
EXECUTE sp_addlinkedserver    @server='LocalLinkedServer', @srvproduct='',
                              @provider='SQLOLEDB', @datasrc='localhost'

--enable the linked server to allow remote procedure calls
EXECUTE  sp_serveroption 'LocalLinkedServer','RPC OUT',True
```

Now we can execute our T-SQL on the linked server by specifying AT and the linked server name:

```
EXECUTE('SELECT * FROM AdventureWorks.Production.Culture') AT LocalLinkedServer
```

The query is executed on the linked server and the results returned. The AT parameter only applies to using EXECUTE on batches of statements, not on explicit stored procedure or function calls.

You can then use sp_dropserver to get rid of the linked server:

```
EXECUTE sp_dropserver LocalLinkedServer
```

■**New Feature** The EXECUTE command allows the specifying of a linked server to send the T-SQL commands to by using the AT keyword.

For completeness, we need to make mention that there already exists a method of executing a batch of commands on another SQL Server, using sp_executesql. It has the added benefit of allowing for parameter and return values. This procedure can also be called remotely as follows:

```
EXECUTE ourLinkedServer.master.dbo.sp_executesql
                @statement = N'SELECT * FROM AdventureWorks.Production.Culture'
```

Code Security Context

The EXECUTE AS clause on a procedure or function declaration allows you to define the security context in which a stored procedure or function (other than inline table-valued functions) is executed. Without this clause, the object executes in the security context of the CALLER. Note that this does not affect the execution of the procedure *unless* there is a break in the ownership chain. Any object owned by the creator of the procedure will be available to the user.

The syntax of this clause is

```
CREATE PROCEDURE <procedureName>
[parameters]
WITH EXECUTE AS <option>
```

```
AS
    <Procedure definition>
```

It is the same syntax when used for functions. There are four possible values for the EXECUTE AS option:

- EXECUTE AS CALLER (the default)
- EXECUTE AS SELF
- EXECUTE AS OWNER
- EXECUTE AS USER=<username>

You can also execute one of these as a stand-alone command to change the context of who is executing the procedure back to the CALLER if needed. One additional statement is included: REVERT to go back to the context set in the WITH clause of the procedure declaration. As an example, we're going to create a user, named barney, and then a procedure that uses the EXECUTE AS option on a procedure to show the basics of EXECUTE AS.

We'll start by creating several users, tables, and procedures:

```
--this user will be the owner of the primary schema
CREATE LOGIN mainOwner WITH PASSWORD = 'mainOwnery'
CREATE USER mainOwner FOR LOGIN mainOwner
GRANT CREATE SCHEMA to mainOwner
GRANT CREATE TABLE to mainOwner

--this will be the procedure creator
CREATE LOGIN secondaryOwner WITH PASSWORD = 'secondaryOwnery'
CREATE USER secondaryOwner FOR LOGIN secondaryOwner
GRANT CREATE SCHEMA to secondaryOwner
GRANT CREATE PROCEDURE to secondaryOwner
GRANT CREATE TABLE to secondaryOwner

--this will be the average user who needs to access data
CREATE LOGIN aveSchlub WITH PASSWORD = 'aveSchluby'
CREATE USER aveSchlub FOR LOGIN aveSchlub
```

Then we change to the context of the main object owner, create a new schema, and then create a table with some rows:

```
EXECUTE AS USER='mainOwner'
GO
CREATE SCHEMA mainOwnersSchema
GO
CREATE TABLE  mainOwnersSchema.person
(
    personId    int constraint PKtestAccess_person primary key,
    firstName   varchar(20),
    lastName    varchar(20)
)
GO

INSERT INTO mainOwnersSchema.person
VALUES (1, 'Paul','McCartney')
INSERT INTO mainOwnersSchema.person
VALUES (2, 'Pete','Townshend')
GO
```

Next, this user gives SELECT permissions to the secondaryOwner user:

```
GRANT SELECT on mainOwnersSchema.person to secondaryOwner
```

Then we set the context to the secondary user to create the procedure:

```
REVERT  --we can step back on the stack of principals,
              --but we can't change directly to secondaryOwner
go
EXECUTE AS USER = 'secondaryOwner'
go
```

Then we create a schema and another table:

```
CREATE SCHEMA secondaryOwnerSchema
GO
CREATE TABLE secondaryOwnerSchema.otherPerson
(
    personId     int constraint PKtestAccess_person primary key,
    firstName    varchar(20),
    lastName     varchar(20)
)
GO

INSERT INTO secondaryOwnerSchema.otherPerson
VALUES (1, 'Rocky','Racoon')
INSERT INTO secondaryOwnerSchema.otherPerson
VALUES (2, 'Sally','Simpson')
GO
```

Then we create two procedures as the secondary users, one for the WITH EXECUTE AS as CALLER, which is the default, then SELF, which puts it in the context of the creator, in this case secondaryOwner:

```
CREATE PROCEDURE   secondaryOwnerSchema.person$asCaller
WITH EXECUTE AS CALLER --this is the default
AS
SELECT   personId, firstName, lastName
FROM     secondaryOwnerSchema.otherPerson --<-- ownership same as proc
SELECT   personId, firstName, lastName
FROM     mainOwnersSchema.person  --<-- breaks ownership chain
GO

CREATE PROCEDURE secondaryOwnerSchema.person$asSelf
WITH EXECUTE AS SELF  --now this runs in context of secondaryOwner,
                      --since it created it
AS
SELECT   personId, firstName, lastName
FROM     secondaryOwnerSchema.otherPerson --<-- ownership same as proc

SELECT   personId, firstName, lastName
FROM     mainOwnersSchema.person  --<-- breaks ownership chain
GO
```

Next, we grant rights on the procedure to the aveSchlub user:

```
GRANT EXECUTE ON secondaryOwnerSchema.person$asCaller to aveSchlub
GRANT EXECUTE ON secondaryOwnerSchema.person$asSelf to aveSchlub
```

Then we change to the context of aveSchlub:

```
REVERT
GO
EXECUTE AS USER = 'aveSchlub'
GO
```

And execute the procedure:

```
--this proc is in context of the caller, in this case, aveSchlub
execute secondaryOwnerSchema.person$asCaller
```

which gives us the following output:

```
personId    firstName             lastName
----------- --------------------- --------------------
1           Rocky                 Racoon
2           Sally                 Simpson
Msg 229, Level 14, State 5, Procedure person$asCaller, Line 4
SELECT permission denied on object 'person', database 'tempdb', schema
'mainOwnersSchema'.
```

Next, we execute the asSelf variant:

```
--secondaryOwner, so it works
execute secondaryOwnerSchema.person$asSelf
```

which gives us the following output:

```
personId    firstName             lastName
----------- --------------------- --------------------
1           Rocky                 Racoon
2           Sally                 Simpson

personId    firstName             lastName
----------- --------------------- --------------------
1           Paul                  McCartney
2           Pete                  Townshend
```

What makes this different is that when the ownership chain is broken, the security context we are in is the secondaryUser, not the context of the caller, aveSchlub. This is a really cool feature, as we can now give users temporary rights that will not even be apparent to them, and will not require granting any permissions.

It is not, however, a feature that should be overused, as it could be all too easy to just build your procedures in the context of the dbo. One nice side effect of this is that we could use it instead of chaining, by setting EXECUTE AS to a user who can access a different database directly, so the system user may have rights to the database, but the executing user cannot. These are just the basics; EXECUTE AS is discussed in more detail in Chapter 10.

.NET Declarations

.NET is tightly integrated with SQL Server 2005. .NET integration is covered in greater depth in Chapter 5, so in this section we are simply going to cover the commands to make assemblies available for use in T-SQL code.

Assembly Maintenance

Prior to using .NET assemblies in T-SQL code, you must declare and load them from the DLL file. `CREATE ASSEMBLY` loads a managed class into SQL Server 2005 memory space so that the CLR database objects can be created. (See the next section for more information on the CLR Database Object declarations.)

The syntax of the `CREATE ASSEMBLY` command is as follows:

```
CREATE ASSEMBLY <assemblyName> FROM <assemblyLocation>
```

For example:

```
CREATE ASSEMBLY dateObject FROM 'C:\projects\bin\Debug\setDate.dll'
```

After loading, the assembly can be subsequently removed using the `DROP ASSEMBLY` command, as shown in this example:

```
DROP ASSEMBLY dateObject
```

An assembly cannot be dropped if any CLR database objects reference it. These references can be seen using Management Studio by right-clicking the Assembly. The assembly commands have more options to them that we will not cover here.

CLR Database Objects

Once an assembly has been created as an OS file and created as a database object, it can then be used to declare objects, including stored procedures, functions, triggers, user-defined types, and user-defined aggregate functions that it has been designed to. The syntax of `CREATE` and `ALTER` for the T-SQL objects also includes the ability to reference CLR objects instead of T-SQL. The basic syntax for these CLR extensions is

```
[CREATE][ALTER] DBOBJECTTYPE ([parameters])
                        AS EXTERNAL NAME assembly_name:class_name
```

For example, to create a procedure that points to a .NET assembly that has been created as an object on the SQL Server, in this case a fictitious one called `getDateValueString`, we could build the following procedure:

```
CREATE PROCEDURE dateString
(
    @dateValue datetime output
) AS EXTERNAL NAME  dateObject:utf8string::getDateValueString
```

The following commands are affected by this change:

- `CREATE/ALTER PROCEDURE`
- `CREATE/ALTER FUNCTION`
- `CREATE/ALTER TRIGGER`
- `CREATE/ALTER TYPE`
- `CREATE/ALTER AGGREGATE`

This has been just a very brief introduction to the new SQL Server commands that revolve around .NET integration. .NET integration is discussed in much more detail in Chapter 5 of this book.

Summary

In this chapter, we looked at a bunch of new features that have been added to T-SQL. The changes are not vast, but several of them will affect the way you code objects in important ways. For example:

- *Error handling*: Error handling had always been pretty bad in T-SQL, and it is vastly improved in SQL Server 2005. Every stored procedure will likely be done differently based on the new error handling.

- *CTEs*: Using them will make some complex queries leaner, and make hierarchies easier to deal with.

- APPLY *join operator*: Table-based user-defined functions can now take columns as parameters so they can be effectively used in the FROM clause of queries.

- *Ranking functions*: Powerful functions that let you add sequence information about your sets.

- .WRITE *on* UPDATE *statement*: Allows for chunked updates of large text objects using T-SQL rather than READTEXT and WRITETEXT. (No pointers to deal with in code!)

- *Output Clause*: Cool way to see what changes are made to a table without a trigger.

- *Synonyms*: Allows you to virtually rename any object in SQL Server.

- INTERSECT *and* EXCEPT: Set-based operators that work like UNION for finding rows that are in both sets (INTERSECT) or the differences between two sets (EXCEPT).

- PIVOT *and* UNPIVOT: Operators that give you the ability to shift the rows of a table to the columns (PIVOT) and back again (UNPIVOT).

All of these changes extend an already good language and make it better, giving you power to manipulate data in faster and more convenient ways.

CHAPTER 4

■ ■ ■

T-SQL Enhancements for DBAs

SQL Server 2005 includes a bevy of new T-SQL commands to make the jobs (and lives) of DBAs easier and working with the database system more efficient. In this chapter, we'll discuss these new features and changes, including replacement of the cryptic system tables with a new set of more usable metadata views, the addition of DDL triggers to simplify auditing of database object changes, a variety of indexing and performance enhancements for tables and views, a new high-concurrency isolation level, and a few new statements to assist with the ever-present question of data integrity.

Metadata Views

Most SQL Server DBAs do not exactly relish the idea of having to crawl through the system tables. Remembering the various types of id columns (which are often misleadingly named) and attempting to decode columns like xtype is often an error-prone task and not a productive use of the DBA's time. It can be surprising to new users of SQL Server 2000 that even a task as mundane as listing all of the tables in a database with their columns and datatypes would require T-SQL as odd as the following:

```
SELECT
    so.name AS theTable,
    sc.name AS theColumn,
    st.name AS theType
FROM sysobjects so
JOIN syscolumns sc ON so.id = sc.id
JOIN systypes st ON sc.xtype = st.xtype
WHERE
    so.type = 'U'
```

The SQL Server 2005 data dictionary situation is quite a bit better. Even for this basic task, the required query is simpler and easier to understand:

```
SELECT
    t.name AS theTable,
    c.name AS theColumn,
    ty.name AS theType
FROM sys.tables t
JOIN sys.columns c ON t.object_id = c.object_id
JOIN sys.types ty ON c.system_type_id = ty.system_type_id
```

It's not just the lack of a WHERE clause that makes this query more readable; it's the little differences, like primary key column names that actually make sense!

In SQL Server 2005, the system tables from SQL Server 2000 are deprecated, having been replaced by two new sets of views. For backward-compatibility purposes, the system tables from previous versions of SQL Server are also still around, in the form of a third set of views. The system tables themselves are now hidden from direct user contact, but should you have legacy code written against them, you'll find that queries will still work and applications will not break; the views do a good job of mimicking the tables' functionality. However, the new metadata views offer much greater usability.

Tables describing objects (e.g., sysobjects and syscolumns) have been replaced by a set of views called the *catalog views*. Tables describing system state (e.g., syscacheobjects and syslocks) are now represented by a set of views called the *dynamic management views*. And the older tables themselves can now be found in a set of views appropriately called the *compatibility views*. The ANSI standard INFORMATION_SCHEMA views are also still around, but due to the fact that so much of the functionality in SQL Server is not ANSI compliant, these views fail to provide much value in SQL Server 2005.

Compatibility Views

All of the SQL Server 2000 system tables have been migrated into a collection of views in the sys schema (see Chapter 11 for more on schemas) called the compatibility views. Their behavior is mostly the same as it was in previous versions of SQL Server, with a few notable changes, primarily to the sysindexes view. You should attempt to migrate existing code away from the compatibility views, and start using the new catalog views instead.

Querying the views is basically the same in SQL Server 2005 as it was in previous versions. SELECT * FROM sysobjects still returns information about objects in the current database. And SELECT * FROM sysindexes still returns information about indexes. However, some columns have been deprecated, so you should carefully test existing code before migrating it to SQL Server 2005. For instance, in SQL Server 2000, the keys column of the sysindexes system table contained a list of the columns that made up the index. But in SQL Server 2005, that column will always be NULL. Other columns in the sys.sysindexes view that are not quite backward compatible are dpages, reserved, used, rowmodctr, maxirow, and statblob. Code that uses these columns should be rewritten to use the sys.indexes view.

Catalog Views

The catalog views are repositories for "static" metadata. They contain data about both serverwide and database-specific objects, including logins, tables, and stored procedures, as opposed to more "dynamic" data, such as locks and the state of the procedure cache. You'll find that they are both more comprehensive and user-friendly than the system tables in SQL Server 2000 were. For instance, the sysindexes table in SQL Server 2000 contained a column called indid that would hold various codes depending on the index type: 0 meant the table was a heap; 1 was a clustered index; and a value greater than 1 was a nonclustered index, unless it was 255, in which case it wasn't an index at all, but an indication that the table had a large object (TEXT or IMAGE) column!

In SQL Server 2005, these cryptic values are gone, and the indid column has been replaced in the sys.indexes catalog view by a column called type_desc. This column can contain the following self-explanatory character values: HEAP, CLUSTERED, NONCLUSTERED, and XML. Quite an improvement. To find a list of all heap tables (tables without clustered indexes) in a SQL Server 2005 database, use the following query:

```
SELECT
    OBJECT_NAME(object_id) AS theTable
FROM sys.indexes
WHERE
    type_desc = 'HEAP'
```

Many other improvements have been made. For instance, almost all code numbers have been replaced by English character strings, and bitmasks and other internal structures have been replaced by normalized tables. One enhancement in particular that many DBAs will enjoy is the addition of a column called modify_date to the sys.objects views and other views that inherit from it (including sys.procedures and sys.views). No more trying to pinpoint the last time someone ran an ALTER on one of the database objects.

Table 4-1 lists some of the key system tables from SQL Server 2000 and the catalog views now present in SQL Server 2005.

Table 4-1. *System Tables and Their Catalog View Equivalents*

System Table	Catalog View(s)	Description
syscolumns	sys.columns sys.computed_columns sys.foreign_key_columns sys.identity_columns	The sys.columns view contains information about every column in every table in the current database. The other views can be used to get information about specific types of columns.
syscomments	sys.sql_modules Also see the OBJECT_DEFINITION function	The sys.sql_modules view and the OBJECT_DEFINITION function allow DBAs to get the definition of T-SQL stored procedures, triggers, functions, and views.
sysconstraints	sys.check_constraints sys.default_constraints sys.key_constraints	These views contain information about column- and table-level CHECK, DEFUALT, PRIMARY KEY, and FOREIGN KEY constraints.
sysdatabases	sys.databases	This view contains information about every database on the server.
sysdepends	sys.sql_dependencies	This view helps DBAs determine which objects are dependent upon other objects in the system. For instance, SQL Server will attempt to determine which tables are referenced by which stored procedures and expose that mapping in this view. Note that this view is not guaranteed to contain all dependencies in the system; due to late binding and dynamic SQL, some references may not be present at the time of object creation.
sysfiles	sys.database_files	This view exposes information about the physical files that back the current database.
sysforeignkeys	sys.foreign_keys sys.foreign_key_columns	These views contain data about FOREIGN KEY constraints.
sysindexes	sys.indexes	This view contains information about which indexes have been created on which tables in the current database.
sysindexkeys	sys.index_columns	This view, used in conjunction with sys.indexes, allows DBAs to determine which columns participate in indexes.
syslogins	sys.sql_logins	This view exposes data about system logins.
sysobjects	sys.objects sys.procedures sys.tables sys.views sys.triggers	The sys.objects view contains information about every user object in the current database. For information about specific object types, the sys.procedures, sys.tables, sys.views, or sys.triggers view can be used.

Table 4-1 is by no means a comprehensive list of the available catalog views. Virtually every type of object available in SQL Server 2005 has an associated catalog view. To see a complete list, navigate to the System Views heading in Object Explorer in SQL Server Management Studio, as shown in Figure 4-1 (note that in this image, Object Explorer's filter is being used to limit results to objects in the sys schema). Throughout the rest of this chapter, we'll mention various catalog views in the context of helping to manage the new features discussed.

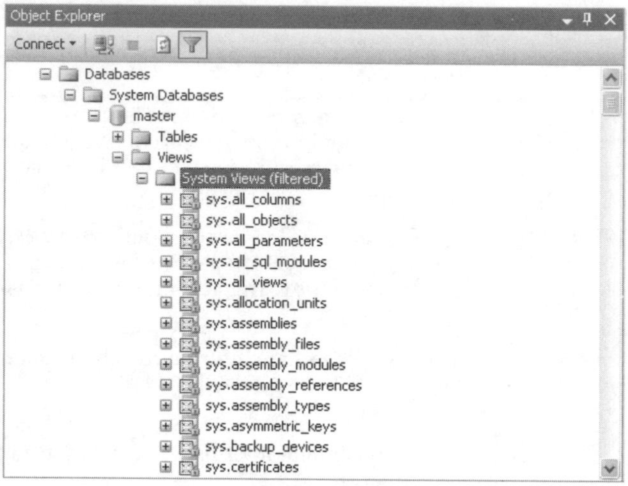

Figure 4-1. *Catalog views appear in Management Studio under the System Views heading in Object Explorer.*

Dynamic Management Views and Functions

Whereas the catalog views contain data about "static" objects, the dynamic management views and functions help the user investigate the ever-changing state of the server. Note that the dynamic management functions are really nothing more than parameterized views—they are not used for modifying data. These views and functions are, like the catalog views, collected in the sys schema, but they are prefixed with dm_. Although these views also replace and improve upon system table functionality from previous versions of SQL Server, the change that will excite most DBAs is the number of new metrics now available.

One of the most useful new functions is dm_exec_query_plan. This function shows an XML representation of query plans for cached and active queries and can take as input the plan_handle value exposed by three of the dynamic management views. The first of these views, dm_exec_requests, exposes information about what queries are active at the time the view is queried. The second, dm_exec_query_stats, stores aggregate statistics about stored procedures and functions, including such statistics as last execution time and total working time—it's a very useful new view! And the dm_exec_cached_plans view replaces the older syscacheobjects system table, with data about compiled query plans.

As an example, to see the query plans for all active requests with valid plan handles, the following T-SQL could be used:

```
SELECT thePlan.query_plan
FROM sys.dm_exec_requests
OUTER APPLY sys.dm_exec_query_plan(plan_handle) thePlan
WHERE plan_handle IS NOT NULL
```

Note See Chapter 3 for information about the new OUTER APPLY relational operator.

Once an XML query plan has been retrieved, it can be saved to a file with the extension .sqlplan. Double-click the file and it will open in SQL Server Management Studio, displayed as a graphical query plan. This feature will prove quite useful for both archiving baseline query plans before performance-tuning work and for remote troubleshooting. The XML can be opened with any instance of SQL Server Management Studio, and it does not require connectivity to the server that generated it for graphical display.

There are many other new dynamic management views—far too many to cover in this chapter. However, they have been named extremely well for browsing. Those prefixed with dm_exec contain data relating to actively executing processes. dm_os views contain operating system–related data. dm_tran views refer to transaction state data. dm_broker and dm_repl views contain data for Service Broker and replication, respectively. The dynamic management views are available in SQL Server Management Studio under the System Views heading, as shown in Figure 4-2 (note that in this image, Object Explorer's filter is being used to limit results to objects with "dm_" in their name).

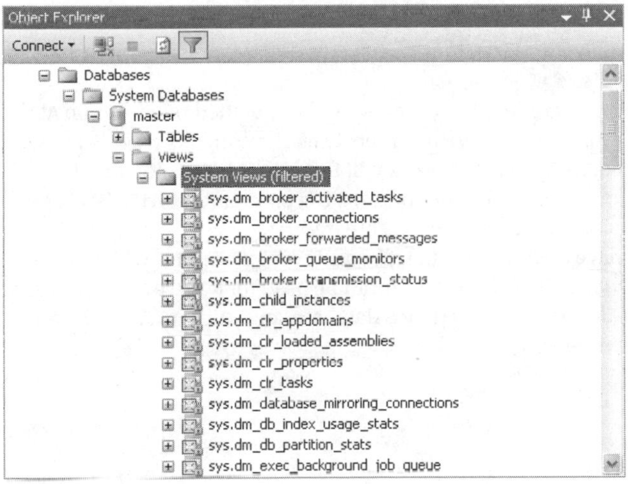

Figure 4-2. *Dynamic management views appear in Management Studio under the System Views heading in Object Explorer.*

DDL Triggers

A common security requirement for database projects is the ability to audit any kind of change to the data. Although triggers as implemented in past versions of SQL Server made this very easy for data modification (inserts and updates), it was quite difficult to audit changes to the underlying schema. DDL triggers are the answer to this problem.

A *DDL trigger* can be defined at either a serverwide or databasewide granularity, and triggers can be set to fire for creation, alteration, or deletion of virtually every SQL Server object type. Unlike DML triggers, there are no inserted or updated tables, and the update() function does not apply. Instead, data about the event that fired the trigger can be obtained via the eventdata() function.

DDL triggers are created, altered, and dropped using the same T-SQL statements as DML triggers, with a slightly different syntax. DDL triggers, like DML triggers, can also be managed using catalog views (more information on this is presented later in the section "Enumerating DDL Triggers Using Catalog Views").

Creating and Altering DDL Triggers

The syntax for creating or altering a DDL trigger is as follows:

```
{ CREATE | ALTER } TRIGGER trigger_name
ON { ALL SERVER | DATABASE }
[ WITH <ddl_trigger_option> [ …,n ] ]
{ FOR | AFTER } { event_type | event_group } [ ,...n ]
AS { sql_statement [ ...n ] | EXTERNAL NAME < method specifier > }
[ ; ]

<ddl_trigger_option> ::=
    [ ENCRYPTION ]
    [ EXECUTE AS Clause ]

<method_specifier> ::=
    assembly_name.class_name.method_name
```

Note that unlike DML triggers, DDL triggers are not defined on database objects and cannot be defined as INSTEAD OF triggers.

The most important things to note here are that the triggers can be specified on either an ALL SERVER or DATABASE level, and that the { event_type | event_group } section controls what event will cause the trigger to fire. If a trigger is created ON ALL SERVER, it will fire for any event for which it's defined, on any database on the entire server. On the other hand, a trigger created on ON DATABASE will fire only if the event occurs in the database in which it was created.

The ALL SERVER and DATABASE levels have their own event types and event groups for which triggers can be defined. Database-level events such as CREATE_TABLE cannot be used for a server-level trigger, and server-level events such as ALTER_LOGIN cannot be used for a database-level trigger. The following server-level events can be used for DDL triggers:

- CREATE|ALTER|DROP LOGIN
- CREATE|DROP HTTP ENDPOINT
- GRANT|DENY|REVOKE SERVER ACCESS
- CREATE|ALTER|DROP CERT

All other events that can be used for DDL triggers are database-level events. These include events such as CREATE|ALTER|DROP TABLE, CREATE|ALTER|DROP TRIGGER, and so on. Every DDL event that can occur in the database can be caught using a DDL trigger. A complete list of the events available to DDL triggers can be found in the SQL Server Books Online topic "Event Groups for Use with DDL Triggers."

One particularly useful event group is the DDL_DATABASE_LEVEL_EVENTS catchall. This group includes all DDL events that can occur in a database, and it is useful for situations in which a DBA might wish to either log, or block, all changes to a database. For instance, the following DDL trigger, which can be created in any database, will roll back any DDL modifications a user attempts to make, unless the trigger itself is dropped or disabled:

```
CREATE TRIGGER NoChanges
ON DATABASE
FOR DDL_DATABASE_LEVEL_EVENTS
AS
```

```
SELECT 'DDL IS NOT ALLOWED IN THE CURRENT DATABASE!'
SELECT 'TO ALLOW DDL, DROP THE NoChanges trigger.'
ROLLBACK
```

Other changes to the trigger syntax that may not seem familiar to SQL Server 2000 DBAs are the inclusion EXTERNAL NAME and EXECUTE AS clauses:

- The EXTERNAL NAME clause allows a trigger to fire a CLR object. More information on this can be found in Chapters 5 and 6, which cover CLR integration.

- The EXECUTE AS clause allows the trigger to impersonate another user's security credentials when it fires. More information on this feature can be found in Chapter 11, which covers security.

Dropping DDL Triggers

Dropping DDL triggers is slightly different than dropping DML triggers, as the trigger's scope must be specified in the statement. The syntax for dropping a DDL trigger is as follows:

```
DROP TRIGGER trigger_name [ ,...n ]
ON { DATABASE | ALL SERVER } [ ; ]
```

It's important to remember the additional ON clause when working with DDL triggers. Failing to include it will yield an error message stating that the specified trigger does not exist. This can be frustrating when you know that the trigger exists, but the system insists that it can't be found.

Enabling and Disabling DDL Triggers

DDL triggers, like DML triggers, can be enabled and disabled. In SQL Server 2005 this is done via two new statements, ENABLE TRIGGER and DISABLE TRIGGER. These statements have similar syntax to DROP TRIGGER:

```
{ ENABLE | DISABLE } TRIGGER trigger_name
ON { DATABASE | SERVER } [ ; ]
```

Note that although DDL triggers can only be enabled or disabled using these statements, DML triggers can still be enabled or disabled using ALTER TABLE.

Enumerating DDL Triggers Using Catalog Views

For obtaining information about database DDL triggers, DBAs can use the catalog views sys.triggers and sys.trigger_events. Server-level triggers can be enumerated using sys.server_triggers and sys.server_trigger_events. The sys.triggers and sys.server_triggers views have the same column definitions, except for two columns in the sys.triggers view that do not apply to DDL triggers: is_not_for_replication and is_instead_of_trigger. The events tables, on the other hand, have the same column definitions.

The parent_class_desc column can be used to differentiate DDL triggers from DML triggers when querying sys.triggers. The following query will return the name and creation date of all DDL triggers in the current database:

```
SELECT
  name,
  create_date
FROM sys.triggers
WHERE parent_class_desc = 'DATABASE'
```

The events views are related to the triggers views by the object_id column. To find out which events the active server-level triggers in the system will be fired on, use the following query:

```
SELECT
  tr.name,
  ev.type_desc
FROM sys.server_triggers tr
JOIN sys.server_trigger_events ev ON tr.object_id = ev.object_id
WHERE tr.is_disabled = 0
```

Programming DDL Triggers with the eventdata() Function

Without a way to figure out under exactly what conditions the trigger fired, DDL triggers would be relatively useless for tasks such as logging what events are taking place in a database and when they are occurring. To provide this functionality, SQL Server 2005 includes the eventdata() function. This function returns an XML document containing information about the event that fired the trigger.

Each event can return data using a different XML schema, but they all share common base schemas. Server-level events use the following base schema:

```
<EVENT_INSTANCE>
  <EventType>name</EventType>
  <PostTime>date-time</PostTime>
  <SPID>spid</SPID>
  <ServerName>server_name</ServerName>
  <LoginName>login</LoginName>
</EVENT_INSTANCE>
```

Database-level events add a UserName element:

```
<EVENT_INSTANCE>
  <EventType>name</EventType>
  <PostTime>date-time</PostTime>
  <SPID>spid</SPID>
  <ServerName>server_name</ServerName>
  <LoginName>login</LoginName>
  <UserName>user</UserName>
</EVENT_INSTANCE>
```

Various elements appear in the schemata for events as appropriate. For instance, the object-based events (CREATE_TABLE, ALTER_PROCEDURE, etc.) add elements for DatabaseName, SchemaName, ObjectName, and ObjectType, and a TSQLCommand element that contains SetOptions and CommandText elements.

By querying the XML document, it's possible to determine every aspect of the event that fired the trigger. For instance, the following trigger echoes back the username, table name, and CREATE TABLE syntax used every time a table is created or altered in the database:

```
CREATE TRIGGER ReturnEventData
ON DATABASE
FOR CREATE_TABLE, ALTER_TABLE
AS
  DECLARE @eventData XML
  SET @eventData = eventdata()

  SELECT
    @eventData.query('data(/EVENT_INSTANCE/UserName)') AS UserName,
    @eventData.query('data(/EVENT_INSTANCE/ObjectName)') AS ObjectName,
    @eventData.query('data(/EVENT_INSTANCE/TSQLCommand/CommandText)') AS CommandText
```

Note For more information on working with XML documents in SQL Server, see Chapters 7 and 8.

Of course, this trigger doesn't have to just select the data back. The data can just as easily be inserted into a logging table:

```
CREATE TABLE DDLEventLog
(
  EventDate DATETIME NOT NULL,
  UserName SYSNAME NOT NULL,
  ObjectName SYSNAME NOT NULL,
  CommandText VARCHAR(MAX) NOT NULL
)
GO

CREATE TRIGGER ReturnEventData
ON DATABASE
FOR CREATE_TABLE, ALTER_TABLE
AS
  DECLARE @eventData XML
  SET @eventData = eventdata()

  INSERT DDLEventLog (EventDate, UserName, ObjectName, CommandText)
  SELECT
    GETDATE() AS EventDate,
    @eventData.value('data(/EVENT_INSTANCE/UserName)[1]', 'SYSNAME')
      AS UserName,
    @eventData.value('data(/EVENT_INSTANCE/ObjectName)[1]', 'SYSNAME')
      AS ObjectName,
    @eventData.value('data(/EVENT_INSTANCE/TSQLCommand/CommandText)[1]',
      'VARCHAR(MAX)') AS CommandText
```

The event data can also be parsed and used to make decisions about what course of action to take. For instance, if you have a table called DontDropMe, you could write the following trigger to keep it from being dropped:

```
CREATE TRIGGER DontDropDontDropMe
ON DATABASE
FOR DROP_TABLE
AS
  DECLARE @eventData XML
  SET @eventData = eventdata()

  DECLARE @objectName VARCHAR(MAX)
  SET @objectName =
    CONVERT(VARCHAR(MAX), @eventData.query('data(/EVENT_INSTANCE/ObjectName)'))

  IF @objectName = 'DontDropMe'
  BEGIN
    PRINT 'You can not drop DontDropMe!'
    ROLLBACK
  END
```

Since the transaction is rolled back if the object name is DontDropMe, it's impossible to drop that table when the DontDropDontDropMe trigger is applied to the database. When using DDL triggers for this type of object-level protection, remember that the trigger fires after the event has finished, but before the transaction has committed. If a large transaction has taken place and needs to be rolled back, excessive locking could occur. Proceed with caution until, hopefully, you see instead-of DDL triggers implemented in a future version of SQL Server.

Indexing and Performance Enhancements

SQL Server 2005 introduces a variety of performance enhancements that DBAs can exploit. These include various indexing improvements, table and index partitioning, and persisted computed columns.

The types of indexes available in the SQL Server 2005 relational engine are the same as those available in SQL Server 2000, with the addition of a specialized XML index type. The basic index types are clustered and nonclustered. Both types of indexes are implemented internally using a variant of a B-Tree data structure. A clustered index reorganizes the base data pages of the indexed table, whereas a nonclustered index is created in separate data pages. A table in SQL Server 2005 can have a single clustered index and up to 249 nonclustered indexes.

Clustered indexes are generally used to support primary keys and should generally be used to index "narrow" columns or groups of columns—many sources recommend that clustered index key columns should not exceed a total of 16 bytes per row. This is due to the fact that the key column data will be repeated in the leaf nodes of every nonclustered index.

Nonclustered indexes are, by default, used to support unique keys. They are also used for other types of indexes added for query performance. It's important for DBAs to remember not to go overboard when creating nonclustered indexes. Each data update of a column that participates in a nonclustered index will have to be written once to the base table and once to the index pages. Creating too many nonclustered indexes can, therefore, have a negative impact on data modification performance.

Although the basic index types and functionality (other than for XML) do not change in SQL Server 2005, index creation and maintenance has been vastly improved. The improvements detailed in this section will mostly help DBAs do their jobs better in high-performance and high-availability environments.

Online Indexing

A common problem in high-availability scenarios is how and when to perform operations such as index creation, which might decrease response times or totally block other transactions. As it's often impossible to predict all indexes that a system might require once it goes live, it's important to be able to apply these changes to the production system. SQL Server 2005 provides this capability using its online indexing feature.

Creating, altering, and dropping clustered indexes produces schema modification locks that block other processes from reading and writing to the table. And creating and altering nonclustered indexes produces shared locks that block other processes from writing. Both of these can be avoided using the online indexing feature. Using the feature will allow other processes to continue normal operations, but performing the indexing operation may be quite a bit slower than in offline mode. If it's important that other processes should be able to continue normal operations during indexing—for instance, when indexing a table in an active OLTP database—this feature should be used. If concurrency is not important, the default offline indexing mode can be used to more quickly complete indexing operations.

To use the online indexing option, use the WITH clause for CREATE INDEX, ALTER INDEX, or DROP INDEX:

```
CREATE INDEX ix_Table
ON Table (Column)
WITH (ONLINE = ON)
```

The default value for the ONLINE option is OFF. It should also be noted that this option is not available for indexing operations on tables containing LOB datatypes (TEXT, NTEXT, and IMAGE) or when creating XML indexes.

Controlling Locking During Index Creation

To further control the effects of indexing on other processes that might be attempting to access the data simultaneously, SQL Server 2005 allows the DBA to specify whether the indexing process can use row- or page-level locks. Tweaking these options can improve concurrency when creating indexes in live production systems, but beware: overriding what might be the query optimizer's best option can mean that index creation will take a much longer time. These options should be used only in specific situations in which problems are occurring due to lock contention during index creation. In most cases, they should be left set to their default values.

The DBA can turn off row locking using the ALLOW_ROW_LOCKS option:

```
CREATE INDEX ix_Table
ON Table (Column)
WITH (ALLOW_ROW_LOCKS = OFF)
```

Page locking can be turned off using the ALLOW_PAGE_LOCKS option:

```
CREATE INDEX ix_Table
ON Table (Column)
WITH (ALLOW_PAGE_LOCKS = OFF)
```

The default value for both of these options is ON, meaning that both row- and page-level locks are allowed. You can combine the options with each other or the ONLINE option by separating the options with a comma:

```
CREATE INDEX ix_Table
ON Table (Column)
WITH (ONLINE = ON, ALLOW_ROW_LOCKS = OFF, ALLOW_PAGE_LOCKS = OFF)
```

Creating Indexes with Additional Columns Included

In previous versions of SQL Server, DBAs could add additional columns to nonclustered indexes to "cover" affected queries. For instance, given the following table and index:

```
CREATE TABLE DatabaseSystems
(
  DatabaseSystemId INT,
  Name VARCHAR(35),
  IsRelational CHAR(1),
  IsObjectOriented CHAR(1),
  SupportsXML CHAR(1),
  FullSpecifications VARCHAR(MAX)
)

CREATE NONCLUSTERED INDEX IX_Name
ON DatabaseSystems (Name)
```

a DBA might want to query this table to find out which databases with names starting with "S" also happened to support XML:

```
SELECT Name, SupportsXML
FROM DatabaseSystems
WHERE Name LIKE 'S%'
AND SupportsXML = 'Y'
```

While the LIKE predicate is satisfied by the index, the database engine still has to do a lookup on the base table to get the SupportsXML column. To eliminate the additional lookup and "cover" the query (i.e., support all columns from the table used in the query) the index can be dropped and a new one created to include the SupportsXML column:

```
DROP INDEX IX_Name
CREATE NONCLUSTERED INDEX IX_Name_SupportsXML
ON DatabaseSystems(Name, SupportsXML)
```

The query engine can now get all of the data to satisfy the query from the nonclustered index—without ever looking up data in the table itself.

But what if IX_Name had been a unique index? Or what if the DBA wanted to cover queries that included the FullSpecifications column? Solving the first problem would require creating a new index and leaving the previous one, a solution that would end up wasting space. And indexing the FullSpecifications column was not possible at all. Indexes in SQL Server 2000 could contain only up to 900 bytes per row. Indexing a large VARCHAR was simply not an option.

SQL Server 2005 includes a new indexing option designed to solve these problems. DBAs can now specify additional columns to be included in a nonclustered index, using the INCLUDE keyword. Included columns are nonindexed but are included in the data pages along with the indexed data, such that they can be used to cover queries. There are no restrictions on width beyond those already enforced at the table level, and uniqueness can be specified for the indexed columns.

To create a unique index that covers the query, use the following:

```
CREATE UNIQUE NONCLUSTERED INDEX IX_Name
ON DatabaseSystems(Name)
INCLUDE (SupportsXML)
```

An index could also be created that would cover queries for either SupportsXML or FullSpecifications—or both:

```
CREATE UNIQUE NONCLUSTERED INDEX IX_Name
ON DatabaseSystems(Name)
INCLUDE (SupportsXML, FullSpecifications)
```

Keep in mind that creating large indexes that include many large columns can both use a lot of disk space and require massive amounts of I/O when updating or inserting new rows. This is due to the fact that any columns included in a nonclustered index will have their data written to disk twice: once in the base table and once in the index. When using this option to eliminate clustered index lookups, test to ensure that the additional disk strain will not be a problem when writing data.

Altering Indexes

SQL Server 2000 introduced a method of altering an existing index by creating a new one in its place, using the WITH DROP_EXISTING option. This option is especially useful for altering existing clustered indexes as it incurs less overhead than dropping and re-creating the index, by allowing the index to be modified without rebuilding existing nonclustered indexes.

SQL Server 2005 upgrades this option by making index alteration a first-class T-SQL operation. The ALTER INDEX syntax, while similar to that of CREATE INDEX, does not support altering an index's column list—the WITH DROP_EXISTING option of CREATE INDEX will still have to be used for that. However, ALTER INDEX offers much additional functionality.

In the following sections, you'll see how a DBA can use ALTER INDEX to defragment an index (replacing DBCC INDEXDEFRAG), rebuild an index (replacing DBCC DBREINDEX), or disable an index (a brand-new feature).

Defragmenting an Index

As indexes age, insertion and deletion of noncontiguous data can take its toll and cause fragmentation to occur. Although minor amounts of fragmentation won't generally hurt performance, it's a good idea to occasionally defragment indexes to keep databases running as smoothly as possible. *Defragmentation*, also known as *index reorganization*, defragments data within data pages, but does not move data pages between extents. Since only data within pages is moved, very little blocking will occur during the defragmentation process, and data can remain available to other processes. However, because extents are not fragmented, this may not be an effective method for defragmenting larger, heavily fragmented indexes. For those situations, index rebuilding is necessary (see the next section, "Rebuilding an Index," for more information).

To determine the level of fragmentation of an index, the dynamic management function sys.dm_db_index_physical_stats can be used. This function replaces the DBCC SHOWCONTIG function, which is deprecated in SQL Server 2005. The column avg_fragmentation_in_percent returns the percentage of fragmented data. Unlike DBCC SHOWCONTIG, extent and logical scan fragmentation are not displayed separately. Instead, the avg_fragmentation_in_percent column shows extent fragmentation for heap tables and logical scan fragmentation for tables with clustered indexes or when displaying information about nonclustered indexes.

Although there is no hard and fast rule, a common recommendation is to keep index fragmentation below 10 percent whenever possible. Microsoft recommends defragmenting indexes that are 30 percent or less fragmented and rebuilding indexes that are more than 30 percent fragmented.

To identify indexes in the current database that have more than 10 percent fragmentation, the following query can be used:

```
SELECT
  OBJECT_NAME(i.object_id) AS TableName,
  i.name AS IndexName,
  ips.avg_fragmentation_in_percent
FROM sys.dm_db_index_physical_stats(DB_ID(), NULL, NULL, NULL, 'DETAILED') ips
JOIN sys.indexes i ON
  i.object_id = ips.object_id
  AND i.index_id = ips.index_id
WHERE ips.avg_fragmentation_in_percent > 10
```

The arguments to the sys.dm_db_index_physical_stats function are database ID, table ID, index ID, partition ID, and scan mode. In this example, DB_ID() is passed for the database ID, which tells the function to scan tables in the current database. NULL is passed for table ID, index ID, and partition ID, so that function does not filter on any of those criteria. Finally, a detailed scan is used. Possible scan modes are LIMITED (the default), SAMPLED, and DETAILED. LIMITED scans only parent-level nodes and is therefore the fastest scan mode. SAMPLED scans parent-level nodes and a percentage of leaf nodes based on the number of rows in the table. DETAILED samples all nodes and is therefore the slowest scan method.

Once a fragmented index is identified, it can be defragmented using ALTER INDEX with the REORGANIZE option. The following query will defragment the index IX_CustomerName on the table Customers:

```
ALTER INDEX IX_CustomerName
ON Customers
REORGANIZE
```

Rebuilding an Index

Index defragmentation only reorganizes the leaf-level nodes of an index. Unfortunately, there are times when that isn't enough to eliminate index fragmentation, and the entire index needs to be rebuilt. The REBUILD option of ALTER INDEX can be used to facilitate this process. This is equivalent to the functionality of the DBCC DBREINDEX function, which is deprecated in SQL Server 2005.

Rebuilding an index is, by default, an offline operation, because pages and extents are being shuffled. When rebuilding a clustered index, the base table will be locked for the duration of the rebuild, and when rebuilding a nonclustered index, the index will be unavailable during the rebuild. However, ALTER INDEX includes an online indexing option to get around this problem. To rebuild the index IX_CustomerName on table Customers using the online indexing option, use the following query:

```
ALTER INDEX IX_CustomerName
ON Customers
REBUILD
WITH (ONLINE=ON)
```

The ONLINE option works by indexing the data outside of the data pages in which the data resides, applying deltas for any data modifications, and then updating pointers from the old index to the new index. Because this operation occurs in a separate area, online re-indexing will use approximately twice as much disk space as offline re-indexing. The process can also be slower, in the case of databases that are very update intensive, due to the additional overhead associated with tracking data changes. This option is therefore best used for databases that require very high availability; if downtime is acceptable, the ONLINE option will provide no benefit.

Disabling an Index

SQL Server 2005 offers an intriguing new feature for indexing, namely the ability to disable indexes. This feature is certain to generate plenty of speculation as to when and where it should be used, but it's best to clear the air up front. The fact is, this feature was not created for DBAs. Rather, Microsoft included it to make updates and service packs easier to apply. There are no performance benefits or any other "hot topic" uses for disabling an index. Nonetheless, this feature can be handy in some situations.

Disabling a nonclustered index deletes the index's data rows, but keeps its metadata—the index's definition—intact. Disabling a clustered index, on the other hand, keeps the data but renders it inaccessible until the index is re-enabled. And disabling a nonclustered index that is being used to enforce a primary key or unique constraint will disable the constraint.

To disable an index, use ALTER INDEX with the DISABLE option:

```
ALTER INDEX IX_CustomerName
ON Customers
DISABLE
```

The index can be re-enabled using the REBUILD option:

```
ALTER INDEX IX_CustomerName
ON Customers
REBUILD
```

Note that rebuilding a disabled index will require only as much disk space as the index requires, whereas rebuilding a nondisabled index requires twice the disk space: disk space for the existing index and disk space for the new, rebuilt index.

So when should index disabling be used? There are a few circumstances in which it will prove useful. A common task during Extract, Transform, and Load (ETL) processes is dropping indexes before doing bulk data loads, and then re-creating the indexes at the end of the process. Index disabling will lead to fewer code changes; there will be no need to update the ETL code when index definitions change.

Another scenario is systems with low disk space that need indexes rebuilt. Since rebuilding a disabled index takes up half the space compared to rebuilding a nondisabled index, this could prove useful in tight situations. However, it should be noted that unlike rebuilding a nondisabled index using the ONLINE option, a disabled index will not be available for online operations during the rebuild process.

A final possible use of index disabling is for testing various index configurations in situations in which the query optimizer isn't necessarily making the correct choice. Disabling and re-enabling indexes should make this process a bit less painful for DBAs, by providing an automatic "backup" of the indexes being worked with.

Using Statistics for Correlated DATETIME Columns

SQL Server 2005 includes an optimization to assist with queries on tables that share similar DATETIME data. When turned on, extra statistics will be generated for DATETIME columns. Joining two tables, each with DATETIME columns that share a foreign key reference, may allow the query optimizer to be able to determine a better plan using the additional statistics.

For instance, the AdventureWorks sample database contains a table of orders called Sales. SalesOrderHeader and a table of corresponding order detail (line items) called Sales.SalesOrderDetail. Each table contains a DATETIME column, ModifiedDate.

Assume that for auditing purposes, it's a business requirement of Adventure Works Cycles that any modification to an order detail row happen within 24 hours of a modification to the corresponding order header row. This would mean that all ModifiedDate values in the Sales.SalesOrderDetail table would fall into a range between the order header's modified date and 24 hours later. The query optimizer could potentially use this fact to improve performance of certain queries.

A requirement for the optimizer being able to use correlated DATETIME statistics is that at least one of the tables' DATETIME columns must be the key column for a clustered index. Since neither table includes the ModifiedDate column in its clustered index, one of the clustered indexes would have to be altered in order to use this optimization.

Once statistics are turned on and the correct indexes are in place, the query optimizer will be able to use the statistics to help drive better query plans. For instance, given the Sales.SalesOrderHeader and Sales.SalesOrderDetail tables, a user might want to see all orders modified in the last 24 hours and their corresponding line items, using the following query:

```
SELECT *
FROM Sales.SalesOrderHeader SOH
JOIN Sales.SalesOrderDetail SOD ON SOH.SalesOrderId = SOD.SalesOrderId
WHERE SOH.ModifiedDate >= DATEADD(hh, 24, GETDATE())
```

If date correlation is enabled an the correct indexes are in place, the query optimizer can analyze the DATETIME statistics for these two tables and determine that data for the ModifiedDate column of the SalesOrderHeader table is always 24 hours or less before the ModifiedDate column of the corresponding rows in the SalesOrderDetail table. This can allow the query to be internally rewritten into the following, possibly more efficient format:

```
SELECT *
FROM Sales.SalesOrderHeader SOH
JOIN Sales.SalesOrderDetail SOD ON SOH.SalesOrderId = SOD.SalesOrderId
WHERE SOH.ModifiedDate >= DATEADD(hh, -24, GETDATE())
AND SOD.ModifiedDate >= DATEADD(hh, -24, GETDATE())
AND SOD.ModifiedDate <= GETDATE()
```

This form of the query can take advantage of a clustered index that involves the SalesOrderDetails ModifiedDate column, thereby possibly avoiding an expensive clustered index lookup operation. This will be especially advantageous the larger the dataset in each table grows and the more highly selective the date columns become.

To turn on date correlation statistics for the AdventureWorks database, the following T-SQL would be used:

```
ALTER DATABASE AdventureWorks
SET DATE_CORRELATION_OPTIMIZATION ON
```

Note that when performing this action, the database must have no users connected or the only connection should be the one running the ALTER DATABASE.

Once the optimization is enabled, it will be automatically maintained by the query engine. Due to the extra work involved, there is a performance penalty for inserts or updates, so make sure to test carefully before rolling this into production environments. To find out if a database has date correlation turned on, query the is_date_correlation_on column of the sys.databases catalog view:

```
SELECT
    Name,
    is_date_correlation_on
FROM sys.databases
```

The column is_date_correlation_on will have a value of 1 if date correlation is turned on for a database; otherwise, it will have a value of 0.

Improving Performance of Ordering for Tertiary Collations

For situations in which string case sensitivity is unimportant from a uniqueness perspective but necessary for sorting purposes, SQL Server supports so-called tertiary collations. String data defined with these collations will be ordered based on case sensitivity (uppercase letters will sort before lowercase letters). However, grouping by or using the distinct operator on such a column will result in uppercase and lowercase letters being treated identically.

For example, take the following table, which includes an indexed tertiary-collated column:

```
CREATE TABLE Characters
(
  CharacterString CHAR(3)
    COLLATE SQL_Latin1_General_CP437_CI_AI
)

CREATE CLUSTERED INDEX IX_Characters
ON Characters (Characterstring)

INSERT Characters VALUES ('aaa')
INSERT Characters VALUES ('Aaa')
```

Selecting the data from this table using an ORDER BY clause on the CharacterString column will result in two rows being returned. The row with the value "Aaa" will sort first, followed by the row with the value "aaa". However, selecting the data from this table using the DISTINCT option returns only a single row. Only sorting is case sensitive. Grouping and uniqueness operations are non-case-sensitive.

Ordering a tertiary collated column requires an intermediate step during which weights for each character are determined. This step is expensive, so SQL Server 2005 provides users the ability to precalculate the weights using the TERTIARY_WEIGHTS function.

Selecting data from the table ordered by CharacterString requires an intermediate computation and sort, even though the data in the index is already sorted, as indicated by the execution plan for on ordered SELECT statement on this table, shown in Figure 4-3.

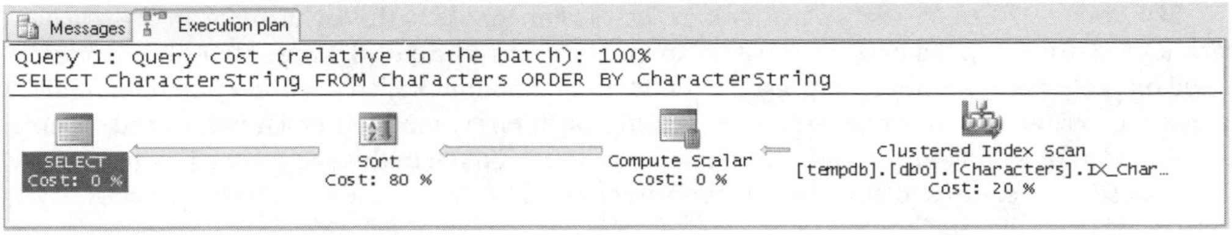

Figure 4-3. *Sorting on tertiary-collated columns requires an intermediate step.*

The solution to this problem in SQL Server 2005 is to create a computed column using the TERTIARY_WEIGHTS function and add it to the index to be used for sorting. The table and index should have been created this way:

```
CREATE TABLE Characters
(
  CharacterString CHAR(3)
    COLLATE SQL_Latin1_General_CP437_CI_AI,
  CharacterWeights AS (TERTIARY_WEIGHTS(CharacterString))
)

CREATE CLUSTERED INDEX IX_Characters
ON Characters
(
  CharacterString,
  CharacterWeights
)
```

As Figure 4-4 illustrates, the intermediate sort is no longer required.

Figure 4-4. *When a computed column using the TERTIARY_WEIGHTS function is used in the index, the intermediate step is no longer required.*

Table and Index Partitioning

A common requirement in dealing with larger datasets is the ability to split the data into smaller chunks to help improve performance. Performance degradation becomes apparent once tables reach larger sizes, and splitting data across files and disks is one way to help databases scale. Although previous versions of SQL Server supported various means of partitioning data—either manually or via features like partitioned views—doing so has always been somewhat of a headache-inducing experience. Partitioning in versions prior to SQL Server 2000 meant splitting data across multiple tables, and then writing application code that could properly navigate the partitions. Things got better with SQL Server 2000's partitioned views feature, but it was difficult to swap data in or out of the partitions without affecting data availability.

SQL Server 2005 makes data partitioning much easier, thanks to the inclusion of an entirely new partitioning strategy that allows the server to automatically handle partitioning of tables and indexes based on range data. Partition ranges are defined using functions called *partition functions*, and ranges are assigned to one or more filegroups using partition schemes. After a function and scheme are created, tables and indexes can use them for partitioning data. In this section we'll examine how to use these new features to build better-performing databases.

■**Note** The new partitioning features are only available in the Enterprise and Developer Editions of SQL Server 2005.

Partition Functions

Partition functions are the means by which the DBA can control which ranges of data will be used to enforce partition boundary values. These functions map partitions based on a datatype and ranges of values for that datatype, but they do not actually partition anything. Due to the fact that they only define partitions, partition functions are reusable; a single function can be used to partition many tables or indexes using the same ranges. The basic syntax for creating a partition function is as follows:

```
CREATE PARTITION FUNCTION partition_function_name(input_parameter_type)
AS RANGE [ LEFT | RIGHT ]
FOR VALUES ( [ boundary_value [ ,...n ] ] )
[ ; ]
```

Partition functions must take a single input parameter (i.e., a column) of a specific datatype—multicolumn partition functions are not supported. The function is defined in terms of ranges, and the LEFT or RIGHT designator controls the placement of the actual boundary value. For a LEFT function, each partition will be defined as containing all values less than or equal to its upper bound. For a RIGHT function, each partition will be defined as containing all values less than its upper bound; the boundary value itself will go into the next partition.

Partition ranges cannot be designed to constrain input values to a given range. Values that fall below the lowest bound will be placed into the lowest partition. Values that fall above the highest bound will be placed into an automatically generated partition for values above that bound. For example, to create a partition function based on fiscal quarters of 2005, the following T-SQL could be used:

```
CREATE PARTITION FUNCTION pf_FiscalQuarter2005 (DATETIME)
AS RANGE RIGHT FOR VALUES
('20050401', '20050701', '20051001', '20060101')
```

This function actually creates five partitions. The first partition contains every value less than April 1, 2005 (remember, RANGE RIGHT defines less than values; if you wanted to include midnight for April 1, 2005, you could use a RANGE LEFT partition). The second, third, and fourth partitions contain all values less than July 1, 2005, October 1, 2005, and January 1, 2006, respectively. The final, implicit partition contains all values greater than or equal to January 1, 2006.

Partition Schemes

Partition schemes are the means by which the boundary values defined in partition functions can be mapped to physical filegroups. The DBA has the option of either mapping all of the partitions from a function into the same filegroup (using the ALL option) or specifying a filegroup for each partition individually. The same filegroup can be used for multiple partitions.

The basic syntax for creating a partition scheme is as follows:

```
CREATE PARTITION SCHEME partition_scheme_name
AS PARTITION partition_function_name
[ ALL ] TO ( { file_group_name | [PRIMARY] } [ ,...n] )
[ ; ]
```

To specify that all partitions from the partition function pf_FiscalQuarter2005 (defined in the preceding section) should be mapped to the primary filegroup, the following T-SQL would be used:

```
CREATE PARTITION SCHEME ps_FiscalQuarter2005_PRIMARY
AS PARTITION pf_FiscalQuarter2005
ALL TO ([PRIMARY])
```

This example uses the ALL option to map all of the partitions to the same filegroup. It should also be noted that the primary filegroup is always specified using square brackets when defining partition schemes.

If the DBA wanted to map the first two partitions to the filegroup Q1Q2_2005 and the other three partitions to the filegroup Q3Q4_2005, the following T-SQL would be used:

```
CREATE PARTITION SCHEME ps_FiscalQuarter2005_Split
AS PARTITION pf_FiscalQuarter2005
TO (Q1Q2_2005, Q1Q2_2005, Q3Q4_2005, Q3Q4_2005, Q3Q4_2005)
```

Note that this example assumes that the filegroups have already been created in the database using ALTER DATABASE ADD FILEGROUP. Also be aware that multiple schemes can be created for a single function, so if there are several objects in a database that should be partitioned using the same data ranges, but that should not share the same filegroups, multiple functions do not need to be created.

Creating Partitioned Tables and Indexes

Once partition functions and schemes have been defined, the DBA can begin using them to partition tables and indexes, which is, of course, the point to this whole exercise. CREATE TABLE and CREATE INDEX both have an ON clause that has been used in previous editions of SQL Server to specify a specific filegroup in which the table or index should be created. That clause still functions as before, but it has now been enhanced to accept a partition scheme.

Given the partition function and schemes created in the previous sections for fiscal quarters in 2005, the following T-SQL could be used to create a partitioned table to record sales amounts, partitioned by the time of the sale:

```
CREATE TABLE SalesAmounts
(
  SalesAmountId INT NOT NULL PRIMARY KEY NONCLUSTERED,
  SalesAmount NUMERIC(9,2) NOT NULL,
  SalesDate DATETIME NOT NULL
)
GO

CREATE CLUSTERED INDEX IX_SalesAmounts_SalesDate
ON SalesAmounts (SalesDate)
  ON ps_FiscalQuarter2005_Split (SalesDate)
```

The table is created using a nonclustered primary key, leaving the table itself available for indexing using a clustered index. Since a table's clustered index organizes the data in the entire table, creating the cluster on the partition range partitions the entire table.

Data from this table will now be partitioned based on the ps_FiscalQuarter2005_Split range function, using SalesDate as the partitioning column. Data for any date less than July 1, 2005, will be put into the Q1Q2_2005 partition; data for any date greater than or equal to July 1, 2005, will be put into the Q3Q4_2005 partition. Likewise, when selecting data from this table using the SalesDate column as a predicate in the WHERE clause, the query engine will need to seek only the necessary partitions for the requested data.

Creating a partitioned index is very similar to creating a partitioned table; the ON clause is used to specify a partition scheme. For instance, to create a nonclustered index on the SalesAmounts table for seeking SalesAmount values, the following T-SQL syntax could be used:

```
CREATE INDEX IX_Amount
ON SalesAmounts
(
  SalesAmount
)
ON ps_FiscalQuarter2005_PRIMARY (SalesDate)
```

This index will be partitioned on the SalesDate column, and because the partition scheme ps_FiscalQuarter2005_PRIMARY was specified, all five partitions will be maintained in the primary filegroup. Note that the partitioning column, SalesDate, need not be included in the index.

Adding and Removing Partitions

In addition to creating new partitioned tables and indexes, SQL Server 2005 also exposes capabilities for DBAs to partition existing tables, modify range boundaries of existing functions and schemes, and swap data in and out of partitions.

Partitioning an existing table can be done in one of two ways. The easier method is to create a clustered index on the table, partitioned using whatever partition scheme the DBA wishes to employ. The other method requires manipulation of partition functions and will be covered in the next section, "Modifying Partition Functions and Schemes."

Assume that in the same database that contains the SalesAmounts table and related partition function and schemes there exists the following table, which contains times that customers visited the store:

```
CREATE TABLE Visitors
(
  VisitorId INT NOT NULL,
  VisitDate DATETIME NOT NULL,
  CONSTRAINT PK_Visitors
    PRIMARY KEY (VisitorId, VisitDate)
)
```

The DBA might wish to partition this table using the same scheme as the sales data, such that data in similar date ranges will share the same filegroups. This table already has a clustered index, implicitly created by the PK_Visitors primary key constraint. To partition the table, the constraint must be dropped. The constraint then must be re-created using a partition scheme. The following T-SQL code accomplishes that:

```
SET XACT_ABORT ON

BEGIN TRANSACTION
  ALTER TABLE Visitors
  DROP CONSTRAINT PK_Visitors
```

```
ALTER TABLE Visitors
ADD CONSTRAINT PK_Visitors
  PRIMARY KEY (VisitorId, VisitDate)
ON ps_FiscalQuarter2005_Split (VisitDate)
COMMIT
```

To avoid inconsistent data, the entire operation should be carried out in a single transaction. SET XACT_ABORT is used in order to guarantee that runtime errors in the transaction will force a rollback.

Converting this table back to a nonpartitioned table can be done using either the reverse operation (i.e., dropping the partitioned clustered index and re-creating the index nonpartitioned) or by modifying the partition function to have only a single partition.

Modifying Partition Functions and Schemes

Partition functions can be altered in two primary ways. Ranges can be "merged" into other ranges (i.e., dropped) or new ranges can be "split" off of existing ranges (i.e., added). Removing ranges using the MERGE keyword is quite straightforward; splitting new ranges using the SPLIT keyword can be a bit more involved, as the partition scheme must also be altered in order to handle the new partition.

For example, if the DBA wished to eliminate the range from pf_FiscalQuarter2005 ending on September 30, thereby creating a larger range that ends on December 31, the following T-SQL would be used:

```
ALTER PARTITION FUNCTION
pf_FiscalQuarter2005()
MERGE RANGE ('20051001')
```

The range specified in a merge must be exactly convertible to a range boundary that exists in the partition function. As a result of a merge operation, the data will be merged into the next partition, and the partition scheme(s) associated with the function will be updated appropriately. As mentioned earlier, this can be one way of departitioning a table: alter the associated partition function, merging the ranges until only a single partition remains.

Splitting a partition function to create new range boundaries requires first altering the associated scheme(s) to provide a "next used" filegroup, which will receive the additional partition range data. Remember that a partition scheme must have exactly the same number of filegroups as its underlying function has ranges.

To add a "next used" filegroup to a partition scheme—in this case, specifying that additional partitions can be placed in the primary filegroup—the following T-SQL could be used:

```
ALTER PARTITION SCHEME ps_FiscalQuarter2005_Split
NEXT USED [PRIMARY]
```

Once the scheme has been appropriately altered, the partition function itself can have an additional range added. To add a range to pf_FiscalQuarter2005 for all of 2006 (not minding that the function is now misnamed), the following T-SQL could be used:

```
ALTER PARTITION FUNCTION
pf_FiscalQuarter2005()
SPLIT RANGE ('20070101')
```

Remember that because the function is a RANGE RIGHT function, this new range boundary ends on December 31, 2006. Data from this range will be placed into the primary filegroup, as that was the next used partition defined before it was created.

Switching Tables into and out of Partitions

The capability exists to move data into partitions from unpartitioned tables and out of partitions back into unpartitioned tables. The former can be useful for data loading processes, as data can be bulk loaded into an unindexed table and then switched into a partitioned structure. The latter can be useful for data archival or other purposes.

Assume that the following staging table has been created for 2006 visitor data:

```
CREATE TABLE VisitorStaging_2006
(
  VisitorId INT NOT NULL,
  VisitDate DATETIME NOT NULL
)
```

This table has the same exact schema as the Visitors table partitioned using the ps_FiscalQuarter2005_split function. It should also have been created on whatever filegroup the DBA wishes it to eventually end up on as part of the partition scheme. For the sake of this example, that will be assumed to be the primary filegroup.

Once data for the 2006 time period has been bulk loaded into the table, the same indexes and constraints must be created on the staging table as exist on the Visitors table. In this case, that's only the PRIMARY KEY constraint:

```
ALTER TABLE VisitorStaging_2006
ADD CONSTRAINT PK_Visitors_2006
  PRIMARY KEY (VisitorId, VisitDate)
```

A CHECK constraint must also be created on the table to guarantee that the data falls within the same range as the partition that the table will be switched into. This can be done with the following T-SQL for this example:

```
ALTER TABLE VisitorStaging_2006
ADD CONSTRAINT CK_Visitors_06012006_12012007
  CHECK (VisitDate >= '20060101' AND VisitDate < '20070101')
```

Once the CHECK constraint is in place, the table is ready to be switched into the new partition. First, the partition boundary number for the new partition should be queried from the sys.partition_functions and sys.partition_range_values catalog views:

```
SELECT rv.boundary_id
FROM sys.partition_functions f
JOIN sys.partition_range_values rv ON f.function_id = rv.function_id
WHERE rv.value = CONVERT(datetime, '20070101')
  AND f.name = 'pf_FiscalQuarter2005'
```

This value can then be plugged into the SWITCH TO option of ALTER TABLE. In this case, the boundary ID is 4, so the following T-SQL switches the VisitorStaging_2006 table into that partition:

```
ALTER TABLE VisitorStaging_2006
SWITCH TO Visitors PARTITION 4
```

The data from the staging table can now be logically queried from the Visitors partitioned table. The staging table can be deleted.

Switching tables out of partitions is much easier. Assuming that the DBA wanted to switch the data back out of the partition just switched into from the staging table, the DBA could re-create the staging table—again, on the same partition and with the same clustered index, but this time with no CHECK constraint necessary. Once the empty table is in place, the data can be switched out of the partition using the following T-SQL:

```
ALTER TABLE Visitors
SWITCH PARTITION 4 TO VisitorStaging_2006
```

Managing Table and Index Partitions

Management of table and index partitions is similar to management of tables and indexes, with one major difference: it's possible to re-index a specific partition in a table, should the DBA not wish to re-index the entire table at once. In addition, SQL Server 2005 includes a series of catalog views to assist with enumerating and viewing data related to partitions.

Rebuilding an index for a specific partition number is very similar to rebuilding an entire index, with the addition of a new clause to the ALTER INDEX syntax: the PARTITION clause. This clause takes a partition number as input. For instance, to rebuild partition 4 of the PK_Visitors index on the Visitors table—assuming that the index is partitioned—the following T-SQL would be used:

```
ALTER INDEX PK_Visitors
ON Visitors
REBUILD
PARTITION = 4
```

The ONLINE option and other indexing options are also available. This functionality can help DBAs to more accurately pinpoint and eliminate performance bottlenecks in large partitioned tables.

Three catalog views are provided to assist with viewing partition function data. The sys.partition_functions view contains data about which partition functions have been created. The sys.partition_range_values view, used with the sys.partition_functions view in an example in a previous section, contains the actual ranges specified for a function. Finally, the sys.partition_parameters function contains information about the parameter datatype used for a function.

The sys.partition_schemes view contains information about schemes. The sys.partitions and sys.partition_counts views contain data about the actual mapping between tables and their partitions, including row counts, used data pages, reserved data pages, and various other statistics.

Complete documentation of these views is beyond the scope of this book. Please refer to SQL Server Books Online for a list of available columns.

Enhancements to Tables and Views

In addition to the indexing and general performance improvements to the SQL Server 2005 relational engine, minor improvements have been made to both views and tables. Indexed views have added capabilities having to do with greater expression-processing capabilities, and tables have been given the ability to persist computed columns. As described in the sections that follow, these additions make these features—which were useful to begin with—even more appealing for use in SQL Server 2005.

Enhancements to Indexed Views

Although indexed views are still fairly restrictive (e.g., DBAs cannot use subqueries, derived tables, and many other constructs), they have been made slightly more flexible in SQL Server 2005 than they were in SQL Server 2000. The query optimizer has been enhanced such that it can now match more query types to indexed views. These include scalar expressions, such as (ColA + ColB) * ColC, and scalar aggregate functions, such as COUNT_BIG(*).

For instance, the following indexed view could be created in the AdventureWorks database, indexed on the OrderTotal column:

```
CREATE VIEW Sales.OrderTotals
WITH SCHEMABINDING
AS
  SELECT
    SalesOrderId,
    SubTotal + TaxAmt + Freight AS OrderTotal
  FROM Sales.SalesOrderHeader
GO

CREATE UNIQUE CLUSTERED INDEX IX_OrderTotals
ON Sales.OrderTotals
(OrderTotal, SalesOrderId)
```

The query optimizer will now be able to consider queries such as the following for optimization by using the indexed view:

```
SELECT SalesOrderId
FROM Sales.SalesOrderHeader
WHERE SubTotal + TaxAmt + Freight > 300
```

This optimization also includes better matching for queries against indexes that use user-defined functions.

Persisted Computed Columns

In certain situations, it can be useful to create columns whose values are computed dynamically by the SQL Server engine when referenced in a query, rather than inserted with an explicit value. Prior versions of SQL Server included the computed column feature for this purpose. Computed columns were able to be indexed, and the data existed within the index to be used for seeking or by queries covered by the index. However, a noncovered query that needed the same data would not be able to use the value persisted within the index, and it would have to be rebuilt dynamically at runtime. For complex computed columns, this can become a serious performance drain.

To eliminate this problem, SQL Server 2005 introduces a new option when creating a computed column, in the form of the PERSIST keyword. Its behavior is simple enough. Instead of the column's value being calculated at runtime, it is calculated only once, at insert or update time, and stored on disk with the rest of the column data.

To add a new persisted computed column to a table, the following T-SQL could be used, assuming that dbo.VeryComplexFunction() is a very complex function that is slowing down SELECT statements:

```
ALTER TABLE SalesData
  ADD ComplexOutput AS
    (dbo.VeryComplexFunction(CustomerId, OrderId))
    PERSISTED
```

Note that existing computed columns cannot be made persisted—they will have to be dropped and re-created as persisted computed columns. Likewise, persisted computed columns cannot be altered back into regular computed columns. They also will need to be dropped and re-created.

To determine which computed columns are persisted, query the is_persisted column of the sys.computed_columns catalog view. is_persisted will have a value of 1 if the column is persisted and 0 otherwise. For instance, the following query shows which columns of which tables in the current database are persisted computed columns:

```
SELECT OBJECT_NAME(object_id), name
FROM sys.computed_columns
WHERE is_persisted = 1
```

Snapshots

A common problem in database systems is that of blocking and concurrency. The system needs to ensure that a reader gets consistent data, so writes cannot take place during a read. Unfortunately, larger systems often fall victim to huge scalability bottlenecks due to blocking problems. DBAs must constantly do battle with queries, attempting to control lock granularities and transaction lengths in order to keep blocking to a minimum. But after a while, many give up and take an easier route, risking getting some inconsistent data from time to time by using "dirty reads," the READ UNCOMMITTED transaction isolation level, or the NOLOCK table hint.

It appears that those days are coming to an end, thanks to two new features in SQL Server 2005: the snapshot isolation level and database snapshots. These features provide mechanisms for readers to get consistent, committed data, while allowing writers to work unabated. Simply put, this means no more blocking and no more inconsistent data.

Snapshots represent the best of both worlds, but they have a cost. DBAs will pay a disk I/O penalty when using these new features due to the overhead of maintaining previous versions of rows.

SNAPSHOT Isolation Level

The SNAPSHOT *isolation level* is a new isolation level in SQL Server 2005 that can best be described as a combination of the consistency of the REPEATABLE READ isolation level with the nonblocking characteristics of the READ UNCOMMITTED isolation level. Transactions in the SNAPSHOT isolation level will not create shared locks on rows being read. And repeated requests for the same data within a SNAPSHOT transaction guarantee the same results.

This nonblocking behavior is achieved by storing previous committed versions of rows in the tempdb database. When an update or delete occurs, the previous version of the row is copied to tempdb and a pointer to the previous version is left with the current version. Readers that started transactions before the write that have already read the previous version will continue to read that version. Meanwhile, the write can occur and other transactions will see the new version.

This is a definite improvement over the behavior of either the REPEATABLE READ or READ UNCOMMITTED isolation levels. The REPEATABLE READ isolation level creates shared locks for the duration of the read transaction, thereby blocking any writers. And the READ UNCOMMITTED isolation level, while not creating locks, will also not return consistent, committed data if there are updates occurring at the same time that the transaction is reading the data.

Due to its being used as a repository for maintaining data changes, the tempdb database will see greatly increased activity when the SNAPSHOT isolation level is used for write-intensive databases. To avoid problems, the isolation level should not be enabled by DBAs arbitrarily. Specific behaviors that indicate that the isolation level may be helpful include performance issues due to blocking, deadlocked transactions, and previous use of the READ UNCOMMITTED isolation level to promote increased concurrency. Before enabling the isolation level in a production environment, test carefully to ensure that tempdb can handle the additional load.

In addition to the snapshot isolation level, SQL Server 2005 also includes the ability to enhance the READ COMMITTED isolation level to behave like snapshot isolation for individual queries not within a transaction. The enhanced version is called READ COMMITTED SNAPSHOT.

Enabling SNAPSHOT Isolation for a Database

Use of the SNAPSHOT isolation level is not allowed by default in SQL Server 2005 databases. Enabling it for production databases should be done only after careful testing in a development or quality assurance environment. The row versioning feature that allows the isolation level to work requires stamping every row in the database with a 14-byte structure that includes a unique identifier and a pointer to the previous versions of the row in tempdb. The extra 14-byte overhead per row and the work required to maintain the previous versions can add up to quite a bit of extra disk I/O, which is why the feature is off by default (except in the master and msdb system databases, in which it is on by default; these databases are small enough that the additional I/O will not cause problems). If you don't actually need row versioning capabilities, do not turn it on.

There are two options available for enabling row version in a database. One is for the SNAPSHOT isolation level itself; the second is for the READ COMMITTED SNAPSHOT isolation level. Both of these are options on ALTER DATABASE, and both are OFF by default. The database must have no users connected when enabling or disabling row versioning.

To allow the SNAPSHOT isolation level to be used for a database called Sales, the following T-SQL would be used:

```
ALTER DATABASE Sales
SET ALLOW_SNAPSHOT_ISOLATION ON
```

For the READ COMMITTED SNAPSHOT isolation level, the following T-SQL would be used:

```
ALTER DATABASE Sales
SET READ_COMMITTED_SNAPSHOT ON
```

Note that these options are independent of each other—either or both can be on for a database. However, since they use the same row versioning mechanism behind the scenes, turning a second one on once the first is enabled will incur no additional overhead. The READ_COMMITTED_SNAPSHOT option cannot be enabled in the master, tempdb, or msdb system databases.

To disable either of these options, simply change the flag to OFF:

```
ALTER DATABASE Sales
SET ALLOW_SNAPSHOT_ISOLATION OFF
```

To find out which databases allow the SNAPSHOT isolation level or use the READ COMMITTED SNAPSHOT isolation level, you can query the sys.databases catalog view. The snapshot_isolation_state and is_read_committed_snapshot_on columns will contain 1 if either option is enabled or 0 otherwise. The view can be queried for the Sales database using the following T-SQL:

```
SELECT
    name,
    snapshot_isolation_state,
    is_read_committed_snapshot_on
FROM sys.databases
```

Enabling SNAPSHOT Isolation for a Transaction

Once the SNAPSHOT isolation level is turned on for a database, it can be set for a transaction using SET TRANSACTION ISOLATION LEVEL SNAPSHOT. Its behavior as compared to other isolation levels is best illustrated with a hands-on example.

The following table is created in a database with row versioning enabled:

```
CREATE TABLE TestSnapshot
(
  ColA INT,
  ColB VARCHAR(20)
)

INSERT TestSnapshot (ColA, ColB)
VALUES (1, 'Original Value')
```

Now assume that two SQL Server Management Studio connections are open to the database. In the first, the following T-SQL is executed:

```
SET TRANSACTION ISOLATION LEVEL SNAPSHOT

BEGIN TRANSACTION

SELECT ColB
FROM TestSnapshot
WHERE ColA = 1
```

This query returns the value 'Original Value' for ColB.

With the transaction still running, the following T-SQL is executed in the second connection:

```
UPDATE TestSnapshot
SET ColB = 'New Value'
WHERE ColA = 1
```

This update will execute successfully and will return the message '(1 row(s) affected)'. Had the REPEATABLE READ isolation level been used in the first connection, the update would have been blocked waiting for the transaction to finish.

Back in the first window, the SELECT can again be run. It will still return the value 'Original Value', even though the actual value has been updated. Had the transaction been using the READ UNCOMMITTED isolation level, results would not be consistent between reads and the value returned the second time would have been 'New Value'.

This is only a very simple example to show the power of the SNAPSHOT isolation level to deliver consistent yet nonblocking results. It represents a very powerful addition to SQL Server 2005's arsenal.

Handling Concurrent Writes in the SNAPSHOT Isolation Level

Although SNAPSHOT provides consistent repeated reads like the REPEATED READ isolation level, it has a very different behavior when it comes to writing data. Should a SNAPSHOT isolated transaction read some data and then attempt to update it after another transaction has updated it, the entire snapshot transaction will be rolled back. This is similar to a deadlock and will have to be handled the same way in production code.

To illustrate this behavior, we'll use the same TestSnapshot table from the previous example. In this case, however, suppose that the goal is to select some data into a temporary table, perform some very complex logic, and then update the table. First, the data is inserted into a temporary table:

```
SET TRANSACTION ISOLATION LEVEL SNAPSHOT

BEGIN TRANSACTION

SELECT ColB
INTO #Temp
FROM TestSnapshot
WHERE ColA = 1
```

The temporary table, #Temp, now contains a row with the value 'Original Value'. As before, another transaction is operating on the TestSnapshot table in another connection with an update:

```
UPDATE TestSnapshot
SET ColB = 'New Value'
WHERE ColA = 1
```

After this, the first transaction has completed its complex logic and goes to do an update of its own:

```
UPDATE TestSnapshot
SET ColB = 'Even Newer Value'
WHERE ColA = 1
```

Unfortunately, this results in the following error:

```
Msg 3960, Level 16, State 1, Line 1
Cannot use snapshot isolation to access table 'TestSnapshot' in database 'Sales'.
Snapshot transaction aborted due to update conflict. Retry transaction.
```

So what's the moral of this story? Treat any snapshot transaction that performs data updates exactly like transactions that are susceptible to deadlocks. Put code in place around these transactions to ensure that when this error occurs, an appropriate course of action will be taken.

Using the READ COMMITTED SNAPSHOT Isolation Level

Similar to the SNAPSHOT isolation level is the READ COMMITTED SNAPSHOT isolation level. This isolation level is actually a modification of the default behavior of the READ COMMITTED isolation level. By turning this option on, any single read query within an implicit or explicit READ COMMITTED transaction will behave like a snapshot read—but only for the duration of the query. So repeatable reads do not occur, but consistency is guaranteed.

Again, this is best illustrated through an example using the TestSnapshot table. Assume the database has READ COMMITTED SNAPSHOT enabled. The following query is run on one connection:

```
SET TRANSACTION ISOLATION LEVEL READ COMMITTED

SELECT ColB
FROM TestSnapshot
WHERE ColA = 1
```

This, of course, returns 'Original Value'. Now in a second connection, another transaction is started, but not committed:

```
BEGIN TRANSACTION

UPDATE TestSnapshot
SET ColB = 'New Value'
WHERE ColA = 1
```

Rerunning the select in the first connection will return 'Original Value' again, because the second transaction has not committed—no blocking occurs, like in the normal READ COMMITTED isolation level. However, as soon as the second transaction commits, the first connection will now see the updated value.

READ COMMITTED SNAPSHOT can be a good balance for databases that have a lot of read activity of data that is regularly updated, where consistency is important but repeatable results within a single transaction are not.

Database Snapshots

Like the SNAPSHOT isolation level, database snapshots give DBAs a way of presenting a consistent view of data at a certain time. However, whereas the SNAPSHOT isolation level provides this only for small amounts of data (that involved in a given transaction), database snapshots provide a frozen replica of the database at the time the snapshot was created. This can be helpful for situations in which DBAs need to provide timestamped data for reporting or auditing purposes.

What differentiates database snapshots from other methods of providing this same functionality (e.g., taking a backup) is that database snapshots have no data when they're first created, and they are therefore created almost instantaneously. This is made possible by a scheme similar to that which allows the SNAPSHOT isolation level to work.

Instead of copying all of the data from the source database, the database snapshot begins life as nothing more than a pointer to the original database. As data changes in that database, the older versions of rows are migrated into the snapshot database, but at any time, the snapshot database is only as large as the amount of data that's changed since it was created. Of course, this works the other way around as well. A database snapshot can grow to be as big as the original database was at the moment the snapshot was created, so ensure that enough disk space exists to provide adequate room for growth should it become necessary. DBAs should also attempt to place snapshot databases on separate physical disks from production databases, to reduce contention due to additional write operations when changes are migrated into the snapshot.

Creating Database Snapshots

Database snapshots are created using CREATE DATABASE with the AS SNAPSHOT OF option. To create a snapshot, each logical filename from the original database must appear in the definition for the snapshot, exactly as it was originally defined. The physical filename should be changed to have the .ss extension, but drives or paths can also be changed.

A recommended naming scheme for database snapshots is the same name as the database, followed by _Snapshot, optionally followed by the date and time the snapshot was created. This naming scheme should help users more quickly determine which snapshot they require for a task. It's also recommended that the snapshot's physical filenames be similarly timestamped, to make disk management easier.

As an example, assume that there is a database called Sales, with two filegroups, SalesPrimary and SalesPrimary_01. It's September 1, 2005. The following T-SQL could be used to create the snapshot:

```
CREATE DATABASE Sales_Snapshot_20050901
ON
  (NAME = SalesPrimary,
    FILENAME = 'F:\Data\SalesPrimary_20040901.ss'),
  (NAME = SalesPrimary_01,
    FILENAME = 'F:\Data\SalesPrimary_01_20040901.ss')
AS SNAPSHOT OF Sales
```

Once a snapshot is created, it will appear to clients to be a read-only database and will persist until it is explicitly dropped using DROP DATABASE. The base database cannot be dropped until all referencing snapshots are dropped. Any number of snapshots can be created for a database, allowing DBAs to keep a running tally of data states, as disk space allows. Remember, these databases will grow as data changes in the base database.

Reverting to a Database Snapshot

One benefit of snapshots, beyond their providing a readily available view of the database at a specific point in time, is that they can be used as a failsafe in case of accidental data corruption. Please note that *using database snapshots is no replacement for a solid backup plan*. However, there are times when reverting to a snapshot could be very useful. For instance, imagine a scenario in which a development team is testing a data upgrade script. These kinds of development tasks generally require the DBA to restore a database, run a version of the update script, regression test, and repeat the process iteratively as bugs are discovered. Using a database snapshot and reverting will decrease a lot of the downtime required for these kinds of tasks and generally make life easier for the DBA.

Reverting to a snapshot is very similar to restoring from a backup. For instance, to revert the Sales database from a snapshot created on September 1, 2005, the following T-SQL could be used:

```
RESTORE DATABASE Sales
FROM
  DATABASE_SNAPSHOT = Sales_Snapshot_20050901
```

A few restrictions apply. A restore from a snapshot can only occur if the database has only one snapshot. So if multiple snapshots have been created, those other than the one to be restored from will have to be dropped. The database can have no full-text indexes. Finally, during the restore process, both the database and the snapshot will be unavailable for use.

Data Integrity Enhancements

Given that SQL Server 2000 is known to be very stable in terms of on-disk data integrity, it should come as no surprise that there are few enhancements in this area in SQL Server 2005. Microsoft has provided two interesting new features: a new checksum-based data page verification scheme in addition to the torn page detection option from previous versions of SQL Server, and the ability to put a database into an emergency, administrator-only access mode. We detail both features in the sections that follow.

Verifying a Database's Pages

SQL Server 2005 adds a new syntax to ALTER DATABASE for page verification, with two options: one option to enable torn page detection and a newer checksum verification option. The checksum verification can detect most of the same types of failures as torn page detection, as well as various hardware-related failures that torn page detection cannot. However, it is more resource intensive than the older option, so as with any other change, careful testing should be done before rolling to production environments.

Enabling the checksum-based page verification scheme for a database called Sales could be done with the following T-SQL:

```
ALTER DATABASE Sales
SET PAGE_VERIFY CHECKSUM
```

To enable torn page detection, use the TORN_PAGE_DETECTION option:

```
ALTER DATABASE Sales
SET PAGE_VERIFY TORN_PAGE_DETECTION
```

Note that only one of the two page verification types can be enabled at any given time.

To turn off page verification altogether, use the NONE option:

```
ALTER DATABASE Sales
SET PAGE_VERIFY NONE
```

To determine the current page verification setting for a given database, use the page_verify_option column of sys.databases:

```
SELECT page_verify_option
FROM sys.databases
WHERE name = 'abc'
```

The column will have a value of 0 if the NONE option is set, 1 for the TORN_PAGE_DETECTION option, and 2 for the CHECKSUM option.

Putting a Database into an Emergency State

Unfortunately, even with data page verification and a very stable DBMS like SQL Server, problems do sometimes occur. Should a problem arise, the DBA can set the database to the new emergency state.

This state makes the database read-only and restricts access to members of the sysadmin fixed server role. Although this sounds like a combination of the read-only and restricted user modes, there is a very important enhancement available with the new emergency state option. This option can be set on databases marked suspect, thereby allowing the DBA to get in and either fix errors or pull out vital data if errors cannot be fixed.

To set the database to the emergency state, use the EMERGENCY option of ALTER DATABASE. To set this mode for a database called Sales, the following T-SQL would be used:

```
ALTER DATABASE Sales
SET EMERGENCY
```

To turn off the emergency state, use the ONLINE option:

```
ALTER DATABASE Sales
SET ONLINE
```

Summary

SQL Server 2005 introduces a large number of new features for DBAs to add to their arsenals: catalog views, performance enhancements, and better data-integrity tools than previous versions of SQL Server. Although the learning curve can be steep with some of these new tools, in the long run use of them will lead to higher-quality, better-performing systems—and more time for DBAs to kick back and take a much-needed break!

CHAPTER 5

■ ■ ■

.NET Integration

Truly devoted (or is it insane?) SQL Server programmers might think back wistfully on days spent debugging extended stored procedures, yearning for those joyfully complicated times. The rest of us, however, remember plunging headfirst into a process that always felt a lot more esoteric than it needed to be and never quite lived up to the functionality we hoped it could provide.

SQL Server 7.0 introduced the idea of *extended stored procedures* (XPs), which are DLLs—usually written in C++—that can be used to programmatically extend SQL Server's functionality. Programming and debugging these is unfortunately quite difficult for most users, and their use gives rise to many issues, such as memory leaks and security concerns, that make them less than desirable. Luckily, extended stored procedures are a thing of the past (or are deprecated, at the very least), and SQL Server 2005 gives programmers much better options with tightly integrated common language runtime (CLR) interoperability. Developers can now use any .NET language they feel comfortable with to create powerful user-defined objects within SQL Server; note, however, that only C#, VB .NET, and Managed C++ are officially supported languages. Although other languages can be used, getting them to work properly may require a bit of additional effort.

In this chapter, programming with CLR objects will be introduced with a step-by-step tour through development of a CLR stored procedure. Also discussed will be the .NET object model provided for SQL Server CLR development, best practices for developing CLR objects, and various deployment issues.

Chapter 6 builds upon this foundation, covering all of the other types of objects that can be created in SQL Server using .NET: CLR user-defined types, CLR user-defined functions, CLR aggregates, and CLR triggers.

Please note that both this chapter and Chapter 6 assume familiarity with .NET programming using the C# language. Those readers who haven't yet picked up .NET skills should consider starting with Andrew Troelsen's excellent book, *C# and the .NET Platform, Second Edition* (Apress, 2003).

Introduction to SQL Server .NET Integration

SQL Server developers have had few choices in the past when it came to doing things in the database that Transact-SQL (T-SQL) wasn't especially well suited for. This includes such things as complex or heavily mathematical logic, connecting to remote services or data stores, and manipulating files and other non–SQL Server–controlled resources. Although many of these tasks are best suited for operation on the client rather than within SQL Server, sometimes system architecture, project funding, or time constraints leave developers with no choice—business problems must be solved in some way, as quickly and cheaply as possible. Extended stored procedures were one option to help with these situations, but as mentioned previously, these were difficult to write and debug, and were known for decreasing server stability. Another option was to use the sp_OA (Object Automation) stored procedures to call COM objects, but this had its own issues, including performance penalties and dealing with COM "DLL hell" if the correct versions weren't registered on the SQL Server.

CLR integration does away with these issues—and provides a structured, easy-to-use methodology for extending SQL Server in a variety of ways.

Why Does SQL Server 2005 Host the CLR?

There are some things that T-SQL just isn't meant to do. For instance, it's not known as a language that excels at accessing data from web services. Although there are some ways that this can be done, T-SQL isn't something we developers would think of as the first choice for this operation. Another good example is data structures; in T-SQL, there is only one data structure: tables. This works fine for most of our data needs, but sometimes something else is needed—an array or a linked list, for instance. And although these things can be simulated using T-SQL, it's messy at best.

The common language runtime is a managed environment, designed with safety and stability in mind. Management means that memory and resources are automatically handled by the runtime—it is very difficult (if not impossible) to write code that will cause a memory leak. Management also means that SQL Server can control the runtime if something goes wrong. If SQL Server detects instability, the hosted runtime can be immediately restarted.

This level of control was impossible with the extended stored procedure functionality that was present in earlier versions of SQL Server. Extended stored procedures were often known for decreasing the stability of SQL Server, as there was no access control—an unwitting developer could all too easily write code that could overwrite some of SQL Server's own memory locations, thereby creating a time bomb that would explode when SQL Server needed to access the memory. Thanks to the CLR's "sandboxing" of process space, this is no longer an issue.

The CLR builds virtual process spaces within its environment, called *application domains*. This lets code running within each domain operate as if it has its own dedicated process, and at the same time isolates virtual processes from each other. The net effect in terms of stability is that if code running within one application domain crashes, the other domains won't be affected—only the domain in which the crash occurred will be restarted by the framework and the entire system won't be compromised. This is especially important in database applications; developers certainly don't want to risk crashing an entire instance of SQL Server because of a bug in a CLR routine.

When to Use CLR Routines

T-SQL is a language that was designed primarily for straightforward data access. Developers are often not comfortable writing complex set-based solutions to problems, and end up using cursors to solve complex logical problems. This is never the best solution in T-SQL. Cursors and row-by-row processing aren't the optimal data access methods. Set-based solutions are preferred.

When non-set-based solutions are absolutely necessary, CLR routines are faster. Looping over a SqlDataReader can be much faster than using a cursor. And complex logic will often perform much better in .NET than in T-SQL. In addition, if routines need to access external resources such as web services, using .NET is an obvious choice. T-SQL is simply not adept at handling these kinds of situations.

When Not to Use CLR Routines

It's important to remember an adage that has become increasingly popular in the fad-ridden world of IT in the past few years: "To a hammer, everything looks like a nail."

Just because you can do something using the CLR, doesn't mean you should. For data access, set-based T-SQL is still the appropriate choice in virtually all cases. Access to external resources from SQL Server, which CLR integration makes much easier, is generally not appropriate from SQL Server's process space. Think carefully about architecture before implementing such solutions. External resources can be unpredictable or unavailable—two factors that aren't supposed to be present in database solutions!

In the end, it's a question of common sense. If something doesn't seem to belong in SQL Server, it probably shouldn't be implemented there. As CLR integration matures, best practices will become more obvious—but for the meantime, take a minimalist approach. Overuse of the technology will cause more problems in the long run than underuse.

How SQL Server Hosts .NET: An Architectural Overview

The CLR is completely hosted by SQL Server. Routines running within SQL Server's process space make requests to SQL Server for all resources, including memory and processor time. SQL Server is free to either grant or deny these requests, depending on server conditions. SQL Server is also free to completely restart the hosted CLR if a process is taking up too many resources. SQL Server itself is in complete control, and the CLR is unable to compromise the basic integrity that SQL Server offers.

Why Managed Objects Perform Well

SQL Server 2005 CLR integration was designed with performance in mind. Compilation of CLR routines for hosting within SQL Server is done using function pointers in order to facilitate high-speed transitions between T-SQL and CLR processes. Type-specific optimizations ensure that once routines are just-in-time compiled (JITted), no further cost is associated with their invocation.

Another optimization is streaming of result sets from CLR *table-valued functions* (which will be covered in detail in the next chapter). Unlike some other rowset-based providers that require the client to accept the entire result set before work can be done, table-valued functions are able to stream data a single row at a time. This enables work to be handled in a piecemeal fashion, thereby reducing both memory and processor overhead.

Why CLR Integration Is Stable

SQL Server both hosts and completely controls the CLR routines running within the SQL Server process space. Since SQL Server is in control of all resources, routines are unable to bog down the server or access unavailable resources, like XPs were able to.

Another important factor is the HostProtection attribute, a new feature in the .NET 2.0 Base Class Library. This attribute allows methods to define their level of cross process resource interaction, mainly from a threading and locking point of view. For instance, synchronized methods and classes (for example, System.Collections.ArrayList.Synchronized) are decorated with the Synchronization parameter of the attribute. These methods and classes, as well as those that expose a shared provider state or manage external processes, are disallowed from use within the SQL Server–hosted CLR environment, based on permission sets chosen by the DBA at deployment time. Permission sets are covered in more detail later in this chapter, in the section "Deploying CLR Routines."

Although an in-depth examination of CLR code safety issues is beyond the scope of this book, it's important that DBAs supporting the CLR features in SQL Server 2005 realize that this is no longer the world of XPs. These objects can be rolled out with a great deal of confidence. And as will be discussed later in this chapter, the DBA has the final say over what access the CLR code will have once it is deployed within the server.

SQL Server .NET Programming Model

ADO.NET, the data access technology used within the .NET Framework, has been enhanced to operate within SQL Server 2005 hosted routines. These enhancements are fairly simple to exploit; for most operations, the only difference between coding on a client layer or within the database will be modification of a connection string. Thanks to this, .NET developers will find a shallow learning curve when picking up SQL CLR skills. And when necessary, moving code between tiers will be relatively simple.

Enhancements to ADO.NET for SQL Server Hosting

CLR stored procedures use ADO.NET objects to retrieve data from and write data to the database. These are the same objects you're already familiar with if you use ADO.NET today: `SqlCommand`, `SqlDataReader`, `DataSet`, etc. The only difference is, these can now be run in SQL Server's process space (in-processes) instead of only on a client.

When accessing SQL Server via an ADO.NET client, the `SqlConnection` object is instantiated, and a connection string is set, either in the constructor or using the `ConnectionString` property. This same process happens when instantiating an in-process connection—but the connection string has been rewired for SQL Server. Using the connection string `"Context connection=true"` tells SQL Server to use the same connection that spawned the CLR method as the connection from which to perform data access.

This means, in essence, that only a single change is all that's necessary for migration of the majority of data access code between tiers. To migrate code into SQL Server, classes and methods will still have to be appropriately decorated with attributes describing how they should function (see the section, "Anatomy of a Stored Procedure"), but the only substantial code change will be to the connection string! Virtually all members of the `SqlClient` namespace—with the notable exception of asynchronous operations—will work within the SQL Server process space.

The other major code difference between CLR routines and ADO.NET programming on clients is that inside of CLR routines the developer will generally want to communicate back to the session that invoked the routine. This communication can take any number of forms, from returning scalar values to sending back a result set from a stored procedure or table-valued function. However, the ADO.NET client has until now included no mechanisms for which to do that.

Overview of the New .NET Namespaces for SQL Server

Two namespaces were added to the .NET Framework for integration with SQL Server 2005. These namespaces contain the methods and attributes necessary to create CLR routines within SQL Server 2005, and perform manipulation of database objects within those routines.

Microsoft.SqlServer.Server

The `Microsoft.SqlServer.Server` namespace contains attributes for defining managed routines, as well as ADO.NET methods specific to the SQL Server provider.

In order for classes and methods to be defined as hosted CLR routines, they must be decorated with attributes to tell SQL Server what they are. These attributes include, among others, the `SqlProcedureAttribute` for defining CLR stored procedures, and the `SqlFunctionAttribute` for CLR user-defined functions. All of these attributes will be explained in detail in the next chapter.

The namespace also contains ADO.NET methods that allow CLR routines to communicate back to the session that invoked them. What can be communicated back depends on the type of CLR routine. For instance, a stored procedure can return messages, errors, result sets, or an integer return value. A table-valued user-defined function, on the other hand, can only return a single result set.

When programming CLR routines that need to return data, an object called `SqlContext` is available. This object represents a connection back to the session that instantiated the CLR routine. Exposed by this object is another object, `SqlPipe`. This is the means by which data is sent back to the caller. Sending properly formatted messages or result sets "down the pipe" means that the calling session will receive the data.

Note that not all `SqlContext` features are available from all routine types. For instance, a scalar user-defined function cannot send back a result set. Developers must remember to carefully test CLR routines; using a feature that's not available won't result in a compile-time error! Instead, an error will occur at runtime when the system attempts to use the unavailable feature. It's very important to keep this in mind during development in order to avoid problems once routines are rolled to production systems.

Programming a CLR Stored Procedure

Now that the basic overview of what's available is complete, it's time to get into some code! The example used in this chapter will be a dynamic cross-tabulation of some sales data in the AdventureWorks sample database that's included with SQL Server 2005. Given the data in the `Sales.SalesOrderHeader` and `Sales.SalesOrderDetail` tables, the goal will be to produce a report based on a user-specified date range, in which the columns are sales months and each row aggregates total sales within each month, by territory.

Before starting work on any CLR routine, the developer should ask the following question: "Why should this routine be programmed using the CLR?" Remember that in most cases, T-SQL is still the preferred method of SQL Server programming—so give this question serious thought before continuing.

In this case, the argument in favor of using a CLR routine is fairly obvious. Although this problem can be solved using only T-SQL, it's a messy prospect at best. In order to accomplish this task, the routine first must determine in which months sales occurred within the input date range. Then, using that set of months, a query must be devised to create a column for each month and aggregate the appropriate data by territory.

This task is made slightly easier than it was in previous versions of SQL Server, thanks to the inclusion of the `PIVOT` operator (see Chapter 3 for more information on this operator). This operator allows T-SQL developers to more easily write queries that transform rows into columns, a common reporting technique known as either *pivoting* or *cross-tabulating*. However, `PIVOT` doesn't provide dynamic capabilities—the developer still needs to perform fairly complex string concatenation in order to get things working. Concatenating strings is tricky and inefficient in T-SQL; using the .NET Framework's `StringBuilder` class is a much nicer prospect—and avoiding complex T-SQL string manipulation is argument enough to do this job within a CLR routine.

Once the determination to use a CLR routine has been made, the developer next must ask, "What is the appropriate type of routine to use for this job?" Generally speaking, this will be a fairly straightforward question; for instance, a CLR user-defined type and a CLR user-defined trigger obviously serve quite different purposes. However, the specific problem for this situation isn't so straightforward. There are two obvious choices: a CLR table-valued function and a CLR stored procedure.

The requirement for this task is to return a result set to the client containing the cross-tabulated data. Both CLR table-valued functions and CLR stored procedures can return result sets to the client. However, as will be discussed in the next chapter, CLR table-valued functions must have their output columns predefined. In this case, the column list is dynamic; if the user enters a three-month date range, up to four columns will appear in the result set—one for each month in which there were sales, and one for the territory sales are being aggregated for. Likewise, if the user enters a one-year date range, up to 13 columns may be returned. Therefore, it isn't possible to predefine the column list, and the only choice is to use a CLR stored procedure.

Starting a Visual Studio 2005 SQL Server Project

Once you have decided to program a CLR routine, the first step is to start Visual Studio 2005 and create a new project. Figure 5-1 shows the menu option to pick in order to launch the New Project Wizard.

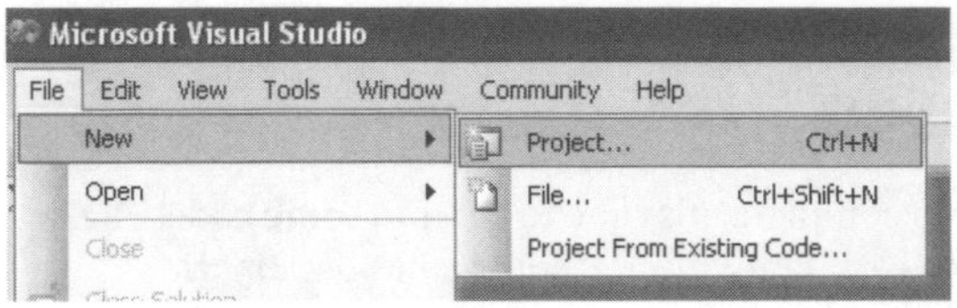

Figure 5-1. *Open a new project in Visual Studio 2005.*

Visual Studio 2005 includes a project template for SQL Server projects, which automatically creates all of the necessary references and can create appropriate empty classes for all of the SQL Server CLR routine types. Although you could use a Class Library template instead and do all of this manually, that's not an especially efficient use of time. So we definitely recommend that you use this template when developing CLR routines.

Figure 5-2 shows the SQL Server Project template being chosen from the available database project templates. On this system, only C# has been installed; on a system with Visual Basic .NET, the same option would appear under that language's option tree.

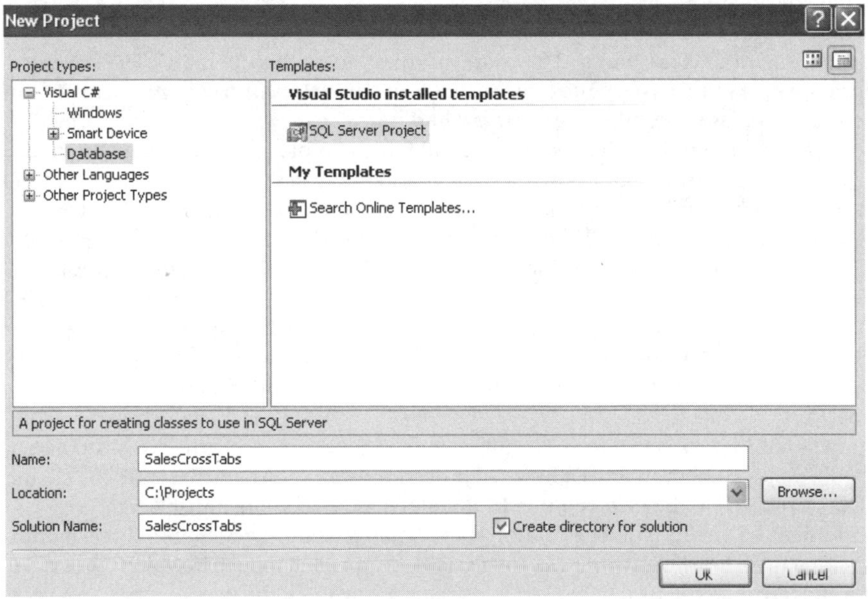

Figure 5-2. *Select the SQL Server Project template.*

This project has been named SalesCrossTabs, since it's going to contain at least one cross-tabulation of sales data—and perhaps more will be added in the future. A single SQL Server project can contain any number of CLR routines. However, it's recommended that any one project logically groups only a small number of routines. If a single change to a single routine is made, you should not have to reapply every assembly referenced by the database.

After clicking the OK button, a dialog box will appear prompting for a database reference, as shown in Figure 5-3. This reference indicates the SQL Server and database to which the project can be automatically deployed by Visual Studio for testing and debugging during the development process.

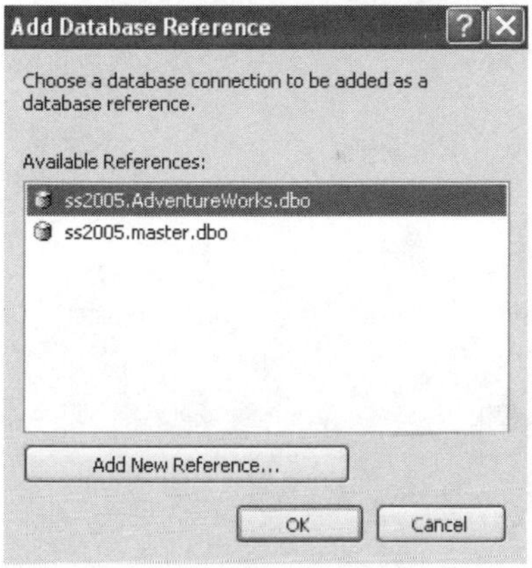

Figure 5-3. *Add a database reference to allow Visual Studio to automatically deploy the routine.*

If the correct reference hasn't already been created, click the Add New Reference button, and the dialog box shown in Figure 5-4 will appear. As development is being done for sales data in the AdventureWorks database, that's what has been selected for this reference. Once the server and database have been selected and the connection has been tested, click the OK button to continue.

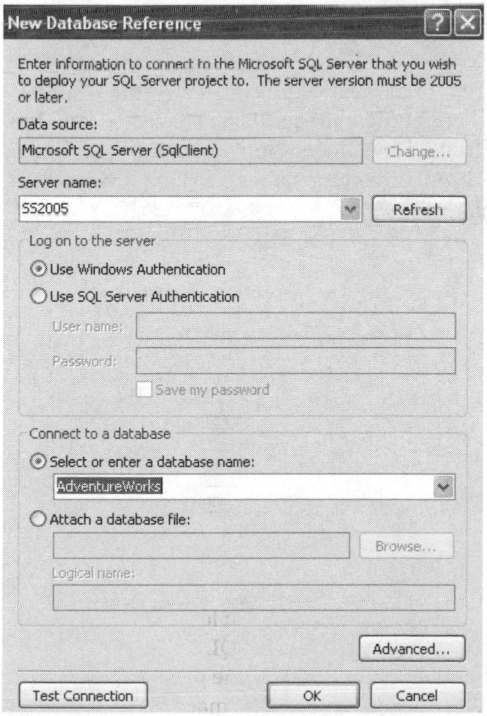

Figure 5-4. *Create a new database reference if the correct one doesn't already exist.*

At this point, a new, blank project has been created and is ready to have some code added. Right-click the project name in the Solution Explorer window, click Add, and then click Stored Procedure, as shown in Figure 5-5.

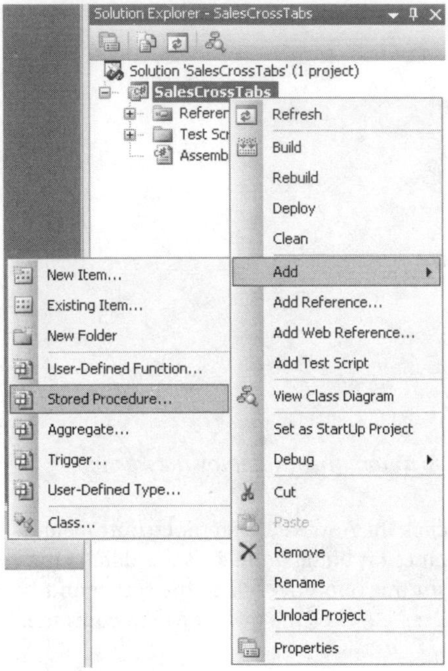

Figure 5-5. *Adding a stored procedure to the project*

The final step in adding the new stored procedure is to name it. Figure 5-6 shows the window that will appear after clicking Stored Procedure. The Stored Procedure template is selected, and the procedure has been named GetSalesPerTerritoryByMonth. Developers should remember that, just as in naming T-SQL stored procedures, descriptive, self-documenting names go a long way towards making development—especially maintenance—easier.

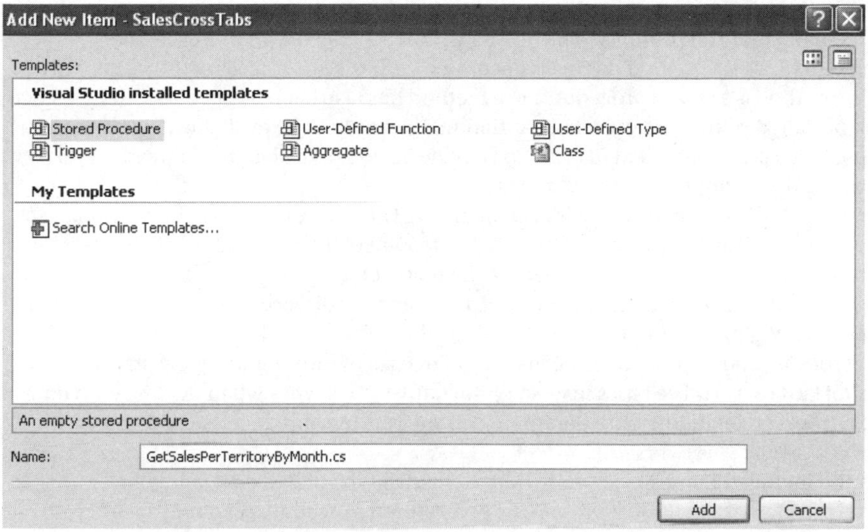

Figure 5-6. *Naming the stored procedure*

Anatomy of a Stored Procedure

After the new stored procedure has been added the project, the following code will be appear in the editing window:

```
using System;
using System.Data;
using System.Data.SqlClient;
using System.Data.SqlTypes;
using Microsoft.SqlServer.Server;


public partial class StoredProcedures
{
    [Microsoft.SqlServer.Server.SqlProcedure]
    public static void GetSalesPerTerritoryByMonth()
    {
        // Put your code here
    }
};
```

There are a few important features to notice here. First of all, note that the Microsoft.SqlServer. Server and System.Data.SqlTypes namespaces have been automatically included in this project. Both of these namespaces have very specific purposes within a routine—and will be necessary within most SQL Server CLR projects.

The `Microsoft.SqlServer.Server` namespace is necessary, as previously mentioned, for the attributes that must decorate all routines to be hosted within SQL Server. In this case, the `GetSalesPerTerritoryByMonth` method has been decorated with the `SqlProcedure` attribute. This indicates that the method is a stored procedure. The method has also been defined as `static`—since this method will be called without an object instantiation, it would not be available if not defined as `static`. The namespace is also included in order to provide access to the calling context, for data access and returning data—but more on that shortly.

The `System.Data.SqlTypes` namespace is also included. This namespace provides datatypes that correspond to each of the SQL Server datatypes. For instance, the equivalent of SQL Server's `INTEGER` datatype isn't .NET's `System.Int32` datatype. Instead, it's `SqlTypes.SqlInt32`. Although these types can be cast between each other freely, not all types have direct equivalents—many of the SQL Server types have slightly different implementations than what would seem to be their .NET siblings. For that reason, and to provide some insulation in case of future underlying structural changes, it's important to use these types instead of the native .NET types when dealing with data returned from SQL Server, including both parameters to the routine and data read using a `SqlDataReader` or `DataSet`.

Aside from the included namespaces, note that the return type of the `GetSalesPerTerritoryByMonth` method is void. SQL Server stored procedures can return either 32-bit integers or nothing at all. In this case, the stored procedure won't have a return value. That's generally a good idea, because SQL Server will override the return value should an error occur within the stored procedure; so output parameters are considered to be a better option for returning scalar values to a client. However, should a developer want to implement a return value from this stored procedure, the allowed datatypes are `SqlInt32` or `SqlInt16`.

Adding Parameters

Most stored procedures will have one or more parameters to allow users to pass in arguments that can tell the stored procedure which data to return. In the case of this particular stored procedure, two parameters will be added in order to facilitate getting data using a date range (one of the requirements outlined in the section "Programming a CLR Stored Procedure"). These parameters will be called `StartDate` and `EndDate`, and each will be defined as type `SqlDateTime`.

These two parameters are added to the method definition, just like parameters to any C# method:

```
[Microsoft.SqlServer.Server.SqlProcedure]
public static void GetSalesPerTerritoryByMonth( SqlDateTime StartDate,
                                                SqlDateTime EndDate)
{
    // Put your code here
}
```

In this case, these parameters are required input parameters. Output parameters can be defined by using the C# ref (reference) keyword before the datatype. This will then allow developers to use SQL Server's `OUTPUT` keyword in order to get back scalar values from the stored procedure.

Unfortunately, neither optional parameters nor default parameter values are currently supported by CLR stored procedures.

Defining the Problem

At this point, the stored procedure is syntactically complete and could be deployed as is; but of course, it wouldn't do anything! It's time to code the meat of the procedure. But first, it's good to take a step back and figure out what it should do.

The final goal, as previously mentioned, is to cross-tabulate sales totals per territory, with a column for each month in which sales took place. This goal can be accomplished using the following steps:

1. Select a list of the months and years in which sales took place, from the Sales.SalesOrderHeader table.

2. Using the list of months, construct a query using the PIVOT operator that returns the desired cross-tabulation.

3. Return the cross-tabulated result set to the client.

The Sales.SalesOrderHeader table contains one row for each sale, and includes a column called OrderDate—the date the sale was made. For the sake of this stored procedure, a distinct list of the months and years in which sales were made will be considered. The following query returns that data:

```
SELECT DISTINCT
    DATEPART(yyyy, OrderDate) AS YearPart,
    DATEPART(mm, OrderDate) AS MonthPart
FROM Sales.SalesOrderHeader
ORDER BY YearPart, MonthPart
```

Once the stored procedure has that data, it needs to create the actual cross-tab query. This query needs to use the dates from Sales.SalesOrderHeader and for each month should calculate the sum of the amounts in the LineTotal column of the Sales.SalesOrderDetail table. And of course, this data should be aggregated per territory. The TerritoryId column of the Sales.SalesOrderHeader table will be used for that purpose.

The first step in creating the cross-tab query is to pull the actual data required. The following query returns the territory ID, order date formatted as YYYY-MM, and total line item amount for each line item in the SalesOrderDetail table:

```
SELECT
    TerritoryId,
    CONVERT(CHAR(7), h.OrderDate, 120) AS theDate,
    d.LineTotal
FROM Sales.SalesOrderHeader h
JOIN Sales.SalesOrderDetail d ON h.SalesOrderID = d.SalesOrderID
```

Figure 5-7 shows a few of the 121,317 rows of data returned by this query.

	TerritoryId	theDate	LineTotal
1	5	2001-07	2024.994000
2	5	2001-07	6074.982000
3	5	2001-07	2024.994000
4	5	2001-07	2039.994000
5	5	2001-07	2039.994000
6	5	2001-07	4079.988000
7	5	2001-07	2039.994000
8	5	2001-07	86.521200
9	5	2001-07	28.840400
10	5	2001-07	34.200000

Figure 5-7. *Unaggregated sales data*

Using the PIVOT operator, this query can be turned into a cross-tab. For instance, to report on sales from June and July of 2004, the following query could be used:

```
SELECT
    TerritoryId,
    [2004-06],
    [2004-07]
FROM
(
    SELECT
        TerritoryId,
        CONVERT(CHAR(7), h.OrderDate, 120) AS YYYY_MM,
        d.LineTotal
    FROM Sales.SalesOrderHeader h
    JOIN Sales.SalesOrderDetail d ON h.SalesOrderID = d.SalesOrderID
) p
PIVOT
(
    SUM (LineTotal)
    FOR YYYY_MM IN
    (
        [2004-06],
        [2004-07]
    )
) AS pvt
ORDER BY TerritoryId
```

Figure 5-8 shows the results of this query. The data has now been aggregated and cross-tabulated. Note that a couple of the values are NULL—this indicates a territory that did not have sales for that month.

	TerritoryId	2004-06	2004-07
1	1	779625.967724	10165.250000
2	2	240725.227509	NULL
3	3	298101.019968	NULL
4	4	993295.830953	9155.300000
5	5	269604.574888	113.960000
6	6	717837.710783	10853.700000
7	7	316740.799297	3491.950000
8	8	349467.104000	3604.830000
9	9	711086.975552	9234.230000
10	10	688354.968664	4221.410000

Figure 5-8. *Cross-tabulated sales data*

In the actual stored procedure, the tokens representing June and July 2004 will be replaced by tokens for the actual months from the input date range, as determined by the StartDate and EndDate parameters and the first query. Then the full cross-tab query will be concatenated. All that's left from the three steps defined previously is to return the results to the caller—but you have a couple of choices for how to tackle that challenge.

Using the SqlPipe

As mentioned in previous sections, SqlContext is an object available from within the scope of CLR routines. This object is defined in the Microsoft.SqlServer.Server namespace as a sealed class with a private constructor—so you don't create an instance of it; rather, you just use it. The following code, for instance, is invalid:

```
//This code does not work -- the constructor for SqlContext is private
SqlContext context = new SqlContext();
```

Instead, just use the object as is. To use the SqlPipe, which is the object we need for this exercise, the following code might be used:

```
//Get a reference to the SqlPipe for this calling context
SqlPipe pipe = SqlContext.Pipe;
```

So what is the SqlPipe? This object allows the developer to send data or commands to be executed from a CLR routine back to the caller.

The Send() Method

The Send() method, which as you can guess is used to actually send the data, has three overloads:

- Send(string message) sends a string, which will be interpreted as a message. Think InfoMessage in ADO.NET or the messages pane in SQL Server Management Studio. Sending strings using Send() has the same effect as using the T-SQL PRINT statement.

- Send(SqlDataRecord record) sends a single record back to the caller. This is used in conjunction with the SendResultsStart() and SendResultsEnd() methods to manually send a table a row at a time. Getting it working can be quite a hassle, and it's really not recommended for most applications. See the section "Table-Valued User-Defined Functions" in the next chapter for a much nicer approach.

- Send(SqlDataReader reader) sends an entire table back to the caller, in one shot. This is much nicer than doing things row-by-row, but also just as difficult to set up for sending back data that isn't already in a SqlDataReader object. Luckily, this particular stored procedure doesn't have that problem—it uses a SqlDataReader, so this method can be used to directly stream back the data read from the SQL Server.

The Send() methods can be called any number of times during the course of a stored procedure. Just like native T-SQL stored procedures, CLR procedures can return multiple result sets and multiple messages or errors. But by far the most common overload used will be the one that accepts SqlDataReader. The following code fragment shows a good example of the utility of this method:

```
command.CommandText = "SELECT * FROM Sales.SalesOrderHeader";
SqlDataReader reader = command.ExecuteReader();
SqlContext.Pipe.Send(reader);
```

In this fragment, it's assumed that the connection and command objects have already been instantiated and the connection has been opened. A reader is populated with the SQL, which selects all columns and all rows from the Sales.SalesOrderHeader table. The SqlDataReader can be passed to the Send() method as is—and the caller will receive the data as a result set.

Although this example is quite simplistic, it illustrates the ease with which the Send() method can be used to return data back to the caller when the data is already in a SqlDataReader object.

Using the ExecuteAndSend() Method

The problem with sending a SqlDataReader back to the caller is that all of the data will be marshaled through the CLR process space on its way back. Since, in this case, the caller generated the data (it came from a table in SQL Server), it would be nice to be able to make the caller return the data on its own—without having to send the data back and forth.

This is where the ExecuteAndSend() method comes into play. This method accepts a SqlCommand object, which should have both CommandText and Parameters (if necessary) defined. This tells the calling context to execute the command and process the output itself.

Letting the caller do the work without sending the data back is quite a bit faster. In some cases, performance can improve by up to 50 percent. Sending all of that data between processes is a lot of work. But this performance improvement comes at a cost; one of the benefits of handling the data within the CLR routine is control. Take the following code fragment, for example:

```
command.CommandText = "SELECT * FROM Sales.ERRORSalesOrderHeader";
try
{
    SqlDataReader reader = command.ExecuteReader();
    SqlContext.Pipe.Send(reader);
}
catch (Exception e)
{
    //Do something smart here
}
```

This fragment is similar to the fragment discussed in the "Using the Send() Method" section. It requests all of the rows and columns from the table, and then sends the data back to the caller using the Send() method. This work is wrapped in a try/catch block—the developer, perhaps, can do something to handle any exceptions that occur. And indeed, in this code block, an exception will occur—the table Sales.ERRORSalesOrderHeader doesn't exist in the AdventureWorks database.

This exception will occur in the CLR routine—the ExecuteReader() method will fail. At that point, the exception will be caught by the catch block. But what about the following code fragment, which uses the ExecuteAndSend() method:

```
command.CommandText = "SELECT * FROM Sales.ERRORSalesOrderHeader";
try
{
    SqlContext.Pipe.ExecuteAndSend(command)
}
catch (Exception e)
{
    //Do something smart here
}
```

Remember that the ExecuteAndSend() method tells the caller to handle all output from whatever T-SQL is sent down the pipe. This includes exceptions; so in this case the catch block is hit, but by then it's already too late. The caller has already received the exception, and catching it in the CLR routine isn't especially useful.

So which method, Send() or ExecuteAndSend(), is appropriate for the sales cross-tabulation stored procedure? Given the simplicity of the example, the ExecuteAndSend() method makes more sense. It has greater performance than Send(), which is always a benefit. And there's really nothing that can be done if an exception is encountered in the final T-SQL to generate the result set.

Putting It All Together: Coding the Body of the Stored Procedure

Now that the techniques have been defined, putting together the complete stored procedure is a relatively straightforward process.

Recall that the first step is to get the list of months and years in which sales took place, within the input date range. Given that the pivot query will use date tokens formatted as YYYY-MM, it will be easier to process the unique tokens in the CLR stored procedure if they're queried from the database in that format—so the query used will be slightly different than the one shown in the "Defining the Problem" section. The following code fragment will be used to get the months and years into a SqlDataReader object:

```
//Get a SqlCommand object
SqlCommand command = new SqlCommand();

//Use the context connection
command.Connection = new SqlConnection("Context connection=true");
command.Connection.Open();

//Define the T-SQL to execute
string sql =
    "SELECT DISTINCT " +
        "CONVERT(CHAR(7), h.OrderDate, 120) AS YYYY_MM " +
    "FROM Sales.SalesOrderHeader h " +
    "WHERE h.OrderDate BETWEEN @StartDate AND @EndDate " +
    "ORDER BY YYYY_MM";
command.CommandText = sql.ToString();

//Assign the StartDate and EndDate parameters
SqlParameter param =
    command.Parameters.Add("@StartDate", SqlDbType.DateTime);
param.Value = StartDate;
param = command.Parameters.Add("@EndDate", SqlDbType.DateTime);
param.Value = EndDate;

//Get the data
SqlDataReader reader = command.ExecuteReader();
```

This code uses the same SqlCommand and SqlDataReader syntax as it would if this were being used for an ADO.NET client; keep in mind that this code won't work unless the System.Data.SqlClient namespace is included with a using directive. The only difference between this example and a client application is the connection string, which tells SQL Server that this should connect back to the caller's context instead of a remote server. Everything else is the same—the connection is even opened, as if this were a client instead of running within SQL Server's process space.

As a result of this code, the reader object will contain one row for each month in which sales took place within the input date range (that is, the range between the values of the StartDate and EndDate parameters). Looking back at the fully formed pivot query, you can see that the tokens for each month need to go into two identical comma-delimited lists: one in the outer SELECT list and one in the FOR clause. Since these are identical lists, they only need to be built once. The following code handles that:

```
//Get a StringBuilder object
System.Text.StringBuilder yearsMonths = new System.Text.StringBuilder();

//Loop through each row in the reader, adding the value to the StringBuilder
while (reader.Read())
{
    yearsMonths.Append("[" + (string)reader["YYYY_MM"] + "], ");
}

//Close the reader
reader.Close();

//Remove the final comma in the list
yearsMonths.Remove(yearsMonths.Length - 2, 1);
```

A StringBuilder is used in this code instead of a System.string. This makes building the list a bit more efficient. For each row, the value of the YYYY_MM column (the only column in the reader) is enclosed in square brackets, as required by the PIVOT operator. Then a comma and a space are appended to the end of the token. The extra comma after the final token is removed after the loop is done. Finally, SqlDataReader is closed. When working with SqlDataReader, it's a good idea to close it as soon as data retrieval is finished in order to disconnect from the database and save resources.

Now that the comma-delimited list is built, all that's left is to build the cross-tab query and send it back to the caller using the ExecuteAndSend() method. The following code shows how that's done:

```
//Define the cross-tab query
sql =
    "SELECT TerritoryId, " +
            yearsMonths.ToString() +
    "FROM " +
    "(" +
        "SELECT " +
            "TerritoryId, " +
            "CONVERT(CHAR(7), h.OrderDate, 120) AS YYYY_MM, " +
            "d.LineTotal " +
        "FROM Sales.SalesOrderHeader h " +
        "JOIN Sales.SalesOrderDetail d " +
            "ON h.SalesOrderID = d.SalesOrderID " +
        "WHERE h.OrderDate BETWEEN @StartDate AND @EndDate " +
    ") p " +
    "PIVOT " +
    "( " +
        "SUM (LineTotal) " +
        "FOR YYYY_MM IN " +
        "( " +
            yearsMonths.ToString() +
        ") " +
    ") AS pvt " +
    "ORDER BY TerritoryId";

//Set the CommandText
command.CommandText = sql.ToString();

//Have the caller execute the cross-tab query
SqlContext.Pipe.ExecuteAndSend(command);

//Close the connection
command.Connection.Close();
```

Note that the same command object is being used as was used for building the comma-delimited list of months in which sales took place. This command object already has the StartDate and EndDate parameters set; since the cross-tab query uses the same parameters, the parameters collection doesn't need to be repopulated. Just like when programming in an ADO.NET client, the connection should be closed when the process is finished with it.

At this point, the CLR stored procedure is completely functional as per the three design goals; so it's ready for a test drive.

Testing the Stored Procedure

Visual Studio 2005 makes deploying the stored procedure to the test SQL Server quite easy. Just right-click the project name (in this case, SalesCrossTabs) and click Deploy. Figure 5-9 shows what the option looks like.

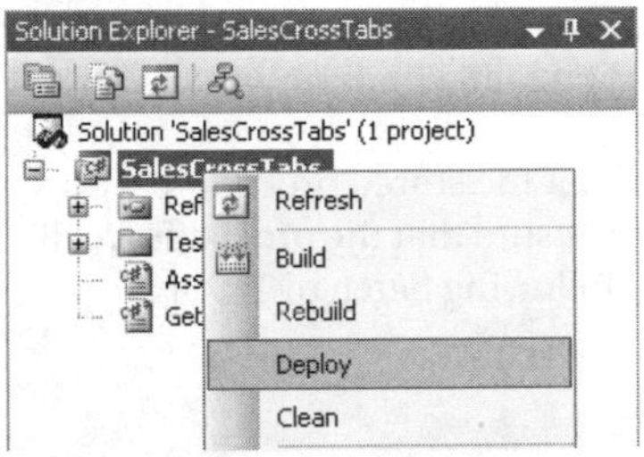

Figure 5-9. *Deploying the assembly to the test server*

Once the procedure is deployed, testing it is simple. Log in to SQL Server Management Studio and execute the following batch of T-SQL:

```
USE AdventureWorks
GO

EXEC GetSalesPerTerritoryByMonth
    @StartDate = '20040501',
    @EndDate = '20040701'
GO
```

If everything is properly compiled and deployed, this should output a result set containing cross-tabulated data for the period between May 1, 2004, and July 1, 2004. Figure 5-10 shows the correct output.

TerritoryId	2004-05	2004-06	2004-07
1	837807.162368	779625.967724	513.140000
2	168740.205705	240725.227509	NULL
3	249727.190221	298101.019968	NULL
4	1007034.715534	993295.830953	248.140000
5	264907.861900	269604.574888	NULL
6	533267.247946	717837.710783	472.150000
7	766232.284720	316740.799297	178.940000
8	407253.815030	349467.104000	149.230000
9	551630.604000	711086.975552	221.730000
10	407520.435480	688354.968664	51.460000

Figure 5-10. *Cross-tabulated sales data for the period between May 1, 2004, and July 1, 2004*

Note that running the stored procedure might result in the message, "Execution of user code in the .NET Framework is disabled. Use sp_configure "clr enabled" to enable execution of user code in the .NET Framework. If this happens, execute the following batch of T-SQL to turn on CLR integration for the SQL Server:

```
USE AdventureWorks
GO

EXEC sp_configure 'clr enabled', 1
RECONFIGURE
GO
```

Running the sp_configure system stored procedure to enable CLR integration is required before CLR routines can be run in any database. Keep in mind that enabling or disabling CLR integration is a server-wide setting.

Once the stored procedure is running properly, it will appear that the stored procedure works as designed! However, perhaps some deeper testing is warranted to ensure that the procedure really is as robust as it should be. Figure 5-11 shows the output from the following batch of T-SQL:

```
USE AdventureWorks
GO

EXEC GetSalesPerTerritoryByMonth
    @StartDate = '20050501',
    @EndDate = '20050701'
GO
```

```
Msg 50000, Level 16, State 1, Line 1
No data present for the input date range.
Msg 6522, Level 16, State 1, Procedure GetSalesPerTerritoryByMonth, Line 0
A .NET Framework error occurred during execution of user defined routine or aggregate
System.Data.SqlClient.SqlException: No data present for the input date range.
System.Data.SqlClient.SqlException:
    at System.Data.SqlClient.SqlConnection.OnError(SqlException exception, Boolean bre
    at System.Data.SqlClient.SqlInternalConnection.OnError(SqlException exception, Boo
    at System.Data.SqlClient.SqlInternalConnectionSmi.ProcessMessages()
    at System.Data.SqlClient.SqlCommand.RunExecuteNonQuerySmi(Boolean sendToPipe)
    at System.Data.SqlClient.SqlCommand.InternalExecuteNonQuery(DbAsyncResult result, 
    at System.Data.SqlClient.SqlCommand.ExecuteToPipe(SmiContext pipeContext)
    at Microsoft.SqlServer.Server.SqlPipe.ExecuteAndSend(SqlCommand command)
    at StoredProcedures.GetSalesPerTerritoryByMonth(SqlDateTime StartDate, SqlDateTime
```

Figure 5-11. *Attempting to cross-tabulate sales data for the period between May 1, 2005, and July 1, 2005*

Debugging the Procedure

What a difference a year makes! Luckily, since this stored procedure is being coded in Visual Studio, the integrated debugging environment can be used to track down the problem. In the Solution Explorer, expand the Test Scripts tree and double-click Test.sql. This will open a template that can contain T-SQL code to invoke CLR routines for debugging. Paste the following T-SQL into the Stored procedure section:

```
EXEC GetSalesPerTerritoryByMonth
    @StartDate = '20050501',
    @EndDate = '20050701'
```

Now return to the code for the managed stored procedure and put the cursor on the first line: SqlCommand command = new SqlCommand();. Pressing the F9 key will toggle a breakpoint for that line.

Before starting the debug session, open the Server Explorer by clicking View ➤ Server Explorer, as shown in Figure 5-12. In the Server Explorer, right-click the database connection being used for this project and make sure that both Application Debugging and Allow SQL/CLR Debugging are checked, as shown in Figure 5-13. Keep in mind that allowing SQL/CLR debugging should not be done on a production SQL Server. During debugging, all managed code running within the SQL Server process will be halted should any breakpoints be hit. This can wreak havoc on a live system that makes use of CLR routines, so make sure to only debug on development systems.

Figure 5-12. *Opening the Server Explorer in Visual Studio*

Figure 5-13. *Allowing SQL/CLR Debugging for the project's database connection*

Once debugging is enabled, press the F5 key, and Visual Studio will enter debug mode. If all is working as it should, the breakpoint should be hit—and code execution will stop on the first line of the stored procedure.

Use the F10 key to step through the stored procedure one line at a time, using the Locals pane to check the value of all of the variables. Stop stepping through on the line `yearsMonths.Remove(yearsMonths.Length - 2, 1);`, and look at the value of the `yearsMonths` variable in the Locals pane—it's empty; no characters can be removed from an empty string!

As it turns out, this stored procedure wasn't coded properly to be able to handle date ranges in which there is no data. This is definitely a big problem, since the output requires a column per each month in the input date range that sales occurred. Without any data, there can be no columns in the output. The stored procedure needs to return an error if no data is present.

Throwing Exceptions in CLR Routines

Any exception that can be thrown from the CLR will bubble up to the SQL Server context if it's not caught within the CLR routine. For instance, the sales cross-tab stored procedure could be made a bit more robust by raising an error if `yearsMonths` is zero characters long, instead of attempting to remove the comma:

```
if (yearsMonths.Length > 0)
{
    //Remove the final comma in the list
    yearsMonths.Remove(yearsMonths.Length - 2, 1);
}
else
{
    throw new ApplicationException("No data present for the input date range.");
}
```

Instead of getting a random error from the routine, a well-defined error is now returned—theoretically. In reality, the error isn't so friendly. As shown in Figure 5-14, these errors can get quite muddled—not only is the error returned as with native T-SQL errors, but the call stack is also included. And although that's useful for debugging, it's overkill for the purpose of a well-defined exception.

```
Msg 6522, Level 16, State 1, Procedure GetSalesPerTerritoryByMonth, Line 0
A .NET Framework error occurred during execution of user defined routine or aggregate 'GetSalesPerTerritoryBy
System.ApplicationException: No data present for the input date range.
System.ApplicationException:
    at StoredProcedures.GetSalesPerTerritoryByMonth(SqlDateTime StartDate, SqlDateTime EndDate)
    .
```

Figure 5-14. *Standard CLR exceptions aren't formatted well for readability.*

A better option, obviously, would be to use a native T-SQL error, invoked with the RAISERROR() function. A batch can be sent using SqlPipe.ExecuteAndSend(), as in the following code fragment:

```
if (yearsMonths.Length > 0)
{
    //Remove the final comma in the list
    yearsMonths.Remove(yearsMonths.Length - 2, 1);
}
else
{
    command.CommandText =
        "RAISERROR('No data present for the input date range.', 16, 1)";
    SqlContext.Pipe.ExecuteAndSend(command);
    return;
}
```

Alas, as shown in Figure 5-15, this produces an even worse output. The T-SQL exception bubbles back into the CLR layer, where a second CLR exception is thrown as a result of the presence of the T-SQL exception.

```
Msg 50000, Level 16, State 1, Line 1
No data present for the input date range.
Msg 6522, Level 16, State 1, Procedure GetSalesPerTerritoryByMonth, Line 0
A .NET Framework error occurred during execution of user defined routine or aggregate 'GetSalesPerTerritoryBy
System.Data.SqlServer.SqlException: No data present for the input date range.
System.Data.SqlServer.SqlException:
    at System.Data.SqlServer.Internal.StandardEventSink.HandleErrors()
    at System.Data.SqlServer.Internal.RequestExecutor.HandleExecute(EventTranslator eventTranslator, SqlConne
    at System.Data.SqlServer.Internal.RequestExecutor.ExecuteToPipe(SqlConnection conn, SqlTransaction tran, (
    at System.Data.SqlServer.SqlPipe.Execute(SqlCommand command)
    at StoredProcedures.GetSalesPerTerritoryByMonth(SqlDateTime StartDate, SqlDateTime EndDate)
    .
```

Figure 5-15. *RAISERROR alone doesn't improve upon the quality of the exception.*

The solution, as strange as it seems, is to raise the error using RAISERROR but catch it so that a second error isn't raised when control is returned to the CLR routine. The following code fragment shows how to accomplish this:

```
if (yearsMonths.Length > 0)
{
    //Remove the final comma in the list
    yearsMonths.Remove(yearsMonths.Length - 2, 1);
}
else
{
    command.CommandText =
        "RAISERROR('No data present for the input date range.', 16, 1)";
    try
    {
        SqlContext.Pipe.ExecuteAndSend(command);
    }
    catch
    {
        return;
    }
}
```

After catching the exception, the method returns—if it were to continue, more exceptions would be thrown by the PIVOT routine, as no pivot columns could be defined. Figure 5-16 shows the output this produces when run with an invalid date range. It's quite a bit easier to read than the previous exceptions.

```
Msg 50000, Level 16, State 1, Line 1
No data present for the input date range.
```

Figure 5-16. *Catching the exception in the CLR routine after firing a RAISERROR yields the most readable exception message.*

The complete code for the sales cross-tab stored procedure, including handling for invalid date ranges, follows:

```
using System;
using System.Data;
using System.Data.SqlClient;
using System.Data.SqlTypes;
using Microsoft.SqlServer.Server;


public partial class StoredProcedures
{
    [Microsoft.SqlServer.Server.SqlProcedure]
    public static void GetSalesPerTerritoryByMonth( SqlDateTime StartDate,
                                                    SqlDateTime EndDate)
    {
        //Get a SqlCommand object
        SqlCommand command = new SqlCommand();
```

```csharp
//Use the context connection
command.Connection = new SqlConnection("Context connection=true");
command.Connection.Open();

//Define the T-SQL to execute
string sql =
    "SELECT DISTINCT " +
        "CONVERT(CHAR(7), h.OrderDate, 120) AS YYYY_MM " +
    "FROM Sales.SalesOrderHeader h " +
    "WHERE h.OrderDate BETWEEN @StartDate AND @EndDate " +
    "ORDER BY YYYY_MM";
command.CommandText = sql.ToString();

//Assign the StartDate and EndDate parameters
SqlParameter param =
    command.Parameters.Add("@StartDate", SqlDbType.DateTime);
param.Value = StartDate;
param = command.Parameters.Add("@EndDate", SqlDbType.DateTime);
param.Value = EndDate;

//Get the data
SqlDataReader reader = command.ExecuteReader();

//Get a StringBuilder object
System.Text.StringBuilder yearsMonths = new System.Text.StringBuilder();

//Loop through each row in the reader, adding the value to the StringBuilder
while (reader.Read())
{
    yearsMonths.Append("[" + (string)reader["YYYY_MM"] + "], ");
}

//Close the reader
reader.Close();

if (yearsMonths.Length > 0)
{
    //Remove the final comma in the list
    yearsMonths.Remove(yearsMonths.Length - 2, 1);
}
else
{
    command.CommandText =
        "RAISERROR('No data present for the input date range.', 16, 1)";
    try
    {
        SqlContext.Pipe.ExecuteAndSend(command);
    }
    catch
    {
        return;
    }
}
```

```
        //Define the cross-tab query
        sql =
            "SELECT TerritoryId, " +
                    yearsMonths.ToString() +
            "FROM " +
            "(" +
                "SELECT " +
                    "TerritoryId, " +
                    "CONVERT(CHAR(7), h.OrderDate, 120) AS YYYY_MM, " +
                    "d.LineTotal " +
                "FROM Sales.SalesOrderHeader h " +
                "JOIN Sales.SalesOrderDetail d " +
                    "ON h.SalesOrderID = d.SalesOrderID " +
                "WHERE h.OrderDate BETWEEN @StartDate AND @EndDate " +
            ") p " +
            "PIVOT " +
            "( " +
                "SUM (LineTotal) " +
                "FOR YYYY_MM IN " +
                "( " +
                    yearsMonths.ToString() +
                ") " +
            ") AS pvt " +
            "ORDER BY TerritoryId";

        //Set the CommandText
        command.CommandText = sql.ToString();

        //Have the caller execute the cross-tab query
        SqlContext.Pipe.ExecuteAndSend(command);

        //Close the connection
        command.Connection.Close();
    }
};
```

Deploying CLR Routines

Once a routine is written, tested, and—if necessary—debugged, it can finally be rolled to production. The process of doing this is quite simple: the release version of the DLL is copied to the server, and a few T-SQL statements are executed.

In order to produce a release version, change the build option on the Standard toolbar from Debug to Release, as shown in Figure 5-17. Once the configuration is set, click Build from the main toolbar, and then click Build Solution. This will produce a release version of the DLL—a version with no debug symbols—in the [Project Root]\bin\Release folder. So if the root folder for the project is C:\Projects\SalesCrossTabs, the DLL will be in C:\Projects\SalesCrossTabs\bin\Release.

Figure 5-17. *Configuring the project for a release build*

The release version of the DLL can be copied from this location onto any production server in order to deploy it. Only the DLL is required in order to deploy the CLR routines compiled within it.

The DLL is registered with SQL Server 2005 using the CREATE ASSEMBLY statement. The syntax for this statement is

```
CREATE ASSEMBLY assembly_name
[ AUTHORIZATION owner_name ]
FROM { <client_assembly_specifier> | <assembly_bits> [,...n] }
[ WITH PERMISSION_SET = { SAFE | EXTERNAL_ACCESS | UNSAFE } ]
[ ; ]
```

The assembly_name represents a user-defined name for the assembly—generally, it's best to use the name of the project. The AUTHORIZATION clause is optional, and allows the DBA to specify a particular owner for the object. The important part of the FROM clause is the client_assembly_specifier—this is the physical path to the DLL file. The assembly_bits option is used for situations in which the DLL has been binary serialized, and won't be covered in this book.

The most important clause of CREATE ASSEMBLY, however, is the optional WITH PERMISSION_SET clause. The DBA is in complete control when it comes to what CLR routines can do. Routines can be assigned to one of three permission sets—SAFE, EXTERNAL_ACCESS, or UNSAFE. Each permission set is progressively less restrictive. By controlling CLR routine permission, the DBA can keep a close watch on what routines are doing—and make sure that none are violating system policies.

The default SAFE permission set restricts routines from accessing any external resources, including files, web services, the registry, or networks. The EXTERNAL_ACCESS permission set opens up access to these external resources. This can be useful for situations in which data from the database needs to be merged with data from other sources. Finally, the UNSAFE permission set opens access to all CLR libraries. It is recommended that this permission set not be used, as there is potential for destabilization of the SQL Server process space if libraries are misused.

Assuming that the SalesCrossTabs DLL was copied to the C:\Assemblies folder on the SQL Server, it could be registered using the following T-SQL:

```
CREATE ASSEMBLY SalesCrossTabs
FROM 'C:\Assemblies\SalesCrossTabs.DLL'
```

Since this assembly doesn't use any external resources, the default permission set doesn't need to be overridden. Keep in mind that if the assembly has already been deployed using Visual Studio, this T-SQL would fail; assembly names must be unique within a database. If there is already an assembly called SalesCrossTabs from a Visual Studio deployment, it can be dropped using the DROP ASSEMBLY statement.

Once CREATE ASSEMBLY has successfully registered the assembly, the physical file is no longer accessed—the assembly is now part of the database it's registered in.

The next step is to tell SQL Server how to use the procedures, functions, and types in the assembly. This is done using slightly modified versions of the CREATE statements for each of these objects. To register the GetSalesPerTerritoryByMonth stored procedure, the following T-SQL would be used:

```
CREATE PROCEDURE GetSalesPerTerritoryByMonth
    @StartDate DATETIME,
    @EndDate DATETIME
AS
EXTERNAL NAME SalesCrossTabs.StoredProcedures.GetSalesPerTerritoryByMonth
```

The parameter list must match the parameters defined on the CLR method. The EXTERNAL NAME clause requires three parameters, delimited by periods: the user-defined name of the assembly, the name of the class defined in assembly (in this case, the default StoredProcedures class), and finally the name of the method defined as the stored procedure in the assembly. This clause is case sensitive, so be careful. Changing the case from that defined in the routine will result in an error.

Once the stored procedure is defined in this way, it can be called just like any native T-SQL stored procedure.

Summary

CLR integration allows developers to extend the functionality of SQL Server 2005 using safe, well-performing methods. Coding CLR stored procedures is an easy way to improve upon some of the things that T-SQL doesn't do especially well.

In the next chapter, we'll cover the other types of CLR objects available to developers: functions, aggregates, user-defined types, and triggers. We'll also present a more in-depth look into managing routines from a DBA's perspective.

Programming Assemblies

In addition to the stored procedures covered in the last chapter, SQL Server 2005 can also host a variety of other types of CLR routines. These include user-defined datatypes, functions (both scalar and table-valued), aggregates, and triggers.

- *User-defined types* allow for special compound type cases, such as point or shape datatypes that can't be modeled naturally using intrinsic scalar types. We present two user-defined type examples in this chapter: a phone number type and an array type.

- *CLR user-defined functions* allow developers to easily integrate any functionality provided by .NET libraries, such as data compression or regular expressions. The example functions in this chapter show how to expose the compression capabilities of the .NET 2.0 base class library, and how to return the elements of the array user-defined type example as a rowset.

- *User-defined aggregates* are an especially exciting new feature. They allow developers to create custom aggregation functions that can be used in queries with GROUP BY clauses—hacking with cursors and (non-CLR) user-defined functions is no longer necessary for defining custom aggregations that go beyond the built-in sum, average, minimum, maximum, count, and standard deviation aggregates. In this chapter, we show a "trimmed mean" example that calculates the average value of a column over a set of rows, disregarding the minimum and maximum values of the column.

- *CLR triggers* behave much like T-SQL triggers, but they can leverage the power of the .NET libraries for more flexible operations. The example in this chapter shows how to create a CLR trigger to validate data on insert or update.

Like CLR stored procedures, each of these types of routines can be built in Visual Studio 2005 using C# or VB .NET. Also like CLR stored procedures, it's important to consider using these routines carefully, as CLR integration is not appropriate for all situations.

For the DBAs of the world, all of this new functionality represents a double-edged sword. On one hand, these features provide incredible power to create functionality within the database that could never before have been imagined. On the other hand, there is quite a bit of room for abuse and misuse. This chapter will help you maneuver through the potential minefields and show how to use the features—as well as how not to use them.

CLR User-Defined Types

Although user-defined types have been available in SQL Server for several years, they were not an especially powerful tool for DBAs and data modelers. T-SQL user-defined types are essentially synonyms for sized type declarations. For instance, you could define a type called ZipCode that maps to a CHAR(5), to be used for representing U.S. 5-digit postal codes. Although this can be useful in some cases, it never really caught on as a widely accepted way of defining data. Most DBAs did not bother to use the feature, and in SQL Server 2005 this functionality has been deprecated.

Slated to replace the not-so-powerful T-SQL user-defined types is a new breed of CLR types that can represent virtually any data structure, as described in the sections that follow. These types are not mere wrappers over the intrinsic SQL Server types, as are T-SQL user-defined types. Rather, these types are full-featured class structures, complete with properties and methods. Implementation of these types can and should include such niceties as data verification and string formatting, which were not possible with T-SQL user-defined types.

Applications for User-Defined Types

User-defined types are excellent candidates for representing complex data that SQL Server's intrinsic types don't deal with well. For instance, a user might want to create a type to represent postal codes, instead of using one of SQL Server's character datatypes. A postal code user-defined type could include logic for digesting and normalizing a variety of input string formats for various countries. Even in the United States alone, postal codes can be represented using five digits, with the format XXXXX, or nine digits, with the format XXXXX-YYYY. By defining logic within a postal code type to parse and process any type of input postal code format, we create a single library to deal with postal codes and thus eliminate repetition. To reduce repetition further, a series of properties or methods could be defined on the type for retrieving the postal code in various string formats.

Another application of CLR user-defined types is to extend the flexibility afforded by T-SQL from a software development perspective. For instance, many projects might benefit from an array datatype within SQL Server. In some situations it's required that small, ordered sets of data be passed between stored procedures or user-defined functions. And although developers could use a variety of hacks to achieve functionality similar to arrays in previous versions of SQL Server, in SQL Server 2005 developers can leverage the .NET Framework to create an actual array that operates safely and efficiently within SQL Server.

Although the ability to create and use custom datatypes brings great power, developers should avoid the temptation to use SQL Server as a serialized object store. This is conceptually possible—business objects would simply need to be decorated with the correct attributes—but it would drive no real value within the database. Member properties of serialized objects cannot be efficiently queried, so any attempt to use the properties as predicates in queries would destroy server performance. Data represented by user-defined types should be atomic from a query perspective; no individual property of a type should be required in order to filter a row containing an instance of the type.

Adding a User-Defined Type to a SQL Server Project

To start a project for user-defined types in Visual Studio 2005, choose Database, and then select the SQL Server Project template, as shown in Figure 6-1. Set the reference to a development database and click OK to launch the project.

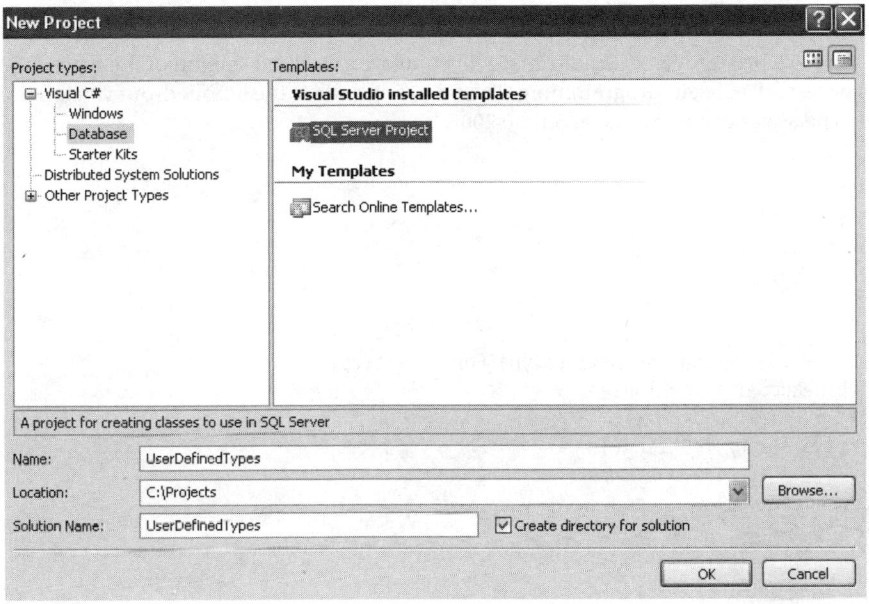

Figure 6-1. *Opening a new project in Visual Studio 2005*

Once the project has been created, right-click the project's name in Solution Explorer, and then select Add ➤ User-Defined Type, as shown in Figure 6-2. The first example type for this chapter will be called PhoneNumber.

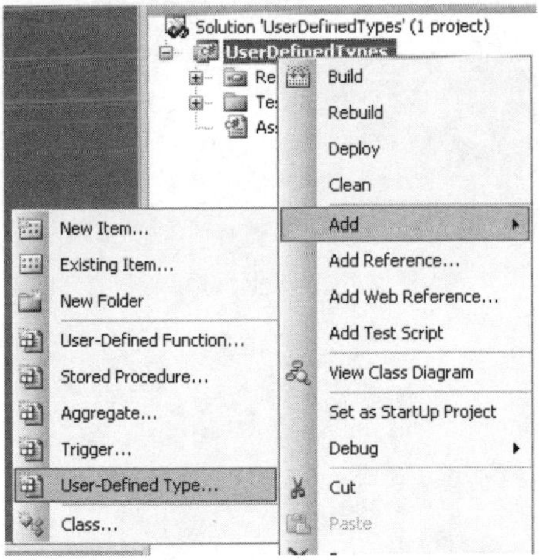

Figure 6-2. *Adding a user-defined type to the project*

Parts of a User-Defined Type

Upon adding a type to a project, Visual Studio 2005 will populate a stubbed version of the type with all of the pieces necessary to begin programming. The following code is the stubbed-out version of the PhoneNumber type as generated by Visual Studio 2005:

```csharp
using System;
using System.Data;
using System.Data.SqlClient;
using System.Data.SqlTypes;
using Microsoft.SqlServer.Server;

[Serializable]
[Microsoft.SqlServer.Server.SqlUserDefinedType(Format.Native)]
public struct PhoneNumber : INullable
{
    public override string ToString()
    {
        // Replace the following code with your code
        return "";
    }

    public bool IsNull
    {
        get
        {
            // Put your code here
            return m_Null;
        }
    }

    public static PhoneNumber Null
    {
        get
        {
            PhoneNumber h = new PhoneNumber();
            h.m_Null = true;
            return h;
        }
    }

    public static PhoneNumber Parse(SqlString s)
    {
        if (s.IsNull)
            return Null;
        PhoneNumber u = new PhoneNumber();
        // Put your code here
        return u;
    }
```

```
    // This is a place-holder method
    public string Method1()
    {
        //Insert method code here
        return "Hello";
    }

    // This is a place-holder static method
    public static SqlString Method2()
    {
        //Insert method code here
        return new SqlString("Hello");
    }

    // This is a place-holder field member
    public int var1;
    // Private member
    private bool m_Null;
}
```

This code is not as complex as it initially looks, and it can be broken down into a few different sections to make analysis easier.

SqlUserDefinedType Attribute

A class or structure will not be treated as a user-defined type unless it is decorated with the SqlUserDefinedType attribute, as shown in the stubbed code. This attribute has a few parameters that define the serialization behavior of the type:

- Format: This is the only required parameter, and it determines the method that will be used for serializing the type (rendering the data as binary so that it can be sent across the network or written to disk). The two choices for this parameter are Native and UserDefined. A value of Native indicates that the CLR runtime should automatically handle the serialization, whereas UserDefined indicates that the serialization is programmed by the developer implementing the IBinarySerialize interface.

  Native serialization will only work if the type is defined as a structure (as opposed to a class) and all members are value types. As such, there are very few nontrivial uses for native serialization of types. The vast majority of cases will be user defined. The complete list of .NET types eligible for native serialization is as follows: bool, byte, sbyte, short, ushort, int, uint, long, ulong, float, double, SqlByte, SqlInt16, SqlInt32, SqlInt64, SqlDateTime, SqlSingle, SqlDouble, SqlMoney, and SqlBoolean.

- IsByteOrdered: For a type to be a candidate for indexing or comparison operations (equal to, less than, greater than, etc.), SQL Server must have a way of comparing one instance of the type to another instance of the type. This is implemented using *byte ordering*. If a type is byte ordered, SQL Server will assume that comparing the raw bytes of the serialized instance of the type is equivalent to comparing the instances of the type. This is much faster than the alternative, which entails deserializing and using IComparable or a similar mechanism to compare instances of the type. Possible values for this parameter are true and false, and for a type to be considered for indexing or comparison, the value must be true. The default value is false.

- IsFixedLength: This parameter can be set to true or false. A value of true tells SQL Server that every serialized instance of this type will always be exactly the same size. The default value is false.

- `MaxByteSize`: This parameter tells SQL Server the maximum size the type can reach. For a fixed-length type, this parameter should indicate the length to which that the type will always serialize. For other types, this size should reflect a realistic estimate on the part of the developer. The value for this parameter can be any integer between 1 and 8,000. Remember that although a value of 8,000 can work for every non-fixed-length type, this can end up hurting performance. The query optimizer can consider a type's maximum length when determining query plans. The default value is 8000.

Note that the stubbed type is also decorated with the `Serializable` attribute. This attribute is also necessary; an instance of a type must be serialized any time it is written to disk or sent across the network.

INullable Interface

A user-defined type must implement the `INullable` interface. This interface defines the `Null` and `IsNull` properties.

The `IsNull` property returns `true` if the type is null, in the SQL Server sense of the term (as opposed to the .NET sense of the term). `null` in C# (`Nothing` in VB .NET) is used to indicate that a reference type does not reference an object. In SQL Server, `NULL` means something different; it is a token used for unknown data, as well as uninitialized variables. Although the two are similar, it's important to remember the distinction when working between the two platforms.

The `IsNull` property is controlled internally in the stubbed type by the value of the `m_Null` private member, but developers are free to implement this property in any way appropriate to the type being developed.

The `Null` property returns a freshly instantiated instance of the type. This instance should be initialized such that the `IsNull` property will return `true`. The `Null` property will be used by SQL Server any time a `new` instance of the type is requested (e.g., when a variable is declared of that type). SQL Server will not call `new`, or an equivalent of `new`, directly. This means that private member initialization code can be put within the `Null` property instead of the constructor, if appropriate.

It's important that user-defined types behave similarly to the intrinsic SQL Server datatypes. Therefore, care should be taken to make sure that the `Null` and `IsNull` properties behave correctly. Developers should make sure that these properties do not incorrectly identify null instances as non-null or non-null instances as null—doing so could severely damage the type's ability to interact properly with the SQL Server engine. This is mainly controlled within the `Parse` method. A simple way to handle the situation is to always return `Null` (that is, the `Null` property of the type) if the string passed in to `Parse` is `NULL` (which you can check using the `IsNull` property of the `SqlString` type).

ToString Method

Every user-defined type must override the `ToString` method (which is inherited from the `object` class by every type defined in .NET). The rationale for this is flexible client interoperability. Although some client libraries may be able to consume a serialized instance of the type, others will only be able to make sense of the type represented as a string.

It is recommended that developers code the `ToString` method such that the string returned is compatible with the `Parse` method, described next. If these two methods are compatible, the string generated by the `ToString` method can be later passed back to SQL Server if necessary, in order to reinstantiate the type.

Parse Method

The Parse method is the exact opposite of the ToString method. Instead of producing a string representation of an instance of the type, this method takes a string as input, returning an instance of the type generated based on the string.

Parse is quite important in the world of user-defined types, as it will be called any time a type's value is set using the assignment operator (aka equals sign). Furthermore, *public mutators* (i.e., public members or public settable properties) cannot be set on null instances; any instance that is null must first be instantiated using Parse.

These concepts are best illustrated using a code example. Assume the presence of a user-defined type called PhoneNumber that has a public, settable property called Number. A user might attempt to define an instance of the type and set Number to a value using the following code:

```
DECLARE @phone PhoneNumber
--Set the number to the Apress business phone line
SET @phone.Number = '5105495930'
```

This code will fail with the error message "Mutator 'Number' on '@phone' cannot be called on a null value." The following code would not result in an error, as it calls Parse internally:

```
DECLARE @phone PhoneNumber
--Set the number to the Apress business phone line
SET @phone = '5105495930'
```

Unfortunately, the developer may have actually wanted to set the phone number using the property. That would require first calling Parse with a fake value to initialize the type, and then calling the property directly:

```
DECLARE @phone PhoneNumber
--Start with a dummy value
SET @phone = '0000000000'
--Set the number to the Apress business phone line
SET @phone.Number = '5105495930'
```

In most cases, it's probably a good idea to assign the value only using the assignment operator (and, therefore, Parse), but in some cases it will be necessary to initialize the type to allow for more straightforward SQL coding. The StringArray type shown later in this chapter provides a good example to illustrate that kind of situation.

A Simple Example: The PhoneNumber Type

A common requirement in virtually every business application is storing contact information. This information usually includes, among other things, names, mailing addresses, e-mail addresses, and phone numbers. Unfortunately, problems can sometimes occur due to formatting irregularities. Some people like to write U.S. phone numbers using parentheses and dashes, as in "(510) 549-5930". Some prefer to use only dashes, as in "510-549-5930". Others feel that periods look cool and will input the number as "510.549.5930".

It's not difficult to handle these differences in format, but properly dealing with them requires that every stored procedure in the system validate the input. There should be exactly ten numerals in any valid U.S. phone number. And preferably, those phone numbers should be stored in the database in exactly the same string format, such that they can be indexed and uniformly formatted for output purposes.

Instead of handling this validation and formatting in every stored procedure that deals with external phone number data, a CLR type can be defined. If every stored procedure uses this type, there will be no need for duplicate logic; all formatting will be handled by one central piece of code. Likewise, it will be guaranteed that the data is stored on disk in a uniform format, and output can be coded however necessary to meet business needs.

Modifying the Stubbed Code

Using the stubbed version generated by Visual Studio as a basis for defining the type, there is surprisingly little work required to develop a complete prototype. The first step is to clean up a bit and stub out the correct members for the project at hand. The following code shows the result of initial modifications:

```
[Serializable]
[Microsoft.SqlServer.Server.SqlUserDefinedType(Format.UserDefined,
IsByteOrdered=true,
IsFixedLength=false,
MaxByteSize=11)]
public struct PhoneNumber : INullable
{
    public override string ToString()
    {
            return this.number;
    }

    public bool IsNull
    {
        get
        {
            if (this.number == "")
                return true;
            else
                return false;
        }
    }

    public static PhoneNumber Null
    {
        get
        {
            PhoneNumber h = new PhoneNumber();
            h.number = "";
            return h;
        }
    }

    public static PhoneNumber Parse(SqlString s)
    {
        if (s.IsNull)
            return Null;
        PhoneNumber u = new PhoneNumber();
```

```
        //Call the Number property for assigning the value
        u.Number = s;
        return u;
    }

    // Public mutator for the number
    public SqlString Number
    {
        get
        {
            return new SqlString(this.number);
        }
        set
        {
            this.number = (string)value;
        }
    }

    // The phone number
    private string number;
}
```

The various placeholder members have been replaced with a single private member, number. This variable is a string, and it will hold the validated phone number for a given instance of the type. The public property Number has also been added. This property currently directly sets the private member to the input value; some validation logic will have to be added in order to make it workable. Parse also now internally calls the Number property—that way, any validation logic for setting numbers will have to live in only one place.

The Null and IsNull properties have also been modified, to reflect the removal of the private member m_Null. Since U.S. phone numbers must be exactly ten digits long, the validation logic will ensure that any number persisted within the type consists of ten digits. Any other time, number will be empty, and this will represent a null value.

ToString has been modified to simply return the value of number, the member variable that contains the phone number data. Since the return type is System.String instead of SqlString, this method cannot return a SqlString.Null value if the type is null, which would be preferable to make the type behave more similarly to the intrinsic SQL Server datatypes.

Finally, the properties of the SqlUserDefinedType attribute are changed to reflect the code. The format will be UserDefined, since strings are not value types in .NET. The serialization will be byte ordered, allowing indexing and comparison on the type (see the next section on IBinarySerialize). The type will not be fixed length, since the empty string (null) case will occupy a single byte in serialized form, whereas properly populated phone numbers will occupy 10 bytes (1 byte per character in the phone number). Since user-defined types occupy 1 byte of overhead, the MaxByteSize parameter is set to 11. Ten bytes are allocated for the member data and 1 byte is allocated for the type.

IBinarySerialize

If you were to compile the code as listed in Visual Studio, it would compile cleanly. And if you were to manually deploy it (using CREATE ASSEMBLY), the resultant assembly would successfully register with SQL Server. However, CREATE TYPE (and, therefore, the Visual Studio deployment task) would fail with the following error:

```
Type "UserDefinedTypes.PhoneNumber" is marked for user-defined serialization, but
does not implement the "System.Data.Microsoft.SqlServer.Server.IBinarySerialize"
interface.
```

To implement the IBinarySerialize interface, add the name of the interface to the inheritance list in the class or structure declaration:

```
public struct PhoneNumber : INullable, IBinarySerialize
```

Visual Studio 2005 has a convenient feature to assist with implementation of interfaces. Right-click the name of the interface after adding it, and a context menu will appear with an Implement Interface option. Click the suboption of the same name, as shown in Figure 6-3, to populate the type with the stubbed methods to implement the routine. Note that either Implement Interface or Implement Interface Explicitly will work. The latter explicitly prefixes methods and properties with the name of the interface to assist with multiple interface situations; however, this is not an issue with the PhoneNumber type.

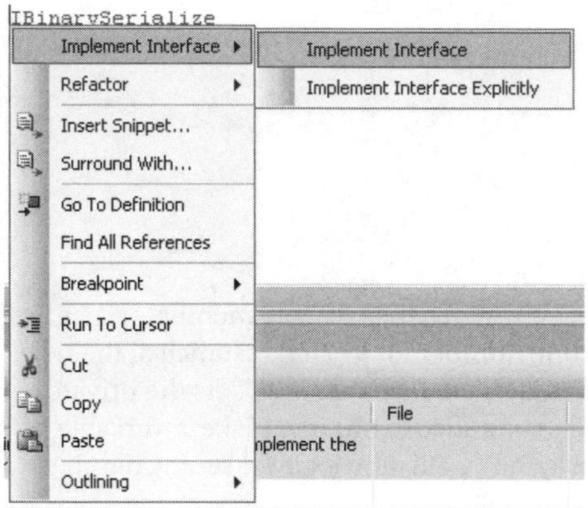

Figure 6-3. *Implementing an interface in the project*

After the interface is implemented, the code for the type will contain a new region similar to the following:

```
#region IBinarySerialize Members

public void Read(System.IO.BinaryReader r)
{
    throw new Exception("The method or operation is not implemented.");
}

public void Write(System.IO.BinaryWriter w)
{
    throw new Exception("The method or operation is not implemented.");
}

#endregion
```

The Read method is responsible for reconstituting an instance of the type from its binary serialized state; the Write method handles the serialization. Although this sounds somewhat complex, the methods of the BinaryReader and BinaryWriter classes are very simple to work with.

The BinaryReader class contains methods that can automatically handle many of the .NET datatypes. These include ReadString, ReadInt16, ReadInt32, and others. Since the PhoneNumber type only deals with a single string (the private member number), the ReadString method alone is sufficient to rebuild an instance of the type from serialized form. The following code is the full representation of the Read method for the type:

```
public void Read(System.IO.BinaryReader r)
{
    this.number = r.ReadString();
}
```

The BinaryWriter class is even simpler than the BinaryReader class, with only a single method that developers will have to concern themselves with in most cases: Write. Several overloads are exposed for this method, such that what it offers is symmetrical to what is offered by the various read methods of the BinaryReader. In the case of the PhoneNumber type, the overload that takes a string can be used:

```
public void Write(System.IO.BinaryWriter w)
{
    w.Write(number);
}
```

Again, this is all that's necessary for implementing the method. And since the string will be serialized as a simple binary stream, this implementation also produces the byte ordering necessary for indexing and comparison.

Although many types will end up with more complex implementations than these, the basic pattern to keep in mind is that each call to one of the BinaryReader methods should have a corresponding call to Write, and vice versa. If you keep this rule in mind when working with the IBinarySerialize interface, development can be simple and efficient.

Implementing the Validation Logic

The final step in defining the PhoneNumber type is to implement the logic to validate the input. For the sake of this exercise, the logic can be quite simplistic: strip out all non-numeric characters from the input string. If the resultant string of numerals is exactly ten characters long, it will be considered valid. Otherwise, it will be rejected with an error.

The following code is the completed Number property for the type:

```
// Public mutator for the number
public SqlString Number
{
    get
    {
        return new SqlString(this.number);
    }
    set
    {
        //If null, don't process any further
        if (value == "")
        {
            this.number = "";
            return;
        }

        //Match groups of 1 or more digits
        Regex regex = new Regex("[0-9]*");
        MatchCollection matches = regex.Matches((string)value);
```

```
            StringBuilder result = new StringBuilder();

            foreach (Match match in matches)
            {
                result.Append(match.Value);
            }

            if (result.Length == 10)
                this.number = result.ToString();
            else
                throw new ArgumentException("Phone numbers must be 10 digits.");
    }
}
```

Note that the Regex, Match, and Matches classes are in the System.Text.RegularExpressions namespace, and the StringBuilder class is in the System.Text namespace. Appropriate using declarations need to be added before the classes to facilitate their use.

The complete code for the PhoneNumber type is as follows:

```
using System;
using System.Data;
using System.Data.SqlClient;
using System.Data.SqlTypes;
using Microsoft.SqlServer.Server;
using System.Text;
using System.Text.RegularExpressions;

[Serializable]
[Microsoft.SqlServer.Server.SqlUserDefinedType(Format.UserDefined,
IsByteOrdered = true,
IsFixedLength = false,
MaxByteSize = 11)]
public struct PhoneNumber : INullable, IBinarySerialize
{
    public override string ToString()
    {
        return this.number;
    }

    public bool IsNull
    {
        get
        {
            if (this.number == "")
                return true;
            else
                return false;
        }
    }
}
```

```csharp
public static PhoneNumber Null
{
    get
    {
        PhoneNumber h = new PhoneNumber();
        h.number = "";
        return h;
    }
}

public static PhoneNumber Parse(SqlString s)
{
    if (s.IsNull)
        return Null;
    PhoneNumber u = new PhoneNumber();

    //Call the Number property for assigning the value
    u.Number = s;
    return u;
}

// Public mutator for the number
public SqlString Number
{
    get
    {
        return new SqlString(this.number);
    }
    set
    {
        //If null, don't process any further
        if (value == "")
        {
            this.number = "";
            return;
        }

        //Match groups of 1 or more digits
        Regex regex = new Regex("[0-9]*");
        MatchCollection matches = regex.Matches((string)value);

        StringBuilder result = new StringBuilder();

        foreach (Match match in matches)
        {
            result.Append(match.Value);
        }

        if (result.Length == 10)
            this.number = result.ToString();
        else
            throw new ArgumentException("Phone numbers must be 10 digits.");
    }
}
```

```
    // The phone number
    private string number;

    #region IBinarySerialize Members

    public void Read(System.IO.BinaryReader r)
    {
        this.number = r.ReadString();
    }

    public void Write(System.IO.BinaryWriter w)
    {
        w.Write(number);
    }

    #endregion
}
```

Deploying and Testing the Type

Once the type is written, it is ready to deploy and test. The type can be deployed for debugging purposes directly from Visual Studio 2005. Right-click the project name in Solution Explorer and click Deploy, as shown in Figure 6-4.

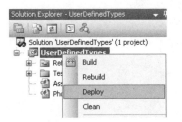

Figure 6-4. *Deploying the user-defined type*

To try out the type, open SQL Server Management Studio and connect to the database that was specified when the project was created. User-defined types, once created, are instantiated using the DECLARE keyword, just like the built-in SQL Server datatypes. Recall the example from earlier in the chapter when we discussed the Parse method:

```
DECLARE @phone PhoneNumber
--Set the number to the Apress business phone line
SET @phone = '510-549-5930'
```

This code creates a variable called @phone of type PhoneNumber. It then sets the value of the variable to the number for the Apress business phone line. Remember that this code is actually calling Parse on a null instance of the type.

To return the string representation of the type (i.e., the ten-digit phone number), the ToString method must be called, as in the following code:

```
PRINT @phone.ToString()
```

Another important thing to remember is that methods and properties on user-defined types are case sensitive, even if the server or database isn't. Note that the capitalization of ToString in the example is the same as the capitalization in the type's definition.

Selecting the type without using `ToString` will return the type in binary serialized form. This form may be usable from a .NET application that has a reference to the assembly in which the type is compiled, but generally speaking, `ToString` will be a more commonly used way of getting a type's data. Printing the type using the T-SQL `PRINT` statement is also possible and requires using either `ToString` or the `CONVERT` function, to convert the type into `NVARCHAR`.

Another Example: The StringArray Type

While the `PhoneNumber` type adequately illustrates the various programming nuances of working with user-defined types, it does not show off much of the power that can be gained from their use.

We'll present here a more interesting example to satisfy a common requirement in SQL Server programming projects: representing data in an array format. This usually falls into the category of a developer needing to pass more than one value into a stored procedure, but arrays can also be used to make the T-SQL language more powerful from a programmatic standpoint. Unfortunately, while many hacks are available for bringing array-like functionality into the world of SQL Sever 2000, they are just that: hacks. CLR user-defined types dramatically change the landscape such that these hacks are no longer necessary. In this example, the power of a .NET collection (the `List` class) will be exposed via a CLR user-defined type, resulting in a fully functional array that can be invoked directly from T-SQL.

Wrapping the Functionality of a Generic List

.NET 2.0 includes support for containers called *generics*, which are strongly typed versions of the object-specific containers available in previous versions of the .NET Framework. Using the `List<T>` type (which is a generic version of the `ArrayList`) as a basis, a CLR user-defined type can be built to deal with collections of strings.

Generics are a new feature in .NET 2.0 that allows developers to easily implement type-safe classes, such as collections. Most of the collection types in .NET 1.*x* were collections of objects. Since every type in .NET is derived from the `object` type, this means that every type can be cast as an object; therefore, every type could benefit from the collections. However, this also meant that a collection could not enforce what kinds of objects it stored. A collection might be incorrectly populated with both integers and strings, for instance. This could lead to exceptions when code meant to deal with integers suddenly encountered strings.

Generics solve this problem by allowing developers to specify a type to be used by a class (or collection) at object creation time. This allows the CLR to enforce type safety, allowing the object to use only the specified class. The syntax for this feature is a pair of angle brackets after the type name. For example, the following code creates an instance of `List` that can only use integers:

```
List<int> myList = new List<int>;
```

Note that when implementing generic classes, a `using` directive for the `System.Collections.Generic` namespace should be included at the top of the source file for the class.

The actual string data will be held in a collection of type `List<string>`. This container will be strongly typed such that it can hold only strings. The following code defines the member:

```
// The actual array
private List<string> arr;
```

Next, the important features that make an array usable should be exposed by properties or methods such that they are accessible from T-SQL. These features include getting a count of strings in the array, adding strings to the array, removing strings from the array, and getting a string at a specific index of the array. The following block of code defines each of those features:

```
public SqlInt32 Count
{
    get
    {
        if (this.IsNull)
            return SqlInt32.Null;
        else
            return (SqlInt32)(this.arr.Count);
    }
}

public SqlString GetAt(int Index)
{
    return (SqlString)(string)(this.arr[Index]);
}

public StringArray AddString(SqlString str)
{
    if (this.IsNull)
        this.arr = new List<string>(1);
    this.arr.Add((string)str);

    return (this);
}

public StringArray RemoveAt(int Index)
{
    this.arr.RemoveAt(Index);
    return this;
}
```

By simply wrapping the List<T>'s methods and properties, they are now accessible from T-SQL.

Implementing Parse and ToString

To instantiate an array, a developer will pass in a comma-delimited list of elements. The Parse method will handle the input, splitting up the list in order to populate the array. The ToString method will do the opposite, to return the contents of the array in a comma-delimited format.

The Parse method for the StringArray type uses the Split method of System.String. This method outputs an array of strings by splitting a delimited list. Once the array is produced, the method trims each element of preceding and trailing white space and puts any nonempty strings into the arr member variable. The following code implements the Parse method:

```
public static StringArray Parse(SqlString s)
{
    if (s.IsNull)
        return Null;

    StringArray u = new StringArray();

    string[] strings = ((string)s).Split(',');
```

```
    for(int i = 0; i < strings.Length; i++)
    {
        strings[i] = strings[i].Trim();
    }

    u.arr = new List<string>(strings.Length);

    foreach (string str in strings)
    {
        if (str != "")
            u.arr.Add(str);
    }

    return u;
}
```

The ToString method does the reverse of Parse, using Join, which has the opposite behavior of Split. An array of strings is input, and a comma-delimited list is output:

```
public override string ToString()
{
    // Replace the following code with your code
    if (this.IsNull)
        return "";
    else
        return String.Join(",", (string[])this.arr.ToArray());
}
```

Defining the SqlUserDefinedType Attribute

Because the private member data for this type will reside in a reference type (List<T>), the format will have to be user defined.

It doesn't make a lot of sense to compare two arrays for the purpose of sorting. There is no clear way to define how two arrays should sort. Should they sort based on number of elements? Based on the elements themselves? As it is nearly impossible to define how arrays would be sorted—and probably not useful for many development challenges—it also does not make sense to index a column of an array type. Indexes are generally helpful for seeking ordered data, but it is unlikely that a developer would want to perform a seek using an array as a key. For these reasons, there is no need to worry about byte ordering, so IsByteOrdered should be set to false.

And since arrays can contain any number of elements, the type is clearly not of a fixed length, nor does it have a maximum byte size, except for the 8,000-byte limit.

The fully populated SqlUserDefinedType attribute for this type is as follows:

```
[Microsoft.SqlServer.Server.SqlUserDefinedType(
    Format.UserDefined,
    IsByteOrdered = false,
    IsFixedLength = false,
    MaxByteSize = 8000)]
```

Implementing IBinarySerialize

Determining how to serialize the data for this type will not be quite as simple as doing so for the PhoneNumber type. Instead of serializing a single piece of data, serialization for this type has to deal with an array containing a variable number of elements.

A simple way of dealing with this situation is to first serialize a count of elements in the array, and then loop over and serialize each array element one by one. The only open issue with such a scheme is serialization of null-valued types. This can be easily taken care of using the following code, which serializes –1 as the count, should the type be null:

```
if (this.IsNull)
{
    w.Write(-1);
}
```

Non-null types, on the other hand, can be written using the following code, which first serializes the count of items and then each element in the array:

```
w.Write(this.arr.Count);

foreach (string str in this.arr)
{
    w.Write(str);
}
```

Reading back the serialized data involves doing the exact opposite. First, the serialized count of items is read back. If it is –1, there is nothing else to do; the type will already be null. If the count is greater than –1, a loop will run to read each element from the serialized binary. Remember that 0 is also a valid count. Empty arrays are not the same as null arrays.

The entire code for implementing IBinarySerialize for the StringArray type is as follows:

```
#region IBinarySerialize Members

public void Read(System.IO.BinaryReader r)
{
    int count = r.ReadInt32();
    if (count > -1)
    {
        this.arr = new List<string>(count);

        for (int i = 0; i < count; i++)
        {
            this.arr.Add(r.ReadString());
        }
    }
}

public void Write(System.IO.BinaryWriter w)
{
    if (this.IsNull)
    {
        w.Write(-1);
    }
    else
    {
        w.Write(this.arr.Count);
```

```
        foreach (string str in this.arr)
        {
            w.Write(str);
        }
    }
}
```

```
#endregion
```

Defining the IsNull and Null Properties

Implementing the INullable interface for the StringArray type is necessary in order to complete development of the type. In keeping with the theme of thinly wrapping the functionality of the .NET List<T> type, the IsNull method can be coded to determine whether the type is NULL based on whether the private member array is null—that is, whether it has been instantiated yet. Due to the fact that the array is not instantiated until data is passed into the Parse method, the Null method can simply call the default constructor and return the instance of the type. The following code implements both of these properties:

```
public bool IsNull
{
    get
    {
        return (this.arr == null);
    }
}

public static StringArray Null
{
    get
    {
        StringArray h = new StringArray();
        return h;
    }
}
```

Complete StringArray Class Sample

The complete code for the StringArray user-defined type is as follows:

```
using System;
using System.Data;
using System.Data.SqlClient;
using System.Data.SqlTypes;
using Microsoft.SqlServer.Server;
using System.Collections.Generic;

[Serializable]
[Microsoft.SqlServer.Server.SqlUserDefinedType(
    Format.UserDefined,
    IsByteOrdered = false,
    IsFixedLength = false,
    MaxByteSize = 8000)]
```

```csharp
public struct StringArray : INullable, IBinarySerialize
{
    public override string ToString()
    {
        // Replace the following code with your code
        if (this.IsNull)
            return "";
        else
            return String.Join(",", (string[])this.arr.ToArray());
    }

    public bool IsNull
    {
        get
        {
            return (this.arr == null);
        }
    }

    public static StringArray Null
    {
        get
        {
            StringArray h = new StringArray();
            return h;
        }
    }

    public static StringArray Parse(SqlString s)
    {
        if (s.IsNull)
            return Null;

        StringArray u = new StringArray();

        string[] strings = ((string)s).Split(',');

        for(int i = 0; i < strings.Length; i++)
        {
            strings[i] = strings[i].Trim();
        }

        u.arr = new List<string>(strings.Length);

        foreach (string str in strings)
        {
            if (str != "")
                u.arr.Add(str);
        }

        return u;
    }
```

```csharp
public SqlInt32 Count
{
    get
    {
        if (this.IsNull)
            return SqlInt32.Null;
        else
            return (SqlInt32)(this.arr.Count);
    }
}

public SqlString GetAt(int Index)
{
    return (SqlString)(string)(this.arr[Index]);
}

public StringArray AddString(SqlString str)
{
    if (this.IsNull)
        this.arr = new List<string>(1);

    this.arr.Add((string)str);

    return (this);
}

public StringArray RemoveAt(int Index)
{
    this.arr.RemoveAt(Index);
    return this;
}

// The actual array
private List<string> arr;

#region IBinarySerialize Members

public void Read(System.IO.BinaryReader r)
{
    int count = r.ReadInt32();
    if (count > -1)
    {
        this.arr = new List<string>(count);

        for (int i = 0; i < count; i++)
        {
            this.arr.Add(r.ReadString());
        }
    }
}
```

```
public void Write(System.IO.BinaryWriter w)
{
    if (this.IsNull)
    {
        w.Write(-1);
    }
    else
    {
        w.Write(this.arr.Count);

        foreach (string str in this.arr)
        {
            w.Write(str);
        }
    }
}

#endregion
}
```

Using the StringArray

The StringArray type can be used to solve development problems that might require the full power
afforded by a CLR function or stored procedure, but are made easier using data structures that are
not built in to SQL Server. An instance of the StringArray can be initially populated from a comma-
delimited list, as in the following code:

```
DECLARE @array StringArray
SET @array = 'a,b,c'
```

As a result of this code, the @array variable contains three elements, which can be retrieved or
deleted using the GetAt or RemoveAt methods. An extension to the type might be to add a SetAt method
to replace existing values in the array, but we'll leave that as an exercise for interested readers.

Interestingly, the SQL CLR engine only blocks modification of null types via public mutators—
public methods that happen to perform modification are allowed. So using the AddString method is
an option at any time, whether or not the type is null. The following code will have the same end
result as the previous:

```
DECLARE @array StringArray
SET @array = @array.AddString('a')
SET @array = @array.AddString('b')
SET @array = @array.AddString('c')
```

Managing User-Defined Types

If an assembly has been loaded into the database using CREATE ASSEMBLY, types can be created or
dropped without using the Visual Studio 2005 deployment task, as assumed in most examples in this
chapter.

To manually create a type that is exposed in an assembly, without using the deployment task,
use the T-SQL CREATE TYPE statement and specify the name of the assembly and name of the structure or class that defines the type. The following code creates the StringArray type from an assembly
called StringArray:

```
CREATE TYPE StringArray
EXTERNAL NAME StringArray.StringArray
```

To drop a type, use DROP TYPE. A type cannot be dropped if it is referenced by a table or function. The following code drops the StringArray type:

```
DROP TYPE StringArray
```

The sys.types catalog view exposes information about both system and user-defined types. To enumerate the data for CLR user-defined type in the database, use the is_assembly_type column:

```
SELECT *
FROM sys.types
WHERE is_assembly_type = 1
```

CLR User-Defined Functions

SQL Server 2000 introduced T-SQL user-defined functions, a feature that has greatly improved the programmability of SQL Server. Scalar user-defined functions allow developers to easily maximize encapsulation and reuse of logic. They return a single, scalar value based on zero or more parameters. These types of functions are useful for defining "black-box" methods; for instance, logic that needs to be used in exactly the same way throughout many stored procedures can be embedded in a scalar function. If the logic ever needs to change, only the function needs to be modified. Table-valued user-defined functions, on the other hand, can be thought of as parameterized views. These functions return a rowset of one or more columns and are useful for situations in which a view can return too much data. Because these functions are parameterized, developers can force users to filter the returned data.

Much like T-SQL user-defined functions, CLR functions come in both scalar and table-valued varieties. *Scalar functions* must return a single value of an intrinsic SQL Server type (i.e., an integer or string). *Table-valued functions*, on the other hand, must return a single, well-defined table. This is in contrast to stored procedures, which can return both an integer value and one or more tables, at the same time. Also unlike stored procedures, functions do not support output parameters.

CLR functions are also similar to T-SQL functions in that data manipulation from within a function is limited. When using the context connection (covered in Chapter 5), data cannot be modified. Connecting via a noncontext connection does allow data modification, but this is not recommended in most scenarios, due to the fact that a scalar function can be called once per row of a table and the data modification could occur on each call, incurring a large performance hit compared to doing a single modification using set-based techniques.

Much like CLR stored procedures, the key to deciding when to use a CLR user-defined function instead of a T-SQL user-defined function is necessity of the power afforded by the .NET base class library. If a T-SQL user-defined function can do the job in question, T-SQL is preferred—most of the time it will deliver better performance and quicker development turnaround. However, for those cases in which additional functionality is required—such as the compression example in this chapter—CLR user-defined functions will prove invaluable.

In this section, we'll look at scalar CLR user-defined functions that enable binary data compression in the database server and table-valued CLR user-defined functions that return rowsets from various sources.

Adding a User-Defined Function to a Visual Studio Project

To add a function to a preexisting SQL Server project in Visual Studio 2005, right-click the project name in Solution Explorer and select Add ➤ User-Defined Function as shown in Figure 6-5.

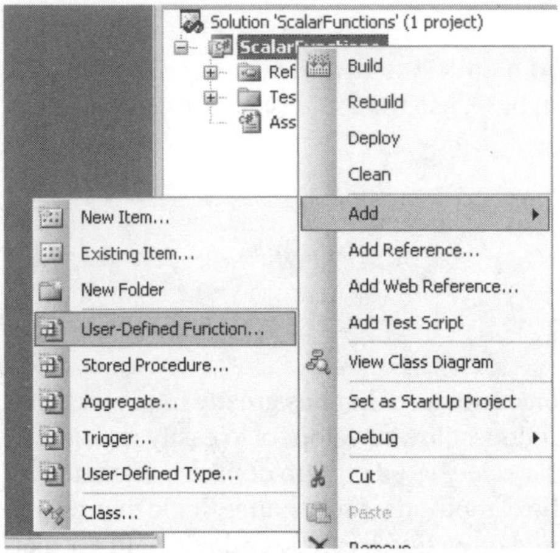

Figure 6-5. *Adding a user-defined function to a SQL Server project*

The Visual Studio 2005 User-Defined Function Template

Adding a user-defined function called NewFunction to a Visual Studio 2005 SQL Server project will produce a template similar to the following:

```
using System;
using System.Data;
using System.Data.SqlClient;
using System.Data.SqlTypes;
using Microsoft.SqlServer.Server;

public partial class UserDefinedFunctions
{
    [Microsoft.SqlServer.Server.SqlFunction]
    public static SqlString NewFunction()
    {
        // Put your code here
        return new SqlString("Hello");
    }
};
```

This template is quite a bit simpler than the user-defined type template shown previously in this chapter. A user-defined function requires nothing more than a public static method decorated with the SqlFunction attribute. The function shown here is a scalar function that returns a SqlString. A few additions are necessary to create a table-valued function. Let's first take a look at the SqlFunction attribute.

The SqlFunction Attribute

The SqlFunction attribute has several parameters, none of which is required:

- DataAccess: This parameter can be set to one of two values of the DataAccessKind enumerator. The possible values are None and Read. A value of None indicates that the function performs no data access, and this is enforced by the SQL Server engine. Attempts to perform data access will be met with an exception. Read indicates that the function is allowed to read data from the context connection (i.e., execute a T-SQL query against the database). User-defined functions cannot modify data in the context connection. The default value for this parameter is None.

- FillRowMethodName: This parameter is used to define a method for outputting rows in a table-valued user-defined function. See the section "Defining a Table-Valued User-Defined Function" later in this chapter for information on building table-valued functions.

- IsDeterministic: This parameter indicates whether a scalar function should be treated by the query optimizer as deterministic. This means that every call with the same exact input parameters will yield the same exact output. For instance, a function that adds 1 to an input integer is deterministic; the output will always be the input value plus 1. On the other hand, the GETDATE function is non-deterministic; a call with the same set of input parameters (none; it has no input parameters) can yield different output as time passes. Certain SQL Server features, such as indexed views, depend on determinism, so treat this parameter carefully. The default value is false.

- IsPrecise: This parameter allows the developer to specify whether the function internally rounds or truncates, thereby eliminating precision of the result. Even a function which does not use floating-point numbers as inputs or outputs may be imprecise if floating-point arithmetic is used within the function. Knowing whether the results are precise can be help the optimizer when calculating values for indexed views and other features. To be on the safe side, always set this parameter's value to false when working with floating-point computations. The default value for this parameter is false.

- Name: This parameter is used by Visual Studio 2005 (and possibly other third-party tools; see the section, "A Note On Visual Studio 2005," later in this chapter) to override the name that will be used for the user-defined function when deployed. If this parameter is set, the name specified in the parameter will be used. Otherwise, the name of the method decorated with the SqlFunctionAttribute will be used.

- SystemDataAccess: This parameter determines whether the function has access to system data from the context connection. Possible values for this parameter are the two values of the SystemDataAccessKind enumerator: None and Read. If the value is set to None, the function will not be able to access views in the sys schema. The default value is None.

- TableDefinition: This parameter is used to define the output table format for table-valued user-defined functions. Its input is a string-literal column list, defined in terms of SQL Server types and/or user-defined types. This parameter is covered in more detail in the section, "Defining a Table-Valued User-Defined Function" later in this chapter.

Scalar User-Defined Functions

When most developers think of functions, they think of scalar functions, which return exactly one value. The utility of such functions is quite obvious. They can be used to encapsulate complex logic such that it doesn't have to be repeated throughout many queries in the database. By using scalar functions, developers can ensure that changes to logic can be made in a single centralized location, which can be a boon for code maintainability.

A somewhat less obvious use for scalar functions, which is made much more desirable by CLR integration, is to expose library functionality not available natively within SQL Server. Examples include such common libraries as regular expressions, enhanced encryption (beyond what SQL

Server 2005 offers), and data compression. The CLR exposes a variety of very useful libraries that are now easy to consume for T-SQL programming projects.

Binary Data Compression Using a Scalar User-Defined Function

The .NET Framework 2.0 base class library exposes a namespace called System.IO.Compression, which includes classes for compressing data streams using the GZip and Deflate algorithms. The power of these algorithms can be harnessed for data applications by defining scalar functions to compress and decompress binary data. These functions can be used in document repositories to greatly reduce disk space, and moving compression into the data layer means that applications need only be concerned with the data itself, not its on-disk storage format. However, there is a downside to moving compression from the application into the data tier. Compression is expensive in terms of processor and memory utilization. Before moving compression into production databases, ensure that the servers can handle the additional load, lest performance suffer.

The first step in modifying the function template to handle compression is to add using directives for the IO and Compression namespaces:

```
using System.IO;
using System.IO.Compression;
```

The System.IO namespace is necessary, as it contains the classes that define streams. A MemoryStream will be used as a temporary holder for the bytes to be compressed and decompressed.

To facilitate the compression using the GZip algorithm, the function will have to create a memory stream using binary data from the SQL Server caller and pass the stream to the specialized GZipStream to get the compressed output. The BinaryCompress function is implemented in the following code:

```
[Microsoft.SqlServer.Server.SqlFunction]
public static SqlBytes BinaryCompress(SqlBytes inputStream)
{
    using (MemoryStream ms = new MemoryStream())
    {
        using (GZipStream x =
            new GZipStream(ms, CompressionMode.Compress, true))
        {
            byte[] inputBytes = (byte[])inputStream.Value;
            x.Write(inputBytes, 0, inputBytes.Length);
        }

        return (new SqlBytes(ms.ToArray()));
    }
}
```

Note that this function uses the SqlBytes datatype for both input and output. The SqlTypes namespace includes definitions of both the SqlBinary and SqlBytes datatypes, and according to the .NET documentation, these are equivalent. However, the Visual Studio SQL Server Project deployment task treats them differently. SqlBinary is mapped to SQL Server's VARBINARY(8000) type, whereas SqlBytes is mapped to VARBINARY(MAX), which can store 2GB of data per instance. Since this function is intended for compression of large documents to be stored in a SQL Server database, VARBINARY(MAX) makes a lot more sense. Limiting the document size to 8,000 bytes would be quite restrictive.

For developers working with character data instead of binary, please also note that this same situation exists with the SqlString and SqlChars types. The former maps to NVARCHAR(4000); the latter maps to NVARCHAR(MAX). Also note that these are mappings as done by Visual Studio only. In the case of manual deployments, these mappings do not apply—SqlString will behave identically to

SqlChars for any size NVARCHAR, and SqlBinary will be interchangeable with SqlBytes for any size VARBINARY.

You should also consider the use of the using statement within the function. This statement defines a scope for the defined object, at the end of which the Dispose method is called on that object, if the type implements IDisposable. It is generally considered a good practice in .NET development to use the using statement when working with types that implement IDisposable, such that a call to Dispose is guaranteed. This is doubly important when working in the SQL Server hosted CLR environment, since both the database engine and the CLR will be contending for the same resources. Calling Dispose helps the CLR to more quickly clean up the memory consumed by the streams, which can be considerable if a large amount of binary data is passed in.

Decompression using the GZipStream is very similar to compression except that two memory streams are used. The following function implements decompression:

```
[Microsoft.SqlServer.Server.SqlFunction]
public static SqlBytes BinaryDecompress(SqlBytes inputBinary)
{
    byte[] inputBytes = (byte[])inputBinary.Value;

    using (MemoryStream memStreamIn = new MemoryStream(inputBytes))
    {
        using (GZipStream s =
            new GZipStream(memStreamIn, CompressionMode.Decompress))
        {
            using (MemoryStream memStreamOut = new MemoryStream())
            {
                for (int num = s.ReadByte(); num != -1; num = s.ReadByte())
                {
                    memStreamOut.WriteByte((byte)num);
                }

                return (new SqlBytes(memStreamOut.ToArray()));
            }
        }
    }
}
```

Using the Compression Routines

The code can now be compiled and deployed using either the Visual Studio 2005 deployment task or manually with the T-SQL CREATE FUNCTION statement (see the upcoming section titled "Managing CLR User-Defined Functions" for more information). To compress data, simply use the BinaryCompression function the same way any T-SQL function would be used. For instance, to get the compressed binary for all of the documents in the Production.Document table in the AdventureWorks database, you could use the following T-SQL:

```
SELECT dbo.BinaryCompress(Document)
FROM Production.Document
```

And, of course, the output of the BinaryCompress function can be passed to BinaryDecompress to get back the original binary.

You should take care to ensure that the data being compressed is data that can be compressed. The nature of the GZip algorithm is such that uncompressable data will actually produce a larger output—the opposite of the goal of compression. For instance, you could use the following query to compare compressed and uncompressed data sizes for documents in the Production.Document table:

```
SELECT
    DATALENGTH(Document),
    DATALENGTH(dbo.BinaryCompress(Document))
FROM Production.Document
```

The results of this query show that, on average, compression rates of around 50 percent are seen. That's not bad. But trying the experiment on the photographs in the `Production.ProductPhoto` table has a slightly different outcome. The results of compressing that data show around a 50 percent increase in data size! The following query can be used to test the photograph data:

```
SELECT
    DATALENGTH(LargePhoto),
    DATALENGTH(dbo.BinaryCompress(LargePhoto))
FROM Production.ProductPhoto
```

The lesson to be learned is to always test carefully. Compression can work very well in many cases, but it can incur hidden costs if developers are not aware of its caveats.

Table-Valued User-Defined Functions

User-defined functions, as mentioned previously, come in two varieties: scalar and table-valued. The former must return exactly one value, whereas the latter can return a table of values, with many columns and rows. A table-valued user-defined function can be thought of as a parameterized view: the query logic is encapsulated within the body of the function, and parameters can be passed in to control the output. In addition, a table-valued function can be used anywhere in T-SQL queries that a view can.

CLR user-defined functions are somewhat different from their T-SQL counterparts, in that they have the capability to stream their data to the client (i.e., the calling SQL Server process) instead of writing it to a temporary table as multistatement T-SQL user-defined functions do. This can mean, in some cases, that CLR user-defined functions will be able to outperform their T-SQL counterparts. Remember, however, that as with any performance boosting methodology, you should test both methods in most cases to ensure that you make the best choice.

Defining a Table-Valued User-Defined Function

Creating a table-valued user-defined function involves defining a function that returns an instance of a collection that implements the `IEnumerable` interface. This collection will be enumerated by the query engine, and that enumeration will result in calling a second function for each member of the collection, in order to map its attributes to a series of output parameters that map to the column list for the table.

This process is better described using a concrete example. Assume that you wish to encapsulate the following query in a user-defined function:

```
SELECT Name, GroupName FROM HumanResources.Department
```

This query can be evaluated and used to populate a `DataTable`. Since the `DataTable` class implements `IEnumerable`, it is a valid return type for a table-valued function. The following code defines a method called `GetDepartments` that retrieves and returns the data using a context connection:

```
[Microsoft.SqlServer.Server.SqlFunction(
    DataAccess=DataAccessKind.Read,
    FillRowMethodName="GetNextDepartment",
    TableDefinition="Name NVARCHAR(50), GroupName NVARCHAR(50)")]
```

```
public static IEnumerable GetDepartments()
{
    using (SqlConnection conn =
        new SqlConnection("context connection=true;"))
    {
        string sql =
            "SELECT Name, GroupName FROM HumanResources.Department";
        conn.Open();
        SqlCommand comm = new SqlCommand(sql, conn);
        SqlDataAdapter adapter = new SqlDataAdapter(comm);
        DataSet dSet = new DataSet();
        adapter.Fill(dSet);
        return (dSet.Tables[0].Rows);
    }
}
```

Aside from the fact that this method contains no exception handling logic—and will behave very poorly if the Department table is empty—the important thing to note in this code listing is the SqlFunction attribute. Since the function is reading data from the database using the context connection, the DataAccess parameter is set to DataAccessKind.Read.

But more important, because this is a table-valued function, both the FillRowMethodName and TableDefinition parameters are used. The FillRowMethodName parameter defines the name of the method that will be used to map each member of the IEnumerable collection returned by the method to a column. The column list that the method must support is defined by the TableDefinition parameter.

In this case, the method is called GetNextDepartment. The method must have a single input parameter of type object, followed by an output parameter for each column defined in the TableDefinition parameter. The following code implements the GetNextDepartment method:

```
public static void GetNextDepartment(object row,
    out string name,
    out string groupName)
{
    DataRow theRow = (DataRow)row;
    name = (string)theRow["Name"];
    groupName = (string)theRow["GroupName"];
}
```

When the user-defined function is called, it will return a reference to the DataTable, which implements IEnumerable. The SQL Server engine will call MoveNext (one of the methods defined in the IEnumerator interface, which is required by IEnumerable) on the DataTable for each row of output. Each call to MoveNext will return an instance of a DataRow, which will then be passed to the GetNextDepartment function. Finally, that function will map the data in the row to the proper output parameters, which will become the columns in the output table.

This architecture is extremely flexible in terms of ability to define output columns. If a DataTable or other collection that implements IEnumerable does not exist in the .NET class library to satisfy a given requirement, it is simple to define a type that does. Keep in mind that the output types can be either intrinsic SQL Server types or user-defined types. This added flexibility is a sign of the tight integration provided by SQL Server 2005 for the hosted CLR environment.

The full code for the GetDepartments function follows:

```csharp
using System;
using System.Data;
using System.Data.SqlClient;
using System.Data.SqlTypes;
using Microsoft.SqlServer.Server;
using System.Collections;

public partial class UserDefinedFunctions
{
    [Microsoft.SqlServer.Server.SqlFunction(
        DataAccess=DataAccessKind.Read,
        FillRowMethodName="GetNextDepartment",
        TableDefinition="Name NVARCHAR(50), GroupName NVARCHAR(50)")]
    public static IEnumerable GetDepartments()
    {
        using (SqlConnection conn =
            new SqlConnection("context connection=true;"))
        {
            string sql =
                "SELECT Name, GroupName FROM HumanResources.Department";
            conn.Open();
            SqlCommand comm = new SqlCommand(sql, conn);
            SqlDataAdapter adaptor = new SqlDataAdapter(comm);
            DataSet dSet = new DataSet();
            adaptor.Fill(dSet);
            return (dSet.Tables[0].Rows);
        }
    }

    public static void GetNextDepartment(object row,
        out string name,
        out string groupName)
    {
        DataRow theRow = (DataRow)row;
        name = (string)theRow["Name"];
        groupName = (string)theRow["GroupName"];
    }
};
```

References in CLR Projects: Splitting the StringArray into a Table

An important feature to be aware of when working with SQL Server 2005's CLR integration is that assemblies loaded into SQL Server databases can reference one another. On top of that, not every assembly loaded into the database need expose SQL Server routines or types. A developer can, therefore, reference third-party libraries within SQL CLR classes or reference other SQL CLR classes.

To reference a third-party assembly within another assembly to be loaded within a SQL Server 2005 database, the third-party assembly must first be loaded using CREATE ASSEMBLY. For instance, assuming an assembly called MyThirdPartyAssembly was in the C:\Assemblies folder, the following code would load it into a SQL Server 2005 database:

```sql
CREATE ASSEMBLY MyThirdPartyAssembly
FROM 'C:\Assemblies\MyThirdPartyAssembly.DLL'
WITH PERMISSION_SET = EXTERNAL_ACCESS
```

Note that the permission set as defined on the assembly will be enforced, even if the referencing assembly is given more permission. Therefore, even if an assembly that references MyThirdPartyAssembly has the UNSAFE permission, any operation that occurs within MyThirdPartyAssembly will be limited to those allowed by EXTERNAL_ACCESS.

When working in Visual Studio 2005, a reference can be added to a SQL Server project only once the assembly to be referenced has been loaded into the database using either CREATE ASSEMBLY or a Visual Studio deployment task. To add a reference to an assembly that has already been loaded, right-click References in Solution Explorer and select Add Reference. A dialog box like the one shown in Figure 6-6 appears. Select the assembly to reference and click OK. Figure 6-6 shows adding a reference to the StringArray assembly defined earlier in this chapter.

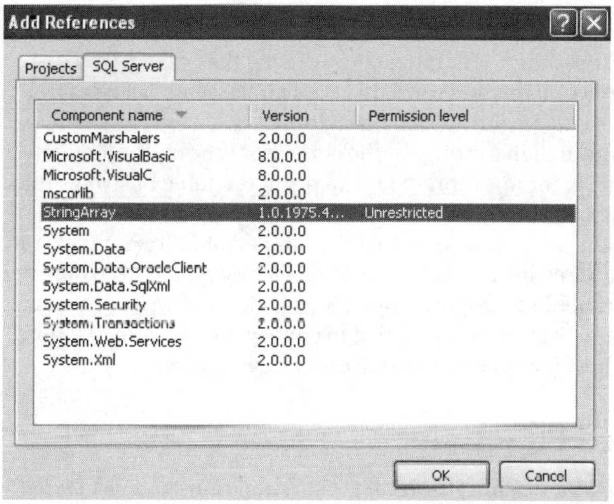

Figure 6-6. *Adding a reference to the StringArray assembly*

Once a reference has been added, the referenced assembly can be treated like any other library. A using directive can be used to alias namespaces, and any public classes, properties, and methods are available.

The following code defines a table-valued user-defined function that takes an instance of the StringArray type as input and outputs a table:

```
using System;
using System.Data;
using System.Data.SqlClient;
using System.Data.SqlTypes;
using Microsoft.SqlServer.Server;
using System.Collections;

public partial class UserDefinedFunctions
{
    [Microsoft.SqlServer.Server.SqlFunction(FillRowMethodName = "GetNextString",
        TableDefinition = "StringCol NVARCHAR(MAX)")]
```

```
    public static IEnumerable GetTableFromStringArray(StringArray strings)
    {
        string csv = strings.ToString();
        string[] arr = csv.Split(',');
        return arr;
    }

    public static void GetNextString(object row, out string theString)
    {
        theString = (string)row;
    }
};
```

The GetTableFromStringArray method retrieves the comma-delimited list of values from the StringArray using the ToString method. This is then split into an array using the String.Split method. Since all arrays are derived from System.Array, and since that class implements IEnumerable, this collection is valid for a return value without any further manipulation.

Each element of the array is nothing more than a string, so the GetNextString method merely needs to cast the row as a string and set theString appropriately. The result is a table of strings that can be joined to another table, inserted into a table, or returned to a client as a result set.

Note that in a real-world scenario, it might make more sense to define the GetTableFromStringArray method to directly consume a comma-delimited list instead of the StringArray type. This would extend the method beyond the 8,000-character limit imposed by CLR user-defined types and make it slightly more flexible. The example listed here is mainly intended to convey the utility of assembly references, and as such, it may not be the best possible solution in every case.

Managing CLR User-Defined Functions

If an assembly has been loaded into the database using CREATE ASSEMBLY, functions can be created or dropped without using the Visual Studio 2005 deployment task.

To create a function that is exposed in an assembly, use CREATE FUNCTION and specify the name of the assembly, the name of the class the function resides on, and the name of the method that defines the function. The following code creates the BinaryCompress type, from an assembly called CompressionRoutines, that contains a class called UserDefinedFunctions:

```
CREATE FUNCTION BinaryCompress(@Input VARBINARY(MAX))
RETURNS VARBINARY(MAX)
AS
EXTERNAL NAME CompressionRoutines.UserDefinedFunctions.BinaryCompress
```

To drop a function, use DROP FUNCTION. A function cannot be dropped if it is referenced by a constraint or schema-bound view. The following code drops the BinaryCompress function:

```
DROP FUNCTION BinaryCompress
```

Functions can also be altered by using ALTER FUNCTION, which is generally used to modify the input or output datatypes. For instance, you may wish to modify the BinaryCompress function, limiting the input to 1,000 bytes:

```
ALTER FUNCTION BinaryCompress(@Input VARBINARY(1000))
RETURNS VARBINARY(MAX)
AS
EXTERNAL NAME CompressionRoutines.UserDefinedFunctions.BinaryCompress
```

Although there is no dedicated view for user-defined functions, they can be enumerated using the sys.objects catalog view. To do so, use the type column and filter on FT for table-valued CLR functions or FS for scalar CLR functions. The following T-SQL will return data about both types:

```
SELECT *
FROM sys.objects
WHERE type in ('FS', 'FT')
```

CLR User-Defined Aggregates

When working with T-SQL, it's often desirable to answer various questions at different levels of granularity. Although it's interesting to know the price of each line item in an order, that information might be more valuable in the form of a total for the entire order. And at the end of the quarter, the sales team might want to know the total for all orders placed during the previous three months; or the average total order price; or the total number of visitors to the website who made a purchase, divided by the total number of visitors, to calculate the percentage of visitors who bought something.

Each of these questions can be easily answered using T-SQL aggregate functions such as SUM, AVG, and COUNT. But there are many questions that are much more difficult to answer with the built-in aggregates. For example, what is the median of the total order prices over the last 90 days? What is the average order price, disregarding the least and most expensive orders? These are but two questions that, while possible to answer with T-SQL aggregates, are quite a bit more difficult than they need be. For instance, the standard algorithm for finding a median involves sorting and counting the set of values, and then returning the value in the middle of the sorted set. Translated to SQL Server, this would most likely mean using a cursor, walking over the result set to find the count, and then backtracking to get the correct value. And while that is a workable solution for a single group, it is not easy to adapt to multiple groups in the same rowset. Imagine writing that cursor to find the median sales amount for every salesperson, split up by month, for the last year. Not a pretty picture.

User-defined aggregates eliminate this problem by giving developers tools to create custom aggregation functions in the .NET language of their choice. These aggregate functions are built to be robust and extensible, with built-in consideration for parallelism and flags that control behavior such that the query optimizer can better integrate the aggregations into query plans. User-defined aggregates can provide powerful support for operations that were previously extremely difficult in SQL Server.

In this section, we'll examine a CLR user-defined aggregate that calculates a "trimmed" mean—an average of a set of numbers minus the smallest and largest input values.

Adding a User-Defined Aggregate to a SQL Server Project

To add a user-defined aggregate to a pre-existing SQL Server project, right-click the project name in Solution Explorer and select Add ➤ Aggregate, as shown in Figure 6-7.

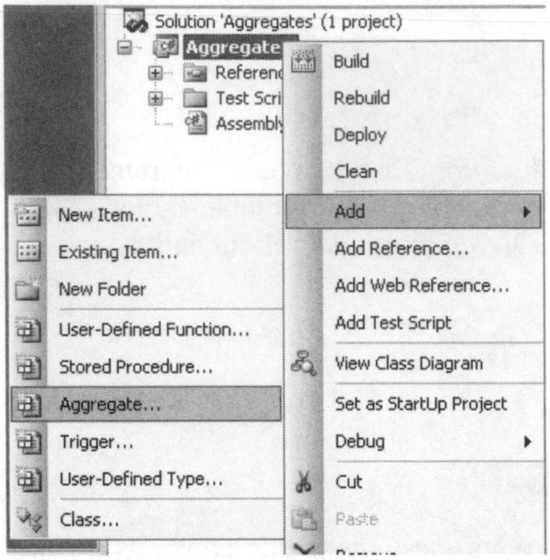

Figure 6-7. *Adding a user-defined aggregate to a SQL Server project*

Once the aggregate has been added to the project, Visual Studio 2005 will add template code. The following code is the result of adding an aggregate called TrimmedMean:

```csharp
using System;
using System.Data;
using System.Data.SqlClient;
using System.Data.SqlTypes;
using Microsoft.SqlServer.Server;


[Serializable]
[Microsoft.SqlServer.Server.SqlUserDefinedAggregate(Format.Native)]
public struct TrimmedMean
{
   public void Init()
   {
      // Put your code here
   }

   public void Accumulate(SqlString Value)
   {
      // Put your code here
   }

   public void Merge(TrimmedMean Group)
   {
      // Put your code here
   }

   public SqlString Terminate()
   {
      // Put your code here
      return new SqlString("");
   }
```

```
// This is a place-holder member field
private int var1;

}
```

Parts of a User-Defined Aggregate

Programming a user-defined aggregate is in many ways similar to programming user-defined types. Both aggregates and types are represented by classes or structures that are serializable. It is important to understand when dealing with aggregates that the intermediate result will be serialized and deserialized once per row of aggregated data. Therefore, it is imperative for performance that serialization and deserialization be as efficient as possible.

SqlUserDefinedAggregate Attribute

The SqlUserDefinedAggregate attribute, much like the SqlUserDefinedType attribute, functions primarily as a way for developers to control serialization behavior. However, the attribute also exposes parameters that can allow the query optimizer to choose better query plans depending on the data requirements of the aggregate. The parameters exposed by the attribute are as follows:

- Format: The Format of a user-defined aggregate indicates what method of serialization will be used. The Native option means that the CLR will control serialization automatically, whereas UserDefined indicates that the developer will control serialization by implementing the IBinarySerialize interface. Native serialization is faster than user-defined serialization, but much more limited: it can only serialize aggregates if all member variables are value types, such as integers and bytes. Reference types such as arrays and strings require user-defined serialization. Given the performance implications of serialization and deserialization on a per-row basis, developers should try to avoid using reference types in aggregates whenever possible.

- IsInvariantToDuplicates: The IsInvariantToDuplicates parameter indicates that the aggregate is able to handle duplicate input values. Setting this parameter to true can help the optimizer formulate better query plans when the aggregate is used. An example of an aggregate that is invariant to duplicates is MIN; no matter how many duplicate values are passed in, only one is the minimum. The default value for this parameter is false.

- IsInvariantToNulls: This parameter indicates to the query optimizer whether the aggregate ignores null inputs. Certain query plans might result in extra nulls being passed into the aggregate; if it ignores them, this will not modify the aggregation. An example of an aggregate with this behavior is SQL Server's SUM aggregate, which ignores nulls if at least one non-null value is processed. The default for this parameter is false.

- IsInvariantToOrder: This parameter is currently unused and will be implemented in a future release of SQL Server.

- IsNullIfEmpty: This parameter indicates whether the aggregate will return null for cases in which no values have been accumulated. This can allow the query engine to take a shortcut in certain cases. The default value for this parameter is true.

- MaxByteSize: This parameter, similar to the same parameter on the SqlUserDefinedType attribute, controls how large, in bytes, the aggregate's intermediate data can grow. The maximum size and default value is 8000.

- Name: This parameter is optionally used by the Visual Studio 2005 deployment task to name the aggregate within the target database differently than the name of the class or structure that defines the aggregate.

Init

The life of an instance of an aggregate begins with a call to Init. Within this method, any private members should be initialized to the correct placeholder values for having processed no rows. There is no guarantee that any data will ever be passed into the aggregate just because Init was called. Care should be taken to ensure that this assumption is never coded into an aggregate. An instance of an aggregate can be reused multiple times for different groups within the result set, so Init should be coded to reset the entire state of the aggregate.

Accumulate

The Accumulate method takes a scalar value as input and appends that value, in the correct way, to the running aggregation. That scalar value is an instance of whatever type is being aggregated. Since these values are coming from the SQL Server engine, they are nullable, and since the method itself has no control over what values are passed in, it must always be coded to properly deal with nulls. Remember that even if the column for the input to the aggregation is defined as NOT NULL, a NULL can result from an OUTER JOIN or a change in project requirements.

Merge

In some cases, query plans can go parallel. This means that two or more operations can occur simultaneously—including aggregation. There is a chance that some aggregation for a given aggregate of a given column will take place in one thread, while the rest will take place in other threads. The Merge method takes an instance of the aggregate as input and must append any intermediate data it contains into its own instance's member data.

Terminate

The final call in an aggregate's life is Terminate. This method returns the end result of the aggregation.

Programming the TrimmedMean Aggregate

T-SQL has long included the AVG aggregate for calculating the mean value of a set of inputs. This is generally quite useful, but for statistical purposes it's often desirable to eliminate the greatest and least values from a mean calculation. Unfortunately, doing this in pure T-SQL is quite difficult, especially if the query also includes other aggregates that should not exclude the rows with the greatest and least amounts. This is a classic problem, and it's the kind that CLR user-defined aggregates excel at solving.

To calculate the mean value excluding the maximum and minimum values, the aggregate will have to keep track of four values:

- A count of the number of values processed so far
- A running sum of all input values
- The minimum value seen so far
- The maximum value seen so far

The final output value can be calculated by subtracting the minimum and maximum values from the running sum, and then dividing that number by the count, minus 2 (to account for the subtracted values). The following private member variables will be used to keep track of these values:

```
private int numValues;
private SqlMoney totalValue;
private SqlMoney minValue;
private SqlMoney maxValue;
```

The Init method will prepopulate each of these variables with the appropriate values. numValues and totalValue will both be initialized to 0, starting the count. minValue will be initialized to SqlMoney.MaxValue, and maxValue to SqlMoney.MinValue. This will ease development of comparison logic for the initial values entered into the aggregate. Note that the SqlMoney datatype is used for this example to facilitate taking averages of order data in the AdventureWorks database. Other applications of such an aggregate may require different datatypes. The following code is the implementation of Init for this aggregate:

```
public void Init()
{
    this.numValues = 0;
    this.totalValue = 0;
    this.minValue = SqlMoney.MaxValue;
    this.maxValue = SqlMoney.MinValue;
}
```

So that the aggregate behaves similarly to intrinsic SQL Server aggregates like AVG, it's important that it ignore nulls. Therefore, the Accumulate method should increment the numValues variable only if the input is non-null. The following code implements Accumulate for this aggregate:

```
public void Accumulate(SqlMoney Value)
{
    if (!Value.IsNull)
    {
        this.numValues++;
        this.totalValue += Value;
        if (Value < this.minValue)
            this.minValue = Value;
        if (Value > this.maxValue)
            this.maxValue = Value;
    }
}
```

Implementing Merge is very similar to implementing Accumulate, except that the value comes from another instance of the aggregate instead of being passed in from the query engine:

```
public void Merge(TrimmedMean Group)
{
    if (Group.numValues > 0)
    {
        this.numValues += Group.numValues;
        this.totalValue += Group.totalValue;
        if (Group.minValue < this.minValue)
            this.minValue = Group.minValue;
        if (Group.maxValue > this.maxValue)
            this.maxValue = Group.maxValue;
    }
}
```

The final step in coding the aggregate is to define the Terminate method. Since the lowest and highest input values will be ignored, the output will be null if numValues is less than 3; it is impossible to ignore values that don't exist! Aside from that, the algorithm employed is as described previously: divide the total value by the number of values after subtracting the minimum and maximum.

```
public SqlDecimal Terminate()
{
    if (this.numValues < 3)
        return (SqlMoney.Null);
    else
    {
        this.numValues -= 2;
        this.totalValue -= this.minValue;
        this.totalValue -= this.maxValue;
        return (this.totalValue / this.numValues);
    }
}
```

Since the aggregate uses only value types as member variables, native serialization will suffice, and the default SqlUserDefinedAggregate attribute will not have to be modified. The complete code for the aggregate follows:

```
using System;
using System.Data;
using System.Data.SqlClient;
using System.Data.SqlTypes;
using Microsoft.SqlServer.Server;


[Serializable]
[Microsoft.SqlServer.Server.SqlUserDefinedAggregate(Format.Native)]
public struct TrimmedMean
{
    public void Init()
    {
        this.numValues = 0;
        this.totalValue = 0;
        this.minValue = SqlMoney.MaxValue;
        this.maxValue = SqlMoney.MinValue;
    }

    public void Accumulate(SqlMoney Value)
    {
        if (!Value.IsNull)
        {
            this.numValues++;
            this.totalValue += Value;
            if (Value < this.minValue)
                this.minValue = Value;
            if (Value > this.maxValue)
                this.maxValue = Value;
        }
    }
```

```
    public void Merge(TrimmedMean Group)
    {
        if (Group.numValues > 0)
        {
            this.numValues += Group.numValues;
            this.totalValue += Group.totalValue;
            if (Group.minValue < this.minValue)
                this.minValue = Group.minValue;
            if (Group.maxValue > this.maxValue)
                this.maxValue = Group.maxValue;
        }
    }

    public SqlMoney Terminate()
    {
        if (this.numValues < 3)
            return (SqlMoney.Null);
        else
        {
            this.numValues -= 2;
            this.totalValue -= this.minValue;
            this.totalValue -= this.maxValue;
            return (this.totalValue / this.numValues);
        }
    }

    private int numValues;
    private SqlMoney totalValue;
    private SqlMoney minValue;
    private SqlMoney maxValue;
}
```

Using the TrimmedMean Aggregate

Once deployed to the database, user-defined aggregate functions can be used just like built-in
aggregates. For instance, to compare the results returned by the T-SQL AVG function to those
returned by TrimmedMean for the total order amounts in the AdventureWorks database, you can use
the following query:

```
SELECT
    AVG(TotalDue) AS AverageTotal,
    dbo.TrimmedMean(TotalDue) AS TrimmedAverageTotal
FROM Sales.SalesOrderHeader
```

The results of this query show a slightly lower average for the trimmed figure: $4,464.88 instead
of $4,471.28 for the normal average.

Managing User-Defined Aggregates

If an assembly has been loaded into the database using CREATE ASSEMBLY, aggregates can be created
or dropped without using the Visual Studio 2005 deployment task.

To create an aggregate that is exposed in an assembly, use CREATE AGGREGATE and specify the
name of the assembly and the name of the structure or class that defines the aggregate. The following
code creates the TrimmedMean aggregate from an assembly called Aggregates:

```
CREATE AGGREGATE TrimmedMean
EXTERNAL NAME Aggregates.TrimmedMean
```

To drop an aggregate, use DROP AGGREGATE. The following code drops the TrimmedMean aggregate:

```
DROP AGGREGATE TrimmedMean
```

There is no catalog view dedicated to aggregates, but some data is exposed in the sys.objects view. To get information about user-defined aggregates, filter the type column for the value AF:

```
SELECT *
FROM sys.objects
WHERE type = 'AF'
```

CLR User-Defined Triggers

Triggers are a very useful construct for T-SQL programmers. A routine can be defined that will automatically fire upon attempted data manipulation, thereby putting the onus for the required logic on the database itself, rather than every stored procedure that needs to manipulate it. An example of this would be a trigger used for auditing. By using a trigger, the logic for copying some of the modified data into another table is centralized. Without the trigger, every stored procedure that did anything with the data would have to have its own copy of this logic, and a developer might forget to include it in one stored procedure, thereby destroying continuity of the audit logs.

CLR triggers behave the same way as T-SQL triggers, bringing the same power to the table: centralization and encapsulation of logic. However, CLR triggers can be written in a .NET language and possibly take advantage of resources not easily accessible from T-SQL, such as regular expressions for data validation. CLR triggers can be used to define both DML (e.g., UPDATE, INSERT, and DELETE) and DDL triggers (e.g., CREATE TABLE).

■**Note** See Chapter 4 for a discussion of DDL triggers.

It's important to remember when working with triggers that speed is of the essence. A trigger fires in the context of the transaction that manipulated the data. Any locks required for that data manipulation are held for the duration of the trigger's lifetime. This means that slow triggers can create blocking problems that can lead to severe performance and scalability issues. This concern is doubly important when working with the CLR. Triggers are not the place to contact web services, send e-mails, work with the file system, or do other synchronous tasks. Developers who need this functionality should investigate using technologies such as SQL Service Broker and SQL Server Notification Services, both of which are covered elsewhere in this book. If you're using CLR triggers, keep them simple!

Adding a CLR User-Defined Trigger to a SQL Server Project

To add a CLR trigger to a pre-existing SQL Server project, right-click the project name in Solution Explorer and select Add ➤ Trigger, as shown in Figure 6-8.

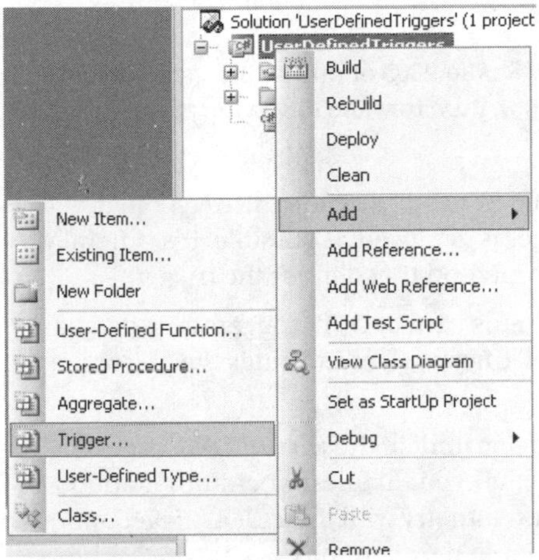

Figure 6-8. *Adding a CLR trigger to a SQL Server project*

Programming CLR Triggers

Once the trigger has been added to the project, Visual Studio 2005 will add template code. The following code is the result of adding a trigger called ValidateYear:

```
using System;
using System.Data;
using System.Data.SqlClient;
using Microsoft.SqlServer.Server;


public partial class Triggers
{
    // Enter existing table or view for the target and uncomment the attribute line
    // [Microsoft.SqlServer.Server.SqlTrigger (Name="ValidateYear",➡
Target="Table1", Event="FOR UPDATE")]
    public static void ValidateYear()
    {
        // Put your code here
    }
}
```

This template is quite simplistic; programming a CLR trigger is very similar to programming a CLR stored procedure. The main differences between the two are the influence of the SqlTrigger attribute and the lack of a return value for triggers—the method that defines the trigger must return void. Aside from those differences, most programming paradigms hold true in both types of routines. CLR triggers, like CLR stored procedures, can make use of SqlPipe to return as many rowsets or messages to the client as the developer requires. See Chapter 5 for a complete discussion on programming with SqlPipe.

SqlTrigger Attribute

The SqlTrigger attribute's primary function is to help Visual Studio 2005 or other third-party deployment tools determine which tables and events the trigger is written for. The following parameters are available for the attribute:

- Name: This parameter indicates the name that should be used to define the trigger in the CREATE TRIGGER statement executed when the trigger is deployed. If possible, it's generally a good idea to keep this in sync with the name of the method that defines the trigger.

- Target: This parameter can indicate a table name in the case of DML triggers, or a database name or the ALL SERVER keyword in the case of DDL triggers. This indicates the object that, when manipulated, will cause the trigger to fire.

- Event: This parameter indicates what event(s) to fire on and, in the case of DML triggers, whether the trigger should fire AFTER or INSTEAD OF the event in question. Another option is FOR, which is equivalent to AFTER and is included for symmetry with the T-SQL trigger options. Note that multiple events can appear in the list, delimited by commas.

TriggerContext

The SqlContext object exposes information about the state of the trigger via the TriggerContext. This object contains properties to assist with determining why the trigger fired. The most important of these are the TriggerAction property, which maps to an enumerator by the same name that contains every possible action that can cause a trigger to fire, and the EventData property, which contains XML data useful in DDL triggers.

For example, the following code fragment would be used to execute code conditionally based on whether the trigger had fired due to an update:

```
if (SqlContext.TriggerContext.TriggerAction == TriggerAction.Update)
{
    // do something
}
```

Validating a Year Using a CLR Trigger

It should be stressed once again that CLR triggers must be kept simple and quick, just like T-SQL triggers. There are few situations in which a pure CLR trigger is appropriate, given that CLR functions can be called from T-SQL triggers. As such, the example here is shown only for the sake of illustrating how to program a CLR trigger—this example is something that should be done in a T-SQL trigger in a production environment.

An example in which a trigger (either CLR or T-SQL) can be helpful is enforcement of business rules that don't fit neatly into CHECK constraints. For instance, a DBA might want to define a rule that any new rows inserted into the HumanResources.Department table must be inserted with a ModifiedDate falling in 2005. A constraint checking the ModifiedDate column would preclude any pre-existing rows from having a date falling in that year; a trigger can be set up to only operate on newly inserted rows and is therefore a better way to enforce the rule.

The rules for this trigger will be simple: if any rows are inserted with a ModifiedDate not falling in 2005, the transaction should be rolled back, and an error should be raised. Otherwise, nothing should happen, and the transaction should be allowed to commit.

Getting the number of rows with years other than 2005 will be accomplished the same way it could be in a T-SQL trigger: The rows will be selected from the INSERTED virtual table. Both INSERTED and DELETED are available from within CLR triggers, using the context connection, as follows:

```
SqlConnection conn =
    new SqlConnection("context connection=true");

//Define the query
string sql =
    "SELECT COUNT(*) " +
    "FROM INSERTED " +
    "WHERE YEAR(ModifiedDate) <> 2005";

SqlCommand comm =
    new SqlCommand(sql, conn);

//Open the connection
conn.Open();

//Get the number of bad rows
int numBadRows = (int)comm.ExecuteScalar();
```

If the number of "bad" rows is greater than zero, an error should be raised. Remember from the last chapter that raising a clean error from the CLR can be tricky—it requires sending a RAISERROR, but wrapping the send in a try/catch block to eliminate a second error bubbling up. Finally, the transaction will be rolled back using the Transaction object. The code to do this follows:

```
if (numBadRows > 0)
{
    //Get the SqlPipe
    SqlPipe pipe = SqlContext.Pipe;

    //Roll back and raise an error
    comm.CommandText =
        "RAISERROR('Modified Date must fall in 2005', 11, 1)";

    //Send the error
    try
    {
        pipe.ExecuteAndSend(comm);
    }
    catch
    {
        //do nothing
    }

    System.Transactions.Transaction.Current.Rollback();
}
```

Note that to use the System.Transactions namespace, a reference to the assembly must be added. To add the reference, right-click References in Solution Explorer, click Add Reference, and select System.Transactions in the Component Name column.

The complete code for the ValidateYear trigger follows:

```csharp
using System;
using System.Data;
using System.Data.SqlClient;
using Microsoft.SqlServer.Server;

public partial class Triggers
{
    // Enter existing table or view for the target and uncomment the attribute line
    [Microsoft.SqlServer.Server.SqlTrigger (
        Name="ValidateYear",
        Target="HumanResources.Department",
        Event="FOR INSERT")]
    public static void ValidateYear()
    {
        SqlConnection conn =
            new SqlConnection("context connection=true");

        //Define the query
        string sql =
            "SELECT COUNT(*) " +
            "FROM INSERTED " +
            "WHERE YEAR(ModifiedDate) <> 2005";

        SqlCommand comm =
            new SqlCommand(sql, conn);

        //Open the connection
        conn.Open();

        //Get the number of bad rows
        int numBadRows = (int)comm.ExecuteScalar();

        if (numBadRows > 0)
        {
            //Get the SqlPipe
            SqlPipe pipe = SqlContext.Pipe;

            //Roll back and raise an error
            comm.CommandText =
                "RAISERROR('Modified Date must fall in 2005', 11, 1)";

            //Send the error
            try
            {
                pipe.ExecuteAndSend(comm);
            }
            catch
            {
                //do nothing
            }
```

```
            System.Transactions.Transaction.Current.Rollback();
        }

        //Close the connection
        conn.Close();
    }
}
```

Managing User-Defined Triggers

If an assembly has been loaded into the database using CREATE ASSEMBLY, triggers can be created or dropped without using the Visual Studio 2005 deployment task.

To create a trigger that is exposed in an assembly, use CREATE TRIGGER and specify the name of the assembly, the name of the class in which the trigger resides, and the name of the method that defines the trigger. The following code creates the ValidateYear trigger, from an assembly called UserDefinedTriggers, containing a class called Triggers:

```
CREATE TRIGGER ValidateYear
ON HumanResources.Department
FOR INSERT
AS
EXTERNAL NAME UserDefinedTriggers.Triggers.ValidateYear
```

To drop a trigger, use DROP TRIGGER. The following code drops the ValidateYear trigger:

```
DROP TRIGGER ValidateYear
```

The sys.triggers catalog view contains information about both T-SQL and CLR triggers. To get information about CLR triggers, filter the type column for the value TA:

```
SELECT *
FROM sys.triggers
WHERE type = 'TA'
```

Managing Assemblies

Several catalog views are available to assist with management and enumeration of assemblies loaded into the database:

- sys.assemblies: This view contains one row for each assembly loaded into the database.

- sys.assembly_files: This view contains information about the files associated with each assembly. Generally, this will only be the file that makes up the assembly (i.e., the actual DLL). However, the Visual Studio 2005 deployment task inserts all of the source files when deploying, so this table can contain many other files per assembly.

- sys.assembly_modules: This view contains one row per function, procedure, aggregate, or trigger created from an assembly.

- sys.assembly_types: This view contains one row per type created from an assembly.

- sys.assembly_references: This view allows developers to determine dependencies among assemblies. When an assembly references another assembly, this view shows the relationship.

A Note Regarding Visual Studio 2005

All examples in this chapter relied upon Visual Studio 2005's project templates and automated deployment functionality. And while this really does assist with creating CLR objects, it is not necessary. Keep in mind that the only things required to create these objects are a text editor and a copy of the .NET Framework. Visual Studio 2005 is only a wrapper over these.

If you are using Visual Studio 2005, there is at least one third-party tool available to assist with making the deployment task more flexible. Niels Berglund has created an add-in deployment step that can assist with certain issues and posted it on his weblog: `http://sqljunkies.com/WebLog/ nielsb/archive/2005/05/03/13379.aspx`.

Summary

When used prudently, CLR routines make powerful additions to SQL Server's toolset. Functions, aggregates, triggers, and types can each be used in a variety of ways to expand SQL Server and make it a better environment for application development. It's important to remember that some caveats exist and that careful testing is required. That said, SQL Server 2005's CLR integration should prove incredibly useful for most software shops.

■ ■ ■

SQL Server and XML

XML is growing in usage everyday. Some relational purists will look at XML and shake their heads. However, XML is complementary to relational technologies. In fact, a lot of XML is structured just like relational data. Is that good? Probably not, since the two models are best at their intended data formats: XML for semistructured data, and relational databases for relational data. Plus, the semantics of storing, querying, and modifying XML is what confuses most relational people. As you'll see, XQuery looks nothing like T-SQL. However, you can use the two technologies together to solve your business problems. Before we dive into what's new in SQL Server 2005 when it comes to XML, we need to first understand what XML is and how SQL Server already leverages XML technologies.

In this chapter, we'll start out with the basics such as what XML is and how the current SQL Server version works with XML including FOR XML, shredding, and support in the .NET Framework FOR XML. We'll also introduce you to XPath and the XPath support in SQL Server. Finally, we'll take a look at SQLXML and how you can use this technology to extend the XML support in SQL Server. If you haven't heard of SQLXML, version 3.0 was a free download off the Web for SQL Server 2000. Version 4.0 of SQLXML is included in SQL Server 2005. In the next chapter, you'll see how SQL Server has evolved to include rich support FOR XML with the new XML datatype and the XQuery language. We'll also look at XML Web Services support in the next chapter, which replaces the ISAPI SQLXML web services support.

What Is XML?

For those of you who have been living in a cave for the last 10 years and haven't heard the hype surrounding XML, it stands for eXtensible Markup Language. XML allows you to structure your data using a standardized schema. The standardization is the most important part since that is the power of XML. Any other system can read or write data that adheres to the standard, of course with the usual caveats that different systems may interpret the data differently sometimes. XML also provides the ability for retrieving certain values from the XML using the XPath standard and transforming your XML using XSLT. You'll learn about both these standards later in the chapter.

One interesting discussion is deciding between XML and relational data. A lot of debate goes back and forth between the value of storing your data in a purely relational model, a hybrid XML/relational model, or a purely XML model. In our opinion, do whatever makes the most sense to the problem you are solving. If your expertise is in relational technology and you are getting great performance from your relational data, there is no need to switch to XML-based storage. You can easily expose your relational data as XML to the outside world, using FOR XML, but you can continue to store your data internally as relational data. Don't fall prey to XML's siren song without good reason to move to it. For example, XML is text based, so it is bigger than its binary equivalents. XML is verbose since it isn't normalized like relational data, so you may have repeating sections of the same data in a single XML document. Finally, XML does have a different programming model than what a relational programmer is used to.

Let's start with some basic XML terminology, and then we can start peeling back the layers of the XML onion so you understand more and more about this technology. You'll hear many people refer to documents, elements, and attributes. The easiest way to think about this is that an entire XML structure is the document, the document contains elements, and elements can contain attributes. The sample XML document here contains one document, three elements, and two attributes:

```
<?xml version="1.0"?>
<customer>
  <name id="10">Tom Rizzo</name>
  <state region="Northwest">WA</state>
</customer>
```

XML has schemas and namespaces. You are not required to put schemas on your XML, but schemas and namespaces help to uniquely define what is valid or invalid structure or data in your XML document. In the relational world, we have our table structures and constraints. You can map some of your relational concepts to XML schemas since XML schemas have datatypes and rules that control order, cardinality, and other aspects of the XML document. Schemas allow you to share your XML data with others but still have the other people understand your XML. An XML namespace is a collection of names, identified by a URI reference, that your element types and attribute names use in an XML document. Namespaces allow you to use the same names from different sources and avoid name collisions. For example, you can use the same element called customer from two different sources if you add namespaces that identify the elements as belonging to different namespaces. Schemas and namespaces will be important when we discuss the new XML datatype in SQL Server 2005 and storing your XML natively in the database.

What Are XPath and the XMLDOM?

Once you have a set of XML documents, you'll obviously want to query them in order to retrieve relevant information. XML Path Language (XPath) is a query language that enables you to define which parts of an XML document you want to select. XPath has a parser that interprets the syntax, reaches into the XML document, and pulls out the relevant parts. For example, you may want to return all customers who live in NY from an XML document. To do this, you would write an XPath statement.

Since XML is hierarchical, you can use XPath to specify the path or paths to the XML that you want to retrieve. Think of XML as a hierarchy of nodes. The root node is normally the XML document entity. Then, a tree structure is created under the root node for all your XML. If we took the XML sample earlier and mapped it to the XML path hierarchy, we would get the tree shown in Figure 7-1.

Not a very exciting tree, but a tree nonetheless. You can see that all elements, attributes, and text have nodes in the tree. There are seven node types you can access in XPath including the root, element, attribute, namespace, processing instruction, comment, and text nodes. You'll find yourself working mostly with element, attribute, processing instruction, and text nodes in your XPath.

You can use XPath to navigate among these different nodes using *XPath axes*. XPath axes describe how to navigate the structure by specifying the starting point and the direction of navigation. There are 13 axes in XPath, but you'll find that you use the child and attribute axes the most. Table 7-1 lists the 13 axes.

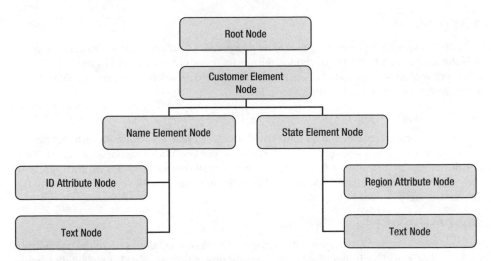

Figure 7-1. *An example XML document tree*

Table 7-1. *XPath Axes*

Name	Description
Ancestor	Contains the parent node of the context node and all subsequent parent nodes of that node all the way to the root node.
Ancestor-or-self	Contains the nodes in the ancestor as well as the context node itself all the way up to the root node.
Attribute	Contains the attributes for the context node if the context node is an element node.
Child	Contains the child nodes of the context node.
Descendant	Contains the child, grandchildren, etc., nodes of the context node.
Descendant-or-self	Contains both the context node itself and all the children, grandchildren, etc., of the context node.
Following	Contains all the nodes in the same document as the context node that are after the context node in document order, but doesn't include any descendent, namespace, or attribute nodes.
Following-sibling	Same as the following axis but contains any nodes that have the same parent node as the context node.
Namespace	Contains the namespace nodes of the context node as long as the context node is an element.
Parent	Contains the parent node of the context node. The root node has no parent. This axis is the inverse of the child axis.
Preceding	Same as the following axis but instead of nodes after the context node, it will be nodes before the context node in document order.
Preceding-sibling	Same as the preceding axis except this will contain all nodes with the same parent as the context node.
Self	Contains just the context node.

XPath Syntax

XPath uses a set of expressions to select nodes to be processed. The most common expression that you'll use is the location path expression, which returns back a set of nodes called a *node set*. You'll find that the syntax of XPath can use both an unabbreviated and an abbreviated syntax. The unabbreviated syntax for a location path is shown as follows:

```
/axisName::nodeTest[predicate]/axisName::nodeTest[predicate]
```

Looking at the sample, you see the forward slash, which refers to the root node as being the context node. Then, the sample shows an axis followed by a nodeTest and an optional predicate. This all can be followed by one or more similar structures to eventually get to the nodes we are interested in retrieving. So, to retrieve all customers, we would use the following unabbreviated XPath syntax. The default axis, if none is provided, is child.

```
/child::root/child::customer
```

Most times, however, you'll use abbreviated syntax. The abbreviated version of the preceding XPath may be //customer. The double slash is the descendent-or-self axis. You'll also find that you'll sometimes use wildcards in XPath. XPath supports three types of wildcards: *, node( ), and @*. * matches any element node regardless of type, except it doesn't return attribute, text, comments, or processing instruction nodes. If you want all nodes, use the node( ) syntax, which will return these back to you. Finally, the @* matches all attribute nodes. Table 7-2 shows you the XPath expression abbreviations that you'll run into.

Table 7-2. *XPath Expression Abbreviations*

Name	Description
"default"	If you provide no axis, the default one used is child.
@	Abbreviation for attributes.
//	Shortcut for descendent-or-self.
.	Shortcut for self.
..	Shortcut for parent.
*	Wildcard that allows for any matches of any element node regardless of type, except it doesn't return attribute, text, comments, or processing instruction nodes.
/	Used as a path separator. Also used for an absolute path from the root of the document.

To return back all the child elements of our customer node earlier or if we wanted all the attributes only, and finally if we wanted only customers with a region equal to Northwest, we would use the following XPath syntax:

```
/customer/*
/customer/@*
/customer[@region = "Northwest"]
```

You'll also find yourself using compound location paths by combining a multitude of path statements. In XPath, there is special syntax beyond the root node syntax of a single slash (/). For example, you can specify all descendents using a double-slash (//). You can also select the parent node using a double period (..). Finally, you can select the current element using a single period (.). The following XPath sample selects all element nodes under the root node that have an ID of 10:

```
//[@id = "10"]
```

You may also want to access attributes. To select attributes, you use the @ syntax. For example, to select the id attribute, you would use /customer/name/@id. Sometimes you'll want to filter element nodes based on the attributes they possess. For example, if we had some customers with no region attribute on their state element, you could filter out those customers by using /customer/state[@name].

XPath Functions

XPath provides functions so that you can return values or manipulate your XML. XPath includes string, node set, number, and Boolean functions. The most common functions you'll use are the position(), count(), contains(), substring(), sum(), and round() functions.

- The position() function returns the position you specify in the document order. For example, /customer[position() = 2] would return the customer element in position 2. You can abbreviate this function by leaving out the position() = portion. For example, /customer[2] is equivalent to the previous example.

- The count() function returns the number of nodes in the node set. For example, if you wanted to count the number of customers, you would use /count(customer). Or, if customers had orders in the XML document, you could use /customer/orders/count(order).

- The contains() function takes two strings and returns true if the second string is contained in the first string. For example, if you wanted to find out whether Tom is contained in a string, you would use /customer/name[contains(.,'Tom')].

- The substring() function returns part of the string specified. The first parameter is the string. The second is the start position, and the final parameter is the length such as /customer/name[substring(.,1,3)].

- The sum() function, as its name suggests, sums numbers together. It takes a node set so if you want to sum all the prices of a set of products, you can use this function to do this, for example, sum(/products/product/price).

- Finally, the round() function will round to the nearest integer.

The XMLDOM–XML Document Object Model

The XMLDOM is a programming interface for XML documents. With the XMLDOM, a developer can load, create, modify, or delete XML information. The easiest way to understand the XMLDOM is to see it in action. For SQL Server folks, you can think of the XMLDOM like the dataset in terms of being an in-memory representation of your parsed XML document.

When using the XMLDOM, the first thing you need to do is declare an object of XMLDocument type. The XMLDocument type extends the XMLNode object, which represents a node of any type in an XML document. After declaring your XMLDocument, you need to load or create your XML document. To load the XML document, you can use the load or loadxml methods as shown here:

```
Imports System.Xml.XmlDocument
Dim oXMLDOM As New System.Xml.XmlDocument

 oXMLDOM.Load("c:\myxml.xml")
 'Or if you already have it as a string
 'oXMLDOM.LoadXml(strXML)
```

Once you have the document loaded, you can traverse the nodes in the document by using an XMLNode object and the ChildNodes property of the DocumentElement. The DocumentElement property returns back the XML document, and the ChildNodes property returns back the collection of nodes that makes up the document. The following code scrolls through an XML document and outputs the nodes in the document:

```
Dim oXMLNode As System.Xml.XmlNode

Dim strResult As String = ""

For Each oXMLNode In oXMLDOM.DocumentElement.ChildNodes
    strResult += oXMLNode.Name & ": " & _
        oXMLNode.InnerText
Next

MsgBox(strResult)
```

As part of the XMLDOM, you can also get elements by tag name using the GetElementsbyTagName function. For example, if you had an element called customer, you could retrieve its value using this code:

```
MsgBox(oXMLDOM.GetElementsByTagName("customer").Item(0).InnerText)
```

The GetElementsbyTagName returns back a node list that you can parse. The code just retrieves the first node in the list, but if you wanted to, you could loop through all the nodes and print them out. The XMLDOM has similar functions such as GetElementByID or GetElementsbyName.

Finally, we'll consider the use of XPath in the XMLDOM. To return a node list that corresponds to our XPath statement using the XMLDOM, we use the SelectNodes method. This method takes an expression that can be an XML Stylesheet Language (XSL) command or an XPath expression. You can also use the SelectSingleNode method to return back just a single node rather than a node list. The code that follows runs a passed-in expression and traverses the returned nodes to print out their value:

```
Dim oNodes As System.Xml.XmlNodeList = oXMLDOM.SelectNodes(txtXPath.Text)
Dim strReturnString as string = ""

Dim oNode As System.Xml.XmlNode
For Each oNode In oNodes
        strReturnString = oNode.OuterXml
Next

Msgbox(strReturnString)
```

The XPathDocument, XPathNavigator, and XPathExpression Classes

While using the XMLDOM for rapid development is OK, if you want a scalable .NET application that uses XPath, you'll use the XPathDocument, XPathExpression, and XPathNavigator classes.

- The XPathDocument is a high-performance, read-only cache FOR XML documents with the explicit purpose of parsing and executing XPath queries against that document.

- The XPathNavigator class is a class based on the XPath data model. This class allows you to query over any data store. You can compile frequently used XPath expressions with the XPathNavigator class.

- Finally, the XPathExpression class is a compiled XPath expression that you can execute from your XPathNavigator class.

The following code instantiates an XPathDocument object and loads some XML into it. Then, the code creates an XPathNavigator using the CreateNavigator method. This method is also supported in the XMLDocument class. To execute our XPath expression, the code calls the Select method and passes in the expression. As you can see, the expression looks for customers with the name Tom Rizzo and then returns the state for customers matching that value.

```
'Instantiate the XPathDocument class.
Dim oXPathDoc As New System.Xml.XPath.XPathDocument("c:\note.xml")

'Instantiate the XPathNavigator class.
Dim oXPathNav As System.Xml.XPath.XPathNavigator = oXPathDoc.CreateNavigator()

'Instantiate the XPathIterator class.
Dim oXPathNodesIt As System.Xml.XPath.XPathNodeIterator = & _
  oXPathNav.Select("//customer/name[. = 'Tom Rizzo']/parent::node()/state")

'Instantiate a string to hold results.
Dim strResult as string = ""

'Use the XPathIterator class to navigate through the generated result set
'and then display the selected Parent Companies.
Do While oXPathNodesIt.MoveNext
    strResult += oXPathNodesIt.Current.Value
Loop

Msgbox(strResult)
```

Getting XML into the Database

Now that you understand a little bit about XML and XPath, we can start talking about how you can get XML into SQL Server. There are a couple of different ways to do this. First, you can just dump your XML into a nvarchar column in the database using a simple INSERT statement. Using this technique is just like entering any text into a column. With SQL Server 2005, you can use the new XML datatype rather than a text column.

Note We'll cover the new XML datatype in the following chapter, where we'll also look at how you can use SQL Server Integration Services (SSIS) to get data into your XML datatype.

There are three other ways of getting XML into your database:

- You may want to shred your XML into multiple columns and rows in a single database call. To do this, you can use the OPENXML rowset provider. OPENXML provides a rowset view over an XML document and allows you to write T-SQL statements that parse XML.

- Another way is to use updategrams. *Updategrams* are data structures that you can use to express changes to your data by representing a before-and-after image. SQLXML takes your updategram and generates the necessary SQL commands to apply your changes.

- The final way is to leverage SQLXML's XML BulkLoad provider. Using this provider, you can take a large set of XML data and quickly load it into your SQL Server.

So you may be wondering which technique is best. Well, they all have their strengths and weaknesses. If you are just looking for the fastest and highest-performance way to get XML data into your SQL Server, you'll want to look at the BulkLoad provider. The BulkLoad provider doesn't attempt to load all your XML into memory, but instead reads your XML data as a stream, interprets it, and loads it into your SQL Server. The BulkLoad provider is a separate component, so if you are looking for something that you can use inside of a stored procedure or in your UDF, you cannot use the BulkLoad provider. You could use it in an extended stored procedure (XP) by calling out to it, but that is an uncommon scenario and has its own set of issues since XPs are complex, hard to debug, and can open up your server to security issues if written incorrectly.

On the other hand, OPENXML can be used in stored procedures and UDFs, since it ships as part of the native T-SQL language. You'll pay a performance penalty for this integration though. OPENXML requires you to use a stored procedure sp_xml_preparedocument to parse the XML for consumption. This SPROC loads a special version of the MSXML parser called MSXMLSQL to process the XML document and, in turn, loads the entire XML document into memory. There is performance overhead and some extra coding required to use OPENXML, as you'll learn later in this chapter in the section "SQLXML: XML Views Using Annotated XML Schemas."

Updategrams are very useful for applications where you want to modify your database and you are OK with building an annotated schema, which you'll learn about later in the chapter, and applying those changes through this annotated schema. SQLXML takes the updategram and translates it to SQL DML statements. The main limitation of updategrams is if you need to apply business logic to the SQL DML statements, then you'll be unable to use updategrams since you cannot access the generated DML statements.

However, before we get going, we need to configure our SQL Server a little bit to learn how to use these technologies.

What Is SQLXML?

SQLXML is an additional set of technologies that shipped separately from SQL Server 2000. These technologies included things like updategram support, the SQLXML BulkLoad provider, client-side FOR XML support, and SOAP support. For SQL Server 2000, the latest version of SQLXML is version 3.0. With SQL Server 2005, SQLXML 4.0 ships with the product but can also be redistributed on its own. Since the technologies in SQLXML don't have to run on the server, the technology needed a name. Don't confuse, which some people do, SQLXML with the XML datatype in SQL Server 2005.

Also, don't confuse SQLXML with the SQL/XML standard, also known as the SQLX standard. SQLX is an ANSI/ISO standard that defines how to make XML data work in relational databases. Microsoft is a member of the working committee for the SQLX standard. SQL Server currently doesn't support the SQLX standard but provides equivalent functionality for the activities covered in the standard. For example, SQLX defines XML publishing, which SQL Server can do using the FOR XML keyword. For the XML decomposition, you can use the XML datatype or OPENXML. Plus, there are things that the standard doesn't define that SQL Server implements such as combining XQuery into relational queries.

Configuring SQL Server

With SQLXML 3.0, SQL Server 2000 required that you have an IIS server to listen for SQL commands using either URL queries or SOAP calls. The ISAPI listener, described later, will parse out the SQL, execute it, and return back a result. With SQL Server 2005, SQL Server can natively listen on a port for HTTP calls, without requiring IIS. As a simple setup for this chapter, we'll create an endpoint so we can send our queries and updategrams to the server. However, for the full web services support information, please refer to the next chapter. If you've used the IIS configuration utility from SQLXML 3.0, you no longer need to use that utility in SQL Server 2005 but can instead use server-side endpoint support. If you still want to keep an IIS server in the mid-tier though, you'll have to continue to use the SQLISAPI listener included with SQLXML 3.0 against your SQL Server 2000 or 2005 backend. You can also call SQLXML from your applications since SQLXML supports a managed object model, as you'll see later in this chapter in the section "Programming SQLXML from .NET and COM."

To configure our server, we'll just issue a CREATE ENDPOINT command and allow our server to listen for T-SQL batches. We'll create a virtual directory called pubs, but remember that this virtual directory will not show up in IIS's virtual directories. Be careful about this, since you may have an endpoint that tries to use the same port as an existing IIS endpoint. You cannot have both SQL and IIS listen on the same ports. The code for this is shown here:

```
CREATE ENDPOINT pubs
  STATE = STARTED
  AS HTTP (
    path='/pubs',
    AUTHENTICATION=(INTEGRATED),
    PORTS = (CLEAR)
  )
  FOR SOAP(
    WSDL = DEFAULT,
    BATCHES=ENABLED
  )
GO
```

OPENXML

Rather than having to parse XML yourself into rows by loading and parsing the XML and the iterating through the XML and generating T-SQL commands, you can use the OPENXML function. The syntax for OPENXML may look difficult at first, but once you try it, you'll see that it is very approachable:

```
OPENXML(idoc int [in],rowpattern nvarchar[in],[flags byte[in]])
[WITH (SchemaDeclaration | TableName)]
```

The first parameter is the integer handle to your XML document. A *handle* is just a unique integer identifier for your document. You can retrieve this using the built-in sp_xml_preparedocument stored procedure. When you pass in your XML document as a parameter, the sp_xml_preparedocument procedure parses it and returns the integer you need to pass to the OPENXML function. The XML document you pass can be text-based, or you can pass the new XML datatype in SQL Server 2005. You can optionally pass the namespace Uniform Resource Identifier (URI) you want for your XPath expressions. Your usage of this parameter will depend on your usage of namespaces in your XML. If you use no namespaces, you won't use this parameter in most of your calls to the stored procedure.

Conversely, the sp_xml_removedocument built-in procedure takes the integer handle to your XML document and removes the internal in-memory representation of your XML document that you created with sp_xml_preparedocument. You should call this stored procedure after you are done with your XML document. If you forget, SQL Server will destroy the in-memory representation once the session that created it disconnects. However, it isn't good practice to rely on this behavior.

The second parameter to OPENXML is the XPath expression that you want to use to parse out the rows. This can be just a simple expression all the way up to a very complex expression.

The third parameter is optional and allows you to switch from attribute- to element-centric mapping. By default, OPENXML uses attribute-centric mapping, which is a value of 0. You'll want to switch this to element-centric mapping if your XML is element centric by specifying a value of 2. By passing a value of 1, you are telling SQL Server to use attribute-centric mappings by default, and for any unprocessed columns, element-centric mapping is used. Finally, a value of 8 specifies to not copy overflow text to the @mp:xmltext metaproperty, which you'll learn about in a minute.

Finally, we have the WITH clause. This clause allows you to specify a schema definition for your newly created rowsets, or you can specify a table if you know your XML will map to the schema in a table that already exists. The schema definition uses this format:

```
ColName ColType [ColPattern | MetaProperty][, ColName ColType
[ColPattern | MetaProperty]...]
```

The parts of this definition are as follows:

- The column name is the name of the column in the table.

- The column type is the SQL datatype you want for the column. If the XML type and the SQL type differ, coercion occurs, which means that SQL Server will try to find the closest native type that can store your data.

- The column pattern is an XPath expression that tells OPENXML how to map the XML value to your SQL column. For example, you may want to explicitly tell OPENXML to use a particular attribute or element of the parent node for a certain column value. If you don't specify the column pattern, the default mapping you specified, attribute or element, will be used.

- The MetaProperty value is the metaproperty attribute that you want to put into the column. *Metaproperty* attributes in an XML document are attributes that describe the properties of an XML item (element, attribute, or any other DOM node). These attributes don't physically exist in the XML document text; however, OPENXML provides these metaproperties for all the XML items. These metaproperties allow you to extract information, such as local positioning and namespace information of XML nodes, which provide more details than are visible in the textual representation. You can map these metaproperties to the rowset columns in an OPENXML statement using the ColPattern parameter.

Table 7-3 shows the different values for the Metaproperty attribute.

Table 7-3. *Metaproperty Values*

Name	Description
@mp:id	A unique identifier for the DOM node, which is valid as long as the document isn't reparsed.
@mp:localname	The local part of the name of a node. You could put this into a column if you need to get the node name at a later point.
@mp:namespaceuri	Returns the namespace URI of the current element.
@mp:prefix	Returns the namespace prefix of the current element.
@mp:prev	Returns the previous sibling's node ID.
@mp:xmltext	Returns a text version of the XML. This is useful for overflow processing, or for handling unknown situations in your database code. For example, if the XML changes, you don't have to change your database code to handle the change if you use this Metaproperty as an overflow.
@mp:parentid	Returns back the ID of the parent node.
@mp:parentlocalname	Returns back the local name of the parent node.
@mp:parentnamespaceuri	Returns back the namespace URI of the parent.
@mp:parentprefix	Returns back the parent prefix.

Let's now take a look at a couple of examples that use the OPENXML function. The XML document that we will be using is quite simple:

```
<ROOT>
  <authors>
    <au_id>172-32-1176</au_id>
    <au_lname>White</au_lname>
    <au_fname>Johnson</au_fname>
    <phone>408 496-7223</phone>
    <address>10932 Bigge Rd.</address>
    <city>Menlo Park</city>
    <state>CA</state>
    <zip>94025</zip>
    <contract>1</contract>
  </authors>
  <authors>
    <au_id>213-46-8915</au_id>
    <au_lname>Green</au_lname>
    <au_fname>Marjorie</au_fname>
    <phone>415 986-7020</phone>
    <address>309 63rd St. #411</address>
    <city>Oakland</city>
    <state>CA</state>
    <zip>94618</zip>
    <contract>1</contract>
  </authors>
</ROOT>. . .
```

■**Note** You may notice our dirty little trick in the XML. No one likes to generate sample XML data so we just used the FOR XML function, which we'll discuss shortly, on the authors table in the pubs database. The only change we made, since we're more element than attribute people, was to have FOR XML spit out our data using element centric formatting.

In this example, we're just going to take our XML document and store it in a relational table. The easiest thing since we're using pubs already is to take the data and store it in a new authorsXML table in pubs. We'll simply accept the defaults and not fill in any optional parameters for the OPENXML function. The code will take our XML document using element-centric mapping, parse the document, and place it into the authorsXML table.

```
CREATE TABLE [authorsXML] (
    [title] [varchar] (20),
    [au_id] [varchar] (11)
) ON [PRIMARY]
GO
DECLARE @idoc int
DECLARE @doc varchar(1000)
SET @doc ='
<ROOT>
  <authors><au_id>172-32-1176</au_id><au_lname>White</au_lname>
<au_fname>Johnson</au_fname><title>book1</title>
<phone>408 496-7223</phone><address>10932 Bigge Rd.</address>
<city>Menlo Park</city><state>CA</state><zip>94025</zip>
<contract>1</contract></authors>
```

```
    <authors><au_id>213-46-8915</au_id><au_lname>Green</au_lname>
<au_fname>Marjorie</au_fname><title>book2</title>
<phone>415 986-7020</phone><address>309 63rd St.
#411</address><city>Oakland</city><state>CA</state>
<zip>94618</zip>
<contract>1</contract></authors>
</ROOT>'
--Create an internal representation of the XML document.
EXEC sp_xml_preparedocument @idoc OUTPUT, @doc
-- Execute a SELECT statement that uses the OPENXML rowset provider.
INSERT AuthorsXML (title, au_id)
SELECT    title, au_id
FROM      OPENXML (@idoc, '/ROOT/authors',2)
            WITH (au_id    varchar(11),
                  au_lname varchar(40),
                  au_fname varchar(20),
                  title varchar(20),
                  phone    char(12)
              )

EXEC sp_xml_removedocument @idoc
```

If we tweaked the preceding statement and removed the INSERT and instead just did a SELECT on our data such as SELECT *, SQL Server would return back our parsed XML as a rowset.

The results would look as follows:

au_id	au_lname	au_fname	phone
172-32-1176	White	Johnson	408 496-7223
213-46-8915	Green	Marjorie	415 986-7020

Now, you may realize that we're leaving some XML unstored such as the address, city, state, zip, and contract values. If we wanted to, we could capture the XML document by creating another column and using the @mp:xmltext command in our schema definition such as

```
catchall nvarchar(1000) '@mp:xmltext'
```

The final OPENXML example shows how you can take OPENXML output and write it into a table. We did this in the last example, except that this time, the sample also demonstrates how to navigate an XML document using an XPath expression in OPENXML. Since OPENXML returns a relational rowset, you could actually join the results with another table and then store this rowset in your table. After calling OPENXML, your XML data can be treated just like any other relational data. Here, we'll use the returned XML rowsets to join data with the publishers table to return back only authors who have the same city as a publisher.

```
DECLARE @idoc int
DECLARE @doc varchar(1000)
SET @doc ='
<ROOT>
  <authors><au_id>172-32-1176</au_id><au_lname>White</au_lname>
<au_fname>Johnson</au_fname>
<phone>408 496-7223</phone><address>10932 Bigge Rd.</address>
<city>Menlo Park</city><state>CA</state><zip>94025</zip>
<contract>1</contract>
```

```
    <books>
      <title>My book1</title>
      <title>My book2</title>
    </books>
  </authors>
  <authors><au_id>213-46-8915</au_id><au_lname>Green</au_lname>
<au_fname>Marjorie</au_fname>
<phone>415 986-7020</phone><address>309 63rd St. #411</address>
<city>Boston</city><state>MA</state>
<zip>94618</zip><contract>1</contract>
    <books>
      <title>My book3</title>
      <title>My book4</title>
    </books>
  </authors>
</ROOT>'
--Create an internal representation of the XML document.
EXEC sp_xml_preparedocument @idoc OUTPUT, @doc

SELECT    a.title, a.au_lname, p.pub_name, p.city
FROM      OPENXML (@idoc, '/ROOT/authors/books',2)
          WITH (title    varchar(20) './title',
                au_id    varchar(11) '../au_id',
                au_lname varchar(40) '../au_lname',
                au_fname varchar(20) '../au_fname',
                phone    char(12)    '../phone',
                city varchar(20) '../city'
               ) AS a
INNER JOIN publishers AS p
  ON a.city = p.city
EXEC sp_xml_removedocument @idoc
```

The results should look as follows:

title	au_lname	pub_name	city
My Book3	Green	New Moon Books	Boston

The best way to use OPENXML is to use it in a stored procedure, especially if you are taking your XML from the mid-tier and putting it into the database. Rather than parsing in the mid-tier, you can send your XML as text to the stored procedure and have the server parse and store it in a single operation. This provides a lot better performance and a lot less wire traffic than parsing the XML in the mid-tier and sending T-SQL commands to the server to store the data.

If you are going to use your newly parsed XML over-and-over again, then, rather than calling OPENXML multiple times, just store the results in a table variable. This will speed up the processing and free up resources on the server for other work. The sample stored procedure that follows implements OPENXML. Notice the use of the new nvarchar(max) datatype. In SQL Server 2000, you would have to use a text datatype. For all new development, use the nvarchar(max) datatype since the text datatype may be removed in future versions.

```
CREATE PROCEDURE update_authors_OPENXML (
    @doc nvarchar(max))

AS
SET NOCOUNT ON
-- document handle:
DECLARE @idoc INT

--Create an internal representation of the XML document.
EXEC sp_xml_preparedocument @idoc OUTPUT, @doc
-- Execute a SELECT statement that uses the OPENXML rowset provider.
INSERT AuthorsXML (title, au_id)
SELECT    title, au_id
FROM      OPENXML (@idoc, '/ROOT/authors/books',2)
          WITH (title    varchar(20) './title',
                au_id    varchar(11) '../au_id',
                au_lname varchar(40) '../au_lname',
                au_fname varchar(20) '../au_fname',
                phone    char(12)    '../phone'
                )

--Execute SPROC

EXEC update_authors_OPENXML '
<ROOT>
  <authors><au_id>172-32-1176</au_id><au_lname>White</au_lname>
<au_fname>Johnson</au_fname><phone>408 496-7223</phone>
<address>10932 Bigge Rd.</address><city>Menlo
Park</city><state>CA</state><zip>94025</zip><contract>1</contract>
    <books>
      <title>My book1</title>
      <title>My book2</title>
    </books>
  </authors>
  <authors><au_id>213-46-8915</au_id><au_lname>Green</au_lname>
<au_fname>Marjorie</au_fname><phone>415 986-7020</phone>
<address>309 63rd St. #411</address><city>Oakland</city><state>CA</state>
<zip>94618</zip><contract>1</contract>
    <books>
      <title>My book3</title>
      <title>My book4</title>
    </books>
  </authors>
</ROOT>'
```

SQLXML: XML Views Using Annotated XML Schemas

XML schemas define the structure of an XML document, in the same way that a relational schema defines the structure of a relational database. With schemas, you can define what makes an XML document legal according to your specifications. For example, you can define the elements, attributes, hierarchy of elements, order of elements, datatypes of your elements and attributes, and any default values for your elements and attributes. Schemas are not required in your XML documents but are recommended, especially if you'll be sharing your XML data with other applications that may not understand your XML data or how to correctly create that XML data without understanding your schema.

The standard for schemas is XML Schema Definition (XSD). You may have heard of older schema technologies from Microsoft called XML Data Reduced (XDR). This was a precursor to XSD and shouldn't be used anymore in your applications.

With SQL Server, you can create an XML schema that maps to your relational structure using some special schema markup. This is useful when you want to create an XML view of your underlying relational data. This view not only allows you to query your relational data into XML, but you can also persist changes using updategrams and SQLXML bulkload. It takes some work to create the annotated schema, but if you are going to be working extensively with XML, the extra work is worth the effort. Plus, you'll want to use annotated schemas with updategrams, which you'll learn about in the section "SQLXML Updategrams" later in this chapter.

■**Note** This chapter will assume you have some knowledge of XML schemas. If you don't, you should read the W3C primer on XML schemas at `http://www.w3.org/TR/xmlschema-0/`.

Visual Studio includes a very capable XML schema editor so that you don't have to generate XML schemas by hand. Following is a typical XML schema for the authors XML that we were using previously. As you can see, the XML schema is an XML document. The system knows it is a schema document because we declare a namespace, xs, that uses the XSD namespace. This namespace is a reference to the W3C XSD namespace, which is `http://www.w3.org/2001/XMLSchema`. This reference is aliased to xs and then all elements use this alias as their prefix inside of the schema.

Also, notice how the schema declares an element called AuthorsXMLNew that contains the rest of your XML data. Then, there is a complex type that declares a sequence of XML elements. These elements include the ID, first name, last name, phone, etc., of the authors. Notice how the elements also declare a type. Schemas can define datatypes for your elements and attributes so you can see that we declare some strings, an unsigned int and an unsigned byte. You can declare other datatypes beyond what this schema has such as dates, Booleans, binary, and other types.

```xml
<?xml version="1.0" encoding="utf-8"?>
<xs:schema attributeFormDefault="unqualified"
elementFormDefault="qualified"
xmlns:xs="http://www.w3.org/2001/XMLSchema">
  <xs:element name="AuthorsXMLNew">
    <xs:complexType>
      <xs:sequence>
        <xs:element name="au_id" type="xs:string" />
        <xs:element name="au_lname" type="xs:string" />
        <xs:element name="au_fname" type="xs:string" />
        <xs:element name="phone" type="xs:string" />
        <xs:element name="address" type="xs:string" />
        <xs:element name="city" type="xs:string" />
        <xs:element name="state" type="xs:string" />
        <xs:element name="zip" type="xs:unsignedInt" />
        <xs:element name="contract" type="xs:unsignedByte" />
      </xs:sequence>
    </xs:complexType>
  </xs:element>
</xs:schema>
```

Now that we have a base schema, if we want to make this annotated schema for use with SQLXML, we need to make some changes. First, we need to add a reference to the XML schema mapping. To do this, we need to modify our XML schema by first adding the namespace for SQL Server's schema mapping, which is `urn:schemas-microsoft-com:mapping-schema`. This schema allows us to map our XML schema to our relational database schema. We'll alias this namespace with `sql` so that we can use the prefix `sql:` when we refer to it. Therefore, if we wanted to modify the preceding schema to support SQL Server mapping, we would use this new schema:

```
<?xml version="1.0" encoding="utf-8" ?>
<xs:schema id="XMLSchema1" targetNamespace="http://tempuri.org/XMLSchema1.xsd"
  elementFormDefault="qualified"
  xmlns="http://tempuri.org/XMLSchema1.xsd"
  xmlns:mstns="http://tempuri.org/XMLSchema1.xsd"
  xmlns:xs="http://www.w3.org/2001/XMLSchema"
  xmlns:sql="urn:schemas-microsoft-com:mapping-schema">
. . .
```

You'll also see the use of the `urn:schemas-microsoft-com:xml-sql` namespace in documents. This namespace provides access to SQLXML functionality that can be used in templates or XPath queries.

Default Mapping

You may notice that the preceding schema just adds the namespace for the mapping. The schema isn't listed since SQL Server supports default mapping between your relational schema and your XML schema. For example, the `authors` complex type would be automatically mapped to the `authors` table. The `au_id` string would automatically map to the `au_id` column and so on.

Explicit Mapping

You can also explicitly map between your schema and your SQL datatypes. For very simple applications, you can use the default mapping. In most cases, you'll use explicit mapping since your XML and relational schemas may be different or you'll want more control over how the mapping is performed or the datatypes used. You use the `sql:relation` markup, which is part of the SQLXML mapping schema, to specify a mapping between an XML item and a SQL table. For columns, you use the `sql:field` markup. We can also include a `sql:datatype` to explicitly map our XML datatype to a SQL datatype so that implicit conversion doesn't happen. Therefore, if we were to add these markups rather than using the default mapping for our schema, our schema would change to look like the following code:

```
<?xml version="1.0" encoding="utf-8"?>
<xs:schema attributeFormDefault="unqualified"
elementFormDefault="qualified"
xmlns:xs="http://www.w3.org/2001/XMLSchema"
xmlns:sql="urn:schemas-microsoft-com:mapping-schema">
  <xs:element name="AuthorsXMLNew" sql:relation="AuthorsXMLNew">
    <xs:complexType>
      <xs:sequence>
        <xs:element name="au_id" type="xs:string" sql:field="au_id" />
        <xs:element name="au_lname" type="xs:string" sql:field="au_lname" />
        <xs:element name="au_fname" type="xs:string" sql:field="au_fname" />
        <xs:element name="phone" type="xs:string" sql:field="phone" />
        <xs:element name="address" type="xs:string" sql:field="address" />
        <xs:element name="city" type="xs:string" sql:field="city" />
```

```
        <xs:element name="state" type="xs:string" sql:field="state" />
        <xs:element name="zip" type="xs:unsignedInt" sql:field="zip" />
        <xs:element name="contract" type="xs:unsignedByte"
                sql:field="contract" sql:datatype="bit" />
      </xs:sequence>
    </xs:complexType>
  </xs:element>
</xs:schema>
```

Relationships

Since in a relational database you can relate data by keys, we can use annotated schemas to describe those relationships in our XML.

However, annotated schema will make those relationships hierarchical through the use of the `sql:relationship` mapping. You can think of this as joining a table. The relationship mapping has a parent element that specifies the parent relation or table. It also has a parent-key element, which specifies the key to use, and this key can encompass multiple columns. Also, you have child and child-key elements to perform the same functionality for the child as the other elements do for the parent.

There is also inverse functionality, so you can flip this relationship. If for some reason your mapping is different from the primary key/foreign key relationship in the underlying table, the inverse attribute will flip this relationship. This is the case with updategrams, which you'll learn about in the section "SQLXML Updategrams" later in this chapter. You'll only use this attribute with updategrams.

Imagine we had our authors and the authors were related to books in our relational schema through the use of an author ID. We would change our schema mapping to understand that relationship by using the following XML schema. Notice how the relationship mapping is in a special section of our XSD schema.

```
<?xml version="1.0" encoding="utf-8" ?>
<xs:schema id="XMLSchema1" targetNamespace="http://tempuri.org/XMLSchema1.xsd"
  elementFormDefault="qualified"
  xmlns="http://tempuri.org/XMLSchema1.xsd"
  xmlns:mstns="http://tempuri.org/XMLSchema1.xsd"
  xmlns:sql="urn:schemas-microsoft-com:mapping-schema"
  xmlns:xs="http://www.w3.org/2001/XMLSchema">
  <xs:element name="Root">
    <xs:complexType>
      <xs:sequence>
        <xs:element name="Authors" sql:relation="Authors">
          <xs:complexType>
            <xs:sequence>
            <xsd:element name="Books" sql:relation="Books">
              <xsd:annotation>
                <xsd:appinfo>
                  <sql:relationship name="BookAuthors"
                          parent="Authors"
                          parent-key="au_id"
                          child="Books"
                          child-key="bk_id" />
                </xsd:appinfo>
              </xsd:annotation>
```

```
                <xsd:complexType>
                    <xsd:attribute name="bk_id" type="xsd:integer" />
                    <xsd:attribute name="au_id" type="xsd:string" />
                </xsd:complexType>
                </xsd:element>
                  <xs:element name="au_id" type="xs:string"
                     sql:field="au_id"></xs:element>
                  <xs:element name="au_lname" type="xs:string"
                      sql:field="au_lname"></xs:element>
                  <xs:element name="au_fname" type="xs:string"
                       sql:field="au_fname"></xs:element>
. . .
                  <xs:element name="contract" type="xs:boolean"
                      sql:field="contract"
                      sql:datatype="bit"></xs:element>
              </xs:sequence>
            </xs:complexType>
          </xs:element>
        </xs:sequence>
      </xs:complexType>
    </xs:element>
</xs:schema>
```

Key Column Mapping Using sql:key-fields

Now that you've seen how to build relationships, you also need to look at how to make SQL Server nest your XML data correctly. For nesting to correctly occur, you'll want to specify the key columns used in your table that make the most sense when creating XML hierarchies. To give SQL hints on the right ordering, use the sql:key-fields mapping, which tells SQL which columns contain key values. The sample that follows lets SQL know that the au_id column is a key column:

```
<?xml version="1.0" encoding="utf-8" ?>
<xs:schema id="XMLSchema1" targetNamespace="http://tempuri.org/XMLSchema1.xsd"
  elementFormDefault="qualified"
  xmlns="http://tempuri.org/XMLSchema1.xsd"
  xmlns:mstns="http://tempuri.org/XMLSchema1.xsd"
  xmlns:xs="http://www.w3.org/2001/XMLSchema">
  <xs:element name="Root">
      <xs:complexType>
          <xs:sequence>
              <xs:element name="Authors" sql:relation="Authors"
                 sql:key-fields="au_id">
. . .
```

Excluding Data from the XML Result Using sql:mapped

Using the sql:mapped syntax, you can specify whether to map an element or attribute in your XSD schema to a database object. If you don't want to have the default mapping occur and you don't want to have the XML appear in your results, you should use the sql:mapped attribute. There may be times when there is extraneous XML that you don't want to appear in your table; for example, if you don't control the XML schema and want to omit the data from your table since a column for the data doesn't exist in the table. This attribute has a Boolean value with true meaning that mapping should occur and false meaning that mapping shouldn't occur.

Creating a Constant Element

If you want an element to be constant in your XML document even if there is no mapping to the underlying database, you should use the sql:is-constant mapping. This mapping is Boolean and a value of true makes the element always appear in your XML document. This mapping is very useful for creating a root element for your XML. An example of using this mapping is as follows:

```
<?xml version="1.0" encoding="utf-8" ?>
<xs:schema id="XMLSchema1"
  targetNamespace="http://tempuri.org/XMLSchema1.xsd" . . .>
  <xs:element name="Root" sql:is-constant="true">
. . .
```

Limiting Values by Using a Filter

You may want to filter the results returned to your XML document by values from your database. The sql:limit-field and sql:limit-value mappings let you do this by allowing you to specify a filter column and the value to limit that column by. You don't have to specify the limit value if you don't want to since SQL Server will default this to null. You can also have multiple limiting values for multiple mappings. The shortened example that follows shows a schema that limits authors who live in Boston:

```
<?xml version="1.0" encoding="utf-8" ?>
<xs:schema id="XMLSchema1"
  targetNamespace="http://tempuri.org/XMLSchema1.xsd" . . .>
  <xs:element name="Root" sql:is-constant="true">
. . .
          <xs:element name="Authors"
               sql:relation="Authors"
               sql:limit-field="city"
               sql:limit-value="Boston">
. . .
```

Other Features in Schema Mapping

The majority of your mapped schemas will use the preceding mappings. For the rest of the mapping technologies, see Table 7-4, a short list that describes the features. To see annotated schemas in action, take a look at the integrated sample at the end of this chapter.

Table 7-4. *Other Schema Mapping Features*

Name	Description
sql:encode	Specifies whether to return back a URL or binary data for a BLOB datatype. Specifying the value URL returns a URL, and specifying the value default returns back the data in a base-64 encoded format.
sql:identity	Allows you to specify a SQL identity column mapping. You can specify a value of ignore, which will allow SQL Server to generate the identity value based on the settings in the relational schema, or you can specify useValue, which will use a different value. Normally, you'll set this to ignore unless you are using updategrams.

Table 7-4. *Other Schema Mapping Features (Continued)*

Name	Description
sql:max-depth	Allows you to specify the depth of recursion to perform in a parent and child relationship. You can specify a number between 1 and 50. An example of using this would be generating an organizational structure where employees work for employees, and you can to go through and generate the hierarchy.
sql:overflow-field	Allows you to specify the database column that will contain any over-flow information. If you have XML data that you haven't mapped into your relational database, this data will go into the overflow column. You specify the column name as the value for this mapping.
sql:use-cdata	Allows you to specify whether the data returned by SQL Server should be wrapped in a CDATA section, which will be treated by XML parsers as plain text. Specify a 1 as the value to turn on this feature.

SQLXML Updategrams

So far, you've seen how to shred data using OPENXML and how to get data out of SQL Server using an annotated schema. We needed to discuss annotated schemas before we talk about XML update-grams, since updategrams build upon the annotated schema concept. Updategrams allow you to change data in SQL Server using an XML format. Rather than writing T-SQL, you specify your changes to your data using before-and-after images specified in an XML format. You can execute these updategrams from ADO or ADO.NET as you'll see in the full sample at the end of this chapter.

The first step towards understanding XML updategrams is to understand the namespace they use, namely urn:schemas-microsoft-com:xml-updategram. This namespace is usually abbreviated to updg as part of your namespace declaration.

Every updategram must contain at least one sync element, which is an XML element that contains the data you want to change in the form of before and after elements. You can have multiple sync elements, and each element is considered a transaction, which means that everything in that sync block is either completely committed or entirely rolled back. The before element contains the data as it was before the change. You'll want to specify a key so that SQL Server can find the data that you want to change. You can only modify one row in your before element.

The after element is the changed data. You can imagine that an insertion will have an after but no before. On the other hand, a delete will have a before but no after. Finally, an update will have both a before and an after. The following is an updategram in its simplest form:

```
<ROOT xmlns:updg="urn:schemas-microsoft-com:xml-updategram">
  <updg:sync [mapping-schema= "AnnotatedSchemaFile.xml"] >
    <updg:before>
      ...
    </updg:before>
    <updg:after>
      ...
    </updg:after>
  </updg:sync>
</ROOT>
```

You'll notice that you can optionally specify an annotated schema file that will map explicitly the elements in your updategram to columns in your tables. If you don't specify an annotated schema file, SQL Server will use default mapping, as you saw in the annotated schema mapping section. It is also important to note that you can mix and match element- or attribute-based mapping. However, for the sake of clarity, our recommendation is to select one style or the other.

To specify a null value with an updategram, you'll use the sync element's nullvalue attribute to specify the placeholder for the null. For example, if you wanted the value of "nothing" to be null, you would use the following updategram, which uses attribute-based syntax:

```
<?xml version="1.0"?>
<authorsupdate xmlns:updg=
    "urn:schemas-microsoft-com:xml-updategram">
  <updg:sync updg:nullvalue="nothing">
    <updg:before>
      <Authors au_id="172-32-1176"/>
    </updg:before>
    <updg:after>
      <Authors state="nothing" phone="nothing"/>
    </updg:after>
  </updg:sync>
</authorsupdate>
```

You can also use parameters with your updategrams by specifying $parametername. For example, if you wanted to create a parameter for the selection of the author, you would use the following updategram:

```
<?xml version="1.0"?>
<authorsupdate xmlns:updg=
    "urn:schemas-microsoft-com:xml-updategram">
  <updg:sync updg:nullvalue="nothing">
    <updg:before>
      <Authors au_id="$AuthorID"/>
    </updg:before>
    <updg:after>
      <Authors state="nothing" phone="nothing"/>
    </updg:after>
  </updg:sync>
</authorsupdate>
```

If you want to use identity columns and you want to pass the identity values between tables, you can use the at-identity attribute. This attribute is a placeholder that you can include, and SQL Server will provide the right value for it when processed. If you want to pass the identity value back to the client, you can use the returnid attribute. SQL Server will then return an XML document containing the identity value after the updategram is applied successfully to the server.

An example will make this all clearer. If we wanted to insert a new author into our authors table, delete an existing author and change the values for yet another author, we would use the following updategram against our authors table. The next section shows how to program in .NET using the SQLXML classes to execute this code.

```
<?xml version="1.0"?>
<authorsupdate xmlns:updg=
    "urn:schemas-microsoft-com:xml-updategram">
  <updg:sync updg:nullvalue="nothing">
    <updg:before>
    </updg:before>
    <updg:after>
      <Authors au_id="123-22-1232" au_fname="Tom" state="WA" phone="425-882-8080"/>
    </updg:after>
```

```
    <updg:before>
        <Authors au_id="267-41-2394"/>
    </updg:before>
    <updg:after>
    </updg:after>
    <updg:before>
        <Authors au_id="238-95-7766"/>
    </updg:before>
    <updg:after>
      <Authors city="Oakland" phone="212-555-1212"/>
    </updg:after>
  </updg:sync>
</authorsupdate>
```

XML BulkLoad

If you want to load a large set of XML data into SQL Server, you'll want to use the XML `BulkLoad` capabilities of SQLXML. Don't—we repeat *don't*—use updategrams or OPENXML. You'll find performance lacking with these two components for loading large amounts of XML data. Of course, you may be wondering what makes up a large amount of XML data. Well, it depends on a number of factors such as size and complexity of your XML. You could be loading hundreds of small XML files, or you could be loading one big XML file. If you have fast processors, lots of memory, and fast disks on your server, you could possibly get away with using OPENXML. Our recommendation is to run a test on your systems to see which method performs acceptably to the data volume that you intend to run.

XML `BulkLoad` is an object that you call as part of the SQLXML object model that in turn calls the bulkload capabilities of SQL Server to load your data from an XML source into SQL Server. Our recommendation is to run a trace while you're bulkloading your XML data, and you'll see the bulkload operations appear as part of that. This will give you insight into the commands that `BulkLoad` is running on your behalf and will allow you to troubleshoot any errors that occur or misshapen data that is imported.

XML `BulkLoad` leverages the mapping schema technology that we've been talking about in this chapter. The mapping schema will tell the `BulkLoad` component where to place your XML data in the database. The object model `FOR XML BulkLoad` is very straightforward. There is one method called `Execute` and a lot of properties that allow you to configure how to handle the bulkload. The `Execute` method takes two parameters. The first is the path to the schema mapping file. The second optional parameter is a path or stream to the XML file you want to import.

Now that we've discussed how to execute the bulkload, first take a look at Table 7-5, which presents the different properties, and then we'll discuss some of the more interesting properties that we recommend you should set.

Table 7-5. *Bulkload Properties*

Name	Description
BulkLoad	A Boolean that specifies whether the bulkload of the data should be performed. If you only want to generate the schema in the database and not load the data, set this property to `false`. The default value is `true`.
CheckConstraints	A Boolean that defaults to `false` and specifies whether to check constraints such as primary key and foreign key constraints. If there is a constraint violation, an error will occur.

Table 7-5. *Bulkload Properties*

Name	Description
ConnectionCommand	Allows you to specify a Command object rather than a ConnectionString with the ConnectionString property. You must set the Transaction property to true if you specify a Command object.
ConnectionString	A string value that allows you to pass a connection string to your SQL Server system.
ErrorLogFile	A string value that allows you to specify a path to where you want to store errors from the bulkload. There will be a record per error with the most recent error at the beginning.
FireTriggers	A Boolean that specifies whether to fire triggers on the target tables when inserting data. The default value is false.
ForceTableLock	A Boolean that specifies whether to lock the entire table during the bulkload operation. The default value is false.
IgnoreDuplicateKeys	A Boolean that specifies whether to ignore when duplicate keys are being inserted into the table. The default value is false, which ignores duplicate keys. If you set this property to true and there is a duplicate key, the record will not be inserted into the table.
KeepIdentity	A Boolean property that specifies whether to keep the identity values from your XML or have SQL Server autogenerate the identity values. By default, this property is true, so BulkLoad keeps your identity values from your XML.
KeepNulls	A Boolean, with a default of true, that specifies whether to place null values in columns where there is no value specified or whether you don't want to use the default value specified for the column.
SchemaGen	A Boolean property, with a default of false, that specifies whether to create the underlying relational tables before performing the bulkload operations. You'll learn more about this property in the upcoming text.
SGDropTables	A Boolean, with a default of false, that specifies whether to drop and re-create tables or to retain existing tables. The property is used with the SchemaGen property. A true value drops and re-creates the tables.
SGUseID	A Boolean, with a default of false, that specifies whether to use an ID from the mapping schema to create the primary key in the relational table. If you set this property to true, you need to set one of your column's datatypes in your mapping schema to be dt:type="id".
TempFilePath	A string that specifies the path to create temp files. If you leave this property blank, temp files will be created wherever the TEMP environment variable points to. This property has no meaning unless you set the next property, Transaction, to true.
Transaction	A Boolean, false by default, that specifies whether a single transaction should be used when bulkloading. If you set this property to true, all your operations are cached in a temporary file before being loaded into SQL Server. If there is an error, the entire bulkload doesn't occur. Please note that the Transaction property cannot be set to true if you are loading binary data.
XMLFragment	This Boolean property specifies whether the XML you are loading is a fragment or not. A *fragment* is an XML document without a root node. Set this to true if your XML is a fragment and leave it alone, since it defaults to false if your XML isn't a fragment.

The first property that you should understand is the Transaction Boolean property. Normally, you want to leave this property false to make the load nontransacted. This will increase your performance at the cost of not being able to roll back if there is a failure.

The next property is the XMLFragment Boolean property. If you set this to true, BulkLoad allows XML fragments, which are XML documents with no root element.

If you are working with constraints and you want those constraints enforced as part of your BulkLoad, you'll want to set the CheckConstraints property to true. By default, BulkLoad turns off constraint checking, which improves performance. Regardless of whether you set this to true or false, you'll want to place primary keys ahead of a table with a foreign key in your mapping schema.

If you want to ignore duplicate keys, you need to set the IgnoreDuplicateKeys Boolean property to true. This is useful if you get data feeds where the person providing the data feed may not know what data is in your database and you don't want the BulkLoad to fail because of duplicate keys. BulkLoad will not commit the row with the duplicate key, but instead just jump over that row in processing.

Many database designers use identity columns to guarantee uniqueness of keys in the table. Sometimes the XML you are loading has an identity-like element that you may want to use rather than having SQL Server generate a value using its own algorithm. To do this, set the KeepIdentity property to true. This is the default value for this property. One thing to remember is that it is a global value, so you cannot have SQL Server generate some identities and have BulkLoad pull from the XML for others.

The KeepNulls property defaults to false with BulkLoad. BulkLoad will not automatically insert null as the value for any column that is missing a corresponding attribute or element in the XML document. If you set this property to true, you have to be careful here since BulkLoad will fail if you don't allow nulls in those columns. BulkLoad will not assign the default value for a column, if one is specified in SQL Server, if the property is true.

One interesting BulkLoad property is ForceTableLock, which locks the table as BulkLoad loads its data. This will speed performance of the load at the cost of locking other users out of the table. The default value is false, so BulkLoad acquires a table lock each time it inserts a record into the table.

If your target tables don't already exist, BulkLoad can create the tables for you. You need to set the SchemaGen property to true to have BulkLoad perform this functionality. BulkLoad will take the datatypes from your schema mapping and autogenerate the correct database schema based on those datatypes. If a table or column already exists with the same name and you want to drop and re-create them, set the SGDropTables property to true.

The next section shows using BulkLoad from a managed environment. BulkLoad supports both COM and .NET so you can program from both environments with this technology.

Getting XML Out of the Database: FOR XML

FOR XML was added in SQL Server 2000 to allow you to get your relational data back in an XML format without having to store that relational data as XML. Given that many developers and DBAs want to keep their relational data as relational but transfer that relational data to other systems as XML due to XML's flexibility and universal support, FOR XML is a very useful addition to SQL Server. In this section, we'll look at using FOR XML both from the server-side and the client-side to understand how to transform your relational data to an XML format.

FOR XML (Server-Side)

You probably use FOR XML today, as it's the easiest way to take data in a relational format from SQL Server and put it into an XML format. A simplified form of the FOR XML query extension syntax is the following:

```
SELECT column list
FROM table list
WHERE filter criteria
FOR XML RAW | AUTO | EXPLICIT [, XMLDATA] [, ELEMENTS]
    [, BINARY BASE64]
```

At the end of this section, we'll focus on how FOR XML has changed in SQL Server 2005, but for this chapter, we'll just take a look at some of the common scenarios where you probably use FOR XML today. The first scenario is using FOR XML in AUTO or RAW mode. Some people use the EXPLICIT mode, but the majority uses the other two modes. The main reason people normally don't use EXPLICIT mode is that the other two meet their needs. The other reason, as you'll see, is EXPLICIT mode is an explicit pain to work with. If you can get away with using the other two modes, we recommend you do that, since you'll find yourself pulling your hair out if you do any complex XML structures with EXPLICIT mode.

RAW Mode

When working in RAW mode, the FOR XML query returns columns as attributes and rows as row elements. An example of FOR XML RAW is shown here:

```
USE pubs
GO
SELECT * FROM Authors FOR XML RAW
```

Truncated Results

```
<row au_id="172-32-1176" au_lname="White" au_fname="Johnson"
phone="408 496-7223" address="10932 Bigge Rd." city="Menlo Park"
state="CA" zip="94025" contract="1"/>
<row au_id="213-46-8915" au_lname="Green" au_fname="Marjorie"
phone="415 986-7020" address="309 63rd St. #411" city="Oakland"
state="CA" zip="94618" contract="1"/>
<row au_id="238-95-7766" au_lname="Carson" au_fname="Cheryl"
phone="415 548-7723" address="589 Darwin Ln." city="Berkeley"
state="CA" zip="94705" contract="1"/>
<row au_id="267-41-2394" au_lname="O&apos;Leary" au_fname="Michael"
phone="408 286-2428" address="22 Cleveland Av. #14" city="San Jose"
state="CA" zip="95128" contract="1"/>
```

As you can see, there is a row element for each row, and each nonnull column has an attribute on the row element. If you are retrieving binary data, you need to specify BINARY BASE64. Also, if you want to retrieve an XML-Data schema with the returned XML, you can specify XMLDATA.

AUTO Mode

When working in AUTO mode, the FOR XML query is the same as RAW mode in that it returns each row as an element with column values as attributes, except the name of the element representing the row is the table name. Therefore, if you run the command shown here, you'll see the following results on the authors table:

```
USE pubs
GO
SELECT * FROM Authors FOR XML AUTO

Truncated Results

<Authors au_id="172-32-1176" au_lname="White" au_fname="Johnson"
phone="408 496-7223" address="10932 Bigge Rd." city="Menlo Park"
state="CA" zip="94025" contract="1"/>
<Authors au_id="213-46-8915" au_lname="Green" au_fname="Marjorie"
phone="415 986-7020" address="309 63rd St. #411" city="Oakland"
state="CA" zip="94618" contract="1"/>
<Authors au_id="238-95-7766" au_lname="Carson" au_fname="Cheryl"
phone="415 548-7723" address="589 Darwin Ln." city="Berkeley"
state="CA" zip="94705" contract="1"/>
<Authors au_id="267-41-2394" au_lname="O&apos;Leary" au_fname="Michael"
phone="408 286-2428" address="22 Cleveland Av. #14" city="San Jose"
state="CA" zip="95128" contract="1"/>
<Authors au_id="274-80-9391" au_lname="Straight" au_fname="Dean"
phone="415 834-2919" address="5420 College Av." city="Oakland"
state="CA" zip="94609" contract="1"/>
<Authors au_id="341-22-1782" au_lname="Smith" au_fname="Meander"
phone="913 843-0462" address="10 Mississippi Dr." city="Lawrence"
state="KS" zip="66044" contract="0"/>
```

The table name is the element for each node with the column values as attributes on that element. The nesting of elements depends on the order in your SELECT clause, so choose your order carefully. Furthermore, you cannot use a GROUP BY, but you can use an ORDER BY in your SELECT statements with FOR XML. The workaround for a GROUP BY is to use a nested SELECT statement to achieve the results you want, but this will have some performance implications. When using joins, you'll find that AUTO will nest the resultset, which is most likely what you want to happen. If you don't want this to happen, you'll have to use the EXPLICIT mode to shape your XML. For example, if we join publishers and titles, and we want all titles nested under their publisher in our XML, we would run the following code:

```
USE pubs
GO
SELECT Publishers.Pub_Name, Titles.Title, Titles.Price
  FROM Titles, Publishers WHERE Publishers.Pub_ID = Titles.Pub_ID
  FOR XML AUTO

Results Truncated

<Publishers Pub_Name="Algodata Infosystems">
  <Titles Title="The Busy Executive&apos;s Database Guide" Price="19.9900"/>
  <Titles Title="Cooking with Computers:
    Surreptitious Balance Sheets"
    Price="11.9500"/>
</Publishers>
<Publishers Pub_Name="New Moon Books">
  <Titles Title="You Can Combat Computer Stress!" Price="2.9900"/>
</Publishers>
<Publishers Pub_Name="Algodata Infosystems">
  <Titles Title="Straight Talk About Computers" Price="19.9900"/>
</Publishers>
```

You can also use the ELEMENTS option with FOR XML AUTO. If you are more of an element than attribute person, you can have AUTO return back element-centric syntax rather than attribute-centric syntax. Personally, we find that element-centric syntax, while making the XML larger in text size because of all the opening and closing tags, results in XML that is easier to read and understand.

Explicit Mode

The last mode is EXPLICIT mode. As the name implies, EXPLICIT mode allows you to completely control the way that your XML is generated. You describe what you want your XML document to look like, and SQL Server fills in that document with the right information. You use a *universal table* to describe your XML document. This table consists of one table column for each value you want to return as well as two additional tags, one that uniquely identifies the tags in your XML and another that identifies your parent-child relationships. The other columns describe your data. An example of a universal table appears in Table 7-6.

Table 7-6. *A Universal Table*

Tag	Parent	Column1's Directive	Column2's Directive
1	Null	Data value	Data value
2	1	Data value	Data value
3	2	Data value	Data value

You use directives to describe how to display your data in the table. Directives are just special commands that you use that SQL Server understands how to parse. The format for these directives is as follows:

Element!Tag!Attribute!Directive

The different pieces of your directive are separated by an exclamation point. So, let's build a simple example table that uses the preceding formatting. Imagine we want to display authors, but make the au_id an attribute on our XML and the rest of our data elements in our output. Well, we can't do that with FOR XML AUTO or RAW, since neither of them can be split between being attribute- or element-centric. Let's see what our query would look like to do this:

```
SELECT 1 as Tag, NULL as Parent,
    au_id as [Authors!1!au_id], au_lname as [Authors!1]
    FROM Authors FOR XML EXPLICIT
```

The first thing you'll notice is that in our column list we have the Tag and Parent columns. We need these columns to identify the tag of the current element, which is an integer from 1 to 255, and also the parent of the current element. In this example, we're not nesting our data, our parent is always null, and our tag is always 1, since we always refer to the same parent. Then, you can see we use the AS clause to rename our data to describe the XML formatting we want to do. The naming for au_id tells SQL Server that we want to use the Authors element, a tag ID of 1, and the name of our attribute. Since we want the other data to be elements, we just rename them to be the element and tag name. At the end, we specify the FOR XML EXPLICIT, since we don't want to get our universal table back, which describes our XML structure, but our actual processed XML structure. The results of this query are shown here:

```
<Authors au_id="409-56-7008">Bennet</Authors>
<Authors au_id="648-92-1872">Blotchet-Halls</Authors>
<Authors au_id="238-95-7766">Carson</Authors>
<Authors au_id="722-51-5454">DeFrance</Authors>
<Authors au_id="712-45-1867">del Castillo</Authors>
<Authors au_id="427-17-2319">Dull</Authors>
. . .
```

You can see that we get the last name returned as element data for our Authors element. We may want to make the last name an element itself nested under the Authors element. To do this, we modify our query slightly to use the element directive as shown here:

```
SELECT 1 as Tag, NULL as Parent, au_id as [Authors!1!au_id],
  au_lname as [Authors!1!au_lname!element]
  FROM Authors FOR XML EXPLICIT
```

Table 7-7 lists all the directives you can use with a description for each.

Table 7-7. *FOR XML EXPLICIT Directives*

Name	Description
cdata	Wraps the data in a CDATA section.
element	Specifies that you want the element entity encoded (for example, > becomes >) and represented as a subelement.
elementxsinil	If you want to generate elements generated for null values, you can specify this directive. This will create an element with an attribute xsi:nil=TRUE.
ID	Allows you to specify an ID for your element. All ID directives require that XMLDATA be requested in your FOR XML clause.
IDREF	Allows attributes to specify ID type attributes to enable intradocument linking.
IDREFS	Similar to IDREF in that it allows you to create intradocument linking, but uses the IDREFS structure rather than IDREF.
hide	Hides the result from the XML rendered.
xml	Same as the element directive, but no encoding takes place.
xmltext	Useful for OPENXML overflow columns in that it retrieves the column and appends it to the document.

Let's look at a more complex example. If we want to return all our authors with their titles and author royalties, we would generate a UNION ALL query to combine together this data from disparate tables, and we would need to nest the results so that our XML hierarchy appears correctly with authors, royalties, and then titles. Before we look at the query and results, we want to give you a couple of tips about troubleshooting FOR XML EXPLICIT queries. First, many people get the error that the parent tag isn't open yet. To troubleshoot your FOR XML EXPLICIT statements, the easiest way to fix problems is to remove the FOR XML EXPLICIT statement and just render the results. This will return the universal table, and you can track down errors. The easiest way we've found to solve the parent tag problem is to make sure to include the tag column in your ORDER BY clause so that you know that no later tags will be rendered before earlier tags, which is the cause of the problem.

OK, let's look at our query for generating the results we wanted earlier. You'll notice that we define a number of parent-child relationships using the Tag and Parent columns. Next, you'll also notice that we use the ORDER BY trick to make sure that the parent tags are in the XML before we process the children tags.

```
SELECT 1 AS Tag, NULL AS Parent,
  Authors.au_fname AS [Authors!1!au_fname!element],
  Authors.au_lname AS [Authors!1!au_lname!element],
  NULL AS [Titleauthor!2!Royaltyper],
  NULL AS [Titles!3!Title!element]
FROM
Authors

UNION ALL

SELECT 2 AS Tag, 1 AS Parent,
  au_fname,
  au_lname,
  royaltyper,
  NULL
FROM Authors INNER JOIN Titleauthor ON
Authors.au_id = Titleauthor.au_id

UNION ALL

SELECT 3 AS Tag, 2 AS Parent,
  au_fname,
  au_lname,
  royaltyper,
  title
FROM Authors INNER JOIN Titleauthor ON Authors.au_id = Titleauthor.au_id
INNER JOIN Titles ON Titles.title_id = Titleauthor.title_id
ORDER BY [Authors!1!au_fname!element], [Authors!1!au_lname!element],
[Titleauthor!2!royaltyper], Tag
FOR XML EXPLICIT
```

Truncated Universal Table

Tag	Parent	Authors!1!au_fname!element	Authors !1 !au_lnameelement
1	NULL	Abraham	Bennet
2	1	Abraham	Bennet
3	2	Abraham	Bennet
1	NULL	Akiko	Yokomoto
2	1	Akiko	Yokomoto
3	2	Akiko	Yokomoto
1	NULL	Albert	Ringer
2	1	Albert	Ringer
3	2	Albert	Ringer
2	1	Albert	Ringer
3	2	Albert	Ringer

Truncated Results

```
<Authors>
  <au_fname>Abraham</au_fname>
  <au_lname>Bennet</au_lname>
  <Titleauthor Royaltyper="60">
    <Titles>
        <Title>The Busy Executive&apos;s Database Guide</Title>
    </Titles>
  </Titleauthor>
</Authors>
<Authors>
  <au_fname>Akiko</au_fname>
  <au_lname>Yokomoto</au_lname>
  <Titleauthor Royaltyper="40">
    <Titles>
        <Title>Sushi, Anyone?</Title>
    </Titles>
  </Titleauthor>
</Authors>
. . .
```

As you've seen, FOR XML EXPLICIT is powerful, yet can be hard to master. If you can get away with using FOR XML AUTO or RAW and can avoid FOR XML EXPLICIT mode, your coding will be much easier. However, for those situations where FOR XML AUTO or RAW don't meet your needs, you can always fall back to EXPLICIT mode.

FOR XML (Client-Side)

Up until now, we have been writing our FOR XML code so that it is processed on the server. However, using SQLXML, you can process your FOR XML code on the client-side. Rather than sending back the formatted XML results from the server, SQL Server sends back the rowsets to SQLXML, and SQLXML formats the results on the client-side. You'll see an example of this in the next section when we explore the SQLXML classes.

Using Templates

You can use templates to execute queries against your SQL Server with SQLXML. Templates are just encapsulation of the technologies we've already looked at in this chapter. These templates can use SQL or XPath queries. You have to use the annotated schema that you create for your XML view with your template. The schema can be inline or loaded via a file. To specify your template, you'll create a file that uses the urn:schemas-microsoft-com:xml-sql namespace. Then, once you set that namespace, you can pass in your SQL or XPath queries in the template. SQLXML will cache your templates in order to improve performance. The following template executes a SQL query:

```
<Root><sql:query xmlns:sql=""urn:schemas-microsoft-com:xml-sql"">
SELECT * FROM Authors FOR XML AUTO</sql:query></Root>
```

To use an XPath query, we would change the sql:query syntax to sql:xpath-query. The sample that follows queries for all authors:

```
<Root><sql:xpath-query xmlns:sql=""urn:schemas-microsoft-com:xml-sql"">/Authors
</sql:xpath-query></Root>
```

You'll see how to use templates from code in the section "Programming SQLXML from .NET and COM" later in this chapter.

Enhancements to FOR XML

To transform relational data into XML data, the FOR XML keyword is still supported in SQL Server 2005 with some enhancements. The major enhancements in FOR XML are support for the XML datatype, enhancements to make writing FOR XML EXPLICIT statements much easier, and support for inline XSD. If you've never worked with FOR XML EXPLICIT, count your blessings. The syntax of using this capability was not for the faint of heart. If you needed to perform any marginally complex XML formatting in SQL Server 2000, you would have to unfortunately resort to FOR XML EXPLICIT.

To support returning values using the XML datatype, FOR XML supports an extra directive called TYPE. By passing this directive to your call, instead of generating the XML and returning it as text, SQL returns back the result as an XML datatype. This means that you can then use XQuery on that returned value to query for information inside of the resultset. Also, you can assign the results to a variable or use it to insert into an XML datatype column. Finally, you can nest FOR XML statements to generate a hierarchy rather than having to resort to using XML EXPLICIT. This capability allows you to quickly convert your relational data or even your data that uses the XML datatype into an XML datatype value. The following code shows how to use the new TYPE directive and then pass the result to an XQuery, which you'll learn about in the next chapter:

```
SELECT (SELECT * FROM authors FOR XML AUTO, ELEMENTS, TYPE).query(
'count(//author)')
```

The new PATH mode allows you to specify where a column's value should appear in your XML hierarchy by using XPath. By having this capability, you can move away from FOR XML EXPLICIT, which is complex and burdensome, and instead generate complex XML using nested FOR XML statements and the new PATH mode. An example of the new PATH mode is shown here. This sample renames the root element to AuthorsNew and also makes a new complex type called Names that stores the first name and the last name.

```
SELECT au_fname "Names/FirstName", au_lname "Names/LastName"
FROM authors FOR XML PATH('AuthorsNew')
```

The final enhancement is the support for inline XSD in RAW and AUTO modes. You can optionally pass this directive, called XMLSCHEMA, in your code. The following code sample shows using the XMLSCHEMA directive and the results returned from the server:

```
SELECT * FROM authors FOR XML RAW('Authors'), XMLSCHEMA('urn:example.com')

<xsd:schema targetNamespace="urn:example.com"
  xmlns:xsd=http://www.w3.org/2001/XMLSchema
  xmlns:sqltypes="http://schemas.microsoft.com/sqlserver/2004/sqltypes"
  elementFormDefault="qualified">
  <xsd:import namespace="http://schemas.microsoft.com/sqlserver/2004/sqltypes"
    schemaLocation=
    "http://schemas.microsoft.com/sqlserver/2004/sqltypes/sqltypes.xsd" />
  <xsd:element name="Authors">
    <xsd:complexType>
  . . .
    </xsd:complexType>
  </xsd:element>
</xsd:schema>


<Authors xmlns="urn:example.com" au_id="172-32-1176"
         au_lname="White" au_fname="Johnson" phone="408 496-7223"
         address="10932 Bigge Rd." city="Menlo Park"
         state="CA" zip="94025" contract="1" />
```

Programming SQLXML from .NET and COM

SQLXML 4.0 provides an object model that allows you to program its capabilities from both managed and unmanaged code. For unmanaged code such as ADO, you use the SQLXMLOLEDB driver. This provider uses the new SQL Native Client. Since space is limited, programming SQLXML from unmanaged code will not be covered. Instead, we'll focus our efforts on managed code. For managed code, you can add a reference to Microsoft.Data.SqlXml in Visual Studio as shown in Figure 7-2.

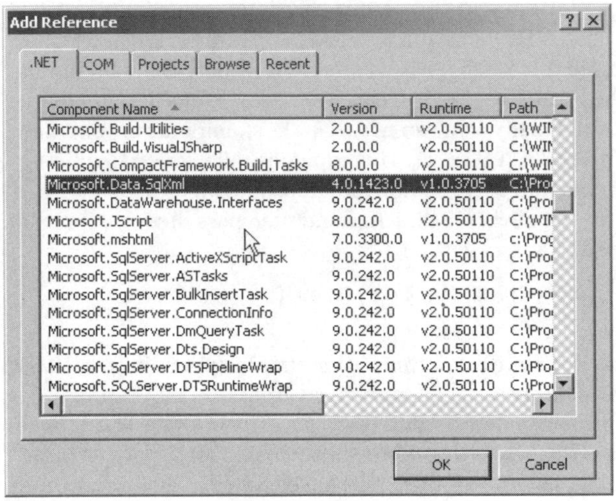

Figure 7-2. *Adding a reference to SQLXML*

The SQLXML-managed assembly has four classes: SqlXmlCommand, SqlXmlParameter, SqlXmlAdapter, and SqlXmlException. Using these classes, you can send commands to SQL Server and process the results on the client-side such as rendering FOR XML statements or executing XML templates. The following section will step through each object, its method and properties, and show you how to program SQLXML.

SqlXmlCommand

SqlXmlCommand is one of the primary classes you'll interact with when using SQLXML functionality. Table 7-8 lists all the methods and Table 7-9 lists all the properties for SqlXmlCommand.

Table 7-8. *SqlXmlCommand Methods*

Name	Description
ClearParameters	Clears all parameters that were created for a particular command object.
CreateParameter	Creates a SqlXmlParameter object from which you can set the name and value for the parameter.
ExecuteNonQuery	Executes the query but doesn't return any value. This is useful if you want to call an updategram that doesn't return a value.
ExecuteToStream	Executes the query and returns the results to an existing Stream object that you pass to the method.

Table 7-8. *SqlXmlCommand Methods*

Name	Description
ExecuteStream	Executes the query and returns the results back as a new Stream object.
ExecuteXMLReader	Executes the query and returns back the results in an XMLReader object.

Table 7-9. *SqlXmlCommand Properties*

Name	Description
BasePath	The base directory path, which is useful for setting paths to XSL, schema mapping, or XSD schema files used in your applications.
ClientSideXML	When set to true, this Boolean property tells SQLXML to convert your rowsets to XML on the client-side.
CommandStream	This property allows you to set your command by using a stream. This is useful if you want to execute a command from a file.
CommandText	Gets or sets the text of the command that you want to execute.
CommandType	Allows you to get or set the command type using the following values: SQLXMLCommandType.Diffgram, SQLXMLCommandType.Sql, SQLXMLCommandType.Template, SQLXMLCommandType.TemplateFile, SQLXMLCommandType.XPath, and SQLXMLCommandType.UpdateGram.
Namespaces	Allows you to specify namespaces for your XML in the format xmlns:x='urn:myschema:Yournamespace'. When using XPath queries that are namespace qualified, you must specify your namespaces using this property.
OutputEncoding	This property specifies the encoding for the results. By default, the encoding is UTF-8, but you could specify ANSI, Unicode, or other valid encoding values.
RootTag	This property specifies the root tag for your XML document, if required. This will normally be the string value root.
SchemaPath	Specifies the directory path and filename for the schema file. If you are using relative paths via the BasePath property, SQLXML will look in the BasePath directory. You can also use absolute paths such as c:\myapp\myschema.xml.
XslPath	Same as the SchemaPath but specifies the path to the XSL transform file rather than the schema file.

SqlXmlParameter

SqlXmlParameter provides the ability to pass parameters to your code. This class is very straightforward since it has only two properties: Name and Value. You specify the name of the parameter such as customerid and the value to be the value for the parameter. You can create a SqlXmlParameter object by calling the CreateParameter method on the SqlXmlCommand object.

SqlXmlAdapter

The SqlXmlAdapter object allows interoperability between .NET datasets and SQLXML functionality. The constructor for this object has three forms. The first form can take a SqlXmlCommand that is populated with the necessary information to connect to your datasource. The second form is the command text as a string, the command type as a SqlXmlCommand object, and finally the connection string as a string. The final form is the same as the second one, except you pass in a Stream object rather than a string for the command text.

Once you've created your adapter, there are only two methods on the object. The first is the Fill method, which you pass an ADO.NET dataset to. SQLXML will fill the ADO.NET dataset with whatever data your commands should return. Then, you can modify your dataset using standard dataset functionality and call the second method, which is Update, with your dataset as a parameter to the method. SQLXML uses an optimistic locking scheme when updating your data in your backend table.

SqlXmlException

This object inherits from the standard SystemException object and allows you to pass back SQLXML exceptions as part of your code. There is an ErrorStream property that you use to return back the error. The following code uses this property to print out any errors caught in an exception:

```
. . .
    Catch ex As Microsoft.Data.SqlXml.SqlXmlException
        ex.ErrorStream.Position = 0
        Dim oSR As New System.IO.StreamReader(ex.ErrorStream)
        Dim strResult As String = oSR.ReadToEnd()
        System.Console.WriteLine(strResult)

    End Try
```

Code Samples

To show you how to use this functionality, let's take a look at a sample application. The sample application allows you to bulk load XML data into SQL and then try out the different functionality discussed in this chapter such as FOR XML, dataset integration, running templates, using updategrams, and also using client-side processing and XMLTextReaders. The user interface for the sample is shown in Figure 7-3.

The sample already has a reference to SQLXML, so we don't have to perform that step again. To start working with our data, we need to load our XML data into our database and shred it into relational columns. The code could have used an OPENXML statement, but instead it uses XML BulkLoad. To start using BulkLoad, we first need to add a reference to the BulkLoad COM object in Visual Studio. The component name is Microsoft SQLXML BulkLoad 4.0 Type Library. Next, we need to create a bulk-load object in our application. The code that follows performs this task:

```
Dim oXMLBulkLoad As New SQLXMLBULKLOADLib.SQLXMLBulkLoad4Class()
```

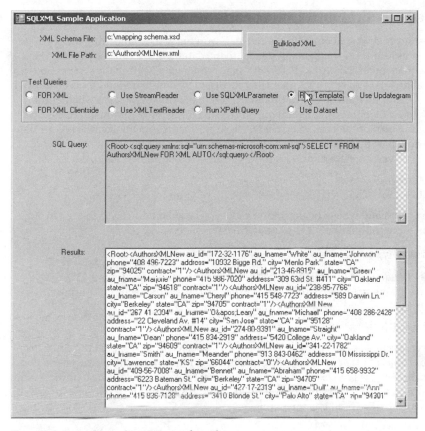

Figure 7-3. *Sample application user interface*

Next, we need to set some properties for our BulkLoad. Since we cannot assume that the table that we are going to bulk load into already exists, the sample sets the SchemaGen property to true. Also, if the tables do exist, we want to drop them, so the sample sets the SGDropTables to true as well. The sample sets other properties such as where to put the error file, whether our XML is a fragment, and whether to keep identities or not. The most important property is the ConnectionString property, since it tells bulkload how to connect to the server. Once we have set all of our properties, the sample calls the execute method of bulkload and passes in the schema mapping file and the XML to bulk load. You'll find all of the schema mapping files and the sample XML files included with the sample application. All this code is shown here:

```
oXMLBulkLoad.ErrorLogFile = "c:\myerrors.log"
oXMLBulkLoad.SchemaGen = True
oXMLBulkLoad.KeepIdentity = False
oXMLBulkLoad.BulkLoad = True
oXMLBulkLoad.SGDropTables = True
oXMLBulkLoad.XMLFragment = True
oXMLBulkLoad.ConnectionString = strConnectionString
oXMLBulkLoad.Execute(txtXMLSchema.Text, txtXMLFile.Text)
```

FOR XML: Server-Side and Client-Side

Once we've successfully bulk loaded our data, we can start working with it. One thing we can do is get our data back out as XML, now that it is shredded into the database. We can use the FOR XML construct to do this. Remember that SQLXML allows you to render your XML on the server or on the client. The sample allows us to select either one. The code uses a common method for executing all queries in the sample. This method takes a number of different parameters such as whether the query coming in is a SQL, template, or diffgram query. The first thing the common query method does is creates a SqlXmlCommand object as shown here. Please note the connection string is your standard connection string that you are probably used to, such as
"Provider=sqloledb;server=localhost;database=pubs;integrated security=SSPI".

```
Dim oSQLXMLCommand As New _
Microsoft.Data.SqlXml.SqlXmlCommand(strConnectionString)
```

Next, it sets the command type to be the appropriate type based on the query coming in. For standard SQL queries, the command type is set to SQL as shown here:

```
oSQLXMLCommand.CommandType = Microsoft.Data.SqlXml.SqlXmlCommandType.Sql
```

To send our FOR XML query to the server, we need to set the command text for our SqlXmlCommand object. Since we pass the query to the method, we use the strQuery variable for this purpose:

```
'Set our Query
oSQLXMLCommand.CommandText = strQuery
```

Since we can render our FOR XML on the server or client, we need to set the ClientSideXml property of our command object to true or false, with true being to render the XML on the client-side. Once we've set this property, we can execute our query and get back the results. The following code uses a StreamReader to get back the results and put them in our results text box. We can also use an XMLTextReader, which you'll see used later on in this section.

```
'See if we need to render client-side
If bUseClientSide = True Then
    oSQLXMLCommand.ClientSideXml = True
End If

Dim oStream As System.IO.Stream
oStream = oSQLXMLCommand.ExecuteStream()

oStream.Position = 0
Dim oStreamReader As New System.IO.StreamReader(oStream)
txtResults.Text = oStreamReader.ReadToEnd()
oStreamReader.Close()
```

As you can see from the code, using FOR XML in SQLXML is very straightforward. The hard part is making sure that you get your FOR XML query correct and returning back the right results.

Using an XMLTextReader

There may be times when you don't want to use a StreamReader to get your results back from your SQLXML queries, but instead want to use an XMLTextReader. The XMLTextReader gives you fast access to XML data and more flexibility in navigating your XML than a StreamReader does. The XMLTextReader parses your XML and allows you to query that XML using XPath. To use an XMLTextReader, you just need to change your ExecuteStream method call to an ExecuteXMLReader method call on your SqlXmlCommand object. Once you get back the reader, you can then use the methods and properties of the XML reader to navigate your XML. The following code executes the XML reader and displays the results to the user in the sample:

```
'Use XMLTextReader
Dim oXMLTextReader As System.Xml.XmlTextReader
oXMLTextReader = oSQLXMLCommand.ExecuteXmlReader()
Dim strXML As String = ""

While oXMLTextReader.Read()
  'We're on an element
  If oXMLTextReader.NodeType = XmlNodeType.Element Then
    strXML += "<" & oXMLTextReader.Name & ""
  ElseIf oXMLTextReader.NodeType = XmlNodeType.EndElement Then
    strXML += "</" & oXMLTextReader.Name & ">"
  End If

'Look for attributes
  If oXMLTextReader.HasAttributes() Then
  Dim i As Integer = 0
  Do While (oXMLTextReader.MoveToNextAttribute())
    i += 1
   strXML += " " & oXMLTextReader.Name & "=" & oXMLTextReader.Value
   If oXMLTextReader.AttributeCount = i Then
    'Last attribute, end the tag
    strXML += " />"
  End If
  Loop

  End If
End While

  txtResults.Text = strXML
  oXMLTextReader.Close()
```

As you can see, the XML reader, for simple operations like just displaying the XML, is overkill since you have to parse the XML to display it. But, if you wanted to figure out information about the XML, such as the number of attributes or elements, or if you wanted to navigate in a richer way, the XML reader is up for the task.

Using Parameters with SQLXML

To use parameters with SQLXML, we need to create a SqlXmlParameter object. Our query must specify that we are going to pass a parameter, and the SqlXmlParameter object must have its properties set correctly. The following code snippets show you how to use a parameter with your SQLXML queries:

```
strQuery = "SELECT * FROM " & strTable & " WHERE city = ? FOR XML AUTO, ELEMENTS"
. . .
Dim oSQLXMLParameter As Microsoft.Data.SqlXml.SqlXmlParameter
oSQLXMLParameter = oSQLXMLCommand.CreateParameter()
oSQLXMLParameter.Name = "city"
oSQLXMLParameter.Value = "Oakland"
. . .
```

Executing XPath or SQL Queries with Templates

With SQLXML, you can execute XPath or SQL queries. The sample application uses a template to execute a SQL query and a straight XPath statement for the XPath query. The sample could have used a template for the XPath query, but the sample demonstrates how to use the XPath command type. The following code sets up the SQL template query:

```
'Load up our query
strQuery = "<Root><sql:query xmlns:sql=""urn:schemas-microsoft-com:xml-sql""> _
SELECT * FROM AuthorsXMLNew FOR XML AUTO</sql:query></Root>"
```

Next, the sample sets the command type to be a template in order to run the SQL template query. The sample also specifies the root node and the path to the annotated XSD schema file.

```
oSQLXMLCommand.CommandType = Microsoft.Data.SqlXml.SqlXmlCommandType.Template
oSQLXMLCommand.SchemaPath = txtXMLSchema.Text
oSQLXMLCommand.RootTag = "ROOT"
```

Since the code uses a `StreamReader` to render the results, that code won't be shown here, since you've seen it already.

To perform the XPath query, again, we set up the query as shown here:

```
'Load up our query
strQuery = "/AuthorsXMLNew[city='Oakland']"
```

Since we are using an XPath query directly, we need to set the command type to be XPath for our `SqlXmlCommand` object. Just like we did for the SQL template query, we want to set our root node and also the path to our annotated XSD schema. After that, we'll again use the `StreamReader` to render our results as we saw earlier.

```
oSQLXMLCommand.CommandType = Microsoft.Data.SqlXml.SqlXmlCommandType.XPath
oSQLXMLCommand.SchemaPath = txtXMLSchema.Text
oSQLXMLCommand.RootTag = "ROOT"
```

Interoperating with the ADO.NET Dataset

SQLXML interoperates with the ADO.NET dataset through the `SqlXmlAdapter` object. You can use the `SqlXmlAdapter` to fill your dataset. Then, you can use the `Dataset` object as you normally would in ADO.NET. The following code, taken from the sample application, creates a query, executes that query using the `SqlXmlAdapter` object, and then fills a dataset with the information. To write out the value returned back, the code uses some stream objects:

```
strQuery = "SELECT * FROM " & strTable & " WHERE city =
  'oakland' FOR XML AUTO, ELEMENTS"
. . .

Dim oSQLXMLDataAdapter As New _
   Microsoft.Data.SqlXml.SqlXmlAdapter(oSQLXMLCommand)
Dim oDS As New System.Data.DataSet()
oSQLXMLDataAdapter.Fill(oDS)
```

```
'Display the underlying XML
Dim oMemStream As New System.IO.MemoryStream()
Dim oStreamWriter As New System.IO.StreamWriter(oMemStream)
oDS.WriteXml(oMemStream, System.Data.XmlWriteMode.IgnoreSchema)
oMemStream.Position = 0
Dim oStreamReader As New System.IO.StreamReader(oMemStream)
txtResults.Text = oStreamReader.ReadToEnd()
oMemStream.Close()
```

Programming Updategrams

The final piece of the sample application we'll look at uses updategrams. Updategrams allow you to update your SQL Server using your existing XML documents. The code creates the updategram using a `StringBuilder` object. Then, the code sets the command type to be `UpdateGram`. Finally, the rest of the code is the same as the original code to execute the command and get the results, so that section is left out.

```
Dim strUpdateGram As New System.Text.StringBuilder()
strUpdateGram.Append("<?xml version='1.0'?><AuthorsXMLNewupdate ")
strUpdateGram.Append("xmlns:updg='urn:schemas-microsoft-com:xml-updategram'>")
strUpdateGram.Append("<updg:sync updg:nullvalue='nothing'>" &
    "<updg:before></updg:before>")
strUpdateGram.Append("<updg:after><AuthorsXMLNew au id='123-22-1232'")
strUpdateGram.Append(" au_fname='Tom' state='WA' phone='425-882-8080'/>")
strUpdateGram.Append("</updg:after>")
strUpdateGram.Append("<updg:before><AuthorsXMLNew")
strUpdateGram.Append(" au_id='267-41-2394'/></updg:before>")
strUpdateGram.Append("<updg:after></updg:after>")
strUpdateGram.Append("<updg:before><AuthorsXMLNew")
strUpdateGram.Append(" au_id='238-95-7766'/></updg:before>")
strUpdateGram.Append("<updg:after><AuthorsXMLNew")
strUpdateGram.Append(" city='Oakland' phone='212-555-1212'/>")
strUpdateGram.Append("</updg:after></updg:sync></AuthorsXMLNewupdate>")

strQuery = strUpdateGram.ToString()
. . .

oSQLXMLCommand.CommandType = _
Microsoft.Data.SqlXml.SqlXmlCommandType.UpdateGram
```

Summary

As you've seen in this chapter, we've established your understanding of XML technologies that work against both SQL Server 2000 and 2005. This includes the OPENXML and FOR XML query extensions, XML BulkLoad, and also the SQLXML technologies. In the next chapter, you'll see some additional new technologies that were added to SQL Server 2005 to support XML and how some of the technologies you've learned about in this chapter have changed.

CHAPTER 8

■ ■ ■

SQL Server 2005 XML and XQuery Support

Convergence is happening all around us. Cell phones are integrating in PDA functionality and cameras. PDAs are becoming cell phones. Convergence is also happening in the world of data. Customers do not want to have to deal with multiple systems to manage their unstructured, semi-structured, and structured data. This is why for years customers have been looking to relational databases to manage all their data, not just their relational data.

There are a number of reasons why a relational database is the best place to work with all your data, rather than other technologies like the file system. First, relational databases have powerful storage technologies that are more granular than what the file system offers. You can do piecemeal backups, you can break apart your data into filegroups—and now even into partitions—and you have a transacted storage mechanism underneath your data. Second, databases have powerful indexing as well as query processors so you can ask complex questions to the system about your data. Finally, databases already store some of your most critical data that you probably want to query across to compare with your other nonrelational data. For example, you may want to show all sales for a particular customer, where your sales data is stored relationally and your customer data is XML. If you use the file system and a relational database, you have to query across those technologies, and if you want to transactionally update across the two for any data changes, you have to write a lot of code. To support these new scenarios that require XML and relational data working seamlessly together, Microsoft added native XML support to SQL Server 2005.

With SQL Server 2005, you work with your nonrelational data in the same way you work with your relational data. The methods might be a little bit different, but the tools and environment are the same. You saw some of this in the last chapter with XPath, OPENXML, and SQLXML support in SQL Server. Beyond these technologies, SQL Server 2005 natively supports storage, querying, and modification of XML data. In this chapter, we will look at the following enhancements in SQL Server 2005:

- *New XML datatype*: The XML datatype brings native XML storage to SQL Server. Rather than shredding your XML data into relational columns, you can now store your XML using the native XML datatype.

- *XQuery*: XML Query Language (XQuery) is a forthcoming standard from the World Wide Web Consortium (W3C) that allows you to query XML data. XQuery is to XML data what the SQL language is to relational data. You can use XQuery inside T-SQL code, as you will see later in this chapter.

- *XML indexes*: Just as you can index relational columns in SQL Server, you can now index XML columns to improve performance. SQL Server supports both primary and secondary indexes on XML columns.

- *Full-text search*: Since XML is text-centric, you may want to combine full-text indexing with the XML datatype to find XML information faster.

- *Dynamic management views for XML*: You may want to understand the usage of XML in your server, such as which XML columns are indexed and what XML schemas you have loaded into your server. Dynamic management views provide this type of information for your XML data.

- *XML web services support*: To support new scenarios for data access, such as retrieving SQL Server information from non-Windows platforms, SQL Server 2005 adds native support for XML web services. Using this capability, you can get or set your data using web services as well as call stored procedures or user-defined functions.

Using the XML Datatype

SQL Server 2005 introduces a new XML datatype you can use to natively store XML data in SQL Server 2005 databases. In SQL Server 2000, you could store XML, but it would have to be in a string-based column, or you would have to shred the data into relational columns using OPENXML or XMLBulkLoad, as you saw in the previous chapter. By adding a native XML type, SQL can support richer operations against your XML data, such as constraints, cross-domain queries that combine relational data and XQuery, and XML indexes.

Another reason for a native XML type is that XML is inherently different from relational data in its structure. XML data is in a hierarchical structure that can be recursive, and XML supports a different query language than relational systems.

There are many scenarios where using relational modeling is a better choice than XML and vice versa. For example, if you have data that is very interrelated, such as customers, their orders, the products in the orders, and the stores that sell those products, you could try and implement a solution using XML. However, you will find that trying to model a solution in XML quickly gets challenging. For example, how do you structure your hierarchy? Do you want a customer to be a top-level node and then have orders for each customer appear underneath? Plus, how do you write a query that returns back all customers with at least five orders, where each order is greater than $1,000, and the name of the store where the customers purchased the products? Plus, in this sort of data, you will repeat data throughout the hierarchy, such as product names, product prices, and so on, because of the hierarchical nature of XML. Plus, if you want to delete a customer but not the products or orders under that customer, you can't do so, because the orders and products are children under the customer element. Using a relational model rather than XML, you can very quickly model your data and query the information.

You may be thinking that in the previous scenario, you should just shred your XML data into the relational database, as you saw in the previous chapter. However, shredding has its own issues, in that you do not always get back what you put in, since you are not guaranteed the same XML when you reconstitute the shredded data. Shredding adds another layer of complexity in terms of code creation and maintenance. Also, any reasonably complex XML document will have to be shredding across many tables, which will require extensive JOIN operations across these tables to reconstitute the XML and a very complex annotated schema to shred into the tables using all the foreign key relations.

Now, there are scenarios where modeling your data using XML is very useful. First, XML can be more flexible than relational models. So, if you need a free-form structure to store data, XML can be a good choice. Also, XML is self-describing and easily portable across applications or even platforms. Plus, if your data has sparse entries or needs rich multivalue functionality, XML makes a good choice as your data format. Finally, if you truly have document-centric data such as Microsoft Office documents, you will want to store this information as XML since Microsoft Office documents lack rigid structures. XML provides the flexibility to store and query the information in the documents in a rich way.

Even if you choose XML as the format for your data, you will need to decide between using the XML datatype, shredding your XML into relational columns, and storing the XML using the new (n)varchar[max] or varbinary[max] type. If you care about the order of elements, and you want the ability to use XML programming paradigms such as XPath and XQuery, you will want to use the XML datatype to store your XML data. If your XML data is best represented using a relational model, you can shred your data into relational columns using annotated schemas, just like you can in SQL Server 2000. Finally, if you need to preserve the XML data exactly as it was created, including white space and attribute ordering, then you will want to store the XML in a (n)varchar[max] or varbinary[max] column. Some scenarios (such as legal documents) may require this.

Finally, SQL Server 2005 can support a hybrid model, whereby you may use the XML datatype but promote certain properties—for example, key document properties such as author, last modification time, or last save time—into relational columns, or you may shred your XML into relational columns but keep the original copy in a nvarchar column. SQL Server 2005 provides the flexibility to meet the needs of your application when working with XML data.

We want to make one thing very clear, though, since this will cause you issues in the long term if you do not remind yourself of it regularly: if your data is quite structured, in that your XML does not look hierarchical and is normalized, you should use the relational model. Do not use XML. XML is targeted at semistructured or unstructured data. If you need to dynamically add schemas or data on the fly that you never expected, XML is your best choice. Do not make the mistake of thinking everything is a nail to bang with the XML hammer in SQL Server 2005,

Understanding How XML Is Stored by SQL Server

Before we discuss how to create a column of type XML, let's first look at how SQL Server stores XML. You may be wondering how, under the covers, SQL Server translates XML into something that is performant when running queries against the XML data. One thing we can guarantee is that XML is not stored as text! When you create a column using the new XML datatype, SQL Server takes the XML and converts it into a binary XML format. One reason for this is that it's faster to index and search binary data than plain text data. A second reason is that you can compress binary data much more easily than plain text data. SQL Server will tokenize the XML and strip out portions of the markup. If you look at many XML documents, they have redundant text throughout for element or attribute markup. With the XML datatype, this redundancy can be removed and your data can be compressed.

The XML datatype is implemented using the new varbinary(max) datatype under the covers to store the binary XML. If the converted binary XML is small enough to fit in the row, SQL Server stores the binary XML in-row. If the XML is too large, a 24-byte pointer is left in the row that points to the binary XML. With the built-in compression, you should expect an average of 20 percent compression of the XML when storing it in the XML datatype. Of course, this will be dependent on the number of tags you have in the document and the redundancy of your text. As you will see, using typed XML is preferable to untyped, since you can get better performance and compression of the XML datatype because SQL Server does not have to do type conversions and can parse data faster when the types are specified.

If you ever want to see how much compression is achieved between storing your XML using nvarchar and using the XML datatype, you can use the DATALENGTH function. The following example compares using nvarchar and the XML datatype with the XML we use as our sample XML in this chapter:

```
select DATALENGTH(N'<?xml version="1.0" standalone="yes"?>
<people>
  <person>
    <name>
      <givenName>Martin</givenName>
      <familyName>Smith</familyName>
    </name>
. . .
') as NVARLEN,
DATALENGTH(CAST(N'<?xml version="1.0" standalone="yes"?>
<people>
  <person>
    <name>
      <givenName>Martin</givenName>
      <familyName>Smith</familyName>
    </name>
. . .
' AS XML)) as XMLLEN
```

```
Results:
NVARLEN: 1154
XMLLEN: 324
```

As you can see, we save about 3.5 times the space using the XML datatype. The reason for this is that many tags in my XML repeat, and the XML datatype can strip these tags when it stores the XML data in SQL Server. Depending on the redundancy in your XML, you should find similar savings in size.

Creating XML Columns

The following code creates a new table that contains a standard relational primary key column as well as an XML column. This example uses untyped XML:

```
CREATE TABLE xmltbl (pk INT IDENTITY PRIMARY KEY, xmlCol XML not null)
```

You can have multiple XML columns in a single table. One thing you will notice is that there is no XML schema associated with the XML column. SQL Server 2005 supports both *untyped* and *typed* XML columns. Untyped columns have no schema associated with them, while typed columns have XML schemas to which the XML documents inserted into the column must conform. Whenever possible, you will want to associate XML schemas with your XML columns, so that SQL Server will validate your XML data, make better optimizations when querying or modifying your data, perform better type checking, and optimize the storage of your XML data, so we'll focus on defining typed XML columns here. As you saw earlier, SQL Server stores XML data in a proprietary binary format for speed and compression. With an index, the server can find the information quicker, but there is a bit of a performance hit when you insert your data.

■**Note** SQL Server 2005 does not support Document Type Definitions (DTDs). DTDs define the document structure of your XML documents. You can use external tools to convert DTDs to an XML Schema Definition (XSD). SQL Server 2005 does support XSD.

Defining Typed XML Columns

To create a typed XML column, you need to load your schema into SQL Server and then associate it with the column in question. Once you've done this, only documents that adhere to your schema can be inserted into the table. You can have one or many schemas associated with an XML column.

The following code creates a new table that uses schema on an XML datatype, hence a *typed* XML column:

```
-- Create a new database for the samples
USE master
DROP DATABASE xmldb

IF NOT EXISTS (SELECT * FROM sys.databases WHERE name = 'xmldb')
        CREATE DATABASE xmldb
GO
--Declare the variable for the XML
declare @x XML
-- Open the XSD Schema
SELECT @x = s
FROM OPENROWSET (
 BULK 'C:\Customer.xsd',
 SINGLE_BLOB) AS TEMP(s)

select @x
-- Make sure the schema does not exist already
IF EXISTS(select * from sys.xml_schema_collections where name='Customer')
  DROP XML SCHEMA COLLECTION Customer
-- Create the schema in the schema collection for the database
CREATE XML SCHEMA COLLECTION Customer AS @x
GO
-- Create a table that uses our schema on an XML datatype
CREATE TABLE xmltbl2 (pk INT IDENTITY PRIMARY KEY,
xmlColWithSchema XML (CONTENT Customer))
GO
```

First, you need to load your XML schema into SQL Server. You can see the use of the OPENROWSET to open the XML schema file stored in the file system. The code assigns the schema to the variable x. Next, the code drops the schema if it exists. Here you will see the use of the new dynamic management views for XML, which we cover later in this chapter. SQL Server 2005 includes views for querying the schema collections, schema namespaces, and XML indexes.

If the schema collection does not exist, the code creates the schema collection in SQL Server. Schema collections are scoped to the database where they are created. Schema collections cannot span databases or instances, so you may have to create the same schema in multiple locations if you use the same schema for multiple, different XML datatypes in different databases. You can have more than one XML schema in your database. In addition, you can assign more than one XML schema to a column that uses the XML datatype. One caveat with schemas is that once you create a schema, you cannot modify or drop it until all references to it are removed from the system. For example, if an XML column in your table references a schema, you will not be able to modify that schema. SQL Server 2005 will return a message stating that the schema is in use and including the name of the components using the schema.

Your schema is loaded into SQL Server's metadata and can be viewed using the sys.xml_ schema_collections metadata view. If you want to retrieve the schema after you load it into the system, you will need to use the xml_schema_namespace function. This function takes two parameters: the first is the relational schema in which your XML schema was created, and the second is the name of the schema you want to retrieve. The following code retrieves the Customer schema created in the previous example:

```
--Return the schema
USE xmldb
go

SELECT xml_schema_namespace(N'dbo',N'Customer')
go
```

Here is the returned XML schema from this call:

```
<xsd:schema xmlns:xsd=http://www.w3.org/2001/XMLSchema
xmlns:t="urn:example/customer" targetNamespace="urn:example/customer"
elementFormDefault="qualified">
  <xsd:element name="NewDataSet">
    <xsd:complexType>
      <xsd:complexContent>
        <xsd:restriction base="xsd:anyType">
          <xsd:choice minOccurs="0" maxOccurs="unbounded">
            <xsd:element ref="t:doc" />
          </xsd:choice>
        </xsd:restriction>
      </xsd:complexContent>
    </xsd:complexType>
  </xsd:element>
 <xsd:element name="doc">
  <xsd:complexType>
    <xsd:complexContent>
      <xsd:restriction base="xsd:anyType">
        <xsd:sequence>
          <xsd:element name="customer" minOccurs="0" maxOccurs="unbounded">
            <xsd:complexType>
              <xsd:complexContent>
                <xsd:restriction base="xsd:anyType">
                  <xsd:sequence>
                    <xsd:element name="name" type="xsd:string" minOccurs="0" />
                    <xsd:element name="order" minOccurs="0"
                     maxOccurs="unbounded">
                      <xsd:complexType>
                        <xsd:complexContent>
                          <xsd:restriction base="xsd:anyType">
                            <xsd:sequence />
                            <xsd:attribute name="id" type="xsd:string" />
                            <xsd:attribute name="year" type="xsd:string" />
                          </xsd:restriction>
                        </xsd:complexContent>
                      </xsd:complexType>
                    </xsd:element>
                    <xsd:element name="notes" minOccurs="0"
                    maxOccurs="unbounded">
```

```
                    <xsd:complexType>
                        <xsd:complexContent>
                            <xsd:restriction base="xsd:anyType">
                                <xsd:sequence>
                                    <xsd:element name="buys" type="xsd:string"
                                    minOccurs="0" />
                                    <xsd:element name="saleslead" type="xsd:string"
                                    minOccurs="0" />
                                    <xsd:element name="competitor" type="xsd:string"
                                    minOccurs="0" />
                                </xsd:sequence>
                            </xsd:restriction>
                        </xsd:complexContent>
                    </xsd:complexType>
                </xsd:element>
            </xsd:sequence>
            <xsd:attribute name="id" type="xsd:string" />
          </xsd:restriction>
      </xsd:complexContent>
    </xsd:complexType>
  </xsd:element>
        </xsd:sequence>
        <xsd:attribute name="id" type="xsd:string" />
      </xsd:restriction>
    </xsd:complexContent>
  </xsd:complexType>
</xsd:element>
</xsd:schema>
```

If you compare the returned XML schema and the original file included with the sample code, you will find that they are different. SQL Server does not guarantee that it will return the same exact XML schema document as you submitted, since it translates your schema into the server metadata catalog. For example, comments, annotations, and white space are removed, and implicit types are made explicit. If you need to keep a copy of your exact schema document, you should store it in a string column, an xml column, or in the file system.

SQL Server defines certain schemas by default; these are common schemas that you may want to use in your XML schemas in addition to your custom schema definitions. The following are the reserved XML schemas with their prefixes. Please note that you cannot create schemas with the same name as the existing predefined schemas in SQL Server.

```
xml = http://www.w3.org/XML/1998/namespace
xs = http://www.w3.org/2001/XMLSchema
xsi = http://www.w3.org/2001/XMLSchema-instance
fn = http://www.w3.org/2004/07/xpath-functions
sqltypes = http://schemas.microsoft.com/sqlserver/2004/sqltypes
xdt = http://www.w3.org/2004/07/xpath-datatypes
(no prefix) = urn:schemas-microsoft-com:xml-sql
(no prefix) = http://schemas.microsoft.com/sqlserver/2004/SOAP
```

One of the interesting schemas just listed is sqltypes. This schema allows you to map your XML data to SQL types such as varchar. You cannot modify these built-in schemas, nor can you serialize these schemas. You can use the import namespace directive to import these schemas into your own XML schema, however, and then use the schema in your own custom schema declarations.

One thing to note about schemas is that you cannot modify an existing schema. You can add new schemas, but then you will have to go through and modify your XML instances to use the new schema. You can drop your schemas and create new schemas, but that will untype your XML, which could be a long operation depending on the number of XML instances contained in your table.

Defining XML Columns Using a GUI

You've seen how to create columns using the XML datatype through code. However, the new SQL Server Management Studio allows you to work with XML in many ways. Figure 8-1 shows creating a new column of type XML. In the Properties area, you can specify the schema you want to associate with the column, if any. Beyond that, all dialog boxes that take types, such as the new stored procedure header dialog box, will take XML as a type since it is a native type in SQL Server 2005.

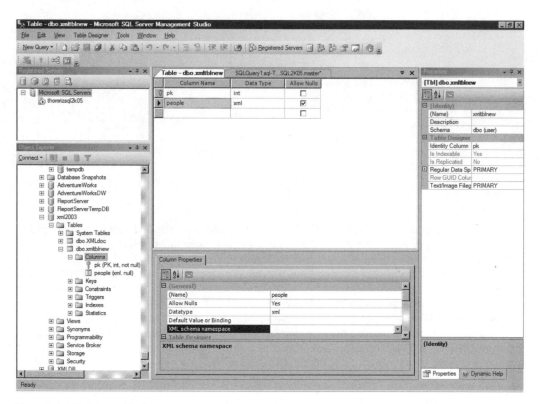

Figure 8-1. *Working with the XML datatype in Management Studio*

Setting Permissions for Schema Creation

The code you walked through earlier for schema creation assumed that you already had permissions to create XML schemas in the server. However, that may not be the case. Since an XML schema is like other objects in a SQL Server database, you can set permissions on schema collections. One thing to note is that users need both permissions on the relational schema and explicit permissions for XML schema creation, since XML schema creation modifies the relational schema as well. The different types of permissions you can grant and their effects are discussed next.

To create an XML schema, you need to be granted the `CREATE XML SCHEMA COLLECTION` permission. You need to grant this permission at the database level.

When you set the `ALTER` permission, users can modify the contents of an existing XML schema collection using the `ALTER XML SCHEMA COLLECTION` statement. Remember that users need permissions on the relational schema as well for this to work.

The `CONTROL` permission allows users to perform any operation on the XML schema collection. This means that users can create, delete, or edit the schema information. To transfer ownership of XML schemas from one user to another, you would set the `TAKE OWNERSHIP` permission.

To use constraints or for typing your XML datatype columns, you would add the `REFERENCE` permission to users. The `REFERENCE` permission is also required when one XML schema collection refers to another.

The `VIEW DEFINITION` permission allows users to query the contents of an XML schema collection either through `XML_SCHEMA_NAMESPACE` or through the XML dynamic management views. Users need to also have `ALTER`, `CONTROL`, or `REFERENCES` permission.

To perform validation against schemas, the `EXECUTE` permission is required. Users also need this permission when querying the XML stored in columns and variables that are typed.

The following code shows how to grant permissions for a user to alter the relational and XML schema inside of a database:

```
-- Grant permissions on the relational schema in the database
GRANT ALTER ON SCHEMA::dbo TO User1
go
-- Grant permission to create xml schema collections in the database
GRANT CREATE XML SCHEMA COLLECTION
TO User1
go
```

Constraining XML Columns

You can use relational constraints on XML columns. There may be times when you will keep your XML data untyped and use constraints instead—for example, if the constraint you want to use is not easily expressed using XML schemas, such as executing an XPath statement. One example of this may be a constraint that makes sure that the order amount is not discounted by more than a certain amount, which is calculated dynamically, depending on the total cost of the order. Bigger order amounts may get larger discounts, but cannot exceed a certain sliding scale of percentages for discounts.

Another reason to use constraints is if you need to constrain the column based on other columns' values. For example, you may want to make sure that another value in another column is filled in before allowing users to insert data into your XML column.

There are limitations to using XML columns, though. For instance, XML columns cannot be primary keys or foreign keys, nor can they have unique constraints, but they can be included in a clustered index or explicitly added to a nonclustered index by using the `INCLUDE` keyword when the nonclustered index is created.

The following example creates a table with an XML column that has a constraint. Please note that this code will work with builds before the June 2005 CTP of SQL Server 2005. If you are using a later version or the release version, use the following code, which wraps the constraint in a UDF:

```
--Create a constraint
CREATE TABLE xmltbl3 (pk INT IDENTITY PRIMARY KEY,
xmlColWithConstraint XML CHECK(xmlColWithConstraint.exist('declare namespace
cust="urn:example/customer";
   /cust:doc/cust:customer/cust:name') = 1
     ))
Go
```

The constraint checks to see if the XML being inserted has a customer name. You could also create constraints against other columns, different datatypes, or information contained in the XML itself. Once you create your table with the constraint, you can then try to insert data into the table. If you insert data that does not meet the constraint, you'll get the following error message:

```
Msg 547, Level 16, State 0, Line 1
INSERT statement conflicted with CHECK constraint 'CK__xmltbl3__xmlColW__0BC6C43E'.
The conflict occurred in database 'xmldb',
 table 'xmltbl3', column 'xmlColWithConstraint'.
The statement has been terminated.
```

Please note that in the final release of SQL Server, you have to wrap your XQuery in a function and then call that function from your constraint. Therefore, you could take the original constraint and rewrite it as follows:

```
create function CheckCustomerName(@x xml)
returns bit
as
begin
  return @x.exist('declare namespace
cust="urn:example/customer";
/cust:doc/cust:customer/cust:name')
end;
Go
--Create a constraint
CREATE TABLE xmltbl3 (pk INT IDENTITY PRIMARY KEY,
xmlColWithConstraint XML CHECK(dbo.CheckCustomerName(xmlColWithConstraint) = 1))
Go
```

Examining the XML Datatype Limitations

There are a number of limitations you should be aware of with the XML datatype. First, the XML datatype is limited to 2GB in size and 128 levels of hierarchy. Furthermore, the XML datatype cannot be compared, sorted, grouped by, part of a view, part of a clustered or nonclustered index, part of a distributed partitioned view, or part of an indexed view. Some of these limitations are due to the fact that XML is not relational data or that the XML datatype has its own way to create indexes or sort its data. Even given these limitations, you should be able to store the majority of your XML data in SQL Server. If you have data that exceeds these limitations, especially the 2GB size limit, we'd love to learn more about that dataset!

SQL Server stores your XML data by default using UTF-16. If you need to use a different encoding, you will cast the results or perform a conversion in your application. For example, you could convert your XML result to a different SQL type such as nvarchar. However, you cannot convert the XML datatype to text or ntext. Your XML data will use the collation settings on your server for the resultset.

XML data employs the same locking mechanism of SQL Server. This means the XML datatype supports row-level locking. This is true as well whether you are using T-SQL or XQuery. Therefore, if the row gets locked, all XML instances in that row are locked as well.

Inserting Data into XML Columns

Now that you know how to create XML columns, we will show you how you get your XML data into those columns. In the last chapter, we saw how to perform this task using SQLXMLBulkLoad. Beyond SQLXML, there are three common ways that you will get your data into your XML column: SQL Server Integration Services (SSIS), bulkloading with OPENROWSET and BCP, and writing queries or applications. We'll discuss each method in the sections that follow.

Using SSIS with XML Data

With SSIS, you can now easily take XML data and move it into SQL Server. SSIS supports pulling XML from file systems or other locations, transforming that XML, and then putting the XML into an XML datatype column in SQL Server 2005 or shredding the XML into relational columns. Figure 8-2 shows a package that pulls data from an XML source and puts the XML into SQL Server.

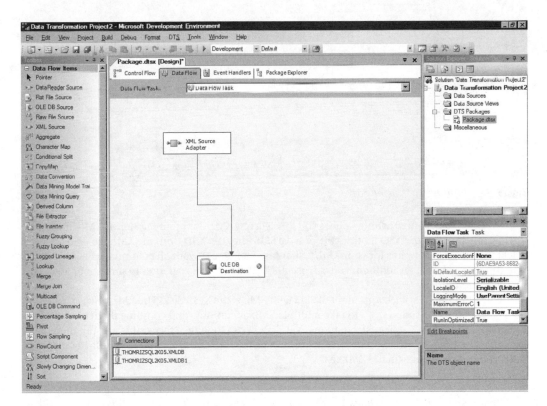

Figure 8-2. *SSIS package that works with XML*

Figure 8-3 shows mapping the data from the XML source to the XML column created earlier. SSIS is probably the easiest way to move XML data between different data sources.

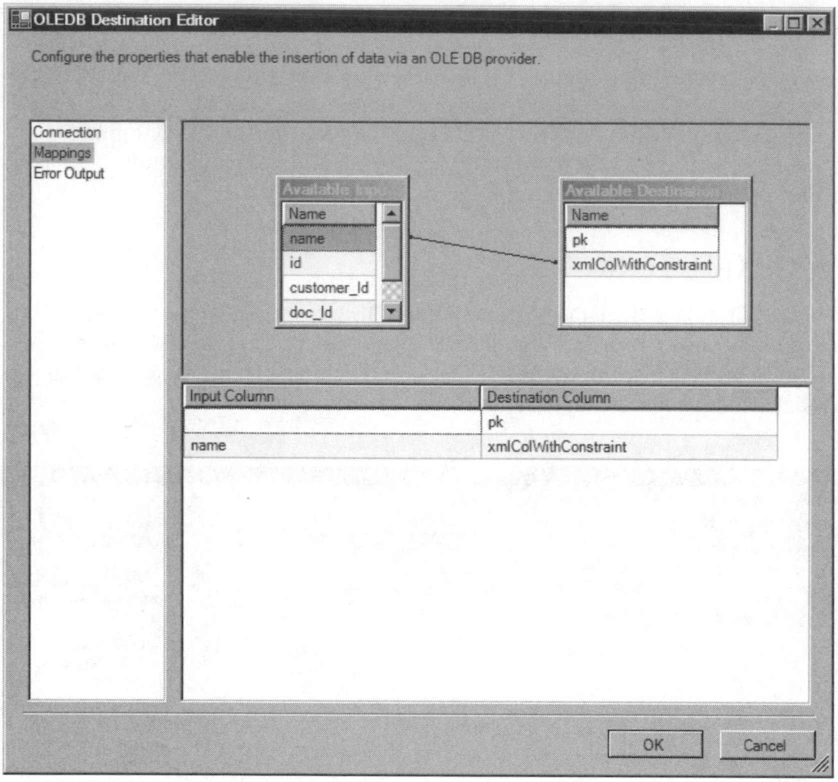

Figure 8-3. *Mapping XML using SSIS*

The XML data source adapter allows you to select any XML data source, such as XML from a file. You can also specify the XSD for the XML or have SSIS infer the XSD from the XML file. You can also select your output columns for your XML just in case you do not want all columns to be imported into the SSIS pipeline. In addition, you can use the XML data source adapter to shred your XML into relational columns.

One other interesting component of SSIS with XML is the XML task. The XML task is part of the SSIS control flow and allows you to take multiple XML documents and combine them or transform the documents using XSL Transformations (XSLT). You can then take the results and put them back into a file or into a SSIS variable that you can use through the rest of your SSIS flow. Table 8-1 outlines the tasks you can perform with the XML task.

Table 8-1. *SSIS Predefined XML Task Methods*

Operation	Description
Diff	Compares two XML documents. The source is the base document, and you specify the XML document to compare the source to. The difference is saved into a DiffGram document. The result is not a new XML document, but just the differences. To apply the DiffGram, use the Patch operation.
Merge	Merges two XML documents together.
Patch	Applies a DiffGram to an XML document. A new document is created with the changes applied.
Validate	Validates the XML against an XML schema or DTD.

Table 8-1. *SSIS Predefined XML Task Methods*

Operation	Description
XPath	Allows you to perform XPath queries against the XML document.
XSLT	Allows you to apply an XSLT transform to your XML document.

You may notice that XQuery is not an option in the XML task. Instead, if you want to perform an XQuery, you will have to use the Execute SQL task feature and use the XQuery methods on a stored XML datatype in your SQL Server database.

Bulkloading XML

Beyond using SSIS, you can bulkload XML data into SQL Server 2005 using the OPENROWSET keyword. The following example takes the data from the file system and inserts it into SQL Server:

```
INSERT INTO xmltbl2 (xmlColWithSchema)
SELECT *
FROM OPENROWSET (
 BULK 'C:\Customer1.xml',
 SINGLE_BLOB) AS TEMP
GO
```

SQL Server 2005 enhances the OPENROWSET with a bulk provider. This provider is similar to the BULK INSERT statement, but you do not have to send the output to a table with the BULK provider. You can specify a format file as you can with bcp.exe. In addition, you can specify inline information about the file properties using the following options: CODEPAGE, DATAFILETYPE, FIELDTERMINATOR, FIRSTROW, LASTROW, and ROWTERMINATOR. You can also specify table hints using the new bulk provider.

Writing a Custom Query or Application

The final way to get your data into your XML columns is to write applications that insert the data. For example, your application could be a simple T-SQL script you run in Management Studio or it could be a full-blown application that inserts XML data into SQL Server using ADO.NET or ADO. No matter which method you use, whether it's using Management Studio directly or writing an application, you will find yourself inserting XML using the INSERT INTO statement. The following code snippet demonstrates inserting XML data inline using T-SQL:

```
--Insert XML directly using inline XML
INSERT INTO xmltbl2(xmlColWithSchema) VALUES(
    '<doc id="d1" xmlns="urn:example/customer">
      <customer id="c7">
        <name>Tom</name>
        <order id="1" year="2002"></order>
        <order id="2" year="2003"></order>
        <notes>
          <buys>gizmos</buys>
          <saleslead>Bob</saleslead>
          <competitor>Acme</competitor>
        </notes>
      </customer>
    </doc>
    ')
Go
```

As you can see, you can pass inline XML directly using an INSERT statement. In your applications, you will either use dynamic SQL to add rows with XML data or create stored procedures.

PRESERVING WHITE SPACE

There may be times when you want to preserve white space in your XML so that the XML data you put in is the same as you get out, with all the white space included. SQL Server by default will discard insignificant white space, such as spaces between tags for elements. If you want to preserve this white space, you can use the CONVERT function and pass the optional style parameter to be 1.

Querying XML Data

Once you get your XML data into SQL Server, you may want to get it back out. The XML datatype provides four methods for you to do this: query(), value(), exist(), and nodes(). The availability of methods to use on the XML datatype is a new capability in SQL Server 2005.

■**Note** There is one more method on the XML datatype called modify(), which we discuss later in the section "Modifying XML Data."

These methods are based on the use of the XQuery language, so we'll start off with a quick XQuery tutorial, and then we'll investigate how to use these methods to query XML data.

XQuery 101

If you currently use XPath or XSLT, XQuery should not be entirely unfamiliar to you. You're used to iterating over hierarchies of data and the semantics of the XPath language. However, if you do only relational work with T-SQL, XQuery may look like a strange new beast. The reason for this is that T-SQL works on rows and columns, not hierarchies of information. XML data is structured differently from relational data, and it will take a bit of time for relational developers to get used to XQuery or even XPath syntax. That should not stop you from starting to learn these different languages, though, since more and more information will be stored in XML over the coming years.

SQL Server 2000 supported XML shredding and XPath 1.0 expressions, and you saw some examples of these technologies in the previous chapter. However, XPath gets you only so far in working with your XML data. It lacks the ability to perform more complex operations on your XML data, as it does not support recursive XML schemas and projection and transformation syntax. XQuery is the big brother of XPath, in that the simplest form of an XQuery is an XPath expression.

Before we dive into XQuery, though, let's take a look at an XPath statement just in case you've never used XPath before or didn't read the previous chapter. We'll work with the following sample XML document. Please note that you can follow along with the samples in this chapter by opening the file XMLSample.sql included with the sample downloads for this book, which you can find in the Source Code area of the Apress website (http://www.apress.com).

```
<?xml version="1.0" encoding="UTF-8" standalone="yes"?>
<people>
  <person>
    <name>
      <givenName>Martin</givenName>
      <familyName>Smith</familyName>
    </name>
    <age>33</age>
    <height>short</height>
  </person>
  <person>
    <name>
      <givenName>Stacy</givenName>
      <familyName>Eckstein</familyName>
    </name>
    <age>40</age>
    <height>short</height>
  </person>
  <person>
    <name>
      <givenName>Tom</givenName>
      <familyName>Rizzo</familyName>
    </name>
    <age>30</age>
    <height>medium</height>
  </person>
</people>
```

To retrieve all the names for all the people, you execute the following XPath statement:

```
/people//name
```

To move this XPath query to an XQuery, you put a curly brace around the query, which tells the XQuery processor that the query is an XQuery expression and not a string literal.

■**Note** It is beyond the scope of this book to provide an in-depth tutorial on XPath; please refer to the previous chapter for an introduction to XPath. If you need more information, the book *Beginning XSLT* by Jeni Tennison (Apress, 2004) provides a good introduction to XPath, or you could check out the articles on sites such as `http:// www.xml.org`.

FLWOR

While you can use XPath expressions in XQuery, the real power of XQuery is through FLWOR. *FLWOR* stands for `For-Let-Where-Order By-Return`. FLWOR is similar to T-SQL's `SELECT`, `FROM`, and `WHERE` statements, in that you can conditionally return back information based on criteria that you set. However, instead of returning relational data like T-SQL, XQuery returns XML data. Let's look in more detail at each of the parts of FLWOR.

The For expression lets you specify the XML that you want to iterate over. The way you specify your XML is by using an XPath expression. Normally, you surround your entire XQuery statement with any beginning or ending XML tags that you want. This will depend on which nodes you iterate in your document and the desired structure of the returned XML document. You can think of this expression as being similar to combining the SELECT and FROM T-SQL statements.

The Let expression is currently not supported in SQL Server 2005. This expression allows you to set a variable to an expression, but does not iterate over the values.

The Where expression is similar to the T-SQL WHERE clause. This expression evaluates to a Boolean, and any value that returns True passes through and any value that returns False is rejected.

The Order By expression is similar to the SQL ORDER BY clause. This expression allows you to sort your resultsets using the sort order you specify.

The Return expression specifies the content that should be returned.

The following is a more complex example of an XQuery statement. The example iterates over the XML contained in a table and returns only the given name of people that have an age element in the XML document.

```
SELECT people.query(
'for $p in //people
where $p//age
return
  <person>
    <name>{$p//givenName}</name>
  </person>
'
)
FROM xmltblnew
```

The following XQuery counts the number of person elements in an XML document. It also shows how to use the query method of the XML datatype with XQuery.

```
SELECT people.query(
'count(//person)
')
FROM XMLtblnew
go
```

Beyond FLWOR, XQuery supports functions such as avg, min, max, ceiling, floor, and round. The following example shows how to calculate the rounded average age of people from an XML document:

```
SELECT people.query(
'round(avg(//age))
')
FROM XMLtblnew
go
```

Finally, XQuery has string functions such as substring, string-length, and contains, and datetime functions such as dateTime-equal, dateTime-less-than, dateTime-greater-than, and individual date and time functions. The example that follows shows some of these functions in use. First, you get all the nodes in the XML document under the people node that have an age. Then, you return the givenName element for each person. If you wanted to only return the data for this element, you could use the data function. Instead, you want to return the full element for the givenName. Next, if there is a match on a particular name, such as Martin, you want to return True; otherwise, you want to return False. Finally, the code figures out the maximum age of all people by using the max function.

```
SELECT people.query(
'for $c in (/people)
where $c//age
return
  <customers>
     <name>
      {$c//givenName}
     </name>
     <match>{contains($c,"Martin")}</match>
     <maxage>{max($c//age)}</maxage>
  </customers>
')
FROM xmltblnew
Go
```

Table 8-2 lists the functions you can use against the XML datatype when using XQuery.

Table 8-2. *XML Datatype XQuery Functions*

Category	Function	Description
Numeric	ceiling	Returns the smallest integer of the values passed to the function that is greater than the value of the argument.
	floor	Returns the largest integer of the values passed to the function that is not greater than the value of the argument.
	round	Rounds to the nearest integer the values passed to the function.
String	concat	Concatenates the strings passed to the function, such as concat($p//givenName[1]/text()[1],$p//familyName[1]/text()[1]).
	contains	Returns a true value if the first argument, the string to test, contains the second argument, the string to search for. Otherwise, it returns false.
	substring	Returns a portion of the first argument, the source string, starting at the location specified in the second argument and optionally for the length in the third argument, such as substring($p//givenName[1]/text()[1], 1, 2).
	string-length	Returns back the length of string passed as an argument.
Boolean	not	Flips the value of the Boolean from true to false and false to true.
Node	number	Returns a number for the value of the node passed as an argument, such as number($p//age[1]/text()[1]).
Context	last	Returns an integer that is the count of the last item in the sequence.
	position	Returns an integer that is the current position in the sequence. This is useful if you want to print the ordinal value of your sequence for identification.
Sequences	empty	Returns true if the argument passed, which is a sequence, is empty.

Table 8-2. *XML Datatype XQuery Functions (Continued)*

Category	Function	Description
	distinct-values	Removes duplicates from your sequence. You must pass a sequence of atomic values to this function, such as distinct-values(data(//people/person/age)).
Aggregate	avg	Returns the average of a sequence of numbers.
	count	Counts the number of items in the sequence and returns an integer.
	min	Returns the minimum value from a sequence of numbers.
	max	Returns the maximum value from a sequence of numbers.
	sum	Returns the sum of a sequence of numbers.
Constructor	various	Allows you to create an XSD type from another type or literal. Depending on the desired type, the constructor function will be different. For example, to construct a string, you would use xs:string("Tom") or a datetime using xs:dateTime("2005-10-01T00:00:00Z").
Data access	data	Returns the typed value of the node. For example, data(/people/person/name/familyName) returns the family name. Data is implicit and does not need to be specified, but doing so can help readability of your XQuery.
	string	Returns the value of the argument as a string. For example, to return just a string of the document node, you would specify string(/).

XQuery in More Depth

If you break apart the XQuery statements shown earlier, XQuery contains a prolog and a body. The prolog contains declarations and definitions that set up the necessary environment to run the body. This setup could include declaring namespaces in the prolog. The body consists of a series of XQuery expressions that will get you your desired result.

To declare a namespace in the prolog, you have two choices. You can either put in an inline declaration in the prolog or use the WITH XMLNAMESPACES keyword. To improve readability of your queries, you will want to use the WITH XMLNAMESPACES approach, since declaring namespaces inline can make a query very hard to understand and read. For example, take a look at the following two queries. You can decide for yourself which one is easier to understand, but most likely you will agree that the second one is the easier of the two.

```
SELECT people.query(
'declare namespace peopleschema="urn:example/people";
round(avg(//peopleschema:age))
')
FROM XMLtblnew
go

WITH XMLNAMESPACES('urn:example/people' AS peopleschema)
SELECT people.query(
'round(avg(//peopleschema:age))
')
FROM XMLtblnew
go
```

As part of the prolog, you can also declare a default namespace. You can then omit element namespace prefixes on all your elements in that namespace. This is useful if you only have one namespace for all elements in your XML document. Either you would use the declare default element namespace syntax if you declared your namespace in the prolog or you would use the WITH XMLNAMESPACES (DEFAULT 'yournamespace') syntax if you declared outside the prolog.

One thing to note is that you can use the WITH XMLNAMESPACES syntax with other operations besides just the XQuery operations. You can also use this syntax with FOR XML if you want to add a namespace to your FOR XML rendered XML documents.

Once you start working with the body of your XQuery, you will start using the literals and operators we discussed previously, such as sum, min, max, for, order by, path expressions, sequence expressions, and so on. One thing to always remember is that comparison operators are XML encoded, which means less than (<) is <, greater than (>) is >, and so forth. Another thing to note is that you can use the built-in types such as xs:string and xs:date in your XQueries. Casting is supported using the cast as operator for explicit casting, but XQuery also supports implicit casting for types it can coerce to be other horizontal types. Numeric types are only supported when doing implicit casting.

XQuery Processing in SQL Server

Because of its modular architecture, SQL Server can leverage the existing query execution and optimization technologies to process XQuery. Rather than building a separate query execution pipeline or optimization infrastructure, SQL Server leverages the same infrastructure for XQuery that it does for T-SQL. Because of this implementation, the level of integration between XQuery and T-SQL is superior. This is what allows you to do rich cross-domain queries between the two languages. For example, when SQL Server encounters an XQuery statement, the XQuery parser is called. The results of the XQuery parser, which is a query tree, is grafted onto any existing query to generate the entire query tree, which may contain both relational and XQuery queries. In effect, the T-SQL query and the XQuery are combined into a single query. The entire query is then passed to the optimizer, and a ShowPlan is created that includes the XQuery operations, as shown in Figure 8-4.

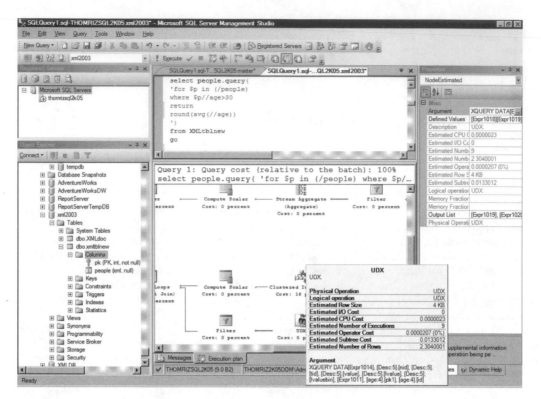

Figure 8-4. *Execution ShowPlan with an XQuery*

Basic XML Query Methods

Let's now examine the four methods for querying XML datatypes:

- query(): Returns the XML that matches your query
- value(): Returns a scalar value from your XML
- exist(): Checks for the existence of the specified XML in your XML datatype
- nodes(): Returns a rowset representation of your XML

query()

The query() method takes an XQuery statement and returns the XML that matches the query. The XML that is returned is untyped XML and can be further parsed if needed.

To see how this works, create a new table, xmltblnew, to store the XML. You'll use this table to learn how to query and modify XML data.

```
-- Create a new table
CREATE TABLE xmltblnew (pk INT IDENTITY PRIMARY KEY, people XML)
GO

--Insert data into the new table
INSERT INTO xmltblnew (people)
SELECT *
FROM OPENROWSET (
```

```
    BULK 'C:\peopleXML.xml',
    SINGLE_BLOB) AS TEMP
GO
```

The following example uses the query() method to look for all people who have an age, and then returns XML that identifies each person by name:

```
SELECT people.query(
'for $p in //people
where $p//age
return
  <person>
    <name>{$p//givenName}</name>
  </person>
'
)
FROM xmltblnew
```

As you look at the preceding XQuery, you will notice that it maps somewhat to T-SQL in the following ways:

- SELECT is equivalent to RETURN.
- FROM is equivalent to FOR.
- WHERE is equivalent to WHERE.
- ORDER BY is equivalent to ORDER BY.

The interesting part is that the semantics of the query are different. Rather than using relational types of operations, you use hierarchical path operations. The XQuery—and for that matter, XPath syntax—takes some getting used to. If you haven't thought in a hierarchical, path-based way before, you should start out with simple queries to learn the language. Once you progress from the simple queries, you will see that XQuery can be almost as complex in terms of functionality as T-SQL.

value()

The value() method returns a scalar value back from the XML instance. This method takes two arguments, with the first being the XQuery you want to use to get the value, and the second being the T-SQL type that you want that value converted to. You cannot convert to a timestamp or the NTEXT, TEXT, or IMAGE types. Also, you can't convert to an XML or sql_variant datatype.

You will want to try and match types between XML and SQL. For example, a string value in XML can be converted to any T-SQL string type. Numbers can be converted to numeric types. In addition, string values that can be coerced into numbers can be converted into numeric or money types. Date, time, or string values that can be valid datetime values can be converted into datetime types.

The following code snippet gets the age of the second person in the XML document and returns it as an integer:

```
SELECT people.value('/people[1]/person[2]/age[1][text()]', 'integer')
 as age FROM XMLtblnew
Go
```

As a quick aside, try running the following code and note the error you get:

```
SELECT people.value('/people[1]/person[2]/age[1][text()]', 'integer')
 as age FROM XMLtblnew
Go
```

You will get an archaic error telling you that the value function requires a singleton or empty sequence and not a operand of type xdt:untypedAtomic. You may be looking at this and thinking, "But I return the text of the first age element, which is a singleton!" Well, when SQL Server goes through its evaluation, it looks at the entire expression to see if any part can return more than a single node. In the code that returns an error, the people path in the expression does not have a position predicate, so it could possibly return more than a single node. The easiest way to fix this common error is to make sure you use position predicates in your expressions.

exist()

The exist() method is used to check for the existence of an XML datatype. This method returns 1 if the XQuery expression returns a non-null result. Otherwise, this method will return 0 if the condition is not met or if the resultset is null. The following example returns the columns in the SELECT statement where the givenName of the person stored in the XML document is equal to Tom.

```
SELECT pk, people FROM xmltblnew
  WHERE people.exist('/people/person/name/givenName[.="Tom"]') = 1
```

nodes()

The nodes() method returns a rowset for each row that is selected by the query. You can then work on that rowset using the built-in functionality of SQL Server. The following example returns the XML in relational form by breaking the XML into individual rows per person using CROSS APPLY. You could also use OUTER APPLY if you like. The nodes() method is similar to OPENXML, except that OPENXML requires you to prepare the document, and it uses the DOM to parse the document, which can slow down performance. The XML datatype is already parsed, so you could see better performance using nodes() than OPENXML.

```
SELECT T2.Person.query('.')
FROM   xmltblnew
CROSS APPLY people.nodes('/people/person') as T2(Person)

Results:
Row 1: <person><name><givenName>Martin</givenName>
<familyName>Smith</familyName>
</name><age>33</age><height>short</height></person>

Row 2: <person><name><givenName>Stacy</givenName>
<familyName>Eckstein</familyName></name><age>40</age>
<height>short</height></person>

Row 3: <person><name><givenName>Tom</givenName>
<familyName>Rizzo</familyName></name>
<age>30</age><height>medium</height></person>
```

Cross-Domain Queries

There may be times when you want to combine your relational and XML data. You've already seen some examples in the previous section of cross-domain queries, whereby you combine relational queries with XML queries or vice versa.

SQL Server provides functionality for you to use your relational data in your XQuery through the `sql:variable()` and `sql:column()` methods. The `sql:variable()` method allows you to apply a SQL variable in your XQuery. The `sql:column()` method allows you to use a SQL column in your XQuery.

The following example uses the `sql:column()` method to retrieve values from relational columns in the table and `sql:variable` to retrieve a T-SQL variable value, and it uses both of these to generate a resultset.

```
USE xmldb
GO

CREATE TABLE xmlTable (id int IDENTITY PRIMARY KEY,
                       CustomerID char(5),
                       Name varchar(50),
                       Address varchar(100),
                       xmlCustomer XML);
GO
INSERT INTO xmlTable
VALUES ('AP', 'Apress LP', 'Berkeley CA', '<Customer />');

GO
DECLARE @numemployees int;
SET @numemployees=500;
SELECT id, xmlCustomer.query('
declare namespace pd="urn:example/customer";
        <Customer
             CustomerID=       "{ sql:column("T.CustomerID") }"
             CustomerName=     "{ sql:column("T.Name") }"
             CustomerAddress=  "{ sql:column("T.Address") }"
             NumEmployees=     "{ sql:variable("@numemployees") }">
        </Customer>
') as Result FROM xmlTable T;
GO
```

Modifying XML Data

Since XQuery does not natively support modifying data yet, SQL Server 2005 includes an extension method to XQuery, the `modify()` method. The `modify()` method allows you to modify parts of your XML data. You can add or delete subtrees, replace values, or perform similar XML modifications. The `modify()` method includes DML commands such as `insert`, `delete`, and `replace value of`.

SQL Server 2005 supports piecemeal XML modification. This means that when you modify your XML document, such as adding elements, changing attributes, or deleting elements, SQL Server performs just the necessary operations on the XML rather than replacing the entire XML document.

With the `insert` command, you can insert XML as the first or last element. You can also specify whether to insert the XML before, after, or as a direct descendant of an existing XML element. You can also insert attributes using this method. Without having to modify the entire document, you can use `insert` to easily put XML into existing documents.

With the `delete` command, you can delete XML elements or attributes from your XML document.

The `replace value of` command allows you to replace a node with a new value that you specify. The node you select must be a single node, not multiple nodes.

The following example inserts and changes the favoritecolor element for person number 3 in the XML document:

```
--First insert a new value
UPDATE xmltblnew SET people.modify(
'insert <favoriteColor>Red</favoriteColor>
  as last into (/people/person[3])[1]')
where pk=1
go

--Select the data to show the change
SELECT * FROM xmltblnew
go

--Modify the value
UPDATE xmltblnew SET people.modify(
'replace value of (/people/person[3]/favoriteColor[1]/text())[1]
  with "Blue"')
where pk=1
go

--Select the data to show the change
SELECT * FROM xmltblnew
go

--Now delete the value
UPDATE xmltblnew SET people.modify(
'delete /people/person[3]/favoriteColor')
where pk=1
go

--Select the data to show the change
SELECT * FROM xmltblnew
Go
```

Limitations of XML Modification

You have some limitations when you modify your XML. For example, for typed or untyped XML, you cannot insert or modify the attributes xmlns, xmlns:*, and xml:base. For typed XML only, the attributes are xsi:nil and xsi:type. For typed or untyped XML, you cannot insert the attribute xml:base. For typed XML, deleting and modifying the xsi:nil attribute will fail, as will modifying the value of the xs:type attribute. For untyped XML, you can modify or delete these attributes.

Indexing XML for Performance

There may be times when you want to increase query performance speed at the cost of data insertion speed by creating an index on your XML columns. SQL Server supports both primary and secondary indexes on XML columns. In addition, your XML column can be typed or untyped. SQL Server 2005 supports indexes on both. SQL Server will index all the tags, values, and paths in reverse order, as path expression searches are faster when the suffix is known.

SQL Server stores the XML datatype in a BLOB field. This field can be up to 2GB in size, and parsing this field at runtime to perform queries without an index can be very time consuming. For this reason, you may want to create an index to speed performance. One thing to note is that the base table must have a clustered index to create an XML index on an XML column. You cannot modify the primary key of the table until you drop all XML indexes on the table. Once you create the XML index, a B+ tree structure is created on all tags, values, and paths on your XML data.

If you do a lot of queries but few inserts on your table with the XML column, you should consider indexing the column with one or more indexes. Also, if your XML data is large but you're often returning only a subset of the data, you will want to create an index. The index will be used when doing XQuery methods, but if you retrieve the entire column using relational methods, such as SELECT xmlCOL from Table, the index will not be used.

Creating the primary index is very straightforward. You can have only one primary XML index per XML column. You can, however, have multiple secondary indexes on an XML column. The following code creates a primary XML index on an XML column called people:

```
CREATE PRIMARY XML INDEX idx_xmlCol on xmltblnew(people)
```

Understanding How XML Indexing Works

Let's take a look under the covers of SQL Server to understand how XML indexing works, since the implementation will affect your system's performance depending on what you do with the XML data after it is indexed. Once you create a primary XML index, SQL Server creates a B+ tree that contains a shredded version of your XML. The XML index does have some redundancy, so you may see your XML index grow on average to about twice the size of the XML data, which means you should plan your disk space usage accordingly.

SQL Server uses ORDPATH, which is a system for labeling nodes in an XML tree that keeps structural fidelity. The easiest way to understand what the underlying index looks like is to consider an example. If we take part of the people XML and look at the structure for the index, Table 8-3 represents the index table.

Table 8-3. *Index Table for Sample XML*

OrdPath	Tag	Node_Type	Value	Path_ID
1	1 (people)	1 (Element)	Null	#1
1.1	2 (person)	1 (Element)	Null	#2#1
1.1.1	3 (name)	1 (Element)	Null	#3#2#1
1.1.1.1	4 (givenName)	1 (Element)	Tom	#4#3#2#1
1.1.1.5	5 (familyName)	1 (Element)	Rizzo	#5#3#2#1
1.1.3	6 (age)	1 (Element)	32	#6#3#2#1
1.1.5	7 (height)	1 (Element)	medium	#7#3#2#1

Of course, this XML is element based, so the index is not as interesting if you also have attributes and free text in your XML. The most important thing to note is not the values of the index, but the structure of the index. If you continued to draw the table out for the XML, you would find that the path ID overlaps with all XML elements that use the same path, such as all the givenNames for people use the path ID of #4#3#2#1, regardless of where they fall in the XML hierarchy in terms of document order. Also, the node type shown in the table is for illustration. SQL Server will map the value to an integer value and only use the integer value, not the string value shown in the table.

You will notice that only odd numbers are used for the ORDPATH. The reason for this is so that in the future, when insertions happen, you do not have to re-create the numbering scheme, but instead can use even numbers. This is not implemented in SQL Server 2005, but it is reserved for future use.

When you have an XML index, the query optimizer decides what will give the best performance when querying your XML. The optimizer can use a top-down approach, where it processes the base table rows before the XML index. Otherwise, it can use a bottom-up approach, where the optimizer does an XML index lookup and then back-joins with the base table. In the most common cases where you are retrieving the entire XML document or using XPath expressions that retrieve most of the data, the optimizer will just shred the XML BLOB at runtime rather than using the index.

One thing to realize is that if you insert or delete nodes that are earlier in the sibling order, you will incur significant cost if you use an XML index, since new rows will have to be inserted or deleted from the primary XML index. Remember that the index costs you time at inserts and deletes, but at query time it can significantly improve performance depending on the types of queries.

Examining Secondary XML Indexes

Once you create the primary XML index, you may want to create a secondary XML index to speed up your applications. There are three types of secondary XML indexes: PATH, PROPERTY, and VALUE. The type of index you will select depends on the types of queries your application uses the most. If you find that you are using one type of XQuery more often than another, and there is a secondary XML index that covers your query type, consider using a secondary XML index. You will not normally gain as much performance as creating a primary XML index on an unindexed table as you will adding a secondary index to a table that already has a primary index. You can have multiple secondary XML indexes on a single column.

If your queries are mostly path expressions to retrieve your data, you will want to use a PATH index. The most common operators that take path expressions are the query() method or the exist() method. If you find yourself using the query() or exist() method regularly in your code, you will want to definitely take a look at the PATH index. Plus, if your XML documents are large and you use path expressions a lot, the primary XML index will walk sequentially through the XML, which will provide slower performance than creating a PATH secondary index.

If you retrieve property values from your XML, you will want to use the PROPERTY index. For example, if you retrieve values in your XML such as the age or name as shown in the last example, you will want to use the PROPERTY index. Also, if you find that in your XQueries that you use the value() method regularly, you will want to use the PROPERTY index.

Finally, if you have a jagged hierarchy or you have imprecise queries using the descendant-or-self axis (//), you will want to use the VALUE index. This index will speed up value-based scans of your data. For example, you may use a wildcard search that will look at every element with an attribute of a certain value. A VALUE index will speed up this type of search.

Listings 8-1 through 8-3 show the creation of an index of each type and a query that will benefit from creating the particular index type.

Listing 8-1. *Creating a PATH Secondary Index*

```
CREATE XML INDEX idx_xmlCol_PATH on xmltblnew(people)
  USING XML INDEX idx_xmlCol FOR PATH
-- Query that would use this index
SELECT people FROM xmltblnew
  WHERE (people.exist('/people/person/name/givenName[.="Tom"]') = 1)
```

Listing 8-2. *Creating a PROPERTY Secondary Index*

```
CREATE XML INDEX idx_xmlCol_PROPERTY on xmltblnew(people)
  USING XML INDEX idx_xmlCol FOR PROPERTY
-- Query that would use this index
SELECT people.value('(/people/person/age)[1]', 'int') FROM xmltblnew
```

Listing 8-3. *Creating a VALUE Secondary Index*

```
CREATE XML INDEX idx_xmlCol_VALUE on xmltblnew(people)
  USING XML INDEX idx_xmlCol FOR VALUE
-- Query that would use this index
SELECT people FROM xmltblnew WHERE people.exist('//age') = 1
```

Full-Text Search and the XML Datatype

Beyond indexing the XML column, you can also full-text index the XML column using the built-in XML IFilter in SQL Server 2005. You can combine the XML column index with the full-text index.

There are a couple of things to understand first about full-text indexing of XML, though. Markup is not indexed, only content. Therefore, the elements are the boundaries of the full-text indexing. Furthermore, attributes are not indexed, since they are considered part of the markup. If you mostly store your values in attributes, you will want to use an XML index, not full-text search. Full-text search also returns back the full XML document, not just the section where the data occurred. If you want to retrieve a particular element that contained the search phrase, you would have to further query the returned XML document with XQuery. Finally, the XQuery contains method and full-text search contains method are different. Full-text search uses token matching and stemming, while XQuery is a substring match.

Other than these differences, the standard full-text restrictions are in effect, such as having a unique key column on the table and executing the correct DDL to create the index. The DDL that follows creates a full-text index on a table containing an XML column. A primary key index called pkft is created in the following code:

```
CREATE FULLTEXT CATALOG ft AS DEFAULT
CREATE FULLTEXT INDEX on xmltblnew(people) KEY INDEX pkft
```

You can combine an XML column index, both primary and secondary, with a full-text index. Whether you do this depends on what your data in the tables looks like, what your application workload does, and the overhead that you want to place on the server for creating and maintaining your index. If you find that you are querying data in your XML column regularly, and a lot of the XML information is not stored as attributes, then creating both a column and full-text index may speed up your query response time. First, you will want to filter based on the full-text index, and then you can use XQuery on the returned data to filter the XML data even more.

For example, the following code uses a full-text search with the CONTAINS keyword and an XQuery that also uses the CONTAINS keyword. Remember that the full-text search CONTAINS keyword is different from the XQuery one. The full-text search is a token match search that uses stemming, whereas the XQuery one is a substring match. Therefore, if you search for "swim" using full-text search, you will also find values for "swimming" and "swam." However, with XQuery, you will find only "swimming" and "swim," since XQuery performs a substring match.

```
SELECT * FROM   xmltblnew
WHERE  CONTAINS(people,'Tom')
AND people.exist('//familyName/text()[contains(.,"Rizzo")]') =1
```

Dynamic Management Views and XML

With SQL Server 2005, there are new views that you can use to peek into the server. These new views are covered in detail in Chapter 2. The XML datatype is represented in these views. For example, you can retrieve all the XML schemas registered in your database instance using the sys.xml_schema_collections view. You can retrieve elements and attributes that are registered by your schemas using the sys.xml_schema_elements and sys.xml_schema_attributes views.

The following code sample uses the dynamic management views to look at all the namespaces in a database instance, all the elements and attributes for a particular namespace, and also any indices on XML columns:

```
SELECT * FROM sys.xml_schema_collections
SELECT * FROM sys.xml_schema_elements
SELECT * FROM sys.xml_schema_attributes
SELECT * FROM sys.xml_schema_namespaces
SELECT * FROM sys.xml_indexes
```

Interesting scenarios for using these views occur when you want to figure out what namespaces exist in your server, what indexes you've created for your different XML types, and what the actual XML looks like across your server using the elements and attributes views. The following example uses the dynamic management views to enumerate all namespaces in your XML schema collections on the server. The code joins together the schema collection and schema namespace views so that you can see the name of your schema namespace. Without this join, if you query the sys.xml_schema_collections view, you would see only the name of the namespace you defined, which may be different from the name of the namespace in your schema.

```
SELECT *
FROM sys.xml_schema_collections xmlSchemaCollection
     JOIN sys.xml_schema_namespaces xmlSchemaName
     ON (xmlSchemaName.xml_collection_id = xmlSchemaName.xml_collection_id)
WHERE xmlSchemaCollection.name = 'Customer'
go
```

Applications and XML

If you use SQLXML or ADO.NET, programming using the XML datatype is simple and does not require much explanation. However, if you use SNAC, you will want to initialize SNAC with the new DataTypeCompatibility keyword in your connection string. You should set this string to be equal to 80, which specifies that you want to use the new SQL Server 2005 datatypes, such as XML. If you continue to use MDAC, there are no required changes to use the XML datatype. Both SNAC and MDAC will return XML as text. You could then load the text into an XML document object to parse the XML. For the richest XML experience, you will want to use .NET with SQLXML. The following code shows how to use ADO with data that uses the new XML datatype:

```
        Imports ADODB
        Const strDataServer = "localhost"
        Const strDatabase = "xmldb"

        'Create objects
        Dim objConn As New Connection
        Dim objRs As Recordset
```

```vb
'Create command text
Dim CommandText As String = "SELECT xmlColWithSchema" & _
            " FROM xmltbl2" & _
            " WHERE pk = 1"

'Create connection string
Dim ConnectionString As String = "Provider=SQLNCLI" & _
                    ";Data Source=" & strDataServer & _
                    ";Initial Catalog=" & strDatabase & _
                    ";Integrated Security=SSPI;" & _
                    "DataTypeCompatibility=80"

'Connect to the data source
objConn.Open(ConnectionString)

'Execute the command
objRs = objConn.Execute(CommandText)

Dim irowcount As Integer = 0

'Go through recordset and display
Do While Not objRs.EOF
    irowcount += 1
    MessageBox.Show("Row " & irowcount & ":" & vbCrLf & vbCrLf & _
     objRs(0).Value())
    objRs.MoveNext()
Loop

'Clean up our objects
objRs.Close()
objConn.Close()
objRs = Nothing
objConn = Nothing
```

XML Web Services Support

The final set of enhancements in SQL Server 2005 that we will look at is the addition of server-side XML web services support. With SQL Server 2000, you could expose your stored procedures as web services using SQLXML. However, this technology required you to run IIS on a mid-tier server. With SQL Server 2005, that requirement is done away with; SQL Server 2005 can expose XML web services directly out of the server without IIS installed. Now, you may be wondering about security concerns, but the web services functionality is explicitly off by default, and SQL Server requires you to create the web service through some code before it turns on.

By supporting web services, SQL Server can support clients that do not have MDAC installed or other platforms that may not even have Windows installed. Through the use of the documented web services protocols and formats, you can even use development environments that may not have native drivers for SQL Server.

The web services support allows you to send T-SQL statements with or without parameters to the server, or you can call stored procedures, extended stored procedures, and scalar UDFs.

You create an *endpoint* to expose your web services functionality. The endpoint needs to have a unique URL that SQL Server will listen on. When that URL receives a request, which is routed to the kernel mode http.sys, http.sys passes this request to the correct SQL Server functionality that the endpoint exposes. By using http.sys, SQL Server does not require IIS. There may be times, however, when you will want to expose your web services through a mid-tier component. For example, if you want to scale out your solution, you may find mid-tier components are easier and sometimes cheaper to scale than your SQL Servers.

You can have multiple endpoints for a single function, or you can expose multiple endpoints for multiple functions. It is up to your application architecture how you use this technology.

Before we look at the technology, we should state that there are times when using web services does not make sense. For example, web services are more verbose than using the native Tabular Data Stream (TDS) protocol, so if size and speed are concerns for you, web services may not make sense. Also, if your application works a lot with BLOB data, you will want to avoid using web services.

Creating an Endpoint

Assume you have a stored procedure existing in your database, and you want to expose it as a web service. The first thing you need to do is call some new DDL to create your endpoints. All endpoints are stored in the master database, and you can use the sys.http_endpoints dynamic management view to query for all the endpoints that exist. To find all the web methods you create, you can use the sys.endpoint_webmethods dynamic management view.

The DDL that follows creates a new endpoint. Please note that endpoints work only on platforms that support http.sys, which is the kernel mode http listener. Windows Server 2003 and Windows XP with Service Pack 2 are the only platforms that support this capability. The CREATE ENDPOINT statement for HTTP endpoints and web services uses the following format:

```
CREATE ENDPOINT endPointName [ AUTHORIZATION login ]
STATE = { STARTED | STOPPED | DISABLED }
AS { HTTP | TCP } (
   <protocol_specific_arguments>
        )
FOR { SOAP | TSQL | SERVICE_BROKER | DATABASE_MIRRORING } (
   <language_specific_arguments>
        )

<AS HTTP_protocol_specific_arguments> ::=
AS HTTP (
  PATH = 'url'
      , AUTHENTICATION =( { BASIC | DIGEST | INTEGRATED
      | NTLM | KERBEROS } [ ,...n ] )
      , PORTS = ( { CLEAR | SSL} [ ,... n ] )
  [ SITE = {'*' | '+' | 'webSite' },]
  [, CLEAR_PORT = clearPort ]
  [, SSL_PORT = SSLPort ]
  [, AUTH_REALM = { 'realm' | NONE } ]
  [, DEFAULT_LOGON_DOMAIN = { 'domain' | NONE } ]
  [, COMPRESSION = { ENABLED | DISABLED } ]
  )
```

```
<FOR SOAP_language_specific_arguments> ::=
FOR SOAP(
  [ { WEBMETHOD [ 'namespace' .] 'method_alias'
    (   NAME = 'database.owner.name'
      [ , SCHEMA = { NONE | STANDARD | DEFAULT } ]
      [ , FORMAT = { ALL_RESULTS | ROWSETS_ONLY } ]
    )


  } [ ,...n ] ]
  [   BATCHES = { ENABLED | DISABLED } ]
  [ , WSDL = { NONE | DEFAULT | 'sp_name' } ]
  [ , SESSIONS = { ENABLED | DISABLED } ]
  [ , LOGIN_TYPE = { MIXED | WINDOWS } ]
  [ , SESSION_TIMEOUT = timeoutInterval | NEVER ]
  [ , DATABASE = { 'database_name' | DEFAULT }
  [ , NAMESPACE = { 'namespace' | DEFAULT } ]
  [ , SCHEMA = { NONE | STANDARD } ]
  [ , CHARACTER SET = { SOL | XML }]
  [ , HEADER_LIMIT = int ]
)
```

If we look at an implementation of `CREATE ENDPOINT`, we get the following:

```
CREATE ENDPOINT SQLWS_endpoint
STATE = STARTED
  AS HTTP(
    PATH = '/sql/sample',
    AUTHENTICATION= ( INTEGRATED ),
    PORTS = ( CLEAR )
  )
FOR SOAP (
  WEBMETHOD
    'http://tempuri.org/'.'SQLWS'
    (NAME = 'xmldb.dbo.usp_SQLWS'),
    BATCHES = ENABLED,
    WSDL = DEFAULT
  )
```

As you can see in the code, you need to pass the name of your endpoint and the type of web authentication you want. You also pass the URL path for your web service, the ports used, the initial state, and finally the method name and whether you want to allow T-SQL batch statements and automatic Web Services Description Language (WSDL) generation.

There are a couple of things to note about creating endpoints. First, endpoints do not allow you to pass credentials unsecured over the wire. Therefore, if you use Basic authentication, you will have to use Secure Sockets Layer (SSL). To enable SSL, you will have to register a certificate on your server. To do so, use the httpcfg.exe utility to register, query, and delete certificates. Also, for testing purposes, you can make self-signed certificates using the makecert.exe utility.

Second, you can also use a subset of WS-Security to authenticate against the server. Specifically, SQL Server web services supports the Username token headers. This is used for SQL Server–based authentication.

Next, you can specify whether you want a complex WSDL, which will use complex XSD types (which some applications do not support), or a simple WSDL, which increases interoperability. To get a simple WSDL, just use `?wsdlsimple` at the end of your URL rather than the standard `?wsdl`. Finally, you can even specify your own custom WSDL by passing in the name of a stored procedure that returns the WSDL. This is useful if you know that the automatically generated WSDL does not work with your applications, and you need to tweak the WSDL.

One other thing to note about creating endpoints is that you can specify the format of the results to return. By default, SQL Server will return all the results, including the results, row count, error messages, and warnings. This is the `ALL_RESULTS` option for the optional `FORMAT` property. If you want only the data, set this option to `ROWSETS_ONLY`. This will return a dataset object rather than an object array.

Endpoints are implicitly reserved with `httpsys` when you use `CREATE ENDPOINT`. If SQL Server is running, `httpsys` will pass requests to SQL Server. However, if SQL Server is not running, other applications can be forwarded the requests rather than SQL Server. You can explicitly request a namespace from `httpsys` by using the system stored procedure `sp_reserve_http_namespace`, which takes the namespace you want to reserve. For example, if you want to reserve the `sql` namespace over port 80, you use `sp_reserve_http_namespace N'http://MyServer:80/sql'`.

Also, you can specify whether to have session support, which allows you to send multiple SOAP messages as a single session with the server. The default is no session support.

The last property that you may want to set is `DATABASE`, which specifies the default database. If you do not specify this property, SQL Server will default to the database specified for the login.

Once you create an endpoint, you can change it using the `ALTER ENDPOINT` statement. You can also drop the endpoint using the `DROP ENDPOINT` statement.

Endpoints are considered applications by SQL Server, in that you must explicitly give your users permissions to execute the endpoint. When you create an endpoint, only those with the sysadmin role or the owner role can execute the endpoint. In addition, endpoints do not skirt SQL Server security. You need permissions on the underlying SQL Server object in order to execute it. If you attempt to call an endpoint that you have permissions on without having permissions on the underlying stored procedure or UDF, you will receive an error.

In addition, endpoints have two levels of security. The first is at the HTTP transport layer, where you can specify web-based authentications such as Integrated, Basic, or Anonymous, and then at the SQL Server layer. The SQL Server layer requires that you are authenticated with SQL Server. Therefore, you could have an anonymous connection at the HTTP layer, but you would not be able to call any SQL Server functionality without passing explicit SQL Server logins and passwords.

To grant execution permissions for users on the endpoint, execute the following code:

```
use MASTER
GRANT CONNECT ON ENDPOINT::SQLWS_endpoint TO [DOMAIN\username]
```

Now that you've created your web service, let's see how to use it from Visual Studio. You can add a reference to the endpoint using the standard web reference dialog box in Visual Studio, as shown in Figure 8-5.

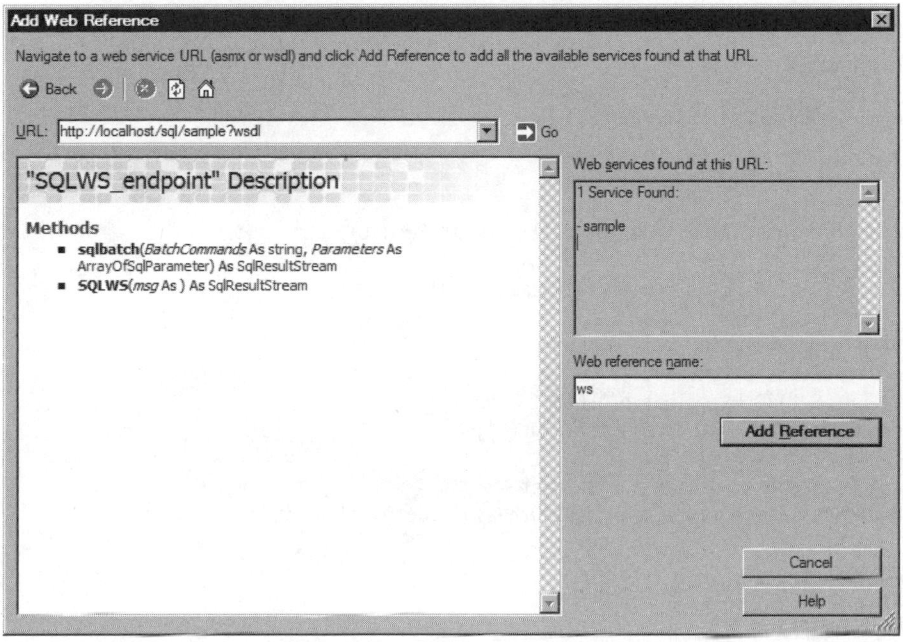

Figure 8-5. *Adding a web reference to a SQL Server web service*

Also, you can just retrieve the WSDL of your endpoint by passing in ?wsdl, just like you do for other web services. The code for getting the WSDL for the previous web service is shown here:

```
http://localhost/sql/sample?wsdl
```

Finally, you can call your web service from code using the standard functionality of Visual Studio or any other development environment that supports web services. Since XML web services use the DiffGram format for their return values, you can easily load the results into a .NET dataset. The following code will call your web services and assume the web service reference is named ws:

```
//Add a reference to SQL WS
ws.SQLWS_endpoint SQLWS = new ws.SQLWS_endpoint();

//Set default credentials to the Windows one
SQLWS.Credentials = CredentialCache.DefaultCredentials;

//Call the sproc through the WS
System.Data.DataSet dsReturnValue =
(System.Data.DataSet)SQLWS.SQLWS("Calling stored proc").GetValue(0);

//Get the reader associated with our Dataset
System.Data.DataTableReader drSQL = dsReturnValue.GetDataReader();
```

```
//Get the result
string strResult = "";
while (drSQL.Read())
    {
        strResult = drSQL[0].ToString();
    }

//Display the results
MessageBox.Show("Return value from SQL call: " + strResult);

ws.SqlParameter[] sqlparams = new ws.SqlParameter[0];

//Send a batch command to SQL
System.Data.DataSet dsReturnValue1 =
(System.Data.DataSet)SQLWS.sqlbatch("SELECT * FROM
sys.http_endpoints", ref sqlparams).GetValue(0);

//Get the reader associated with the Dataset
System.Data.DataTableReader drSQL1 = dsReturnValue1.GetDataReader();

//Get the result
string strResult1 = "";
while (drSQL1.Read())
    {
        strResult1 = drSQL1[0].ToString();
    }

//Display the results
MessageBox.Show("Return value from SQL call: " + strResult1);
```

As you can see, you need to create a new instance of your web service. Then, you need to set the default credentials for your web service calls. The code uses the default Windows credentials by using the CredentialCache class's DefaultCredentials property.

Once you set the credentials, you can make the call to your web service. Since you exposed a stored procedure, the code calls that first. Without casting the result, an object type would be returned by the server. Instead of just getting a generic object, the code casts the return value to a Dataset object. From the Dataset object, the code gets a DataTableReader object and then gets the results. The DataTableReader object provides a forward-only, read-only iterator over the data in your resultsets.

In the second example in the code, since the endpoint allowed batch commands, the code can send up T-SQL to the server to have it execute. Since the master database is the default database in this code, the dynamic management view for endpoints is queried and returned.

The code uses the built-in web services technologies in Visual Studio, but you could call this code from other environments and create the SOAP headers and body yourself. For example, you could use the Web Services Toolkit from VB6 or the XMLHTTP or ServerXMLHTTP objects directly to make raw HTTP calls to the server. This is the flexibility and power SQL Server gives you with the new web services integration.

Using Advanced Web Services

Most times, you will find yourself using the built-in capabilities of Visual Studio and SQL Server web services to do your web services programming. However, there may be times when you want to leverage the advanced functionality of SQL Server web services. For example, you may want to support sessions, transactions, SQL authentication, and other functionality.

To use the advanced functionality, you will need to dive into writing part of the SOAP envelope that will be delivered to SQL Server. The reason for this is that SQL Server uses some special extension headers to implement its functionality. Before we talk about how to achieve this functionality, let's look at a piece of what a typical SOAP request looks like. (Please note that only a portion of the SOAP request is shown for space reasons.)

```
<?xml version="1.0" encoding="utf-8" ?>
<soap:Envelope
    xmlns:soap="http://schemas.xmlsoap.org/soap/envelope/"
    xmlns:xsi="http://www.w3.org/2001/XMLSchema-instance"
    xmlns:xsd="http://www.w3.org/2001/XMLSchema">
 <soap:Body>
   <MySP xmlns="http://tempUri.org/">
<Param1>1</Param1>
<OutputParam />
  </MySP>
</soap:Body>
</soap:Envelope>
```

As you can see, SOAP messages are XML messages with an envelope and a body. The body contains the payload, which is the stored procedure, UDF, or even T-SQL batch you want to send to the server. SQL Server extends the envelope with some special headers to achieve more advanced functionality. Table 8-4 shows the SQL Server optional header extensions. The table assumes that you have declared the namespace for the header extensions as xmlns:sqloptions="http://schemas.microsoft.com/sqlserver/2004/SOAP/Options. Assume sqloptions: appears before each header name.

Table 8-4. *SQL Server XML Web Services Header Extensions*

Name	Description
applicationName	User-defined application name. You could use this to limit applications that call your web service.
clientInterface	User-defined client interface. For example, you could limit applications to only certain interfaces, such as ADO.NET 2.0.
clientNetworkID	User-defined network ID.
clientPID	User-defined process ID.
databaseMirroringPartner	The name of the database mirroring partner for this server. This is returned by SQL Server when you use the environmentChangeNotification("partnerChange") request.
environmentChangeNotifications	Allows you to specify that you want to be notified of environment changes. Valid environment changes include language changes using languageChange, database mirroring changes using partnerChange, database changes using databaseChange, and transaction usage changes using transactionChange.
hostName	User-defined hostname.

Table 8-4. *SQL Server XML Web Services Header Extensions (Continued)*

Name	Description
initialDatabase	Allows you to specify the initial database for your SOAP request. You can also pass the database filename using the filename attribute for this header. You must set this in your initial session request to the server if using sessions.
initialLanguage	Allows you to specify the language, similar to the SET LANGUAGE T-SQL command. You must set this in your initial session request to the server if using sessions.
notificationRequest	Allows you to use query notifications. You must specify the attributes notificationId and deliveryService, which specify the unique notification ID for the query notification already created and the delivery service that will deliver the notifications.
prepExec	Allows you to prepare and execute operations.
sqlSession	Allows you to maintain a session across multiple SOAP requests. This header has attributes, which are initiate, terminate, sessionId, timeout, and transacationDescriptor.

While just looking at the header descriptions may be confusing at first, seeing some of them in action will make the concepts clearer, as you'll see shortly. Before we do that, we need to look at non-SQL extension headers. SQL Server supports some parts of the WS-Security standard, specifically the ability to pass usernames and passwords using WS-Security. This is also the way that you specify SQL authentication information if you want to use that rather than Windows-based authentication. Remember that to use SQL authentication, you must set LOGIN_TYPE to mixed and PORTS must be set to SSL in your CREATE ENDPOINT statement. SQL Server will not let you send usernames and passwords over unencrypted channels!

To use WS-Security for your web services, you need to pass WS-Security–specific information in your headers. The following code shows how to perform a SQL-based authentication when calling a SQL Server web service:

```
<SOAP-ENV:Header>
        <wsse:Security  xmlns:wsse=
                "http://docs.oasis-open.org/wss/2004/01/
                  oasis-200401-wss-wssecurity-secext-1.0.xsd">
        <wsse:UsernameToken>
                <wsse:Username>thomriz</wsse:Username>
        <wsse:Password Type=
                "http://docs.oasis-open.org/wss/2004/01/
                  oasis-200401-wss-username-token-profile-
                1.0#PasswordText">Passw0rd!@11</wsse:Password>
        </wsse:UsernameToken>
        </wsse:Security>
</SOAP-ENV:Header>
```

As you can see, you pass the username using the Username element and the password using the Password element. You can even change passwords using WS-Security with SQL Server by adding the oldpassword element as follows:

. . .

```
        <wsse:UsernameToken>
        <sql:OldPassword Type="http://docs.oasis-open.org/wss/2004/01/
          oasis-200401-wss-username-token-profile-1.0#PasswordText"
         xmlns:sql="http://schemas.microsoft.com/sqlserver/2004/SOAP">pass
         word1</sql:OldPassword>
```

. . .

Using Sessions and Transactions with Web Services

Since the Web is asynchronous and loosely coupled in nature, SQL Server web services are that way as well by default. When you send a request via web services, each request is a new session and transaction with the server. In fact, there is an implicit transaction created when you send your requests. There may be times, though, when you want to keep a session alive across multiple requests, or you may want to be able to do transactions across session boundaries. To support this, SQL Server has the ability to initiate sessions and transactions as part of its web services support. To enable this, you must use the SOAP extension headers discussed earlier.

Before you can start using sessions, the endpoint you create must have sessions enabled. You can also specify session timeout and header limits. The following statement alters an endpoint to enable session support:

```
ALTER ENDPOINT default_endpoint_clear
FOR SOAP  (
                             SESSIONS = ENABLED,
                             SESSION_TIMEOUT = 1200,
                             HEADER_LIMIT = 65536
)
go
```

The next step is to send a SOAP header on your first request to the server that tells the server to enable session support, which you do by using the SOAP extension headers. The following is the header you send to start a session with SQL Server:

```
<SOAP-ENV:Envelope xmlns:SOAP-ENV="http://schemas.xmlsoap.org/soap/envelope/"
xmlns:sql="http://schemas.microsoft.com/sqlserver/2004/SOAP"
xmlns:xsi="http://www.w3.org/2001/XMLSchema-instance"
xmlns:sqlparam="http://schemas.microsoft.com/sqlserver/2004/SOAP/types/SqlParameter"
xmlns:sqlsoaptypes="http://schemas.microsoft.com/sqlserver/2004/SOAP/types"
xmlns:sqloptions="http://schemas.microsoft.com/sqlserver/2004/SOAP/Options"
>
<SOAP-ENV:Header>
<sqloptions:sqlSession SOAP-ENV:mustUnderstand="1" initiate="true" />
</SOAP-ENV:Header>
  <SOAP-ENV:Body>
    <sql:sqlbatch>
     <sql:BatchCommands>use Northwind
     </sql:BatchCommands>
    </sql:sqlbatch>
  </SOAP-ENV:Body>
</SOAP-ENV:Envelope>
```

The response from SQL Server will contain the GUID sessionId returned in the headers. You need to retrieve that sessionId and pass it along in subsequent requests to make sure you continue over the same session. The following is the response from the server:

```
<SOAP-ENV:Envelope xml:space="preserve" xmlns:xsd="http://www.w3.org/2001/XMLSchema"
xmlns:xsi="http://www.w3.org/2001/XMLSchema-instance" xmlns:SOAP-
ENV="http://schemas.xmlsoap.org/soap/envelope/"
xmlns:sql="http://schemas.microsoft.com/sqlserver/2004/SOAP"
 xmlns:sqlsoaptypes="http://schemas.microsoft.com/sqlserver/2004/SOAP/types"
xmlns:sqlrowcount=
   "http://schemas.microsoft.com/sqlserver/2004/SOAP/types/SqlRowCount"
xmlns:sqlmessage=
   "http://schemas.microsoft.com/sqlserver/2004/SOAP/types/SqlMessage"
mlns:sqlresultstream=
   "http://schemas.microsoft.com/sqlserver/2004/SOAP/types/SqlResultStream"
mlns:sqltransaction=
   "http://schemas.microsoft.com/sqlserver/2004/SOAP/types/SqlTransaction"
xmlns:sqltypes="http://schemas.microsoft.com/sqlserver/2004/sqltypes">
<SOAP-ENV:Header xmlns:sqloptions=
   "http://schemas.microsoft.com/sqlserver/2004/SOAP/Options">
   <sqloptions:sqlSession sessionId="SESSIONIDGUID">
</sqloptions:sqlSession>
   </SOAP-ENV:Header>
   <SOAP-ENV:Body>
     <sql:sqlbatchResponse>
     <sql:sqlbatchResult>
     </sql:sqlbatchResult>
     </sql:sqlbatchResponse>
   </SOAP-ENV:Body>
</SOAP-ENV:Envelope>
```

Please note that you must pass the sessionId to continue using a session. You must also continue to use the same endpoint and the same user context. If you change any of this, sessions will not work.

To terminate the session, send the terminate command and pass the sessionId to the server. Instead of showing the full SOAP request here, we show the terminate SQL header:

```
<sqloptions:sqlSession terminate="true" sessionId="SESSIONIDGUID" />
```

To use transactions, you must use sessions. However, you will want to make sure that in your headers, the transaction request comes before the session initiation. Please note that explicit transactions are supported only with SQL batches and not when calling web methods. If you want to support transactions with your web method calls, put the transaction into the functionality called by the web method. For example, if you expose a stored procedure as a web method, put your transaction context code in the stored procedure.

The following code is a snippet of the header you will want to pass to start transactions. You have to set the transactionBoundary attribute of the environmentChangeNotifications header to true to use transactions. Then you can use the BEGIN TRANSACTION statement in your T-SQL batch.

```
. . .
<sqloptions:environmentChangeNotifications transactionBoundary="true" />
<sqloptions:sqlSession initiate="true" timeout="60"/>
. . .
<sql:BatchCommands>
        USE MyDB
        BEGIN TRANSACTION
        INSERT INTO MyTable (MyColumn) VALUES ('MyValue');
     </sql:BatchCommands>
. . .
```

The server will let you know whether or not the transaction was successfully begun and will send back a transactionDescriptor. This is similar to the sessionId in that you need to send this transactionDescriptor with every request that wants to perform an action that uses that transaction context. The following code is a snippet of the response from the server:

```
<SOAP-ENV:Body>
    <sql:sqlbatchResponse>
        <sql:sqlbatchResult>
            <sqlresultstream:SqlTransaction xsi:type="sqltransaction:SqlTransaction">
                <sqltransaction:Descriptor>BQCCCDMABCD=</sqltransaction:Descriptor>
                <sqltransaction:Type>Begin</sqltransaction:Type>
            </sqlresultstream:SqlTransaction>
        </sql:sqlbatchResult>
    </sql:sqlbatchResponse>
</SOAP-ENV:Body>
```

The following code snippet is the next request, with the sessionId and the transactionDescriptor passed along with the request:

```
. . .
sqloptions:sqlSession sessionId="SessionGUID"
  transactionDescriptor=" BQCCCDMABCD="/>
. . .
```

Over one session, you can have multiple transactions. Just make sure to keep track of the different transactionDescriptor values that are sent back from SQL Server.

Adding SOAP Headers Using Visual Studio

The easiest way to add custom headers to your Visual Studio applications is to use the sample class included with SQL Server Books Online. This class makes it easy for you to take an existing SOAP call and add the headers to it. Since Books Online includes all the information you need to start using this class, we refer you there to get the sample code and the instructions for using that sample code.

Monitoring Performance of XML Web Services

The XML web services in SQL Server have a number of performance counters that you can monitor to understand how your web services are performing. The web services counters are under the SQL Server: General Statistics object. Table 8-5 lists the performance counters included.

Table 8-5. *XML Web Services Performance Counters*

Name	Description
HTTP Anonymous Requests	Number of anonymous requests per second
HTTP Authenticated Requests	Number of authenticated requests per second
SOAP Empty Requests	Number of empty SOAP requests per second
SOAP Method Invocations	Number of SOAP method invocations per second
SOAP Session Initiate Requests	Number of SOAP session initiations per second
SOAP Session Terminate Requests	Number of SOAP session terminations per second
SOAP SQL Requests	Number of batch SQL requests per second
SOAP WSDL Requests	Number of WSDL requests per second

Summary

In this chapter, you saw many examples of using XML in SQL Server 2005. With the addition of a new native XML datatype, which allows you to store your XML data right alongside your relational data, and support for the XQuery language and native XML web services, SQL Server 2005 should provide the level of XML support you need for most applications.

SQL Server 2005 Reporting Services

The runaway hit for SQL Server in 2004 was SQL Server 2000 Reporting Services. Reporting Services represented Microsoft's foray into the enterprise reporting market and introduced a very mature product, even though it was just the first version to the market. With its tight integration with Visual Studio and Microsoft Office, Reporting Services was a welcome addition to the SQL Server family, especially for all the customers and partners who were, and possibly still are, waiting for SQL Server 2005 to be released.

The Reporting Services technology allows you to design rich reports that can pull from multiple data sources; display the data from those data sources in a rich way using tables, matrixes, and charts; and also export your reports to a number of formats such as Excel, PDF, XML, or HTML without your writing any code. Reporting Services also provides an extensibility model that lets you extend the designer, exporting formats and delivery mechanisms for your reports. Finally, Reporting Services has an API that you can call using web services so you can automate almost any part of your reports through your own scripts or programs.

This chapter will describe the major components of the 2000 version of Reporting Services, and will then focus on the new features introduced in SQL Server 2005, such as the following:

- Tight integration with both the SQL Server Management Studio and also with Analysis Services. From a single report, you can easily build both relational and OLAP queries to access your data.

- New report design and execution capabilities such as an enhanced expression editor, multi-valued parameters, and a calendar picker.

- Additional Visual Studio integration and ReportViewer controls that allow reporting to be embedded directly within an application.

- End-user ad hoc (on-the-fly) query and reporting capabilities in Report Builder.

Reporting Services Components

Most companies store a vast array of data that can form the basis of many critical decisions affecting the performance and direction of the business. However, up until now, the creation of reports based on this data has involved the use of, often expensive, third-party tools that most frequently used proprietary formats for the definition of a report.

One of the goals of SSRS was to provide a single, standard platform for the design, creation, deployment, and management of all reports, and to promote interoperability between different reporting environments by adopting a standard XML-based language to define the reports, namely Report Definition Language (RDL).

The main architecture components of Reporting Services are as follows:

- *Report Server*: A web service API, responsible for every client request, either to render a report or to perform a management request

- *Metadata Catalog*: Stores all of the information related to reports, such as report definitions, data sources, report parameters, cached reports, security settings, scheduling and delivery information, and report execution log information

- *Report Designer*: A graphical client, embedded in Visual Studio, that allows you to design and deploy reports in a "drag-and-drop" environment

- *Report Manager web application*: A browser-based tool for viewing and rendering reports, creating report subscriptions, modifying report properties, configuring security, as well as a host of other tasks

You'll get a chance to take a look at each one in a bit more detail, but before you do, let's see Reporting Services laid out in an architectural diagram:

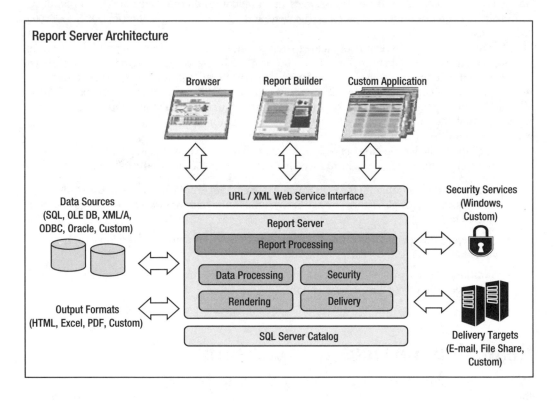

As you can see in the illustration, Reporting Services is made up of a Report Server, which contains the processing power of the server; a Metadata Catalog stored in SQL Server; a web services interface for applications or clients to call; and then a number of built-in but extensibility services in the Report Server. We'll take a look at the components of Reporting Services is more detail next and also look at what was in SQL Server 2000 Reporting Services to ascertain its level set before we go into what's in SQL Server 2005 Reporting Services.

Report Server

The Report Server is the main component of Reporting Services. It is a web service that uses subcomponents to retrieve data, combine that data with the report layout, and render the information into the requested format.

All the other components interact with the Report Server. For example, to deploy reports, the Report Designer calls the methods exposed by the Report Server's web service. The Report Manager web application instigates management operation via the web service. Client or server applications could call the web service to automate Reporting Services.

The Report Server also supports URL addressability so that you can embed reports in your application using a web browser. By passing different parameters along the URL, you can control different aspects of your reports. For example, the following URL retrieves a report called employees, the RDL file for which is stored in the HR subfolder of the reportserver virtual root directory (which points to the web service) of a Report Server called SRS03, and instructs it to render the report (the rs:Command parameter) in PDF format (via the rs:Format parameter):

```
http://SRS03/reportserver?/hr/employees&rs:Command=Render&rs:Format=PDF
```

Metadata Catalog

Reporting Services requires that you have a SQL Server database to store metadata information. The Metadata Catalog, created as part of the SSRS installation, stores information such as data sources, report snapshots that contain the layout and data for a report at a specific point in time, and report history and credential information for authentication, if you have Reporting Services store that information. This Metadata Catalog can be on the same server as your Reporting Services server, but most people deploy it on a separate server for performance reasons and for high availability using clustering.

Report Designer

One place where you will spend a lot of your time when working with Reporting Services is inside of Visual Studio .NET 2003, and the Report Designer. Reporting Services extends VS with a graphical Report Designer that you can use to connect to your data, write your queries, and design and deploy your reports, all in a drag-and-drop environment. Figure 9-1 shows a query being created in SQL Server 2000 Report Designer.

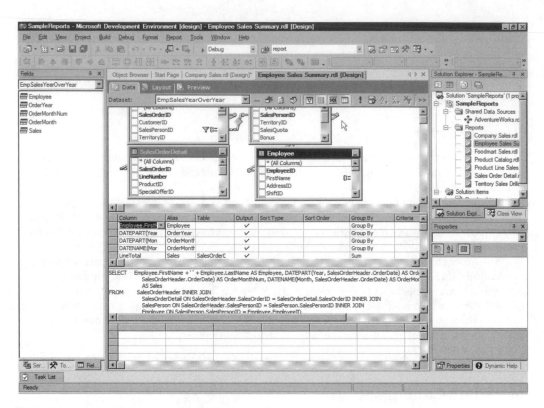

Figure 9-1. *Designing a query in the SQL Server 2000 Report Designer*

The Report Designer has a number of controls that you can use to add a user interface to your form. The Report Designer supports controls such as text boxes, tables, matrices, images, lines, charts, rectangles, and lists.

The Report Designer allows you to extend any of your reports using VB .NET expressions, or even to call code in a custom .NET assembly that you have associated with the report. Figure 9-2 shows a sample report included with Reporting Services. It demonstrates the use of an expression to set the background color for a cell in a table. Expressions are based on VB .NET and can be used in many different properties in Reporting Services.

As noted previously, your reports can also use custom .NET code. You can write script code using VB. NET and embed it directly in your report, or you can write a custom .NET assembly and call it from your report.

Use of embedded script code is the simpler of the two techniques, and you get the highest level of portability, since the custom .NET code is saved with the report definition file. To add your custom VB .NET code, you simply open the Report Properties window of your report from within Report Designer, and paste the code into the Custom Code window in the Code tab. Methods in embedded code are available through a globally defined `Code` member that you can access in any expression by referring to the `Code` member and method name (in other words, `Code.methodname`).

Use of a .NET assembly adds to the complexity of deployment: assemblies are deployed as a separate file and must be on every server where the report runs. However, the payback is flexibility. The assemblies can be written in any .NET language and, once installed, are available to all reports that run on that server.

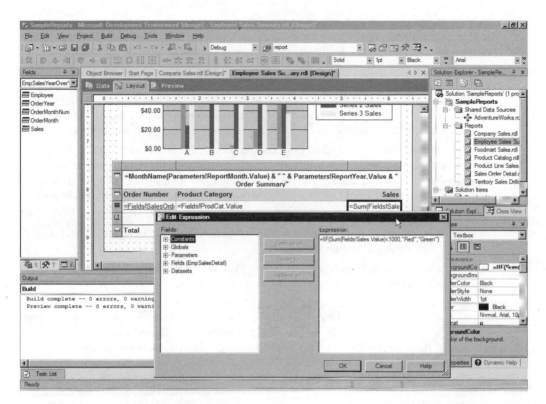

Figure 9-2. *A report that shows using controls and expressions in the Report Designer in SQL Server 2000*

■**Note** A full discussion of using custom assemblies with SSRS is beyond the scope of this chapter. The topic is covered in full detail in *Pro SQL Server Reporting Services* by Rodney Landrum and Walter J. Voytek II (Apress, 2004).

If you look at the source for your report, you will see that the report definition is an XML file. This XML file uses a standard schema for reports that Microsoft created called the *Report Definition Language*. You can find the complete schema at `http://www.microsoft.com/sql/reporting/ techinfo/rdlspec.mspx`. You could edit your report's XML by hand, but the Report Designer is a much better interface to create your reports! Since RDL is a published format, third-party tools can create RDL, and Reporting Services will consume that RDL.

Report Manager Web Application

The Report Manager web application allows you to browse, manage, and view your reports. Inside of the Report Manager interface, you can view the report hierarchy, select a single report to view, and then export that report to the multitude of formats that Reporting Services supports such as HTML, Excel, images such as TIFF, PDF, comma-delimited files (CSV), and XML. You can also manage your reports by performing actions such as managing your data sources, report parameters, execution properties, and subscriptions.

Three interesting pieces of functionality that Reporting Services provides and that you can manage through Report Manager are *caching*, *report snapshots*, and *subscriptions*, which are covered as follows:

- *Caching* allows you to increase the performance of your reporting solution. With caching enabled, a report can be added to the cache on its first execution and then retrieved from the cache, rather than the SSRS database, for subsequent requests.

- A report *snapshot* is a point-in-time representation of both the layout of a report and its data. The rendering of a large report (one that contains a lot of data) can consume valuable resources, and you may not want to perform this action every time a different user requests the report. Instead, you can create a snapshot of the report and allow users to access that. You can also use report snapshots to keep a history of your report and see how it changes over time.

- Finally, you can create *subscriptions* to reports. Subscriptions provide a means of delivering reports to a specified location, whether an e-mail account, a fileshare, or a custom delivery location you code, at a specified time (for example, to the e-mail account of a department manager on the last Friday of every month). There are two types of subscriptions in Reporting Services:

  - Standard subscriptions, which are statically set up for one or more users and can be created and managed by individual users

  - Data-driven subscriptions, which are system-generated and where subscriber lists can be dynamically generated from multiple data source locations

Data-driven subscriptions are great in scenarios where you have a very large list of subscribers who may want personalized data and report formats, and where the subscriber list may change over time. For example, you may want to deliver personalized reports for a thousand salespeople based on their own sales data. Each salesperson may want his or her report delivered in a different format, with some wanting HTML and others wanting PDF. Rather than creating and managing a thousand individual subscriptions for these salespeople, you can create one data-driven subscription that queries a database for the list of salespeople, their e-mail addresses, and the format in which they wish to get the report.

As part of subscriptions, you can select the delivery mechanism. Reporting Services supports delivering reports via e-mail or posting to fileshares. You can extend the delivery system in Reporting Services to deliver reports to other locations via a set of extensions called *delivery extensions*.

Reporting Services Security

The final piece of Reporting Services that we will discuss, before diving into SQL Server 2005 enhancements, is security. Reporting Services supports role-based security. The default roles in the server are as follows:

- *Browser*: Users assigned to the Browser role may only view reports, folders, and resources. They may also manage their own subscriptions.

- *Content Manager*: Administrators are assigned to the Content Manager role by default. This role allows a user to perform every task available for SRS objects such as folders, reports, and data sources.

- *My Reports*: When the My Reports feature enabled, this is the role that is automatically assigned to a user. It creates individual report folders specific to each Windows user, and allows that user to create and manage his or her own reports.

- *Publisher*: Typically this role is used for report authors who work with Report Designer to create and deploy reports. It provides the privileges required to publish reports and data sources to the Report Server.

- *System User*: Allows a user to view the schedule information in a shared schedule and view other basic information about the Report Server.

- *System Administrator*: This role can enable features and set defaults. You can set site-wide security and define role definitions. This role can also manage jobs on the server.

Additionally, you can create your own roles by combining individual permissions. For your reports themselves, when you use either the Report Manager interface or the web services interfaces, Reporting Services supports standard web authentication methods such as Basic, Digest, Integrated for authentication, and then you can encrypt the communication channel using SSL.

Building a Basic Report with SSRS 2000

Let's build a basic report that lists all employees from Northwind so that you can see how SSRS works in action. If you already are familiar with SSRS report design, you can skip this section and continue on to learn how SSRS has changed in 2005. This section will show you the SSRS 2000 experience so you can compare and contrast it to the enhancements in SSRS 2005.

Launching the Designer

Your SSRS report design will begin with Visual Studio. Note, if you are using SSRS 2005, you can use either Visual Studio or the new Business Intelligence Development Studio. For this walkthrough, we will assume that you are using Visual Studio. After launching Visual Studio, you should create a new project. In the project type list, you should see Business Intelligence projects. If they are not there, you need to install the Report Designer for SSRS, which you can do by running SSRS setup. In the BI project type, select Report Project on the right-hand side and type in **Basic Report** as the name. Click OK.

Working with Data Sources and Datasets

Now that you have your project up, you need to add a data source to your report. Without data, you will not have very much to report on! To do this, right-click the Shared Data Sources node in the Solution Explorer on the right-hand side and select Add New Data Source. For this example, use Northwind as your data source, so in the dialog box that appears, type in your server name for your SQL Server and select the Northwind database from the database drop-down list. Click OK, and you now have a data source.

However, you can't stop there because the data source defines what data you want to connect to, but you really haven't defined the data you want to report on. Now, you need to create a dataset from your data source. To do this, you first need to add a new report to your project. Right-click the Reports node in the Solution Explorer, select Add, select Add New Item, and finally in the dialog box select Report and click Open. The Report Designer should launch in the main window, and you should see a dataset drop-down list at the top. From the drop-down list, select <New Dataset...>. In the dialog box for the dataset, just click OK.

The first thing you will notice is that a new user interface appears. This is the Query Designer interface. SSRS drops you into the generic Query Designer by default, which is used for handwriting your queries. Normally, you would use this for queries against nonrelational data sources such as Exchange, Active Directory, or Analysis Services. Please note that you will see a graphical Query Designer for SSAS later in this chapter that is new in SSRS 2005. Let's switch the Query Designer into the graphical one, since we're working against a relational data source. To do this, just click the Generic Query Designer button on the dataset toolbar.

You should now see the graphical Query Designer with four distinct windows. Right-click in the top window and select Add Table. From this dialog box, you can select the tables, views, or functions you want to call from your data source. Select the Employees table, click Add, and then click Close. Now you can select the columns from the Employees table that you want to include in your report. You could also just write your T-SQL statement that you want to pass as well and paste it into the SQL window in the middle of the page. To make it easier, that is exactly what you will do. You could graphically build your SELECT statement, create GROUP BY clauses and other SQL functionality, but for simplicity, paste the following SQL statement into the third window in the designer:

```
SELECT    LastName, FirstName, Country
FROM      Employees
```

To test your query, you can click the Run button on the toolbar, represented by the exclamation point icon, to see what results you would get back. As you build more and more reports, you will appreciate the graphical Query Designer and the ability to execute your queries to see what data is returned. This report has a simple query, but you could write distributed queries across multiple data sources that will work with SSRS.

Laying Out and Previewing the Report

The next step is to lay out your report. Click the Layout tab at the top, and a blank grid should appear. This is your report body. Creating the layout is a matter of dragging Report Item controls such as Table, Lists, Matrices, or other controls onto the grid. Make sure you have selected the Toolbox on the left-hand side and can see the different layout controls. Drag and drop a Table control onto your report. You will see that SSRS automatically sizes the table to the width of your report and the table has a header, detail, and footer.

Next, select the Fields tab on the left-hand side. SSRS creates fields for the data that is returned in your dataset. You can also create calculated fields, which do not exist in the dataset but instead are created by writing VB .NET expressions. For example, you could have created a fullname field that combines first and last name together. You need to drag and drop your fields onto your table. Drag FirstName into the detail cell in the first column. Drag LastName into the middle detail cell. Finally, drag Country in the last detail cell. Notice how SSRS creates automatic headers for you as you do this.

Now that you have your simple report laid out, preview it. To do this, click the Preview tab at the top of the designer. SSRS allows you to preview the report before you deploy it to your server. This is useful so that you can find and fix any errors in your report.

Working with Expressions

The final piece of work on your report that you will do is add a little splash of color using VB .NET expressions. Go back to your design by clicking the Layout tab. You may want your rows to alternate colors so that they are easier to read. To do this, you need to make sure every even row is a different color than an odd row. SSRS supports expressions on many different properties in your reports. One such property that you'll create an expression on is the background color for your detail row in your report. Select the entire detail row by clicking the rightmost icon for the row, which should be a three bars icon. Next, in the Properties window, find the BackgroundColor property, click its drop-down list, and select <Expression...>. In the Expression dialog box, paste in the following expression in the right-hand side and click OK.

```
=iif(RowNumber(Nothing) Mod 2,"LightGreen","White")
```

This expression will check the row number in your report, RowNumber is a built-in function with SSRS, and if it's an odd row number, then the BackgroundColor will be LightGreen; otherwise the color will be White. Click the Preview tab at the top of the form to see what you have. You should see a lovely greenbar report like in the old greenbar printer days.

Deploying Your Report

You need to deploy your report to your server so that other users can use your report. To do this, you need to set some properties on your project to define where to place the report. To set your properties, right-click the report solution in the Solution Explorer called Basic Report and select Properties. In the dialog box, type in the TargetServerURL text box the path to your server. This path should be something like http://servername/reportserver/. Click OK. To deploy your report, from the Build menu, select Deploy Basic Report. You will see status information at the bottom of your screen on how the deployment is going. Once deployed, your report is now ready to be used by all users to whom you assign permissions for viewing the report.

Upgrading from SQL Server 2000 Reporting Services

The move from SQL Server 2000 Reporting Services to SQL Server 2005 Reporting Services is a very seamless one. Since the product was released only in early 2004, the format for RDL files has basically stayed the same. In fact, SSRS 2005 will support running SSRS 2000 reports. For example, the simple report created in the previous example will easily upgrade to SSRS 2005 by just opening the report in the new SSRS 2005 Report Designer. You need to modify your reports to take advantage of the new enhancements in RDL that support some of the new 2005 functionality. However, once you do that, your reports will not run on the 2000 version.

One of the interesting enhancements in setup for Reporting Services was the addition of *default values*. A lot of DBA users of SSRS 2000 did not want to have to enter in all the values for their website, e-mail address, or other information that the 2000 version consistently asked for. To remove this annoyance, SSRS 2005 by default sets values for you, which you can modify in setup when installing SSRS 2005. However, you cannot use the default values if you are not installing a local database engine at the same time or you want to perform a more advanced configuration that does not use the default values. Instead, you should select the Install but do not configure the server option, and then you can use the Reporting Services Configuration Tool, which you will learn about later in this chapter, to configure your server. Figure 9-3 shows the default values portion of SSRS 2005 setup.

The other things you will notice when setting up the 2005 version is that SSRS supports both multi-instancing and 64-bit SQL Server, both x64 and Itanium-based 64-bit. In 2000, you could only have a single instance of SSRS on a server, and the SSRS server did not fully support 64-bit. You could have your SSRS database sit on a 64-bit SQL Server, but you could not have your web services and SSRS runtime on a 64-bit machine. With this new support, you can break out your SSRS instances to allow more granular control and administration rather than having to set up completely new servers.

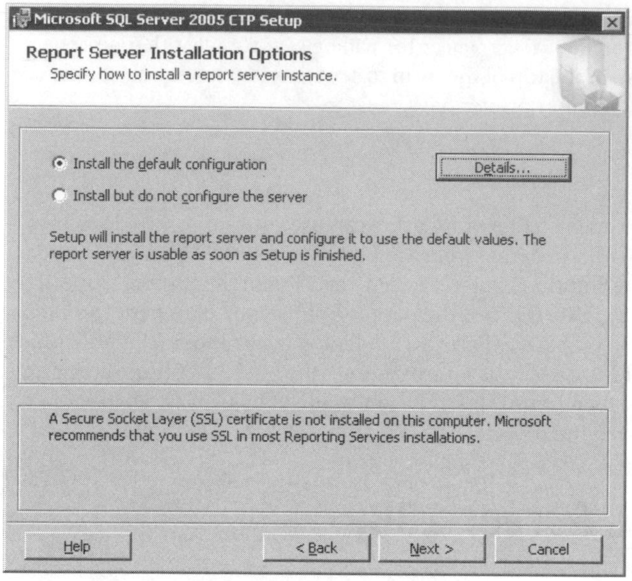

Figure 9-3. *Default values in SSRS 2005 setup*

Licensing Changes for Reporting Services

Some of the other changes you will see in Reporting Services are licensing related. Many will be happy that Reporting Services, at least the server-side pieces, are in all editions of SQL Server, from Express through Enterprise. You will find some restrictions such as Express and Workgroup only being able to access the local SQL Server as a data source.

This change is important, especially for developers who build SSRS applications. Today, developers need to write two different applications for SQL Server depending on the edition that they are targeting. The different editions will need to be SSRS enabled or not. The ReportViewer controls that you will learn about later in this chapter allow you to generate reports on all editions of SQL Server, but there is a problem with the controls from an application standpoint. The controls are designed to work against user-supplied data sources, such as an ADO.NET dataset, and do not write RDL that is compatible with the server RDL. Therefore, if you want to move from the ReportViewer controls to a Report Server, you will need to migrate your report application, or support two different versions of the application. With Reporting Services in all editions, you can write your report application once and scale it from Express Edition to Enterprise Edition.

Custom authentication has been extended to the Workgroup Edition. Based on feedback from customers, custom authentication is required to build ASP.NET forms-based authentication or custom authentication against other directory services such as an LDAP source; but providing the functionality only in Enterprise Edition was a major blocker due to the cost of Enterprise Edition. With this change, Internet-based scenarios for Reporting Services will become easier to buy and implement since many Internet scenarios use custom authentication instead of Windows-based authentication.

Another major change is that Report Builder, the end-user ad hoc query and reporting tool you will learn about later on, will be in Workgroup, Standard, and Enterprise Editions. Previously, you could only get Report Builder in Enterprise Edition. This is great news, since any paid-for edition now has this capability. For the lower editions such as Workgroup, Report Builder is limited in connectivity to only the relational databases on the local Workgroup SQL Server instance.

The main benefits you will get in the Enterprise Edition of Reporting Services are scale-out support, data-driven subscriptions, and infinite click-through in Report Builder. You will learn about infinite click-through later in this chapter when we look at the new Report Builder model.

SQL Server Management Studio Integration

In SSRS 2000, Report Manager was used to perform all management tasks, such as creating folders, managing data sources and report parameters, managing security, deploying RDL files, and setting up schedules for caching and snapshots.

SQL 2005 introduces a new integrated management tool called the SQL Server Management Studio (which we introduced in Chapter 2). Management Studio can manage SQL Server, Analysis Services, SQL Mobile Edition, and Reporting Services. All of the reporting management tasks just listed can now be performed using SSMS.

Report Manager still exists in SQL Server 2005, and you'll continue to use it if you have only browser access to your Report Server. However, you may find that the advantages inherent in using a single, integrated management tool may push you to use SQL Server Management Studio.

Figure 9-4 shows browsing the objects in a Reporting Services installation from Management Studio.

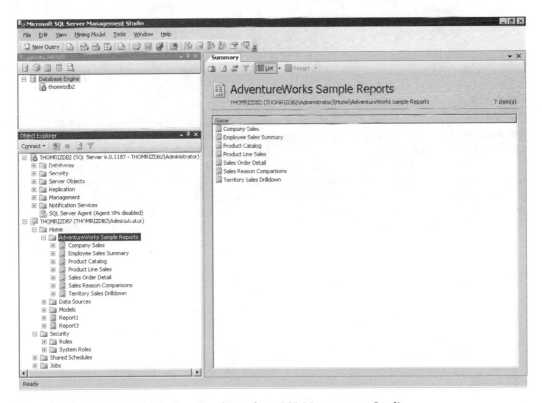

Figure 9-4. *Browsing Reporting Services objects from SQL Management Studio*

To get more intimate with managing a Reporting Services solution with Management Studio, the following walkthrough will demonstrate how to add a RDL file to the Report Server and then modify it, in the process highlighting some of the more common tasks that you'll need to perform in your environment, such as configuring a data source, managing parameters, and so on.

Walkthrough: Management Studio and Reporting Services

Imagine you're a DBA, and you've just been given the requirement to take a report that a developer has created and saved as an RDL, and add that report to your new SQL Server 2005 Report Server. How would you do this?

Well, the first step is to fire up Management Studio and connect to your Report Server as shown in Figure 9-5.

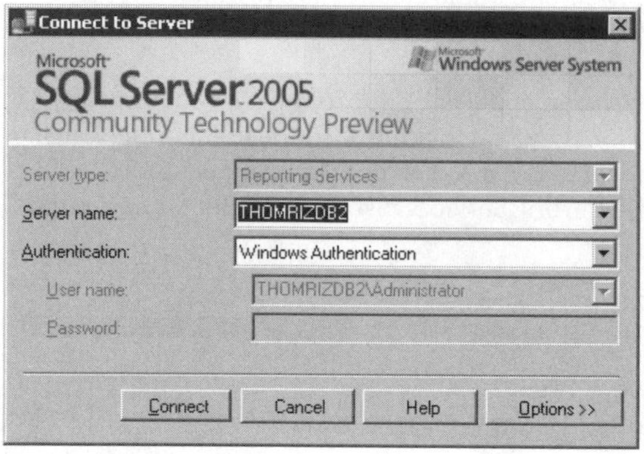

Figure 9-5. *Connecting to Reporting Services from Management Studio*

Once you have the connection, you may want to create a new folder to hold your report. To do this, right-click the folder underneath which you want to create the new folder. In this case, click the Home folder as shown in Figure 9-6.

Next, you will want to create whatever data sources you need for the report. You can have multiple data sources in a single report, but in this case, let's assume you have a single data source. By right-clicking your folder, you can add a new data source, and the New Data Source property page appears. In this property page, you can name your data source and select the connection information as shown in Figure 9-7.

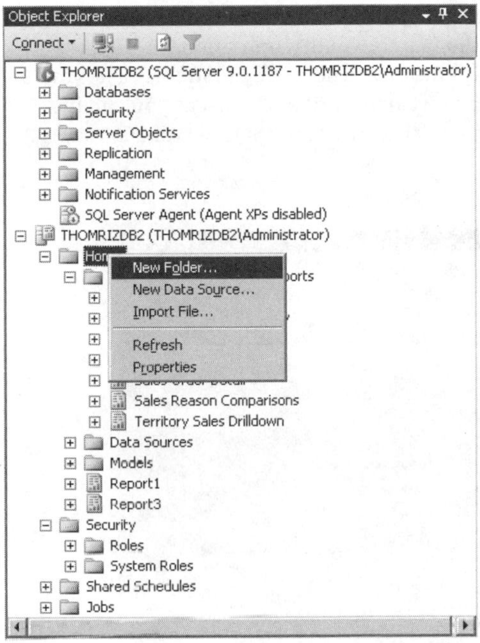

Figure 9-6. *Creating a new folder*

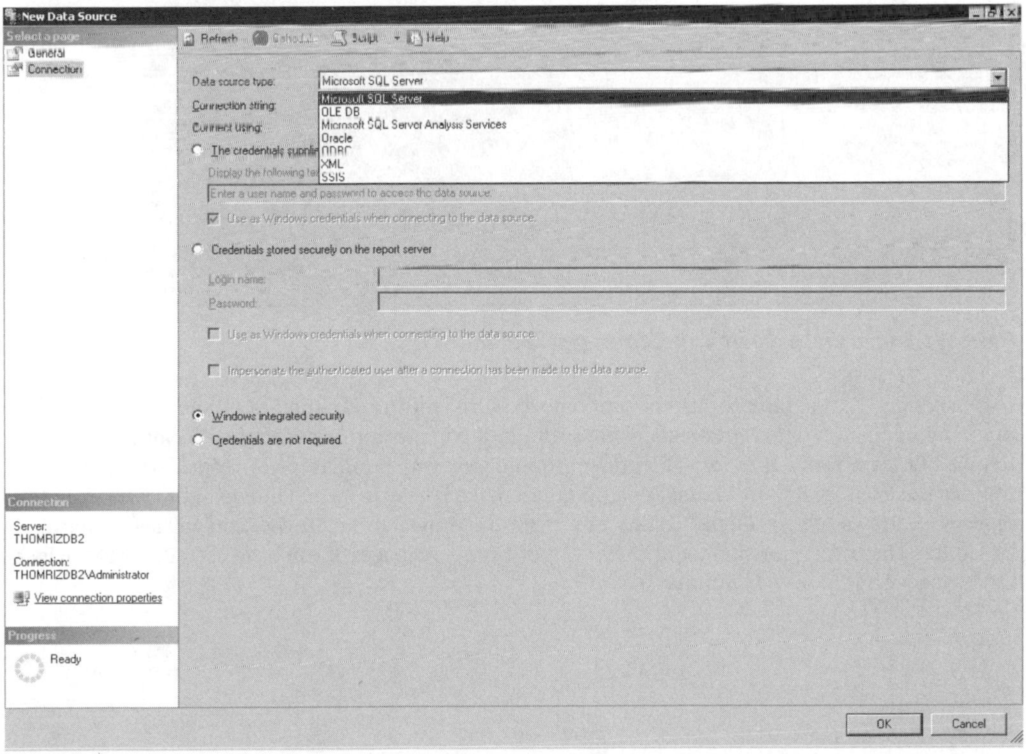

Figure 9-7. *Selecting a data source in Management Studio*

Now that you have your data sources, you need to get your report imported into the server. If you were the developer, you could just use Visual Studio to perform this operation through the Reporting Services deployment services integrated with the developer tool, but in this case, you'll use Management Studio. By right-clicking your folder, you can import a file, just as you can in Report Manager. Figure 9-8 shows importing an existing RDL file from the SQL Server 2005 samples into Reporting Services.

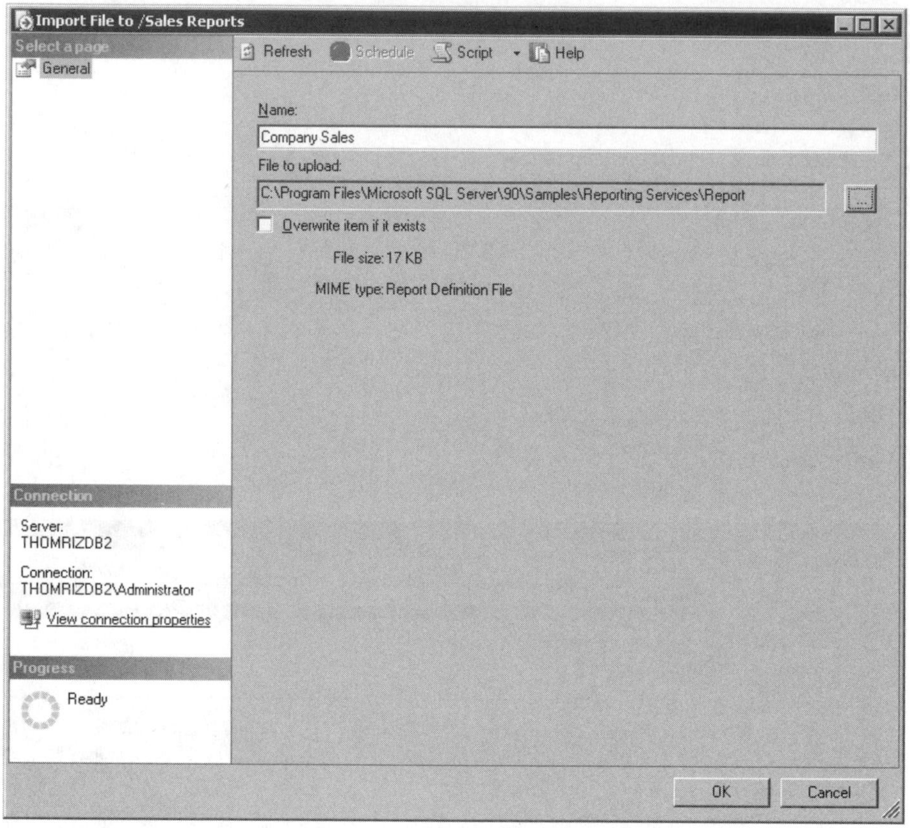

Figure 9-8. *Importing a report using Management Studio*

You may want to modify parts of your report such as setting parameters, changing data sources, or changing history or execution snapshot settings. If you are familiar with the Properties tab in Report Manager for your reports, Figure 9-9 should look very familiar to you. Management Studio mimics the existing Report Manager paradigm to make it easy to switch between the two tools. Figure 9-9 shows setting the properties for a report in Management Studio. You will see General, Execution, History, Permissions, and Linked Reports property pages. If you have used Report Manager, these pages should be very familiar to you.

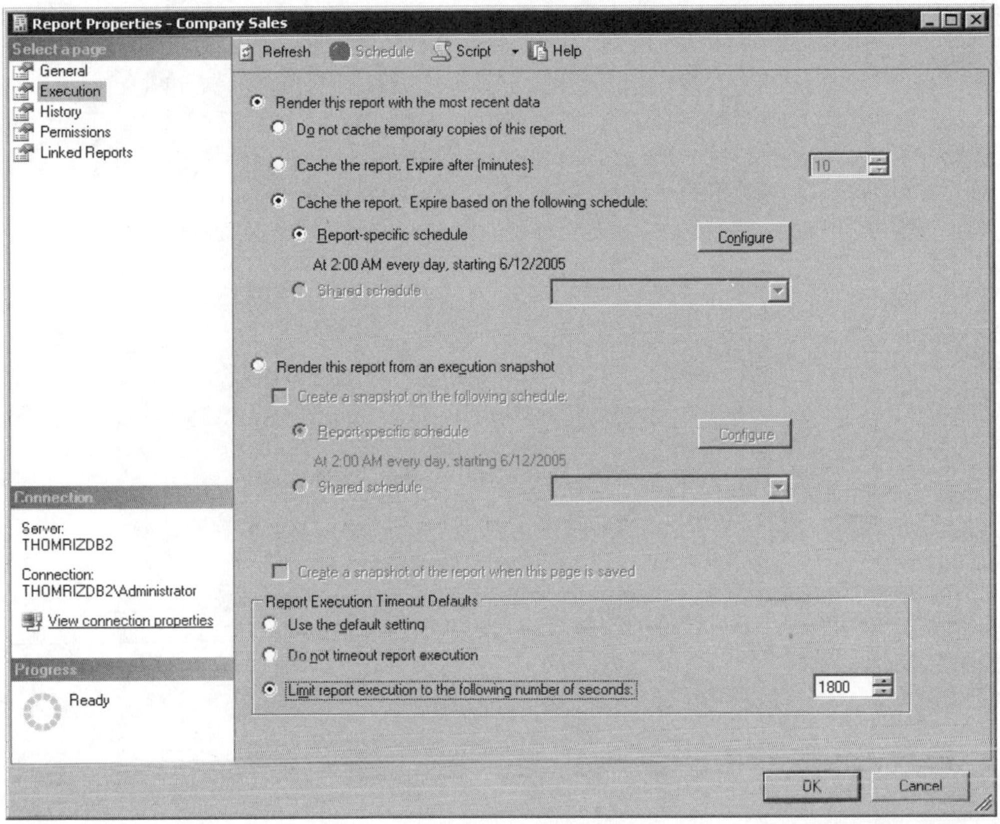

Figure 9-9. *Managing execution parameters using Management Studio*

Next, you may want to create a shared subscription schedule for your report. To create a shared schedule, right-click the Shared Schedules folder and select New Schedule. Shared schedules, as their name implies, can be shared among many reports just like shared data sources. Please note that SSRS uses SQL Server Agent to run scheduled reports, so SQL Server Agent must be installed and running on your server. Figure 9-10 shows the dialog box for creating the shared schedule. As you can see in the dialog box, you can set recurrence patterns and start and stop dates.

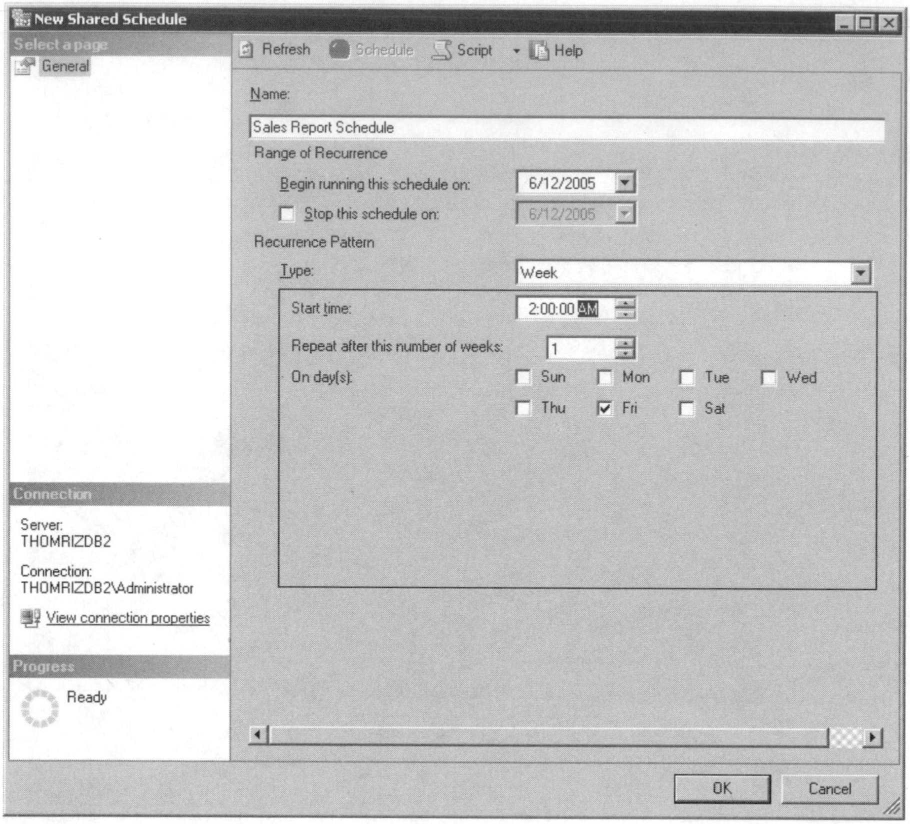

Figure 9-10. *Creating a shared schedule for report execution*

Now that you have your shared schedule, you can create snapshots or subscriptions that follow that schedule. Please note that in order to create subscriptions, you need to store the credentials with your data source when you create it or use no credentials at all. To create your subscription, you expand your report, and right-click the Subscriptions folder. Then, you can select the type of delivery you want for your subscription. All installed delivery extensions are displayed in the delivery extension drop-down list. You can write your own delivery extensions beyond the built-in ones, which include fileshares and e-mail. Delivery extensions are .NET components that implement the IDeliveryExtension interface. Figure 9-11 shows setting the properties for a subscription.

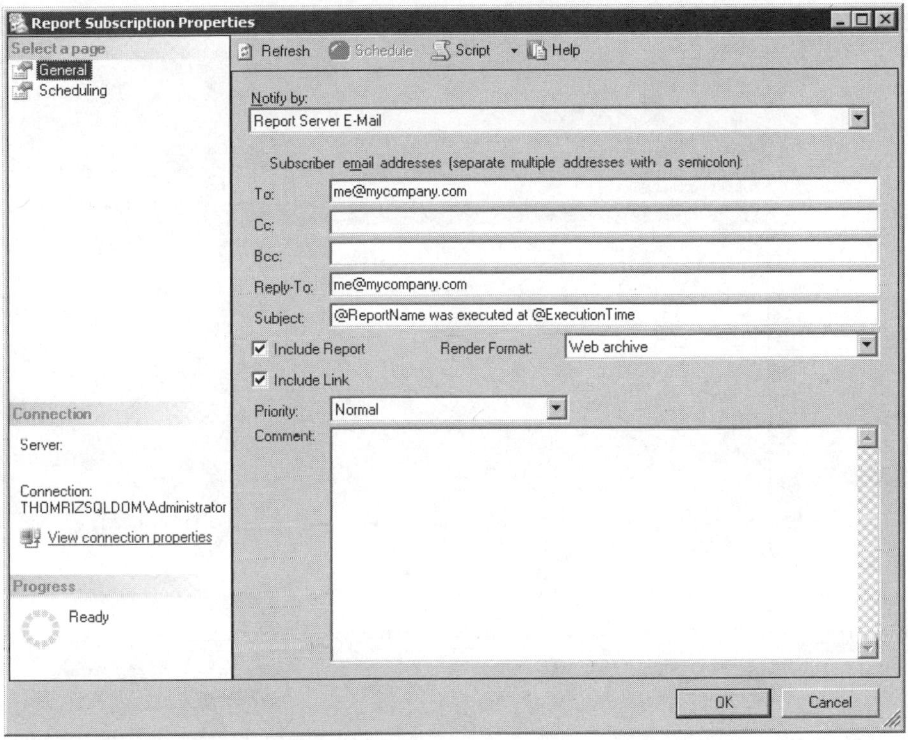

Figure 9-11. *Creating a subscription for a report*

The final step is to give your users permissions on the report. The standard roles that you found in SQL 2000 Reporting Services are included with SQL 2005 such as Browser, Content Manager, My Reports, Publisher, System Administrator, and System User. We will not be showing you how to create a custom role, even though you could do that in Management Studio; instead you will be adding users to your report through the user interface. To do this, you can right-click your report and select Properties. Under the Permissions page, you can add, remove, or change users and permissions on your report, as shown in Figure 9-12.

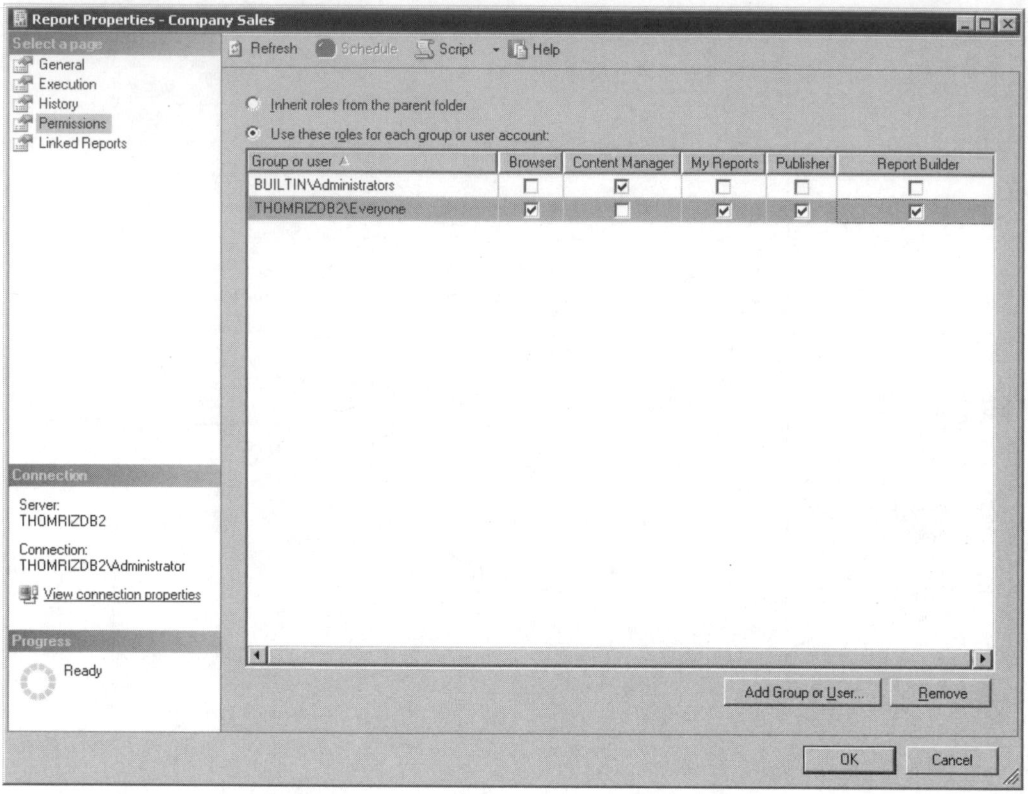

Figure 9-12. *Working with Reporting Services permissions in Management Studio*

You can also delete any of the objects you've created in this walkthrough such as your reports, data sources, or users. Management Studio combines your experience of managing your SQL Server assets with the addition of the ability to view and modify Reporting Services.

Management Changes

Another change has been made to SSRS when it comes to managing your server, even beyond the SSMS integration. There is a revised WMI provider for SSRS. This revised provider allows more granular control and querying of both SSRS and some parts of IIS that SSRS depends upon. You can use these new capabilities to build your own administration tool or script the management of Reporting Services. While the list of WMI classes and properties is too big to present here, let's take a look at performing some common operations using the WMI provider. From there, you will get the sense of how to use the WMI provider and then can apply that knowledge across the rest of the WMI classes for SSRS.

WMI Provider

We will look at an example that retrieves information about a particular instance of Reporting Services. The full sample is included in the samples for this chapter (downloadable from the Apress site at http://www.apress.com) so we will look at snippets of code from the full sample. What we will do is enumerate all the properties and methods for the instances of Reporting Services that you can call via WMI. Then, we will call one of those methods to perform functionality. Following this paradigm, you can call any of the other WMI methods provided.

The first thing to realize is that WMI is implemented in the System.Management namespace. The easiest way to browse WMI namespaces, rather than writing code, is to use the Server Explorer in Visual Studio. From the Server Explorer, you can see default WMI classes. Then, you can browse and add new WMI classes to the Server Explorer. However, we will be writing code to browse WMI namespaces.

The code snippet that follows sets some variables and then connects to WMI. As you can see, the code uses the new My namespace in VB, which is a lifesaver. WMI is implemented using namespaces, classes, and scopes.

```
Dim WmiNamespace As String = "\\" & My.Computer.Name & _
"\root\Microsoft\SqlServer\ReportServer\v9"
    Dim WmiRSClass As String = "\\" & My.Computer.Name & _
 "\ROOT\Microsoft\SqlServer\ReportServer\v9\Admin: " & _
 "MSReportServer_ConfigurationSetting"
    Dim serverClass As ManagementClass
    Dim scope As ManagementScope

    Private Function ConnecttoWMI() As Boolean
        scope = New ManagementScope(WmiNamespace)

        'Connect to the Reporting Services namespace.
        scope.Connect()
        'Create the server class.
        serverClass = New ManagementClass(WmiRSClass)
        'Connect to the management object.
        serverClass.Get()

        If (serverClass Is Nothing) Then
            ConnecttoWMI = False
        Else
            ConnecttoWMI = True
        End If
    End Function
```

After you connect to the WMI server class for Reporting Services, you then retrieve all instances of that server class that represent instances of Reporting Services. Then, to enumerate properties and methods, you just use the built-in properties and methods properties as you scroll through each instance. If you already know the method or properties you want to call, you do not have to perform all these steps, as you will see in the next example.

```
'Loop through the instances of the server class.
Dim instances As ManagementObjectCollection = serverClass.GetInstances()
Dim instance As ManagementObject
For Each instance In instances

    Dim instProps As PropertyDataCollection = instance.Properties
    Dim prop As PropertyData
    For Each prop In instProps
        strItemtoAdd = ""
        name = prop.Name
        val = prop.Value

        strItemtoAdd = name & ": "
        If Not (val Is Nothing) Then
            strItemtoAdd += val.ToString()
        Else
            strItemtoAdd += "<null>"
        End If
        listResults.Items.Add(strItemtoAdd)
    Next
Next

Dim methods As MethodDataCollection = serverClass.Methods()
Dim method As MethodData
For Each method In methods
    strItemtoAdd = method.Name
    listMethods.Items.Add(strItemtoAdd)
Next
```

If you want to call a method, which is more difficult than calling a property, you just need to set your in-parameters, which are the values you need to pass to the method. In the example that follows, we're going to show you how to back up your encryption key for your SSRS instances just in case you ever have to restore it. To set your in-parameters, you need to first get those parameters using the GetMethodParameters method and pass in the name of the method you are interested in. Next, you can set individual in-parameters via name and pass the values for the parameters. You need to pass a password for encrypting the encryption key to this parameter. Then, you use the InvokeMethod method to call the method with your parameters. You pass your object for out-parameters as part of that call so you can retrieve whatever comes back. In this case, you get back the HRESULT and the encrypted key, which eventually you display to the screen. You could easily store this key to disk so that you could back it up to hardened storage.

```
'Back up the encryption key for each instance using the
'BackupEncryptionKeyMethod
Dim instances As ManagementObjectCollection = serverClass.GetInstances()
Dim instance As ManagementObject

For Each instance In instances

    Dim inParams As ManagementBaseObject = & _
instance.GetMethodParameters("BackupEncryptionKey")

    inParams("Password") = "Tom15892!!"
```

```
              Dim outParams As ManagementBaseObject = & _
instance.InvokeMethod("BackupEncryptionKey", inParams, Nothing)

              Dim strKeyFile As String = ""

              Dim arrKeyfile As System.Array

              arrKeyfile = outParams("KeyFile")
              Dim i As Integer = 0
              For i = 0 To arrKeyfile.Length - 1
                  strKeyFile += Hex(arrKeyfile(i))
              Next


              MsgBox("HResult: " & outParams("HRESULT") & " Value: " & strKeyFile)
        Next
```

Management and Execution Web Services

The other change is the addition of two new web services that break out the management and execution management for developers who want to programmatically perform fine-grained control of both these functions. From the management web service, you can create folders, data sources, roles and list subscriptions, reports, and histories. From the execution web service, you can process and render reports. To access the report management web service, point to http://yourserver/ReportServer/ReportService2005.asmx?wsdl. To access the report execution web service, point to http://yourserverReportServer/ReportExecution2005.asmx?wsdl. Both have extensive object models, so we will point you to the documentation for all the different properties and methods you can use. Look for the section titled "Introducing the Report Server Web Service" in Books Online.

Reporting Services Configuration Tool

Previously, one of the hardest things for DBAs to understand was how to configure Reporting Services. If you have used Reporting Services in the past, I bet you have run into issues with the master key on your Report Server. This is one of the most common configuration errors that folks see with Reporting Services. To help with the task of configuring your Report Server after setup, you can use the new SSRS Configuration Tool. This tool allows you to work with SSRS virtual directories, service accounts, report metadata databases, encryptions keys, e-mail settings, and scale-out settings. Many of the things you would normally use the rsconfig command-line tool for are now included in the Configuration Tool. Figure 9-13 shows the main interface for the SSRS Configuration Tool.

You can also use the SQL Server Configuration Manager to manage some elements of your Reporting Services deployment, such as the report service and the service account. Furthermore, you may find that using the existing command-line tool actually continues to provide you with the most flexibility, especially in scripting scenarios where GUIs will not meet your needs. Finally, there are also web services that you can use to manage your SSRS environment. The reason for all these different tools and techniques is to provide a multitude of capabilities depending on your environment. If you are mostly a GUI person, you will find yourself using SSMS and the SSRS Configuration Tool most of the time.

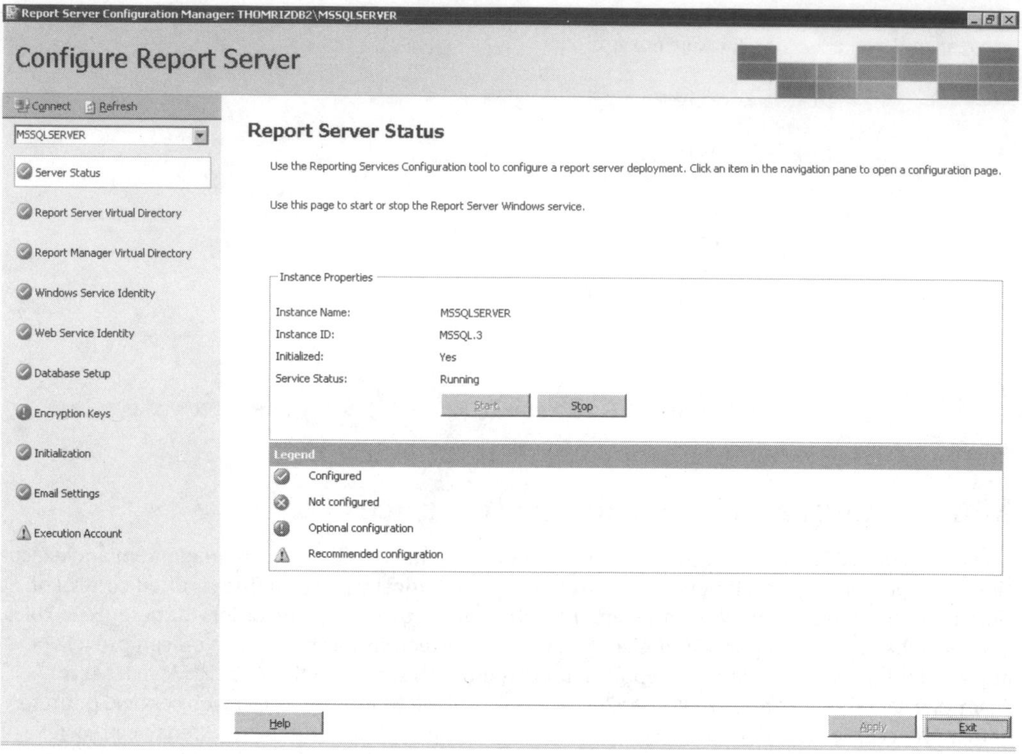

Figure 9-13. *SSRS Configuration Tool*

Report Design and Execution Improvements

Based on customer feedback on the top requested improvements, SSRS adds changes to both the design-time and runtime execution environment. SSRS design work is now part of the *Business Intelligence Development Studio* (BIDS). From BIDS, you can work with SSIS, SSAS, or SSRS. For SSRS in particular, you can create a new report project, run the Report Project Wizard, or create a new Report Builder model project, which we will discuss a little later on in the "Walkthrough: Report Builder" section. Figure 9-14 shows the new project user interface in BIDS that supports SSRS.

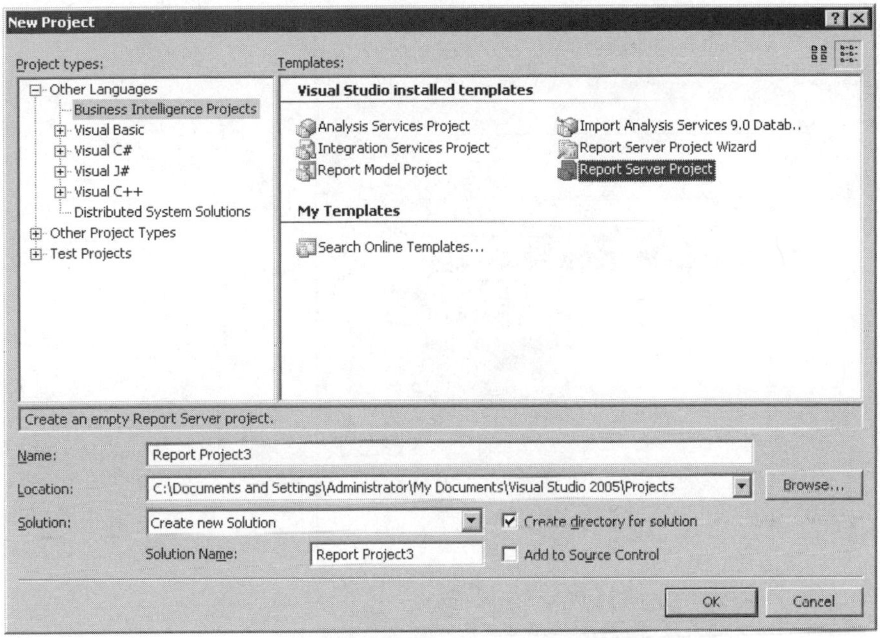

Figure 9-14. *Creating a report project in Business Intelligence Development Studio*

Expression Editor

As part of the new BIDS design-time environment, you will find new capabilities in the designer. The first one is that the designer now has an Expression Editor. Yes, you did read that correctly. You do not have to use Notepad-like functionality anymore to edit your expressions. You now get color coding, the ability to select functions from a list, syntax checking, intellisense for parameters, and even statement completion. One common question with regard to expressions in SSRS 2000 was the functions that SSRS supported. Figure 9-15 shows the new Expression Editor in SSRS 2005.

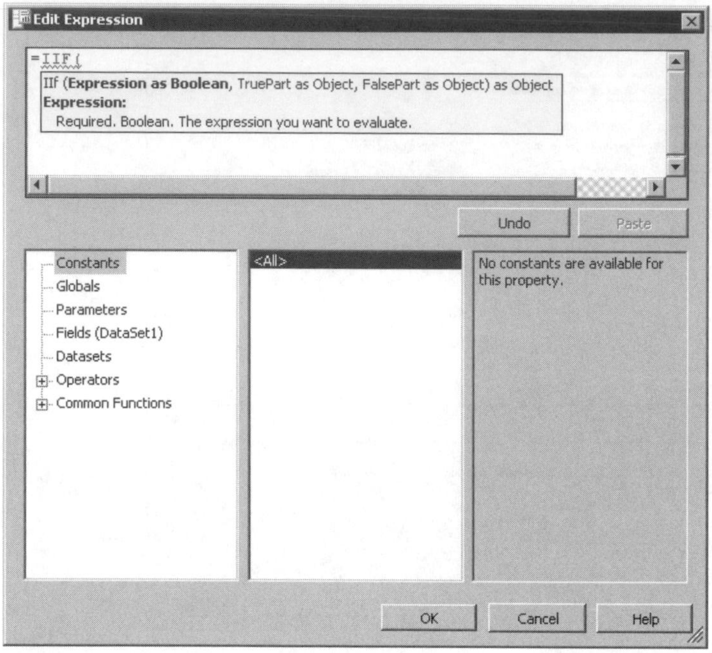

Figure 9-15. *The new Expression Editor*

Multivalued Parameters

SSRS 2005 introduces the concept of multivalued parameters. In SSRS 2000, you had to create this functionality either by passing delimited text that you would parse or by embedding SSRS into your application and wrapping it with your own parameter UI. Multivalued parameters are very useful in reporting applications. Imagine the scenario where you want to be able to select customers based on the state in which they live. However, you may have sales reps who cover multiple states, so they want to access their customers from multiple states at once. With multivalued parameters, you can provide this capability.

To create a multivalued parameter, you create your parameters as you normally would except you also check the multi-value check box option in the report parameters user interface as shown in Figure 9-16.

Also notice the new Internal check box in this figure. This is to support parameters that cannot be changed at runtime. They appear nowhere in the report or on the URL, unlike hidden parameters. These parameters only appear in the report definition. Enough on this digression, though. Once you have specified your parameter will be multivalued, the SSRS runtime takes care of displaying the parameters as check box options in the user interface for users to select the different values. There is even a Select All option that will select and deselect all parameter values. Figure 9-17 shows the runtime interface for multivalued parameters.

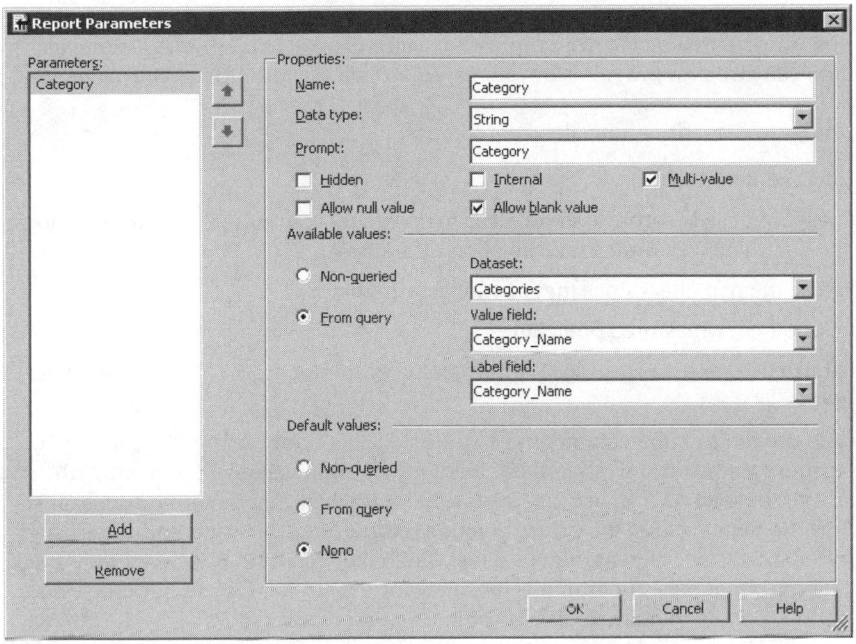

Figure 9-16. *Creating multivalued parameters*

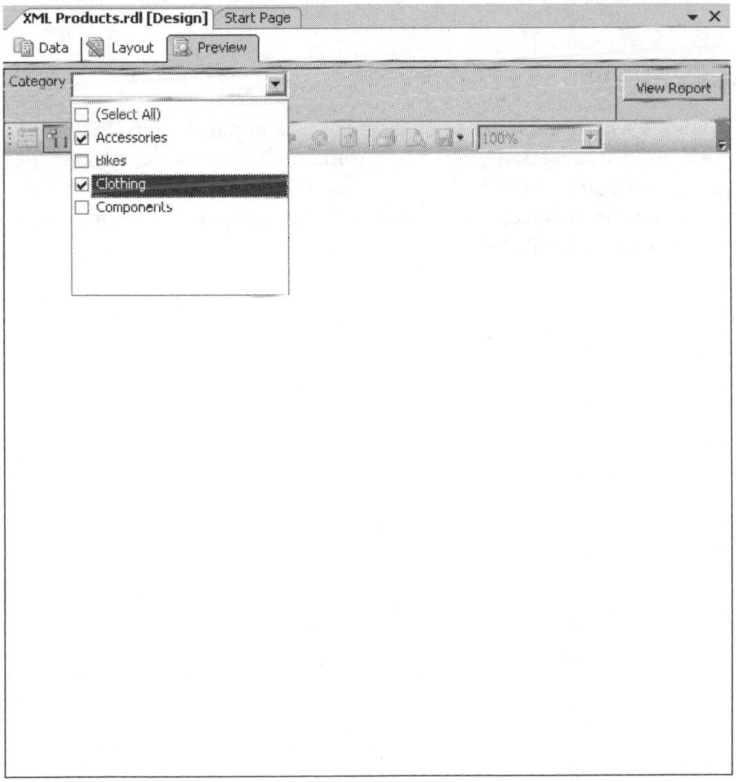

Figure 9-17. *Runtime UI for multivalued parameters*

When a user selects a multivalued parameter, SSRS returns back the selected values as a comma-delimited list. If you want to use that list in an expression, you will need to parse that list into its different values. You can also pass the value for your parameters along the URL to SSRS using a comma-delimited list.

A few other things to note with multivalued parameters:

- They cannot accept null values.

- They are always returned as strings, so you need to make sure your stored procedures or logic that uses the parameter can understand and parse the string.

- You cannot use them in filters since they are not deterministic.

- You cannot use them with stored procedures.

- Your query must use an IN clause to specify the parameter such as SELECT * FROM table WHERE name IN (@NameMVParam).

- If you want to use multivalued parameters in expressions, you can use the JOIN and SPLIT functions to join together or split apart the values for your multivalued parameter. With multivalued parameters, you can use the Label, Value, and Count functions to return back the names of the parameter values; the values function returns back the values for the selected parameters that might be different from the label, and finally count returns back the count of the values for the parameter. For example, the following expression returns back the values for a multivalued parameter named Cities: =Join(Parameters!Cities.Value, ", ")).

Finally, as with any parameters, make sure to not overdo the number of options you allow in your parameter. Limit it to the list that is required for the user to make the right selections; otherwise your performance will suffer.

DatePicker for Date Values

To support making it easier for end users to select date values when used in parameters, SSRS adds a DatePicker runtime control. A couple of caveats, though. The parameter has to use a datetime type, and it cannot be selected for a multivalued parameter. If you specify a multivalued parameter, you will get a drop-down list for your parameter value selection and not a DatePicker control. Figure 9-18 shows selecting a parameter that uses the DatePicker control.

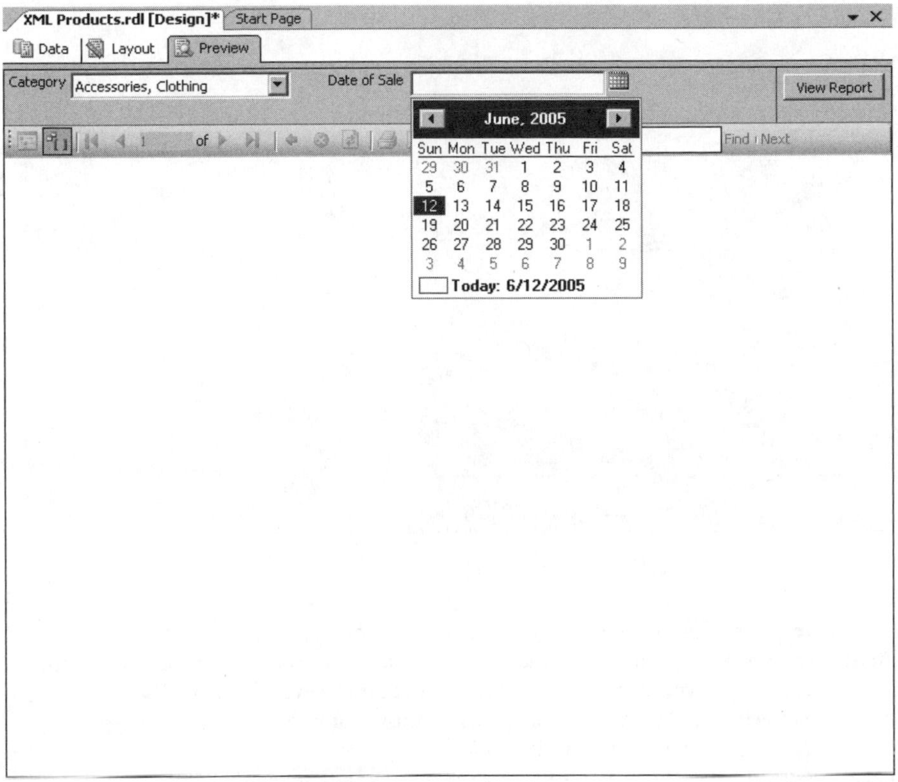

Figure 9-18. *Runtime UI for date parameters*

Interactive Sorting

While SSRS 2000 had some good levels of interactivity using features such as visibility toggles, one missing built-in feature was interactive sorting. If you have ever clicked a column heading in Outlook and saw your e-mail re sort according to that column heading in ascending or descending order, you have used interactive sorting. Again, you could hack your way around this limitation using parameters and data region sorting techniques, but that was for the SSRS expert, not the person who wanted to just click a check box or fill out a simple form to get the functionality. With 2005, interactive sorting is now a core feature of the product. Interactive sorting is done through text box properties in SSRS 2005. This means that you do not select an entire column to view the interactive sort properties, but instead click the text box that is the column heading in a table. Interactive sorting works with tables, lists, and matrixes as well as grouped or nested data in those containers. In addition, you can sort different multiple columns as well using this technology. Figure 9-19 shows the property page for interactive sorting.

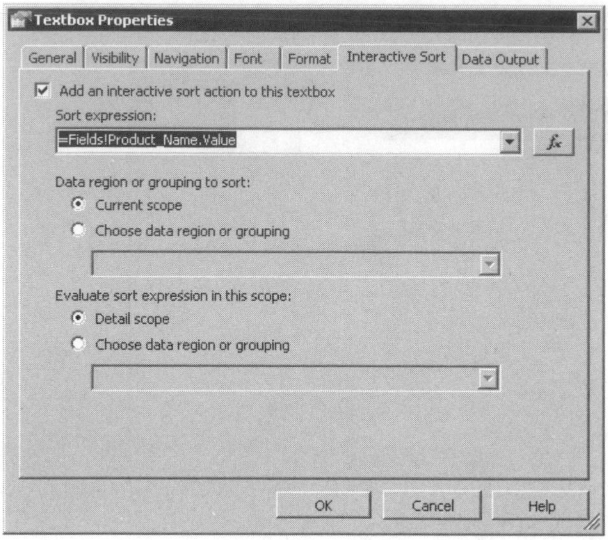

Figure 9-19. *Setting interactive sort settings at design time*

As you can see from the screenshot, you need to fill out the sort expression. For most scenarios, this will just be the expression that evaluates to the column of data that you want to sort. For example, if you are sorting on last names, you will put in an expression that will evaluate to the last name field in your report. There may be times when your sort may be more complex. For example, you may want to sort based on the relative value of another field.

You can also specify the data region or grouping to sort or where to evaluate the scope of the sort expression. This is useful if you want independent sorting based on grouping or not. For example, you could have a sales report grouped by country and then by city. You may not want to have changing of sort order of countries to affect the sort order of the cities in those countries. If you use the default settings, this is the default behavior. However, you could make re-sorting the countries affect the sorting of the cities as well.

The user interface for the sort is an up arrow or a down arrow depending on the sort order. When you do the sort inside of the user interface, a request is actually sent back to the server to redo the sort. It is not a client-side sort only, so you have to be careful about performance implications of users re-sorting on many columns in your report.

Analysis Services Integration

One of the pieces missing from SSRS 2000 was tight integration with Analysis Services. While you could manually write MDX into the generic Query Designer and query your AS cubes, this experience was no better than typing code in Notepad. You had no integrated Query Designer, and getting the query and report right on the first attempt was difficult, if not close to impossible. However, if you were working against relational sources, you could use the integrated visual data tools included with Visual Studio to add tables, create groupings, and preview the returned results.

With SSRS 2005, the deficit of AS integration is removed. By having SSRS integrate with BIDS, you now have one place where you can create and manage your Analysis Services technologies, such as cubes, key performance indicators (KPIs), and data mining settings. Plus, you can create your SSIS packages in BIDS. Finally, you can create and deploy your reports from BIDS. Figure 9-20 shows the interface for the Analysis Services in BIDS.

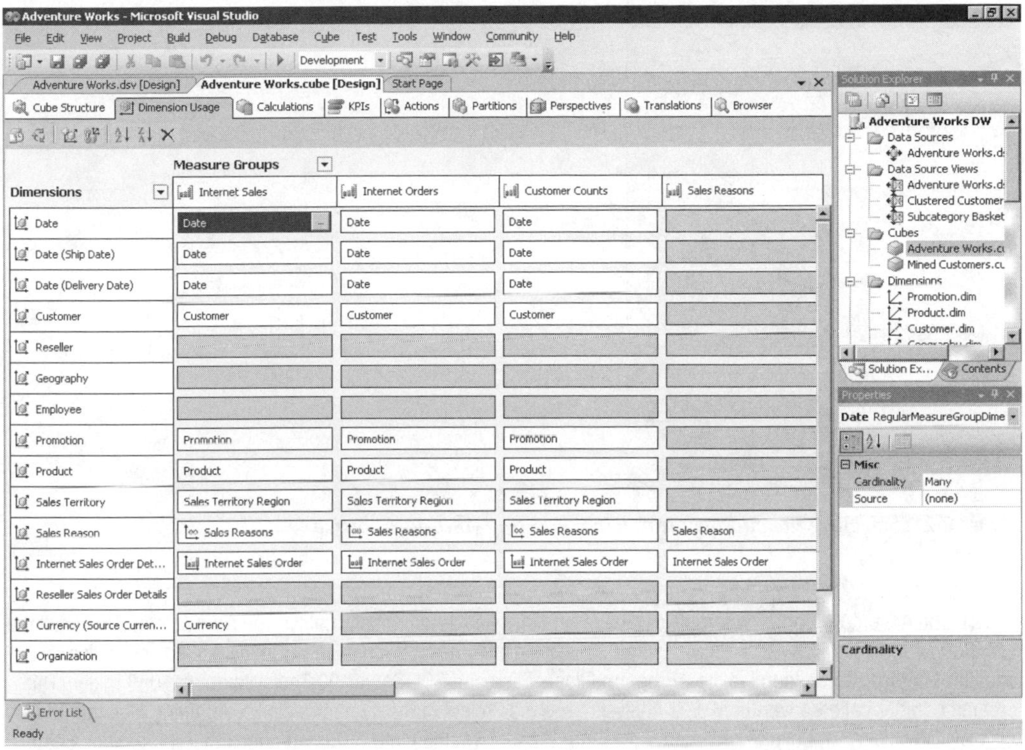

Figure 9-20. *SSAS interface in BIDS*

With Reporting Services, you can easily add your Analysis Services cubes to a report. Let's walk through the creation of a new report that uses OLAP technologies in SQL Server 2005 to give you a better understanding how the Analysis Services integration works. The walkthrough assumes you already have an existing Analysis Services cube. For the purposes of the walkthrough, the AdventureWorks sample database and cubes included with SQL 2005 will be used.

Walkthrough: Building a Report in BIDS

First, fire up BIDS. From the File menu, you can create a new project. If you select the Report Project Wizard, you will get the same wizard you have seen in SQL 2000. The only difference is that Analysis Services is a top-level data source and has a built-in Query Designer that you can launch from the wizard. Instead of using the wizard, use the generic Report Project type.

Once you select the report project and give it a name, you're dropped into the design environment, which is very similar to Visual Studio. Since BIDS builds on the Visual Studio shell, you will want to become familiar with the layout and commands of Visual Studio. In the Solution Explorer, you will add a new data source by right-clicking the Shared Datasources node and selecting Add New Datasource, just like you do in SQL 2000. For the provider, you will use the .NET Framework Provider for Microsoft Analysis Services, which is called SQL Server Analysis Services in the user interface, and fill out the location of your data as shown in Figure 9-21. You can find the AdventureWorks samples as part of your SQL Server 2005 installation, which you will use here.

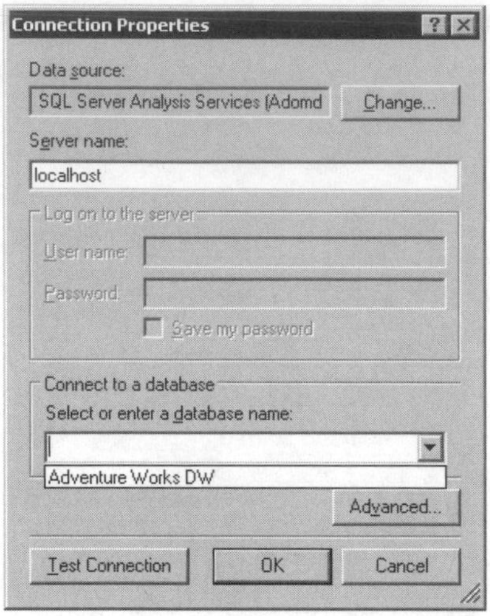

Figure 9-21. *Selecting the cube location when creating your data source*

Tip The AdventureWorksDW sample database isn't installed automatically unless you have selected to install the SQL Server 2005 samples as part of your setup. To install it after the fact, you need to run the SqlServerSamples.MSI installer file that can be found in the <Program Files>\Microsoft SQL Server\90\Tools\Samples\1033 folder. This creates a folder called AdventureWorks Analysis Services Project in the same directory containing files that make up a BI Tools solution. Load the solution (Adventure Works DW.slnbi) into BIDS and check that the project's data source matches your setup. If it's different, you'll need to change both the adventure_works.ds data source and the project settings (select Project ➤ AdventureWorksAS Properties on the main menu and then change the target server on the Deployment page of the Configuration Properties dialog box). Finally, deploy the database by right-clicking the solution name in Solution Explorer and selecting Deploy Solution. This may take some time . . .

If you double-click your data source after you create it, you will see that Analysis Services appears as a top-level data source, just like SQL Server, Oracle, OLEDB, and ODBC. The property page for the data source is shown in Figure 9-22.

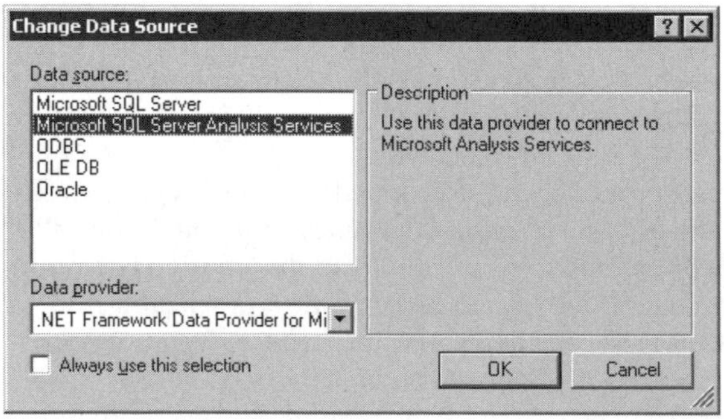

Figure 9-22. *Analysis Services as a top-level data source*

Next, you add a new report. Instead of using the Report Wizard, you just add a new item by right-clicking Reports and selecting Add ➤ Add New Item ➤ Report, which creates a blank report. Type in your report name, such as Report1.rdl, and click Add. Once the report is created, you can add a new dataset to the report by clicking the Dataset drop-down list and selecting <New Dataset…>. This new dataset will be based off your Analysis Services data source. Once you select the AS data source you created earlier and click OK, you are dropped into the AS Query Designer. This is a new feature in SQL 2005. Instead of having to write MDX by hand, you can drag and drop measures in the new Query Designer. The MDX is automatically generated for you based on your interaction with the Query Designer. If you are a power MDX user, you can still go into the generic Query Designer and write MDX by hand. The new Query Designer is shown in Figure 9-23.

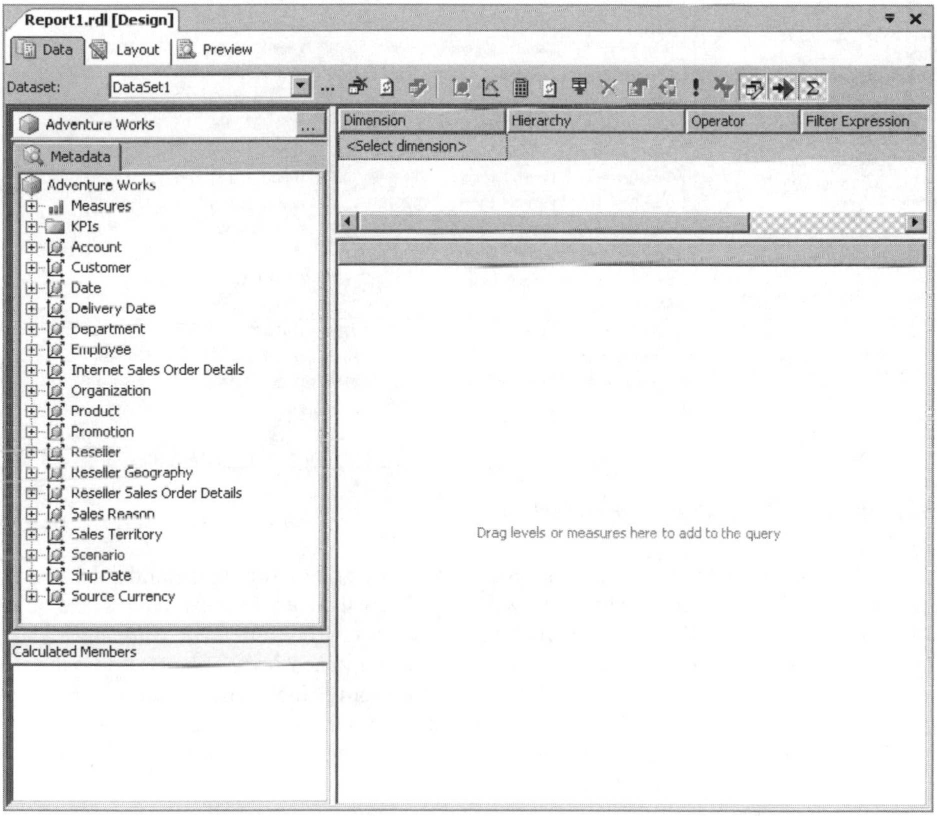

Figure 9-23. *The new AS Query Designer in Reporting Services*

Since you want to create a quick report that shows your salespeople how much they have sold, the total cost of the sales, and then the total profit each salesperson has brought into your company, you need to create your queries. The first step is to drag and drop from your measures, KPIs, or AS hierarchy over to your query window on the right-hand side. The first level in the hierarchy that you'll add to the report is the Employees level. When you drag and drop, the Query Designer executes the query to return a preview of your result set, as shown in Figure 9-24, once once you complete the steps that follow.

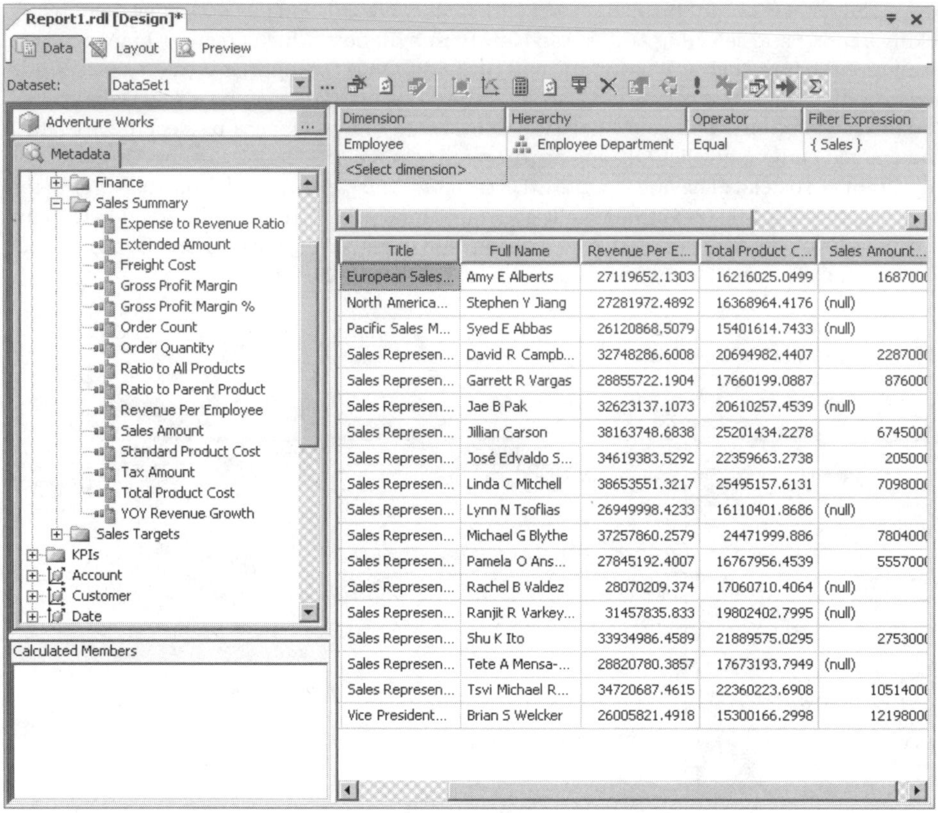

Figure 9-24. *Previewing the result set in the Query Designer*

First, drag and drop the dimension called Employee onto the grid on the right-hand side. You can find this dimension under the AdventureWorks cube. This will create the Department Name, Title, and Full Name columns. You can remove the Department Name column if you want since you will filter on it later anyway. Next, you need to drag and drop some measures. The first one is the Revenue Per Employee measure. You can find this under the Measures hierarchy, then under Sales Summary. Drag and drop the Revenue Per Employee measure onto the grid. Then, drag and drop the Total Product Cost measure from the same hierarchy. Finally, drag and drop the Sales Amount measure from the same location onto the grid.

Since right now this returns all employees, not just the sales employees, you need to refine your query a little bit. Rather than writing the MDX by hand, all you need to do is select the dimension on which you wish to filter in the top filter dialog box, the hierarchy in that dimension that you want to use, the operator, and finally the value. Here, you will select the Employee dimension, the Employee

Department hierarchy, and check to see whether the Employee Department name is equal to "Sales". Optionally, you can make the filter expression a parameter to the report by clicking the check box called Parameters, which could be off the screen to the right in some cases. Since you do not want to make this a parameter because you just want one value for this filter, you will leave the check box unchecked. This entire action is shown in Figure 9-25.

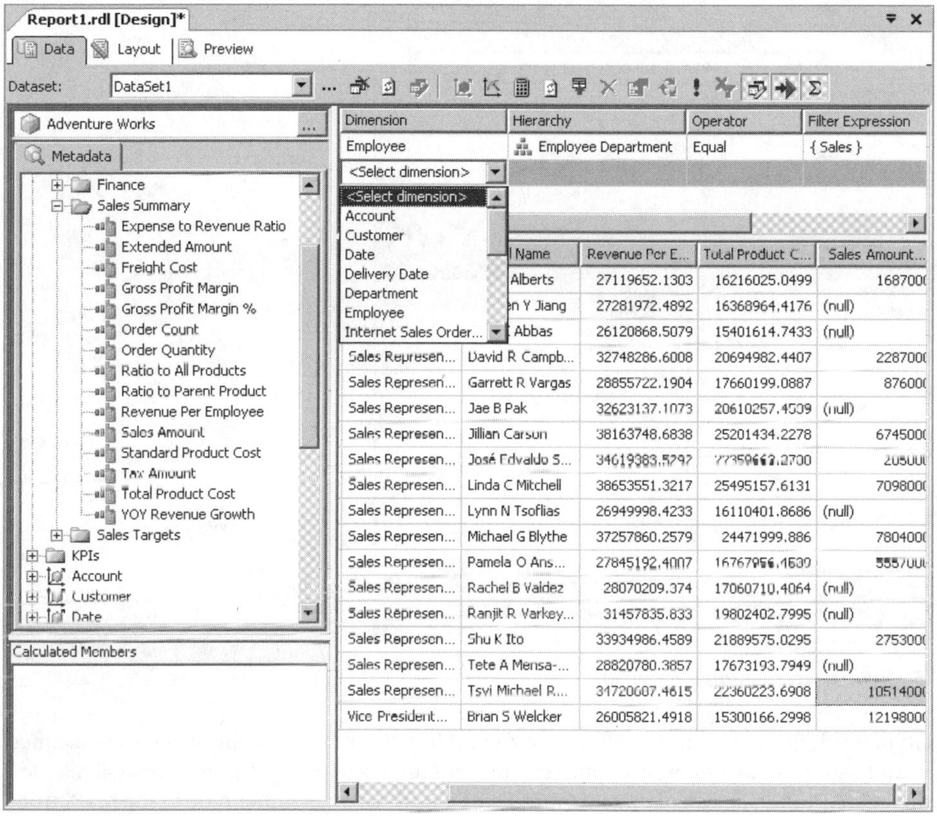

Figure 9-25. *Creating filters in the Query Designer*

Finally, you need to calculate the total profit from each employee. To do this, you need to create a *calculated member* in the Query Designer. A calculated member is a member that you use an expression to create, and the member does not exist in the underlying data sources but in the metadata model for Analysis Services. You can right-click in the calculated member section of the Query Designer and select New Calculated Member. The Calculated Member Builder appears, as shown in Figure 9-26.

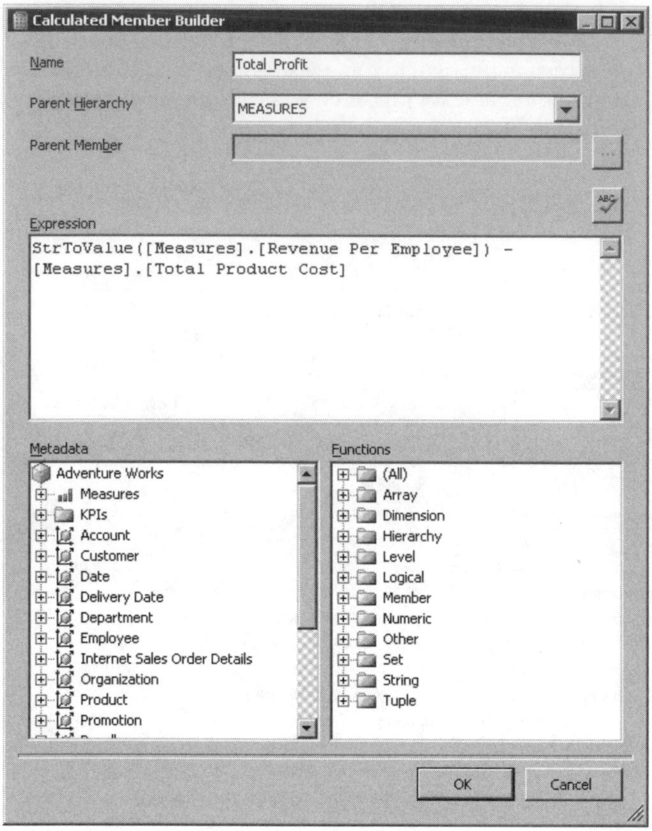

Figure 9-26. *Creating a calculated member*

As part of the dialog box, you can select the different functions that MDX provides for you. Since you just want to subtract two numbers, total revenue and total cost, this is a pretty easy calculated member to create. Name the calculated member Total_Profit. You can either type in the MDX from the screenshot or follow the steps described next to create the calculated member. First, find Revenue Per Employee in the Measures hierarchy under Sales Summary and drop it into the Expression window. Put a minus sign after the Revenue Per Employee and drag and drop the Total Product Cost from the same part of the hierarchy. You can optionally put the StrToValue function around the Revenue Per Employee member. I did this just to show you how you can use different functions in the designer. Click OK.

If you look at the MDX that the designer generates for you for the entire query, you can see that you would not want to do this by hand!

```
WITH MEMBER [Measures].[Total_Profit] AS
'StrToValue([Measures].[Revenue Per Employee]) -
[Measures].[Total Product Cost]' SELECT NON EMPTY {
[Measures].[Revenue Per Employee], [Measures].[Sales Amount Quota],
[Measures].[Total Product Cost], [Measures].[Total_Profit] } ON COLUMNS,
NON EMPTY { ([Employee].[Employee Department].[Full Name].ALLMEMBERS ) }
DIMENSION PROPERTIES MEMBER_CAPTION ON ROWS FROM ( SELECT (
STRTOSET(@EmployeeEmployeeDepartment, CONSTRAINED), * ) ON COLUMNS
FROM [Adventure Works]) CELL PROPERTIES VALUE
```

Now that you have your dataset, switch to the design view of Reporting Services by clicking the Layout tab. You will notice that the fields from your cube are available in the field list. You can drag and drop your fields onto controls that you add to your report. You'll use the Table control and also the Chart control to display your data.

By dragging on a Table control from the Toolbox tab, you can add your information to the report. You could also use the Matrix control if you wanted to hide and show your information or export it out to the Office Web Components for slicing and dicing. In the table, you'll just drop some fields from the Dataset tab into the details, such as the Full_Name, Revenue_Per_Employee and Total_Product_Cost columns. Next, right-click the table and select Insert Column to the Right. In the header for this new column, type in **Percentage Profit**. In the detail cell for this new column, find the Value property in the right-hand Properties window and click the drop-down list in the Value property. Select <Expression…> and add an expression to show how much the cost of goods is percentage-wise to total revenue for each employee, which would be the expression =(Fields!Total_Profit.Value / Fields!Total_Product_Cost.Value). Click OK. For example, if a salesperson sold $10 of goods, and it cost $5 to make the goods, cost would be 50 percent of total revenue. In the Properties window for the cell with your expression, find the Format property and put a **P** in for the value that specifies you want the result formatted as a percentage. You could have entered P1 or P3 to tell SSRS to render one or three places in your percentage if you wanted to. By default, SSRS will render out two places in a percentage. Figure 9-27 shows the form design with just the table added.

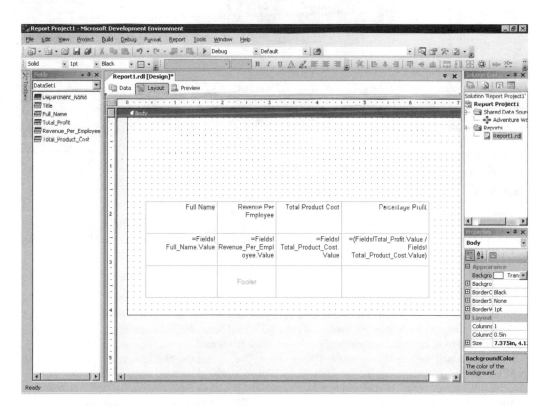

Figure 9-27. *A table layout with OLAP information*

Next, you may want to chart the information to see how each employee is doing. The charting technology is the same between SQL 2000 and SQL 2005. To add OLAP fields to a chart, it's just a drag-and-drop operation. Drag and drop a Chart control from the Toolbox tab onto your report.

From the Datasets tab, drag and drop the Full_Name field onto the category fields drop target on the chart. Drag and drop the Revenue_Per_Employee field onto the data field drop target on your chart and do the same action for the Total_Product_Cost field. Figure 9-28 shows a chart that will show total revenue and total product cost per employee.

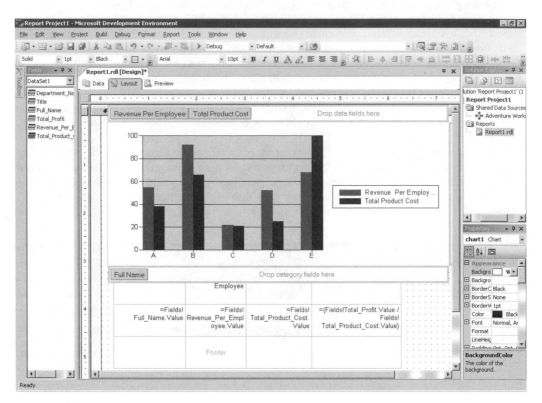

Figure 9-28. *A chart with OLAP information*

You can then preview or deploy your new report using the built-in previewing or deployment support of the BIDS. In this walkthrough, you've seen how you can leverage your OLAP information as easily as your relational information in SQL Server 2005.

Floating Headers

When working with the Matrix and Table controls, you may want to have a floating header so that as users scroll through their data, the header for the grouping floats with the scrolling. This makes the data easier to read for end users since they do not have to try and remember what each column header is or scroll back up continuously if they forget. To create these headers, you just need to set a property in the property page for your particular control under the group properties. Please note that floating headers only work in interactive renderers, which are the web- and Windows-based renderers. This means that if you export out to Excel, PDF, or other formats, your floating headers will not work, and you'll just get the standard nonfloating header. Figure 9-29 shows setting the floating headers property.

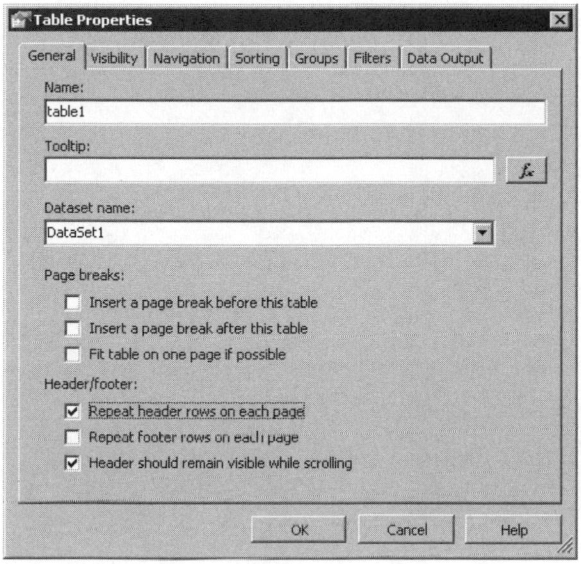

Figure 9-29. *Setting the properties for a floating header*

Data Source Changes: Expressions, XML/Web Services, SSIS, and SAP

Some data source changes in SSRS 2005 help you solve some issues when using multiple data sources and also allow you to connect to new data sources. The first change is the support of expression-based data sources. Imagine a scenario in which you want to deploy your report but change your data source at runtime rather than at design time or deployment time. This could be because you want to connect to your test environment with your report rather than a deployment environment. Or you could want to connect to different servers based on locality of the end user running the report. There may be a replicated data source that is closer than the default data source that you put into the report. The second change is some new data sources that you can take advantage of.

Data Source Expressions

To use a data source expression, you should create your data source as you normally would using a static connection string. Please note that expression-based connection strings only work with nonshared data sources. Design your report since you can only use a static connection string to get back your fields and lay out the report the way you want. Next, add a parameter that will specify your data source. You can either make this parameter use static values or pull from a data source to get its values. Once you have set the parameter, you can go back to your data source definition and replace the static value with a parameter. An example of a connection string using a data source expression is shown here:

```
="data source=" & Parameters!Datasource.Value & ";initial catalog=AdventureWorks"
```

Figure 9-30 shows setting a data source using an expression. Again, please note that you must use a report-specific data source and not a shared data source in order for expression-based data sources to work.

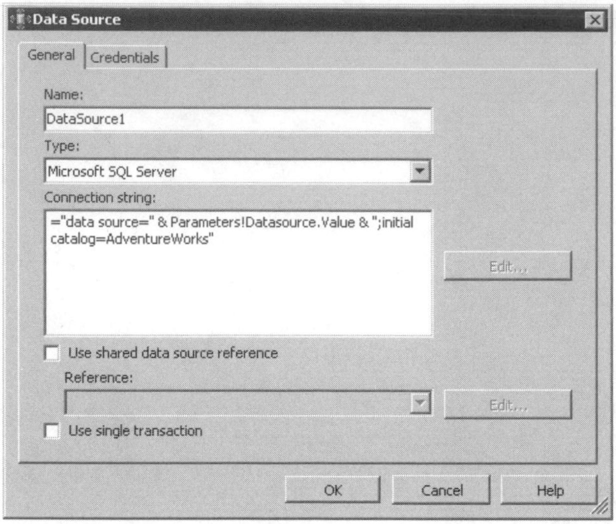

Figure 9-30. *A data source that uses an expression*

Data Sources for XML/Web Services, SSIS, and SAP

The other change is three new data sources: XML/web services, SSIS, and SAP. The XML/web services data source lets you connect to SOAP data sources and report off them. The SSIS data source connects to and runs an SSIS package and returns back the results so you can report off the results. The SAP data source lets you report directly off of an SAP data source so that you can provide rich reporting for SAP applications without having to extract the data into another intermediary data source.

XML/Web Services Data Source

The XML/web services data source, called XML in the Datasource type drop-down list (this may change in the final release), allows you to connect to an XML document, web service, or web application that returns back XML data. You simply specify the endpoint URL to which you wish to connect. For example, if you wanted to connect to a web service, you would input the URL to the ASMX or WSDL file for the web service. Some interesting web services that Reporting Services supports connecting to are

- SQL web services using the new native web services technology in SQL Server 2005
- The Google, Amazon, and eBay web services
- Web services that you create using Visual Studio or other development environments

You can also connect to just pure XML data sources, so if you have a web application that you can address via URL and that returns back an XML document, you can use that application to retrieve information to your report. Please note that the XML data source does not work with file:// URLs; you must use http:// URLs.

To try this technology, you need to create a new data source and specify XML as the type. The completed sample application is available with the samples in this chapter, so you will see a shortened step-through of using the XML data source in the text here. For full setup instructions, please refer to the readme file included with the sample application. In the Connection string property, enter the URL to your data source. In the example we'll use here, we'll create a web service using ASP .NET that returns the product categories from the AdventureWorks database. So, we will put in the URL to our web service. This is shown in Figure 9-31.

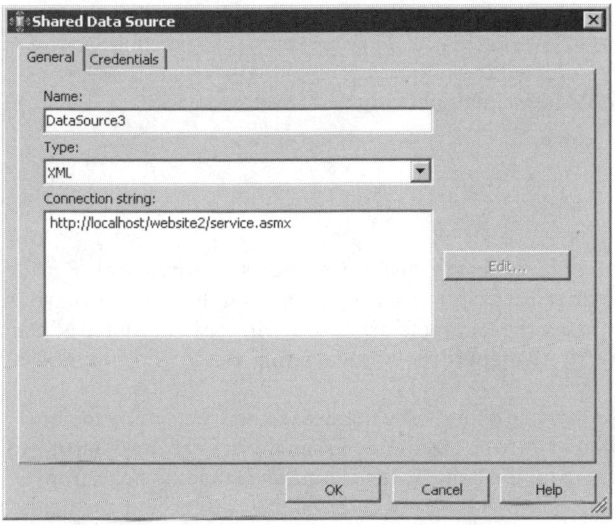

Figure 9-31. *Connecting to a web service in SSRS*

■**Note** Please note that you can only use integrated security or no credentials with the XML data source.

Now that you have your data source, you need to create your report. The dataset for your report is where you can specify different options, such as the fields you want to retrieve for the XML data source. You can only use the generic Query Designer with this provider. The query you write is itself an XML document that is rooted by the <Query> element. If you leave out the query element, SSRS will call your web service, expecting back an XML document from the default call. Even though we are using a custom web service in this example, you could just use SSRS itself to test this feature. Many times, we just use a sample report and just have it render out to XML. If you did the same, you could then take the URL to the report, place it into connection string, and query the XML returned back in your new report.

In the Query element, you can create the SoapAction element, which specifies the particular SOAP method to call. In our example, we pass in the fully qualified method name using our XML namespace. The query element for the sample is shown here:

```
<Query><SoapAction>http://AdventureWorks.org/GetProducts</SoapAction></Query>
```

Besides using just the SoapAction element, we can also pass in an ElementPath element, which allows us to specify the sequence of nodes to traverse within our XML document to retrieve the fields of data. For example, if we only wanted to return back the category for each product in our sample, we would use the following query:

```
<Query><SoapAction>http://AdventureWorks.org/GetProducts</SoapAction>
<ElementPath IgnoreNamespaces="true">
GetProductsResponse/GetProductsResult/Category
</ElementPath></Query>
```

You will notice that we can pass an attribute, IgnoreNamespaces. This gets us out of providing the XML namespace for the document we want to traverse. If you wanted to pass the namespace to your query, you would specify it as an attribute on the query element.

There is also a Method element that you can use rather than the SoapAction element. To show you using a different web service, the query that follows works with the web services of Reporting Services itself. So, the connection string is http://localhost/reportserver/ReportService2005.asmx. The method call that follows will call the ListChildren method on the SSRS web services:

```
<Query>
  <Method Name="ListChildren">
  </Method>
</Query>
```

You can also pass parameters to your data sources to customize what is returned back. For example, you may want to allow end users to select a city or user as a parameter that you pass to your web service. The easiest way to do this is to use the Parameters dialog box in the data source editor. You can also embed your parameters as XML elements in your query string, but the first method is easier and quicker for you to do.

So, let's see a report that uses the web service data source that we created. One thing to note is that after you have created your connection to the web service, try to run the query before starting to design your report layout. Also, make sure to hit the Refresh Fields button so that the fields from your data source are added to the field list, since SSRS will not automatically discover all the fields from your data source until you do this. Figure 9-32 shows a simple report that we created that shows the products grouped by category and then subcategory. Notice that we also use a multivalued parameter that is fed by the elementpath we created earlier to allow us to select the category that we are interested in rendering in our report.

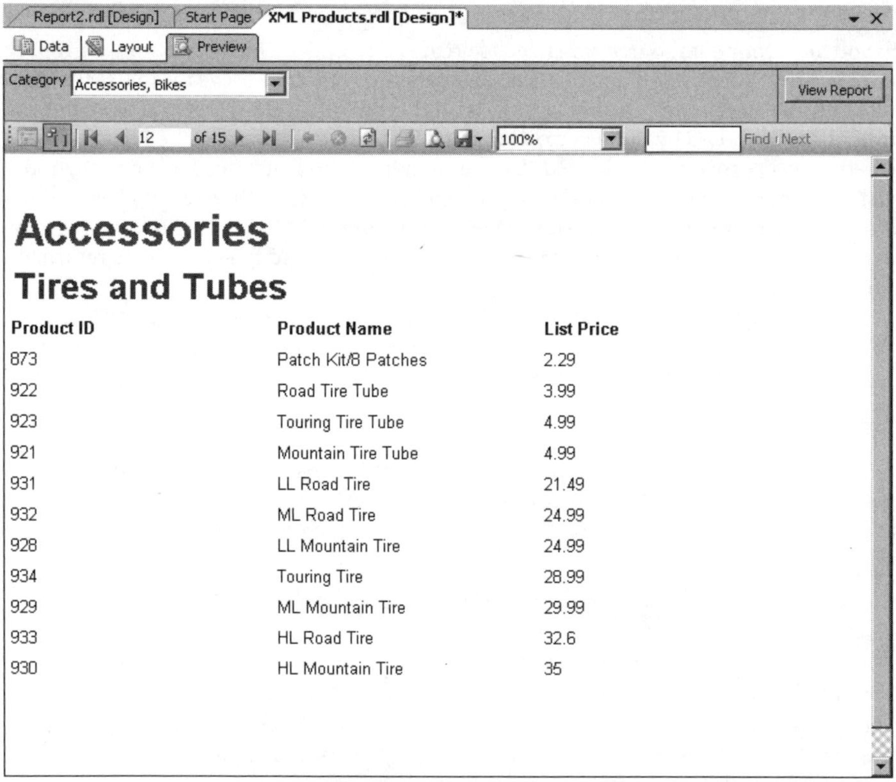

Figure 9-32. *Rendering XML data in a report*

SSIS Data Source

SQL Server Integration Services (SSIS) provides a new integration server and design environment for you to integrate all your different data together. With SSRS 2005, you can combine SSIS and SSRS to build reports on the real-time data that your SSIS packages process. Essentially, you can trigger SSIS to run on your server and have SSRS report off the results of the package. This provides real-time reporting on data transformed or integrated together with SSIS. The SSIS data source is great for volatile data sources that may not keep the same schema or may need to be cleansed in real time, such as logs or other data that may change over time. One thing to realize is that report and package processing happen sequentially when you use this feature. SSRS triggers the package to run, SSIS performs its actions, and then passes the data to SSRS. SSIS cannot trigger a report to run, but instead SSRS always triggers SSIS to execute. When you design your package, you must have the output be a DataReader destination. This is the only output type that SSRS can pick up from SSIS. The following are general steps to create a report with SSIS as the data source.

The first step is to create your new SSIS data source. Create a data source like you normally would in SSRS, but select SSIS as the type. In the connection string, add an -f and then the path to your package that you want to run. If there are spaces in the path, please enclose the path in double-quotes. SSRS uses the DTExec utility to execute your package, which is why you need the -f before the path to your package.

Then, you can create your report. Create a new dataset, which you've seen how to do previously in the chapter. For the query in your dataset, type in the name of the output DataReader that you created in your SSIS package. By default, the DataReader is called DataReaderDest. You can modify this name in SSIS, but if you do this, you also must modify it in SSRS. Make sure to click the Refresh Fields button to get a refreshed list of fields from your SSIS data source. Run your query to make sure your data source is working, and then you can design your report using SSIS just like any other report you have designed. Figure 9-33 shows querying SSIS from the Query Designer in SSRS. A full sample that uses SSIS is included with the samples for this chapter.

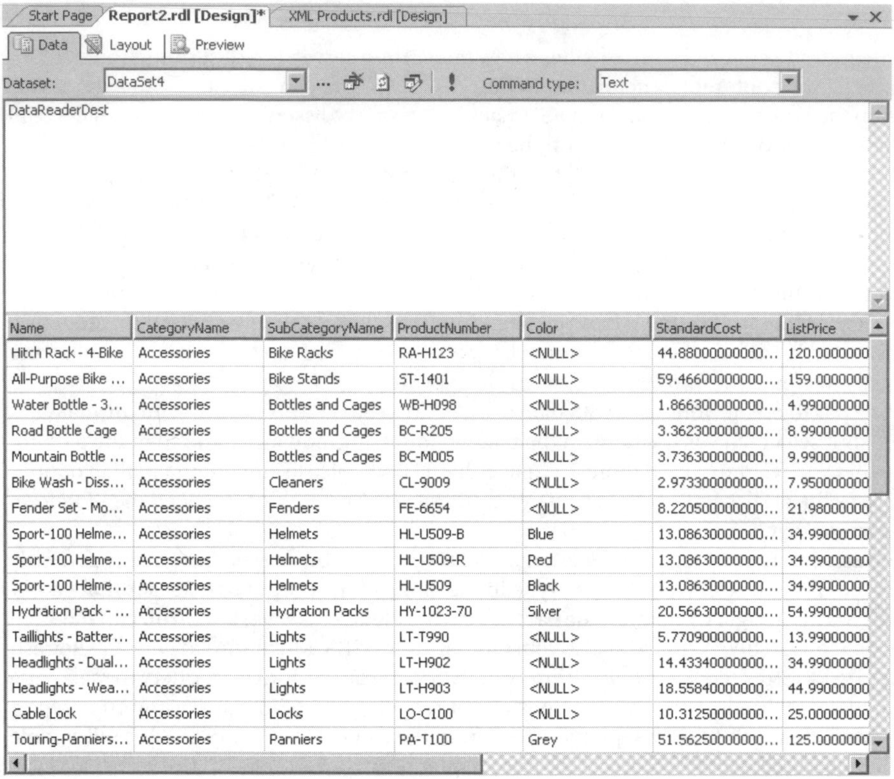

Name	CategoryName	SubCategoryName	ProductNumber	Color	StandardCost	ListPrice
Hitch Rack - 4-Bike	Accessories	Bike Racks	RA-H123	<NULL>	44.88000000000...	120.0000000
All-Purpose Bike ...	Accessories	Bike Stands	ST-1401	<NULL>	59.46600000000...	159.0000000
Water Bottle - 3...	Accessories	Bottles and Cages	WB-H098	<NULL>	1.866300000000...	4.990000000
Road Bottle Cage	Accessories	Bottles and Cages	BC-R205	<NULL>	3.362300000000...	8.990000000
Mountain Bottle ...	Accessories	Bottles and Cages	BC-M005	<NULL>	3.736300000000...	9.990000000
Bike Wash - Diss...	Accessories	Cleaners	CL-9009	<NULL>	2.973300000000...	7.950000000
Fender Set - Mo...	Accessories	Fenders	FE-6654	<NULL>	8.220500000000...	21.98000000
Sport-100 Helme...	Accessories	Helmets	HL-U509-B	Blue	13.08630000000...	34.99000000
Sport-100 Helme...	Accessories	Helmets	HL-U509-R	Red	13.08630000000...	34.99000000
Sport-100 Helme...	Accessories	Helmets	HL-U509	Black	13.08630000000...	34.99000000
Hydration Pack - ...	Accessories	Hydration Packs	HY-1023-70	Silver	20.56630000000...	54.99000000
Taillights - Batter...	Accessories	Lights	LT-T990	<NULL>	5.770900000000...	13.99000000
Headlights - Dual...	Accessories	Lights	LT-H902	<NULL>	14.43340000000...	34.99000000
Headlights - Wea...	Accessories	Lights	LT-H903	<NULL>	18.55840000000...	44.99000000
Cable Lock	Accessories	Locks	LO-C100	<NULL>	10.31250000000...	25.00000000
Touring-Panniers...	Accessories	Panniers	PA-T100	Grey	51.56250000000...	125.0000000

Figure 9-33. *Querying SSIS data from SSRS*

SAP Data Source

The final new data source is SAP. SQL Server 2005 introduces a new SAP ADO.NET provider in the Enterprise Edition. You need to download the provider from `http://msdn.microsoft.com/downloads`. Once you have downloaded the provider, you can start executing queries against your SAP system from any environment that uses ADO.NET, including SSRS. There are two query commands you can send to this data source. The first executes RFCs/BAPI, which is the API for SAP. The second executes SQL queries against SAP tables. We will point you to the documentation, in particular the Microsoft .NET Data Provider for SAP topic, to learn more about this data source.

Custom Report Items

Custom report items are primarily targeted at partners who want to extend SSRS with custom controls that get processed when the report gets processed, and then output an image onto the report. These controls allow the enterprise developer to build, in any .NET language, and deploy more sophisticated custom controls. For example, if you wanted to add a new chart type that SSRS does not support, such as one that shows advanced financial or statistical analysis, you can write a custom report item (sometimes called a *custom ReportViewer control*) that integrates with the design-time and run-time SSRS experience. Do not confuse this with the ability to drop custom controls, like .NET controls, onto a report. With the image you produce on the report, you can create an image map so that you can provide interactivity with your control. Most likely you will not create custom report items, but you will probably consume them in your reports from third-party providers.

Visual Studio Integration and ReportViewer Controls

One of the big questions that customers and partners always ask is how they can embed reports in their applications. Reporting Services 2000 provided customizability along the URL, such as sending rendering formats or parameters and the ability to embed reports into applications by using a browser control and URLs to your reports. Unfortunately, SSRS 2000 did not have an embeddable WinForm or WebForm control. Therefore, you have no way, without having a full Reporting Services installation available when you run your report, to take your reports and embed them into existing applications. This means that if you are running offline and you try to execute a report, you will get a failure since your SSRS server is not available. Other products, such as Crystal Reports, have these capabilities, and SQL 2005 Reporting Services has added embeddable and offline reporting technology as part of the continuing improvement of the product.

SSRS 2005 includes both a WebForm and a WinForm rendering control that can be embedded inside of custom web or Windows application. The controls take an RDL source and some data and perform the processing on the local machine, rather than having to go back to the Report Server to process the information. The controls support background processing and will start streaming the report onto the screen as the report is processed. When users want to view reports offline using a report snapshot, or a developer needs report rendering but can't guarantee that the customer has Reporting Services, the controls are very useful. However, when the workload of the application gets too large for the controls to handle, moving the controls from local processing to using a Report Server is very easy. In addition, the Report Server provides capabilities that the control does not have such as the ability to have subscriptions, caching, execution history, and better manageability of reports.

The controls support both local execution as well as server-side execution against a Reporting Services server. At times you may want to switch between the different execution modes. For example, your application may need to work both online and offline. When online, you may want to leverage the Reporting Services infrastructure, but when you're offline, you may want to render from a snapshot, since you may not have a connection to the SSRS server.

The main differences between using these controls and customizing SSRS using URLs are as follows:

- The controls do not support exporting to all SSRS formats when working with client-side reports. Only HTML and Excel are supported through client-side reports. With server-side reports, all formats are supported.

- The controls do not prompt for parameters in local execution mode—you must pass parameters programmatically to the controls.

- The controls do not support the advanced features of Reporting Services such as caching and subscriptions.

Using WinForm Controls

If you've seen the preview pane in the Report Designer, WinForm control will look familiar. It's pretty much the same control, but has the ability to run outside the Visual Studio environment. Plus, the control has an object model that you can program against. We're going to cover the WinForm control here since the WinForm and WebForm controls have very similar object models.

Adding the control to your application is a drag-and-drop operation. In Visual Studio, just drag and drop the ReportViewer control, which you can find under the Data group on the Toolbox tab for your WinForm application. Figure 9-34 shows the WinForm control in an application.

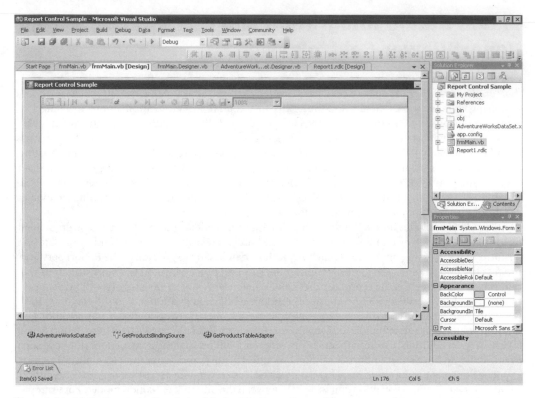

Figure 9-34. *A WinForm application with the WinForm ReportViewer control*

Once you have the control on the page, you need to set some properties, either through the user interface or programmatically. Using the new smart tags in VS, you can select your report location. The controls allow for either creating a new report or selecting a server report to render from. If you select the Report Server, you need to pass the URL and report path to the control in order for the rendering to work. If you select a new report, you will be creating a client-side report, denoted by an rdlc extension to specify client-side, that will use a different data source mechanism than what server reports use. If you want to move this report to the Report Server, you will have to perform some work to do this since the data source and query mechanisms are different between the two. The main benefits of using the local data source versus the server is that you can pass arbitrary ADO.NET data tables to the ReportViewer controls and they do not require a Report Server to work, which means that the ReportViewer controls can work offline.

When using local, client-side processing, the control takes ADO.NET datatables or objects that implement the IEnumerable interface as data sources to the report. The easiest way to get your data for your report is to use the Data Source dialog boxes and wizards inside of VS. From the wizards, you can select your data source and the actual data that you want returned back to your report. Figure 9-35 shows using the data source wizard.

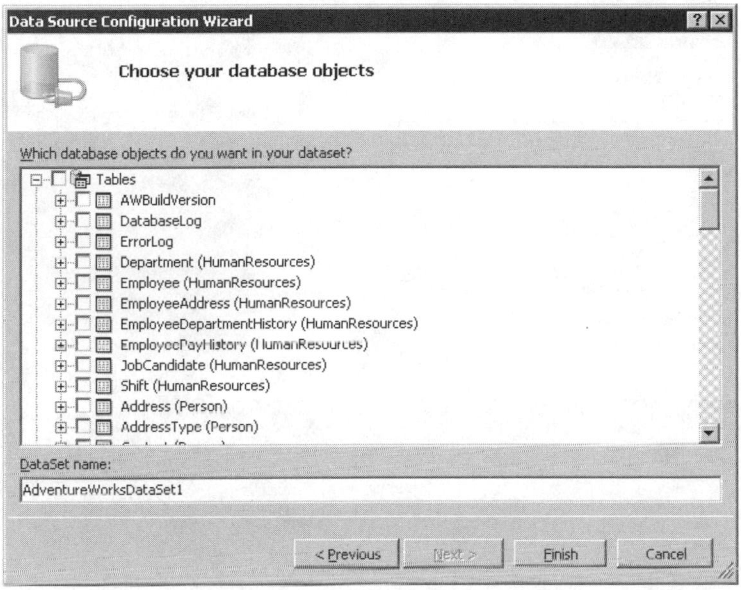

Figure 9-35. *Using the Data Source Configuraton Wizard*

As part of Visual Studio, you get the SSRS Report Designer so that you can design reports for the controls. After you create your data source, you can use the Report Designer to drag and drop your fields onto your report. The Report Designer is the same as you have already seen, so we won't describe it again here. You will notice that the extension for your local report is rdlc, not rdl. This is how it is differentiated from the server-side RDL code. Once you have created your data source, designed your report, and dragged and dropped the ReportViewer control onto your application, you are set to go. To try out your application, just run the application as you normally would from VS. To make this easier for you, we've included a full working sample application with the samples for this chapter. You may notice that in the load event for your form, SSRS adds some code to load your data and render your report. We will explore how to programmatically perform the same steps in the UI in a moment. Figure 9-36 shows running a simple form with two ReportViewer controls, which is demonstrated in the included sample application. One pulls from the server, the other renders reports locally.

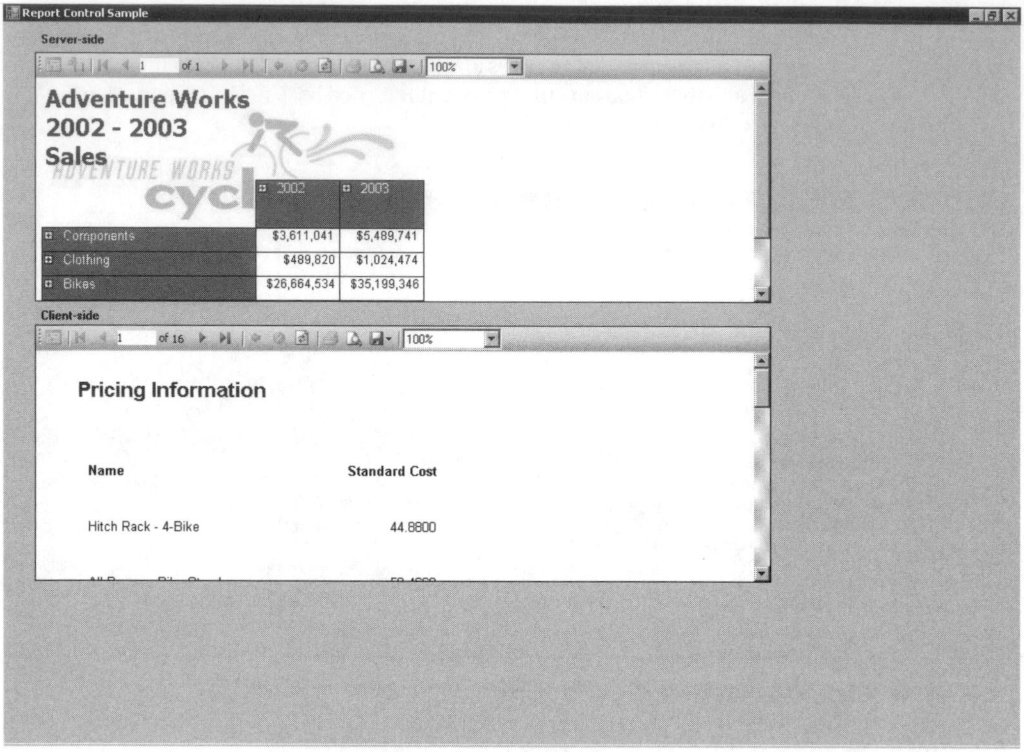

Figure 9-36. *Combining local and remote processing using the WinForm ReportViewer control*

Working with the ReportViewer Controls Programmatically

Rather than doing everything through the user interface, you may want to programmatically pass your data and render the report from code inside of your application. The ReportViewer controls support a rich API to allow you to do this. If you want to perform the same steps we did through the UI earlier, you would first pass your data through the Datasources collection of the control. Next, you have to pass the RDL for the report that you want to render. This can come as an embedded resource from the project itself by just passing the fully qualified project and then report name, with underscores replacing spaces, or it can be read from the file system. Then, you can set some of the properties on the control such as whether to display the toolbar, document map, context menu, or parameters. Finally, you need to render the report. One thing to note is if you already have a data source in the report, make sure to name your data source programmatically the same name as your existing data source. Otherwise, you will receive errors from the control. The following code shows how to program the control:

```vb
Private Function GetData() As System.Data.DataSet

        con = New System.Data.SqlClient.SqlConnection( _
          "server=localhost;Database=AdventureWorks;Integrated Security=SSPI")

        Using con

            con.Open()


            Dim sda As New System.Data.SqlClient.SqlDataAdapter( _
              "EXEC dbo.GetProducts", con)

            Dim ds As New System.Data.DataSet
            sda.Fill(ds)
            con.Close()
            Return ds
        End Using
    End Function
    Private Sub Button1_Click(ByVal sender As System.Object, ByVal e _
      As System.EventArgs) Handles Button1.Click

        Dim ds As System.Data.DataSet
        ds = GetData()
        Dim dt As System.Data.DataTable
        dt = ds.Tables(0)

        ReportViewer3.ProcessingMode = _
          Microsoft.Reporting.WinForms.ProcessingMode.Local

        ReportViewer3.LocalReport.ReportEmbeddedResource = _
            "Report_Control_Sample.Report1.rdlc"
        ReportViewer3.LocalReport.ReportPath = Nothing

        ReportViewer3.ShowToolBar = True
        ReportViewer3.ShowDocumentMap = True
        ReportViewer3.ShowContextMenu = True
        ReportViewer3.ShowParameterPrompts = True
        ReportViewer3.Name = "My Report"
        Dim rds As New Microsoft.Reporting.WinForms.ReportDataSource( _
            "AdventureWorksDataSet_GetProducts", dt)
        ReportViewer3.LocalReport.DataSources.Add(rds)
        ReportViewer3.RefreshReport()

    End Sub
```

Figure 9-37 shows the form running with the results.

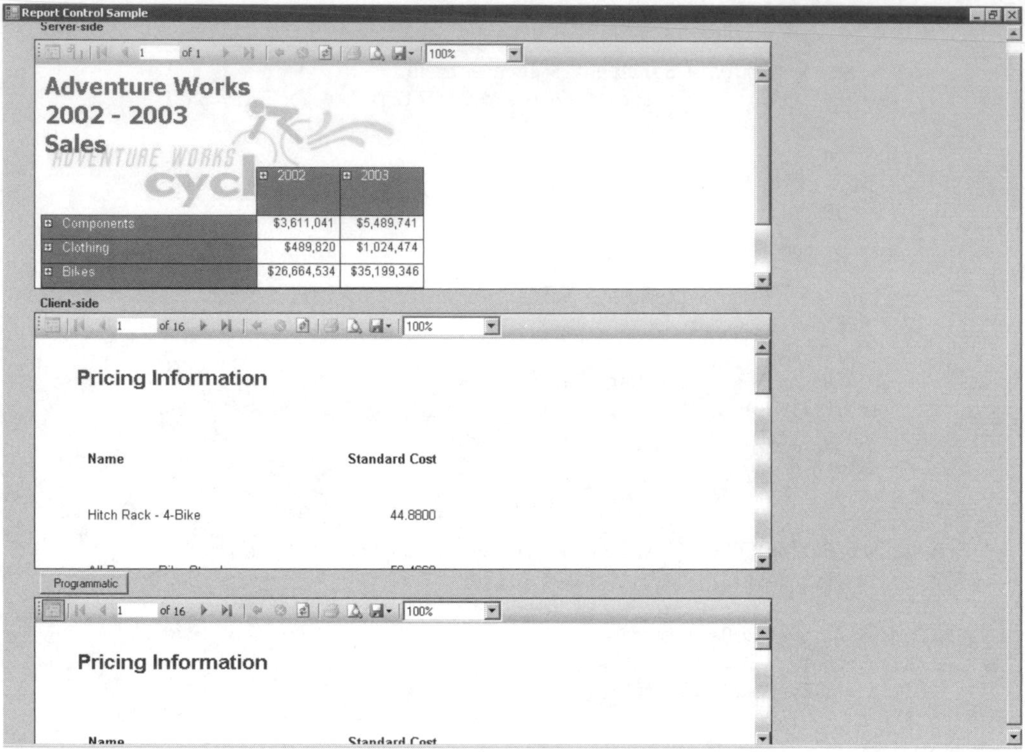

Figure 9-37. *Programming the WinForm ReportViewer control*

Table 9-1 outlines the most common properties you will use with the ReportViewer control.

Table 9-1. *Properties of the Winform ReportViewer Control*

Name	Type	Description
CurrentPage	Int32	Gets or sets the current page displayed in the report.
LocalReport	LocalReport	Returns a LocalReport object from which you can load report definitions, set data sources, perform actions such as document map navigation, and render reports.
ShowDocumentMap	Boolean	Gets or sets whether the document map is visible.
ShowParameterPrompts	Boolean	Gets or sets whether the parameters area is visible.
ShowCredentialPrompts	Boolean	Gets or sets whether the credentials area is visible.
ShowToolbar	Boolean	Gets or sets whether the toolbar is visible.
ShowContextMenu	Boolean	Gets or sets whether the context menu is visible.

Table 9-1. *Properties of the Winform ReportViewer Control*

Name	Type	Description
ShowDocumentMapButton	Boolean	Gets or sets whether the Document Map button is visible.
ShowExportButton	Boolean	Gets or sets whether the Export button is visible to export to other formats.
ShowPageNavigationControls	Boolean	Gets or sets whether the page navigation controls are visible.
ShowPrintButton	Boolean	Gets or sets whether the Print button is visible.
ShowProgress	Boolean	Gets or sets whether the progress animation is visible when rendering.
ShowRefreshButton	Boolean	Gets or sets whether the Refresh button is visible.
ShowZoomButton	Boolean	Gets or sets whether the zoom button is visible.
ServerReport	ServerReport	Returns back a ServerReport object, which allows you to perform similar tasks as the LocalReport object except in the context of a server report. For example, you cannot add new data sources with the ServerReport, but you can retrieve the list of data sources.
ZoomMode	Enum	Gets or sets the zoom factor such as FullPage, PageWidth, or ZoomPercent.
ZoomPercent	Int32	The zoom percentage.

Table 9-2 shows the methods on the WinForm ReportViewer control.

Table 9-2. *Methods for the WinForm ReportViewer Control*

Name	Description
Back	Goes back if the report is a drill-through report
Clear	Clears the report
Find	Searches the report for the given text
FindNext	Continues the search for the given text from the current search point
GetPrintDocument	Returns back a print document for printing the report
PrintDialog	Brings up the Print dialog box and then prints the report
Refresh	Refreshes the report, which reprocesses the report with any new data
Render	Processes and renders the report
RenderStream	Returns a stream associated with the report
SaveSnapshot	Saves a snapshot
Stop	Stops background processing of the report

LocalReport and ServerReport Objects

Beyond learning the ReportViewer control's methods and properties, you should also look at both the LocalReport and ServerReport objects. Due to space limitations, we will only discuss the common LocalReport methods and properties, since the ServerReport is simpler in its design. Plus, the ServerReport has less functionality because you are using the control just as a rendering engine and not passing data sources to it. The tables that follow show you the most common properties and methods for the LocalReport object only. Please note that you retrieve this object from the ReportViewer control using the `LocalReport` property.

Table 9-3 shows the methods on the properties for the LocalReport object.

Table 9-3. *Properties for the LocalReport Object*

Name	Type	Description
Datasources	ReportDatasourceCollection	Returns back the `Datasource` collection so you can get and set data sources for your report.
ReportEmbeddedResource	String	Name of the embedded report within the application. This must be a fully qualified name with the project and report name. Replace all spaces with underscores.
ReportPath	String	Fully qualified path to the report definition in the file system.

Table 9-4 shows the methods on the LocalReport object.

Table 9-4. *Methods on the LocalReport Object*

Name	Description
GetDocumentMap	Returns a `DocumentMapNode` object so you can traverse your document map in your report.
GetParameters	This property returns a `ReportParameterInfoCollection` so that you can then get information about parameters in your report. Use this in conjunction with `SetParameters`.
GetTotalPages	Gets the total number of pages in the report.
ListRenderingExtensions	Lists the rendering extensions that are available.
LoadReportDefinition	Loads the specified RDL file, which you pass either as a `TextReader` or a `Stream` object.
LoadSubReportDefinition	Loads the specified RDL file for subreports, which you pass either as a `TextReader` or a `Stream` object.
PerformBookmarkNavigation	Navigates to the specified bookmark that you pass the ID and name for.
PerformDocumentMapNavigation	Navigates to the document map node that you specify the ID for.

Table 9-4. *Methods on the LocalReport Object*

Name	Description
PerformDrillThrough	Performs a drill-through to another report, which you specify in the call to this method. You can also listen for drill-through events in the control and perform the correct actions to drill to another report.
Render	Renders the report and returns back either a byte array or a stream, which is the end result. You need to pass in the format, device info, mime type, and encoding.
SetParameters	Allows you to pass an array of ReportParameter objects, which will set the parameters for your report. ReportParameter objects are effectively just a named key/value pair.

Finally, the ReportViewer controls support events so your application can listen for events such as page navigation, printing, drill-through, searching, zooming, and other activities in the control. In this overview, you've seen how you can get started with the new ReportViewer controls in your own applications and leverage the power of Reporting Services, even without the Report Server.

SharePoint Integration

Based on what was added in SP2 of Reporting Services 2000, SSRS 2005 continues to support SharePoint integration. Since no new features for SharePoint integration are included in SSRS 2005, we will not cover this integration that deeply. The main thing to note is that the SSRS web parts for SharePoint, the report explorer and report viewer, are implemented as IFrames that wrap Report Manager. A more interesting implementation may be using the new ReportViewer controls in SharePoint web parts to display report information. However, if you are just looking for the ability to drag and drop web parts from your SharePoint web part gallery onto your page, set some properties, and have reports appear, the web parts that ship with SSRS 2005 should easily meet your needs.

End-User Ad Hoc Query and Reporting

The final piece of new technology that we will look at in Reporting Services is the new ActiveViews technology. Microsoft acquired this technology in the spring of 2004. With this addition, Reporting Services now has a client tool called Report Builder that end users can use to connect to their data, create queries, create filters, view reports, and export to multiple formats. While Visual Studio or the BIDS is a great place for a developer or DBA to create reports, no end user will understand those environments. This is why the Report Builder client was created. From a technology standpoint, Report Builder uses Reporting Services on the back end to create and show the reports. What is actually produced by Report Builder is RDL that is executed on the server. For this reason, Report Builder only works when a user is online.

The way Report Builder works is that there is a metadata model, called the Semantic Model Definition Language (SMDL), that sits between the end user and the data he or she accesses. Since most end users do not understand relational databases or even sometimes OLAP structures, the metadata model takes the complexity of the database and puts it in terms that the end user understands such as entities, relationships, and aggregates. This means that the full power of the relational database and your OLAP systems are used, but the complexity is lessened for end users to get the data they need. Plus, end users do not have to depend on IT folks or developers to build reports for them; they can now self-service their needs through the Report Builder client.

So, the different pieces of the Report Builder architecture are the Report Builder client, the Semantic Data Model and its designer, and the server-side of Reporting Services. Let's step through in a little more detail for each of these pieces before we walk through how to build a report using the Report Builder client and its components.

The Report Builder Client

The Report Builder client is a Windows Form application built using .NET. You may be wondering how you could deploy this application to all your different end users, since it is Windows based. Well, the Report Builder client actually leverages some new deployment technology in .NET 2.0 called Click-Once. ClickOnce gives you Windows-based interactivity and applications, but the deployment model of web applications. When an end user clicks the Report Builder button in Report Manager, ClickOnce checks his or her machine to make sure that the system has the .NET 2.0 Framework and also that the latest version of the Report Builder client that is published on the server. If the system does not, these components are download and installed—making for a very easy deployment experience. You could also deploy the client via standard mechanisms, though, such as SMS, and when the end user clicks, if the versions match, nothing will be downloaded.

Please note that you can have different versions of the client on the same machine. For example, you may have SP1 of Report Builder on one server and just the RTM version on another. Since Report Builder data sources are server dependent and the client bits are installed from the server, one end-user machine may have both versions of the client. This is OK and no cause for alarm. When the other server is updated to SP1 and the end user clicks the Report Builder button, the new version will be downloaded.

The client is a report designer that at the end creates RDL on the fly that gets passed to the server. One thing you have to realize is that the Report Builder client is not Report Designer. It does not have all the power and flexibility that Report Designer has. There is a good reason for this, since that power and flexibility is a liability for an end-user tool that is supposed to be simple and easy to use. Therefore, you may be frustrated by the supposed lack of flexibility in the tool, but end users will find it easier to create reports because it is structured and works only in a certain way.

You can take a report that an end user creates into Report Designer, though. You will be working against the Semantic Data Model and not the data source underneath, however, so do not be confused by that. Also, any reports that you modify in Report Designer may not be able to go back to Report Builder due to the differences in functionality. It is usually a one-way street between the two.

The Semantic Model Definition Language

SMDL is an XML-based grammar that describes your data sources in human-readable terms. Think of it as a universal translator for your data sources from geek to end user. Building a SMDL uses the other pieces of SQL Server 2005 that both SSIS and SSAS use, which are data sources and data source views. Data sources are straightforward. The only caveat is that currently SMDL only supports SQL Server data sources, in particular, the relational database and Analysis Services. The reason for this is that the queries in SMDL must be translated to data-specific queries for the underlying source. However, the query translator that is built into SSRS is pluggable so that in future versions, Microsoft could add more data sources. Also, only one data source, in fact if you are working with databases only one database, is supported per model. So, you cannot query relational and OLAP data sources together, only OLAP or relational databases in a single model.

Data Source Views (DSVs) allow you to separate physical schema from virtual schema. Think of it this way: you may have underlying schema in your relational database that you cannot modify, but in order to make the schema better for end users, you need to add schema or modify schema. With

DSVs, you can perform these actions in the metadata for the DSV rather than in the underlying data source. You can create calculated columns, virtual tables, and other schema changes in DSVs without modifying the original data source.

SDML is made up on entities, folders, attributes, expressions, perspectives, and roles. Entities correspond to a table or query view in the underlying data source. For example, you may have a product entity that maps to the product table in your database. Folders are just containment vehicles for entities. If you want to group entities together, put them in a folder. Attributes correspond to columns or named calculations on an entity. For example, the price attribute on the product entity could just be the price column in the products table, or it could be a calculated aggregate that only exists in the DSV.

Expressions are what they sound like, calculated fields in your model. You can create expressions that create aggregates, do string manipulation, perform conversions, as well as other functions. You control the creation of expressions while the Report Model generator creates attributes for you automatically.

Perspectives provide the ability to break a large model into smaller models. You can create perspectives that contain a subset of an existing model. End users can then see the perspectives they have permissions on from the client. You can think of perspectives like relational database views. With views, you can hide your underlying tables and only display back information to users who have permissions on the view.

Roles define relationships among your data. For example, an employee has an address or a customer has orders. You can define roles to have a one-to-one, one-to-many, or many-to-many relationship. Customers do not have one order but have many orders. The way roles are surfaced in the client is through the navigation. Please note that these roles should not be confused with role-level security in Reporting Services. Report Builder does support role-level security so that you can lock down parts of the model based on user roles. This is useful to secure sensitive and confidential data such as salaries, social security numbers, etc.

The reason for having this semantic data model, beyond the simplicity it presents to the end user while still providing a powerful model for the DBA and developer, is the ability to provide rich relationships and infinite drill-through. Say you enable infinite drill-through on your data model, and you own the Enterprise Edition of SQL Server (since infinite drill-through is only supported there); when a report is rendered, if there is a path through the model, users can click attributes that send queries, which in turn generate drill-through reports. End users do not have to create each individual report themselves, and DBAs do not have to manually link together reports since they can just mark relationships in the model.

Walkthrough: Report Builder

The easiest way to understand the Report Builder technology is to do a walkthrough of a scenario that uses it. The full sample for this section is included with the samples for this chapter. When beginning to work with the Report Builder technology, the first tool that you will use is the same tool you use to create reports: BIDS. This is the tool that allows you to create your metadata models, tweak those models, and set the security on your model. The tool includes the ability to automatically scan your relational databases and auto-generate the metadata model from the scan. You can then go in and tweak the metadata based on your particular needs. Please note to create a model over an OLAP data source, you need to use either the Report Manager tool or SQL Server Management Studio. BIDS does not support connecting to OLAP data sources yet for Report Builder models.

Figure 9-38 shows the Report Model Wizard. To get to the wizard, you first need to create a Report Model Project in BIDS. Then, you need to create a new data source, a Data Source View, and then finally, you can right-click the Report Model node and select Add New Report Model. Through the wizard you can tell Report Builder whether to ignore system tables, system views, or both. You also decide how to deal with foreign key constraints.

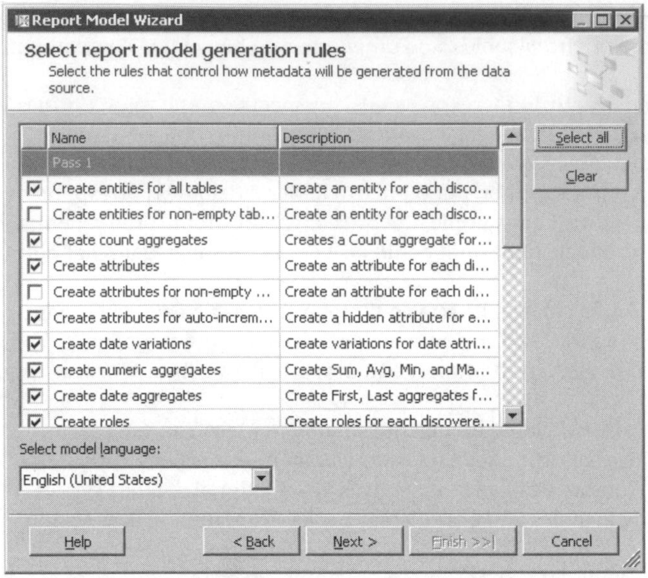

Figure 9-38. *The Report Model Wizard*

Once the metadata model is generated using the default rules, you can view it through the management tool. By browsing the auto-generated model, you can see what fields, aggregates, and relations the wizard has created. Figure 9-39 shows the auto-generated metadata for the Northwind database. You may wonder why we do not use AdventureWorks. Well, frankly, the AdventureWorks auto-generated model is horrible. That is why Microsoft publishes a downloadable version of that model for you that is modified from the auto-generated one. The wizard is not foolproof. Northwind generates a much better model from the wizard because the schema for Northwind is easier. You will want to test, tweak, and change the model the wizard generates, or you may get some strange results when you go to design your reports.

Relations in the metadata model allow the model to hide the complexity of the underlying relational data for the end user. Through a role, you can create lookup values and infinite drill-throughs. When a user clicks a role in a report, the relation links to the new metadata class that the role points to. Figure 9-40 shows the properties for the Orders role that is related to Customers in Northwind.

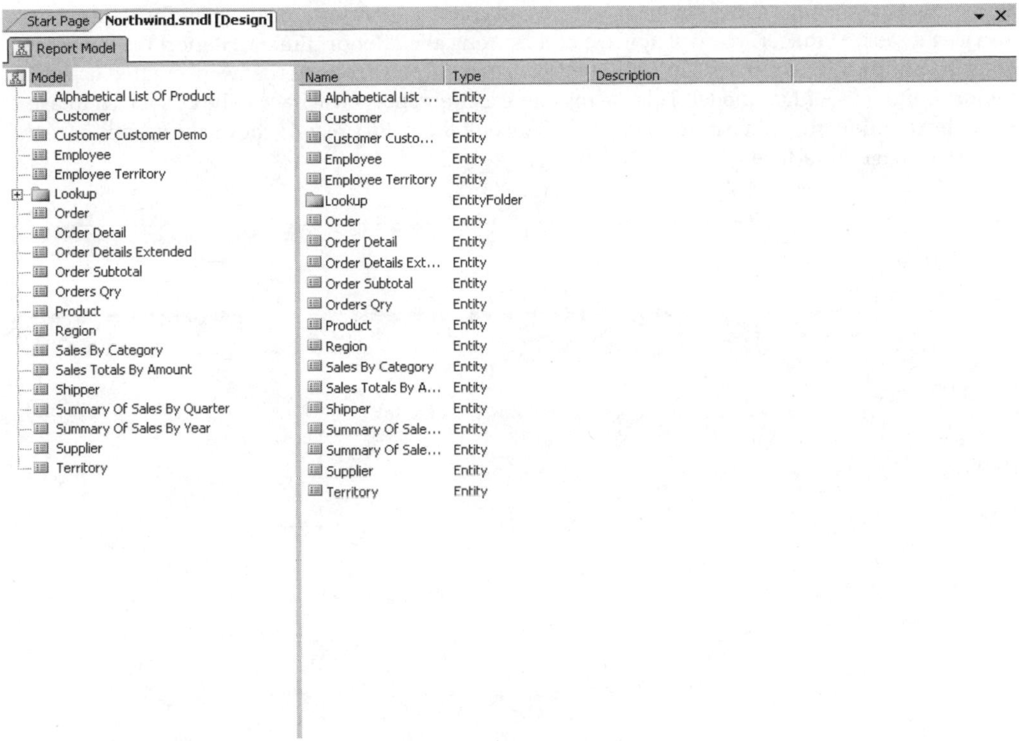

Figure 9-39. *Northwind database auto-generated metadata*

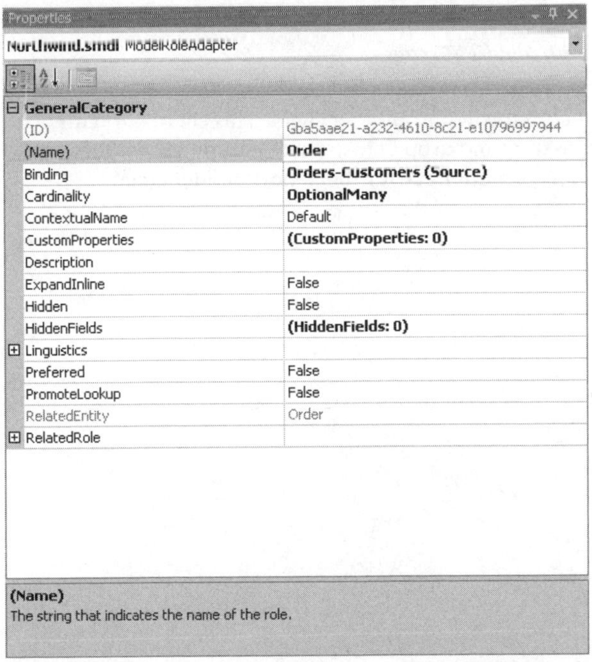

Figure 9-40. *The properties of a role in Northwind*

Now that you have a metadata model, you can create your report. If you go to the Reporting Services Report Manager, you will notice a new button called Report Builder. Report Builder also adds the ability to edit reports. Unfortunately, you can only edit reports that were created using the Report Builder metadata model. This means that existing reports will have to be converted to use the Report Builder metadata model before you can edit them. Figure 9-41 shows the additions to the Report Manager interface.

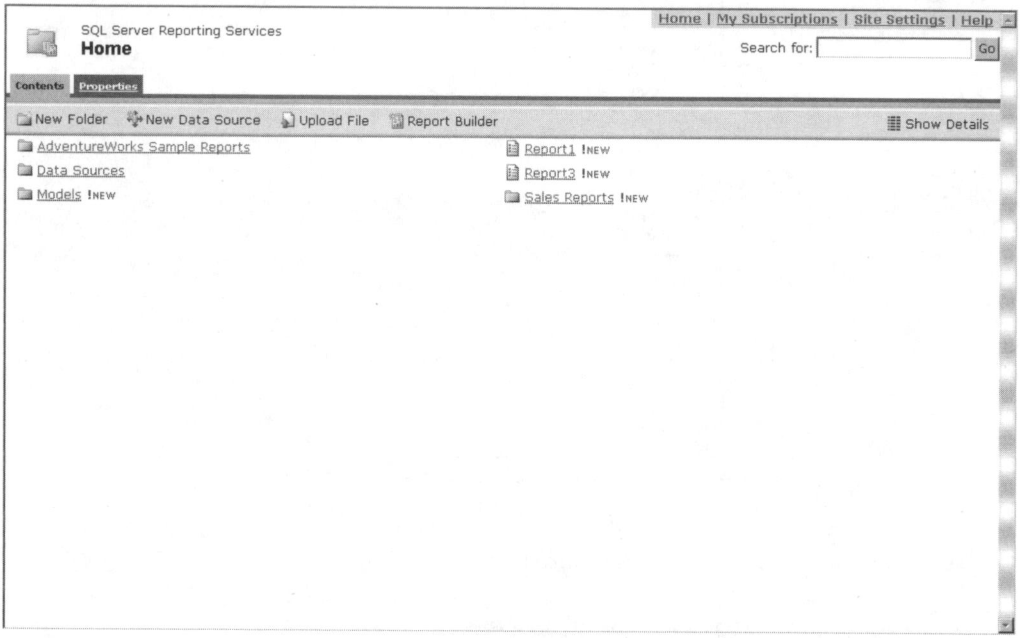

Figure 9-41. *The new Report Builder button with Report Manager*

Clicking the Report Builder button launches the Report Builder client. This client is a WinForm application and makes it easy for end users to drag and drop fields, create groupings, and even set criteria for their reports. Figure 9-42 shows the user interface for the Report Builder client.

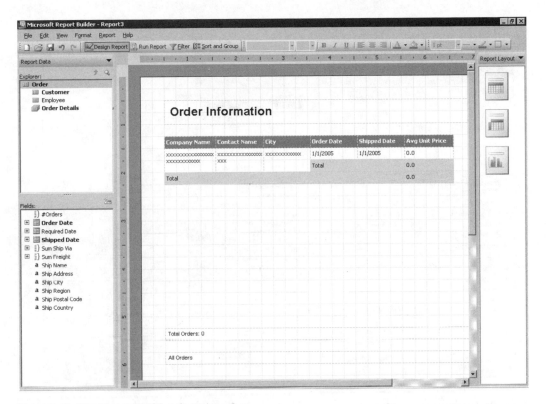

Figure 9-42. *The Report Builder client interface*

You can build complex criteria in your reports through the Report Builder client by dragging and dropping information in the Criteria window. Report Builder supports simple equality criteria or complex grouping of criteria terms. Plus, if a field has a role, Report Builder will do a lookup to find the values to limit the criteria selection. Figure 9-43 shows adding criteria to a report.

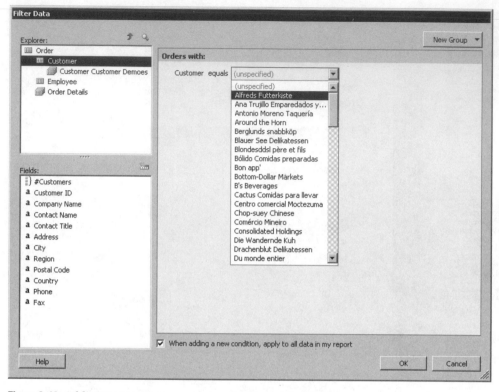

Figure 9-43. *Adding criteria to your reports using Report Builder*

The final piece that end users may want to do is preview their reports before saving them back to the Report Server. Under the covers, the Report Builder client generates RDL, sends it to the server, and views the results in the client. Figure 9-44 shows previewing a report in the Report Builder client.

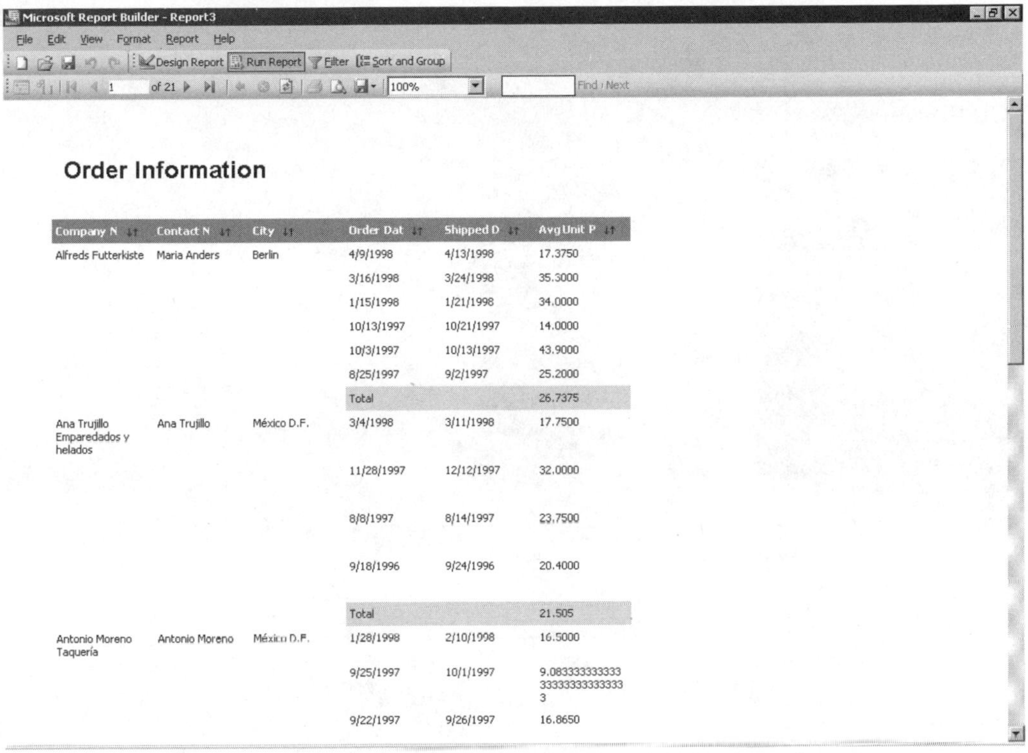

Figure 9-44. *Previewing a report in the Report Builder client*

The last interesting piece of Report Builder that we will cover in this chapter is infinite drill-through. Through the use of roles, you can click a hyperlinked field in Report Builder. Report Builder, through its metadata layer and built-in templates, auto-generates a drill-through report. For example, when you click the company name from the previous figure, the customer information report is as shown in Figure 9-45. This infinite drill-through allows end users to keep searching for more details about their data without having to know the intricacies of the data relationships inside the database.

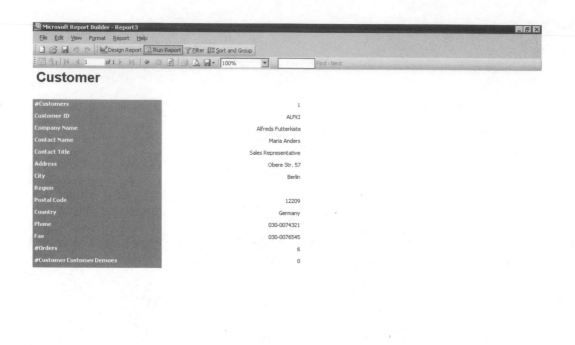

Figure 9-45. *Infinite drill-through in the Report Builder client*

You can save your reports out to a Report Server and even export your reports to other formats using the Report Builder client. All formats that Reporting Services supports are supported by Report Builder, since in the end, it calls the Reporting Services server to render the reports. A quick note about permissions with Report Builder: to launch Report Builder, a user must have permission for the server-wide Execute Report Definitions task. Therefore, you can lock down who can use Report Builder through this permission. To create a report with Report Builder, a user must have item-level permissions for the View Models task for at least one model on the server. To open an existing report with Report Builder, a user must have item-level permission for the Consume Reports task for the specified report, as well as permission for the View Models task for the corresponding model.

As the walkthrough shows you, Report Builder is a powerful addition to Reporting Services. No longer will you have to build reports for your end users but instead you can empower them, through the models you create for them, to build their own reports.

Summary

Phew! In this chapter, you have seen how Reporting Services has matured in SQL Server 2005. We started by looking at what SSRS 2000 provided as a level set. Then, we went on to see what was new in SSRS 2005. In a little over a year, the SSRS team has added a lot of new functionality that will make any developer or DBA who has to create reports very happy. Finally, with the new integration with SQL Management Studio, tighter integration with Analysis Services, and newfound developer and end-user enhancements, you should be able to find a use for Reporting Services in any of your Business Intelligence projects.

CHAPTER 10

■ ■ ■

Analysis Services

Databases store data, but they are truly profitable (think ROI) when their data can interpreted to make accurate business decisions (e.g., should a firm expand, are new products going to be practical, or is out sourcing cost efficient?). Data interpretation and the massaging of said data to be interpretable is referred to as *business intelligence (BI)*. Under the generic heading of business intelligence, SQL Server 2005 introduces a suite of technologies designed to support the development and administration of BI applications. Reporting Services and Integration Services (SSIS) can be classified as elements of BI, but the cornerstone of this database's BI services is SQL Server 2005 Analysis Services (SSAS, where within Microsoft each letter is pronounced es-es-ay-es). Within Analysis Services are mechanisms for exploiting Online Analytical Processing (OLAP) and data mining. The functionality associated with just the OLAP features of Analysis Services is daunting in scale, and hence OLAP is the Analysis Services mechanism reviewed in this chapter.

Any Analysis Services endeavor can be broken down into a set of tasks associated with application administration and with application development. As has been discussed previously, SQL Server 2005 ships with two tools designed to facilitate these tasks:

- *SQL Server Management Studio (SSMS)*: This tool supports application administration including the viewing of data and the creation of Multidimensional Expressions (MDX), Data Mining Extensions (DMX), and XML for Analysis (XML/A).

- *Business Intelligence Development Studio (BIDS)*: This tool supports application development by allowing the core components of an Analysis Service project to be defined (data sources, data views, dimensions, value, cubes, etc.). This tool also allows data within the analyzed environment to be viewed from a variety of perspectives.

SSMS and BIDS support a broader set of technologies than those just mentioned. As this chapter focuses on Analysis Services only the features of SSMS and BIDS related to Analysis Services will be presented.

SSAS 2005 Enhancements

Let's start the discussion with a look at some of the major differences between SSAS 2000 and SSAS 2005. Essentially, the 2005 enhancements can be broken down into one of the following categories:

- *Architecture*: Flexible web-services-oriented architecture based on the new *Unified Dimensional Model*

- *Performance, Scalability, Availability*: Introduction of proactive caching and support for fault-tolerant clustering

- *Usability*: Improved tools, including the introduction of Business Intelligence Development Studio

- *Development*: Standardized and improved programmatic access

Let's take a look at each in turn.

Architecture

Figure 10-1 gives a high-level view of the SSAS 205 architecture:

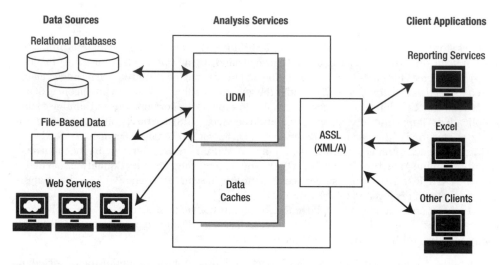

Figure 10-1. *SSAS 2005 Architecture*

Unified Dimensional Model (UDM)

The purpose of UDM is to provide a cohesive dimensional model representing relational and multi-dimensional data repositories. The UDM provides a bridge (standard representation) from a client such as Excel or Reporting Services to a diverse set of heterogeneous data sources. Rather than accessing the data sources in their native languages (specific SQL dialects, etc.), the UDM allows client applications to issue commands against the UDM.

A large number of Analysis Services features presented are implemented using the UDM including hierarchies, categorizations, time representations, language translations, and perspectives. Even proactive caching and analytics are intrinsically part of the Unified Dimensional Model and therefore available to Analysis Services 2005.

XML, XML/A, ASSL, and Web Services

When Analysis Server 2000 was released, the web was not nearly as pervasive, XML was not nearly as refined and commonplace, and web services were not the norm in standardized administration and programmatic access. Analysis Services 2005 heavily leverages these contemporary technical mainstays. An Analysis Services 2005 server behaves as a web service, and it should come as no surprise that the language for administering this server is XML based. All client communication with the Analysis Services server is via the standards-based XML for Analysis (XML/A) protocol.

Microsoft is continuing to support a variety of technologies aimed at backwards compatibility with the functionality provided by XML/A (ADOMD, ADOMDB.NET, OLE DB for OLAP, and Win32).

XML/A is actually a subset Analysis Services Scripting Language (ASSL), where XML/A sends action commands such as Create, Alter, or Process (create a cube, alter a cube, or process a cube). ASSL is also the language used to specify the objects within Analysis Services. XML/A handles commands while the rest of ASSL is a data definition language (DDL) for Analysis Services objects.

BIDS uses Visual Studio's style of development (solutions, projects, and source files). The source files associated with a BIDS Analysis Services project contain the metadata associated with Analysis Services objects. These files can be checked into standard source code control (such as Visual SourceSafe or Team Foundation Services). In SQL Server 2000, Analysis Services metadata was stored in a specific database. In Analysis Services 2005, the metadata language is XML-based and is stored in files. The XML-based language is ASSL. The command protocols used by SQL Server Management Studio and BIDS to communicate with Analysis Services are XML/A.

Performance, Scalability, Availability

Analysis Services no longer contains a client-side cache. In order to improve overall performance and reduce the client-side footprint, all computations are performed on the server. A new feature of SSAS 2005 is *proactive caching*. Rather than having each query execute against the underlying data source (a potential performance bottleneck), Analysis Services data is cached. Proactive caching lets low-latency applications be developed with minimal managerial overhead. The primary purpose of proactive caching is the management of data obsolescence. For example, the proactive cache could be configured to update when the underlying data is modified. If the cache is in the process of updating, Analysis Services is sophisticated enough to direct a query not to the cache, but instead to run said query against the underlying data source. Proactive caching works optimally against a relational database that provides notifications when the underlying data has changed.

Unlike SSAS 2000, the 2005 version does not cache entire dimensions in memory. Just as an operating system keeps certain pages in memory and has certain pages swapped out to disk, SSAS 2005 uses physical memory and disk space. The benefit of this conventional approach is that Analysis Services 2005 now supports unlimited dimension sizes. In order to understand this, consider the implication of Analysis Services 2000 storing all dimensions in memory. Analysis Services 2000 is constrained by the amount of physical memory on the machine, while Analysis Services 2005 can take advantage of caching (keeping results partially on disk) and is therefore not RAM-bound.

In recognition of the critical nature of Analysis Services, failover clustering now supports Analysis Services. Built on top of windows Clustering Services, fault tolerant clustering provided a failover, where a failover is a backup operation that automatically switches to a standby database/server in the event of catastrophic failure. Additionally, fault tolerant clustering extends to Notification Service and SQL Server replication.

Usability

As of SSAS 2005, developers do not need to connect to Analysis Services in order to perform development. BIDS supports offline development before an Analysis Services project is ultimately deployed to an Analysis Services server. This offline development is accomplished because BIDS works with snapshots of the schemas from the data sources accessed. The Analysis Services objects it creates (cubes, dimensions, fact tables, etc.) are just locally copies of said object that must be deployed in order to be recognized by a specific Analysis Services server. The true benefit of this is that development can take place even if Analysis Server is not running locally and if a developer is completely disconnected from the network.

On top of offline development, BIDS provides administrative dialog boxes and wizard-based support for the creation of computations. These user interface enhancements automate the manipulation of computations ranging from time manipulation and interpretation, to account intelligence, financial aggregation, support for multiple currencies, including conversion, and semi-additive measures. The alternatives to the dialog box and wizard-based support would be the hand coding of computations. Understanding the term "semi-additive measures" requires some understanding of Analysis Services objects. Computations in Analysis Services are performed on cubes composed of dimensions. Fully additive measures are computed against all dimensions of a cube, while semi-additive measures are additive across some but not all dimensions of a cube.

In addition to automating the creation of computations, Business Intelligence Development Studio automates the development of cubes by evaluating the underlying architecture and potentially creating what is referred to as a *one-click cube*—a cube created through heuristic analysis rather than having a developer define said cube's attributes.

Another usability-related perk of BIDS is support for multiple configurations. This allows projects to be deployed against multiple instances of Analysis Services. Also supported are localized objects and translations, which means Analysis Services 2005 supports deployments in multiple languages.

Development

There have been many advancements in the general areas of "development" and improvements in the business intelligence capabilities of SSAS. In this section, we provide a brief overview of some of the most significant enhancements—and then you'll get to see many of them in action a little later.

Key Performance Indicator (KPI) Framework and Perspectives

SSAS 2005 introduces key performance indicators (KPIs). These server-side objects, are a graphic representation of a value, goal, current status, and trend. For example, a brokerage house could use a thumb-is-up or thumb-is-down graphic to indicate whether a stock should be purchased or sold. The underling algorithm to determine this could be quite complex (value, goal, current status, and trend), but the KPI (the corporate measure) can be quite simple: buy (thumb-is-up) or sell (thumb-is-down). Additionally, a KPI can be associated with a trend that includes a graphic representing the trend (a thermometer, a fuel gauge, an array up/down, etc.). A trend is directional behavior KPI. For example, a car might be winning a race (the status of KPI), but another car could be gaining rapidly (the trend). Using graphics such as a smiling face, indifferent face, and sad face, a business analyst can use a KPI to make quick decision about KPI (the status) and where it is heading (the trend).

Another new feature that supports a user-specific context of information is perspectives. A *perspective* is a logical collection of attributes, user-defined hierarchies, actions, and measure groups optimized to provide a given category of user a highly sophisticated, customized view of the underlying data.

Data Source Views

Data Source Views form a virtual layer on top of a data source and contain a subset (just the pertinent elements) of the objects associated with a data source. For example, a Data Source View could contain a subset of the tables and views pertaining to payroll processing. This virtualization allows objects to be renamed, calculated columns to be added, and name queries to be supported (analogous to database views). An added benefit of named query support is developers gain access to what are fundamentally views without requiring a user to have CREATE VIEW permissions on the data source.

Multiple Fact Tables

The fundamental object used by Analysis Services is a cube. As of Analysis Services 2005, a cube can contain multiple fact tables. For example, business measures related to both sales (product cost, shipping, revenue, tax, and profit) and employees (salary, commission, and benefits) could be analyzed simultaneously. In Analysis Services 2000, only a single fact table was supported (what is referred to as a Start or Snowflake schema). In Analysis Services 2005, arbitrary schemas can be defined.

Multidimensional Expressions (MDX)

Multidimensional Expressions is the language supported by Analysis Services 2000 that is used to implement calculations and security rules. The consensus opinion on MDX for Analysis Services 2000 is that it is vastly too complex. Analysis Services 2005 introduces a powerful but simpler version of MDX scripting (simpler constructs, simpler syntax). MDX scripting will be covered in more detail when the infrastructure of cube calculations is decomposed.

CLR Integration and SSAS

From a programmatic standpoint, Analysis Services 2005 has advanced significantly from Analysis Services 2000. In the previous version of Analysis Services, user-defined functions were added using COM objects. For example, if an algorithm was too complex for SQL, it was developed in a high-level language such as VB 6.0 or C++, and the interface to this high-level language's code was COM. Using this approach, part of an Analysis Services 2000 application was developed using Analysis Services and part of the application was in a different environment (e.g., Visual Basic 6.0 or Visual C++ 6).

Analysis Services projects still at times need to take advantage of computations performed in a high-level language such as the common language runtime (CLR) languages C# and VB .NET. As of SQL Server 2005, SQL Server objects such as user-defined functions can be created using CLR languages such as VB .NET and C#. This CLR language support extends not only to user-defined functions, but also to stored procedures and triggers as well. Such CLR add-ons to SQL Server can be developed using Visual Studio 2005. It would be possible for the same Visual Studio .NET solution to contain both an Analysis Services 2005 project and the C# or VB .NET project for the user-defined functions utilized by the Analysis Services 2005 project—one application and one development environment.

Analysis Management Objects (AMO)

From an administrative standpoint, Analysis Management Objects (AMO) have been added to create and manipulate business objects programmatically. AMO is the successor to Analysis Server 2000's Decision Support Object (DSO) programming model. The functionality exposed by AMO allows for the creating and maintenance of data mining objects. AMO can handle administrative tasks for data mining including security and processing. It even handles backup and restore within this area of Analysis Services.

Auditing

Analysis Services 2005 supports SQL Server 2005's server trace events. Using this construct SQL Server Profiler can now audit the behavior of an Analysis Services application. Using trace events, an application can be more readily debugged because of basic error logging. Additionally, server trace events improve overall manageability and can be used to audit who is using an Analysis Services object when the object is accessed.

Installation

When installing SQL Server 2005, the option is available to install or not install Analysis Services. You can also choose whether or not the Windows service associated with Analysis Services should be started by default. In order for Analysis Services to function, this Windows service must be running.

It is not necessary to run the Analysis Services Windows service on a developer's machine. Ultimately, Analysis Services would run on a production host. Developers could connect to a server on which Analysis Services is installed and running. For ease of development, it is simplest to install and run Analysis Services locally on the development machine and publish Analysis Services projects to staging or production hosts after they have been developed and debugged. As was previously discussed, using BIDS, it is possible to develop Analysis Services projects offline, meaning that an active connection to Analysis Services is not required for development.

What Is Analysis?

In order to justify Analysis Services, consider that you're a developer working for Adventure Works (as in the SQL Server 2005 demo database). Someone from accounting stops at your office and asks for a breakdown of product sales. So you write a query in Management Studio, joining the Production.Product table to the Sales.SalesOrderDetail table, as shown in Figure 10-2.

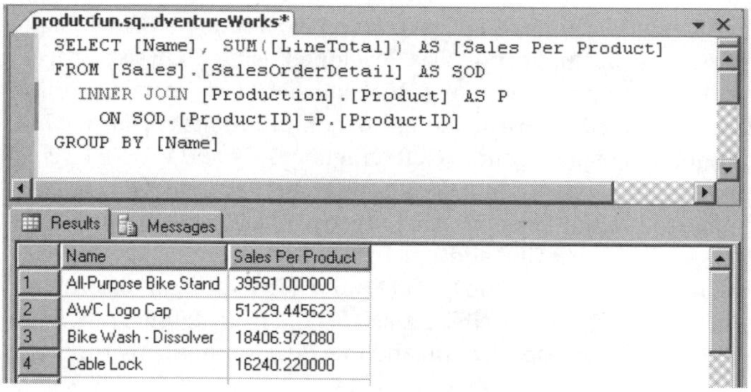

Figure 10-2. *Query and result: total sales by product*

The task completed, you start your real work again, but then someone from manufacturing stops by and wants to see a sales breakdown by Production.DaysToManufacture, soon followed by a design team member who wants to see sales by Production.Color. Just as you're about to start writing these queries, the accounting guy returns, wanting to see a further breakdown of the product sales according to sales period (by month, quarter, and year) and also wanting you to include a breakdown by SalesPerson, Product, ProductCategory, ProductSubCategory, and Customer. Rather than writing custom query after custom query, the solution is to use Analysis Services.

OLAP, OLTP, and Data Warehouses

The previous examples of data interpretation fall under the heading of Online Analytical Processing. An OLAP database is optimized for analysis and decision making. Before data can be interpreted, it needs to be created and quite often updated and deleted. Such a database environment is referred to as an Online Transaction Process (OLTP) system. For example, a retail establishment needs to record purchases, process returns, add new products, and receive new inventory. All this falls under the heading of an OLTP system, and AdventureWorks is an example of a typical OLTP database. After the store closes, the data in the AdventureWorks database is potentially copied to a separate repository and subject to OLAP to determine if denim jackets are profitable to sell and if plaid skirts sell more than striped shorts. SQL Server 2005 ships with the AdventureWorksDW database, a database optimized for OLAP, where the DW in the database name stands for Data Warehouse.

Given their differing characteristics, OLAP and OLTP environments may be configured differently. Within an OLAP environment, it might make sense to have more indexes so as to optimize data for reading, while in an OLTP system each additional index can negatively impact insert, delete, and update performance. In order to make data simpler to interpret, an OLAP data system could have demoralized data. As we have all learned the hard way, fully normalized data can get extremely complex. In an OLAP environment optimized for easy of analysis, it is a simpler to know an employee is part of the accounting department rather than knowing the employee belongs to DepartmentID=398. And OLTP would favor normalization for performance and design clarity reasons. A single database system could be used for both OLAP and OLTP.

A separate repository in which analysis-centric data is placed is referred to as a *data warehouse*. Such repositories are often large (terabytes) and optimized for the delivery and analysis of copious amounts of information. OLAP does not require a data warehouse, but OLAP is often associated with data warehouses because OLAP is the technique for interpreting copious amounts of data. Integration Services facilitates populating the data warehouse. Analysis Services organizes and places the data in accessible constructs. Reporting Services allows this data to be presented in a meaningful form targeted to those who need to make the business decisions based on this data.

OLAP Concepts

Working with Analysis Server requires the understanding of certain key OLAP terminology including *cubes*, *dimensions*, and *measures*. These concepts correspond to objects used within Analysis Services and its related technologies.

Cubes

Core amongst these concepts is the cube. Figure 10-3 shows an example of this derived from the AdventureWorksDW database.

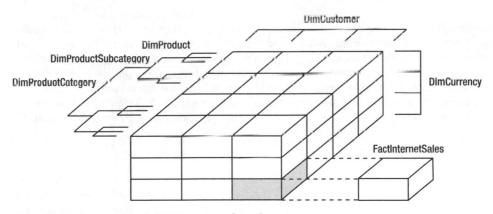

Figure 10-3. *AdventureWorksDW Internet sales cube*

A cube is a multidimensional representation of the quantitative values to be analyzed. The data to be analyzed is contained in the FactInternetSales table. The elements within this fact table are not shown in the previous diagram but include OrderQuantity, SalesAmount, DiscountAmount, and TaxAmount. The mechanisms for administering and accessing these values are what Analysis Services provides.

In conventional terms, a cube is thought of as containing three dimensions: height, width, and depth. Within Analysis Services a cube is not limited to three dimensions. Sales and Quantity are measures that could readily be associated with five dimensions: DimProduct, DimCustomer, DimSalesPerson, DimCreditCardType, and DimCurrency. The cube diagram in Figure 10-3 contains three dimensions (DimProduct, DimCustomer, and DimCurrency) because they are simpler to draw, but this in no way means that an Analysis Services cube is limited to three dimensions.

Cells

Irrespective of the number of dimensions, a cube is composed of cells. A cell is the atomic unit of an Analysis Service's cube and is specified by identifying its position within the cube in terms of dimensions. A Sales cell measure could be uniquely identified by its Customer, Sales Person, Credit Card Type, Currency, and Product, where Product is specified across each of its members (Product, Subcategory, and Category).

Measures and Fact Tables

Within a cube, measures such as `FactInternetSales` are quantitative values such as `OrderQuantity` and `SalesAmount` that can be used to assess business activity. By managing and allowing the manipulation of measures, Analysis Services allows a score to be associated with data (much like a football match has a score associated with it). Often numeric in value, measures tend to be aggregated (show sales aggregated by product category, sales by product color, or sales by customer). Date/Time, monetary units, and quantity are all examples of potential measures.

Measures are contained in a fact table, which is a database table containing one or more measures. The aptly named table `FactInternetSales` is the fact table of the previously displayed cube. The term "measure" is synonymous with the term "fact," hence the term "fact table."

A measure may not a database column but could be a calculation (sales less commission, sales plus tax, etc). Within Analysis Services, Multidimensional Expressions are used to generate calculated measures.

Dimensions and Attributes

The previous example cube had three dimensions (DimProduct, DimCustomer, and DimCurrency). What is a dimension? The formal definition of an Analysis Services dimension is "a dimension categorizes measures." The currency dimension categorizes the measures in the `FactInternetSales` fact table by Hong Kong Dollar, Ruble, and Euro. The DimCustomer dimension is completely independent of the DimCurrency dimension and categorizes based on which customer purchased the product.

In a more traditional database sense, dimensions are often the foreign keys of a fact table.

Each dimension is composed of descriptive characteristics. For example, a DimProduct may be red in color. Color is an attribute of the dimension and can be used to select data within said dimension.

Hierarchies

Dimensions are ordered by hierarchies, where the levels of the hierarchy could be classified as Category, Subcategory, and Product. The tables associated with Category, Subcategory, and Product compose all levels of the DimProduct dimension. Hierarchies are broken down into balanced hierarchies and unbalanced hierarchies. In order to understand this, consider the Category, Subcategory, and Product levels shown in Figure 10-4.

At the base of the previous hierarchy are specific products (Logo Cap or Stock Vest, S). These values represent the leaves of the hierarchy. Each leaf is the same distance from the root level of the hierarchy, which means it is a balanced hierarchy.

Analysis Services allows results to be returned that are cognizant of the hierarchical levels in each dimension. Results could be returned such as Internet sales for all products, Internet sales by category, Internet sales for category starting with the letter "Q," or product sales by category and subcategory.

Hierarchies can also be unbalanced, such as the geographic hierarchy shown in Figure 10-5 (which is not based on the previously drawn cube diagram).

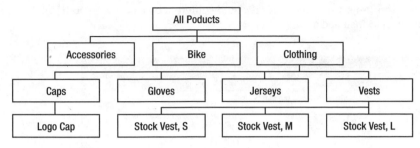

Figure 10-4. *Production dimension: balanced hierarchy*

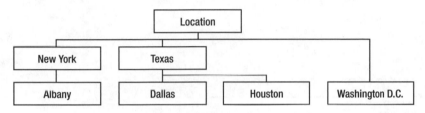

Figure 10-5. *Location dimension: unbalanced hierarchy*

The leaf nodes are cities, and the city of Washington D.C. is not affiliated with a state. The distance between this leaf node and the hierarchy room differs from that of the other leaf nodes. Why this emphasis on balanced and unbalanced hierarchies? Analysis Services 2005 supports both types of hierarchies, though this is not the case with comparable tools from other database vendors.

Analysis Services Projects

Recall the cube diagram in Figure 10-3 which contained the dimensions of DimProduct, DimCurrency, and DimCustomer. This cube also contained a fact table, FactInternetSales. This cube will be implemented using an Analysis Services project within BIDS in order to show off BIDS capabilities in the Analysis Services arena. The cube in the previous diagram will be modified in that it will be created with a fourth dimension, DimTime.

In order to create Analysis Services objects (cubes, dimensions, measures, etc.), a developer could code natively in Analysis Service Scripting Language, the XML-based language used by client applications to communicate with Analysis Services. Writing raw XML (regardless of how well designed) is tedious and error prone. SQL Server 2005 ships with Business Intelligence Development Studio, and this integrated development environment (IDE) supports Analysis Services projects. This project type is ASSL under the covers (the source files of the project are ASSL XML), but BIDS IDE streamlines development by generating ASSL while developers get to work with a sophisticated user interface.

Analysis Services project are accessed using BIDS (Microsoft SQL Server 2005 ➤ Business Intelligence Development Studio). This application is actually a version of Visual Studio 2005 that ships at no extra cost with SQL Server 2005. The types of projects available in Business Intelligence Development Studio will depend on whether SQL Server is installed on a host with or without Visual Studio 2005. If Visual Studio 2005 is installed on the same host as SQL Server, then the Business Intelligence Development Studio will contain all projects installed with Visual Studio 2005 (Window Application, Console Applications, etc.). The discussion in this section assumes that SQL Server 2005 is installed without Visual Studio 2005.

In order to create an Analyst Services project with BIDS, select File ➤ New, and from the New Project dialog box, shown in Figure 10-6, navigate as follows: Other Languages ➤ Business Intelligence

Projects ➤ Analysis Services Project (this sequence is slightly different on a host with both SQL
Server and Visual Studio 2005 installed on it).

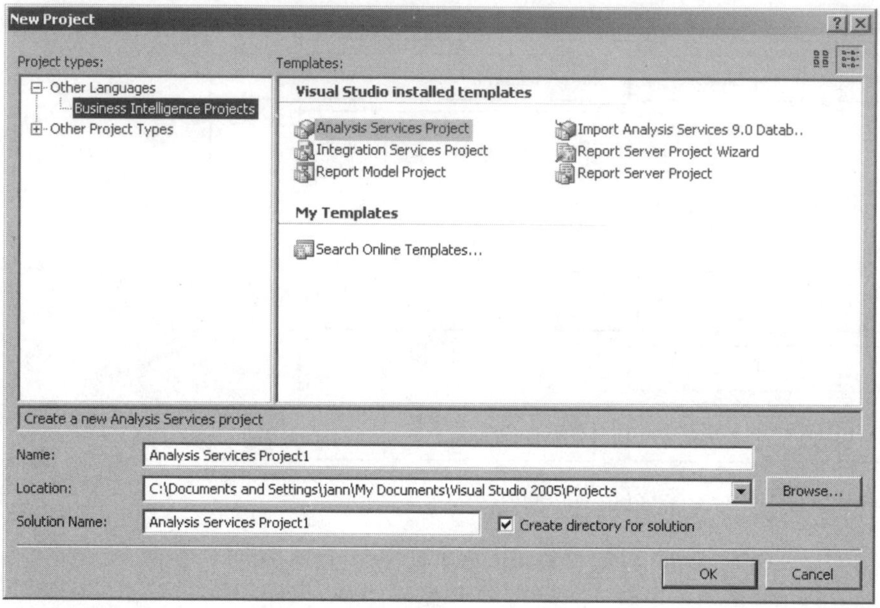

Figure 10-6. *Business Intelligence Development Studio: New Project dialog box*

By default, the name of the project and solution will contain a generic name such as Analysis
Services Project1. To more readily identify the project, enter **Internet Sales** in the Name text box and
click OK for the New Project dialog box.

The model used by Business Intelligence Development Studio is that of a solution containing
one or more projects. For this scenario, there is one solution and one Analysis Services project. It
would be possible within the same solution to create additional projects such as a Report Server
project and an Integration Services project.

Defining Data Sources

Once an Analysis Services project is created, a data source needs to be created. This data source
refers to the database from whence our project will access data. This data source may be associated
with SQL Server or could be any flavor of data source accessible as a managed provider, OLE DB, or
ODBC. In order to create a data source, within Solution Explorer (View ➤ Solution Explorer) right-
click the Data Sources folder within the Internet Sales project and select New Data Source from the
context menu, as you see in Figure 10-7.

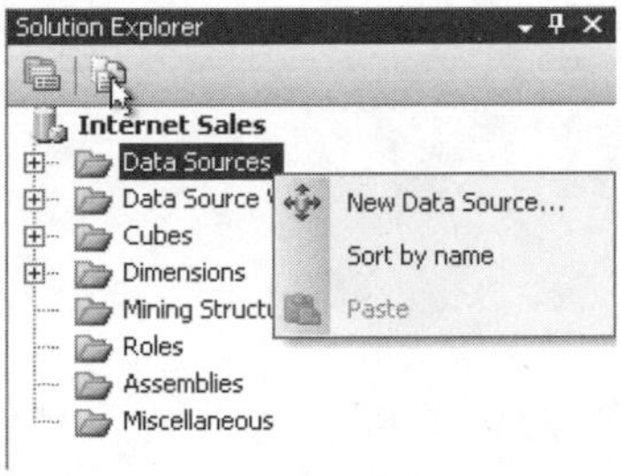

Figure 10-7. *Data Sources context menu*

Right-clicking New Data Source displays the Data Source Wizard, where we can click Next immediately to move from the start page. The second screen of the Data Source Wizard, shown in Figure 10-8, allows the data source to be created.

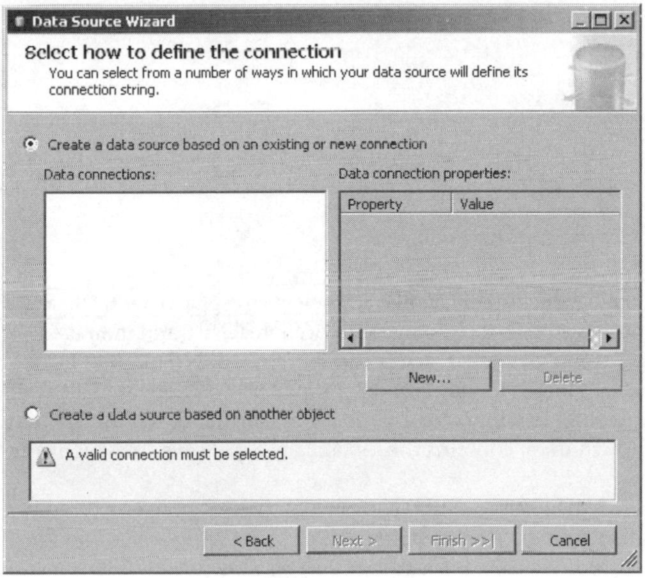

Figure 10-8. *Defining the data source*

A data source is associated with a data connection (data provider, host, database, security credentials, etc.). Creating a data connection, and thus allowing a data source to be created, is achieved by clicking the New button, which displays the Connection Manager dialog box, shown in Figure 10-9.

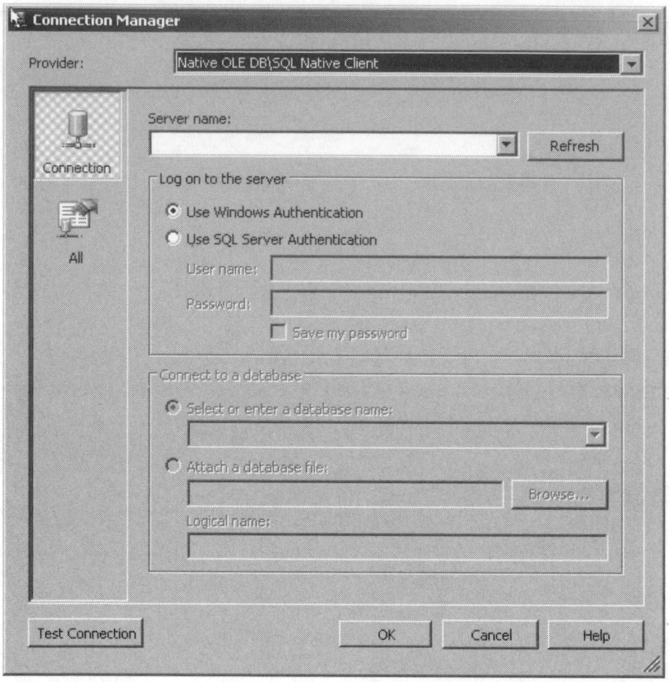

Figure 10-9. *Data Source Wizard: Connection Manager dialog box*

When the Connection Manager dialog box initially displays, it selects the Native OLE DB\SQL Native Client by default. OLE DB is the data access technology that predates .NET and managed providers. In order to most efficiently access SQL Server, select the .Net Providers\SqlClient Data Provider from the Provider combo box. Under Server name, a drop-down list will appear of all available hosts running SQL Server. You can enter **localhost** (or a period, for shorthand) to indicate that the machine on which BIDS is presently running contains the instance of SQL Server to which you wish to connect.

At this point the type of security needs to be selected, and you need to choose either Use Windows Authentication or Use SQL Server Authentication. Microsoft advocates using Windows Authentication so SQL Server adopts the same, uniform security infrastructure as Windows. Native SQL Server Authentication has one advantage over Windows Authentication and that is that it means developers do not need to submit a formal request with their MIS department in order to get their Windows accounts associated with specific SQL Server roles/permissions. If you have a username and login to SQL Server, there is no need to deal with MIS bureaucracy.

One clue that your security is set up correctly is that when the Select or enter a database name drop-down list is selected, it will display all accessible databases on the server for the specific user credentials. If security is not working correctly, then this list will be empty. From the drop-down list, select the database AdventureWorksDW, the data warehouse variant of the AdventureWorks database. As a double check, click the Test Connection button in order to verify that the server, security credential, and database all combine to make a valid database connection. Once the connection is validated, click OK, thus creating a data connection.

The connection name displayed on the Data Source Wizard dialog box will take the following form if it was created using Windows Authentication: Hostname.Databasename. If the connection was created using SQL Server Authentication, the connection will be named as follows: Hostname.Databasename.Username.

With the data connection created, click Next from the Data Source Wizard dialog box that handles data connections. This displays the Data Source Wizard Impersonation Information dialog (see Figure 10-10), which is where the credentials are specified that are used by Analysis Services to connect to the specific data source.

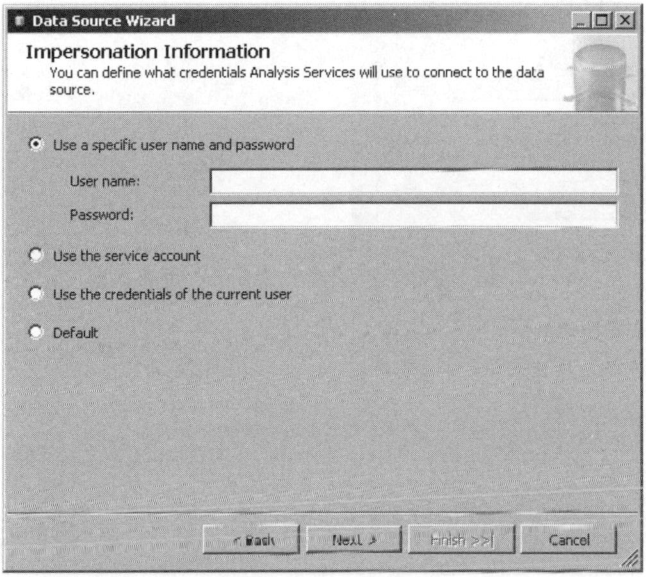

Figure 10-10. *Data Source Wizard: Impersonation Information dialog box*

The Impersonation Information dialog box is needed because Analysis Services, and not the user currently working with BIDS, ultimately connects to the data source. Within the previous dialog box, it is best not to select the option Use the credentials of the current user. Under certain circumstances (such as when a data source is used for training data mining structures/modules), it is not permissible according to the documentation to use this impersonation mode. For the purposes of this exercise, specify the option Use the service account. Selecting this radio button option assumes that the account under which Analysis Services runs (the service account) has access to the data source.

There is no mandate that the data source point to a SQL Server 2005 database. The purpose of Analysis Services's UDM is to allow heterogeneous data sources to be accessed in a manner seamless to the end user. For the sake of convenience, AdventureWorksDW, a SQL Server 2005 database, was used. The data source could have easily been a SQL Server 2000 database such as Northwind or a Jet database named Pubs. The data source could have been DB2, Oracle, Excel, or any heterogeneous data source supported by a managed provider, OLE DB, or ODBC.

Designers vs. Wizards

By double-clicking a newly created data source within Solution Explorer, we launch the Data Source Designer, shown in Figure 10-11, thus allowing us to edit the data source.

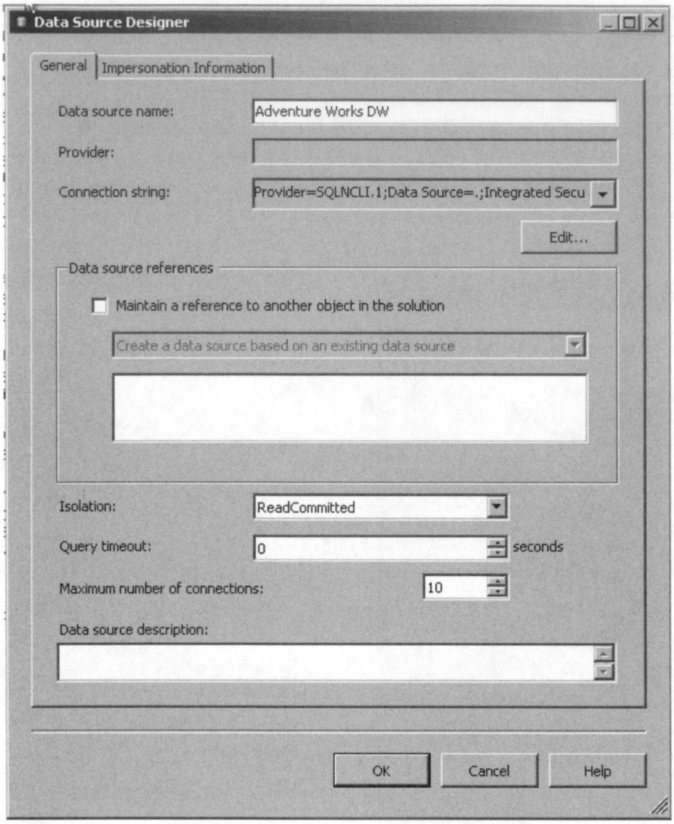

Figure 10-11. *Data Source Designer dialog box*

Using the Data Source Designer, we can change the name of the data source, alter the connection string, or modify other properties associated with the data source. In fact, the designer has access to features not exposed by the wizard. The Edit button is useful if the underlying host, data, or security credentials change for the data source. This may sound trivial and obvious, but it is quite significant. Imagine the connection string initially points to a SQL Server 2000 database running on Host A. As part of an upgrade, the same data is moved to a SQL Server 2005 database running on Host B. There is no need to delete the data source and the other Analysis Services objects in the project associated with this data source. The data source can be mapped to a different type of database, different database name, or different host without requiring the project to be reworked. This would even work using non-Microsoft data sources such as DB2 on an OS 390 mainframe being moved to Oracle on a Linux box. The Impersonation Information tab is also handy in case the security credentials used by Analysis Services when connecting to the data source need to be changed.

Every object within BIDS Data Source Views, cubes, and dimensions all have wizards and designers associated with them.

Defining Data Source Views

The core premise of Analysis Services is to get the metadata correct and the data will fall into place. In keeping with this philosophy, a Data Source View needs to be created within an Analysis Services project. A Data Source View is an offline repository of the metadata associated with tables or views used by the Analysis Services project. The idea is to allow development to proceed by allowing access to the required metatdata without having to maintain a persistent connection to the data source.

A Data Source View is created by right-clicking the Data Source Views folder for the Analysis Services project within Solution Explorer. The right-click displays a context menu containing the New Data Source View menu item, as you see in Figure 10-12.

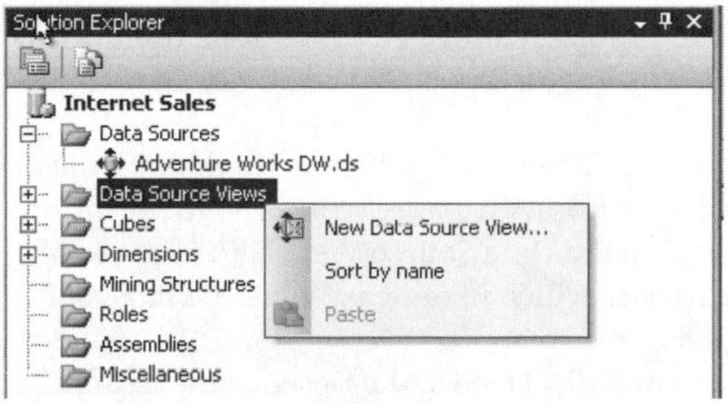

Figure 10-12. *Data Sources Views: context menu*

Clicking the New Data Source View menu item displays the Data Source View Wizard. Click Next to move the wizard off the generic start page. The second page of the wizard allows a data source to be selected. For this exercise, we select the data source previously created, Adventure-WorksDW, and then click the Next button s to bring up the Select Tables and Views screen shown in Figure 10-13.

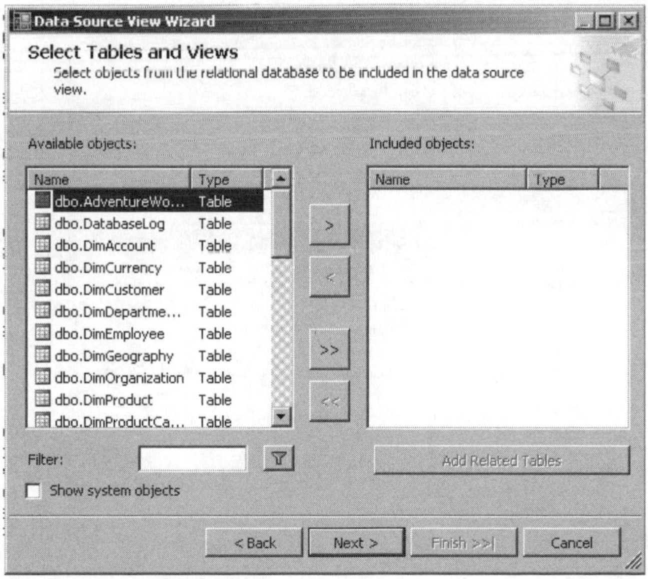

Figure 10-13. *Data Source View Wizard: Select Tables and Views dialog box*

Here, the tables and views of interest for our Analysis Services exercise can be selected. Do so by double-clicking the DimProductCategory, DimProductSubCategory, DimProduct, DimCustomer, DimCurrency, DimTime and FactInternetSales tables, thus moving them to the Included objects list.

■Note The previous dialog box contains a major enhancement found in numerous SQL Server 2005 and Visual Studio 2005 dialog boxes, namely that the dialog box can be resized. The three lines forming the triangle in the lower-right portion of the screen indicate that the dialog box can be resized. In previous products, almost all such screens were fixed size, making seeing the full names of the available objects and included objects a tedious process.

Although not used in this example, the Add Related Tables feature can prove quite useful. This button will move tables from the Available objects list that have a foreign key relationship with the tables and views of the Included objects list.

Once the desired tables have been selected, click Next. When the final screen of the wizard is displayed, change the default name of the Data Source View from Adventure Works DW to **Adventure Works Internet Sales** and then click Finish, thus creating the Data Source View. The purpose of the view is to isolate a pertinent subset of the information, which in our case were the tables of AdventureWorksDW related to sales generated via the Internet.

Once the Data Source View is created, a data diagram is displayed in the Design view associated with the newly created Data Source View (see Figure 10-14).

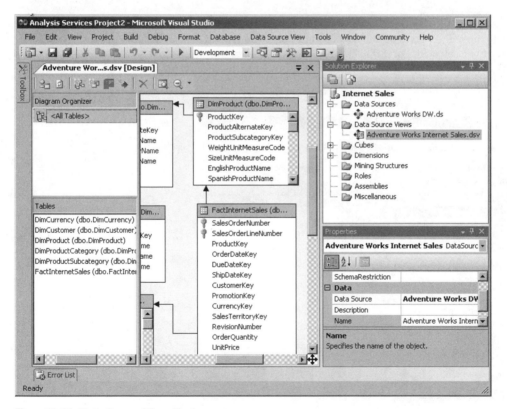

Figure 10-14. *Data Source View: Design screen*

You can see in this figure that it is possible to select a table from the Design window. The properties of a table (such as FactInternetSales) can be changed in Properties window. For example, a friendly name could be associated with the otherwise cryptically named table/view. (There is a large brokerage house headquartered near San Francisco that could have used this feature in a product that contained the (misspelled) Receivables table.) It is also possible to drag one table/view on top of another such that the relationship between these entities can be created.

Right-clicking the Design window displays a context menu that allows additional manipulations to be made of the Data Source View. Tables and views can be added or removed. For example, if we had forgotten the `DimProduct` table when traversing the new Data Source View, a significant piece of the model would be missing. This oversight could be corrected using the context menu's Add/Remove Tables option.

Using the Designer window's context menu, it is also possible to specify a named query for the data source. Recall that a named query is a query associated with a specific data access command (a `SELECT` in SQL terminology). This named query would show up in the designer as a table. As mentioned previously, a named query is what in a relational database is considered to be a view, but a named query does not reside in the underlying data source and therefore does not require `CREATE VIEW` permission on the data source. It also could be the case that the underlying data source is not a relational database, and therefore does not even support the concept of a view. The named query resides in the local metadata associated with the Data Source View.

New relationships can be created using the context menu. A new relationship can also be created by dragging a foreign key from one table and dropping it onto the primary of the table referenced by the foreign key. This technique might prove useful if the foreign key relationships are not defined in the underlying data source or if the underlying data source does not provide access to its metadata, preventing the BIDS Wizard from automatically setting up the table relations. This latter scenario is quite common where a user will be given access to data but not given access to metadata definitions for constructs such as indexes, foreign keys, and view definitions.

Creating a new relationship would be a necessity with using a named query. A named query has no underlying metadata defining its relationship to the other tables in the data source. Creating a new relationship would provide this missing critical information.

It is possible to right-click the newly created Data Source View and toggle between Design and Code view. Code for any object in an Analysis Services project object is just the XML representation of the object. This XML is the Analysis Services Scripting Language (ASSL) previously introduced. The code view is handy for globally changing names within an Analysis Services project object. For example, if a developer mistakenly used the term Sails as the friendly name for each sale-related object, a global replace in the code can easily remedy the mistake without bring up the designer dialog box. For developers who need to work directly with ASSL, the various source files of an Analysis Services project can serve as a tutorial.

■**Note** When creating a Data Source View, the wizard does not create the relationships between tables. These can be manually added in the Designer. When adding a relationship (say dragging `ProductKey` from one table to another), be sure to drag and drop in the correct direction (from the table containing the foreign key to the table containing the primary key). If the direction is reversed (set up incorrectly), the Cube wizard will confuse fact tables with dimension tables.

Defining Cubes

Creating a new cube is a matter of right-clicking the project's Cubes folder within Solution Explorer and selecting New Cube from the context menu. Cubes are highly configurable, but for the first four screens of the Cube Wizard just click Next until the Identifying Fact and Dimensions Tables screen is displayed (see Figure 10-15).

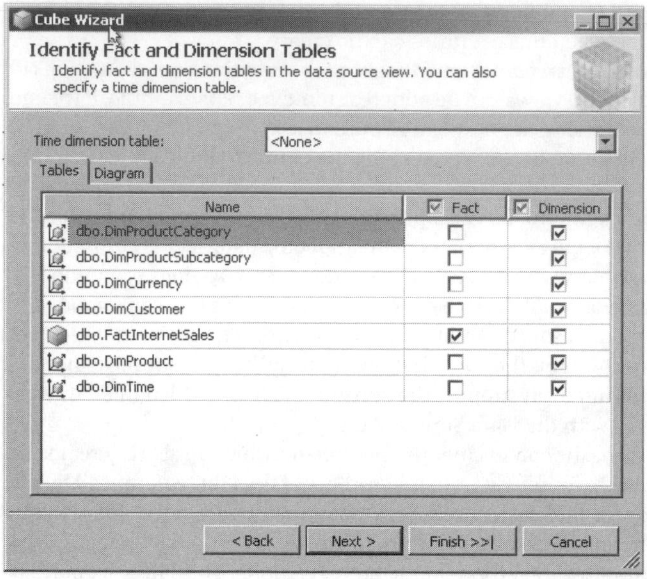

Figure 10-15. *Cube Wizard: Identity Fact and Dimension Tables dialog box*

As we expect, the FactInternetSales table contains the potential measures (OrderQuantity, UnitPrice, SalesAmount, TaxAmount, Freight, and TotalProductCost) and is hence the fact table. A fact table need only contain one measure, but could contain more than one. The DimCurrency and DimCustomer tables serve as dimensions but do not contain a hierarchy, as their dimension contains but one table. For the DimCurrent table, the CurrencyName column is used to identify the measure, while for the DimCustomer table, identification is through the FirstName, MiddleName, and LastName columns. The third dimension, which is hierarchal in nature, is composed of DimProductSubcategory, DimProductCategory, and DimProduct tables.

Note Recall that special emphasis was placed on correctly manually creating intertable relationships (drag from the table containing the foreign key to the table containing the primary key). The Identity Fact and Dimension Tables dialog box will contain incorrect fact and dimension checked boxes if the relationships were not set up correctly or were for some reason omitted (not set up by the wizard and then set up manually by the developer).

This screen contains an entry for Time dimension table. The DimTime table contains a variety of DATETIME columns that reference date fields in the FactinternetTable (OrderDateKey, DueDateKey, and ShipDateKey), and hence the DimTime table can be selected in the Time dimension table drop-down list. When the DimTime table is selected as the Time dimension, the Dimension check box next to this table is selected.

When we click the Next button from the Identity Fact and Dimension Tables screen, we get the dialog box shown in Figure 10-16.

The previous dialog box is only displayed as part of the wizard when a time dimension table is selected in the Identity Facts and Dimension Tables dialog box. The Select Time Periods dialog box enables us to specify the time hierarchy or the Time dimension. If the company assesses sales on a quarterly basis, then the time property name Quarter should be associated with a time table column (DimTime.TimeKey), thus resulting in a hierarchy of year, quarter, and month with each quarter containing three leaf nodes corresponding to each month in the quarter.

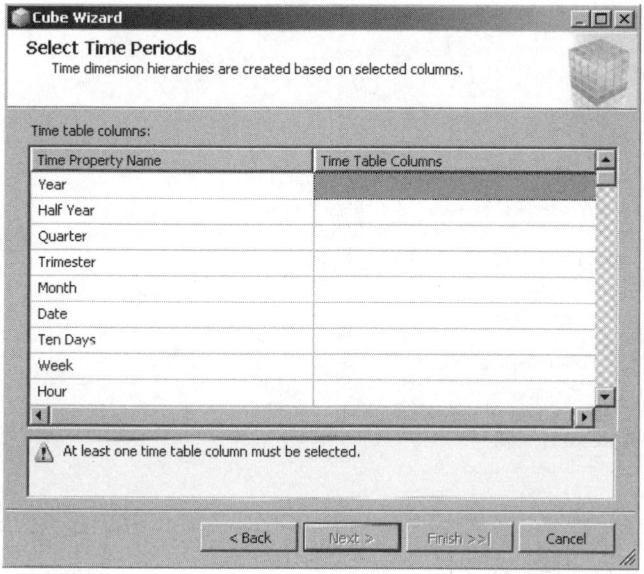

Figure 10-16. *Cube Wizard: Select Time Periods dialog box*

The screen in Figure 10-17 is used to specify the dimensions of the cube by moving the following from the Available dimensions list to the Cube dimensions list: DimCustomer, DimCurrency, DimProduct (whose hierarchy includes subcategory and category) and DimTime. With the dimensions specified, clicking Next displays the screen used to specify which measures will be used in the fact table (see Figure 10-18).

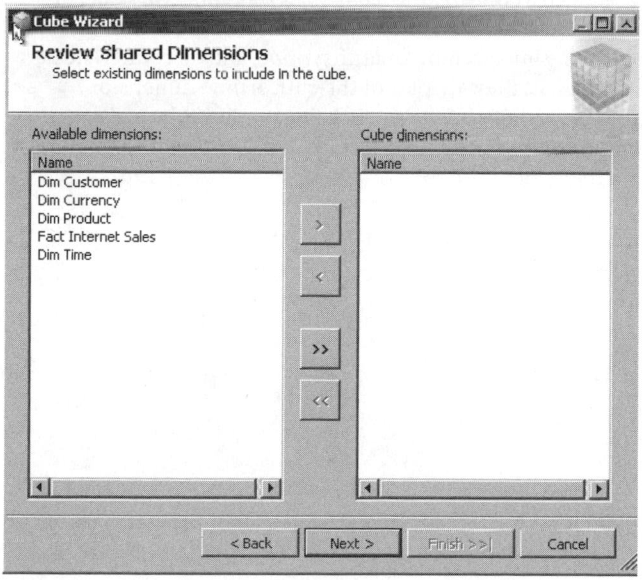

Figure 10-17. *Cube Wizard: Review Shared Dimensions*

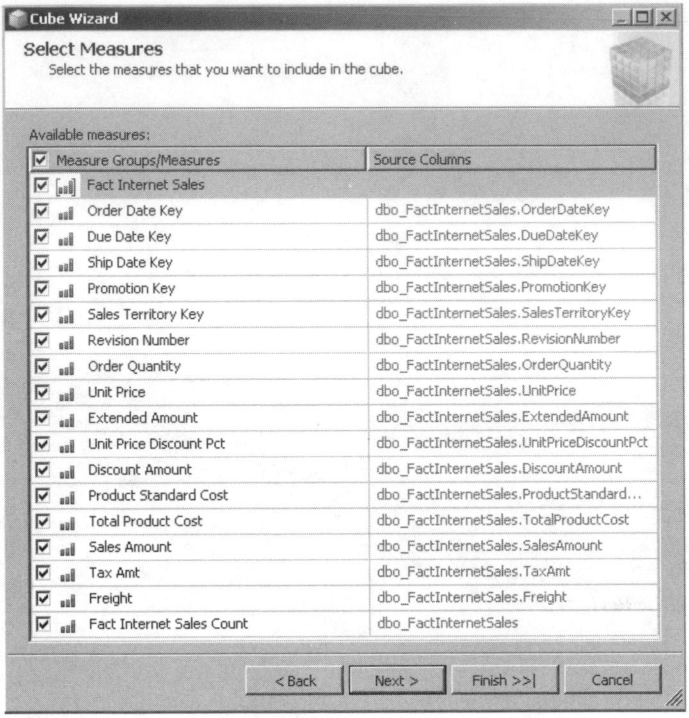

Figure 10-18. *Cube Wizard: Select Measures dialog box*

This screen was resized to accommodate all the potential measure columns. The Select Measures dialog box allows the measures associated with a cube to be selected. For this cube, we select Order Quantity, Sales Amount, Tax Amt, and Freight. All other columns will be unchecked. The Sales Amount column is the total cost of the goods sold taking into account quantity, price, and discount. The date-related columns were deliberately unchecked, as they are part of the cube's time dimension.

To complete the cube, hit Next three more times and then click Finish. The cube picks up the name of the Data Source View, and hence the cube is called Adventure Works Internet Sales.cube as can be seen in the view of Solution Explorer in Figure 10-19.

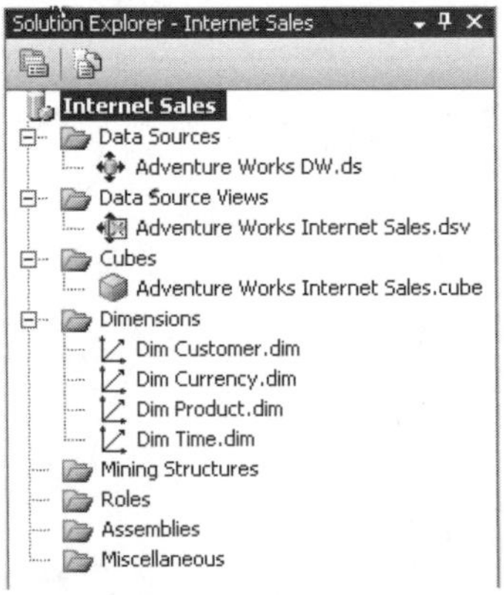

Figure 10-19. *Solution Explorer with dimension and cube*

For both cubes and dimensions, it is possible to select the Properties window with either of these items highlighted and hence change the cube or dimension name. Right-clicking a cube or dimension can launch the Business Intelligence Wizard, which lets us perform more intricate manipulation of the cube or dimension.

At this point, the cube needs to be deployed to Analysis Services. The rationale for this is that BIDS contains an incomplete view of the constructs at this stage of the game. For example, if a cube is selected in Solution Explorer, the Measures and Dimensions windows within BIDS will not contain the cube's measures and dimensions until the cube is deployed.

■**Note** The screens discussed only apply when adding a cube to a virgin product. If a new cube was created within the exact same project, the Cube Wizard does not require as much information. The dimensions are already defined, so a developer will not be prompted again to specify the dimensions.

Deploying Projects and Configuring Projects for Deployment

It is important to recognize that a project is a local representation of ultimately what Analysis Services will manipulate. The Analysis Services projects exist locally, and the SSAL in the project files has thus far not been processed by Analysis Services using XML/A. The underpinnings of the project may be XML-based SSAL and XML/A, but no XML-script-level development is required in order to deploy the project to Analysis Services. Deploying a project makes constructs such as cubes become visible to Analysis Services. Projects are deployed either from Build ➤ Deploy or by right-clicking the project from within Solution Explorer and selecting Deploy from the context menu. In a real-world situation, a developer might deploy to their local machine or a training/development host in order to debug their project. Once a project was behaving correctly, it could then be deployed to a staging or production server.

In order to change the host to which a project is deployed, select Project ➤ Properties. From the Property Pages dialog box, select Configuration Properties ➤ Deployment and specify the server to which the project should be deployed. An example of the Project ➤ Properties dialog box appears in Figure 10-20.

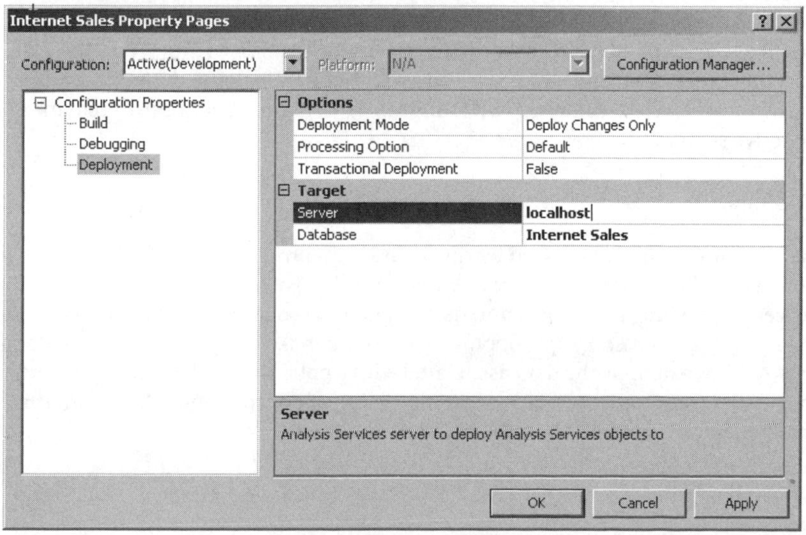

Figure 10-20. *Internet Sales Property Pages dialog box*

In this dialog box you will see the button Configuration Manager. C# and VB .NET developers will recognize what this button does. Clicking Configuration Manager allows a BIDS developer to create a production configuration (for example) in addition to the standard development configuration associated with the project. The development configuration could utilize localhost, while the production configuration could access BigMainCorporate host. The standard toolbar of Business Intelligence Development Studio has a drop-down list that displays the current configuration, as shown in Figure 10-21.

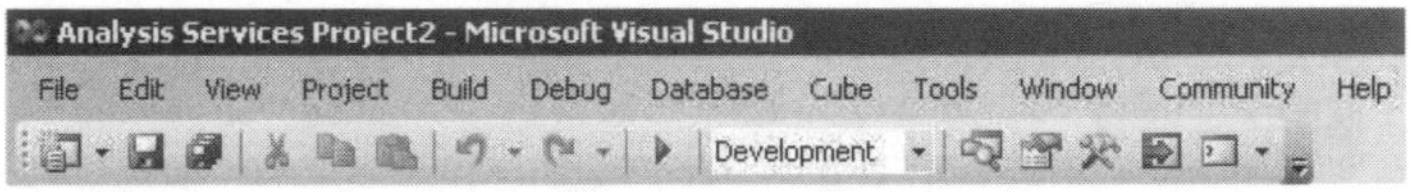

Figure 10-21. *BIDS standard toolbar with Configuration drop-down list*

By default, the previous toolbar's configuration drop-down list is set to Development. This drop-down list can also be changed to select an alternate configuration (say the production configuration that was just created). Selecting an alternate configuration is how developers can deploy an Analysis Services project to an alternate host without having to change Configuration Properties ➤ Deployment ➤ Server with each alternate deployment.

Deploying the Internet Sales Project

The reason for discussing project configurations and deployments is because our example project must be deployed in order to demonstrate some advanced features of cube manipulation. Deploying a project is achieved using the BIDS menu item Build ➤ Deploy Solution of Build "project name." For our example, as Internet Sales is the name of the project, so we would see the option Build Internet Sales after selecting the Build menu option. Right-clicking the project within Solution Explorer exposes a context menu that contains a Deploy option (deploy project).

Deployment is not an instantaneous process. The status of the deployment can be observed using the BIDS output window visible via View ➤ Other Windows ➤ Output. The process of deployment could involve more than just the Analysis Services project. If we select Build ➤ Deploy Solution, then all deployable projects within the solution will be deployed. This could include Analysis Services projects, Reporting Services projects, Integration Services projects, and CLR projects such as a C# or VB .NET DLL that contains user-defined functions used by the Analysis Services project. In the case of a CLR project, deployment would be to the SQL Server on which the user-defined function was to reside. In the case of other project types (Analysis, Reporting, and Integration Services), deployment would be to their respective servers.

Deployment vs. Processing

The BIDS Build menu and context menu accessed by right-clicking a product within Solution Explorer exposed options to either deploy or process a cube. Thus far, we have discussed deployment, which is the process of pushing the project and its objects (data sources, dimensions, cubes, etc.) to a specific Analysis Services server. Simply deploying does not make the underlying data associated with the cube visible. For example, the data associated with a cube will not be browsable until it is processed. When an object such as a cube is processed, Analysis Services copies data from the underlying data source or data sources into the cube objects.

Cube Operations

When the Design window for a cube is displayed, a set of tabs are available to further enhance the cube. Following is a list of a subset of these tabs and the functionality they expose:

- *Calculations*: Although they can be created using the BIDS UI, calculations are MDX scripts or expressions. Calculations let entities such as computed members (e.g., a member computed using arithmetic expressions) and name sets (e.g., a set of dimension members) be defined.

- *KPIs*: As discussed earlier, key performance indicators are graphical representations of a value, goal, current status, and trend.

- *Actions*: An action is an MDX statement used by client applications. An action is capable of running an OLE DB command or another style of operation. An action can return a dateset or rowset, or report. The latter is returned after submitting a URL to Report Server.

- *Partitions*: Managed the data and metadata for the aggregations of measure groups.

- *Perspectives*: Recall from our earlier discussion that this is a per-user (simplified) view of the cube's information.

- *Translations*: Facilitates client applications that localize content such as presenting the data for English ➤ Canadian and French ➤ Canadian.

- *Browser*: Browses the contents of the cube, meaning the actual data associated with each element within a cube. The browser allows the data to be presented in a meaningful way.

Accessing the previous options only makes sense after a cube has been deployed to Analysis Services. The contents of the previous tabs will not be accessible until a project is deployed. By default, the Cube Structure tab is selected, and when this tab option is selected, the Measures and Dimensions windows shown in Figure 10-22 is displayed.

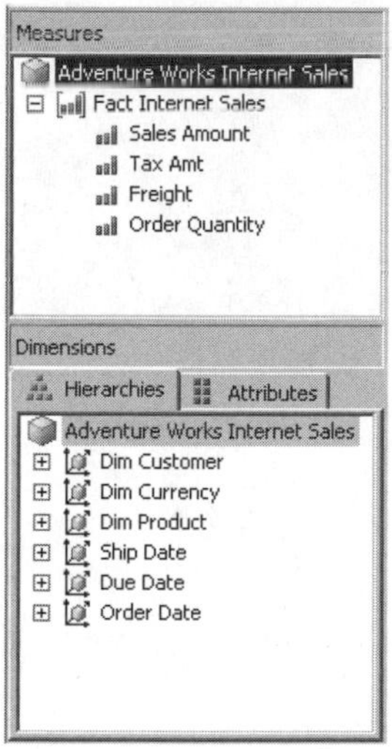

Figure 10-22. *Measures and Dimensions windows*

The Measures and Dimensions windows identify the fundamental structure of the created cube. Under Measures, we could click Fact Internet Sales and add new measures such as Unit Cost and Total Product Cost using the context menu. Using the Measures context menu, we could add measure groups, which are an organizational approach to categorizing what could potentially be hundreds of attributes (cost measure groups or tax measure groups or income measure groups).

The Dimensions window's Hierarchies tab allows us to access DimCustomer and, if we so desire, the Geographic key of the DimCustomer table could be used to create a geographic layer in the hierarchy of the dimension. By adding the DimGeography table to the DimCustomer hierarchy, new types of aggregation would be available to the developer such as to aggregate the data in the cube by a customer's state, city, or postal code.

The Attributes tab of the Dimensions window allows the attributes of the dimension to be seen. The attributes include the columns within each member of a dimension. For the DimProduct dimension, the product-related columns would be available, but so would the columns associated with the category and subcategory members of the product hierarchy.

Browsing Cubes

So far, a lot of work has been put into the process of creating a cube (specifically the metadata associated with a cube) with very little to show for it from a data standpoint. In order to see the data associated with a cube, the cube must first be processed (select Build ➤ Process, or right-click the project in Solution Explorer and select Process). Once the cube has been processed successfully, the underlying data can be browsed.

Browsing is achieved by clicking a cube instance to display the Designer for said cube. From the Designer, select the Browser tab, and now the measures and dimensions of the cube are displayed to the left of the Browser window, as you see in Figure 10-23.

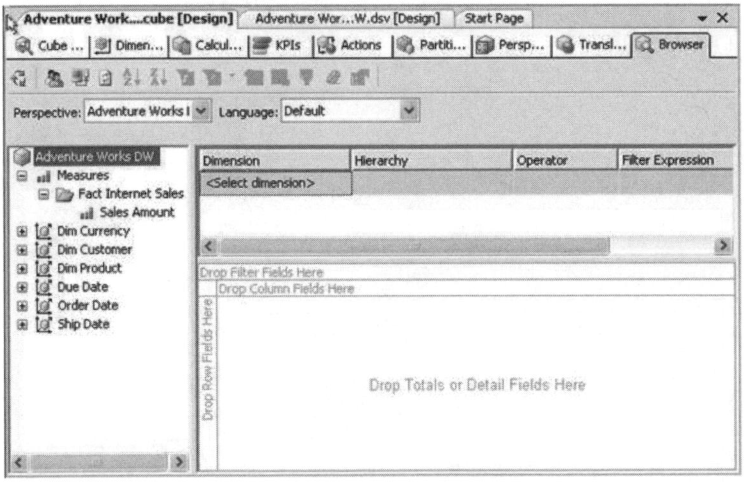

Figure 10-23. *Browser window before data is displayed*

To show off the browser's ability to display a cube's data, open the DimProduct dimension, drag the English Product Name attribute from Explorer window, and drop the product on the Drop Row Fields Here region of the browser. Then drag from Measures ➤ Fact Internet Sales ➤ Sales Amount to the Browser window's region labeled Drop Total or Detail Fields Here (see Figure 10-24).

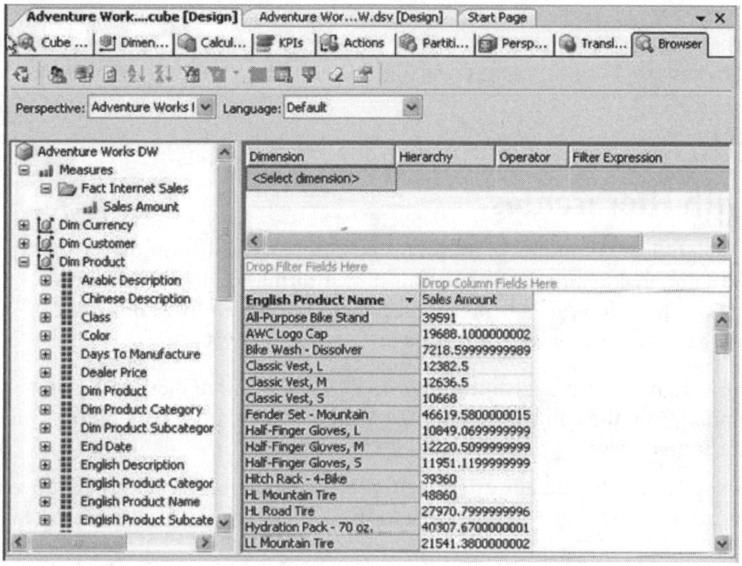

Figure 10-24. *Product.Name sales figures for Adventure Works DW*

The information displayed in the browser is actually the information initially requested by the chap in accounting. Recall that your coworker from the design team wanted to see sales based on product colors. From within the browser window, select Products and then hit the Delete key. Products are no longer the value used to interpret the sales measure. Drag Product ➤ Color and drop it on the Drop Row Fields Here region of the browser (see Figure 10-25).

Color	Sales Amount
Black	0838411.9576015
Blue	2279096.28000007
Multi	106470.740000006
NA	435116.689999853
Red	7724330.52400018
Silver	5113389.08160051
White	5106.31999999993
Yellow	4856755.62750044
Grand Total	29358677.2206503

Figure 10-25. *Product.Color sales figures for Adventure Works DW*

With a click, a drag, and a drop, the question raised by the design department has been answered. There was no SQL used at all in this manipulation of how the data was displayed (at least not SQL visible to the developer). Best of all, the Universal Dimension Model (which is what Fact and Dimension Explorer exposes) indicates that the data was displayed without a data-store-specific command being executed. There was no Transact SQL or PL/SQL or any other homogeneous language required to access the cube's underlying data.

Note Removing dimensions and measures from the browser window is performed using the Delete key. The browser window is for display purposes only. This delete action in no way deletes or alters the underlying data associated with the cube.

Browsing Cubes with Hierarchies

Although our cube contained significant amounts of useful information, we will demonstrate adding a level of hierarchy to a dimension and then using this new information to browse more complicated data. The dimension to be altered is DimCustomer, and the hierarchy to be added is from the DimGeography table. This more elaborate scenario is initiated as follows:

1. From Solution Explorer, right-click the Adventure Works DW Data Source View and select the View Designer option from the context menu. This displays the relational diagram of all the tables in the Data Source View.

2. Within the View Designer, right-click an empty space in the Designer and select Add/Remove Tables from the context menu. This will allow us to add the DimGeography table to the Data Source View.

3. From the Add/Remove Tables dialog box, double-click DimGeography to move this table from the Available objects list to the Included objects list.

4. Click OK on the Add/Remote Tables dialog box to add the DimGeography table to the Data Source View.

5. After the DimGeography table has been added to the Designer, visually inspect the table to make sure that the foreign key was created such that the DimGeography table's GeographyKey columns are one-of-many columns in the DimCustomer table. If this relationship is not set up automatically, then manually created it.

6. Just because the DimGeography table is part of the data source does not mean it is added to the DimCustomer dimension of the cube. In order to add this new table to the DimCustomer dimension, double-click the Adventure Works Internet Sales cube and select the Cube Structure tab. This will display the Cube Explorer, and from this window we can expand the DimCustomer dimension, thus exposing a rather useful link, Edit DimCustomer, shown in Figure 10-26.

From this point forward, adding the Dim Geography level to the DimCustomer cube is a straightforward process supported by BIDS. After adding the DimGeography table to the customer region, it is necessary to redeploy the project in order for the cube browser to access the underlying data.

Tip Even after successful deployment, the Design window for a cube may say that it cannot verify that the cube has been deployed. Close the Design window for the cube (click the X in the upper-right corner) and then double-click the cube in Solution Explorer in order to display the cube's Design window again. This refreshing of the cube's Design window will allow you to manipulate the cube.

It is now possible to drag items from the Customer Hierarchy English Country Region Name and Last Name onto the Drop Row Fields Here region of the Browser. Drag the measures Sales Amount and Order Quantity to the browser window's region labeled Drop Total or Detail Fields Here (see Figure 10-27).

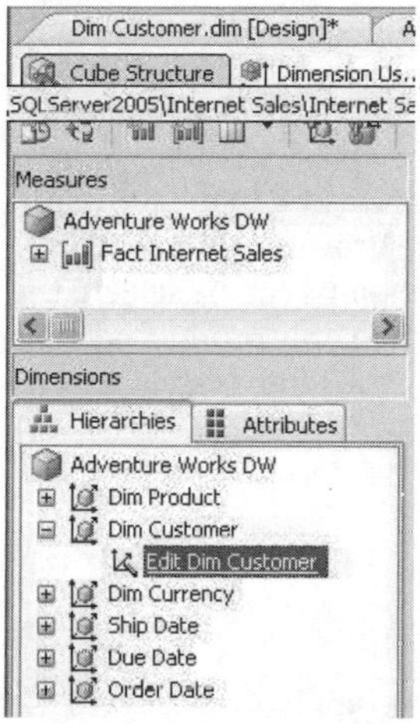

Figure 10-26. *Edit DimCustomer: launching the Dimension Editor*

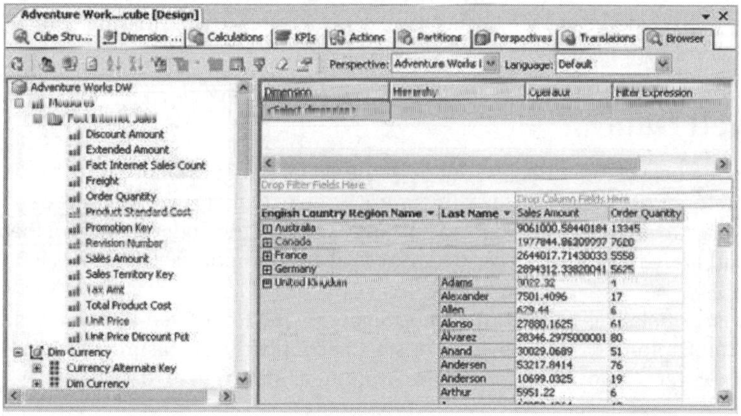

Figure 10-27. *Customer Country, Customer Last Name for Adventure Works*

The previous example demonstrated the simplicity with which hierarchal data can be aggregated and displayed in a meaningful fashion using the cube browser. Based on which nodes are expanded within the browser, totals for Sales Amount and Order Quantity are summed based on customer country or customer country and last name.

The browser window is vastly more powerful than even this. For example, drag Customer Birth Date on the Drop Filter Fields Here region. The results in the browser window can now be set up to include or exclude ranges of birthdays. Using this approach, the septuagenarian customers could be clustered in order in preparation for a marketing campaign aimed at active senior citizens (see Figure 10-28).

Figure 10-28. *Filtering data*

Thus far our browser has behaved like a Tree View control (like the Folder View in Windows Explorer). By dragging dimension members onto the Drop Column Fields Here region of the browser, the browser can now show detailed information across the horizontal dimension much like Windows Explorer does when configured to View ➤ Details.

We can apply filtering even more elaborate than that just previously discussed to the browser window. This more extensive filtering is made available along the top of the browser window. Using this filter, zero or more dimensions, hierarchies, operators, and filter expressions can be selected. For example, when browsing product-related data, it would be possible to see only product categories whose names begin with C (Clothing and Components). Just configure the filter as shown in Figure 10-29.

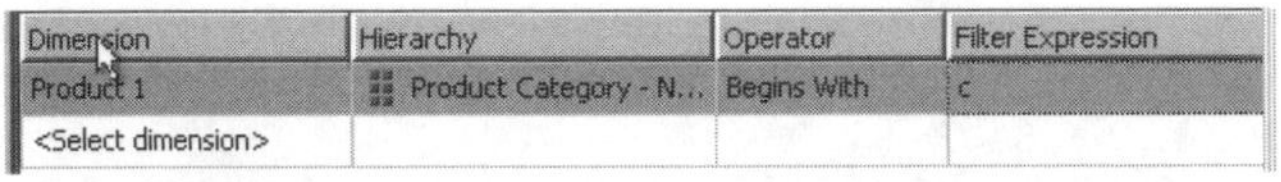

Dimension	Hierarchy	Operator	Filter Expression
Product 1	▦ Product Category - N...	Begins With	c
<Select dimension>			

Figure 10-29. *Filtering category, subcategory, and product sales data for Adventure Works*

The aforementioned filtering can become quite sophisticated, given multiple cube dimensions with intricate hierarchies. The operators supported include Not Equal, In, Not In, Contains, Begins With, Range (Included), Range (Excluded), and MDX. This last operator refers to a Multidimensional Expression (a rather pervasive concept in Analysis Services).

Managing Displayed Data

The Browser tab provides a good deal of functionality, but from the visual esthetics standpoint, a few things were missed. First and foremost is that the measures were not particularly well formatted. Sales Amount, for example, is a currency, but contains no currency symbol (the dollar sign), and the column is left justified instead of right justified. Order Quantity is also a numeric value, but it is left justified instead of right justified.

The remedy to this numeric malady is to select the Cube Structure tab for a given cube. The Cube Structure tab contains an Explorer window that lets us select an individual measure or dimension member. Expand this Explorer window and select Sales Amount as shown in Figure 10-30.

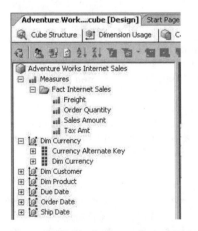

Figure 10-30. *Exploring cube structure: Sales Amount measure*

Once Sales Amount is selected, then display the Properties window for this measure (View ➤ Properties), as shown in Figure 10-31.

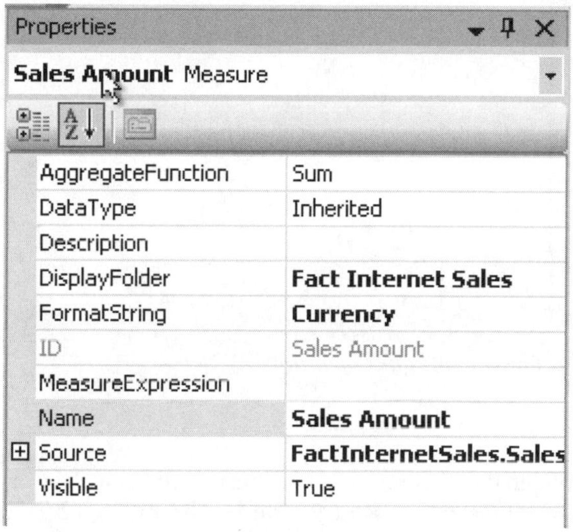

Figure 10-31. *Properties window: Sales Amount measure*

In the previous screenshot, the FormatString of the Sales Amount has been set to Currency. We could have set it to Percentage (though this makes no sense), Short Date, or Short Time. A format taking into account thousands separators and/or decimal places could have also been specified (# or #,# or #,#.0 or #,#.00).

Within the Properties window, we can also set the AggregateFunction property. For the line item, the aggregate function is Sum, which makes intuitive sense since this value represents the sales figure over a category or subcategory or product aggregation. It might make sense to set the Name property to Sales.

For measures such as UnitPrice or UnitDiscount, Sum is not an appropriate aggregate function. The choices for the AggregateFunction property include Sum, Count, Min, Max, DistinctCount, None, FirstNonEmpty, and LastNonEmpty, leaving developers with a diverse suite of options.

After modifying any of the aforementioned properties or any measure/member properties for that matter, the project must be deployed again. If the project is not redeployed, then the browser window will generate errors.

■**Note** When the Browser tab is selected, you will see there is also an Explorer window that contains measures including Sales Amount. Displaying the Properties window (View ➤ Properties) will show the properties for the cube. In order to select per-measure or per-member properties, you must select the Cube Structure tab.

Using the Properties window to format measures or members does not handle all display-related issues. Within the Browser tab, it is possible to alter the data's appearance. From within the browser window, right-click the item to be formatted (measure or member) and select the Commands and Options menu item from the context menu. This menu item displays a dialog box that is fundamentally a mini word processor capable of formatting the data (see Figure 10-32). Using this, it would be possible to right-justify numeric values and do more risqué maneuvers such as changing the font, color, or column width.

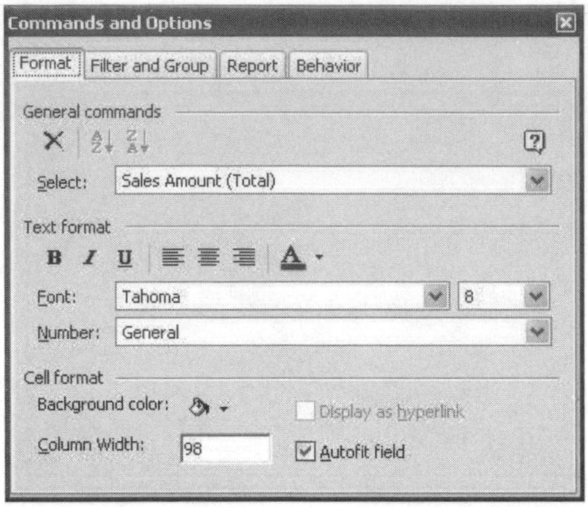

Figure 10-32. *Commands and Options dialog box for Sales Amount measure*

Many-to-Many Hierarchies

Thus far, when discussing hierarchies, each child in the hierarchy has had one parent (snowflake or star schema) such as each product belonging to at most one subcategory and each subcategory belonging to at most one category. There are hierarchies, called many-to-many hierarchies, where this is not the case. In order to understand this, consider a product: a yogurt breakfast drink. If this were defined under a category, it might fall under beverage and breakfast. The category is beverage because the yogurt is a liquid, and breakfast because the yogurt serves as a meal. If this yogurt drink was sold by Adventure Works, how would it get computed given that it could reside in two categories? It would not make sense to include the data twice. The sales figures would be off.

The question is, does Analysis Services 2005 handle many-to-many relationships in dimensional hierarchies? We actually saw how to handle this scenario. One of the properties not discussed was MeasureExpression. Using this property, a weighting could be given to any computation involving a jointly parented product (say 50-50). These numbers would be used in the weighting the computations performed against each of these separately aggregately categories, since they frankly can't both be 100 percent. This same weighting concept and the use of the MeasureExpression property can apply to any many-to-many hierarchy. Consider a piece of land owned 50 percent by a parent and 25 percent each by two children. An ownership percentage would have be read from a separate table and used to determine measure weightings.

Calculations and MDX

The dimensions and measures of a cube provide one view of the data. It is often useful to perform a calculation on this data in order to create a data value that is easier to interpret. For example, the Customer dimension contains LastName and FirstName, which could be represented as a calculated member, FullName, whose calculation is as follows: LastName + ", " + Firstname. Calculations can be performed on the members of dimensions or measures.

Calculations are in actuality (under the covers) Multidimensional Expressions. BIDS provides a sophisticated UI that aids in developing Multidimensional Expressions. Recall that double-clicking a cube within Solution Explorer displayed an array of versatile tabs including the Calculations tab. For the purpose of this example, a calculation will be created in order to determine the average cost per product sold. Once the Calculations tab has been selected on the Cube Design window and this computation has been set up, you will see a display within BIDS like the one in Figure 10-33.

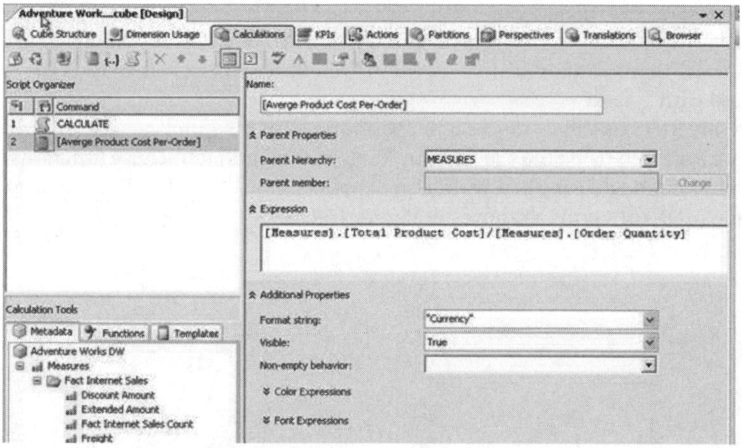

Figure 10-33. *Calculations: Average Product Cost Per-Order*

We create the Average Cost Per-Order calculation as follows:

1. Right-click the body area of the Script Organizer window and select New Calculated Member. This displays a window like the one in Figure 10-33 save that the data fields of the window have yet to be filled in.

2. In the Name text box, give the calculation the name Average Product Cost Per-Order, but in order to allow spaces and special characters (the dash is a special character as it is an operator), wrap the name in square brackets.

3. By default, the MEASURES parent hierarchy is selected. If (for example) the computation had been FullName, then we would have picked a parent hierarchy such as DimProduct. Since this computation is a measure, leave the Parent Hierarchy drop-down list set to MEASURES.

4. From the Calculation Tools window, select the Metadata tab and expand the Measures node and its child node, Fact Internet Sales.

5. From the list of measures displayed in Fact Internet Sales, drag Total Product Costs and drop it on the Expressions text box of the new Calculations window.

6. Repeat this step, but this time drag Order Quantity and drop it on the Expression text box after the Total Product Cost text.

7. Place the division operator, "/", between the Total Product Cost and the Order Quantity members, thus creating the calculation expression.

8. From the Format string drop-down list, select Currency as the average product cost per order is a monetary value.

9. In order to work with the calculated member, deploy the project. Once deployed, calculated members (such as Average Product Cost Per-Order) will appear under Calculation Tools ➤ Metadata under their appropriate parent. For example, Average Product Cost Per-Order will appear under the Measures node, as this was the parent of this calculation.

It is possible to use a calculation as part of other calculations. It is also possible to use the calculation in the computation of KPIs and to browse the contents of the calculated member using Cube Designer's Browser tab.

The previous calculation utilized the division operator. As far as Multidimensional Expressions go, there are vastly more elaborate operations that can be utilized, including string concatenation, cross joins, multiplication greater than, and Boolean XOR. MDX even includes the standard SQL comment operators (/* paired with */ and --).

In addition to operators, the BIDS Calculations designer supports all of the functions associated with MDX. These functions are accessed using the Calculation Tools ➤ Function tab. These functions can be dragged from the Function tab and dropped within an Expression text box. The Functions tab's root level categorizes the MDX functions as shown in Figure 10-34.

Figure 10-34. *Calculation Tools: functions*

Using the Functions tab, functions, including those that manipulate and expose key performance indicators, hierarchy navigation, statistics, and string/time manipulation, can be used as part of Multidimensional Expressions.

Given the Calculations form designer and the Calculation Tools (including the Metadata and Functions tabs), it should be clear that BIDS provides significant assistance in the creating and maintaining of Multidimensional Expressions.

The Calculation Tools window contains one more tab, Templates. This tab offers a variety of standard template computations including topics such as Analytics, Budgeting, Financial, Forecasting, Internet, and Time Series. For example, the Internet topic includes templates for computing average page loads, distinct visitors over time, downloads over time, etc. When a template is selected by double-clicking the template name, the contents of the Form View are filled in with seed values (calculation name, expression, format string, etc.) For example, clicking Financial ➤ Net Income fills in the Expression text box with the following computational template:

```
<<Gross Profit>> - (<<Operating Expenses>> + <<Tax Expense>> + <<Interest>>
+ <<Depreciation>>)
```

The previous snippet is simply a template. A developer is still responsible for filling in the dimension members that are used to compute values such as gross profit, operating expense, tax expense, interest, and depreciation. A crafty developer might use techniques such as named queries, aliased member names, and calculations (such as a calculation for gross profit) in order to already have values for gross profit, operation expenses, etc. precomputed so they could simply be plugged into the template.

MDX

The Calculations tab of the Cube Designer hid a tremendous about of the complexity associated with the MDX language. In a formal sense, the MDX scripting language is used to populate a cube with calculations. The specific form of the language is that it is composed of statements separated by semicolons. The MDX scripts are actually parts of cubes just like dimensions and measures.

In order to see the raw MDX of a calculation, click the Script View icon in the Calculations toolbar. To return the friendly user interface that facilitates the creation of calculations, click the Form View icon. When the Script View icon for the Average Product Cost Per-Order is selected, we get the following:

```
CALCULATE;
CREATE MEMBER CURRENTCUBE.[MEASURES].[Averge Product Cost Per-Order] AS
[Measures].[Total Product Cost]/[Measures].[Order Quantity],
FORMAT_STRING = "Currency", VISIBLE = 1  ;
```

The previous snippet of MDX script is composed of two statements:

- CALCULATE: This statement computes the value of a subcube or determines the order of how the dimensions in a subcube are computed.

- CREATE MEMBER: This is a data definition statement in MDX used to create a calculated member.

The benefits of the BIDS UI should be clear when compared against raw MDX scripting. Extremely sophisticated developers can code directly in MDX. This can be accomplished using the View Script (as was just demonstrated) or within SQL Server Management Studio using File ➤ New ➤ Analysis Services MDX Query.

As a scripting language, MDX is broken down into scripting statements (such as CALCULATE, CASE, FREEZE, and IF), data definition statements (CREATE CUBE, ALTER CUBE, CREATE SET, CREATE DIMENSION, CREATE MEMBER, etc.) and data manipulation statements (INSERT INTO, SELECT, UPDATE, etc.). As is the case with any language, MDX exposes operators (mathematical, comparative, Boolean, and join manipulations), and an incredible suite of functions encompassing metadata manipulation, set operations, statistical computation, date/time computations, string manipulation, etc. These functions were presently previously in that they are contained on the Functions tab of the Calculation Tools window.

Key Performance Indicators (KPIs)

Surf to any website that evaluates stocks, and you will be immediately exposed to a KPI, namely that a given stock is rated based on Strong Buy, Buy, Hold, Sell, and Strong Sell. Rating a stock involves a tremendous amount of financial data that is somehow boiled down to five distinct values. To add some spice to the website, rather than simply saying Strong Buy, a thermometer could be displayed that is fiery red and shooting through the top. Rather than simply saying Strong Sell, a thermometer could be displayed with the line sunk down to the bottom and the thermometer covered in cold blue ice.

A KPI as a quantifiable value (e.g., Strong Buy or Strong Sell) used to assess a business's performance. From an Analysis Services standpoint, a KPI is a set of computations performed using Multidimensional Expressions. These computations are associated with additional information indicating how their results are to be displayed. When the computations determine a company's stock in a Strong Buy, then that bursting red thermometer is displayed. Although visual in nature, KPI is a server-side object. This means that the company website developed in C# and ASP.NET would get the same thermometer displayed as the company's annual report, which was put together with Microsoft Word, VB .NET and Visual Studio Tools for Office. There is a single version of the KPI on the server, and it is accessible to different clients (such as ASP.NET or Microsoft Office).

Within an Analysis Services project, KPIs are created by selecting the Cube Designer's KPIs tab. The toolbar of this tab contains an icon that, when clicked, creates a new KPI. The icons are best identified by dangling the mouse cursor over each icon and reading the tool tip that is displayed. When the New KPI icon is clicked, you will see the dialog box shown in Figure 10-35.

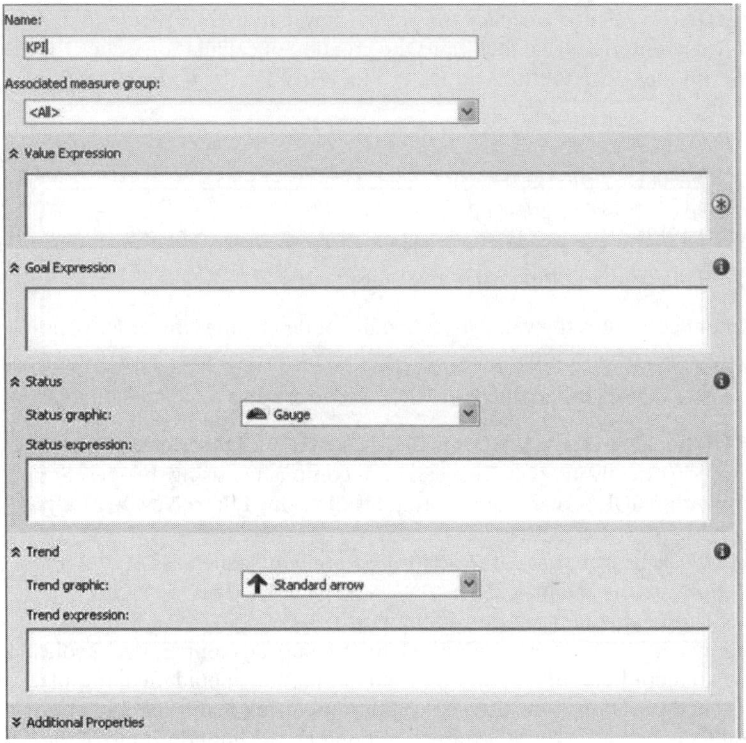

Figure 10-35. *Cube Designer, KPI, Form View*

For demonstration purposes, we will create a KPI that can measure the profitability of a product. For example, software has a fixed cost, and costs next to nothing to manufacture (potentially high profitability). A game console is sold at cost or near cost for competitive reasons, and hence has a low profitability. For the purposes of simplicity, profitability is a measure of the sales compared to cost.

In the dialog box shown in Figure 10-35, we fill in the name value with Profitability (see the Name text box in this screen). A KPI is associated with all measure groups or a specific measure group. Potentially, there could be measure groups for sales, marketing, and human resources. These measure groups are set up in advance and are just categorizations of measures targeted to a specific audience (the accounting department, the human resources department, etc.). This example will just use <All> as the value for the Associated measure group drop-down list.

Each KPI contains two expressions, value and goal. MDX is used to specify these expressions. The value expression is a physical measure, while the goal expression is objective. For our example, the value expression is defined as profitability:

```
(
    ([Measures].[Sales Amount] -[Measures].[Total Product Cost])
    / [Measures].[Sales Amount]
)
```

Like the Calculations tab, the KPIs tab contains a Calculation Tools window. The measures Sales Amount and Total Product Cost were dragged from the Calculation Tools window and placed in the Value Expression text box. The formula was put together with some junior high math skills. If the cost equals the amount of the sale, the profit is zero (0% profit). If the cost is zero, then the profit is 1 (100 %). The Goal Expression text box is set to 0.80, which means that it is desirable that costs represent no more than 20 percent of a sale.

BIDS provides a set of status graphics that include a traffic light, a gauge similar to a car's fuel gauge, a thermometer, and faces with various expressions (ranging from smiling to indifferent to sad). Each graphic gauges business performance across a range of values from –1 (e.g., WorldCom, Enron) to 1 (e.g., Berkshire Hathaway, Microsoft). For the purpose of this example, the smiley face will be selected.

A certain type of expression, called a status expression, is needed to generate the values used by the status graphic when displaying the KPI. Given that a range of values from –1 to 1 needs to be produced for the status expression, MDX's CASE scripting statement is ideal, as it behaves just like CASE in standard SQL. The status expression for our example is as follows:

```
CASE
  WHEN /* 60% looking good so 1 */
    ((([Measures].[Sales Amount] -  [Measures].[Total Product Cost])
          / [Measures].[Sales Amount])> 0.60) THEN 1
  WHEN /* between 30 and 60 percent profit, okay but not great  so zero */
    ((([Measures].[Sales Amount] - [Measures].[Total Product Cost])
          / [Measures].[Sales Amount])> 0.30) THEN 0
  WHEN /* between 10 and 30 percent profit, okay but not great  so -0.5 */
    ((([Measures].[Sales Amount] - [Measures].[Total Product Cost])
          / [Measures].[Sales Amount])> 0.10) THEN -0.5
  ELSE -1 /* less 10% or less profit or maybe even a loss so -1 */
END
```

The comments in the previous status expression explain what each WHEN clause of the CASE statement is looking to indicate. For example, 60 percent profit is good, while less than 10 percent profit is extremely bad.

An additional measure is provided with a KPI, namely a trend expression. This expression represents the current behavior of the value expression as compared to the goal expression. The trend expression allows a quick assessment to be made with respect to the KPI's momentum. In order to understand this, consider a football (soccer) game. One team might be leading 3 to 1 (hence the status expression is a smiley face); however, having 5 players on the team in the lead come down with nausea would result in a trend expression indicated by a down arrow, as there could be 11 players facing only 6 opponents. The trend would indicate that a 3-to-1 lead might not be safe if half the players on the team in the lead are unable to play due to illness.

For a trend graphic, we will select the standard arrow for our example. Indicating how a trend behaves requires that the past be compared to the present values, which can be seen in the following trend expression used for our example:

```
CASE
  WHEN
    ((([Measures].[Sales Amount] - [Measures].[Total Product Cost]) >
((([Order Date].[Fiscal Time].PrevMember, [Measures].[Sales Amount]) -
      ([Order Date].[Fiscal Time].PrevMember, [Measures].[Total Product Cost]))
  THEN 1
  ELSE -1
END
```

A trend expression is an MDX that Analysis Services uses to evaluate the current trend of the value expression compared to the goal expression. The trend expression helps the business user to quickly determine whether the value expression is getting better or worse relative to the goal expression. You can associate one of several graphics with the trend expression to help business users be able to quickly understand the trend.

Browsing KPIs

The toolbar for the Cube Designer's KPIs tab contains an icon whose functionality is defined to be Browser View. Clicking this icon, which looks like a magnifying glass in front a stack of folded towels, displays the current status of the KPI and allows filters to be associated with the KPI (to fine-tune the range of value over which the KPI applies). An example of the KPI created in this section is shown in Figure 10-36.

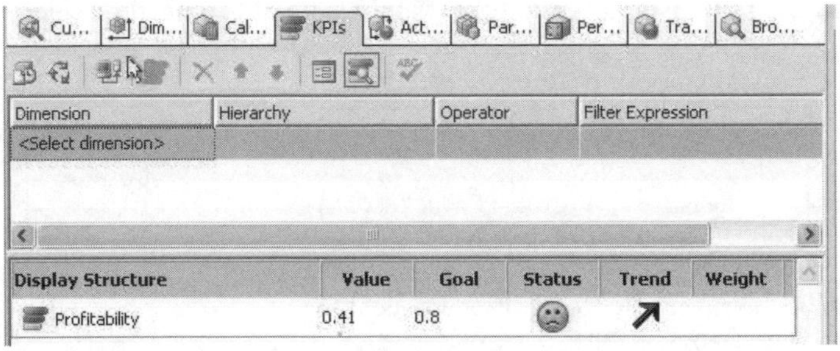

Figure 10-36. *Cube Desginer, KPI Browser View*

It should be evident from the sad face the status of profitability goal is not being met. Over time, the trend is positive (meaning we are becoming more profitable). Still, the goal is 0.80 (80 percent) and the present profitability is 0.41 (41 percent).

It might benefit the Adventure Works Bicycle Company to jettison their least profitable products (accessories, bikes, clothing, etc.). Using the Dimension column above the displayed KPI, a filter could be created to explorer the profitability of each catalog, subcatalog, or profit. The behavior of these filters directly parallels that of the Cube Designer's browser functionality.

Analysis Services Scripting Language (ASSL)

Touted as a useful new feature of Analysis Services 2005, ASSL is the scripting language used by clients to communicate with Analysis Services 2005. SQL Server Management Studio and BIDS both use ASSL and its command subdialect, XML/A. ASSL could also be used by developers as a means to programmatically communicate with Analysis Services.

Before decomposing an ASSL command, we will create an object whose underlying representation is ASSL. In order to accomplish this, we will modify a Data Source View object within an Analysis Services project. As each object type within a project (data source, Data Source View, dimension, cube, etc.) is represented by ASSL, using the BIDS UI to indirectly manipulate ASSL will allow us to explore the complexities and power associated with ASSL. The ASSL base object to manipulate will be a Data Source View, and the modification made to this object will be to add a named query to said object.

Example ASSL Object: A Data Source View with a Named Query

When browsing data, a customer's LastName was displayed in conjunction with Sales Amount. It would have been possible to display both the LastName and the FirstName columns, but this is not the most convenient way to view named data (show me all people named Patel who bought bike helmets). It might make more sense to include a full name (LastName + ", " + FirstName) so customers could be uniquely identified, say, Preshant Patel versus Baiju Patel. A mechanism that can be used to perform this merging of data within a measure is a named query. Remember that a named query is defined for a Data Source View where a named query is functionally equivalent to a view within a relational database. The benefit of a named query is that it does not require the metadata of an underlying data source to be updated because the expression defining the named query is stored within Analysis Services.

Named queries are created by double-clicking a Data Source View within Solution Explorer. This double-clicking should display the Designer window (View ➤ Designer) for the Data Source View (the database diagram of tables and name queries for the Data Source View). To create a named query, right-click an empty region in the Designer and select the New Named Query option. Selecting this context menu option will display the dialog box shown in Figure 10-37.

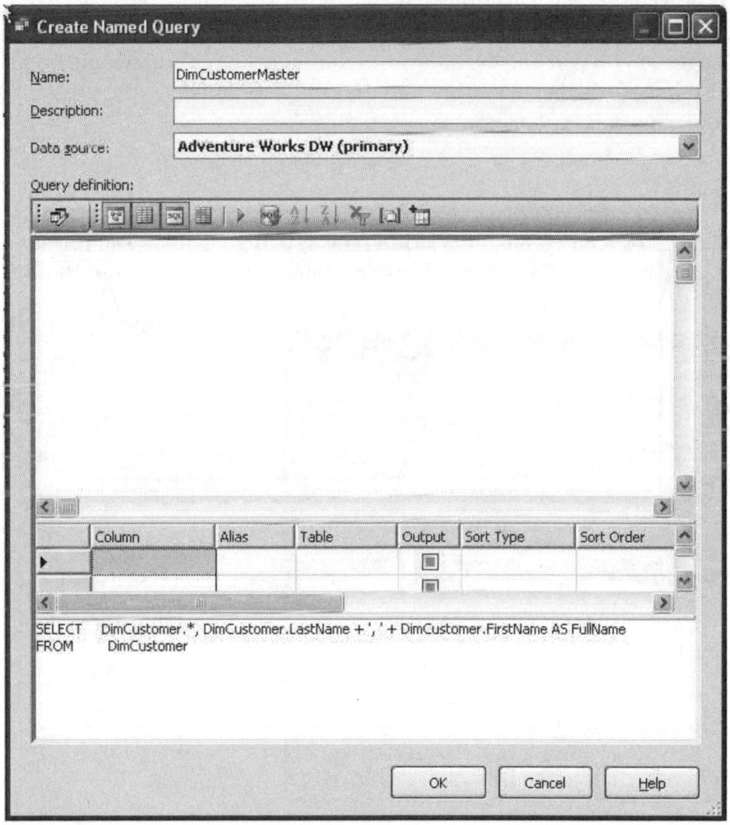

Figure 10-37. *Create Named Query dialog box*

This dialog box has been tweaked to contain the named query to be created. The Name text box contains the name of our named query, DimCustomerMaster, and the code associated with generating the named query is at the bottom of the dialog box. Once the appropriate SQL code has been specified, click OK, and the named query will be added to Designer for the Data Source View.

When the new named query it added to the Designer for the Data Source View, the named query is missing certain database elements it needs so that it can be used in a cube. Specifically, the named query does not contain a primary key and does not have relationships set up to other tables in the diagram. To remedy these, missing entities, we do the following:

1. Right-click the `CustomerKey` column of the DimCustomerMaster name query. From the context menu, select Set Logical Primary Key, thus causing this named view to mirror the primary key of the `DimCustomer` table.

2. Drag the `DimCustomerMaster.GeographyKey` column and drop it on the like-named column in the `DimGeography` table. This sets up the GeographyKey foreign key in the DimCustomer-Master name query.

3. Drag the `FactInternetSales.CustomerKey` column and drop it onto the primary key for the DimCustomerMaster named query (DimCustomerMaster.CustomerKey).

In order to use this newly create named query, a new cube must be created or the Customer dimension for an existing cube must be edited. If every cube in the Analysis Services project used the named query instead of the underlying table, `DimCustomer`, it would be possible to delete the table from the Data Source View. The reason for deleting the table from the Data Source View would be so that the view only contains the database elements pertinent to the cubes contained in the project (no superfluous entities hanging about).

ASSL Drilldown

The best way to experience the raw power and raw complexity of ASSL is to highlight our Data Source View in Solution Explorer and display the code windows: (View ➤ Code) as shown in Figure 10-38.

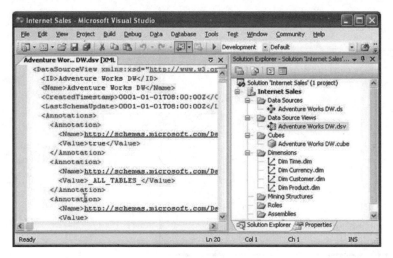

Figure 10-38. *ASSL for a Data Source View*

Given the readability of XML, the previous ASSL snippet should be understandable because it is composed of elements such as <DataSourceView>, <ID>, <Name>, etc. Each of these elements is fully documented in MSDN along with aptly named elements such as <DataSource>, <Cube>, <Dimension>, and <Measure>. Looking though the file for our named query, the name DimCustomerMaster would be found inside the hierarchy of a <Diagram> element, representing the Designer view associated with the Data Source View.

```
<xs:element name="DimCustomerMaster"
  msprop:QueryDefinition="SELECT CustomerKey, GeographyKey,
     CustomerAlternateKey, Title, FirstName,
```

Like most XML formats, ASSL is simple to understand but lengthy to write. SQL Server Management Studio is used to develop such code (File ➤ New ➤ Analysis Services XMLA Query). Clearly this highly granular type of development is designed for a very narrow group of applications.

In all, the AdventureWorksDW Data Source View has over eleven hundred lines of XML in it. The cube developed for the Analysis Services project has over a thousand lines. The time it would take to work programmatically with raw XML at the ASSL level including XML/A to pass commands to Analysis Server is far greater than working with the UI-driven client applications such as SQL Server Management Studio and BIDS. Developers requiring a low level of granular access to Analysis Server and companies such as Computer Associates, which makes Erwin data modeling software, are candidates for using ASSL and XML/A.

Summary

This chapter focused on Analysis Services 2005 by exploring its core features in the environment in which most developers will use Analysis Services 2005, Business Intelligence Development Studio. We introduced the key concepts of Analysis Services including the architecture, enhancements since Analysis Services 2000, and the core objects used by Analysis Services (cubes, measures, and dimensions). Also presented were the common components of Analysis Services projects within BIDS (data sources, Data Source Views, cubes, dimensions, cube structures, and browsers). A great deal of time was spent on the various features available to an Analysis Services project. This included project deployment, ongoing project maintenance, data formatting, calculated measures/members, KPI, and MDX. It is not uncommon for developers to be overwhelmed by the number of features exposed by Analysis Services projects within BIDS (menu items, toolbars, submenu toolbars, various configuration windows, tabs, and context menus). The simplest rule of Analysis Services is to build a house of wood before attempting to construct the Taj Mahal, meaning it easier to start with a simple cube than to utilize the plethora of features associated with Analysis Services and BIDS.

We also presented the administration of Analysis Services and touched upon ASSL and XML/A. As our text made clear, ASSL is extremely powerful and should be utilized by developers who need precise, programmatic administration of their Analysis Services 2005 environment. Similarly, we touched on MDX in the context of calculations and KPIs. Like ASSL, MDX is an extremely powerful and complex language. BIDS dramatically simplifies development using MDX scripting, and where possible BIDS should be used simply in order to save time in this arena.

Business intelligence, which encompasses Analysis Services, Integration Services, and Reporting Services, is an incredibly complex arena. In order to shed some more light on this topic, consider picking up *Pro SQL Server 2005 Reporting Services* (Apress, 2005). Analysis Services is a lot more exciting when interfaced using the slick presentation environment exposed by Reporting Services 2005.

■ ■ ■

Security

As with most areas of SQL Server, the security features built into SQL Server 2005 have undergone a fairly radical overhaul. In this chapter, we'll show you the new features for granting and denying permissions to access resources in the database, and the new system of schemas, which now resemble ANSI SQL schemas far more closely. Schemas provide a new level in the security hierarchy (below the database level), with each database object now belonging to a schema rather than being owned by an individual user.

As well as these recastings of familiar aspects of SQL Server technology, there are entirely new features: the Surface Area Configuration feature that disables certain functionality that could open security liabilities unless it's explicitly enabled; and the new encryption functions that allow us to encrypt and decrypt data from within T-SQL code. In addition, the new functionality of SQL Server brings new security challenges, so you'll see how you can use Code Access Security with .NET assemblies in SQL Server, and how to use certificates to secure HTTP web services. In summary, in this chapter we'll look at

- Surface Area Configuration
- Principals and securables
- Permissions
- Code Access Security
- Encryption
- Certificates and web services

But first:

A Word about sa

The sa account still exists in SQL Server 2005, but, as in SQL Server 2000, Microsoft recommends that you use the sysadmin fixed server role instead, which has the same (unlimited) powers. In addition, SQL Server installation now enforces a password for the sa account, so SQL Server installations with a blank sa password are at last a thing of the past!

Surface Area Configuration

To ensure that SQL Server is as secure as possible out of the box, a number of features that represent potential security risks are disabled by default, and must be explicitly enabled before they can be used. These features include the following:

- Remote connections
- .NET Framework
- Database Mail
- SQLMail
- Service Broker
- HTTP connectivity
- Database mirroring
- Web tasks

These features and services can be enabled graphically through the Surface Area Configuration (SAC) tool (as described briefly in Chapter 2), or programmatically through the `sp_configure` system stored procedure (although the latter option isn't available for all features and services).

Remote Connections

By default, SQL Server 2005 installations don't accept remote connections, only connections from the local machine. This clearly reduces risks considerably, as hackers will need access to the machine, or access to another enabled service that accepts remote connections (such as an HTTP endpoint), but unfortunately it also dramatically reduces the usefulness of SQL Server! If your server really doesn't need to accept remote connections (e.g., if it's only ever accessed from ASP.NET web pages on that machine), then it will be a good idea to keep this setting. However, most SQL Server instances will need to be accessed from client machines that are running data entry applications etc., so in most cases you'll need to enable remote connections.

If you do enable this, there are three possible options, depending on the protocols used to access the SQL Server: TCP/IP only, Named Pipes only, or both TCP/IP and Named Pipes. Naturally, it makes sense only to enable the protocol you need, and only enable both if you really do need to access the server both via TCP/IP and Named Pipes. Microsoft recommends TCP/IP over Named Pipes, as this requires communications over fewer ports, and therefore fewer ports need to be opened across the firewall.

Use the Surface Area Configuration for Services and Connections tool to enable remote TCP/IP and/or Named Pipes connections. The dedicated administrator connection is configured separately (see the next section).

Dedicated Administrator Connection

You saw in Chapter 2 that SQL Server introduces a new dedicated administrator connection (DAC). It listens on a dedicated port that members of the `sysadmin` server role can use to troubleshoot a SQL Server instance that isn't responding to standard connections. By default, it's only possible to connect via the DAC from the local machine, but remote connections over the DAC can be enabled through the SAC tool or through the `sp_configure` procedure:

```
EXEC sp_configure 'remote admin connections', 1
GO
reconfigure
GO
```

.NET Framework

Although having the CLR enabled for a database server brings much new functionality to SQL Server, it also brings potential security loopholes if not administered correctly. There are few limits to the tasks that an unsafe SQL assembly can perform if the appropriate security code isn't put in place (see the section "Code Access Security" later in this chapter); for example, with poor security, a SQL assembly could have access to the entire file system on the database server. Therefore, DBAs need to be especially vigilant on what actions .NET code is allowed to perform.

For this reason, the CLR is disabled by default on a SQL Server 2005 database server, and needs to be explicitly enabled before SQL assemblies can be executed on that server. CLR support can be enabled either through the Surface Area Configuration for Features tool, or by executing the `sp_configure` stored procedure with the `'clr enabled'` option. You also need to run `reconfigure` to activate this change:

```
sp_configure 'clr enabled', 1
GO
RECONFIGURE
GO
```

Database Mail

Database Mail is SQL Server 2005's SMTP-based system for sending e-mails from within T-SQL stored procedures and triggers. The security weakness of enabling Database Mail is twofold. First, the DBA has no intrinsic control over what data is sent via e-mail, but must rely on the database developer writing code that can't inadvertently send sensitive data to an unintended recipient. Second, the SMTP server may not require Transport-Layer Security (TLS), in which case messages will be sent unencrypted. If you enable Database Mail and have procedures that send sensitive data, you should ensure that the SMTP server used is configured for TLS.

Database Mail can be enabled through the SAC tool. Note that Database Mail relies on Service Broker, so it will only work if it's run in a database for which Service Broker has been enabled.

SQLMail

SQLMail is the traditional mail technology built into SQL Server, and is set to be replaced to a large extent by Database Mail. SQLMail poses the same potential security vulnerabilities as Database Mail, but with the added risk that, because it's based on MAPI rather than being based directly on SMTP, SQLMail can read as well as send mail. This means that you need to make sure not only that any stored procedures that use SQLMail can't send data from SQL Server to people who aren't intended to access it, but also that it can't be misused to access data stored in the e-mail account of the MSSQLServer service. Even worse, because it's MAPI-based, SQLMail requires Outlook to be installed on the SQL Server machine, with all the attendant risks of viruses and worms transmitted through e-mail. Finally, SQLMail runs as an extended stored procedure in the same address space as the SQL Server process, so any failure could impact on the entire server.

SQLMail can be enabled either through the SAC tool, or programmatically:

```
EXEC sp_configure 'SQL Mail XPs', 1
GO
RECONFIGURE
GO
```

Service Broker

Service Broker is SQL Server's new asynchronous messaging technology. We will look at using Service Broker in detail in Chapter 12, including enabling it for a specific database.

HTTP Connectivity

If you want to create additional SQL Server services, such as Service Broker or web services, by default SQL Server won't accept connections. To enable these, you need explicitly to create an endpoint telling SQL Server to listen or talk on a specific port. You'll see a few examples of HTTP connectivity later in this chapter, and in Chapter 12.

Database Mirroring

Database mirroring is an easy-to-manage alternative to log shipping and failover clustering, and involves creating an exact copy of a database on another SQL Server instance that can be used if the primary database fails. Any updates to the primary database are replicated to the mirror database, so the copy remains exact. Again, the security liability here is that data must be transmitted over the network to the mirror server, and therefore also requires HTTP endpoints to be configured and active. For more information on configuring database mirroring, please see Chapter 15.

Web Assistant

Web Assistant is a set of stored procedures that create HTML pages based on a database query. In general, Web Assistant will be replaced in SQL Server 2005 by Reporting Services, but it is still supported for backward compatibility. To enable Web Assistant, use the SAC tool or run the following command:

```
EXEC sp_configure 'Web Assistant Procedures', 1
GO
RECONFIGURE
GO
```

xp_cmdshell

The xp_cmdshell extended stored procedure allows operating system commands to be executed from within the database environment. The dangers of this are obvious, from both accidental and malicious misuse, so this procedure is disabled by default. It can be enabled through the SAC tool, or through the sp_configure procedure:

```
EXEC sp_configure 'xp_cmdshell', 1
GO
RECONFIGURE
GO
```

Ad Hoc Remote Queries

If Ad Hoc Remote Queries are enabled, the OPENROWSET and OPENDATASOURCE functions can be used to query a remote SQL Server without setting up a linked server. These queries are harder to keep track of than linked or remote servers, as they will be buried in T-SQL code, so Ad Hoc Remote Queries should only be enabled if your stored procedures actually make such queries. They can be enabled using the SAC tool.

OLE Automation XPs

By default, extended stored procedures aren't permitted to call custom OLE Automation objects. In time, .NET assemblies will hopefully begin to replace C++ XPs, and DBAs will have more control over what code is running in the database. In the meantime, the DBA has no control whatsoever (except for the assurances of the developer!) over what these objects do, so OLE Automation XPs should be permitted only if necessary. To do this, you can either use the SAC tool or sp_configure:

```
EXEC sp_configure 'Ole Automation Procedures', 1
GO
RECONFIGURE
GO
```

SMO and DMO XPs

SMO, and its predecessor DMO, provide APIs for developers to perform automated administration tasks on SQL Server. There is naturally some security risk involved in permitting these, as both SMO and DMO can be used in external applications for managing SQL Server, over which the DBA has little or no control.

However, SMO and DMO are enabled by default, as two of SQL Server's management tools, Management Studio and the Database Tuning Adviser, rely on them. You should therefore only disable them if you don't need these tools and neither SMO nor DMO are used by any existing applications. They can be disabled using sp_configure:

```
EXEC sp_configure 'SMO and DMO XPs', 0
GO
RECONFIGURE
GO
```

Principals and Securables

The SQL Server 2005 security model relies on two fairly straightforward concepts: *principals* and *securables*. Principals are those objects that may be granted permission to access particular database objects, while securables are those objects to which access can be controlled.

Principals

Principals may represent a *specific user*, a *role* that may be adopted by multiple users, or an *application*. SQL Server divides principals into three classes:

- *Windows principals*: These represent Windows user accounts or groups, authenticated using Windows security.

- *SQL Server principals*: These are server-level logins or groups that are authenticated using SQL Server security.

- *Database principals*: These include database users, groups, and roles, as well as application roles.

Note that SQL Server and Windows logins apply only at the server level: you can't grant permissions on these to specific database objects. To do this, you need to create a user associated with the login. You'll see how to do this when we look at database principals.

Windows Principals

SQL Server allows us to create logins from Windows user accounts or groups. These can belong either to the local machine or to the domain. When users log on to SQL Server using Windows authentication, their current user account must either be created as a login in SQL Server, or they must belong to a Windows user group that exists as a login.

To create a login from a Windows account, we use the FROM WINDOWS clause in the CREATE LOGIN statement. For example:

```
CREATE LOGIN [apress\AdventureWorks Reader]
FROM WINDOWS
WITH DEFAULT_DATABASE = AdventureWorks;
```

This will create a login for a previously set up Windows user called "AdventureWorks Reader" in the apress domain, and sets the default database for this login to AdventureWorks. We can also specify a DEFAULT_LANGUAGE in the WITH clause. Note that the login must have the same name as the actual Windows account.

SQL Server Principals

Whereas Windows authentication relies on the underlying operating system to perform authentication (determining who a particular user is), and SQL Server only performs authorization (determining what actions an authenticated user is entitled to perform), with SQL Server authentication, SQL Server itself performs both authentication and authorization.

As in previous versions of SQL Server, SQL Server 2005 supports both individual logins and server roles, which multiple individual users can be assigned to.

SQL Server Logins

When users connect to SQL Server using SQL Server authentication, they supply a username and password that SQL Server uses to authenticate that user and determine the appropriate access rights. These user credentials are stored in SQL Server and are not connected at all to Windows user accounts.

In general, Windows authentication is preferred to SQL Server authentication. Because Windows authentication relies on the underlying operating system security mechanism, it doesn't require an extra password that could be compromised. In order to access SQL Server, users need to log on to Windows with an appropriate account, rather than merely supplying a username/password combination.

However, in some cases it's not possible to use Windows authentication (for example, if you're accessing SQL Server from a non-Windows operating system), and for this reason (and also for backward compatibility), SQL Server authentication is still supported, and has even been slightly enhanced in SQL Server 2005, for example, by allowing Windows 2003 password policies to be enforced.

To create a SQL Server login, we use the CREATE LOGIN command with a WITH PASSWORD clause; for example:

```
CREATE LOGIN [AdventureWorks Editor]
WITH PASSWORD = 'gsd45QK^*%demt',
    DEFAULT_DATABASE = AdventureWorks,
    CHECK_EXPIRATION = ON,
    CHECK_POLICY = ON;
```

If the password is supplied to the statement as a hash, add the HASHED keyword immediately after it; otherwise, the password will be hashed before it is stored. You can also add the MUST_CHANGE keyword after the password to stipulate that users must change their password the first time they log in. As with Windows logins, we can also specify the DEFAULT_DATABASE and/or DEFAULT_LANGUAGE for the login. Finally, we can specify whether we want domain password expiration policies and/or password complexity policies to be applied to the password (these are both ON by default); we'll look at SQL Server logins and Windows 2003 password policies shortly.

Server Roles

Server roles are predefined server-level principals that are granted a fixed set of permissions. Both SQL Server and Windows logins can be added as members of a server role, in which case they inherit the role's permissions. To do this, we call the sp_addsrvrolemember system stored procedure, exactly as in SQL Server 2000. If a user's permissions conflict with those granted by a server role of which the user is a member, those of the server role take precedence.

Note The server roles available in SQL Server 2005 are the same as those available in SQL Server 2000. The sp_srvrolepermission stored procedure that is used to discover what permissions are granted to a particular server role still exists, but unfortunately still returns the permissions of the role in SQL Server 2000, not the updated permissions for SQL Server 2005.

Creating Logins from Certificates and Asymmetric Keys

SQL Server 2005 also allows us to create logins from certificates and asymmetric keys. For example, the following code creates a SQL Server certificate and then uses this to create a login:

```
CREATE CERTIFICATE awCert
ENCRYPTION BY PASSWORD = 'gwp;&569DVLq'
WITH START_DATE = '04/04/2005',
     EXPIRY_DATE = '04/04/2006',
     SUBJECT = 'caserver.apress.com'
GO

CREATE LOGIN [awCertifiedLogin]
FROM CERTIFICATE awCert
GO
```

A server login created in this way will be associated with the supplied certificate/asymmetric key. When the certificate or key is used to log on to SQL Server (for example, via an HTTPS or Service Broker endpoint), it will be in the security context of this login. See Chapter 12 for an example of creating logins in this way to identify two Service Broker instances to each other. A login created in this way can't be used to log on to SQL Server in the normal way through ADO.NET or Management Studio.

We'll look at creating and using certificates and asymmetric keys in more detail later in the chapter.

Windows 2003 Server Policies

For SQL Server 2005 installations on Windows Server 2003 (currently Enterprise edition or above only), SQL Server can use the Windows security policies for SQL Server authentication. This means that the system administrator can stipulate that SQL Server security must meet the same standards as Windows security with regard to

- *Password complexity*: Ensures that passwords used with SQL Server authentication meet a set of requirements such as containing nonalphanumeric characters.

- *Password length*: Specifies the minimum number of characters that a valid password can contain. Passwords with fewer characters won't be accepted.

- *Password history*: Ensures that users don't reuse recent passwords when their password expires and they are forced to change it.

- *Account lockout threshold*: Specifies how many chances users get to enter their password correctly before the account is locked.

- *Account lockout duration*: Specifies how long an account will be locked for after users have incorrectly entered their password the number of times specified in the account lockout threshold.

- *Password age*: Specifies the maximum and minimum allowed age for a password (respectively how long a password will be valid for before the user is forced to change it, and the earliest time that a user will be allowed to change the password).

These policies will be applied only on SQL Server installations running on Windows Server 2003: this feature is unavailable on Windows 2000 or XP (even if the machine is on a Windows 2003 domain).

To test this, we'll demonstrate how to enforce a minimum length for SQL Server passwords. First, we need to set the policy on the local machine, so open the Local Security Settings MMC snap-in (Start ➤ Programs ➤ Administrative Tools ➤ Local Security Policy) or Default Domain Controller Security Settings (Start ➤ Programs ➤ Administrative Tools ➤ Domain Controller Security Policy), depending on whether or not the SQL Server machine is a domain controller.

Open up the Account Policies node, and then the Password Policy node, and double-click the Minimum Password Length policy, as you see in Figure 11-1.

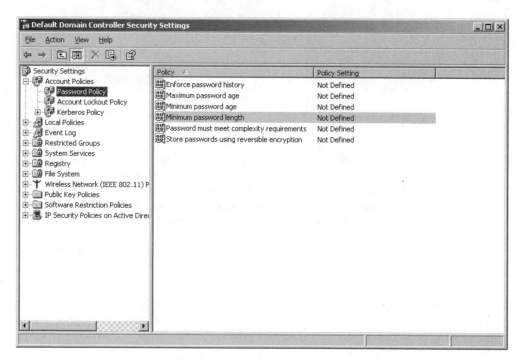

Figure 11-1. *The default Domain Controller Security settings in Windows Server 2003*

Check the Define this policy setting box and set the minimum length to six characters, as in Figure 11-2.

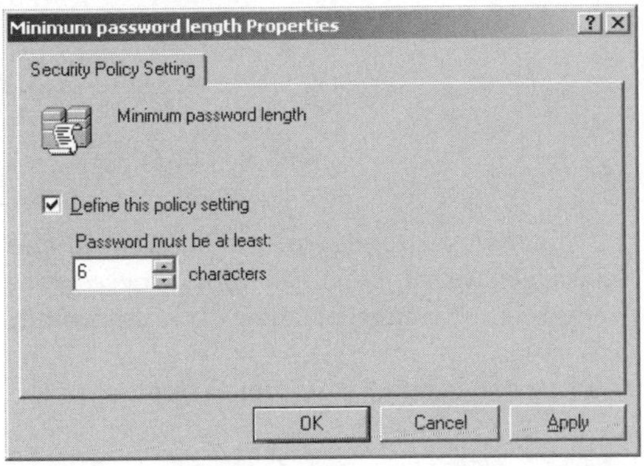

Figure 11-2. *Setting the minimum password length in Windows Server 2003*

Now if we attempt to create a SQL Server login, SQL Server will check the password against the local Windows security policy, and if the password doesn't meet the requirements of the password, the attempt will fail. To test this, create a user with an invalid password:

```
CREATE LOGIN Bob WITH PASSWORD = 'bob'
```

SQL Server will reject this command and won't create the login, because the password doesn't meet the criteria stipulated in the local Windows policy. You should now see an error message like this:

```
.Net SqlClient Data Provider: Msg 15116, Level 16, State 1, Line 1
Password validation failed. The password does not meet policy requirements
because it is too short.
```

Database Principals

Database principals are the objects that represent users to which we can assign permissions to access databases or particular objects within a database. Whereas logins operate at the server level and allow us to perform actions such as connecting to a SQL Server, database principals operate at the database level, allowing us to select or manipulate data, to perform DDL statements on objects within the database, or to manage users' permissions at the database level.

SQL Server 2005 recognizes four different types of database principals:

- Database users
- Database roles
- Database groups
- Application roles

Database Users

Database user principals are the database-level security context under which requests within the database are executed, and are associated with either SQL Server or Windows logins. To create a database user, we should no longer use the sp_adduser system stored procedure, which is now deprecated, but instead issue the CREATE USER command within the target database; for example:

```
USE AdventureWorks
GO

CREATE USER awEditor
FOR LOGIN [AdventureWorks Editor];
GO
```

This will create a new user within the AdventureWorks database and associate this user with the AdventureWorks Editor login we created earlier. When a user with this login attempts to access the AdventureWorks database, that user will do so under the security context of the awEditor user within that database.

We can also create a user associated with a certificate or asymmetric key; for example:

```
CREATE USER [awCertifiedUser]
FOR CERTIFICATE awCert;
```

In this case, if a user (or application) identified by a particular certificate or asymmetric key logs on to a web service, the query will be run in the security context of the user associated with that certificate or key.

Database Roles

As in SQL Server 2000, database role principals may be either a user-defined role, or a fixed database role. They can be created and have permissions assigned to them (although, of course, the permissions of fixed database roles are fixed).

The fixed database roles in SQL Server 2005 are the same as those in SQL Server 2000.

To create a database role, we now use the CREATE ROLE T-SQL statement, instead of the sp_addrole system stored procedure:

```
CREATE ROLE [AdventureWorks Editor]
AUTHORIZATION dbo;
```

The (optional) AUTHORIZATION clause corresponds to the @ownername parameter of sp_addrole, and indicates the owner of the database role. Note that we still use the system stored procedure sp_addrolemember to add users to a user-defined role.

Database Groups

Database groups, deprecated since SQL Server 7, are still just about supported in SQL Server 2005 for backwards compatibility, but will apparently be removed in the next release. As in previous versions, you can add groups to a database using the sp_addgroup system stored procedure, but this *really* shouldn't be used any more.

Application Roles

Application roles allow us to define a security context for a specific application. After the application has connected to SQL Server, it calls the sp_setapprole system stored procedure, and from that point has the permissions assigned to the application role, rather than those of the user account under which the application is running. In SQL Server 2005, application roles are now created using the CREATE APPLICATION ROLE statement, rather than the sp_addapprole stored procedure:

```
CREATE APPLICATION ROLE DataEntryAppRole
WITH PASSWORD = 'gSLi87po(&$dK',
DEFAULT_SCHEMA = Sales;
```

The DEFAULT_SCHEMA clause is optional. We'll look at SQL Server 2005 schemas shortly.

Object Ownership

Apart from the separation of schemas from users, which we'll look at when we consider schema-scoped securables, object ownership isn't too different in SQL Server 2005. There are a couple of extra features worth mentioning, however. First is the new optional AUTHORIZATION clause in many CREATE statements that allows us to set the owner of the created object. For example, to specify that we want the new object to be owned by a user called John rather than the user who is executing the statement when creating a new database role, we use the following:

```
CREATE ROLE NewDbRole
AUTHORIZATION John;
```

We can also change the owner of an object using the new ALTER AUTHORIZATION SQL statement. This takes the following form:

```
ALTER AUTHORIZATION
ON <entity_type>::<entity_name>
TO <principal_name>
```

Instead of providing the name of a principal as the new owner, we can specify SCHEMA OWNER, which will set the owner of the object to the owner of the schema to which it belongs.

For example, to change the owner of the role we created previously from John to a user called Fred, we would use the following command:

```
ALTER AUTHORIZATION
ON ROLE::NewDbRole
TO Fred;
```

Impersonation

SQL Server 2005 allows a user to impersonate another user for a specific block of code. This is achieved using the EXECUTE AS clause, which is added to the CREATE/ALTER statements for procedures, functions, triggers, and Service Broker queues. Unlike the existing SETUSER, EXECUTE AS isn't restricted to members of the sysadmin fixed server role or the db_owner database role.

This is important, because the impersonating account doesn't need to have access to the objects referenced in the module (the procedure, function, etc.), so long as it has permission to execute the module, and the impersonated account has the requisite permissions to access the referenced objects. This means that we can force access to data through particular database objects, rather than directly through the database tables. Note that the default is for modules to be executed under the caller's account, so without impersonation, the caller wouldn't be able to access the data at all.

To see how this works, open up a query window in Management Studio and create a couple of new users in the AdventureWorks database:

```
USE AdventureWorks
GO

CREATE LOGIN John WITH PASSWORD = '34r%*Fs$lK!9';
CREATE LOGIN Jane WITH PASSWORD = '4LWcm&(^o!HXk';

CREATE USER John FOR LOGIN John;
CREATE USER Jane FOR LOGIN Jane;
GO
```

Now give John SELECT permission on the database by adding that account to the db_datareader fixed database role, and permission to create stored procedures by adding him to the db_ddladmin role:

```
EXEC sp_addrolemember 'db_datareader', 'John';
EXEC sp_addrolemember 'db_ddladmin', 'John';
GO
```

Now we can create a new stored procedure that reads some data from the database. We set the EXECUTE AS clause so that the procedure will always impersonate John:

```
CREATE PROCEDURE usp_GetAddresses
WITH EXECUTE AS 'John'
AS
SELECT * FROM Person.Address;
GO
```

We'll use the new ALTER AUTHORIZATION command to set the owner of this procedure to the new user, John, to create this, so that the procedure has a different owner from the underlying tables. This breaks the chain of ownership, and forces SQL Server to check the permissions on the underlying objects:

```
ALTER AUTHORIZATION ON usp_GetAddresses
TO John;
```

Finally, let's give Jane permission to execute this procedure (but not to access the data directly):

```
SETUSER
GRANT EXECUTE ON usp_GetAddresses TO Jane;
```

To test that this has worked, switch to the user Jane and verify that you can't read data in it:

```
SETUSER 'Jane'
SELECT * FROM Person.Address;
```

You should see this error message, confirming that Jane can't access the data directly:

```
SELECT permission denied on object 'Address', database 'AdventureWorks',
schema 'Person'.
```

Now execute the stored procedure we just created:

```
EXEC usp_GetAddresses;
```

This should run fine and return the data as expected, proving that we've forced Jane to access the data through the stored procedure by not granting her SELECT permission on the table. We can use this technique regardless of whether the ownership chain is broken between the stored procedure and the table.

As well as specifying the actual name of a user, we can also stipulate that a module should run as the CALLER (the default), the object's OWNER, or SELF (a shortcut for the name of the user account under which the object is being created or modified). This provides a great deal more flexibility than SQL Server 2000 when it comes to chains of ownership (when modules call other modules), as it allows us to specify in advance exactly what user account each module should run under.

Securables

Securables are the database objects to which you can control access and to which you can grant principals permissions. SQL Server 2005 distinguishes between three scopes at which different objects can be secured:

- *Server scope*: Server-scoped securables include logins, HTTP endpoints, event notifications, and databases. These are objects that exist at the server level, outside of any individual database, and to which access is controlled on a server-wide basis.

- *Database scope*: Securables with database scope are objects such as users, roles, and CLR assemblies, that exist inside a particular database, but not within a schema.

- *Schema scope*: This group includes those objects that reside within a schema within a database, such as tables, views, and stored procedures. A SQL Server 2005 schema corresponds roughly to the owner of a set of objects (such as dbo) in SQL Server 2000.

Server-scoped Securables

Server-scoped securables are objects that are unique within a SQL Server instance (for example, an instance can only contain one database of a given name, and there can only be one service listening on a given port). The server-scoped objects are

- Connections
- Databases
- Event notifications
- HTTP endpoints
- Linked servers
- Logins

Permissions on server-scoped securables can only be granted to server-level principals (that is, either SQL Server logins or Windows logins), not to database-level principals such as users or roles. Also, these permissions must be granted in the master database—any attempt to grant them within another database produces the following error:

```
Permissions at the server scope can only be granted when the current database is
master
```

Database-scoped Securables

Database-level securables are unique to a specific database. The database securables in SQL Server 2005 are

- Application roles
- Assemblies
- Certificates and asymmetric/symmetric keys
- DDL events
- Full-text catalogs
- Message types
- Remote Service Bindings
- Roles
- Routes
- Schemas
- Service contracts
- Service
- Users

You can apply permissions on each of these securables to the database-level security principals. However, if you grant permissions to a SQL Server or Windows login that doesn't have a corresponding database user principal, SQL Server will create a user with the same name for you in the current database. This doesn't apply to logins created from certificates or asymmetric keys.

Schema-scoped Securables

A schema is a new layer within the SQL Server security hierarchy, but is a standard object in ANSI SQL. While schemas did exist in SQL Server 2000, they weren't distinct from the database user; each user had a corresponding schema of objects of which they were the owner, and schemas couldn't be explicitly created or named.

In SQL Server 2005, a schema is still a collection of objects owned by a database user, but there is no longer a one-to-one link between users and schemas. A user can own more than one schema, and schemas can, if they are owned by a SQL Server role or a Windows group, be owned by more than one user. The following objects are securable at the schema level:

- Defaults
- Functions
- Procedures
- Queues
- Rules
- Synonyms
- Tables
- Types
- User-defined aggregates
- Views
- XML Schema Collections

How Schema-level Security Works

A look at the schemas in the AdventureWorks database is instructive if you want to see how schemas are intended to be used. Each schema contains a set of objects commonly accessed by the same set of users: in this case, a department of the company such as Sales, Production, or HumanResources. You can get a list of the schemas in a database from the sys.schemas system view:

```
USE [AdventureWorks]
SELECT * FROM sys.schemas;
```

When we add a user, we can assign a default schema for that user. For example, let's drop and re-create our user Jane from the previous example, and set her DEFAULT_SCHEMA to Sales (while we're at it, we'll also add her to the db_ddladmin fixed role, so that she can create procedures in this database):

```
USE AdventureWorks
DROP USER Jane;

CREATE USER Jane FOR LOGIN Jane
WITH DEFAULT_SCHEMA = Sales;

EXEC sp_addrolemember 'db_ddladmin', 'Jane';
```

Setting the default schema means that anything Jane does will by default occur in this schema, so any objects she creates will be placed in the Sales schema, and any objects she references will be assumed to be in the Sales schema unless the object name is explicitly qualified by the name of the schema it resides in. So, when Jane runs this CREATE PROCEDURE statement:

```
USE AdventureWorks
GO

CREATE PROCEDURE usp_GetCustomers
AS
SELECT * FROM Customer
```

The new procedure will be placed in the Sales schema, and any user with a different default schema will need to refer to it as Sales.usp_GetCustomers. Also note that Jane can refer to the Customer table without explicitly prefixing the schema name, because it's in her default schema. If no default schema is given in the CREATE USER command, it will default to dbo, as in SQL Server 2000.

Creating a New Schema

To create a schema, we issue the CREATE SCHEMA command. For example, to create a schema named Finance, we would use the command

```
CREATE SCHEMA Finance
```

We can also specify the database principal that owns the schema:

```
CREATE SCHEMA Finance AUTHORIZATION Jane
```

This gives Jane ownership of the schema and implicitly access to all the database objects within it, even if these aren't granted elsewhere. However, it doesn't give her permission to create objects within the schema, because DDL events are scoped at the database level, not at the schema level. See the section "Managing Schema Permissions" later in this chapter for information on how to do that.

One final point to note on the CREATE SCHEMA statement is that it can include nested CREATE TABLE and CREATE VIEW statements for creating tables and views within the schema, so the entire schema can be created in one go. We can also include GRANT, DENY, and REVOKE statements within the CREATE SCHEMA command.

Permissions

Permissions are the individual rights, granted (or denied) to a principal, to access a securable. As in previous versions, we can GRANT permissions, DENY them, or REVOKE permissions that have already been granted. What's changed is the sheer number of permissions that we can grant—there are 181 combinations of permissions and securables!

Types of Permission

The exact permissions that can be granted, and the format for the GRANT and DENY commands, vary according to the securable; these can be broken down into 12 different groups:

- *Server permissions*: These are permissions that apply to the server as a whole, such as permission to connect to the server or to an endpoint, permission to create or alter DDL or other events, and permission to access resources external to SQL Server. The controlling permission is CONTROL SERVER, which gives the grantee authority to perform any action and is effectively equivalent to adding the login to the sysadmin fixed server role.

- *HTTP endpoint permissions*: These include permissions to connect to the endpoint, and to control, alter, view the definition of, or take ownership of the object.

- *Certificate permissions*: Permissions to alter or control a specific certificate.

- *Database permissions*: These are database-wide permissions that apply to all objects in the current database, for example, permissions to create, alter, or execute objects in the database; to perform selects, inserts, updates, or deletes in any object in the database; and to control or take ownership of the database.

- *Schema permissions*: These are permissions that apply to a named schema or to all objects within the schema. They include the ability to perform selects, inserts, updates, and deletes on any object in the schema, to execute any procedure or function in the schema, or to control, alter, or take ownership of the schema.

- *Assembly permissions*: Permissions on a specific assembly, such as permission to execute, control, alter, or take ownership of the assembly.

- *Type permissions*: Permissions on a specific user-defined type, such as permission to execute, control, or take ownership of the type.

- *Full-text catalog permissions*: Permissions to reference, take ownership of, view the definition of, or control the catalog.

- *Service Broker permissions*: Permissions on a specific Service Broker object. These vary slightly depending on the type of object.

- *Server principal permissions*: These are permissions to impersonate a given login account, or to alter, view the definition of, take ownership of, or control the login.

- *Database principal permissions*: Permissions to impersonate a given user, or to alter, control, or view the definition of a specific database principal.

- *Object permissions*: These are permissions granted on a schema-scoped securable such as a table, view, or stored procedure, for example, to execute or to perform selects, deletes, etc. on the object. You can also specify ALL (or ALL PRIVILEGES) to grant all available permissions on the object.

We can't cover every permission here, so please consult Books Online for a full list of the permissions supported by each type of object.

The Data Control Language (DCL) statements for granting and revoking permissions to users in SQL Server 2005 are much the same as in SQL Server 2000. The basic syntax for the GRANT statement is as follows:

```
GRANT <permission>
[ON [<securable type>::]<securable>]
TO <principal>
[WITH GRANT OPTION]
[AS {<group> | <role> }]
```

The ON clause is omitted for database permissions and server permissions, which apply to the current database or server respectively as a whole, and the <securable type>:: syntax is not used for permissions on database objects such as tables, views, and stored procedures. The WITH GRANT OPTION and AS {<group> | <role> } clauses are optional in all cases. The former gives the grantee the ability to grant the permission in turn to other principals, and the latter indicates the name of a database group or role that the granter belongs to and that has the authority to grant permissions on the securable.

The syntax for DENY and REVOKE follows the same format, so we won't show those here: they shouldn't give any additional problems to anyone used to using them in SQL Server 2000.

Managing Permissions

The preceding (necessarily somewhat condensed) information shows how much more control the DBA now has in granting permissions on specific objects. There's a much wider range of permissions available than in SQL Server 2000, and the addition of the schema to the security hierarchy facilitates a finer degree of control. However, in the real world, of course, permissions don't occur singly, and managing permissions has two major complications:

1. Many permissions implicitly grant other permissions, and permissions combine so that there may be multiple permissions on the same object.

2. Objects call other objects, on which the principal may or may not have permissions.

The way permissions work in these respects is not fundamentally different from SQL Server 2000, so we'll concentrate here on a couple of issues that are new to SQL Server 2005: managing schema permissions, and cross-database ownership chaining.

Managing Schema Permissions

Schemas provide an extra layer in the authorization hierarchy that didn't exist in earlier versions of SQL Server. For example, the database-level permission to create tables or other objects doesn't actually mean anything unless you also have permission to add those objects to a specific schema, as database objects must now exist within a schema in the database. Conversely, as we saw earlier, the owner of a schema automatically has the right to perform selects, etc., from objects within it, but not to create new objects in it. In order to do that, we'd need to give the user the relevant permission at database level; for example:

```
USE AdventureWorks
GRANT CREATE TABLE TO Jane
```

This gives Jane the right to create tables in the database, and assuming she's the owner of the Finance schema we created previously, she can now create new tables there. In order to create objects in a schema, a user needs ALTER permission on the schema, so for example Jane can't create tables in the Sales schema unless we grant her this permission:

```
GRANT ALTER
ON SCHEMA::Sales
TO Jane
```

As you would expect, if there's a conflict in permissions between the schema itself and an object in the schema, DENY overrides GRANT. For example, try to run this T-SQL code that denies Jane access to the HumanResources schema, but tries to grant access to the Department table within it, and then switches to the Jane user and tries to read from the table:

```
DENY SELECT ON SCHEMA::HumanResources TO Jane
GRANT SELECT ON HumanResources.Department TO Jane

SETUSER 'Jane'
SELECT * FROM HumanResources.Department
SETUSER
```

This gives the following error message:

```
SELECT permission denied on object 'Department', database 'AdventureWorks',
schema 'HumanResources'.
```

This means that there's no way to explicitly deny access to all but a specific set of objects in a schema: you need either to grant access only to the required object, without configuring access to the remaining objects, or to explicitly deny access to each of the objects that you don't want the principal to access.

Chains of Ownership and Cross-database Ownership Chaining

Chains of ownership in SQL Server 2005 are similar to those in SQL Server 2000. If a database object (such as a stored procedure) accesses another object (such as a table), SQL Server will skip permission checking for performance reasons if the owner of the two objects is the same. If the two objects have different owners, the chain of ownership will be broken, and SQL Server will check the permissions on the accessed object.

However, there are a couple of differences. First, SQL Server 2005 lets us bypass the chain of ownership by using the EXECUTE AS clause to specify exactly what security context we want a module such as a stored procedure or function to run in, as you saw in the section "Impersonation" earlier in this chapter. Second, it allows us to continue the chain of ownership even across database boundaries.

Before we use cross-database chaining in our SQL Server instance, we need to enable it using the sp_configure stored procedure, and then run RECONFIGURE:

```
sp_configure 'cross db ownership chaining', 1
GO
RECONFIGURE
GO
```

To try this out, we'll create a new login called William and a couple of new databases and add a simple table to each of them. These tables contain data on actual customers and on recipients who have signed up for our mailing list, for whom we have only an e-mail address. Once we've added some data to our tables, we'll write a view that performs a union query on the two tables. We also create a user based on the William login to whom we grant permission to access the view, but neither of the tables directly. Notice that the William user has to exist in both of the databases, or the query will fail.

```
CREATE DATABASE CustomerData
WITH DB_CHAINING ON

CREATE DATABASE MailingList
WITH DB_CHAINING ON
GO
CREATE LOGIN William WITH PASSWORD = '?sdj7JS3&*(%sdp_';

USE CustomerData
CREATE TABLE Customers
(
    CustomerID int IDENTITY PRIMARY KEY,
    FirstName nvarchar(255) NOT NULL,
    LastName nvarchar(255) NOT NULL,
    Email varchar(255) NOT NULL
);

INSERT INTO Customers VALUES ('John', 'Smith', 'John.Smith@somewhere.com');
INSERT INTO Customers VALUES ('Jane', 'Jones', 'JaneJ@somewhereelse.com');
GO

CREATE USER William FOR LOGIN William;
GO
```

```
USE MailingList
CREATE TABLE EmailAddresses
(
    ContactID int IDENTITY PRIMARY KEY,
    Email varchar(255) NOT NULL
);

INSERT INTO EmailAddresses VALUES('gprice@somedomain.com');
INSERT INTO EmailAddresses VALUES('fredb@anotherdomain.com');
GO

CREATE VIEW vGetAllContactEmails
AS
SELECT Email FROM EmailAddresses
UNION
SELECT Email FROM CustomerData.dbo.Customers;
GO

CREATE USER William FOR LOGIN William;
GRANT SELECT ON vGetAllContactEmails TO William;
GO

SETUSER 'William'
SELECT * FROM vGetAllContactEmails
SETUSER
```

When we set the current user to William, we should be able to access the view, even though it accesses data in another database, because the view and the two tables it selects data from are all owned by the same user, so the chain of ownership isn't broken.

Code Access Security

While T-SQL now has far more granular permissions than previously, it's still relatively crude compared to the control available with .NET. From the point of view of security, the most important aspect of .NET–SQL Server integration is that it allows the database developer to take advantage of Code Access Security (CAS). CAS is the .NET mechanism that allows developers to state explicitly what permissions their code needs to run (for example, the permission to access unmanaged code or the permission to access some part of the file system), and also to grant or deny permission to specific code to perform some action.

There are four fundamental actions that can be performed with CAS permissions:

- *Assert*: Asserting a permission allows a section of code to perform a given action, even if the method (which may be in a different assembly) that called the current method doesn't have that permission. The current code itself must have permission to perform the action, or the assert will fail.

- *Deny*: Denying a permission will cause any attempts further down the method call stack to perform the prohibited action or to demand the same permission to fail. However, the denial may be overridden by a subsequent call to Assert or PermitOnly.

- *Demand*: Demanding a permission signals that the code requires this permission to run. The demand will be granted only if hasn't been denied higher up the call stack, or permitted only on a different resource.

- *PermitOnly*: This is used to grant access only to a specific resource, and to refuse access to other resources that require the same permission. PermitOnly can be overridden by an assert or deny permission, but not by another PermitOnly.

Imperative and Declarative CAS

CAS can be implemented in two ways: declaratively, using attributes to demand and assert permissions; and imperatively, by calling methods on individual permission objects (these are defined in the System.Security.Permissions namespace, and derive from the CodeAccessPermission base class). Permissions can also be configured for entire assemblies, groups of assemblies, or even the entire local machine or domain using the Code Access Security policy management application, caspol.exe, or the .NET Configuration Wizard.

CAS permissions are in fact slightly misnamed—in many cases they're actually broad groups of permissions that contain individual permissions. For example, the Security permission contains subpermissions to enable assembly execution, to allow calls to unmanaged code, and so on. To request a specific permission using imperative security, we instantiate the corresponding .NET class, passing in any parameters we need to identify precisely what our code needs permission to do, and then call the appropriate Demand(), Assert(), Deny(), or PermitOnly() method on the instance. For example, to demand Read permission on the file C:\temp.txt, we would use

```
FileIOPermission perm = new FileIOPermission(FileIOPermissionAccess.Read,
    @"C:\temp.txt");
perm.Demand();
```

To do the same using declarative security, we place .NET attributes in front of the assembly, class, or method that requires the permission, passing in the appropriate action as a SecurityAction enum member:

```
[FileIOPermission(SecurityAction.Demand, Read=@"C:\temp.txt")]
public static string ReadTempData()
{
    // Method body...
}
```

Using CAS with SQL Server

To see how this works in practice, let's look at a simple example. We'll write a C# DLL called FileReader.dll that reads a list of names of sales representatives in a text file line by line, and returns the contents as a string array. This will be called by a SQL Server assembly (GetSalesAssem.dll), also written in C#, which looks up these names in the AdventureWorks database and extracts the sales figures for the year to date and last year, and returns these as a result set.

The code for FileReader.cs is shown here:

```
using System.Collections;
using System.IO;
using System.Security.Permissions;

namespace Apress.SqlServer2005.SecurityChapter
{
    public class FileReader
    {
```

```
    public static string[] ReadFile(string filename)
    {
        FileIOPermission perm = new FileIOPermission(
                                FileIOPermissionAccess.Read, filename);
        perm.Demand();

        ArrayList names = new ArrayList();
        FileStream fs = new FileStream(filename, FileMode.Open,
                                FileAccess.Read);
        StreamReader sr = new StreamReader(fs);
        while (sr.Peek() >= 0)
            names.Add(sr.ReadLine());
        sr.Close();
        fs.Close();

        return (string[])names.ToArray(typeof(string));
    }
  }
}
```

We use CAS to demand permission to read the file that's passed in as a parameter to the method that does the file reading. If the caller doesn't have permission to access the file, this line will throw an exception. We don't handle this exception in this class, because we want the exception to be available to the caller. We could, of course, create a new exception with its InnerException set to the original Exception object, but this involves creating an extra object that we don't really need.

Compile this C# file at the command-line using the following statement:

```
csc /t:library FileReader.cs
```

Next comes the SQL Server assembly. This reads the names from the file specified in the parameter and uses these to construct a SQL statement that gathers the sales data for each employee. We then execute this statement against the server and return the results as a data reader to SQL Server:

```
using System;
using System.Data;
using System.Data.SqlClient;
using System.Data.SqlTypes;
using System.Security;
using System.Security.Permissions;
using System.Text;
using Microsoft.SqlServer.Server;

namespace Apress.SqlServer2005.SecurityChapter
{
    public class SalesFetcher
    {
        public static void GetSalesForNames(SqlString filename)
        {
            try
            {
                // Create a PermissionSet to hold the permissions we want to grant
                PermissionSet perms = new PermissionSet(PermissionState.None);
```

```csharp
// Ensure that only correct file can be accessed through this method
FileIOPermission ioPerm = new FileIOPermission(
    FileIOPermissionAccess.Read, @"C:\names.txt");
perms.AddPermission(ioPerm);

// Permit access to SQL Server data
SqlClientPermission sqlPerm = new SqlClientPermission(
                                    PermissionState.None);
sqlPerm.Add("context connection=true", "",
        KeyRestrictionBehavior.AllowOnly);
perms.AddPermission(sqlPerm);
perms.PermitOnly();

// Get the names from the text file as a string array
string[] names = FileReader.ReadFile(filename.ToString());

// Build SQL statement
StringBuilder sb = new StringBuilder();
sb.Append(@"SELECT emp.EmployeeID,
                sp.SalesYTD + sp.SalesLastYear AS RecentSales
        FROM Sales.SalesPerson sp
            INNER JOIN HumanResources.Employee emp
            ON emp.EmployeeID = sp.SalesPersonID
        WHERE sp.SalesPersonID IN
        (
            SELECT emp.EmployeeID
            FROM HumanResources.Employee emp
                INNER JOIN Person.Contact c
                ON c.ContactID = emp.ContactID
            WHERE c.FirstName + ' ' + c.MiddleName + ' ' +
                c.LastName
            IN (");

// Concatenate array into single string for WHERE clause
foreach (string name in names)
{
    sb.Append("'");
    sb.Append(name);
    sb.Append("', ");
}
sb.Remove(sb.Length - 2, 2);
sb.Append("))");

// Execute the SQL statement and get back a SqlResultSet
using (SqlConnection cn = new SqlConnection(
                                "context connection=true"))
{
    cn.Open();
    SqlCommand cmd = new SqlCommand(sb.ToString(), cn);
    SqlDataReader dr = cmd.ExecuteReader();
```

```
                // Send success message to SQL Server and return SqlDataReader
                SqlPipe pipe = SqlContext.Pipe;
                pipe.Send(dr);
                pipe.Send("Command(s) completed successfully.");
                cn.Close();
            }
        }
        catch (Exception e)
        {
            SqlPipe pipe = SqlContext.Pipe;
            pipe.Send(e.Message);
            pipe.Send(e.StackTrace);
            pipe.Send("Error executing assembly");
        }
    }
}
}
```

This is where the power of CAS really shows itself, because we grant access only to one specific file (here, C:\names.txt) by calling PermitOnly() on our FileIOPermission object. Any attempt to access any other file through this assembly will fail. Now, in this case, we could have just hard-coded the value into the method call on our FileReader class, but CAS also lets us specify an array of files we want to permit access to through this method, in which case hard-coding the filename wouldn't have been an option.

As well as the FileIOPermission, notice that we also require a SqlClientPermission, which permits us to connect to SQL Server via the context connection—otherwise calling PermitOnly on the FileIOPermission would prevent us accessing SQL Server data. We create a new SqlClientPermission object with no permissions to connect to any SQL Server, and then call the Add method on this permission object, allowing connection on the context connection with no exceptions. It's not possible to call PermitOnly individually on more than one permission in a method, so we need to create a PermissionSet object, add these two permissions to it, and then call PermitOnly on the PermissionSet.

To compile this file, run the following command:

```
csc /t:library /r:FileReader.dll /r:"<path to sqlaccess.dll>" GetSalesAssem.cs
```

where <path to sqlaccess.dll> is

```
<Program Files>\Microsoft SQL Server\<MSSQL instance>\MSSQL\Binn\sqlaccess.dll
```

For example, on our system, this is

```
C:\Program Files\Microsoft SQL Server\MSSQL.1\MSSQL\Binn\sqlaccess.dll
```

Now we just need to register the assembly in SQL Server and create a procedure that will call this method. The stored procedure has one parameter, of type nvarchar, which will automatically be converted by the CLR to the corresponding .NET type (System.String)—which is the type of the parameter to our .NET method:

```
USE AdventureWorks
GO

CREATE ASSEMBLY GetSalesAssem
FROM 'C:\Apress\ProSqlServer\Chapter11\GetSalesAssem.dll'
WITH PERMISSION_SET = EXTERNAL_ACCESS
GO
```

```
CREATE PROCEDURE uspGetSalesForNames @filename nvarchar(255)
AS EXTERNAL NAME GetSalesAssem.
    [Apress.SqlServer2005.SecurityChapter.SalesFetcher].GetSalesForNames
GO
```

To test this out, create a new text file called names.txt in the root of the C:\ folder that contains the following names:

```
Michael G Blythe
Garrett R Vargas
Amy E Alberts
```

and call the new procedure

```
EXEC uspGetSalesForNames 'C:\names.txt'
```

You should see the EmployeeID and sales data for each of these employees. You can check that the Code Access Security is working by making a copy of this file called names2.txt and running the procedure against that. You'll see an error message and stack trace indicating that the attempt to demand the FileIOPermission failed.

Encryption

Another major new feature of SQL Server 2005 that helps improve the security of your data is the provision of a number of functions that allow us to encrypt and decrypt data within T-SQL statements. These can be used to encrypt sensitive data such as credit card details before storing it in the database (so that if the security of the database is compromised, sensitive data will remain safe). Although it would generally make sense for any complex encryption processing to be performed in a .NET assembly, as .NET has far more powerful methods for manipulation of strings and byte streams, simpler tasks can be performed within T-SQL; this has the advantage of not opening up the database to any potential security vulnerabilities from misuse of the .NET methods (.NET cryptography relies heavily on unmanaged code).

SQL Server 2005 provides four pairs of encryption/decryption functions, each pair using a specific encryption technique:

- *Password encryption*: This is the simplest and weakest type of encryption. The data is encrypted with a user-supplied password string, with no checks on the strength of the chosen password.

- *Asymmetric key encryption*: This is the most secure form of encryption, as it uses different keys for encrypting and decrypting the data. However, it is also much slower than weaker forms of encryption, and shouldn't generally be used for large quantities of data unless security is all-important and performance isn't an issue.

- *Symmetric key encryption*: Symmetric key encryption uses a single key for both encryption and decryption. SQL Server 2005 provides two sets of functions for symmetric key encryption: using a user-provided password as the key, and using a key stored as an object in SQL Server.

- *Certificate encryption*: Certificates are issued by trusted certificate authorities, and are used to provide proof of the identity of the author of some code or the sender of some data. They are widely known from their use in Secure Sockets Layer (SSL), which is used to secure HTTPS. SQL Server 2005 can issue its own certificates.

The SQL Server 2005 Encryption Hierarchy

Before we discuss the encryption functions, we need to look briefly at the encryption hierarchy of SQL Server 2005. At the top of this hierarchy is the *Service Master Key*, which is created when a SQL Server instance is installed, and which is encrypted with the Windows Data Protection API (DPAPI) using the password of the Windows service account under which the key was created.

This key exists at the server level, but each database can also contain a *database master key*, which is used to encrypt the private keys of certificates and asymmetric keys stored in the database. The database master key is a symmetric key encrypted using the Triple DES algorithm with the password supplied when the key is created:

```
CREATE MASTER KEY
ENCRYPTION BY PASSWORD = '<password>';
```

However, by default copies of the key encrypted with the Service Master Key are also stored in the database and in the master database, so that the key can be opened without supplying the password. You can change this behavior using the ALTER MASTER KEY command:

```
ALTER MASTER KEY
DROP ENCRYPTION BY SERVICE MASTER KEY;
```

If you change this default, you will need to OPEN the master key before using it. Creating, opening, or backing up the master key requires CONTROL permission on the database.

Below the database master key in the encryption hierarchy are the certificates and asymmetric keys that are stored in the database and whose private keys are encrypted with the database master key. These can be used directly to encrypt data, or to encrypt symmetric keys stored in the database to provide a higher level of security than simple symmetric key encryption. Symmetric keys form the bottom level of the encryption hierarchy, and may be used to secure data or other symmetric keys.

Encryption with a User-supplied Password

The simplest pair of these functions is used to encrypt/decrypt data with a key supplied by the user. This is useful when the password isn't stored on the system at all, but is a string known only to the user. The advantage of this approach is, of course, that if the password isn't kept on the system, we don't need to worry about storing it securely. The disadvantages are that we may need to send it across the network more often (which requires further encryption, and therefore potentially a performance hit), and that we don't know how secure the user keeps the password himself. SQL Server also won't enforce strong passwords in these functions, so unless the front-end application validates the password when it is chosen, there's no guarantee that it isn't something as lame as "secret". For added security, this should be used in conjunction with another encryption method.

To encrypt data with a user-supplied password, we call the EncryptByPassPhrase() function, which takes as parameters the value to be encrypted and the pass phrase, both of which may either be string literals or values of a string type (char, nchar, wchar, varchar, or nvarchar). Then, to decrypt, we call the DecryptByPassPhrase() function, passing in the pass phrase followed by the cipher text we want to decrypt:

```
DECLARE @creditCardNum varchar(20),
    @passPhrase varchar(255),
    @cipherText varchar(1000),
    @clearText varchar(1000);
SET @creditCardNum = '34324521093872';
SET @passPhrase = 'fe34&*$PO2hs';
SET @cipherText = EncryptByPassPhrase(@passPhrase, @creditCardNum);
PRINT 'Cipher text = ' + @cipherText;
```

```
SET @clearText = DecryptByPassPhrase(@passPhrase, @cipherText);
PRINT 'Clear text = ' + @clearText;
```

The output of this will be something like the following:

```
Cipher text = ÂJn}û£¯ÞŠW4÷áê"U†«¨â^$…ð'19_{æìz    È
Clear text = 34324521093872
```

Note that the cipher is salted with an arbitrary value, so that the cipher text will be different each time you run this. However, this does not affect the decryption process.

Encryption with a Symmetric Key

The next most simple (and the next fastest) method is to encrypt the data with a symmetric key that is stored in the database. Because a single key is used both for encrypting and decrypting data, the two sides of a conversation that is encrypted with a symmetric key need some way to pass the key between them securely, as both sides need the same key. However, this may not be a problem in a SQL Server context if the function is used to encrypt data immediately before it is stored in the database, and decrypt it immediately after the data has been extracted, as in this case the key won't need to be sent across the wire.

To create a symmetric key in the database, we use the CREATE SYMMETRIC KEY statement:

```
CREATE SYMMETRIC KEY CreditCardKey
WITH ALGORITHM = TRIPLE_DES
ENCRYPTION BY PASSWORD = 'fe34&*$PO2hs';
```

The possible algorithms for symmetric key encryption are DES, TRIPLE_DES, RC2, RC4, DESX, AES128, AES192, and AES256. As well as (or instead of) password-protecting the key in the database, we can also encrypt it using a certificate or another symmetric key. If the key is a temporary key, we don't need to encrypt it at all. Lastly, there are two other options we can include in the WITH clause: DERIVED_FROM allows us to derive the key from a pass phrase supplied by the user; and IDENTIFIED_BY lets us specify a phrase that we can use to identify data encrypted with this key.

In order to encrypt or decrypt data using a symmetric key, we first need to open the key using the OPEN SYMMETRIC KEY statement. The EncryptByKey() function takes the GUID of the key to use, which we can obtain from the Key_GUID() function, as well as the clear text to encrypt. We can optionally supply a column name or value to use to create a hash that is attached to the cipher text. When decrypting, SQL Server can recognize the key used to encrypt the data, so we only supply the cipher text to the DecryptByKey() function. Finally, we need to close the key:

```
DECLARE @keyGuid UNIQUEIDENTIFIER,
    @creditCardNum varchar(20),
    @password varchar(255),
    @cipherText varchar(1000),
    @clearText varchar(1000);
SET @keyGuid = Key_GUID('CreditCardKey');
SET @creditCardNum = '12345678';

OPEN SYMMETRIC KEY CreditCardKey
    DECRYPTION BY PASSWORD = 'fe34&*$PO2hs';
SET @cipherText = EncryptByKey(@keyGuid, @creditCardNum);
PRINT 'Cipher text = ' + @cipherText;
SET @clearText = DecryptByKey(@cipherText);
PRINT 'Clear text = ' + @clearText;
CLOSE SYMMETRIC KEY CreditCardKey;
```

Asymmetric Key Encryption

Asymmetric key encryption actually uses two keys: a private key, which is stored locally and shouldn't be revealed to anyone, and a related public key that can be revealed to the world at large. Data encrypted with the public key can only be decrypted with the corresponding private key, and vice versa. This solves the major problem of symmetric key encryption, because the private key never has to be transmitted over the network. We can encrypt data with the intended recipient's public key, and only he will be able to decrypt it with his private key.

However, this doesn't provide any guarantee of the sender's identity, as anyone can encrypt data with a public key. In order to provide truly secure communication, we need to use two sets of keys: we need to encrypt the message with our own private key (which proves that we are the sender), and then encrypt the cipher text with the recipient's public key. The recipient can then decrypt the message with his own private key, and again with our public key.

This model provides very good security, but unfortunately very poor performance, so it's never used for large quantities of data. In practice, you need to use this technique in conjunction with other encryption techniques. For example, you can create a temporary symmetric key, transmit that using asymmetric key encryption, and then encrypt the rest of the conversation with the symmetric key.

The CREATE ASYMMETRIC KEY statement has two basic forms: we can create a new asymmetric key pair from scratch using a specified algorithm, or we can load one from an existing file. To create a new asymmetric key, we use the WITH ALGORITHM clause:

```
CREATE ASYMMETRIC KEY PpeKey
WITH ALGORITHM = RSA_512
ENCRYPTION BY PASSWORD = 'fe34&*$PO2hs';
```

The possible algorithms are RSA_512, RSA_1024, and RSA_2048.

Alternatively, we can create the key from an existing key file, signed assembly file, or .NET assembly. For example, to create an asymmetric key from a key file generated with the sn.exe command-line utility:

```
CREATE ASYMMETRIC KEY PpeKey
FROM FILE = 'C:\Apress\SqlServer2005\SecurityChapter\Encryption\keyfile.key'
ENCRYPTION BY PASSWORD = 'fe34&*$PO2hs';
```

Both the EncryptByAsymKey() and DecryptByAsymKey() functions take as parameters the GUID for the key (available from the AsymKey_ID() function), the text to be encrypted/decrypted, and, for decryption, the password used to encrypt the key (if applicable). Note that this last parameter needs to be of type nvarchar rather than varchar. Unlike symmetric keys, we don't need to open the key prior to using it:

```
DECLARE @keyId int,
    @creditCardNum varchar(20),
    @password varchar(255),
    @cipherText varchar(1000),
    @clearText varchar(1000);
SET @keyId = AsymKey_ID('PpeKey');
SET @creditCardNum = '12345678';

SET @cipherText = EncryptByAsymKey(@keyId, @creditCardNum);
PRINT 'Cipher text = ' + @cipherText;
SET @clearText = DecryptByAsymKey(@keyId, @cipherText,
    CAST('fe34&*$PO2hs' AS nvarchar));
PRINT 'Clear text = ' + @clearText;
```

Encryption with a Certificate

Certificates are used to identify a particular person or organization, and are best known for their use in securing websites using Secure Sockets Layer. They contain a public key, and additional data such as information on the owner of the key, and start and expiry dates. Certificates are issued by certificate authorities (CAs) such as VeriSign, Thawte, and GlobalSign. These companies perform background checks on anyone who applies for a certificate to ensure that all the data they supply is correct, so certificates issued by these authorities will be trusted on most systems. However, it's also possible to issue your own certificates (for example, using Certificate Services in Windows 2000/2003); these self-issued certificates will generally be trusted within your own organization, but not by anyone outside it. SQL Server 2005 also has the ability to issue certificates, which can be used to encrypt data and to create HTTPS endpoints for secure web services (we'll look at an example of that in the next section).

The CREATE CERTIFICATE T-SQL statement is similar to CREATE ASYMMETRIC KEY, in that you can either create a new certificate from scratch, or load one from an existing certificate file, .NET assembly, or assembly file. If creating a new certificate, you need to specify the start date, expiry date, and subject (the server that issued the certificate), as well as the password to encrypt the private key associated with the certificate:

```
CREATE CERTIFICATE TestCertificate
ENCRYPTION BY PASSWORD = 'fe34&*$PO2hs'
WITH START_DATE = '04/04/2005',
    EXPIRY_DATE = '04/04/2006',
    SUBJECT = 'certserver.apress.com';
```

Alternatively, it's possible to specify a file from which to load the private key. We can also indicate that the certificate is to be made available for initiating Service Broker conversations using the clause:

```
ACTIVE FOR BEGIN_DIALOG = ON
```

The default is OFF, so without this clause the certificate won't be available.

Finally, if you simply omit the ENCRYPTION BY PASSWORD clause, the certificate will be encrypted with the master key for the current database. This is required in certain situations, such as when creating a certificate to authenticate a Service Broker endpoint.

Once you have your certificate, you can use it to encrypt data with the EncryptByCert() function. Again, this takes as parameters the GUID for the certificate (obtainable from the Cert_ID() function) and the clear text to be encrypted. We can decrypt certificate-encrypted text using the DecryptByCert() function:

```
DECLARE @certId int,
    @creditCardNum varchar(20),
    @password varchar(255),
    @cipherText varchar(1000),
    @clearText varchar(1000);
SET @certId = Cert_ID('TestCertificate');
SET @creditCardNum = '12345678';

SET @cipherText = EncryptByCert(@certId, @creditCardNum);
PRINT 'Cipher text = ' + @cipherText;
SET @clearText = DecryptByCert(@certId, @cipherText,
    CAST('fe34&*$PO2hs' AS nvarchar));
PRINT 'Clear text = ' + @clearText;
```

Certificates and Web Services

As we mentioned previously, certificates can also be used for securing web service endpoints, so that the service can only be accessed using HTTPS instead of HTTP. To see how this works, let's run through a simple example. Unfortunately, it's not possible to create a certificate that's valid for SSL within SQL Server, so we'll need to resort to an external tool to create an appropriate certificate.

■**Note** This example will only work on SQL Server 2005 installations running on Windows 2003. At the time of writing, Windows 2000 and XP don't support SQL Server 2005 web services without IIS.

First, we need to create a stored procedure that we'll use as the basis for our web service:

```
USE AdventureWorks
GO

CREATE PROCEDURE usp_SQLWS
AS
SELECT * FROM HumanResources.Employee;
GO
```

Now we have to create an endpoint for the web service. This is basically the same as the example in the Chapter 7, but notice the PORTS - (SSL) clause that indicates that this service will only be available over HTTPS. We also specify the SSL port, although 443 is the default, and that we'll be using integrated authentication:

```
CREATE ENDPOINT SQLWS_endpoint
STATE = STARTED
  AS HTTP
  (
     PATH = '/sql/sample',
     AUTHENTICATION = (INTEGRATED),
     PORTS = (SSL),
     SSL_PORT = 443
  )
  FOR SOAP
  (
     WEBMETHOD
        'http://tempuri.org/'.'SQLWS'
        (NAME = 'AdventureWorks.dbo.usp_SQLWS'),
        BATCHES = ENABLED,
        WSDL = DEFAULT
  );
```

Next, we need to obtain a certificate. For a live web service, you would need to obtain a certificate from a trusted certificate authority, but for the purposes of this example, we'll use a self-signed certificate created with makecert.exe. From a command prompt on the SQL Server machine, run the following command:

```
makecert -r -pe -n CN="servername" -eku 1.3.6.1.5.5.7.3.1 -ss my -sr localmachine
-sky exchange -sp "Microsoft RSA SChannel Cryptographic Provider" -sy 12
```

The makecert command-line tool is used to generate test certificates and ships with the .NET Framework SDK and with the Platform SDK, but it doesn't come with the .NET redistributable or with SQL Server 2005, so you may need to download one of these SDKs from MSDN.

This command will create a new certificate and install it the into the "My" certificate store on the local machine. We won't go through all the options in detail here, although the full list of options can be found on MSDN, and the list of options required for SQL Server can be found in Books Online. The only option you need to change is -n, which should be set to your server name in the form CN="servername".

Next, we need to register the certificate for use with SSL. However, in order to configure SSL to use this certificate, we first need to know the hash that identifies it. This can be found using the certutil.exe utility, which ships with Windows Server 2003. Use the command

```
certutil -store MY servername
```

to display details of the certificates in the "My" store with the issuer *servername*. This will print something like the following to the console:

```
================ Certificate 3 ================
Serial Number: 30d872a4b44eb88e4525181b5ffdde44
Issuer: CN=Daufiltri
Subject: CN=Daufiltri
Signature matches Public Key
Root Certificate: Subject matches Issuer
Cert Hash(sha1): 5d a1 ca e8 6c 21 a9 fd 2b 2f 39 1e 4a 84 a4 0d 44 f8 19 3e
  Key Container = cf714cd5-886b-4a9f-b67f-f0238d08bff3
  Provider = Microsoft RSA SChannel Cryptographic Provider
Encryption test passed
```

The hash for the certificate is displayed in the Cert Hash line, but you'll need to remove the spaces from the hash before using it to register the certificate for SSL.

Next, you need a GUID to identify the entity that is registering the certificate. Microsoft recommends creating one GUID per SQL Server instance, and using that for all certificates registered by that instance. GUIDs can be generated with guidgen.exe, another tool that comes with the Platform SDK, or in .NET code by calling the System.Guid.NewGuid static method.

Once you have the hash and GUID, you can register the certificate for SSL using another command-line tool, httpcfg.exe. This ships as one of the Support Tools for Windows Server 2003. The command you need is in the format

```
httpcfg set ssl /i <ip_address>:<port> /h <certificate_hash>
/g "<guid>"
```

where the /i option specifies the IP address and TCP port that the web service will be running on, the /h option indicates the hash of the certificate you want to register (minus spaces), and the /g option the GUID you've just generated. For example:

```
httpcfg set ssl /i 192.168.16.2:443 /h 5da1cae86c21a9fd2b2f391e4a84a40d44f8193e
/g "{E95F971C-513F-4133-948D-D896B07EBA0A}"
```

All being well, you should now be able to access the web service over HTTPS; you can view the WSDL file for the web service by browsing to the URL https://x.x.x.x/sql/sample?WSDL, where x.x.x.x is the IP address that the service is running on.

Summary

SQL Server 2005 has many new security enhancements, touching almost every area of SQL Server. We haven't been able to look at everything in this chapter, but we've looked at the main security changes with regard to the database engine itself. In particular, we covered

- *Surface area configuration*: The disabling of certain features that could represent a security liability until they're explicitly enabled by the DBA.

- *Principals and securables*: You learned how SQL Server 2005 supports Windows, server, and database-level principals, and how it adds an extra layer to the authorization model through schemas.

- *Permissions*: SQL Server 2005 has a far more granular permission structure than SQL Server 2000, allowing you more control over exactly what actions each user can perform.

- *Code Access Security*: You learned how you can achieve even greater control over code running in .NET assemblies using Code Access Security.

- *Encryption*: We showed you the new functions that allow you to encrypt data within T-SQL code, and the new objects representing symmetric and asymmetric keys and certificates. You also learned how you can use certificates to secure web services over SSL.

CHAPTER 12

■■■

Service Broker

One of the most important new features of SQL Server 2005 is Service Broker. Service Broker is a message queuing technology that is native to SQL Server and allows developers to integrate SQL Server fully into distributed applications. Service Broker provides an asynchronous system for database-to-database communication; it allows a database to send a message to another database without waiting for the response, so the application will continue to function if the remote database is temporarily unavailable.

As with all message queuing systems, Service Broker applications work by sending messages containing data to a queue. The messages will be stored on the queue until the system has the resources available to process them and perform any actions that the messages demand. This helps to ensure the scalability of the application by using resources efficiently, as messages are guaranteed to be processed at some point, even if they can't be processed immediately.

In this chapter, we'll start by taking a high-level look at Service Broker, discussing the architecture of Service Broker applications and examining some sample scenarios where Service Broker can help you improve the robustness or scalability of your applications. We'll then get down to the details of creating Service Broker applications, looking at the new objects that you need to create in SQL Server and writing a simple example to show how to use these in practice. We'll then drill down into a couple of more advanced topics, including how to specify the way Service Broker should route messages and how it provides security for messages. We'll finish up with a more complex example that demonstrates these advanced techniques.

To summarize, in this chapter we'll cover

- The Service Broker architecture
- Scenarios for using Service Broker
- Using the new SQL Server Service Broker objects
- Service Broker routing
- Service Broker security

What Is Service Broker?

As intimated in the chapter introduction, Service Broker is message queuing for SQL Server. It provides a means by which you can send an asynchronous, transactional message from within a database to a queue, where it will be picked up and processed by another service. The sending and receiving services could be in separate instances of SQL Server, so the availability of the receiving service can't be guaranteed. However, because Service Broker places the message in a queue, you know that the message will eventually be picked up, even if the remote service isn't currently online.

Service Broker Architecture

The Service Broker architecture is essentially a straightforward client/server architecture: a Service Broker application consists of a client service that initiates a conversation and a receiving service that receives and processes the messages. Each service is associated with a particular queue, which it can send messages to, retrieve messages from, or both. The relationship between the services and the queue is defined by a *contract*, which specifies what type of messages the initiating and target services can send to the queue. The exchange of messages between the two services is called a *dialog conversation* (or simply a *dialog*). The fundamental architecture of a Service Broker application is shown in Figure 12-1.

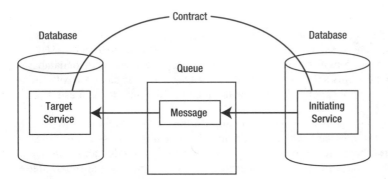

Figure 12-1. *The Service Broker architecture*

Services

A service is an endpoint for a Service Broker conversation. A service can be either an initiating service, which starts the conversation by sending a message to the queue, or a target service, which retrieves messages from the queue. A service is associated with a single queue (although queues can be associated with multiple services) and with a contract, which stipulates what type of messages it can send to the queue. Thus, the service is used to enforce the contract for a conversation. SQL Server also uses services to identify the queues to deliver messages to and to route messages through, and to authorize connections to remote services.

Queues

A queue is a depository for messages. Queues can be associated with multiple services, which can send and/or retrieve messages in the queue. A queue can also be associated with a stored procedure, which will execute when a message arrives in the queue. This gives you the option of processing messages as soon as they arrive in the queue, but it is also possible to process the messages by scheduling a SQL Server Agent job to run recurrently, or when the CPUs are idle.

   If the receiving service and sending service are in the same SQL Server instance, they can share the same queue; otherwise, they will need to be associated with different queues. If the receiving queue is in another instance of SQL Server, or if it isn't active for message receipt, the message will be placed in the *transmission queue* for the database that the sending service belongs to until the message can be delivered to the queue. Similarly, incoming messages will be sent to the transmission queue of the receiving database if the target queue isn't active for message receipt. You can see the messages currently in the transmission queue through the sys.transmission_queue system view. It's useful to check this queue when debugging Service Broker applications, as unsent messages remain here and the transmission_status column may contain an error message explaining why the message wasn't sent.

Messages

Each message is represented by a row in the queue. The format of messages is defined by the message type, which is specified in the contract between two services. The message type can require that messages be empty, well-formed XML; or XML that is valid according to a specific schema; or that no validation is to occur, in which case the messages in a conversation can contain any data, including binary data. There are also special messages that all services receive, regardless of the contract:

- *Error messages*: These are defined as messages of type `http://schemas.microsoft.com/SQL/ServiceBroker/Error`, and they are validated as well-formed XML. They consist of a root element called `<Error>`, with child elements representing the code and description of the error. Once an error has been generated for a conversation, no further messages can be sent on that conversation.

- *End Dialog messages*: These are empty messages of type `http://schemas.microsoft.com/SQL/ServiceBroker/EndDialog` and indicate that a service is ending the conversation without error.

- *Dialog Timer messages*: These are empty messages of type `http://schemas.Microsoft.com/SQL/ServiceBroker/DialogTimer`, which are placed in a queue to indicate that a conversation timer has expired.

Dialog Conversations

A dialog conversation represents the exchange of messages between two services. Messages in a dialog are delivered to the queue in the order in which they are sent. When an application processes a message from a queue, it may send another message to the queue, and it can indicate that this forms part of the same conversation. The conversation continues until one of the participating applications explicitly ends the conversation or sends an error message. However, each participant in the conversation must issue an END CONVERSATION command, or the dialog will remain in the database (you can view the active conversations through the `sys.conversation_endpoints` system view).

The initiating application can indicate a maximum lifetime for the application, after which each side will place a timeout error in the queue and refuse further messages. Each participant in a conversation can also specify one *conversation timer* per conversation. When a conversation timer expires, SQL Server places a Dialog Timer message in the queue, as a prompt for the application to perform a specific action (such as executing a stored procedure).

Conversation Groups

Each dialog belongs to a conversation group. If an application accesses information from two or more services, it may need to relate these conversations to each other; it can do this by including the second conversation in the same conversation group as the first (this doesn't affect the applications at the other end of the conversations, as conversation groups aren't shared and the other applications may group the conversations as they wish). Service Broker includes the ID for the conversation group in all incoming messages in that conversation, so that the application can determine which messages from the remote services belong together.

For example, suppose you have a service that is used to process employee vacation requests and that retrieves information about the employee making the request from one service and information about the timelines for current projects from another service. It uses the data from these two services to decide whether or not to grant the request for that employee at that time. This application can use the conversation group ID to ensure that it processes the correct employee data together with the related project data.

Conversation groups are locked when a message is being sent or retrieved on that group. This helps to ensure exactly once in order (EOIO) delivery.

Contracts

The message types that each participant in a conversation is permitted to send are specified in the contract for that conversation. The two services in the conversation will be bound by the same contract; if the two services are in different databases, then identical contracts must be created in each database. The contract stipulates what types of messages the initiating service and the receiving service can send, and what types can be sent by either service. The contract *must* include at least one message type that can be sent by the initiating service (or by either service, which obviously includes the initiating service); otherwise, there is no way for the conversation to be initiated.

The Service Broker Endpoint

If the two services in a conversation are in different instances of SQL Server, then you need to create a Service Broker endpoint, which will accept incoming and outgoing TCP/IP connections on a specific port. A SQL Server instance can only contain one Service Broker endpoint, which is shared between all services in the instance. We will look at remote service connections later in the chapter.

Remote Service Bindings

Remote Service Bindings are used to establish the security context under which an initiating service connects to a remote service in a different instance of SQL Server. The Remote Service Binding uses a certificate associated with the specified database user account to connect to the remote instance.

Routes

Service Broker uses routes to locate a service that it is sending a message to. If no route is explicitly associated with a service, then by default Service Broker will deliver the message within the current instance. A route contains the name of the service it is used to connect to, the ID of the Service Broker instance that hosts the service, and the network address of the remote Service Broker endpoint.

Service Broker Scenarios

Now that you've seen the various parts that make up a Service Broker application, and you've seen how Service Broker works at a high level, a basic question remains: what do you actually use Service Broker for? Service Broker brings two things to the table that ordinary SQL Server modules don't possess: guaranteed delivery of messages and asynchronicity. Without Service Broker, if you attempt to connect to a remote instance of SQL Server (e.g., using a linked server), and that server isn't available, you have to roll back the transaction and let the operation fail. With Service Broker, you can simply send a message to the queue and go on about your business, safe in the knowledge that when the server comes back online, it will be able to pick up the message and process it. Also, if you want to execute some complex processing within a module without Service Broker, you need to wait until that processing has completed before the module will continue executing. Service Broker allows the module to send a message and continue executing. The message can be processed at a later time, perhaps when the CPU is idle or during out-of-office hours.

Naturally, Service Broker also comes with an overhead, so it isn't an appropriate solution if you need an immediate response or if an application is time-critical. It wouldn't make any sense to use Service Broker to perform a simple SELECT query on a remote database. It's also worth bearing in mind that, if you use Service Broker for database updates, it could create result in data conflicts, as the update may not be performed immediately.

Possible scenarios for Service Broker applications include

- *Asynchronous triggers*: If a trigger requires resource-intensive processing that isn't time-critical, then it makes sense to use Service Broker. The trigger can simply place a message on the queue and return without needing to wait for the processing to complete.

- *Bulk processing*: If a module is run that requires extensive processing, such as bulk data processing, then Service Broker can avoid the potential performance degradation of running this immediately at busy times of the day. Instead, it can send a message to a queue, and a stored procedure can run as a SQL Server Agent job that will process any messages in the queue at a more convenient time.

- *Distributed order processing*: The other advantage of Service Broker—the guaranteed delivery of messages—makes it a good option for applications that involve order processing, where the order doesn't need to be fulfilled immediately, but it's vital that the order be delivered. This is particularly the case if orders are taken and fulfilled by different systems (e.g., if orders are taken at a local branch and dispatched from a central warehouse), where the availability of the remote system isn't guaranteed at the time the order is taken.

Creating Service Broker Applications

Now that you've learned what Service Broker is and what it's for, let's delve into the details of creating Service Broker applications. The exact number of steps you need to perform to do this varies, for example, on whether the conversation takes place within a single instance of SQL Server or whether the messages that will be sent are defined by an XML schema. For a single-instance application with validated XML messages, ten steps are involved:

1. Enable Service Broker for the database.
2. Create a master key for the database.
3. Create one or more XML SCHEMA COLLECTIONs to validate messages sent to the queue.
4. Define message types based on the schema(s).
5. Define the contract for the application.
6. Create a Service Broker program (e.g., a stored procedure) to process messages that are sent to the queue.
7. Create the queue.
8. Create the target service.
9. Create the initiating service.
10. Create a program to initiate the conversation by sending a message to the queue.

Let's look at these individual steps before putting everything together into a simple Service Broker application. We'll skip steps 2 and 3 until we actually get to the example, as there's nothing specific to Service Broker about these, and we'll also cover creating the target and initiating services (steps 8 and 9) and their associated stored procedures together.

Enabling Service Broker

Before Service Broker can be used in a database, we need to alter the database to enable Service Broker:

```
ALTER DATABASE database_name SET ENABLE_BROKER;
```

There's obviously some security risk in this, simply because it opens up another possible line of attack for a hacker trying to get into your database. However, unless you explicitly create a Service Broker endpoint, Service Broker won't accept connections from outside the instance. You also need to enable Service Broker in a database if you want to use Database Mail within that database.

Creating Message Types

Before we can create a contract for our Service Broker application, we need to define the message types that can be used in the conversation. The syntax for the CREATE MESSAGE TYPE command is

```
CREATE MESSAGE TYPE message_type_name
VALIDATION = validation_type
```

The VALIDATION clause has four possible options:

- EMPTY: The message must not contain any data.

- NONE: The message is not validated and may contain any or no data.

- WELL_FORMED_XML: The message must consist of a well-formed XML document.

- VALID_XML WITH SCHEMA COLLECTION schema collection name: Messages of this type must conform to the schema(s) contained in the specified collection. If a message doesn't conform to this schema, it will be rejected and not placed on the queue; instead, an XML-formatted error message will be sent to the queue.

Creating Contracts

A *contract* consists of a list of the message types that can be included in the conversation, together with the service(s) that can send them. The basic syntax for creating a contract is as follows:

```
CREATE CONTRACT contract_name
  message_type_name SENT BY sending_service [, ...]
```

The CREATE CONTRACT statement specifies the message types that a conversation can accept and the service(s) that can send those messages. For each message type, we must also include a SENT BY clause, which indicates the services that can send messages of that type. The possible values for this are as follows:

- INITIATOR: Only the service that started the conversation can post messages of this type.

- TARGET: Only the service that processes the messages on the queue can post messages of this type.

- ANY: Either of the two services in the conversation can send this type of message.

Instead of specifying a named message type, we can alternatively use the identifier [DEFAULT], which indicates a default message type (with no validation) sent by either of the two services. As we noted earlier, each contract must include at least one message type that may be sent by the initiator (i.e., is SENT BY either INITIATOR or ANY).

Creating Queues

The command for creating a queue is perhaps the most complex of the new T-SQL commands used to create Service Broker objects:

```
CREATE QUEUE queue_name
WITH
    STATUS = ON | OFF,
    RETENTION = ON | OFF,
    ACTIVATION
    (
        STATUS = ON | OFF,
        PROCEDURE_NAME = queue_sproc_name,
        MAX_QUEUE_READERS = integer,
        EXECUTE AS SELF | OWNER | user_name
    )
ON [DEFAULT] | filegroup_name
```

The WITH clause is optional, but if included it can have a number of subclauses (again, all of these are optional):

- STATUS: This subclause indicates whether or not the queue is originally enabled.

- RETENTION: If this subclause is set to OFF (the default), any messages that are processed will be removed from the queue. Otherwise, the messages will be left on the queue, but their status will be updated to indicate that they have been processed.

- ACTIVATION: This subclause indicates whether a procedure will be executed on the arrival of a message in the queue. Here we can specify the STATUS (whether the procedure will be activated automatically or not), the PROCEDURE_NAME (the SQL Server identifier for the service program), the maximum number of instances of the service program that can be created to process the queue, and the user to execute the procedure as. This can be one of SELF (the currently logged-in user), OWNER (the user account that owns the queue), or a username as a string.

Lastly, we can also optionally specify an ON clause, which specifies the filegroup on which to create the queue. Alternatively, we can use [DEFAULT] to specify the default filegroup for the database.

Creating Services

We need to specify two pieces of information when we create a service: the queue with which the service is associated and the conversations in which it can participate. The latter are specified through the contracts, so the CREATE SERVICE command looks like this:

```
CREATE SERVICE service_name
    ON QUEUE queue_name
    contract_name [, ...]
```

Contracts are used to indicate to other services what conversations the service can take part in, so they only need to be supplied if the service receives messages. If no contracts are specified, the service will be able to initiate conversations, but not to retrieve any responses.

Instead of naming a user-defined contract, we can use the identifier [DEFAULT] to use the default contract, which allows either service to send unvalidated messages.

Creating Service Broker Stored Procedures

The most complex part of writing a Service Broker application unsurprisingly is creating the programs (typically stored procedures or triggers) that send and receive the messages. Initiating and target service applications obviously differ in that only the initiating service needs to begin a conversation, but otherwise the tasks that they need to perform are similar.

Initiating a Conversation

The first task in a conversation is for the initiating service to open up a dialog using the BEGIN DIALOG CONVERSATION command. This takes a local variable of type UNIQUEIDENTIFIER that will be populated with a handle we can use to identify the new conversation; we use this when we actually send a message on the conversation. BEGIN DIALOG CONVERSATION has three mandatory clauses:

- FROM SERVICE: The SQL Server identifier for the initiator service. Note that this is *not* surrounded by quotes.
- TO SERVICE: The name of the receiving service, as a string.
- ON CONTRACT: The SQL Server identifier for the contract that binds the two services.

Optionally, we can also specify that this conversation will belong to an existing conversation group. To associate a new dialog with an existing conversation group, we can supply either the ID for that group or the ID for another conversation in the group:

```
BEGIN DIALOG CONVERSATION @dialogHandle
    FROM SERVICE initiating_service
    TO SERVICE receiving_service
    ON CONTRACT contract_name
    WITH RELATED_CONVERSATION = conversation_ID
```

or

```
    ...
    WITH RELATED_CONVERSATION_GROUP = conversation_group_ID
```

There are two other pieces of information we can include in the WITH clause. We can specify a LIFETIME timeout period, after which the conversation will be closed, and we can include an ENCRYPTION option to state whether the message must be encrypted. By default, this is ON, which means that an error will occur if encryption isn't correctly configured. If it is OFF, encryption will still be used if configured, but otherwise the messages will be sent unencrypted. Messages sent to another service in the same SQL Service instance are never encrypted.

Sending Messages to a Queue

Once our conversation dialog is open, we can start to send messages to the queue. To do this, we use the SEND command:

```
SEND
    ON CONVERSATION dialog_handle
    MESSAGE TYPE message_type_name
    (message_body)
```

The dialog handle will be the variable that we received from the BEGIN DIALOG CONVERSATION command or from a RECEIVE command that was used to retrieve messages from a queue. Both the message_type_name and the message_body can be omitted. The former can be omitted if the message is of the default type (requiring no validation); the message_body should be omitted if the message type is EMPTY. Otherwise, the message body is enclosed in parentheses, and it can contain any data, including binary data.

Retrieving Messages from a Queue

To retrieve a message from a queue, we use the RECEIVE statement:

```
RECEIVE [TOP n]
  column_name [, ...]
  FROM queue_name
  INTO table_variable
  [WHERE conversation_handle = dialog_handle |
       conversation_group_id = conversation_group_id]
```

This retrieves the messages in the queue as rows into the supplied table variable. We can optionally limit the messages retrieved by specifying the maximum number of messages in the TOP clause and by restricting the messages returned to a specific conversation or conversation group.

The information about each message is contained in columns in the returned result set, and we specify the information we want to retrieve just as we do for a SELECT statement: by including the column names in the RECEIVE statement. The full list of columns in the result set returned from the RECEIVE command is shown in Table 12-1.

Table 12-1. *Columns Returned from the RECEIVE Command*

Column	Datatype	Description
status	tinyint	The status of the message. This will always be 0 for a message that has been retrieved. The full list of values is as follows: 0: Ready 1: Received message 2: Not yet complete 3: Retained sent message
queuing_order	bigint	The number of the message within the queue.
conversation_group_id	uniqueidentifier	The ID of the conversation group to which this message belongs.
conversation_handle	uniqueidentifier	The dialog handle for the conversation to which this message belongs.
message_sequence_number	bigint	The sequence number of the message within the conversation.
service_name	nvarchar(512)	The name of the conversation target service.
service_id	int	The ID of the conversation target service.
service_contract_name	nvarchar(256)	The name of the contract for the conversation.
service_contract_id	int	The ID of the contract for the conversation.
message_type_name	nvarchar(256)	The name of the message type for the message.
message_type_id	int	The ID of the message type for the message.
validation	nchar(2)	The type of validation used for the message. The possible values are as follows: E: Empty N: None X: XML
message_body	varbinary(MAX)	The body of the message.
message_id	uniqueidentifier	The ID of the message.

By default, the RECEIVE statement will return an empty result set if no messages are present in the queue. We can alter this behavior by wrapping the statement in a WAITFOR statement:

```
WAITFOR
(
    RECEIVE ...
) [, TIMEOUT timeout]
```

This causes the RECEIVE statement to wait for the timeout period (in milliseconds) until a message arrives; if the timeout period expires, an empty result set will be returned. To wait indefinitely, omit the TIMEOUT clause, or specify a value of –1.

Ending a Conversation

When your application wants to close the conversation, both sides should explicitly end the dialog:

```
END CONVERSATION dialog_handle
    [WITH ERROR = error_code DESCRIPTION = error_description]
    [WITH CLEANUP]
```

Use the WITH ERROR clause if you want to throw an error, passing in an error code (of type int) and description (of type nvarchar(3000)). This will cause Service Broker to send an Error message to the queue, which can then be handled by the other participant in the conversation. If the END CONVERSATION command is issued without a WITH ERROR clause, Service Broker places an End Dialog message on the queue to inform the remote service that the conversation is closed. However, the remote application still needs to end its side of the conversation. Once it has done this, Service Broker will remove all messages belonging to this conversation from the queue.

The WITH CLEANUP clause is used to remove any messages from a queue when it isn't possible to end the conversation normally, usually because the remote service isn't available. If the conversation is ended WITH CLEANUP, the remote service isn't informed that the conversation is ending.

Conversation Timeouts

We stated earlier in the chapter that a Service Broker application can issue one conversation timer per dialog, which will cause Service Broker to place a Dialog Timer message in the queue after a specific timeout period has elapsed. To do this, we use the BEGIN CONVERSATION TIMER command:

```
BEGIN CONVERSATION TIMER(dialog_handle)
    TIMEOUT = timeout
```

Here, dialog_handle is the ID for the conversation that the timer will be placed on, and timeout is timeout period in seconds, after which the message will be placed in the queue.

A Simple Service Broker Example

The easiest way to see how these components relate to each other is to walk through an example. To demonstrate the concepts, we'll start with a very simple example. We use only one database, although Service Broker has been designed to aid asynchronous communications distributed across multiple databases. Our Service Broker application will process vacation requests from employees. Employees will call a stored procedure, passing in their employee ID number, their e-mail address, the number of hours of vacation they want to take, and the start time and date they plan to take the vacation. This will send a message to a specially created queue. When this message is processed, we will merely perform some rudimentary validation and then use Database Mail (which itself uses Service Broker) to send an e-mail to the employee, indicating whether or not the request was successful.

Our Service Broker application will have the following components:

- A MESSAGE TYPE to represent the XML-formatted messages that will be stored on our queue.

- An XML SCHEMA COLLECTION that will be used to validate messages as they arrive on the queue.

- A QUEUE to store the vacation requests before they are processed.

- A CONTRACT to define the message types that can be stored on the queue and the services that can send messages to the queue.

- One SERVICE that acts as the endpoint that initiates a conversation by sending a message to a queue and another that acts as the endpoint for retrieving messages from the queue.

- A stored procedure that will be called by an end user (or, more likely, an application) to make a vacation request.

- Another stored procedure for processing messages on the queue; this will be called automatically by Service Broker whenever messages arrive on the queue.

Before we create these objects, we need to enable Service Broker in the AdventureWorks database:

```
ALTER DATABASE AdventureWorks SET ENABLE_BROKER;
```

We then have to create a master key for the AdventureWorks database, which Service Broker will use as the session key for the conversation:

```
CREATE MASTER KEY
ENCRYPTION BY PASSWORD = 'sl38!Gk$^&wMv';
```

Next, we need to create the schema that we will use to validate the holiday requests:

```
CREATE XML SCHEMA COLLECTION
[http://schemas.apress.com/prosqlserver/HolidayRequestSchema]
AS N'<?xml version="1.0" ?>
<xs:schema xmlns:xs="http://www.w3.org/2001/XMLSchema">
   <xs:element name="vacationRequest">
      <xs:complexType>
         <xs:sequence minOccurs="1" maxOccurs="1">
            <xs:element name="employeeId" type="xs:integer" />
            <xs:element name="email" type="xs:string" />
            <xs:element name="startTime" type="xs:dateTime" />
            <xs:element name="hours" type="xs:integer" />
         </xs:sequence>
      </xs:complexType>
   </xs:element>
</xs:schema>';
```

Note that, as its name suggests, an XML SCHEMA COLLECTION can hold more than one schema, so we can validate an XML document against multiple schemas in one go. In this case, however, we just need to ensure that our messages meet the simple criteria laid out in this single schema. Also notice that, following Microsoft's practice, we've named the schema using a Uniform Resource Name (URN).

This schema specifies that each message will consist of a root element called <vacationRequest>, which contains one instance each of the child elements <employeeId>, <email>, <startTime>, and <hours>. For example, the following message requests one day's vacation (8 hours) starting on July 26, 2004, for the employee with an ID of 140 and e-mail address of laura1@adventure-works.com:

```
<?xml version="1.0" encoding="utf-16"?>
<vacationRequest>
    <employeeId>140</employeeId>
    <email>laura1@adventure-works.com</email>
    <startTime>2004-08-01T09:00:00+00:00</startTime>
    <hours>8</hours>
</vacationRequest>
```

Now we can create a MESSAGE TYPE object from this schema collection:

```
CREATE MESSAGE TYPE [http://schemas.apress.com/prosqlserver/HolidayRequest]
VALIDATION = VALID_XML WITH SCHEMA COLLECTION
   [http://schemas.apress.com/prosqlserver/HolidayRequestSchema];
```

We want validation to occur against our schema, so we set the VALIDATION to VALID_XML WITH SCHEMA COLLECTION, passing in the name of the XML SCHEMA COLLECTION that we've just created.

Next, we define the contract for the conversations that will take place between our initiating service and receiving service:

```
CREATE CONTRACT [http://schemas.apress.com/prosqlserver/HolidayRequestContract]
(
   [http://schemas.apress.com/prosqlserver/HolidayRequest]
   SENT BY INITIATOR
);
```

This contract stipulates that only the initiating service will be sending messages to the queue and that it will only send messages of our HolidayRequest type.

Receiving Service

Now we need to define the two services that will be used to send and process the messages. First, we'll create a stored procedure to handle any messages that are sent to the queue. Once we have the message, we'll just close the conversation, as we don't want to send any information back to the initiating service.

As stated at the outset, the processing we'll perform is minimal; we'll simply check whether the employee has enough hours of vacation entitlement left (assuming an annual entitlement of 20 days or 160 hours, which we just made up for the purposes of this example), and that the employee has given enough notice (at least one week in advance of the desired vacation start date). We then e-mail the employee, either stating that the request has been granted or giving the reason for rejecting it.

```
CREATE PROCEDURE usp_ProcessHolidayRequest
AS
DECLARE @msgBody    XML(
  [http://schemas.apress.com/prosqlserver/HolidayRequestSchema]),
        @convID     uniqueidentifier,
        @email      varchar(50),
        @employeeID int,
        @hours      int,
        @startTime  DateTime,
        @hoursTaken int,
        @msgType    nvarchar(256);
```

```
DECLARE @msgTable TABLE
(
    message_body         varbinary(max),
    conversation_handle uniqueidentifier,
    message_type_name    nvarchar(256)
);
BEGIN
    WAITFOR
    (
        RECEIVE TOP (1) message_body, conversation_handle, message_type_name
        FROM HolidayRequestQueue
        INTO @msgTable
    ), TIMEOUT 2000;

    SET @msgBody = (SELECT TOP (1) CAST(message_body AS XML) FROM @msgTable);
    SET @convID = (SELECT TOP (1) conversation_handle FROM @msgTable);
    SET @msgType = (SELECT TOP (1) message_type_name FROM @msgTable);
    END CONVERSATION @convID;

    IF @msgType = 'http://schemas.apress.com/prosqlserver/HolidayRequest'
        BEGIN
            SET @email = @msgBody.value('data(//email)[1]', 'varchar(50)');
            SET @hours = @msgBody.value('data(//hours)[1]', 'int');
            SET @startTime = @msgBody.value('data(//startTime)[1]', 'datetime');
            SET @employeeID = @msgBody.value('data(//employeeId)[1]', 'int');
            SET @hoursTaken = (SELECT VacationHours FROM HumanResources.Employee
                                WHERE EmployeeID = @employeeID);

            IF @hoursTaken + @hours > 160
                EXEC msdb.dbo.sp_send_dbmail
                    @profile_name = 'Default Profile',
                    @recipients = @email,
                    @subject = 'Vacation request',
                    @body = 'Your request for vacation has been refused because you
have insufficient hours remaining of your holiday entitlement.';
            ELSE IF @startTime < DATEADD(Week, 1, GETDATE())
                EXEC msdb.dbo.sp_send_dbmail
                    @profile_name = 'Default Profile',
                    @recipients = @email,
                    @subject = 'Vacation request',
                    @body = 'Your request for vacation has been refused because you
have not given sufficient notice. Please request holiday at least a week in
advance.';
            ELSE
                BEGIN
                    UPDATE HumanResources.Employee
                        SET VacationHours = VacationHours + @hours;
                    EXEC msdb.dbo.sp_send_dbmail
                        @profile_name = 'Default Profile',
                        @recipients = @email,
                        @subject = 'Vacation request',
                        @body = 'Your request for vacation has been granted.';
                END
        END
END
```

The first task here is to retrieve the message from the queue, which we do with a RECEIVE statement:

```
WAITFOR (
        RECEIVE TOP (1) message_body, conversation_handle, message_type_name
        FROM HolidayRequestQueue
        INTO @msgTable
), TIMEOUT 2000;
```

Note that we wrap the RECEIVE statement in a WAITFOR statement to ensure that the procedure will wait for the specified TIMEOUT value (in milliseconds, so two seconds in this case) for a message to arrive. Our RECEIVE clause retrieves the body and type of the first message in the queue and the ID of the conversation it belongs to into a table variable called @msgTable.

Once we have the message shredded into a table variable, we can extract the message body from it and cast it to the XML datatype, and we can also retrieve the message type to ensure we have the right sort of message, and the dialog handle, which we need to close the conversation:

```
SET @msgBody = (SELECT TOP (1) CAST(message_body AS XML) FROM @msgTable);
SET @convID = (SELECT TOP (1) conversation_handle FROM @msgTable);
SET @msgType = (SELECT TOP (1) message_type_name FROM @msgTable);
END CONVERSATION @convID;
```

Then we check that the message is of the correct type. If so, we use XQuery and the value() method of the XML datatype to extract the individual values (the employee's ID and e-mail address, and the start time and duration of the planned vacation) into local variables.

Next, we query the HumanResources.Employee table to see how many hours of vacation the employee has already taken, and we perform checks to determine whether or not to grant the vacation. If the vacation is granted, we update the VacationHours of that employee and e-mail the employee to confirm we're granting the request; otherwise, we just e-mail the employee stating the reason why we're refusing the request.

■**Note** Database Mail must be enabled, or this procedure won't compile. See Chapter 13 for information about installing Database Mail.

Once we've defined the message type for our service and the stored procedure that will process the messages, we can create the queue to hold the messages:

```
CREATE QUEUE HolidayRequestQueue
WITH
    STATUS = ON,
    RETENTION = OFF,
    ACTIVATION
    (
        STATUS = ON,
        PROCEDURE_NAME = usp_ProcessHolidayRequest,
        MAX_QUEUE_READERS = 5,
        EXECUTE AS SELF
    );
```

We set the queue to activate immediately and not to retain messages when they are retrieved by our stored procedure. The ACTIVATION clause ensures that our service program will execute whenever a message is sent to the queue.

We're now ready to create the service itself:

```
CREATE SERVICE
        [http://schemas.apress.com/prosqlserver/HolidayRequestProcessorService]
ON QUEUE HolidayRequestQueue
(
    [http://schemas.apress.com/prosqlserver/HolidayRequestContract]
);
```

The service simply acts as a link between the queue and one or more contracts, so no new information is introduced here and the syntax is self-explanatory.

Initiating Service

We've now done everything we have to do to process messages in our queue, but as yet we don't have any way to send messages to it. To do this, we need to create another service and a procedure that initiates a dialog and sends a message to the queue when an employee requests a vacation.

First the service. The code to create the initiator service is identical (except for the name) to the code for the processor service:

```
CREATE SERVICE
    [http://schemas.apress.com/prosqlserver/HolidayRequestInitiatorService]
ON QUEUE HolidayRequestQueue
(
    [http://schemas.apress.com/prosqlserver/HolidayRequestContract]
);
```

Again, we're simply associating the HolidayRequestContract with our queue.

Our last task is to create the stored procedure that will send a message to the queue:

```
CREATE PROCEDURE usp_RequestHoliday
    @employeeId int,
    @email varchar(50),
    @hours int,
    @startDate varchar(50)
AS
DECLARE @dialogHandle uniqueidentifier,
        @body           nvarchar(1000),
        @msg            XML,
        @date           nvarchar(100)
BEGIN
    SET @body = N'<?xml version="1.0"?>
<vacationRequest>
    <employeeId>' + CAST(@employeeID AS varchar) + '</employeeId>
    <email>' + @email + '</email>
    <startTime>' + @startDate + '</startTime>
    <hours>' + CAST(@hours AS nvarchar) + '</hours>
</vacationRequest>';
    SET @msg = CAST(@body AS XML)

    BEGIN DIALOG CONVERSATION @dialogHandle
        FROM SERVICE
          [http://schemas.apress.com/prosqlserver/HolidayRequestInitiatorService]
        TO SERVICE
          'http://schemas.apress.com/prosqlserver/HolidayRequestProcessorService'
        ON CONTRACT
          [http://schemas.apress.com/prosqlserver/HolidayRequestContract];
```

```
SEND ON CONVERSATION @dialogHandle
  MESSAGE TYPE [http://schemas.apress.com/prosqlserver/HolidayRequest]
  (@msg);
END CONVERSATION @dialogHandle;
END
```

This procedure takes four parameters—the information that we'll pass into the message. We use this information to build an XML document that conforms to the schema we specified for our message type as nvarchar, and then cast this to the XML datatype.

Now we're ready to start the conversation. To do this, we use the BEGIN DIALOG [CONVERSATION] statement, specifying the initiating and target services and the contract, and retaining a reference to the ID for the conversation. We use this ID to send a message to the remote service, specifying our HolidayRequest message type and passing in the XML-typed variable that contains the body of the message. Once we've sent this, our sproc has done its work, so we just close the conversation.

This completes our simple Service Broker example. To test it, execute this stored procedure, for example:

```
EXEC usp_RequestHoliday 140, 'someone@somewhere.com', 8,
                  '2004-08-01T09:00:00+00:00'
```

Note that, to make testing much easier, the e-mail address is passed in separately, instead of being looked up in the database. This means you can supply your own e-mail address instead of using the one that corresponds to the EmployeeID you pass in. Also, note that the start date is passed in as a string in XSD dateTime format (i.e., 'yyyy-mm-ddThh:mm:ss+timezone offset').

Service Broker Routing and Security

Although we demonstrated the fundamental concepts of Service Broker using a single database on a single instance of SQL Server, Service Broker is designed to be able to communicate between different instances. At this point, security also becomes an issue, because we need to ensure that we can authenticate users from another instance of SQL Server. And since we're possibly transferring sensitive data over the network, the data sent between the two services may need to be encrypted.

Creating Distributed Service Broker Applications

There are three extra things we need to do to create a secure distributed Service Broker application:

- Create a Service Broker endpoint in each instance to allow Service Broker to listen for incoming messages and send messages outside the instance.

- Create a route to tell Service Broker where to find the remote service.

- Create a Remote Service Binding to provide the security credentials that the initiating service will provide so that the remote service can authenticate it.

We'll also need to create certificates and database master keys in order to provide the credentials that will be used for authentication to the remote service and for encryption of the messages sent over the network. Service Broker distinguished between two types of security: *transport security*, which is used to specify which Service Broker instances can communicate with each other, and *dialog security*, which is used to encrypt messages in a conversation and operates at the user level. The type of transport security we use is specified when we create the Service Broker endpoint, while dialog security is configured using Remote Service Bindings.

Creating a Service Broker Endpoint

The syntax for creating a Service Broker endpoint is as follows:

```
CREATE ENDPOINT endpoint_name
STATE = STARTED | STOPPED | DISABLED
AS TCP
(
   LISTENER_PORT = port_number,
   LISTENER_IP = ALL | (ip_address)
)
FOR SERVICE_BROKER
(
   AUTHENTICATION = authentication_options,
   ENCRYPTION = DISABLED | SUPPORTED | REQUIRED
      ALGORITH algorithm,
   MESSAGE_FORWARDING = ENABLED | DISABLED,
   MESSAGE_FORWARD_SIZE = forward_size
)
```

All the Service Broker subclauses are optional, as is the LISTENER_IP subclause. If this subclause is omitted, Service Broker will listen on all available IP addresses; if an IP address is given, it can be either a traditional four-part IP address, or an IPv6 address. The default TCP port for Service Broker is 4022.

The AUTHENTICATION subclause allows you to specify whether to use Windows authentication (the default) or a named certificate to provide credentials to the remote service. It takes the following form:

```
AUTHENTICATION = WINDOWS [NTLM | KERBEROS | NEGOTIATE] |
                CERTIFICATE cert_name |
                WINDOWS [NTLM | KERBEROS | NEGOTIATE] CERTIFICATE cert_name |
                CERTIFICATE cert_name WINDOWS [NTLM | KERBEROS | NEGOTIATE]
```

If you choose Windows authentication, you can also specify whether to use the NTLM or KERBEROS protocol, or let Windows NEGOTIATE which protocol to use. The default is NEGOTIATE. If you use a named certificate, that certificate must be a valid certificate in the master database, it must be signed with the database master key, and the current date must be between its start and expiration dates. If both Windows and a certificate are specified, Service Broker will attempt to use the first authentication method in the list, and if that fails, it will try the second one.

The ENCRYPTION options are fairly self-explanatory. If it's DISABLED, Service Broker will never encrypt dialogs; if it's REQUIRED, dialogs will always be encrypted; and if it's SUPPORTED, dialogs will be encrypted only when the remote endpoint supports encryption. If encryption is used, a Remote Service Binding *must* exist in the database for the remote service, or the dialog will fail.

If you're using encryption, you can also specify the algorithm(s) that will be supported. This can be one of the following:

- RC4 (the default)
- AES
- RC4 AES
- AES RC4

As with the authentication options, if two algorithms are listed, preference will be given to the one listed first.

Finally, you can also specify whether or not Service Broker will forward on messages received by this endpoint to another address (MESSAGE_FORWARDING = ENABLED) or simply discard any messages it receives that are intended for another instance. If message forwarding is enabled, you can additionally specify the maximum space (in megabytes) that may be used to store messages for forwarding.

Creating Routes

Service Broker uses routes to determine where to send messages destined for a particular service that isn't hosted on the current instance of SQL Server. If the remote endpoint supports message forwarding, the route doesn't need to point to the actual destination—it can point simply to the next hop, and from there it will be forwarded using another route.

The syntax for creating a route is as follows:

```
CREATE ROUTE route_name
WITH
    SERVICE_NAME = remote_service_name,
    BROKER_INSTANCE = uniqueidentifier,
    LIFETIME = route_lifetime,
    ADDRESS = next_hop_address,
    MIRROR_ADDRESS = mirror_address
```

The only option that's actually required is the address for the next hop. This takes the form 'TCP://hostaddress:port', where hostaddress is the hostname, IP address, or NetBIOS name of the machine that hosts the remote Service Broker instance, and port is the TCP port number that the remote Service Broker endpoint is listening on. You can also specify 'LOCAL' for the local SQL Server instance or 'TRANSPORT' for an address specified in the name of the remote service. If 'TRANSPORT' is used, you cannot specify the service name or broker instance ID in the CREATE ROUTE command.

If the database that hosts the remote service is mirrored, you should also specify the MIRROR_ADDRESS, to ensure that messages will be sent to the mirror database if the other database can't be reached. If the MIRROR_ADDRESS is specified, you *must* include the service name and the broker instance ID.

The SERVICE_NAME is the name of the remote service that this route is used to send messages to. If included, this must be exactly the same as the name of the service in the remote database. However, it can also be omitted, in which case this route will match all services, but it will have a lower priority than routes that name a service, so it won't be used to send messages to a service that is explicitly associated with a specific route.

The BROKER_INSTANCE specifies the ID of the remote instance of Service Broker that this route points to. You can find this ID by running the following query in the remote database:

```
SELECT service_broker_guid
FROM sys.databases
WHERE database_id = DB_ID()
```

Finally, the LIFETIME clause allows you to stipulate the number of seconds that this route will remain active for. After this time has elapsed, SQL Server will discard the route. By default, routes never expire.

Creating Remote Service Bindings

The last new Service Broker object we need to look at is the Remote Service Binding, which contains the security credentials that Service Broker uses to connect to a remote service (Remote Service Bindings are never used to connect to a service in the local instance).

The syntax for the CREATE REMOTE SERVICE BINDING command is as follows:

```
CREATE REMOTE SERVICE BINDING binding_name
    TO SERVICE remote_service_name
    WITH USER = user_name, ANONYMOUS = ON | OFF
```

This creates a binding between the specified service and the given database user (or application role), so that whenever Service Broker connects to the service, it will exchange the session encryption key for the dialog using a certificate associated with the specified database principal.

The only optional part of this statement is the ANONYMOUS clause, which allows you to indicate whether Service Broker should connect to the remote service as the specified user (ANONYMOUS = OFF) or it should connect as a member of the public fixed server role. The default is OFF.

Distributed Service Broker Example

Now that you've seen how to create the new objects you'll need for dialog security and message routing, let's build a more complex application that uses these objects to communicate between services in separate instances of SQL Server on different machines. This example builds on the previous vacation request example, but as well as adding an extra service to demonstrate routing and dialog security, we'll also combine two conversations into a conversation group to show off this functionality too.

As in the previous example, the application will be started by calling a stored procedure within the AdventureWorks database that sends a message to a VacationRequestService including the ID and e-mail address of the employee, and the start time and number of hours of the planned vacation. This fires the service program stored procedure, which starts off two new Service Broker conversations: one to request the number of hours' leave remaining for that employee and another requesting the number of active projects that that employee will be working on over the period. This latter service is hosted in a Projects database, on another machine. These services send messages back to the processing service, and another stored procedure is run on the queue for this service to retrieve the response messages and as before send an e-mail to the employee, depending on the responses from the two services. Figure 12-2 shows the architecture for this application. (Admittedly, this is somewhat more complex than it really needs to be, but that's the only way to see more of Service Broker's functionality and to understand how services communicate with each other in more realistic scenarios.)

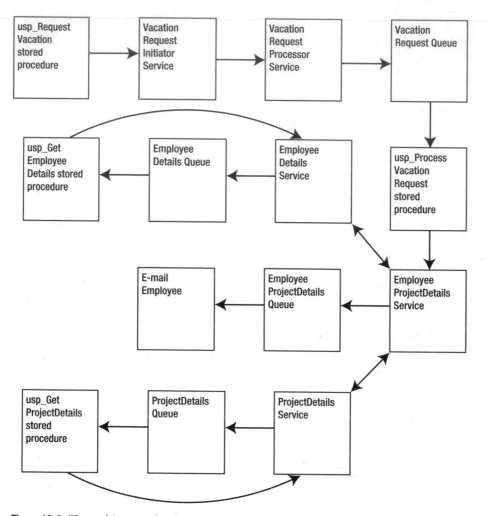

Figure 12-2. *The architecture for the distributed Service Broker example*

As our application will be distributed over two machines, we'll look at the objects that need to be created on each machine in turn. The majority of the objects will be in the instance that hosts the AdventureWorks database (in this case, this machine is called ecspi.julianskinner.local), so we'll look at the Projects database (on our example system, this is on a machine called peiriantprawf. julianskinner.local) before we tackle AdventureWorks. However, first we need to set up the Service Broker endpoints on the two machines.

Setting Up the Service Broker Endpoints

Before we create the Projects database, let's first create the Service Broker endpoint for the instance that will host this database. We'll use certificates to authenticate between the two instances, so before we do this, we need to create a certificate that's signed with the master key for the master database:

```
USE master
GO

CREATE MASTER KEY ENCRYPTION BY PASSWORD = 'gs53&"f"!385';
GO

CREATE CERTIFICATE projEndpointCert
WITH SUBJECT = 'peiriantprawf.julianskinner.local',
     START_DATE = '01/01/2005',
     EXPIRY_DATE = '01/01/2006'
ACTIVE FOR BEGIN_DIALOG = ON;
GO
```

When we create a new certificate without specifying a password or a file to take the key from, it will be signed with the database master key.

Now we can create the endpoint:

```
CREATE ENDPOINT ServiceBrokerEndpoint
   STATE = STARTED
   AS TCP (LISTENER_PORT = 4022)
   FOR SERVICE_BROKER
   (
      AUTHENTICATION = CERTIFICATE projEndpointCert,
      ENCRYPTION = SUPPORTED
   );
```

We start the endpoint listening right away using the STATE clause and use the default TCP port of 4022. If your machine has a firewall, you'll need to allow traffic through this port. We'll use the certificate we've just created to authenticate, and we'll support but not require encryption of the dialogs over this endpoint. We won't allow anonymous connections, so we don't include an ANONYMOUS subclause in the SERVICE_BROKER options.

In order for the two instances to authenticate each other, we need to install this certificate in the instance that hosts AdventureWorks and also create a certificate there that we install in the Projects instance. So first, we'll save the certificate we just created to a file so we can copy it to the AdventureWorks machine:

```
BACKUP CERTIFICATE projEndpointCert TO FILE =
        'C:\Apress\ProSqlServer\Chapter12\projEndpointCert.cer';
```

Now we'll copy this file to the AdventureWorks machine and install it into that instance of SQL Server:

```
USE master
GO

CREATE CERTIFICATE projEndpointCert
FROM FILE = 'C:\Apress\ProSqlServer\Chapter12\projEndpointCert.cer';
```

Next, we need to create the Service Broker endpoint for this instance:

```
CREATE MASTER KEY ENCRYPTION BY PASSWORD = '45Gme*3^&fwu';
GO
```

```
CREATE CERTIFICATE awEndpointCert
WITH SUBJECT = 'ecspi.julianskinner.local',
    START_DATE = '01/01/2005',
    EXPIRY_DATE = '01/01/2006'
ACTIVE FOR BEGIN_DIALOG = ON;
GO

CREATE ENDPOINT ServiceBrokerEndpoint
  STATE = STARTED
  AS TCP (LISTENER_PORT=4022)
  FOR SERVICE_BROKER
  (
    AUTHENTICATION = CERTIFICATE awEndpointCert,
    ENCRYPTION = SUPPORTED
  );
```

We can now grant permissions to the remote service to connect to this endpoint. To do this, we need to create a login from the certificate and then grant that login CONNECT permission on the endpoint:

```
CREATE LOGIN sbLogin
FROM CERTIFICATE projEndpointCert;
GO

GRANT CONNECT ON ENDPOINT::ServiceBrokerEndpoint TO sbLogin;
GO
```

We need to repeat these steps back in the Projects instance, so we'll back up this certificate to a file:

```
BACKUP CERTIFICATE awEndpointCert
TO FILE = 'C:\Apress\ProSqlServer\Chapter12\awEndpointCert.cer';
```

Then we'll copy the awEndpointCert.cer file generated over to the Projects machine, install it in SQL Server, create a login from the certificate, and grant it permission to connect to the Service Broker endpoint:

```
CREATE CERTIFICATE awEndpointCert
FROM FILE = 'C:\Apress\ProSqlServer\Chapter12\awEndpointCert.cer';
GO

CREATE LOGIN sbLogin
FROM CERTIFICATE awEndpointCert;
GO

GRANT CONNECT ON ENDPOINT::ServiceBrokerEndpoint
TO sbLogin;
GO
```

We now have certificates installed in both instances that allow the two Service Broker instances to authenticate each other, so they can make the initial connection. This provides transport security, but it doesn't yet allow messages to be sent with dialog security. To do this, we need to create yet more certificates—this time associated with database users—and again install these in both instances. We first need to create the Projects database, however.

The Projects Database and ProjectDetailsService

We've set up the endpoints, and now we can start to create the database-level objects. As mentioned earlier, there are far fewer objects we need to create in the Projects database, so we'll start there.

The Projects Database

The Projects database consists of three tables: a project table with columns for the project's name, start date, and end date; an employee table that contains the first and last names of the employee and the employee's e-mail address; and a projectemployee table that's used to join the other two tables in a many-to-many relationship. We'll also add one row to each table, so we have some data to play with. The e-mail address you use for the employee should be a real address you can receive mail with:

```
CREATE DATABASE Projects;
GO

USE Projects
GO

ALTER DATABASE Projects SET ENABLE_BROKER;
GO

CREATE TABLE Project
(
    ProjectID   int IDENTITY PRIMARY KEY,
    ProjectName nvarchar(100),
    StartDate   datetime,
    EndDate     datetime
);

CREATE TABLE Employee
(
    EmployeeID  int IDENTITY PRIMARY KEY,
    FirstName   nvarchar(256),
    LastName    nvarchar(256),
    Email       nvarchar(512)
);

CREATE TABLE ProjectEmployee
(
    ProjectID   int FOREIGN KEY REFERENCES Project(ProjectID),
    EmployeeID  int FOREIGN KEY REFERENCES Employee(EmployeeID)
);
GO

INSERT INTO Project VALUES ('Pro SQL Server 2005', '01/01/2005', '10/15/2005');
INSERT INTO Employee VALUES ('John', 'Doe', 'JohnDoe@apress.com');
INSERT INTO ProjectEmployee VALUES (1, 1);
GO
```

The ProjectDetailsService

Now we can start to create the ProjectDetailsService. First, we'll create the message types handled by this service and their associated schemas. There will be one message type for the request, which is basically very similar to the HolidayRequest type in the previous example, except that we don't include the EmployeeID, as the IDs in the Projects database are unrelated to those in AdventureWorks. The second message type is sent in response and will contain a <projectResponse> root element, under which will be an <activeProjects> element that will contain the number of projects the employee is working on over the time spanned by the planned vacation, as well as the e-mail address and the start time, which we return in the response so that the procedure that processes the responses has access to this data:

```
CREATE XML SCHEMA COLLECTION
    [http://schemas.apress.com/prosqlserver/ProjectRequestSchema]
AS N'<?xml version="1.0" ?>
<xs:schema xmlns:xs="http://www.w3.org/2001/XMLSchema">
   <xs:element name="projectRequest">
      <xs:complexType>
         <xs:sequence minOccurs="1" maxOccurs="1">
            <xs:element name="email" type="xs:string" />
            <xs:element name="startTime" type="xs:dateTime" />
            <xs:element name="hours" type="xs:integer" />
         </xs:sequence>
      </xs:complexType>
   </xs:element>
</xs:schema>';

CREATE XML SCHEMA COLLECTION
    [http://schemas.apress.com/prosqlserver/ProjectResponseSchema]
AS N'<?xml version="1.0" ?>
<xs:schema xmlns:xs="http://www.w3.org/2001/XMLSchema">
   <xs:element name="projectResponse">
      <xs:complexType>
         <xs:sequence minOccurs="1" maxOccurs="1">
            <xs:element name="email" type="xs:string" />
            <xs:element name="startTime" type="xs:dateTime" />
            <xs:element name="activeProjects" type="xs:integer" />
         </xs:sequence>
      </xs:complexType>
   </xs:element>
</xs:schema>';

CREATE MESSAGE TYPE
    [http://schemas.apress.com/prosqlserver/ProjectRequestMessage]
VALIDATION = VALID_XML WITH SCHEMA COLLECTION
    [http://schemas.apress.com/prosqlserver/ProjectRequestSchema];

CREATE MESSAGE TYPE
    [http://schemas.apress.com/prosqlserver/ProjectResponseMessage]
VALIDATION = VALID_XML WITH SCHEMA COLLECTION
    [http://schemas.apress.com/prosqlserver/ProjectResponseSchema];
```

Next, we'll create the contract for the service:

```
CREATE CONTRACT
    [http://schemas.apress.com/prosqlserver/ProjectServiceContract]
(
   [http://schemas.apress.com/prosqlserver/ProjectRequestMessage]
      SENT BY INITIATOR,
   [http://schemas.apress.com/prosqlserver/ProjectResponseMessage] SENT BY TARGET
);
```

   This stipulates that the only messages that can be sent on this conversation are the
ProjectRequestMessage, sent only by the initiator, and the ProjectReponseMessage, sent only by the
receiving service.
   The next task is to write the activation stored procedure, which will be called whenever a
message arrives on the queue:

```
CREATE PROCEDURE usp_GetProjectDetailsForEmployee
AS
DECLARE @msgBody      XML(
          [http://schemas.apress.com/prosqlserver/ProjectRequestSchema]),
       @convID        uniqueidentifier,
       @email         varchar(512),
       @hours         int,
       @startTime     datetime,
       @endTime       datetime,
       @projectCount  int,
       @response      XML(
          [http://schemas.apress.com/prosqlserver/ProjectResponseSchema]),
       @respText      nvarchar(1000),
       @msgType       nvarchar(256);

DECLARE @msgTable TABLE
(
   message_body        varbinary(max),
   conversation_handle uniqueidentifier,
   message_type_name   nvarchar(256)
);
BEGIN
   WAITFOR
   (
      RECEIVE TOP (1) message_body, conversation_handle, message_type_name
      FROM ProjectServiceQueue INTO @msgTable
   ), TIMEOUT 2000;

   SET @msgBody = (SELECT TOP (1) CAST(message_body AS XML) FROM @msgTable);
   SET @msgType = (SELECT TOP (1) message_type_name FROM @msgTable);
   SET @convID = (SELECT TOP (1) conversation_handle FROM @msgTable);
   IF @msgType = 'http://schemas.apress.com/prosqlserver/ProjectRequestMessage'
   BEGIN
      SET @email = @msgBody.value('data(//email)[1]', 'varchar(50)');
      SET @hours = @msgBody.value('data(//hours)[1]', 'int');
      SET @startTime = @msgBody.value('data(//startTime)[1]', 'datetime');
      SET @endTime = DATEADD(week, @hours/40, @startTime)

      SET @projectCount = (SELECT COUNT(*)
      FROM Project p
         INNER JOIN ProjectEmployee pe
         ON p.ProjectID = pe.ProjectID
            INNER JOIN Employee e
            ON pe.EmployeeID = e.EmployeeID
      WHERE e.Email = @email
        AND (p.StartDate < @startTime AND p.EndDate > @startTime)
         OR (p.StartDate < @endTime AND p.EndDate > @endTime)
         OR (p.StartDate > @startTime AND p.EndDate < @endTime));
```

```
        SET @respText = N'<?xml version="1.0"?>
<projectResponse>
   <email>' + @email + '</email>
   <startTime>' + CONVERT(nvarchar, @startTime, 126) + '+00:00</startTime>
   <activeProjects>' + CAST(@projectCount AS nvarchar) + '</activeProjects>
</projectResponse>';

        SET @response = CAST(@respText AS XML);
        SEND ON CONVERSATION @convID
            MESSAGE TYPE
                [http://schemas.apress.com/prosqlserver/ProjectResponseMessage]
            (@response);

        END CONVERSATION @convID;
    END;
END;
GO
```

This isn't too different from the activation stored procedure from the first example. We retrieve the body of the first message on the queue and the ID for the conversation it belongs to, read the data into variables and, if the message is of the correct type, use this to work out how many projects that employee will be working on at that time (using the e-mail address to identify the employee). Once we have that, we embed it in a ProjectDetailsResponseMessage and send the data back to the initiator service on the same conversation. Finally, we end the dialog.

Note that, because of an apparent bug in the current version of SQL Server at the time of writing, we hard-code the timezone offset (+00:00 for GMT) into the string when we convert the start time into character data. The format designated by the number 126 (yyyy-mm-ddThh:mm:ss.mmm) used with the CONVERT function is designed specifically for XML dates, but doesn't include the timezone offset in the required format.

Once we have the activation sproc, we can create the queue and the service:

```
CREATE QUEUE ProjectServiceQueue
WITH
    STATUS = ON,
    RETENTION = OFF,
    ACTIVATION
    (
        STATUS = ON,
        PROCEDURE_NAME = usp_GetProjectDetailsForEmployee,
        MAX_QUEUE_READERS = 5,
        EXECUTE AS SELF
    )

CREATE SERVICE [http://schemas.apress.com/prosqlserver/ProjectDetailsService]
ON QUEUE ProjectServiceQueue
(
    [http://schemas.apress.com/prosqlserver/ProjectServiceContract]
);
```

Next, we need to create a route, so that Service Broker knows where to find the initiating service to send replies to:

```
CREATE ROUTE EmployeeProjectDetailsRoute
WITH
   SERVICE_NAME =
      'http://schemas.apress.com/prosqlserver/EmployeeProjectDetailsService',
   ADDRESS = 'TCP://ecspi:4022';
GO
```

This associates the name of the remote service—this must be exactly the same as its name in the AdventureWorks database (service names are case sensitive)—with a TCP address, including the name or IP address of the host machine and the port that the SQL Server endpoint for the instance is configured to listen on. For both instances, we use the default port 4022.

That almost ties up our work on this instance of SQL Server, except for the little matter of dialog security, which we'll address shortly.

The AdventureWorks Side of the Conversation

We'll look at creating the EmployeeProjectDetailsService that initiates the conversation with the ProjectDetailsService later, but for now there are a couple of objects we need to create in the AdventureWorks database for our two services to be able to talk to each other.

First, we need to create the message types and contract for the conversation in the AdventureWorks database, using exactly the same code as for the Projects database. It's important that the names of these objects are exactly the same in both databases, or the messages won't be sent to the queue.

Next, we create the route so this instance of Service Broker will be able to find the ProjectDetailsService. The code for this is very similar to the code for the route we just created in the Projects database:

```
CREATE ROUTE ProjectDetailsRoute
WITH
   SERVICE_NAME =
               'http://schemas.apress.com/prosqlserver/ProjectDetailsService',
   ADDRESS = 'TCP://peiriantprawf:4022';
GO
```

The EmployeeDetailsService

Next let's turn our attention to the EmployeeDetailsService. The conversation architecture for this service is similar to that for the ProjectDetailsProcessorService, except that here both initiating and target services will be in the same database. Our application will send an EmployeeRequestMessage giving an employee ID and the number of hours requested, and the service will return an EmployeeResponseMessage indicating the total number of hours' vacation that employee will have taken if it's granted.

We'll start by creating the message types and associated XML schemas:

```
USE AdventureWorks
GO

CREATE XML SCHEMA COLLECTION
    [http://schemas.apress.com/prosqlserver/EmployeeRequestSchema]
AS N'<?xml version="1.0" ?>
<xs:schema xmlns:xs="http://www.w3.org/2001/XMLSchema">
   <xs:element name="employeeRequest">
      <xs:complexType>
         <xs:sequence minOccurs="1" maxOccurs="1">
            <xs:element name="id" type="xs:integer" />
            <xs:element name="hours" type="xs:integer" />
         </xs:sequence>
      </xs:complexType>
   </xs:element>
</xs:schema>';

CREATE XML SCHEMA COLLECTION
    [http://schemas.apress.com/prosqlserver/EmployeeResponseSchema]
AS N'<?xml version="1.0" ?>
<xs:schema xmlns:xs="http://www.w3.org/2001/XMLSchema">
   <xs:element name="employeeResponse">
      <xs:complexType>
         <xs:sequence minOccurs="1" maxOccurs="1">
            <xs:element name="id" type="xs:integer" />
            <xs:element name="hoursVacation" type="xs:integer" />
         </xs:sequence>
      </xs:complexType>
   </xs:element>
</xs:schema>';

CREATE MESSAGE TYPE
    [http://schemas.apress.com/prosqlserver/EmployeeRequestMessage]
VALIDATION = VALID_XML WITH SCHEMA COLLECTION
    [http://schemas.apress.com/prosqlserver/EmployeeRequestSchema];

CREATE MESSAGE TYPE
    [http://schemas.apress.com/prosqlserver/EmployeeResponseMessage]
VALIDATION = VALID_XML WITH SCHEMA COLLECTION
    [http://schemas.apress.com/prosqlserver/EmployeeResponseSchema];
```

The contract that conversations on this service will follow looks like this:

```
CREATE CONTRACT
    [http://schemas.apress.com/prosqlserver/EmployeeServiceContract]
(
   [http://schemas.apress.com/prosqlserver/EmployeeRequestMessage]
        SENT BY INITIATOR,
   [http://schemas.apress.com/prosqlserver/EmployeeResponseMessage]
        SENT BY TARGET
);
```

The activation stored procedure for this service simply takes the employee ID from the top message in the queue and uses this to find the number of hours vacation taken by that employee.

We then add this value to the number of hours of vacation request, wrap up the total in an EmployeeResponseMessage together with the employee's ID, and send it back to the initiating service:

```
CREATE PROCEDURE usp_GetHoursVacation
AS
DECLARE @msgBody      XML(
            [http://schemas.apress.com/prosqlserver/EmployeeRequestSchema]),
        @response     XML(
            [http://schemas.apress.com/prosqlserver/EmployeeResponseSchema]),
        @convID       uniqueidentifier,
        @empID        int,
        @hours        int,
        @hoursTaken   int,
        @totalHours   int,
        @msgType      nvarchar(256),
        @respText     nvarchar(1000);

DECLARE @msgTable TABLE
(
    message_body        varbinary(max),
    conversation_handle uniqueidentifier,
    message_type_name   nvarchar(256)
);
BEGIN
    WAITFOR
    (
        RECEIVE TOP (1) message_body, conversation_handle, message_type_name
        FROM EmployeeDetailsQueue INTO @msgTable
    ), TIMEOUT 2000;

    SET @msgBody = (SELECT TOP (1) CAST(message_body AS XML) FROM @msgTable);
    SET @convID = (SELECT TOP (1) conversation_handle FROM @msgTable);
    SET @msgType = (SELECT TOP (1) message_type_name FROM @msgTable);

    IF @msgType = 'http://schemas.apress.com/prosqlserver/EmployeeRequestMessage'
    BEGIN
        SET @empID = @msgBody.value('data(//id)[1]', 'int');
        SET @hours = @msgBody.value('data(//id)[1]', 'int');
        SET @hoursTaken = (SELECT VacationHours FROM HumanResources.Employee
                            WHERE EmployeeID = @empID);
        SET @totalHours = @hoursTaken + @hours;
        SET @respText = N'<?xml version="1.0"?>
<employeeResponse>
    <id>' + CAST(@empID AS nvarchar) + '</id>
    <hoursVacation>' + CAST(@totalHours AS nvarchar) + '</hoursVacation>
</employeeResponse>';

        SET @response = CAST(@respText AS XML);
        SEND ON CONVERSATION @convID
            MESSAGE TYPE
[http://schemas.apress.com/prosqlserver/EmployeeResponseMessage]
            (@response);
```

```
        END CONVERSATION @convID;
    END;
END;
GO
```

Finally, we can create the queue and the service:

```
CREATE QUEUE EmployeeDetailsQueue
WITH
    STATUS = ON,
    RETENTION = OFF,
    ACTIVATION
    (
        STATUS = ON,
        PROCEDURE_NAME = usp_GetHoursVacation,
        MAX_QUEUE_READERS = 5,
        EXECUTE AS SELF
    )

CREATE SERVICE [http://schemas.apress.com/prosqlserver/EmployeeDetailsService]
ON QUEUE EmployeeDetailsQueue
(
    [http://schemas.apress.com/prosqlserver/EmployeeServiceContract]
);
```

The Main Service Program

The next task is to write another service that will initiate conversations with these two services within a conversation group. This conversation is similar to the one in the first example in this chapter, so the message type, schema, and contract should look pretty familiar:

```
CREATE XML SCHEMA COLLECTION
     [http://schemas.apress.com/prosqlserver/VacationRequestSchema]
AS N'<?xml version="1.0" ?>
<xs:schema xmlns:xs="http://www.w3.org/2001/XMLSchema">
    <xs:element name="vacationRequest">
        <xs:complexType>
            <xs:sequence minOccurs="1" maxOccurs="1">
                <xs:element name="employeeId" type="xs:integer" />
                <xs:element name="email" type="xs:string" />
                <xs:element name="startTime" type="xs:dateTime" />
                <xs:element name="hours" type="xs:integer" />
            </xs:sequence>
        </xs:complexType>
    </xs:element>
</xs:schema>'

CREATE MESSAGE TYPE [http://schemas.apress.com/prosqlserver/VacationRequest]
VALIDATION = VALID_XML WITH SCHEMA COLLECTION
     [http://schemas.apress.com/prosqlserver/VacationRequestSchema]

CREATE CONTRACT [http://schemas.apress.com/prosqlserver/VacationRequestContract]
(
    [http://schemas.apress.com/prosqlserver/VacationRequest]
    SENT BY INITIATOR
)
GO
```

Then comes the activation stored procedure. Here we read the first message from the VacationRequestQueue and read the data in the message into local variables. We begin a new dialog with the EmployeeDetailsService and send a message including the employee ID and the number of hours of vacation request. We then open up another conversation within the same group to find out from the remote ProjectDetails service how many projects the employee will be working on during the vacation period. Including these two conversations in the same group ensures that Service Broker will match the two pieces of data for the same employee. As you've seen, these two services send response messages on the same conversations containing the data we asked for. These messages will be placed on the queue associated with the EmployeeProjectDetailsService and will be picked up later by another stored procedure. Therefore, we don't end the conversations at this time:

```
CREATE PROCEDURE usp_ProcessVacationRequest
AS
DECLARE @msgBody        XML(
            [http://schemas.apress.com/prosqlserver/VacationRequestSchema]),
        @empRequest     XML(
            [http://schemas.apress.com/prosqlserver/EmployeeRequestSchema]),
        @projRequest    XML(
            [http://schemas.apress.com/prosqlserver/ProjectRequestSchema]),
        @empRequestBody  nvarchar(1000),
        @projRequestBody nvarchar(1000),
        @msgType        nvarchar(256),
        @convID         uniqueidentifier,
        @empConvID      uniqueidentifier,
        @projConvID     uniqueidentifier,
        @email          varchar(50),
        @employeeID     int,
        @hours          int,
        @startTime      DateTime;

DECLARE @msgTable TABLE
(
    message_body          varbinary(max),
    conversation_handle   uniqueidentifier,
    message_type_name     nvarchar(256)
);

BEGIN
    WAITFOR
    (
        RECEIVE TOP (1) message_body, conversation_handle, message_type_name
        FROM VacationRequestQueue INTO @msgTable
    ), TIMEOUT 2000;

    SET @msgBody = (SELECT TOP (1) CAST(message_body AS XML) FROM @msgTable);
    SET @convID = (SELECT TOP (1) conversation_handle FROM @msgTable);
    SET @msgType = (SELECT TOP (1) message_type_name FROM @msgTable);
    END CONVERSATION @convID;

    IF @msgType = 'http://schemas.apress.com/prosqlserver/VacationRequest'
    BEGIN
        SET @email = @msgBody.value('data(//email)[1]', 'varchar(50)');
        SET @hours = @msgBody.value('data(//hours)[1]', 'int');
        SET @startTime = @msgBody.value('data(//startTime)[1]', 'datetime');
        SET @employeeID = @msgBody.value('data(//employeeId)[1]', 'int');
```

```
        SET @empRequestBody = N'<?xml version="1.0"?><employeeRequest>
    <id>' + CAST(@employeeID AS varchar) + '</id>
    <hours>' + CAST(@hours AS varchar) + '</hours>
</employeeRequest>';
        SET @empRequest = CAST(@empRequestBody AS XML)

        SET @projRequestBody = N'<projectRequest>
    <email>' + @email + '</email>
    <startTime>' + CONVERT(nvarchar, @startTime, 126) + '+00:00</startTime>
    <hours>' + CAST(@hours AS varchar) + '</hours>
</projectRequest>';
        SET @projRequest = CAST(@projRequestBody AS XML)

        BEGIN DIALOG CONVERSATION @empConvID
            FROM SERVICE
              [http://schemas.apress.com/prosqlserver/EmployeeProjectDetailsService]
            TO SERVICE
              'http://schemas.apress.com/prosqlserver/EmployeeDetailsService'
            ON CONTRACT
              [http://schemas.apress.com/prosqlserver/EmployeeServiceContract];

        SEND ON CONVERSATION @empConvID
            MESSAGE TYPE
                [http://schemas.apress.com/prosqlserver/EmployeeRequestMessage]
            (@empRequest);

        BEGIN DIALOG CONVERSATION @projConvID
            FROM SERVICE
              [http://schemas.apress.com/prosqlserver/EmployeeProjectDetailsService]
            TO SERVICE
              'http://schemas.apress.com/prosqlserver/ProjectDetailsService'
            ON CONTRACT
              [http://schemas.apress.com/prosqlserver/ProjectServiceContract]
            WITH RELATED_CONVERSATION = @empConvID, ENCRYPTION=OFF;

        SEND ON CONVERSATION @projConvID
            MESSAGE TYPE
                [http://schemas.apress.com/prosqlserver/ProjectRequestMessage]
            (@projRequest);
    END
END;
GO
```

We now create the EmployeeProjectDetailsService and its associated queue where the response messages will be sent:

```
CREATE QUEUE EmployeeProjectDetailsQueue
WITH STATUS = ON, RETENTION = OFF;

CREATE SERVICE
          [http://schemas.apress.com/prosqlserver/EmployeeProjectDetailsService]
ON QUEUE EmployeeProjectDetailsQueue
(
    [http://schemas.apress.com/prosqlserver/EmployeeServiceContract],
    [http://schemas.apress.com/prosqlserver/ProjectServiceContract]
);
```

We don't set an activation procedure for the queue because we'll pick up messages at set times. The service has two contracts, as it communicates with both the EmployeeDetailsService and the ProjectDetailsService.

We also need to create the queue that the initial message that makes the vacation request is sent to and the receiving service for this conversation:

```
CREATE QUEUE VacationRequestQueue
WITH
    STATUS = ON,
    RETENTION = OFF,
    ACTIVATION
    (
        STATUS = ON,
        PROCEDURE_NAME = usp_ProcessVacationRequest,
        MAX_QUEUE_READERS = 5,
        EXECUTE AS SELF
    );

CREATE SERVICE
    [http://schemas.apress.com/prosqlserver/VacationRequestProcessorService]
ON QUEUE VacationRequestQueue
(
    [http://schemas.apress.com/prosqlserver/VacationRequestContract]
);
GO
```

With that done, only a few tasks are left. We need to create procedure that will process the response messages sent to the EmployeeProjectDetailsQueue, and we need to set up dialog security so that our two databases know who they're talking to. Finally, we need to create the initiating service and the stored procedure that kicks the whole thing off.

Reading the Response Messages

The real processing for the example is performed in the usp_ReadResponseMessages stored procedure, which reads the messages in the EmployeeProjectDetailsQueue by conversation group, stores the data from these messages into local variables, determines whether to grant the vacation, and e-mails the employee with the verdict:

```
CREATE PROCEDURE usp_ReadResponseMessages
AS
DECLARE @empMsgBody   XML(
          [http://schemas.apress.com/prosqlserver/EmployeeResponseSchema]),
        @projMsgBody  XML(
          [http://schemas.apress.com/prosqlserver/ProjectResponseSchema]),
        @groupId      uniqueidentifier,
        @empConvId    uniqueidentifier,
        @projConvId   uniqueidentifier,
        @activeProj   int,
        @hours        int,
        @empId        int,
        @email        nvarchar(50),
        @startTime    datetime;
```

```
DECLARE @msgTable TABLE
(
    message_body         varbinary(max),
    message_type_name    nvarchar(256),
    conversation_handle  uniqueidentifier
);
BEGIN
    WAITFOR
    (
        GET CONVERSATION GROUP @groupID
        FROM EmployeeProjectDetailsQueue
    ), TIMEOUT 500;
    WHILE @groupID IS NOT NULL
    BEGIN
        WAITFOR
        (
            RECEIVE message_body, message_type_name, conversation_handle
            FROM EmployeeProjectDetailsQueue INTO @msgTable
        ), TIMEOUT 2000;

        IF (SELECT COUNT(*) FROM @msgTable) > 0
        BEGIN
            SET @empMsgBody = (SELECT TOP (1) CAST(message_body AS XML)
                FROM @msgTable
                WHERE message_type_name =
                    'http://schemas.apress.com/prosqlserver/EmployeeResponseMessage');
            SET @empConvID = (SELECT TOP (1) conversation_handle FROM @msgTable
                WHERE message_type_name =
                    'http://schemas.apress.com/prosqlserver/EmployeeResponseMessage');
            SET @hours = @empMsgBody.value('data(//hoursVacation)[1]', 'int');
            SET @empId = @empMsgBody.value('data(//id)[1]', 'int');

            SET @projMsgBody = (SELECT TOP (1) CAST(message_body AS XML)
                FROM @msgTable
                WHERE message_type_name =
                    'http://schemas.apress.com/prosqlserver/ProjectResponseMessage');
            SET @projConvID = (SELECT TOP (1) conversation_handle FROM @msgTable
                WHERE message_type_name =
                    'http://schemas.apress.com/prosqlserver/ProjectResponseMessage');
            SET @activeProj = @projMsgBody.value('data(//activeProjects)[1]',
                                                'int');
            SET @email = @projMsgBody.value('data(//email)[1]', 'varchar(50)');
            SET @startTime = @projMsgBody.value('data(//startTime)[1]', 'datetime');

            IF @hours > 160
                EXEC msdb.dbo.sp_send_dbmail
                    @profile_name = 'Default Profile',
                    @recipients = @email,
                    @subject = 'Vacation request',
                    @body = 'Your request for vacation has been refused because you
```

```
have insufficient hours remaining of your holiday entitlement.';
        ELSE IF @startTime < DATEADD(Week, 1, GETDATE())
          EXEC msdb.dbo.sp_send_dbmail
              @profile_name = 'Default Profile',
              @recipients = @email,
              @subject = 'Default Profile',
              @body = 'Your request for vacation has been refused because you
have not given sufficient notice. Please request holiday at least a week in
advance.';
        ELSE IF @activeProj > 1
          EXEC msdb.dbo.sp_send_dbmail
              @profile_name = 'Default Profile',
              @recipients = @email,
              @subject = 'Vacation request',
              @body = 'Your request for vacation has been refused because you
have too many active projects at that time.';
        ELSE
          BEGIN
              UPDATE HumanResources.Employee
                SET VacationHours = @hours
                WHERE EmployeeID = @empId;
              EXEC msdb.dbo.sp_send_dbmail
                @profile_name = 'Default Profile',
                @recipients = @email,
                @subject = 'Vacation request',
                @body = 'Your request for vacation has been granted.';
          END

      END CONVERSATION @empConvID;
      END CONVERSATION @projConvID;
    END;

    WAITFOR
    (
      GET CONVERSATION GROUP @groupID
      FROM EmployeeProjectDetailsQueue
    ), TIMEOUT 500;
  END;
END;
GO
```

We use a new command in this procedure, GET CONVERSATION GROUP, which populates a variable of type uniqueidentifier with the ID for the next available conversation group in the queue. Like RECEIVE, this command can be enclosed in a WAITFOR statement to wait for messages to be sent to the queue if none are already on it. We therefore start by calling GET CONVERSATION GROUP and iterating through the available conversation groups until this returns null. For each conversation group, we receive all available messages into a table variable. Note that the RECEIVE command retrieves messages from only one conversation group. Once we have retrieved the messages, we select the messages of the EmployeeResponseMessage and ProjectResponseMessage types (there should only be one each of these for each conversation group), store the data in these messages into local variables, make a decision based on these values whether or not to grant the vacation, and e-mail the result to the employee.

You would probably run this procedure at set times as a SQL Server Agent job, but for convenience we'll just run it manually to test the example.

Let's now proceed to set up dialog security.

Setting Up Dialog Security

The certificates that we created earlier exist at the server level and identify the two Service Brokers to each other, but they don't identify the users in the database, nor are they used to encrypt individual messages. To do that, we need to configure dialog security for our conversation.

Dialog security requires us to create a user in each database that corresponds to a user in the remote database. This user must have connect permission to the remote database, as well as send permission on the service. For our example, we'll connect as dbo in each case. This means that we need to create a user (which we'll call projUser) in the AdventureWorks database that represents dbo in the Projects database, and a user (called awUser) in the Projects database that represents dbo in AdventureWorks. These dbo users must be the owners of the services that participate in the conversation, and must own private keys. The corresponding remote users, projUser and awUser, must be the owners of certificates that correspond to these private keys, so that Service Broker can identify the certificate sent by the remote service with a local user. These users need to have send permission on the service and connect permission on the database that they belong to. Note that the activation stored procedures for a queue don't execute in the caller's context, so these remote users don't need permission to access data. Finally, we also need to create a Remote Service Binding in the initiating service to tell Service Broker which user to connect to the remote service as.

This process should become clearer as we walk through the steps needed to set up dialog security. To start with, we'll create a certificate for the dbo user in the Projects database and save that to file so we can install it into AdventureWorks. The certificate is not permitted to be password protected, so we'll encrypt it with the master key for the database (which we need to create in any case for dialog security to work):

```
USE Projects
GO

CREATE MASTER KEY ENCRYPTION BY PASSWORD = 'gs53&"f"!385';
GO

CREATE CERTIFICATE projUserCert
WITH SUBJECT = 'peiriantprawf.julianskinner.local',
     START_DATE = '01/01/2005',
     EXPIRY_DATE = '01/01/2006'
ACTIVE FOR BEGIN_DIALOG = ON;
GO

BACKUP CERTIFICATE projUserCert TO FILE =
          'C:\Apress\ProSqlServer\Chapter12\projUserCert.cer'
```

Next, we'll create the projUser user in the AdventureWorks database, install this certificate with that user as its owner (using the AUTHORIZATION clause to set the owner), and grant the user the necessary permissions. In this case, we've created the user from an existing login:

```
USE AdventureWorks
GO

CREATE USER projUser FOR LOGIN login_name;
GO
```

```
CREATE CERTIFICATE projUserCert
AUTHORIZATION projUser
FROM FILE = 'C:\Apress\ProSqlServer\Chapter12\projUserCert.cer';
GO

GRANT CONNECT TO projUser;
GRANT SEND ON
  SERVICE::[http://schemas.apress.com/prosqlserver/EmployeeProjectDetailsService]
TO projUser;
```

We also need to create a certificate to identify the dbo user in AdventureWorks, which will be associated with the awUser user in the Projects database, and save this to file so that it can be installed into Projects. The remote service needs to identify itself to the initiating service as the owner of that service (dbo in our case), so this user must own a certificate containing a private key in the AdventureWorks database that has a corresponding certificate in Projects. Again, we'll encrypt this with the master key for the database, so we need to create that first (obviously, don't include this step if you've already created a master key for the AdventureWorks database):

```
CREATE MASTER KEY ENCRYPTION BY PASSWORD = '45Gme*3^&fwu';
GO

CREATE CERTIFICATE awUserCert
WITH SUBJECT = 'ecspi.julianskinner.local',
    START_DATE = '01/01/2005',
    EXPIRY_DATE = '01/01/2006'

BACKUP CERTIFICATE awUserCert TO FILE =
        'C:\Apress\ProSqlServer\Chapter12\awUserCert.cer';
```

While we're in AdventureWorks, we also need to create a Remote Service Binding to tell Service Broker which user to connect as:

```
CREATE REMOTE SERVICE BINDING ProjectDetailsServiceBinding
TO SERVICE 'http://schemas.apress.com/prosqlserver/ProjectDetailsService'
WITH USER = projUser;
```

This tells Service Broker to identify itself to the ProjectDetailsService using the certificate owned by the projUser database user.

Finally, we need to create a new user in the Projects database to represent dbo in AdventureWorks, install the awUserCert certificate in the Projects database with our new user as its owner, and grant the user permissions to connect to the database and send messages to the ProjectDetailsService service. Again, we'll create the user from a preexisting login:

```
CREATE USER awUser FOR LOGIN login_name;
GO

CREATE CERTIFICATE awUserCert
AUTHORIZATION awUser
FROM FILE = 'C:\Apress\ProSqlServer\Chapter12\awUserCert.cer';
GO

GRANT CONNECT TO awUser;
GRANT SEND ON
  SERVICE::[http://schemas.apress.com/prosqlserver/ProjectDetailsService]
TO awUser;
GO
```

Note If the database user who owns the EmployeeProjectDetailsService already owns a certificate in the AdventureWorks database, that certificate may be sent to the ProjectDetailsService instead of the certificate we've just created. In that case, dialog security will fail, as the remote Service Broker instance won't recognize the certificate and thus won't be able to associate it with a user. To rectify this, either install any existing certificates in the Projects database or change their owner in the AdventureWorks database with the ALTER AUTHENTICATION statement.

The Initiator Service

The final tasks are to create the initiator service and the stored procedure that will send the initial message. In both cases, these are practically identical to the equivalent objects in the first example—only the names have changed:

```
CREATE SERVICE
    [http://schemas.apress.com/prosqlserver/VacationRequestInitiatorService]
ON QUEUE VacationRequestQueue
(
    [http://schemas.apress.com/prosqlserver/VacationRequestContract]
);
GO

CREATE PROCEDURE usp_RequestVacation
    @employeeId int,
    @email varchar(50),
    @hours int,
    @startDate varchar(50)
AS
DECLARE @dialogHandle uniqueidentifier,
        @body           nvarchar(1000),
        @msg            XML,
        @date           nvarchar(100)
BEGIN
    SET @body = N'<?xml version="1.0"?>
<vacationRequest>
    <employeeId>' + CAST(@employeeID AS varchar) + '</employeeId>
    <email>' + @email + '</email>
    <startTime>' + @startDate + '</startTime>
    <hours>' + CAST(@hours AS nvarchar) + '</hours>
</vacationRequest>';
    SET @msg = CAST(@body AS XML)

    BEGIN DIALOG CONVERSATION @dialogHandle
        FROM SERVICE
            [http://schemas.apress.com/prosqlserver/VacationRequestInitiatorService]
        TO SERVICE
            'http://schemas.apress.com/prosqlserver/VacationRequestProcessorService'
        ON CONTRACT
            [http://schemas.apress.com/prosqlserver/VacationRequestContract];

    SEND ON CONVERSATION @dialogHandle
        MESSAGE TYPE [http://schemas.apress.com/prosqlserver/VacationRequest]
        (@msg);
    END CONVERSATION @dialogHandle;
END;
```

We run the application by executing this stored procedure within the AdventureWorks database:

```
EXEC usp_RequestVacation 140, 'someone@somewhere.com', 8,
                    '2005-08-01T09:00:00+00:00'
```

The e-mail address we pass in should be the one entered into the `Employee` table of the Projects database.

After waiting a short while, we run the `usp_ReadResponseMessages` procedure to process the responses that should have been sent to the `EmployeeProjectDetailsQueue`:

```
EXEC usp_ReadResponseMessages
```

As before, the address we passed in should shortly receive an e-mail granting or denying the request.

Summary

In this chapter, we've taken a fairly superficial look at Service Broker (out of necessity). Service Broker is a complex new message queuing technology for SQL Server, and in the space of one chapter it's not possible to go into great depth. Instead, we've concentrated on the main elements of creating Service Broker applications, with a couple of reasonably practical examples to get you started with the technology as quickly as possible. In this chapter, we covered the following topics:

- What Service Broker is and situations it can be used in
- The Service Broker architecture and the new database objects for building Service Broker applications
- A simple, single-instance Service Broker application
- Service Broker routing and security
- A more complex, cross-instance Service Broker application

CHAPTER 13

■ ■ ■

Automation and Monitoring

SQL Server 2005 brings us advancements in many areas that will make the daily administration and maintenance of SQL Server much easier. In addition to these functional enhancements, moves have been made to address the plethora of concerns surrounding security. Features like SQL Server Agent aren't available after a default installation unless the system administrator explicitly asks the setup to start the service automatically. Even after the SQL Server Agent service is started, users who aren't system administrators will still not have access to SQL Agent unless they are associated with one of the new SQL Agent roles. Other features like Profiler have also made feature access enhancements. System administrators will be relieved to know that they no longer have to give sysadmin rights to developers to use the Profiler tool. By granting the ALTER TRACE permission, users can now create and replay trace files These are just a few of the many changes and enhancements made to SQL Server in this latest version. This chapter will explore the following automation and monitoring enhancements:

- *SQL Server Agent*: The task scheduling service used by SQL Server to execute a variety of jobs, including T-SQL, replication, and maintenance tasks. This service is also used in multiserver administration as well as monitoring and responding to events such as SQL Server alerts, performance conditions, and WMI events.

- *Maintenance Plan feature*: This is a brand new feature in SQL Server 2005 that replaces the Database Maintenance Wizard of SQL Server 2000. Not only is the wizard replaced, but you'll find the ability to create a powerful custom workflow that can handle almost any T-SQL-based maintenance scenario.

- SQLCMD: Short for *SQL Command*, this is a command-line tool used to connect to SQL Server and submit T-SQL queries and commands. It's a replacement for the existing ISQL and OSQL utilities found previously in SQL Server. SQLCMD takes the functionality of these tools and adds powerful features such as variables and multiple connections.

- *Database Mail*: Database Mail is an enterprise solution for your database applications to send e-mail messages to users. These messages can contain a variety of contents, including query results and file attachments. Database Mail, unlike its predecessor, is an asynchronous mail application designed for reliability, scalability, security, and supportability.

- *Profiler*: The usefulness of one of the best performance, tuning, and optimization tools in SQL Server has improved greatly with features like performance log correlation and replay.

SQL Server Agent

Picture this scenario: you've been recently hired by a startup company as the only database administrator for their SQL Server. After helping out the developers with their table schema designs, you retreat to your desk and contemplate how to maintain the database in the long term. Naturally, the need for a backup solution pops into your mind, and you decide on performing a full database backup at midnight, followed by a differential backup 12 hours later at noon. Since the database is mostly read-only, you imagine this solution to be best. But you then ask yourself how a backup database command can be issued at midnight. Although this is a startup, and hopefully one day you imagine yourself relaxing on a Maui beach with a nice cold glass of fermented wheat and hops in your hand, you realize that sitting around until midnight every night isn't that appealing. Here is where SQL Server Agent might help you. SQL Server Agent is a Windows Service that runs continuously. Through defining and scheduling actions called *jobs*, Agent can automatically perform work against your SQL Server. In this case, SQL Server Agent can handle both scheduled backups. SQL Server Agent can also be used for a variety of other reasons, including to alert you if any performance events happen such as the occurrence of any deadlocks. Before we get into what is new in SQL Server 2005, let's continue our example and walk through how you would create these backup jobs in SQL Agent.

First, we want to create a job that performs a full database backup everyday at midnight. We can either create this job via stored procedures or by using the dialog boxes in SQL Server Management Studio (SSMS). For the purposes of this example, we will explore this creation through SSMS.

Step 1: Connect to SQL Server

Once you connect to the SQL Server database engine, you'll notice one of three different states of the SQL Server Agent node in Object Explorer. First, if you don't see the Agent node there at all, then you probably are not a member of the sysadmin role nor are you granted any specific access to Agent. See the "Permissions for Executing Agent Jobs" section later in this chapter for more information on how to gain access to SQL Server Agent. The second state that Agent could be in is the off state. If you perform a default installation of SQL Server and don't explicitly tell the setup to start SQL Server Agent, you'll see the following node in Object Explorer:

SQL Server Agent (Agent XPs disabled)

It's important to briefly discuss what is meant by "Agent XPs disabled." In SQL Server 2005, a large effort was placed on restricting the surface area for security-related attacks. One of the features that was implemented was the ability to disable execution of extended stored procedures like `xp_cmdshell`, `xp_sendmail`, and in this case, `xp_sqlagent_notify`. These extended stored procedures are logically grouped inside SQL Server. You can list these groups by issuing an `sp_configure` statement as shown here:

```
SP_CONFIGURE 'show advanced', 1
GO
RECONFIGURE
GO
SP_CONFIGURE
```

The result set returns about 60 different global configuration settings. Although most of these settings aren't related to the enabling and disabling of extended stored procedures, if you look through this list, you'll see "Agent XPs" listed. When the value is 1, Agent-specific extended stored procedures, like `xp_sqlagent_notify`, as well as other procedures, like those found in SMO calls, will be enabled. At this point, you might be wondering whether you have to manually go to the Query Editor and issue a call to enable Agent XPs when you want your SQL Agent to work. Thankfully, this isn't the case. When the SQL Server Agent service is started, it will automatically enable the Agent

XPs, and when it's stopped, it will automatically disable the Agent XPs. Note that this is the only time these extended stored procedure groupings will be automatically enabled and disabled. For normal use of SQL Agent, you'll never need to worry about manually changing this setting. However, for all other features, such as Database Mail and `xp_cmdshell`, you'll have to manually enable/disable these or use the Surface Area Configuration tool, which you see in Figure 13-1.

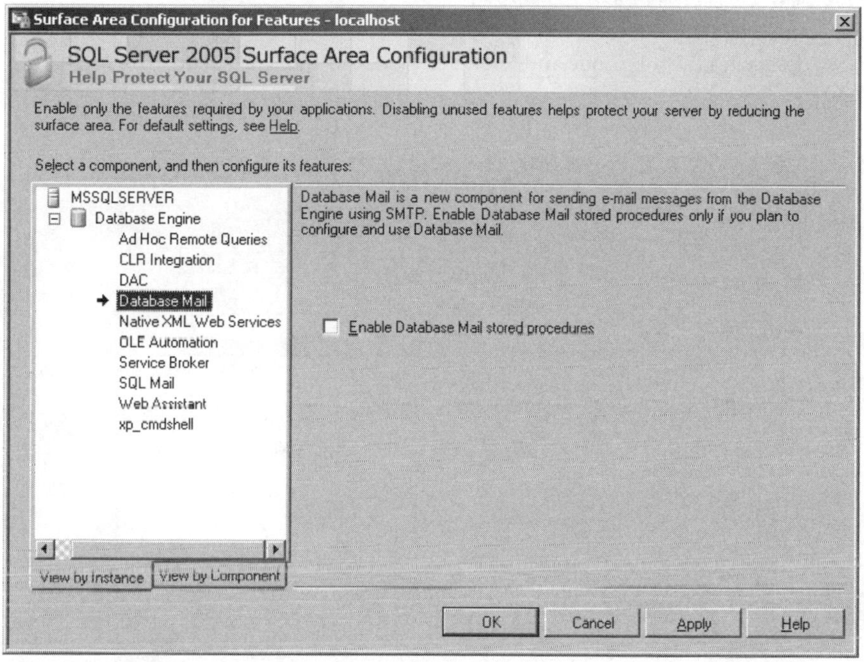

Figure 13-1. *Surface Area Configuration tool*

The changes that are made through this tool or by calling `sp_configure` directly are persistent; that is, they survive server reboots and service restarts.

Going back to our example, in Object Explorer, you see the SQL Agent node with the words, "Agent XPs disabled." As previously mentioned, if you right-click this and select Start, the Agent service will automatically enable the Agent XPs, and you can now use SQL Server Agent. When SQL Server Agent is started and the Agent XPs group is enabled, Object Explorer will show the Agent node as enabled, as you see here:

SQL Server Agent

At this point, you're ready to create your Agent job.

Step 2: Create the Agent Job

Once you're connected to SQL Server and have started the SQL Server Agent service (if need be), expand the SQL Server Agent node. Your screen should appear as shown in Figure 13-2.

Figure 13-2. *Agent node in Object Explorer*

To create a job, right-click the Jobs node and select New job. This will launch the New Job dialog box shown in Figure 13-3.

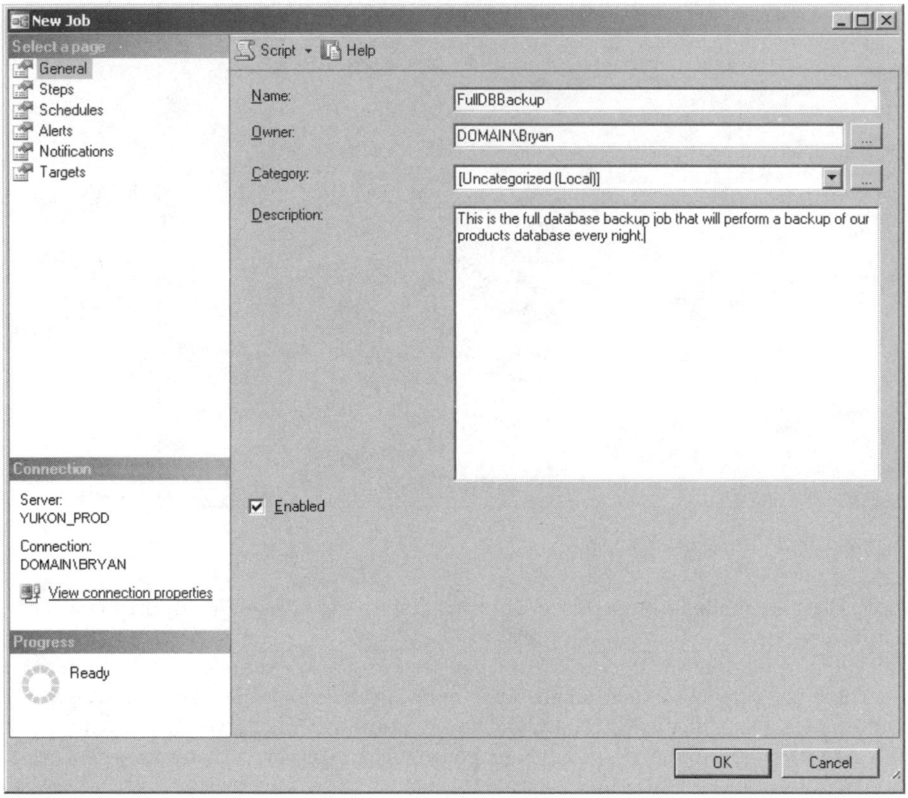

Figure 13-3. *General tab in the New Job dialog box*

The General tab allows you to enter some metadata about the job, such as its name, description, and who the owner of the job is.

■**Note** Only members of the sysadmin role can change the owner of a job.

Referring to our original backup scenario, let's give it an appropriate name like FullDBBackup. Once you've given the job a name, you can proceed to add steps to this job. Jobs can have one or more steps to them, and each step can be of one of more of the following types: T-SQL, ActiveX Script, Operating System (CmdExec), Replication (there are actually five Replication subsystems, but for the most part these are configured using Replication wizards and dialog boxes, and users usually don't manually create replication job steps), SQL Server Analysis Services Command and Query, and SQL Server Integration Services (SSIS) Package. Since jobs don't have to contain the same job step types, it's possible to have a job that first executes some T-SQL against SQL Server, then runs an SSIS package, and finally processes an Analysis Services cube. In this example, all we need is a single T-SQL job step. When we click the Steps tab, we're presented with a grid listing the steps within our job, as shown in Figure 13-4.

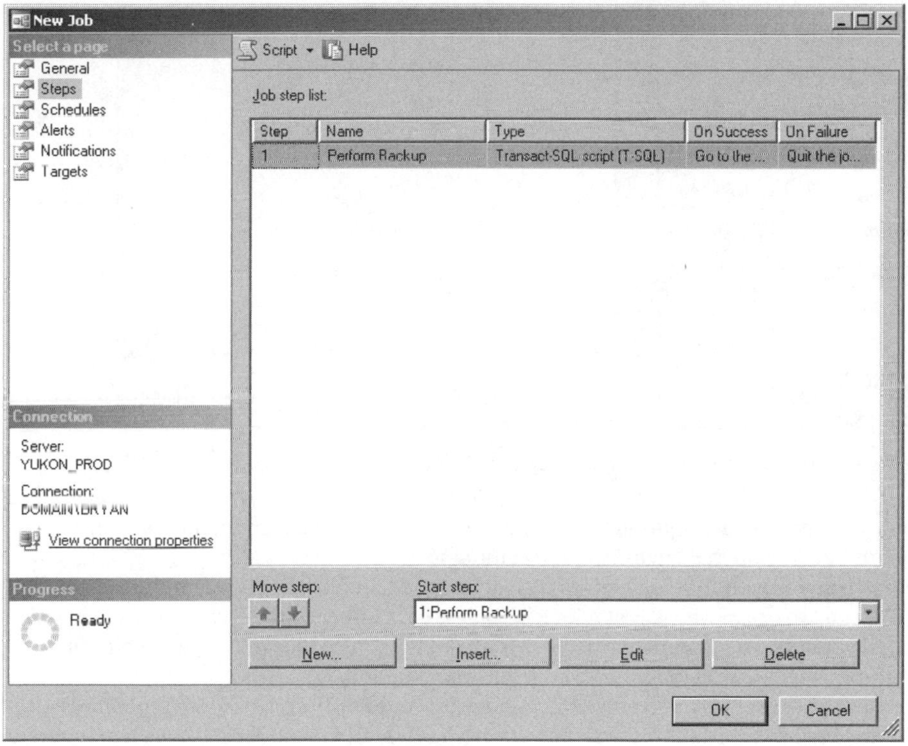

Figure 13-4. *Steps tab in the New Job dialog box*

This tab allows you to add, remove, and edit job steps as well as define which job step will be executed first. Since we only have one job step in our example, the backup of the database itself, the first step will be the starting step. If you add or edit a step, you'll be presented with the New Job Step dialog box shown in Figure 13-5.

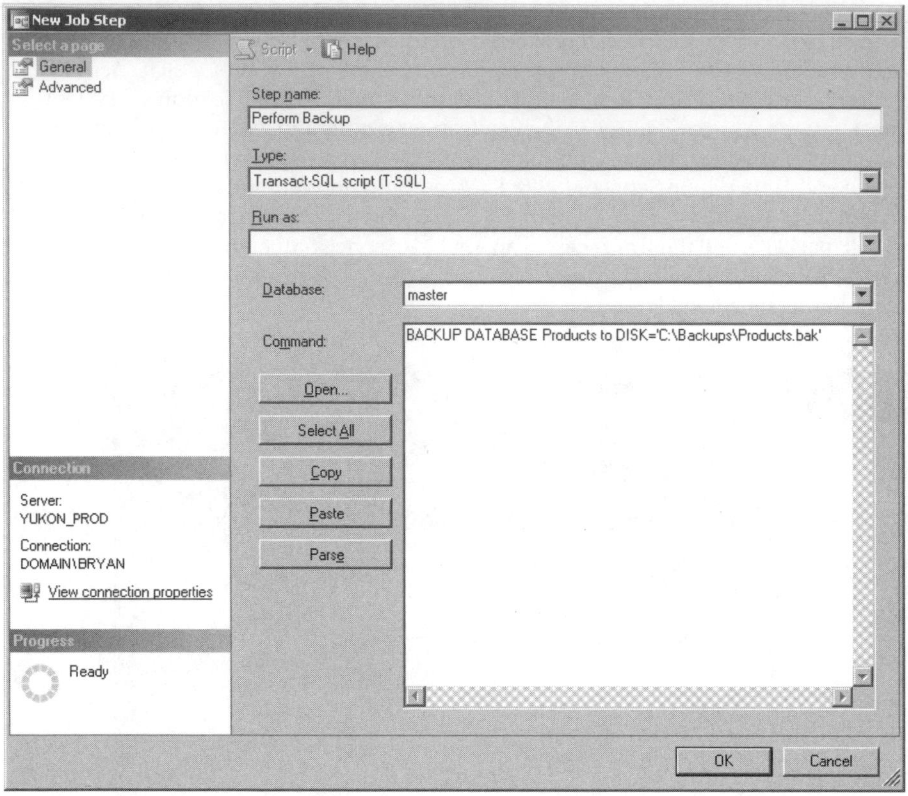

Figure 13-5. *General tab in New Job Step dialog box*

Every job step requires a unique name. Once we give this particular step a name, we can add the T-SQL script for backing up the database as the command.

Once you've added the job step(s), it's time to define the schedule. In our example, we want the full database backup to occur every day at midnight. On the New Job dialog box, you'll find a Schedule tab. Clicking this tab, you see another grid that lists all the schedules that will execute your job. Figure 13-6 shows how our grid looks for our database backup job.

In previous versions of SQL Server Agent, a single job could have zero or more schedules defined, and no two jobs could share the same schedule (although they could still have two separate schedules that are defined with the same time period). In SQL Server 2005, the same schedule can be shared among any jobs that the user owns. For more information about shared schedules, see the "Sharing Job Schedules" section later in this chapter. Once we've defined a schedule and clicked OK on the New Job dialog box, our database backup job is now ready for automatic execution.

As you can see from the previous example, SQL Server Agent provides an easy-to-use solution for routine maintenance and monitoring of SQL Server. This section of the chapter will dive into the key changes in SQL Server 2005 and provide you with potential issues related to the design and limitations to consider.

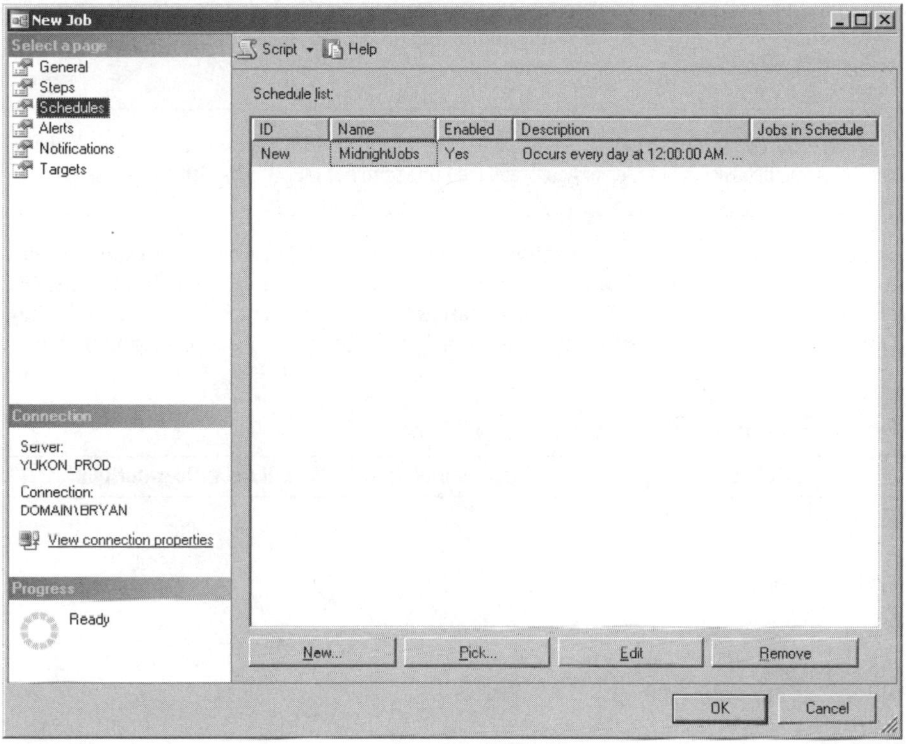

Figure 13-6. *Grid displayed on Schedule tab in New Job dialog box*

Security Enhancements

There are significant security enhancements that come with SQL Server Agent. These features allow the system administrator more granularity and control. It's important to note that they don't come for free though. As with any product, the more options there are, the harder the product is to learn and manage.

Microsoft has made an attempt to make it relatively easy to manage; however, we could imagine that in future releases there will be more wizards and UI dialog boxes to assist system administrators in this sensitive area.

Note One of the options provided when installing SQL Server is whether to set the startup of the SQL Agent service to automatic or manual. By default, SQL Server setup won't set the Agent service to start up automatically. In the event that the user chooses the Automatic setting, this will cause the SQL Agent service to be started when the operating system starts, else the user will have to manually start the service either through the SQL Server Configuration Manager or through the Services applet in the Control Panel. Remember to change the startup type to automatic in this applet if you plan on using the SQL Agent service.

Permissions for Executing Agent Jobs

SQL Server database administrators will be pleased to note that on a default installation of SQL Server 2005, only members of the sysadmin role can create, manage, or execute SQL Server Agent jobs. Ordinary SQL users won't even find the SQL Server Agent node visible in the Object Explorer tree when connected to a SQL Server 2005 instance. If a user isn't a sysadmin, then in order to use SQL Server Agent, that user will need to be added to one of three predefined database roles in the MSDB database: SQLAgentUserRole, SQLAgentReaderRole, or SQLAgentOperatorRole.

■**Tip** In SQL Server 2000, all MSDB database users had the ability to create, edit, and execute SQL Agent jobs by default. To obtain this same behavior in SQL Server Agent, add the Public role in MSDB to the SQLAgentUserRole.

Each one of these new roles provides additional privileges within SQL Server Agent starting with the most restrictive role, SQLAgentUserRole, followed by the SQLAgentReaderRole, and finally the least restrictive role, SQLAgentOperatorRole. The following tables list these new roles and the actions they can perform on Agent objects, starting with Table 13-1, which describes user role access for alert objects.

Table 13-1. *SQL Server Agent User Role Access for Alert Objects*

Action	SQLAgentUserRole	SQLAgentReaderRole	SQLAgentOperatorRole
Create			
Modify			
Delete			
Enumerate			Yes
Enable/Disable			
View Properties			Yes

SQL Server Agent alerts read events generated by SQL Server and from the Windows application log. Alerts can be configured so that, based on certain criteria being met, an action will be automatically performed. These actions can be either starting an Agent job or notifying an Operator. An Operator is a SQL Agent-specific object that is basically an arbitrary name, such as BryanTheDBA, and has at least one of the following pieces of information defined: e-mail address, pager address, or net send address. An Operator can be defined on a job to be notified of job failure, or, in the case of an alert, when the alert criteria are met.

■**Note** Operators have no ties to Windows user accounts or SQL logins, and most importantly the Operators we discuss here having nothing to do with the SQLAgentOperatorRole.

Table 13-2 lists user role access for Operator objects.

Table 13-2. *SQL Server Agent User Role Access for Operator Objects*

Action	SQLAgentReaderRole	SQLAgentUserRole	SQLAgentOperatorRole
Create			
Modify			
Delete			
Enumerate	Yes	Yes	Yes

Table 13-2. *SQL Server Agent User Role Access for Operator Objects*

Action	SQLAgentReaderRole	SQLAgentUserRole	SQLAgentOperatorRole
Enable/Disable			
View Properties			Yes

Jobs are what define the work to do in SQL Server Agent. Jobs can be run locally on the same server where SQL Server Agent is installed or remotely. When a job is set to run remotely, the sysadmin has to configure one server to be the master (SQL Server Books Online documentation refers to this as the *MSX server*) and source of the jobs, and the rest of the servers will be targets (also known as *TSX servers*). Tables 13-3 and 13-4 list role access based on local or remote jobs.

Table 13-3. *SQL Server Agent User Role Access for Job Objects (Local Jobs Specifically)*

Action	SQLAgentReaderRole	SQLAgentUserRole	SQLAgentOperatorRole	Comments
Create	Yes	Yes	Yes	No non-sysadmin users can change the owner of the job.
Modify	Yes	Yes	Yes	Users can only modify jobs they own.
Delete	Yes	Yes	Yes	Users can only delete jobs they own.
Enumerate	Yes	Yes	Yes	For SQLAgentReaderRole and SQLAgentOperatorRole: users can enumerate all jobs, including those owned by different users. For SQLAgentUserRole: users can only enumerate jobs they own.
Enable/ Disable	Yes	Yes	Yes	For SQLAgentOperatorRole: action is only supported by calling the sp_update_job stored procedure. Users can enable/disable jobs they own. Users who are SQLAgentOperators can enable/disable all jobs but have to do this by calling sp_update_job directly.
Start Job	Yes	Yes	Yes	For SQLAgentOperatorRole: user can start any job.
Stop Job	Yes	Yes	Yes	For SQLAgentOperatorRole: user can stop any job.
View History	Yes	Yes	Yes	For SQLAgentReaderRole and SQLAgentOperatorRole: user can view history for any job. For SQLAgentUserRole: users can only view history for jobs they own.

Table 13-3. *SQL Server Agent User Role Access for Job Objects (Local Jobs Specifically) (Continued)*

Action	SQLAgentReaderRole	SQLAgentUserRole	SQLAgentOperatorRole	Comments
Delete History	Yes	Yes	Yes	For SQLAgentReaderRole and SQLAgentUserRole: users can delete job history from jobs they own. For SQLAgentOperatorRole: users can delete history of any job.
View Properties	Yes	Yes	Yes	For SQLAgentReaderRole and SQLAgentOperatorRole: read-only access to all jobs.

Table 13-4. *SQL Server Agent User Role Access for Job Objects (Multiserver Jobs Specifically)*

Action	SQLAgentReaderRole	SQLAgentUserRole	SQLAgentOperatorRole	Comments
Create				
Modify				
Delete				
Enumerate	Yes		Yes	
Enable/ Disable				
Start Job			Yes	
Stop Job			Yes	
View History	Yes		Yes	For SQLAgentReaderRole and SQLAgentOperatorRole: users can view history for any multiserver job.
Delete History				
Manage Target Servers				
Manage Job Categories				
View Properties	Yes		Yes	For SQLAgentReaderRole and SQLAgentOperatorRole: read-only access to all multiserver jobs.

As mentioned previously, schedules can be shared among jobs that are owned by the same user. Even sysadmins can't mix and match schedules from different users; all job and schedule "pairs" must have the same owner. Table 13-5 lists the role access for schedule objects.

Table 13-5. *SQL Server Agent User Role Access for Schedule Objects*

Action	SQLAgentReaderRole	SQLAgentUserRole	SQLAgentOperatorRole	Comments
Create	Yes	Yes	Yes	No non-sysadmin users can change the owner of the schedule.
Modify	Yes	Yes	Yes	Users can only modify schedules they own.
Delete	Yes	Yes	Yes	Users can only delete schedules they own.
Enumerate	Yes	Yes	Yes	For SQLAgentReaderRole and SQLAgentOperatorRole: users can enumerate all schedules, including those owned by different users. For SQLAgentUserRole: users can only enumerate schedules they own.
Enable/ Disable	Yes	Yes	Yes	For SQLAgentOperatorRole: action only supported by calling sp_update_schedule stored procedure. Again, this enable/ disable for Reader and User role is applicable only to jobs they own.
Attach and Detach	Yes	Yes	Yes	Users can only attach and detach schedules they own.
View Properties	Yes	Yes	Yes	For SQLAgentReaderRole and SQLAgentOperatorRole: read-only access to all schedules. User role can only see properties of jobs they own.

In the introduction of this chapter, we explored the SQL Server Agent job and its ability to have one or more job steps of different types. As a sysadmin, you're free to add job steps of any type. What is important to note is that for all job step types except T-SQL, when the job step is run, it's executed under the context of the SQL Server Agent service account. T-SQL job steps are a special case: they are always run under the job owner. So given this information, what if we wanted our developers who aren't sysadmins on our server to be able to schedule and execute SSIS packages? In this case, we would want to create a proxy account in SQL Server Agent for the developers. A *proxy account* is a friendly name and a Windows credential that is stored in SQL Server. The sysadmin can grant access to this proxy to any SQL login, MSDB role, or system role. Also, this proxy can be assigned to one or more job step types (sometimes referred to as *Agent subsystems*). More information about proxies is available in the "Multiple Proxy Accounts" section later in this chapter.

Table 13-6 lists the user role access for proxy objects.

Table 13-6. *SQL Server Agent User Role Access for Proxy Objects*

Action	SQLAgentReaderRole	SQLAgentUserRole	SQLAgentOperatorRole	Comments
Create				
Modify				
Delete				
Enumerate	Yes	Yes	Yes	For SQLAgentReaderRole and SQLAgentUserRole: users can only enumerate proxies that they have explicit access to. For SQLAgentOperatorRole: users can enumerate all proxies.
View Properties			Yes	Read-only access to all proxies.

> **Note** SQL Server Agent error logs can be read by using the sp_readerrorlog stored procedure. However, the user must be a member of the security admin role in order to execute this stored procedure. By default, no one but sysadmins can read SQL Server Agent error logs.

If you're upgrading from a previous version of SQL Server to SQL Server 2005 and had Agent jobs already defined, the upgrade behavior is as follows: non-sysadmin users who owned jobs will automatically be included in the SQLAgentUserRole. This will allow the jobs to continue to run after upgrade. It's important to note that there are some corner-case issues with respect to upgrades that should be taken into consideration. Refer to the "Agent Upgrade" section later in this chapter for important information about this topic.

Multiple Proxy Accounts

Storing credentials has traditionally been an interesting design problem. In the interest of consistency within the SQL Server products, SQL Server Agent has moved from storing credentials in the registry-based Windows Local System Authority (LSA) store to utilizing the new credential store inside SQL Server.

This design change has made it easier to create multiple proxy accounts. In previous versions of SQL Server, the administrator had to define a single proxy account that would be shared among all users. This proxy account defined a set of windows credentials (for example, username and password) that SQL Agent would impersonate when performing certain operations, such as executing command shell job steps or writing the job step output to a text file on the file system. You can see the obvious security issue here: as soon as this single proxy account was defined, then any SQL user could utilize these credentials in their Agent jobs.

In SQL Server Agent, administrators can define multiple proxy accounts. Each one of these proxy accounts can be used in one or more subsystems. In addition, you can explicitly grant permission to use a particular proxy account to individual SQL logins, MSDB database roles, and/or system roles. For example, say the administrator creates a proxy account called SSISDevProxy.

Note Similar to the SQL Server 2000 proxy account, a proxy account in SQL Server Agent contains a valid Windows credential.

The administrator then assigns this new proxy account to the SQL Server Integration Services (SSIS) subsystem. He grants the SQL login, "Tammie," the right to use this new proxy account. At this point, the next time Tammie logs in to SQL Server, she will be able to create a SQL Agent job with a job step of type SQL Server Integration Services Package. Under the Run As combo box, she will have the option to select SSISDevProxy as the proxy account to use when SQL Agent executes this SSIS package.

When this Agent job is executed, the SQL Agent service will impersonate the credentials of SSISDevProxy and proceed to execute the package. In this example, there was a one-to-one-to-one relationship between user, proxy, and subsystem. However, SQL Server Agent supports a many-to-many-to-many relationship. That is, the administrator can set up many logins to many proxies to many subsystems. Figure 13-7 depicts the possibilities of defining proxy accounts.

If we set up SQL Server Agent as represented by the previous figure, the experiences for the three SQL logins, Tammie, Gary, and George, would be as follows:

When Tammie creates an Agent job with a SQL Server Integration Services Package job step type, she will only be able to select SSISDevProxy as a proxy to use.

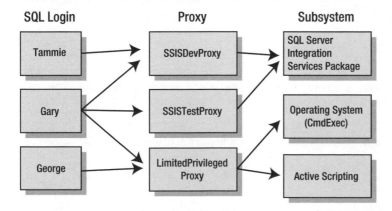

Figure 13-7. *Multiple proxy example*

When Gary creates an Agent job with a SQL Server Integration Services Package job step type, he can select between SSISDevProxy and SSISTestProxy because the system administrator has given him access to both of these proxies assigned to the SQL Server Integration Services Package subsystem.

Proxy accounts themselves don't need to be assigned to just one subsystem. When George creates an Agent job with an Operating System (CmdExec) job step type, he can select the LimitedPrivilegedProxy for use as the proxy account. However, if he created a job step of type ActiveX Script, he could also select this proxy because the system administrator had assigned this proxy to both the ActiveX Script and Operating System (CmdExec) subsystems.

The intent of the multiple proxy account feature in SQL Server Agent is to provide flexible, secure access to the Agent features.

System administrators can create proxy accounts through the Object Explorer in SQL Server Management Studio or through T-SQL code.

■**Note** You'll have to create a credential first before you can create a proxy. If you're using Object Explorer, then you can create a credential by launching the New Credential dialog box and selecting New Credential from the Credentials node of the Security node.

The following is a T-SQL example of creating a proxy account:

First, we must create a credential in the SQL Server secure store. This credential is the actual Windows identity that the SQL Server Agent service will impersonate before it executes the job step.

```
CREATE CREDENTIAL [DevCredential]
 WITH IDENTITY='<<Domain\Username>>',
 SECRET='<<password>>'
```

Having created the credential in SQL Server, we can now create the Agent proxy account that references this credential as follows:

```
USE MSDB
GO
sp_add_proxy @proxy_name = 'SSISDevProxy',
@enabled = 1,
@description = 'proxy account used by developers to test their SSIS packages',
@credential_name = 'DevCredential'
```

At this point, the proxy account is neither assigned to any subsystems nor accessible by anyone except members of the sysadmin roles. We assign the proxy account to the SSIS subsystem as follows:

```
sp_grant_proxy_to_subsystem
    @proxy_name = N'SSISDevProxy',
    @subsystem_name = N'SSIS'
```

■**Note** SQL Server Integration Services is the new name for what used to be called Data Transformation Services, or DTS, in previous versions of SQL Server.

Finally, we will grant the SQL login "Tammie" the ability to use this new proxy account, as follows:

```
sp_grant_login_to_proxy
    @login_name = N'Tammie',
    @proxy_name = N'SSISDevProxy'
```

At this point, the SQL login Tammie will be able to create a new job step of type SQL Server Integration Services Package and select SSISDevProxy as the proxy account under which to run when her package is executed.

Now that we have gone over the details of proxy accounts, it's important to note that all subsystems use proxy accounts with the exception of the T-SQL subsystem. In this case, the Agent service can impersonate the job owner through T-SQL and doesn't need to store the user's Windows credentials separately. System administrators won't need to create a proxy account for job steps of type T-SQL.

■Note Although we have shown the T-SQL for creating and assigning proxies, the SQL Server Management Studio tool has a UI that makes it easier to create and manage proxy accounts.

Agent Subsytems

SQL Server 2005 includes major advancements in Data Transformation Services (now known as SQL Server Integration Services) and Analysis Services. Agent in SQL Server 2005 has added three new subsystems to accommodate the growing number of users who execute SSIS packages and Analysis Services jobs. These new subsystems are as follows:

- *SQL Server Integration Services Package*: Allows the user to create job steps that execute SSIS packages

- *Analysis Services Command*: Allows the user to submit XML/A to an Analysis server

- *Analysis Services Query*: Allows the user to submit MDX to an Analysis server

SQL Server Integration Services Package Subsystem

In SQL Server 2000, it was possible to execute DTS packages within Agent jobs. The administrator would have to create a command shell job step and call dtsrun.exe (that is, the DTS 2000 runtime executable). In SQL Server Agent, a separate subsystem called SQL Server Integration Services Package is available. This allows administrators to give users the ability to create jobs that call SSIS packages without giving them access to the Command Shell subsystem. For those users who like executing packages from the command line, there still is a command-line executable to run SSIS packages in SQL Server 2005: dtexec.exe. In addition, there is another executable that provides a user interface to help in setting the right parameters for dtexec.exe, and it's called dtexecui.exe. When creating an Agent job, you don't need to use these executables, though, since the Agent user interface provides the same options as you'll find in the dtexecui application.

■Note If a user still wants to execute DTS 2000 packages in SQL Server 2005, he can still call create a command shell job step and call the old dtsrun.exe. The user will only be able to execute DTS 2000 packages.

Analysis Services Subsystems

Previous versions of SQL Server Agent had no concept of OLAP or Analysis Services job steps. It was difficult to schedule the processing of a cube or to back up an OLAP database. In SQL Server Agent, there are two subsystems specifically for Analysis Services: Analysis Services Query and Analysis Services Command.

Analysis Services Query is a subsystem that accepts MDX scripts for its command text. This allows OLAP users to schedule Analysis Services stored procedure calls within SQL Agent.

The Analysis Services Command is a subsystem that accepts XML/A scripts for its command text. This form of script is unique to Analysis Services, and can be obtained by scripting almost any Analysis Services dialog. XML/A is used to issue commands to Analysis Services such as back up database or process cube.

Sharing Job Schedules

Job schedules can now be shared among jobs that are owned by the same user. For example, the administrator has a series of jobs that she would like to run every day at midnight. In previous versions of SQL Server, she would create a job and then create a separate schedule for each job, each executing at the same schedule time. In SQL Server Agent, she can create a single schedule (in this case, occurring every day at midnight), and attach it to one or more jobs, provided she is the owner of the jobs.

This concept is easily seen from the UI supplied by SQL Server Management Studio. Consider the following example:

Greg creates a job, Job1, with a schedule, Schedule1. Since he was told only to run jobs starting at the time defined in Schedule1 by his system administrator, Greg wants to create his second job, called Job2, with this same schedule.

Greg launches the New Job dialog box in SQL Server Management Studio and, after supplying the name, clicks the Schedules tab and is presented with the dialog box you see in Figure 13-8.

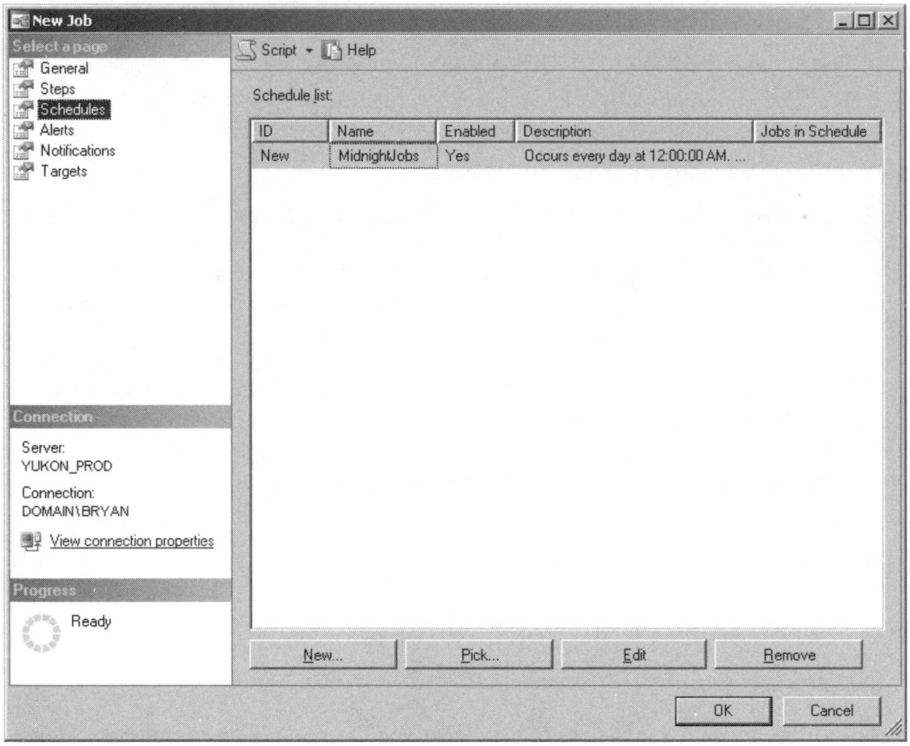

Figure 13-8. *Schedules tab of the New Job dialog box*

Below the schedule list grid there are two buttons, New and Pick. If Greg wanted to create a separate schedule for this job, he simply clicks the New button and is presented with the New Job Schedule dialog box. However, since he wants to reuse the schedule he already created for in Job1, he clicks the Pick button and is presented with the dialog box shown in Figure 13-9.

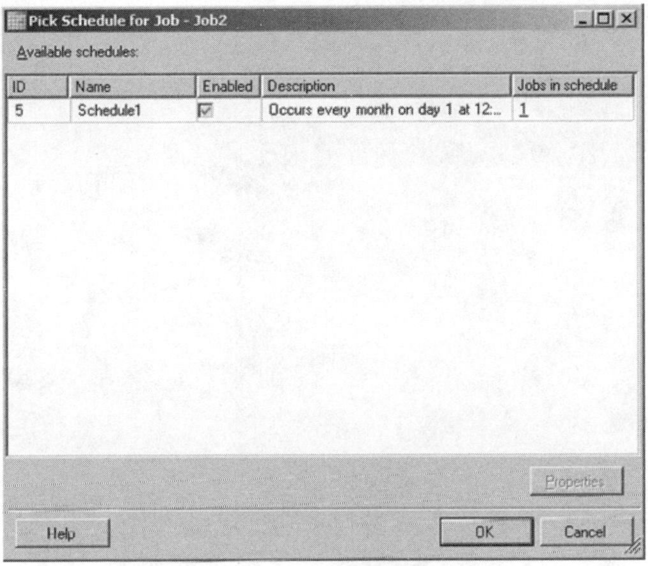

Figure 13-9. *Picking an existing schedule throught the Pick Schedule for Job dialog box*

At this point, Greg can view all the jobs that are assigned to a schedule by clicking the hyperlinked number in the Jobs in schedule column. Clicking this will pop up the dialog box shown in Figure 13-10.

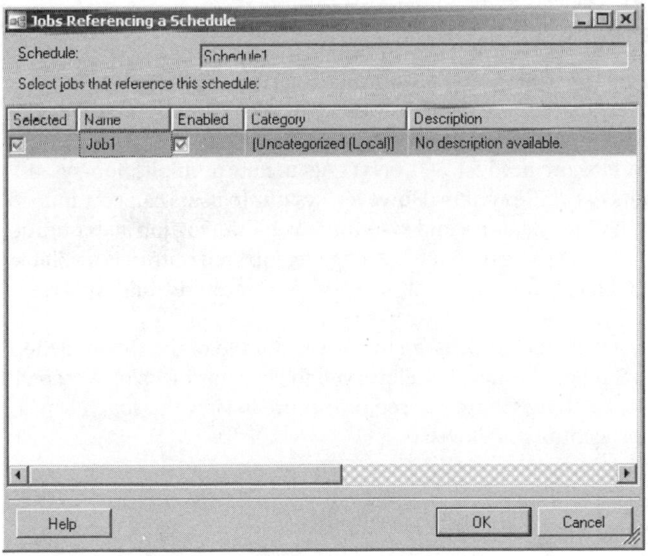

Figure 13-10. *Dialog box showing jobs that are referencing a particular schedule*

Greg can now confirm that this is the schedule he wants to reuse, as well as view the other jobs that also reference this schedule.

SQL Server Management Studio also provides a separate dialog box launched from the Jobs container node called Manage Schedules, which is shown in Figure 13-11.

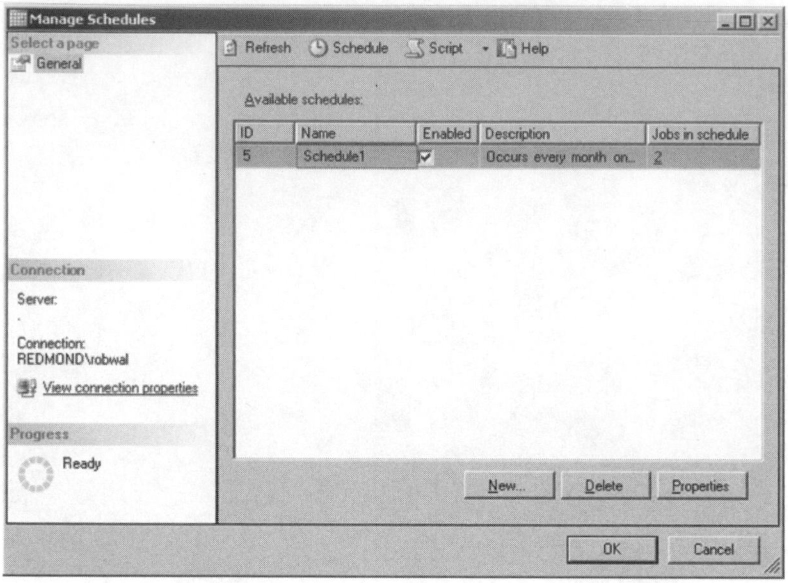

Figure 13-11. *Manage Schedules dialog box*

From this dialog box, users can see all the schedules they created and find out which other jobs reference these schedules. Users will only be able to see schedules and jobs that they own. System administrators, however, will be able to see all schedules and jobs that exist in SQL Server Agent.

Logging to the sysjobstepslogs Table

In previous versions of SQL Server, it was possible to log the output of certain job steps to a file. Sysadmin users could do this without any additional configuration. However, if a non-sysadmin user wanted to write the output to a file, the sysadmin needed to configure the global proxy account to allow this action. In the spirit of a more secure product, SQL Server Agent now prohibits non-sysadmins from logging their job step outputs to the file system. However, sysadmin users can continue to use this feature. As a replacement, both non-sysadmin and sysadmin users can log job step output to a well-known table, sysjobstepslogs, in the MSDB database. Logging job step output is available only on these specific job step types: T-SQL, CmdExec, Analysis Services Command, and Analysis Services Query.

Logging to the table is an option that can be set through the Advanced tab of the New Job Step dialog box in SQL Server Management Studio. This tab also allows you to view the log using Notepad. Alternatively, you could use the new sp_help_jobsteplog stored procedure to view this log. Just pass the job ID or job name to this stored procedure as follows:

```
USE MSDB
GO
sp_help_jobsteplog @job_name='FullDBBackup'
GO
```

WMI Events and Agent Alerts

Tokens are character placeholders within T-SQL code. The use of tokens within SQL Server Agent job steps has been around in previous versions of SQL Server. At runtime, SQL Agent replaces these tokens with values such as the current date or the computer name.

■**Note** SQL Server Agent has changed the token nomenclature from brackets, [ ], to $( ). It was found that using the brackets for tokens like [DATE] could clash with SQL Server's use of brackets to group object names that contain special characters.

SQL Agent now responds to WMI event notifications raised by SQL Server 2005, as well as any other WMI event provider (one restriction is that events must be raised from the local server on which the Agent resides).

Therefore, in addition to providing the same token list as in SQL Server 2000, SQL Server Agent introduces a new token that provides the user the ability to return properties of WMI events. This token is called out by the following:

```
$(WMI(X))
```

where X is the desired WMI property of the WMI event that the user wishes to insert.

SQL Server 2005 event notifications can raise WMI events off of various DDL and DML statements. The following example shows how the administrator can now raise an Agent alert when someone creates a new database.

■**Note** This example can also be easily done through the SQL Server Management Studio user interface, but in the interest of introducing the new parameters for the WMI events, we show it as a series of T-SQL commands.

First, let's create an Agent Operator:

```
EXEC msdb.dbo.sp_add_operator @name=N'MyAgentOperator',
                              @enabled=1,
                              @pager_days=0,
                              @netsend_address=N'robs_laptop'
GO
```

Since we supplied the netsend_address parameter, this Operator should be notified of the database creation via net send. Note that the Messenger service must be started in order for the Agent to send network messages.

Next, we'll create an Agent alert using built-in system stored procedures called sp_add_alert and sp_add_notification. Together this code will notify an Operator if anyone issues a CREATE DATABASE statement to SQL Server.

```
EXEC msdb.dbo.sp_add_alert @name=N'Create_Database_Alert',
                           @enabled=1,
                           @delay_between_responses=0,
                           @include_event_description_in=0,
@wmi_namespace=N'\\.\root\Microsoft\SqlServer\ServerEvents\MSSQLSERVER',
                           @wmi_query=N'SELECT * FROM CREATE_DATABASE'
GO
EXEC msdb.dbo.sp_add_notification
    @alert_name=N'Create_Database_Alert',
    @operator_name=N'MyAgentOperator',
    @notification_method = 4
GO
```

Note In order for SQL Server Agent to raise WMI event-based alerts, SQL Service broker must be enabled for MSDB. If the previous example resulted in an error, try executing the following command:

```
IF(SELECT is_broker_enabled FROM sys.databases WHERE name = 'msdb')=1
ALTER DATABASE msdb SET ENABLE_BROKER
GO
```

There are two new optional parameters in the sp_add_alert stored procedure:

- @wmi_namespace is the namespace of the desired WMI event object. If you were to create this alert through the user interface provided by SQL Server Management Studio, the default path of \\.\root\Microsoft\SqlServer\ServerEvents\MSSQLSERVER is already in place for you. You may have noticed that even though the SQL Server event namespace is prepopulated, there is nothing stopping you from replacing it with any other WMI event provider. Thus, it's possible to raise Agent events on things like free disk space and all the other Win32 event providers installed on your server.

- @wmi_query is the actual Windows Management Instrumentation Query Language (WQL) query that the Agent will issue when looking for this event. In the case of this example, we're interested in the CREATE_DATABASE event that is raised by SQL Server, so we entered SELECT * FROM CREATE_DATABASE. Although this WQL resembles T-SQL, it isn't the same.

A lot of resources are available on MSDN that describe how to write and use WQL. WQL resembles SQL in its syntax. In fact, it's a subset of the standard American National Standards Institute Structured Query Language (ANSI SQL) with minor semantic changes to support WMI. It's definitely worth taking the time to get to know this Windows feature. Additional information can be found online at http://msdn.microsoft.com (search for "Querying with WQL").

Once the preceding script has been executed, the Operator will be notified as shown in Figure 13-12 via a net send alert whenever a new database is created on the server.

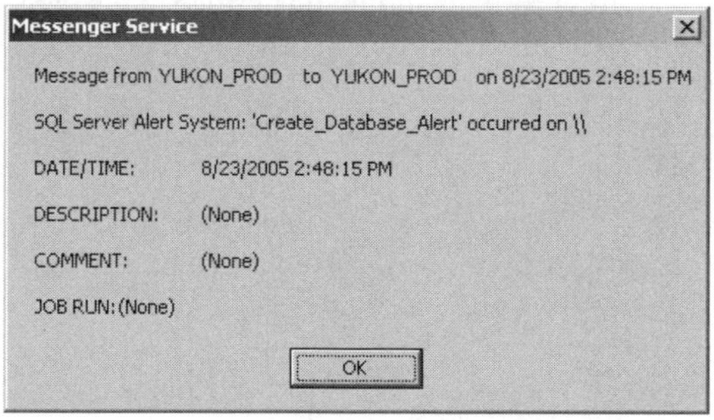

Figure 13-12. *Net send alert notification*

Agent Performance Counters

The SQL Server Agent service now has a set of performance counters installed on the server. There are four performance objects for each instance of SQL Server Agent that is installed on the server, which are defined as follows:

- SQLAgent:Alerts: This performance object provides information such as number of alerts activated since the Agent service started and how many alerts are raised within the last minute.

- `SQLAgent:Jobs`: This performance object describes a variety of job states, such as number of active jobs, how many jobs are queued, and the job success/failure rate as a percentage of successful/failed jobs from the total number of executed jobs.

- `SQLAgent:JobSteps`: This performance object can determine the active and queued job steps per subsystem, in addition to total number of step retries.

- `SQLAgent:Statistics`: Perhaps one of the more simple performance objects, this one has just one counter, Server Restarted, and describes how many times the SQL Server service was restarted during the life of the current Agent service process.

Although not an exhaustive list of everything inside the Agent service, these counters should be a starting point in monitoring the Agent service activity through Performance Monitor (Perfmon).

Most of the instances for these performance objects are self-explanatory, except for the `Jobs` object. When you select the `Jobs` object, you'll have the option to pick all counters or specific ones, as you can see from Figure 13-13.

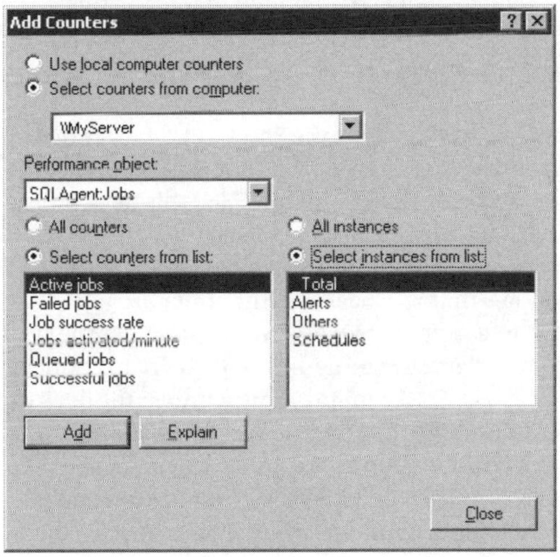

Figure 13-13. *Add Counters dialog box from Perfmon application*

In the case of the job instances, Alerts means jobs that were started by an alert, Schedules means jobs that were started by a schedule, Others means jobs that were started manually via `sp_start_job`, and _Total means jobs that were started by any one of these.

Agent Upgrade

Now that you've been exposed to the significant changes and new features in SQL Agent, it's now important to talk about the upgrade experience. If you're planning a new install of SQL Server 2005, this section doesn't directly apply to you; however, you may find this information educational.

Previously in this chapter, we discussed the addition of the three new database roles in the MSDB database: `SQLAgentReaderRole`, `SQLAgentUserRole`, and `SQLAgentOperatorRole`. As with a new install, an upgrade of SQL Agent also restricts default access to only sysadmin users. The exception to this, in the case of an upgrade, is that users who owned jobs prior to the upgrade will be automatically granted access to the `SQLAgentUserRole` database role in MSDB. This will allow these jobs to continue to execute after upgrade. In most cases, the jobs will continue to execute as before without any issues. There are a few exceptions that relate to jobs when the single global proxy account was set and used in the job.

In previous versions of SQL Server Agent, the sysadmin could define a single proxy account to use to allow non-sysadmin users to perform any of these functions:

- Execute active scripting job steps.

- Execute command shell job steps.

- Log job step output to the file system.

- Execute the xp_cmdshell extended stored procedure.

Once this account was defined, any SQL login could use this proxy account. As discussed earlier, in order to lock down the box, administrators could use the multiple proxies feature in SQL Server 2005 to hand pick which users can use which proxies. On an upgrade, the single global proxy, if defined, is created on the upgraded server and is called UpgradedProxy. Job owners who either had active scripting or command shell jobs will have access to this proxy after upgrade. Those non-sysadmin users who were logging their job output to the file system will now be upgraded to logging this output to a table. These changes will allow the jobs to continue to execute as they did previously and now provides the sysadmin the ability to configure the security context of the job step to a more granular level.

Another important note about proxies is with respect to the use of the xp_cmdshell extended stored procedure. In previous versions of SQL Server, sysadmins set the proxy for this via a SQL Agent extended stored procedure, xp_sqlagent_proxy_account. In SQL Server 2005, this behavior has changed; if any of your scripts call this XP, they will have to be changed to use the new stored procedure, sp_xp_cmdshell_proxy_account, to set the proxy account for the xp_cmdshell. The link between Agent's global proxy account and the credentials that xp_cmdshell run under are now broken, which makes sense since you should not have to configure SQL Agent to use xp_cmdshell.

Another minor surprise you may notice is if you had originally configured SQL Agent to connect to SQL server using SQL Authentication. In SQL Server 2005, SQL Agent prohibits connecting back to SQL Server using SQL Authentication. With the move to multiple proxies, Agent did away with storing credentials in the registry and now only accepts Windows Authentication, which means that the Agent service account must be sysadmin on SQL Server. If you had SQL Authentication and upgraded to SQL Server 2005, Agent will use the Agent service account to connect back to SQL Server after the upgrade is complete.

Maintenance Plans

A *maintenance plan* is a workflow of T-SQL tasks that can be scheduled to run or be executed on demand. In previous versions of SQL Server, the *Database Maintenance Plan* feature attempted to cover the most common database maintenance tasks, like backing up a database and reindexing tables. The user would accomplish this through the use of a wizard that would create an agent job whose only job step was to call the SQL Maintenance utility. This utility is an executable called sqlmaint.exe that can be called directly from the command line or by the extended stored procedure xp_sqlmaint in T-SQL.

Even though the original idea was to capture most of the main tasks of an administrator, the feature itself was limited in functionality, and users ended up having some issues with the design, some of which included the following:

- It wasn't easy to tell exactly what T-SQL would be sent by the sqlmaint.exe application to the server. You could set up a Profiler trace, but this was tedious just to obtain some relatively simple information.

- The tasks themselves weren't customizable; the user was stuck with whatever options the UI provided.

- Performing workflow within maintenance plans was tedious. In previous versions of SQL Server, it wasn't possible from the Database Maintenance Wizard to conditionally say, "If the Check Database fails, then skip over the Backup Database Task and continue with reindexing a table."

In SQL Server 2005, all of this is now possible with the new Maintenance Plan feature. Built upon the SSIS engine, maintenance plans now provide an easy way to create workflow within your plans, to add custom T-SQL tasks in case the UI doesn't provide the specific option you need, and to tell the user at design time what the T-SQL will look like. The term "Database" was removed from its name because the function of the tool isn't just maintaining databases, rather maintaining your server in general.

Figure 13-14 shows a maintenance plan that was created to first check a database's integrity and then issue a backup database statement. If the check database integrity task failed, it would notify an Agent Operator.

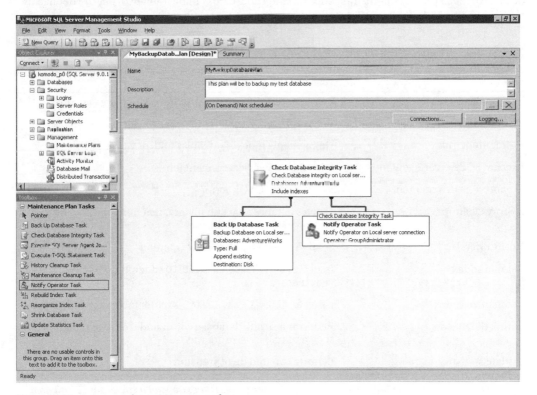

Figure 13-14. *An example maintenance plan*

Creating a Maintenance Plan

There are two ways to create a maintenance plan using SQL Server Management Studio:

- Via the Maintenance Plan Wizard
- By directly creating a new plan through the Maintenance Plan Designer

You can launch the Maintenance Plan Wizard by selecting Maintenance Plan Wizard from the context menu of the Maintenance Plans Node in Object Explorer. To create a new plan using the Maintenance Plan Designer, simply select New Maintenance Plan from this same context menu.

Launching the Maintenance Plan Wizard will take you through a series of dialog boxes that allow you to pick and choose which tasks you would like to include as part of your plan. The wizard is similar to SQL Server 2000's Database Maintenance Wizard, except that when you're finished with the wizard, you'll effectively have created a maintenance plan that can be executed or modified in the Maintenance Plan Designer.

If you modify an existing plan or create a new plan, the Maintenance Plan Designer will open as a *document window* inside the Management Studio shell. In addition, the *toolbox* will also become visible and it will, by default, locate itself beneath the Object Explorer as shown in Figure 13-14. The toolbox contains the list of all the available tasks in SQL Server 2005. Before we walk through creating an actual plan, let's start by defining each of these tasks.

Toolbox

SQL Server 2005 provides 11 maintenance tasks to choose from in the toolbox. They are defined as shown in Table 13-7.

Table 13-7. *Maintenance Task List*

Task	Function
Backup database	Performs full, differential, and transaction log backups
Check database integrity	Performs a database integrity check using DBCC CHECKDB
Defragment index	Defragments indexes on tables and/or views
Execute SQL Server Agent Job	Launches a SQL Server Agent job
Execute T-SQL Statement	Executes any T-SQL script
History cleanup	Deletes database backup history, maintenance plan history, and/or SQL Agent job history
Notify operator	Sends a message to an Agent Operator
Rebuild Index	Issues an ALTER INDEX...REBUILD statement for table and view indexes
Reorganize Index	Issues an ALTER INDEX...REORGANIZE for table and view indexes
Shrink database	Performs a shrink database command if certain parameters such as database size are met
Update statistics	Performs an update of statistics

*Table Footnote   To use the Notify Operator task, you must have Database Mail installed and configured with a default profile. For more information on using Database Mail, see the "Database Mail" section later in this chapter.

If you accidentally closed the toolbox, or it doesn't show up, you can always enable the toolbox from the View menu on the toolbar.

Maintenance Plan Designer Document Window

Next we'll look at the designer document window that opens when you either create a new plan or modify an existing plan. This document window has two sections. The bottom half is the designer, where the actual workflow is defined, while the top half is for metadata about the plan and resembles what you see in Figure 13-15.

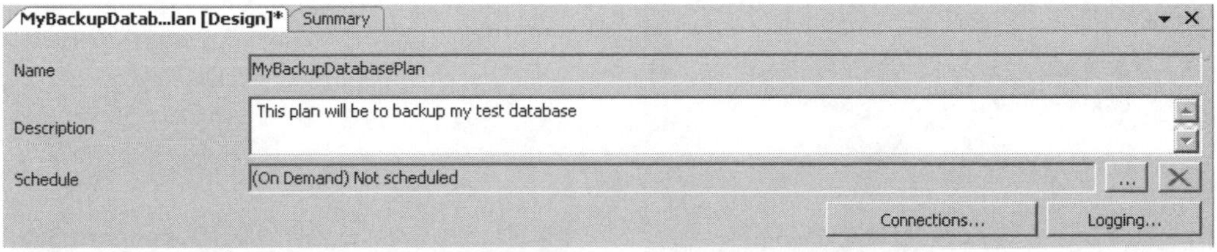

Figure 13-15. *The top half of the Maintenance Plan Designer document window*

The first issue you'll notice with this section of the designer is that the name field is read-only. When you create a new plan, you'll be asked for a plan name before you even see the designer. If you use the default, MaintenancePlan, and later decide you want to change it, then you'll have to use the Rename context menu off of the Object Explorer. You can't change the name of the maintenance plan directly through the designer.

The Description field is editable and can take up to 512 characters.

The Schedule label by default shows (On Demand) Not scheduled. This indicates that the maintenance plan can be run on demand but isn't scheduled via SQL Agent at this time. To schedule this plan, you click the browse button (the one sporting an ellipsis) to launch the Schedule dialog box. In the event that you want to remove a schedule and have the plan be an on-demand plan only, then click the X button. This will delete the schedule associated with this maintenance plan.

Manage Connections Dialog Box

A single server connection is generated for each maintenance plan you create. This connection is to the local SQL Server on which the plan is created. If you want to perform tasks on other instances of SQL Server, you'll need to add additional connections. Each plan doesn't have to contain tasks that all connect to the same server; you could have a plan whereby every task uses a different connection. This design makes it easier to manage and maintain multiple servers. To manage these connections, click the Connections button. This will bring up the dialog box you see in Figure 13-16.

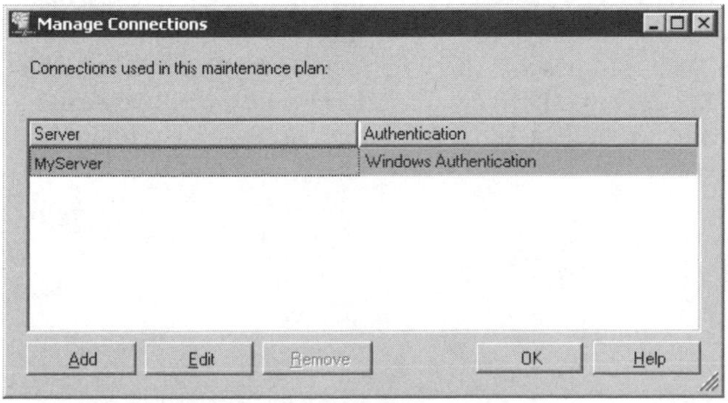

Figure 13-16. *The Manage Connections dialog box*

In Figure 13-16, notice that the Remove button is disabled for MyServer; this is because each maintenance plan requires you to have at lease one connection for the plan itself.

Suppose we want to perform tasks on our other SQL Server instance, MyServer\Instance1. First we add this connection by clicking the Add button, which would launch the dialog box in Figure 13-17.

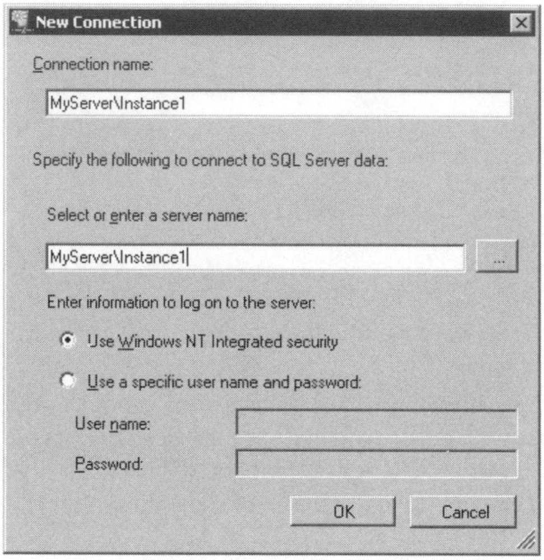

Figure 13-17. *New connection dialog box*

By default the connection name will be blank. You're free to put in any name you would like for this connection. However, we find it easier to enter the actual server name. Once this connection is added, we can use it in any of the existing tasks as well as any new tasks that we drop on the designer surface.

Reporting and Logging Dialog Box

The last button that needs explaining on the designer is the Logging button. This button, when clicked, brings up the Reporting and Logging dialog box as shown in Figure 13-18.

As with SQL Server 2000's Database Maintenance Plan implementation, in SQL Server 2005 you can generate text file reports of the plan as well as send the report to an e-mail recipient. Note that you'll need to install Database Mail in order to send the report to an Agent Operator. One check box item that may not seem so obvious is the Log extended information option. When this item is checked, all the T-SQL that gets submitted to SQL Server will be included in the maintenance plan history. It's checked by default and is useful for debugging any issues that arise from plan execution. However, depending on how large the T-SQL script is that was being executed, this could add a lot of data to your MSDB database. To make sure your MSDB database doesn't get too full, you can either uncheck this option or add a History Cleanup task that will automatically remove mainte-nance plan history tasks older than a certain date.

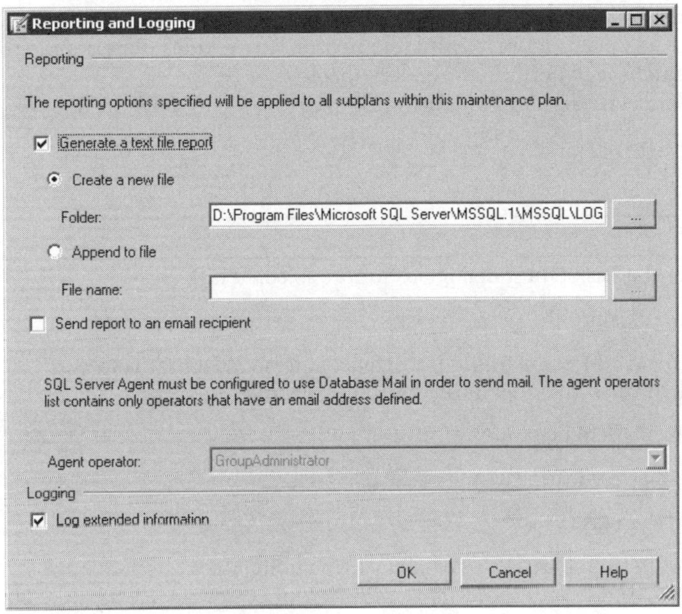

Figure 13-18. *Reporting and Logging dialog box*

Using the Designer Surface

The designer surface is where you actually define what tasks are performed in your maintenance plan. To add a task, simply drag the task from the toolbar onto the designer surface. For purposes of illustration, let's create a maintenance plan for the AdventureWorks database that first checks the database integrity (for example, whether it will issue a DBCC CHECKDB() against SQL Server) , then on success performs a database backup. In addition, on failure of the check, the database would notify an Agent Operator.

First, let's drag the Check Database Integrity, Backup Database, and Notify Operator tasks onto the designer surface. The designer would display the tasks as shown in Figure 13-19.

Figure 13-19. *Maintenance Plan Designer*

One of the first things you may notice is the red X to the right of each of these tasks. This indicates that the task isn't configured and needs more information in order to execute—for example, which connection to use, which database to perform the action on, etc.

Right-clicking a task brings up a context menu with the options presented in Table 13-8.

Table 13-8. *Context Menu for a Task*

Menu Item	Function
Edit	Launches the Task Editor dialog box for the selected task.
Disable/Enable	Enables or disables the selected task.
Add Precedence Constraint	Allows you to add a constraint through a dialog box; alternatively, you can click the task and drag the arrow to the destination task.
Group	Allows the tasks to be groups together.
Zoom	Changes the visual appearance of the designer.
Cut	Cuts the select task.
Copy	Copies to the clipboard the selected task, including the tasks configuration information.
Paste	Pastes the task from the clipboard.
Rename	Renames the task.
Delete	Deletes the selected task.
Select All	Selects all tasks in the designer.

To edit a task, select Edit or double-click the task. For the purposes of this example, we choose to edit the Check Database Integrity task; double-clicking this task brings up the dialog box shown in Figure 13-20.

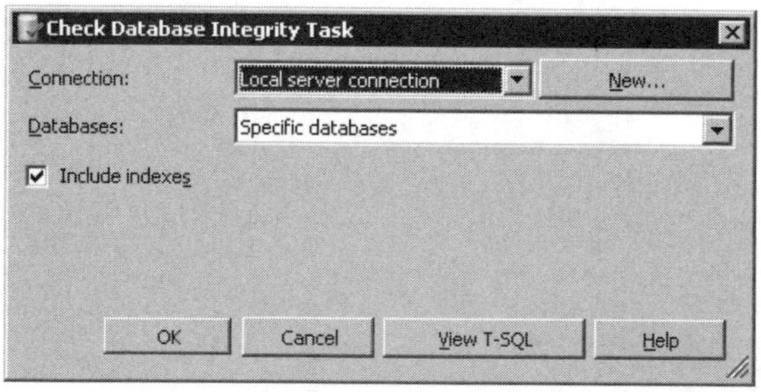

Figure 13-20. *Check Database Integrity Task dialog box*

In each task, there will always be at least two (sometimes three depending on the task) controls on the task editor: Connection, Databases, and Tables (or View). In the case of Check Database Integrity, the task only needs to know the connection and which database to check. By default, the local connection is selected; however, if we defined multiple connections, we could select one of these connections from the drop-down list or create a new connection by clicking the New button, which would bring up the connection dialog box shown in Figure 13-17.

The Databases combo box, when dropped, shows a subdialog box, shown in Figure 13-21, that allows the user to pick the databases on which to perform the action.

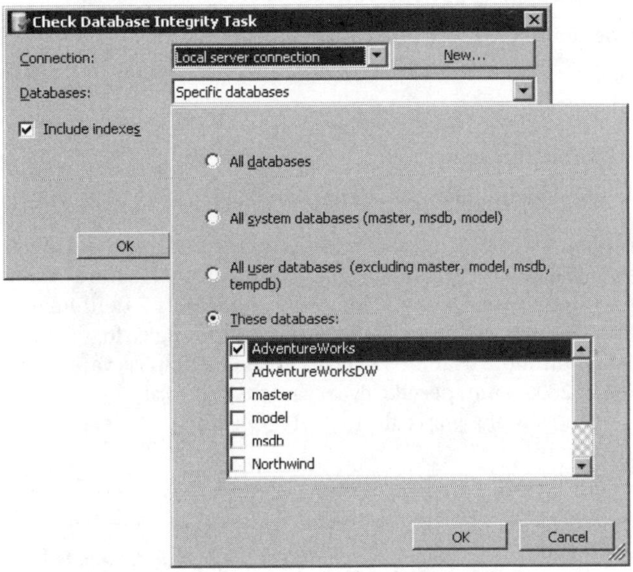

Figure 13-21. *Databases drop-down combo box*

Once you select the database or databases to perform the action on, the task may enable or disable options in the dialog box based on whether you're performing the action on more than one database. This is more apparent from the backup database task than this task though, but its worth mentioning, as you might wonder why all of a sudden some controls on the UI are disabled.

Once the task is configured (that is, a connection is defined and you've selected a database and tables or views as appropriate), you may view the T-SQL that will most likely be executed at runtime against the connection. We say "most likely" because some tasks have conditions that need to be met before they are run, For example, in the case of the Shrink Database task, the user defines how large the database has to be before shrinking, but the View TSQL button will still always show you the T-SQL that would be executed.

Once you configure the task, the red X will disappear, and you can continue editing the other tasks.

One of the most powerful features of a maintenance plan is its ability to create workflow among the tasks. To do this, select a task, click and hold the green arrow at the bottom of the task, and drag this to another task. By default, the arrow is green, indicating On success. To change this, simply right-click the green line and select Error or Completion for On Error or On Completion, respectively.

Once you've defined your workflow and configured the rest of your tasks, you should be able to execute your plan either via Agent by scheduling it or on demand by right-clicking the plan name in Object Explorer and choosing Execute.

Maintenance plans are an important part of a database administrator's daily routine. This new version of maintenance plans combines the power of the SSIS workflow engine with the usefulness of specific maintenance tasks wrapped in an easy-to-use feature.

SQLCMD

SQLCMD, pronounced "SQL command," is a command-line tool used to connect to SQL Server and submit T-SQL queries and commands. With SQLCMD, you can perform the following:

- Execute SQL scripts against any SQL Server.
- Define and pass variables from the command line as well as within scripts.
- Use of predefined system variables.
- Include multiple SQL scripts inline.
- Dynamically change connections within the same script.
- Connect to SQL Server via the dedicated administrator connection (DAC).

SQLCMD was designed as a replacement to the existing osql and isql utilities. Of these two older utilities, osql will still ship in SQL Server 2005; however, it's still tagged as a deprecated feature, so no new development will be done on osql. Switching to SQLCMD from these older tools is definitely worth your time. The SQLCMD code was written from scratch, and it appears as though a lot of effort was put into performance and features that promote usability, such as the ability to pass variables. SQLCMD also supports the new SQL Server 2005 datatypes like nvarchar(max) and xml.

SQLCMD is designed so that the user can simply swap calls to osql.exe with SQLCMD.exe and have the script work without any modifications.

■**Note** If you're directly replacing calls to SQLCMD.exe instead of osql.exe or isql.exe, take note that some parameters aren't supported and are ignored if placed on the command line. They are as follows:

```
-D      ODBC DSN name
-O      use old ISQL behavior
```

Connecting to SQL Server

Unlike osql and isql, which used ODBC to connect to SQL Server, SQLCMD now uses an OLE DB connection and allows users to make multiple connections to different servers within the same script. For example, suppose we had a few simple backup database scripts that each backed up a database on a specific server. On SERVERONE, the administrator would run this backup script to back up the ReportServer database:

```
File: backup_ReportServer.sql
BACKUP DATABASE [ReportServer] TO DISK='C:\backups\ReportServer.bak'
```

On SERVERTWO, the administrator would run this backup script to back up the Products database:

```
File: backup_Products.sql
BACKUP DATABASE [Products] TO DISK='D:\SQLServer\Backups\Products.bak'
```

In the real world, we know that administrators tend to have lots of scripts that each perform their own functions on a specific server. With SQLCMD, you can now consolidate these into a single script using the :CONNECT command. Let's see this same scenario of backing up multiple databases using a single script:

```
File: backup_databases.sql
--Make a connection to SERVERONE using Windows Authentication
:CONNECT SERVERONE -E
--Issue a backup database command for ReportServer
BACKUP DATABASE [ReportServer] TO DISK='C:\backups\ReportServer.bak'
GO

--Make a connection to SERVERTWO using Windows Authentication
:CONNECT SERVERTWO -E
--Issue a backup database command for Products database
BACKUP DATABASE [Products] TO DISK='D:\SQLServer\Backups\Products.bak'
GO
```

Issuing the SQLCMD command sqlcmd -E -i backup_databases.sql yields the following result:

```
Sqlcmd: Successfully connected to server 'SERVERONE'.
Processed 280 pages for database 'ReportServer', file 'ReportServer' on file 4.
Processed 1 pages for database 'ReportServer', file 'ReportServer_log' on file 4.
BACKUP DATABASE successfully processed 281 pages in 0.369 seconds (6.238 MB/sec).
Sqlcmd: Successfully connected to server 'SERVERTWO'.
Processed 144 pages for database 'Products', file 'Products' on file 6.
Processed 1 pages for database 'Products', file 'Products_log' on file 6.
BACKUP DATABASE successfully processed 145 pages in 0.237 seconds (5.011 MB/sec)
```

Passing Variables

SQLCMD also provides the ability to pass variables from the command line and within the script itself. For example, assume you have a generic "backup database" script, called backup_database_generic.sql, that could be reused:

```
File: backup_database_generic.sql
:CONNECT $(myConnection)
BACKUP DATABASE $(myDatabase) TO DISK='C:\backups\$(myDatabase).bak'
```

At this point, we could call this script from the command line using the new -v parameter. This parameter tells SQLCMD that the following text is a variable, an example of which is shown here:

```
C:\>SQLCMD -E -i backup_database_generic.sql
 -v myConnection="." myDatabase="ReportServer"
```

When the backup_database_generic.sql script is run, it will have two variables defined: myConnection, which is equal to "." and myDatabase, which is equal to "ReportServer". Alternatively, if we wanted to use variables, we also could have set the parameters within another script as shown here:

```
File: backup_database_main.sql
:SETVAR myConnection .
:SETVAR myDatabase ReportServer

:R "backup_database_generic.sql"

GO
```

When this script is executed, SQLCMD will set the myConnection variable to "." (the period is an alias for the local server—we could have used "localhost" or the actual name of the server as well), the myDatabase variable to "ReportServer", and then insert the contents of the backup_database_generic.sql script inline.

Using the Dedicated Admin Connection

SQL Server 2005 now spawns a separate thread called the *dedicated administrator connection* (DAC). This connection was designed to be used by members of the sysadmin role in the event that they can't connect to SQL Server under normal operating conditions. There is only one connection of this type allowed per instance of SQL Server available, and it can only be accessed through SQLCMD.

To connect to SQL Server 2005 on the DAC, use the -A parameter in SQLCMD.

```
C:\>SQLCMD -E -S. -A
```

Creating Scripts

Although some might claim Notepad is the best text editor around, writing scripts for SQLCMD can sometimes be tedious using even this robust text editor application. For this reason, SQL Server Management Studio supports writing SQLCMD scripts.

To create a new SQL Script, open the SQL Server Management Studio, connect to your server, and select the New Query button. On the context menu, select New SQL Server Query. You'll now have a query editor window open, as shown in Figure 13-22. If you start typing SQLCMD commands in this window, you'll notice that the editor will complain, and you'll get errors if you try and execute the script.

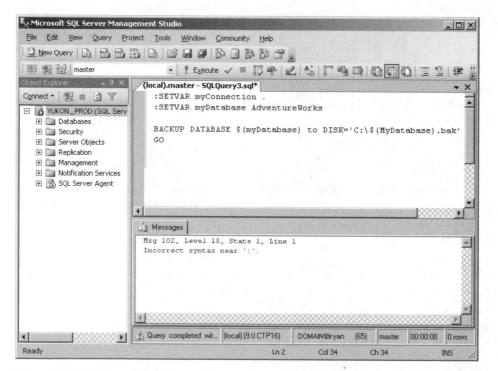

Figure 13-22. *SQL Server Management Studio not in SQLCMD mode*

These errors occur because you first need to enable SQLCMD mode in the editor. You can enable this mode by selecting SQLCMD mode from the Query menu in SQL Server Management Studio. When the editor is in SQLCMD mode, you'll notice that SQLCMD-specific commands such as :SETVAR and :CONNECT are highlighted in the editor, as demonstrated in Figure 13-23. This is to differentiate them from traditional T-SQL. Once the SQLCMD mode is enabled on the editor, the script can be executed by clicking the Execute button. This will pass the script to the SQLCMD application to be interpreted instead of submitting it to the SQL Server database engine directly.

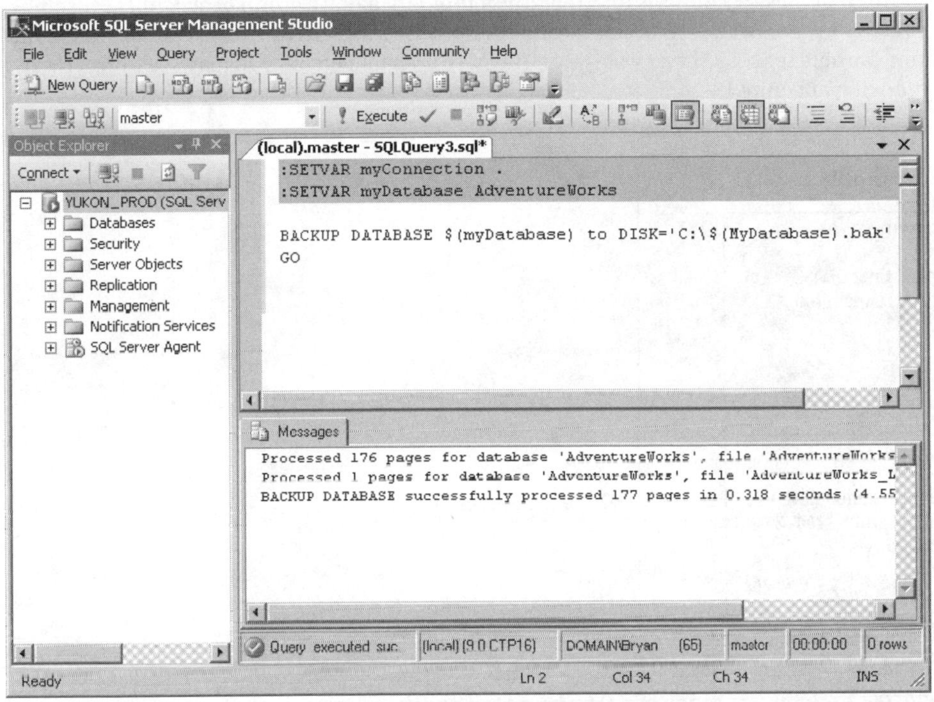

Figure 13-23. *SQL Server Management Studio in SQLCMD mode*

SQLCMD is a complete rewrite of the existing osql command prompt utility. Within its design came many performance-related improvements. At the time of writing, there are no published numbers to report, but preliminary tests suggest SQLCMD will process the script multiple times faster than osql.

Database Mail

Warning: mentioning SQLMail to some database administrators may cause undesirable reactions. The notoriously bad press that surrounded the SQLMail feature in previous versions of SQL Server can now come to an end. So can the hassles of configuring MAPI profiles, installing the Outlook client on your production server, and living with the risk of a disruptive xp_sendmail call taking down the SQL Server process.

Database Mail is a completely new SMTP-based e-mail solution for SQL Server 2005, replacing SQL Mail as the solution for sending mail from SQL Server. This new mail feature provides users with the following:

- Asynchronous mail solution
- Restricted user access to Database Mail
- Scalable SMTP server configuration
- Attachment and query restrictions

Overview

Before we dive into the Database Mail internals, let's define a few basic concepts in the Database Mail world. An *account* is a name, description, and authentication information for a specific SMTP account. A group of these accounts is referred to as a *profile*. Having a group of accounts is useful, since this adds a layer of reliability, because the mail would still be sent by a different account in the profile if one particular SMTP server was down. If you're a visual person, you may see things more clearly by looking at Figure 13-24.

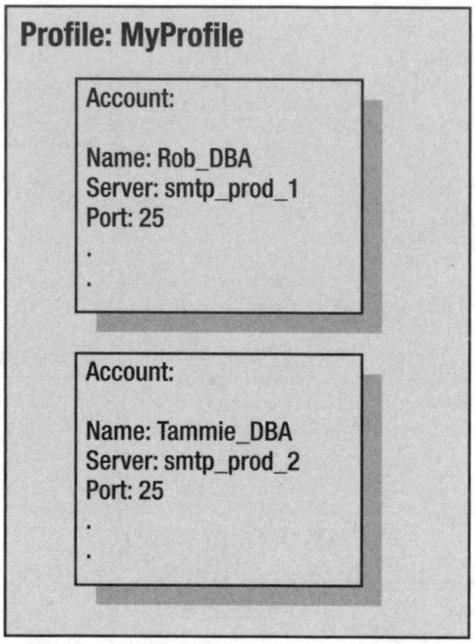

Figure 13-24. *Pictoral representation of a Database Mail profile*

As shown in Figure 13-24, there is one profile defined as MyProfile. This profile has two accounts created within it: Rob_DBA and Tammie_DBA, respectively.

When users send mail using Database Mail, they use the new stored procedure `sp_send_dbmail`. An example is shown here:

```
sp_send_dbmail      @profile_name='MyProfile',
@recipients='testuser@apress.com',
@subject='Test Message',
@body='This is the body of the message.',
@importance='HIGH'
```

One of the parameters in this stored procedure is `@profile_name`. When the user specifies a profile, Database Mail looks at the first account that is defined for the particular profile and attempts to send the e-mail using this account. If for whatever reason the send fails, such as when the SMTP server is offline, Database Mail will wait 100 seconds (the default Account Retry Delay setting), and then proceed down the account list and attempt to send the mail using the second account. If this account fails, it will continue to the next account, and so on. When it has reached the end of the account list, the send will fail. If the administrator wanted Database Mail to loop back around and attempt the first account again, he can set the Account Retry Attempts setting to the number of times Database Mail will "round-robin" the account list. These global settings will be described in detail in the upcoming section, "Configuring Database Mail."

So are profiles just a way to group accounts? Well, sort of. There are two types of profiles: public and private. Public profiles can be accessed by any valid MSDB database user. With private profiles, administrators can limit which users can use a specific profile.

Database Mail installs both configuration and mail item information in the MSDB database. In SQL Server 2005, it isn't possible to install Database Mail on any other database.

Configuring Database Mail

The Database Mail Wizard can be accessed from the Configure Database Mail context menu off of the Database Mail node. This wizard is used to manage accounts, profiles, and Database Mail global settings. Clicking Next on the welcome screen will bring you to the Select Configuration Task page. This page, which is shown in Figure 13-25, will determine which function the wizard should perform.

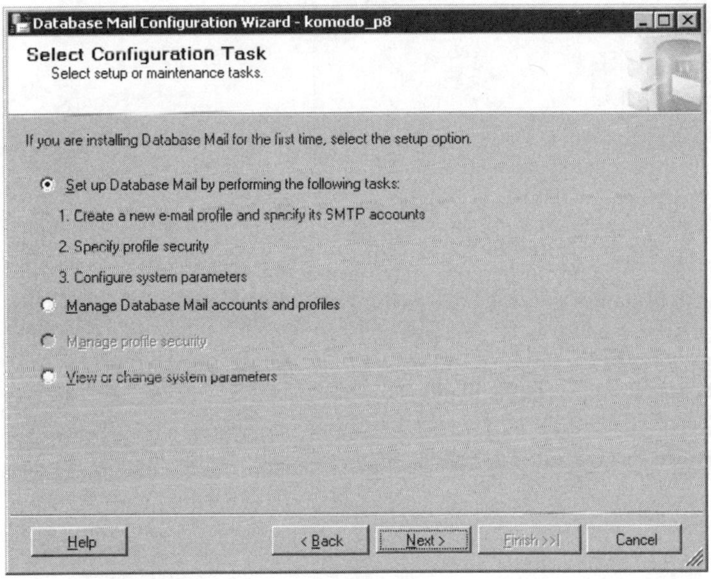

Figure 13-25. *Select Configuration Task page*

By default, configuring the mail host database is selected. Since we are interested in configuring the mail host database, we can simply click the Next button.

■**Note** At one point, Database Mail could be installed on any database, but sometime after Beta 2 of SQL Server 2005, a decision was made to restrict its use to just the MSDB database. Thus, the Database Mail mail host database is MSDB.

At this point we need to have at least one profile configured in order to use Database Mail, which we do through the New Profile page, shown in Figure 13-26. The profile name is what users will use when sending e-mail, so make sure it's easy to remember. The description is optional and is used to provide a more descriptive purpose for the profile.

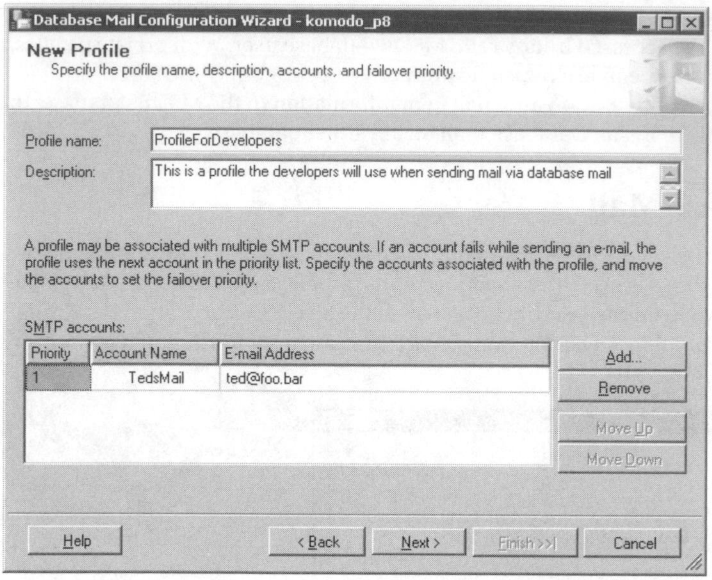

Figure 13-26. *New Profile page*

At the bottom of this page, you can define one or more accounts that this profile will use. Clicking Add will pop up a dialog box that will allow you to select an existing account or create a new account.

Once an account is defined, it's available for all profiles.

Clicking Next now brings us to one of the more interesting UI conglomerations without SQL Server. The "Manage Profile Security" page is shown in Figure 13-27.

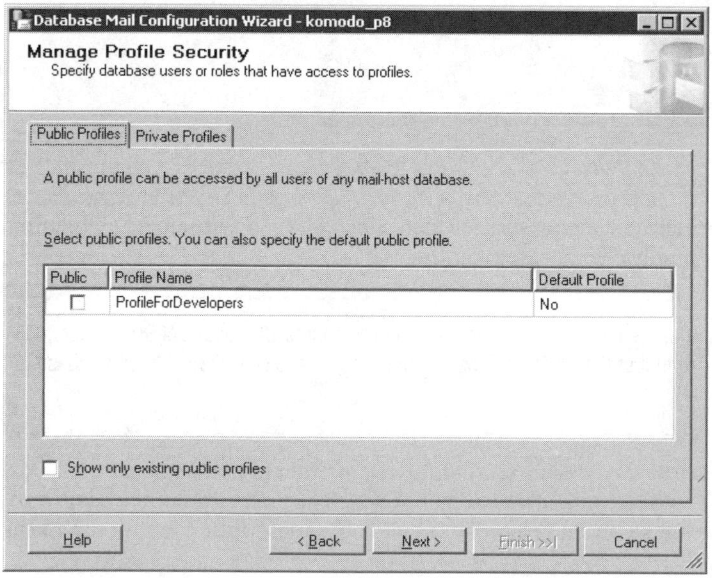

Figure 13-27. *Manage Profile Security page*

The first thing to notice about this page is it has two tabs: Public profiles and Private profiles. When a new profile is created it's neither public nor private; basically only sysadmins can use this profile. If the sysadmin marks a profile as public, then any database user in the MSDB database can send mail using this profile.

Note In an effort to increase security, any non-sysadmin user who wants to use Database Mail must be added to the DatabaseMailUserRole database user role in MSDB.

If you click the Private profile tab, you'll notice a combo box that allows you to specify a database user, as shown in Figure 13-28.

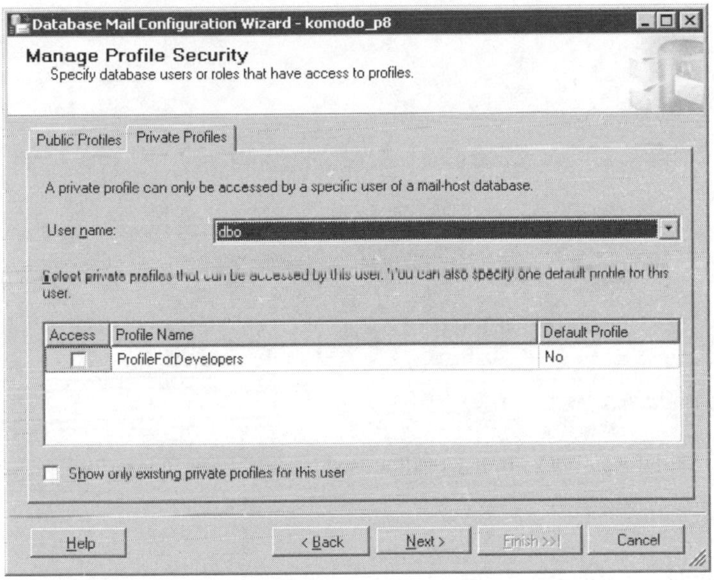

Figure 13-28. *Manage Profile Security, Private Profile page*

From the user name combo box, you can select any user name and check the profiles to which to grant them access. Once you finish the wizard, the private profile won't generally show up unless you have the user name selected in the combo box.

The last significant property that needs to be set on a profile is the default profile. If there are no profiles that are set for the default, then users will always have to specify the @profile_name parameter in the sp_send_dbmail stored procedure call. If the sysadmin has a default profile defined, users can omit the profile and Database Mail will use the default profile that is defined.

Clicking Next on the wizard will bring you to the last configuration page called Configure System Parameters, shown in Figure 13-29.

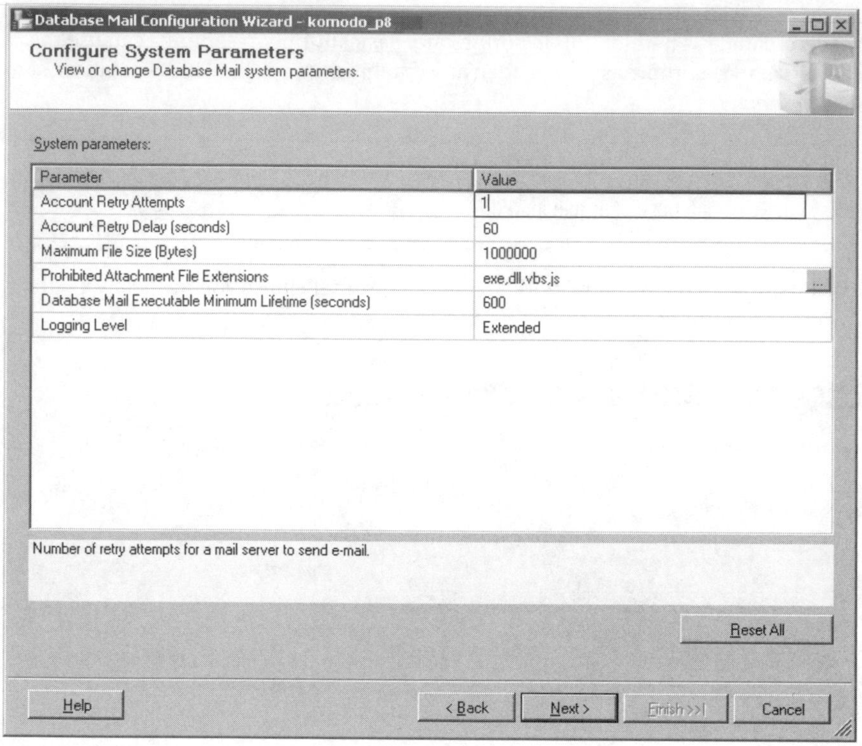

Figure 13-29. *Configure System Parameters page*

This page allows the user to set the global settings of Database Mail. Table 13-9 describes each of these parameters.

Table 13-9. *Database Mail System Parameters*

Parameter	Description
Account Retry Attempts	This is the number of times Database Mail will try to send the mail before declaring failure.
Account Retry Delay (seconds)	This is the delay in-between attempts to resend mail.
Maximum File Size (Bytes)	This is the maximum file size for attachments allowed per mail.
Prohibited Attachment File Extensions	This determines which file extensions won't be sent.
Logging level	This is the amount of information saved in the log.
Database Mail Executable Minimum Lifetime (seconds)	This is a performance-tuning option and specifies how long the Database Mail process will live for before terminating due to no activity.

The next page on the wizard is the summary page describing the actions that will be performed. Following that page is a progress page that will show you the live status of the actions being performed on your database.

Depending on which options you selected, you'll have a variable number of actions to be performed. In the event of a failure, the status would read "Failed," and there would be an error message hyperlink in the message column. Clicking this hyperlink may provide you with additional information about this error, provided you have an active Internet connection. This online error help feature can be seen throughout all of the SQL Server Management Studio dialog boxes and wizards.

The Database Mail feature isn't enabled by default on SQL Server. As we've seen in the wizard, this feature can be enabled via the wizard or through the SQL Server Surface Area Configuration tool. If you're planning on configuring Database Mail entirely through scripts and want to enable Database Mail, simply enable the Database Mail XPs parameter through the `sp_configure` stored procedure as shown here:

```
SP_CONFIGURE 'show advanced', 1
GO
RECONFIGURE
GO
SP_CONFIGURE 'Database Mail XPs", 1
GO
RECONFIGURE
GO
```

So now that we've finished the wizard, we're ready to send mail.

Sending Mail

For purposes of this discussion, consider an example where the administrator has created a single profile called `MyDatabaseMailProfile`. This profile contains two accounts: `Rob_DBA` using SMTP server `SMTP_SVR1`, and `Tammie_DBA` using SMTP server `SMTP_SVR2`.

At this point, the administrator issues the following T-SQL command:

```
Use msdb
GO
EXEC sp_send_dbmail @profile_name='MyDatabaseMailProfile',
@recipients='username@foo.bar',
@subject='Test message',
@body='This is the body of the test message.'
```

The stored procedure will first validate that the required parameters are entered, and then write the message in the `sysmail_mailitems` table. Having an immediate copy of the mail before it's "sent" allows the administrator to easily troubleshoot mail problems. After the `mailitems` entry is created, the stored procedure will call another stored procedure to create an XML document that wraps the mail. At this point this XML document is sent to a predefined SQL Service Broker queue. SQL Service Broker in SQL Server 2005 provides queuing and reliable messaging. Using this feature allows Database Mail to asynchronously send large amounts of e-mail without disrupting other server operations.

When messages are placed on this queue, a SQL event notification is raised. At this point, another Service Broker queue is listening for this event, and upon reception it will spawn the `DatabaseMail90.exe` process. When this process is instantiated, it obtains configuration information from MSDB, pulls messages from the queue, and sends the mail. Upon completion, it will update the `sysmail_mailitems` table with delivery status and update the `sysmail_log` table. Since spawning a process is an expensive operation, the process itself will stay alive after processing all the mail items for a time period that is defined in the Database Mail global configuration settings as Database Mail Executable Minimum

Lifetime. The default value is 600 seconds, or 10 minutes, and can be changed through the Database Mail wizard.

SQL Profiler

SQL Profiler (aka Profiler) is the primary tool for use in performance analysis and tuning for SQL Server. It can be used to capture queries and statement events that are sent to a specific server. For example, imagine that you're a database administrator in a large organization and are tasked to find out why a particular database application is running slow. The application is an inventory management tool. This tool is a Win32 application that uses SQL Server as its data storage engine. Users had reported that most of the time the application works well except for when they try to obtain a report for the quantity of SKUs left in their inventory. You start troubleshooting this by launching SQL Profiler located in the Performance Tools menu of Microsoft SQL Server 2005.

When Profiler is launched, you essentially have a blank screen and a menu bar. From here, we can start a new trace or load an existing trace. Since this is our first time troubleshooting, let's choose New Trace from the File menu. This will cause a Connection dialog box to pop up asking which server we want to perform a trace on. We make a connection to the server that contains the Products database, which is the database that the Inventory management tool is using. Once connected, we are presented with the Trace Properties dialog box as shown in Figure 13-30.

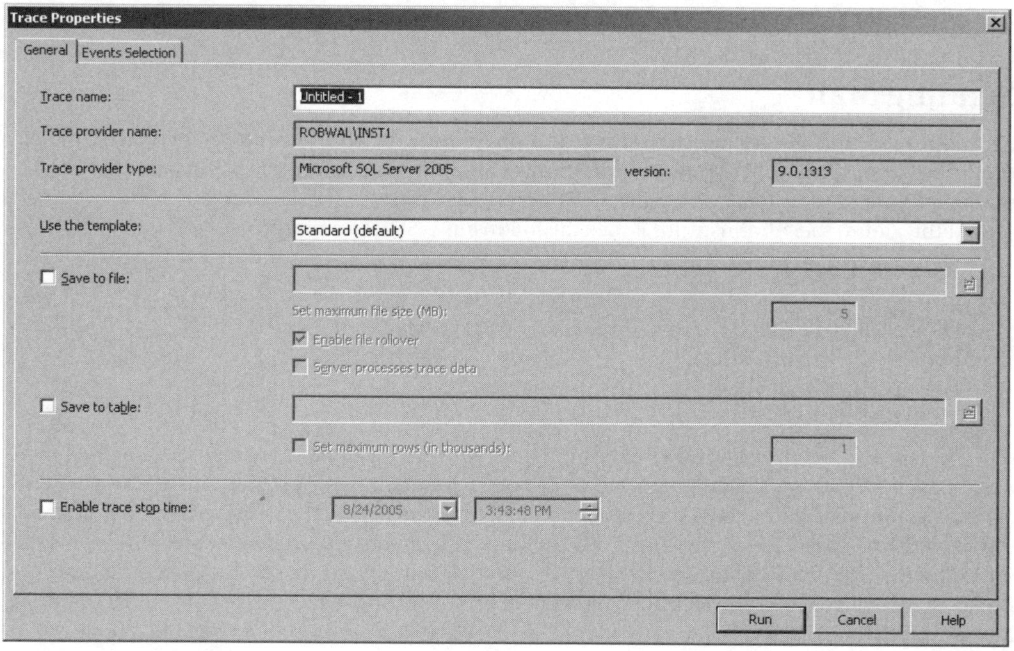

Figure 13-30. *Trace Properties, General tab*

Here we are able to give the trace a name and specify where the trace should be created either on file or in a table. Traces can also be configured to stop at a certain time, so if you had an issue that occurred at irregular intervals, you could set up a trace to run for a certain period of time in hopes of capturing some useful information. Predefined templates are also available to help sort out which events to listen to. Eight templates are available, and if none of these eight are right for you, you can create your own templates to use. For the purposes of this example, we will use the Standard

(Default) template. If you click the Events Selection tab, you'll notice which events and columns that this particular template is using. You can add or remove any addition events from this tab as shown in Figure 13-31.

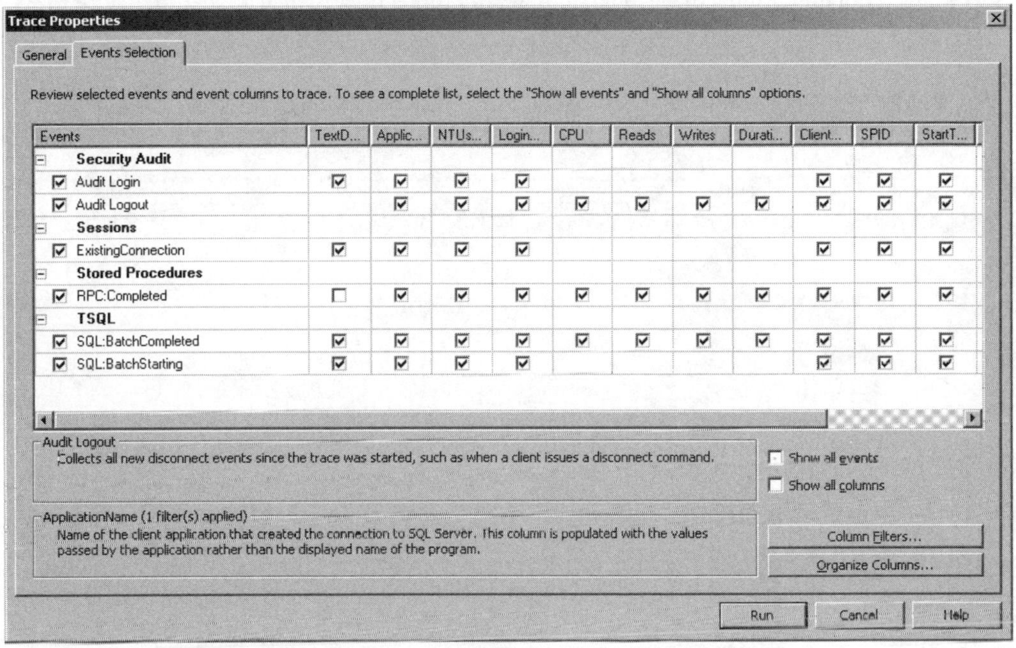

Figure 13-31. *Trace Properties, Event selection tab*

You can notice the plethora of choices available by clicking the Show all events and Show all columns check boxes. To assist in trying to reduce the amount of unneeded data, you can optionally filter your columns by clicking the Column Filters button. Since we are looking for long running queries, let's put a filter on the Duration column to only show events that are longer than 2 seconds in duration, as shown in Figure 13-32.

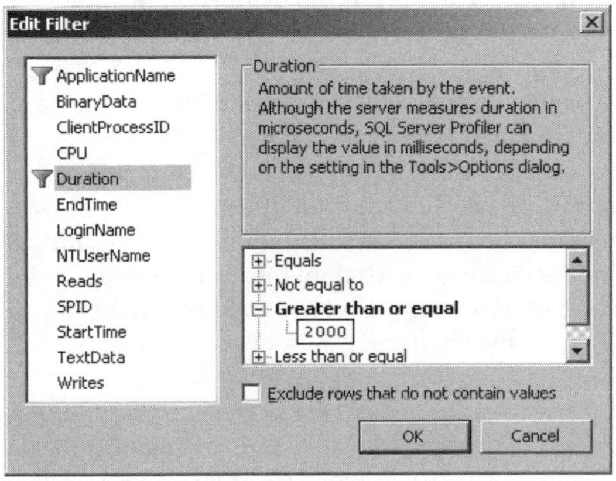

Figure 13-32. *Column Filter dialog box*

Now that we've defined the trace, we can click Run on the Trace Properties dialog box to start recording. Once we have SQL Profiler tracing SQL Server, we can now run the problematic database application.

Assume that we ran the database application and noticed the performance problem that our users were complaining about. If we took a look at our Profiler trace, which appears in Figure 13-33, we can see the problematic T-SQL statement.

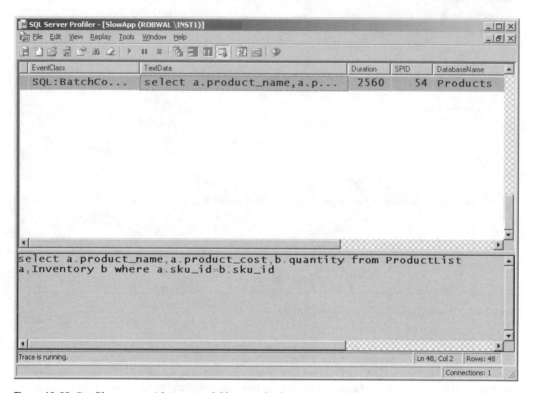

Figure 13-33. *Profiler trace with 2-second filter applied*

If you click the row, the complete T-SQL will be displayed at the bottom of the tool. Now that we see that this select statement was the problem, we can notify the developer of this issue or take a look at optimizing the schema using indexes.

Profiler for SQL Server 2005 contains a lot of new functionality. Most of the enhancements have come as a result of utilizing XML heavily throughout the feature set. The extensibility that XML provides allows Profiler to become more extensible and dynamic, as we will show in this section.

In SQL Server 2005, trace definitions are now dynamically loaded from the server. This allows Profiler to adjust its event selection based on the server it's connecting to. For example, if in a future service pack a new event is created or modified, Profiler will be able to adapt these new settings to its list of available events. Having a dynamic trace definition also made it easier to add new server types to capture traces from. In SQL Server 2005, Profiler can now trace and replay events from Analysis Services 2005 as well.

There could be times when a Profiler user would want to automate trace collection, trace manipulation, and trace replay. This would allow users to establish performance benchmarks against their applications. There is now a set of objects under the Microsoft.SqlServer.Management.Trace namespace that allows users to programmatically achieve this.

Performance Monitor Correlation

Perhaps one of the more useful features in Profiler for SQL Server 2005 is the ability to import Performance Monitor data and correlate it to a specific trace. The combination of these two technologies gives users a useful way to observe system performance and trace events simultaneously.

One thing you should note is that you can't correlate both Performance Monitor and trace events live; you must have already captured the trace file and Performance Monitor data before you can correlate them in Profiler. The following example demonstrates a quick way to get started with this feature.

In this example, we want to see if sending large amounts of Database Mail affects the CPU process. First we set up a Profiler trace to capture the Database Mail stored procedure calls, just as we did previously in this chapter by selecting the New Trace menu option from File menu. On the Events Selection tab, make sure to include at least the SQL:BatchCompleted event.

Before we start the trace, we need to define the Performance Monitor counter log that will be used to capture our Performance Monitor objects. To create a new counter log, open the Performance Monitor tool and select New Log Settings from the Counter Log node. Since we are interested in processor utilization but aren't quite sure which counter to include, let's include the Processor object of the local server, as shown in Figure 13-34.

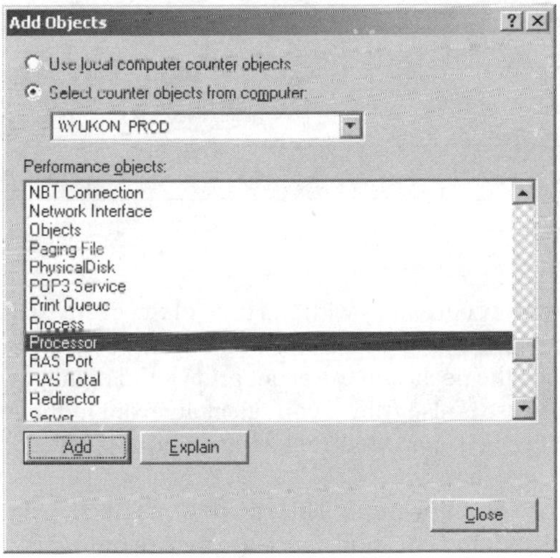

Figure 13-34. *Add Objects dialog box*

This can be selected by clicking the Add Objects button. Also include the Database Mail objects using the same Add Object dialog box. At this point, we can now start both the Profiler trace and Windows Performance Log. Our environment is now set up so that we can execute a Database Mail script that will send 100 e-mails. After the script is executed, we stop the Performance Monitor log and save the trace file.

Now that we have both a performance log and trace file, we can now use Profiler to correlate these two logs based on time. To do this, we first load the trace file using Profiler.

To load Performance Monitor data, we select the Import Performance Data option on the File menu. Next we select the performance counter log file that was just created. Profiler asks us which counters we want to correlate at this point. For this example, we'll select % Processor Time and SendMailRequests. Once this selection is made, notice that Profiler now contains both the trace file and performance counters on the same screen as shown in Figure 13-35.

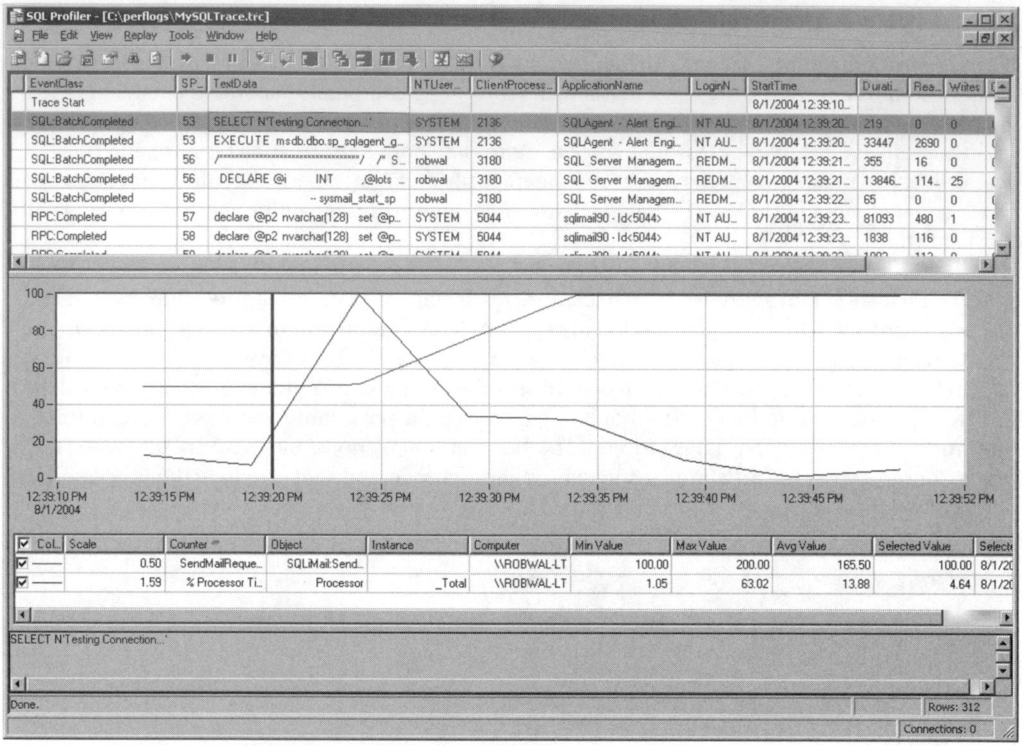

Figure 13-35. *Profiler showing Perfmon correlation*

The vertical line on the performance counter window correlates with the time of the event that is selected in the event grid. For example, if the user wanted to know what statement was being executed when the CPU was at its peak, she could click the peak, and the event grid would highlight the statement that executed at that time. The reverse case is also true: if you select an event in the grid, the red line will move to the time period in the Performance Monitor log that contained this event.

Users can also zoom in and out of the Performance Monitor graph. This can be done by clicking the start time and dragging the mouse to the desired end time location. Once the mouse button is released, the Performance Monitor graph will adjust and only show you the selected time period. The context menu of the Performance Monitor graph gives you the ability to zoom out or to show all the Performance Monitor data available.

ShowPlan

ShowPlan is a feature of SQL Server that allows the user to obtain information about the data retrieval methods chosen by the SQL Server query optimizer. ShowPlan appears in the form of an execution plan that includes information such as the execution cost of specific statements and queries. The actual plan information comes in the form of XML from the SQL Database Engine. The Profiler user interface interprets this information and forms the familiar ShowPlan execution as seen in the SQL Server Management Studio.

To enable the ShowPlan feature in Profiler, as it appears in Figure 13-36, select the ShowPlan XML event under the Performance category. Once this event is selected, the Events Extraction Settings tab will show up on the Trace Properties dialog box. This tab will allow users to save the XML

ShowPlan data separately to a file. Users can also load the ShowPlan data in SQL Server Management Studio for further analysis.

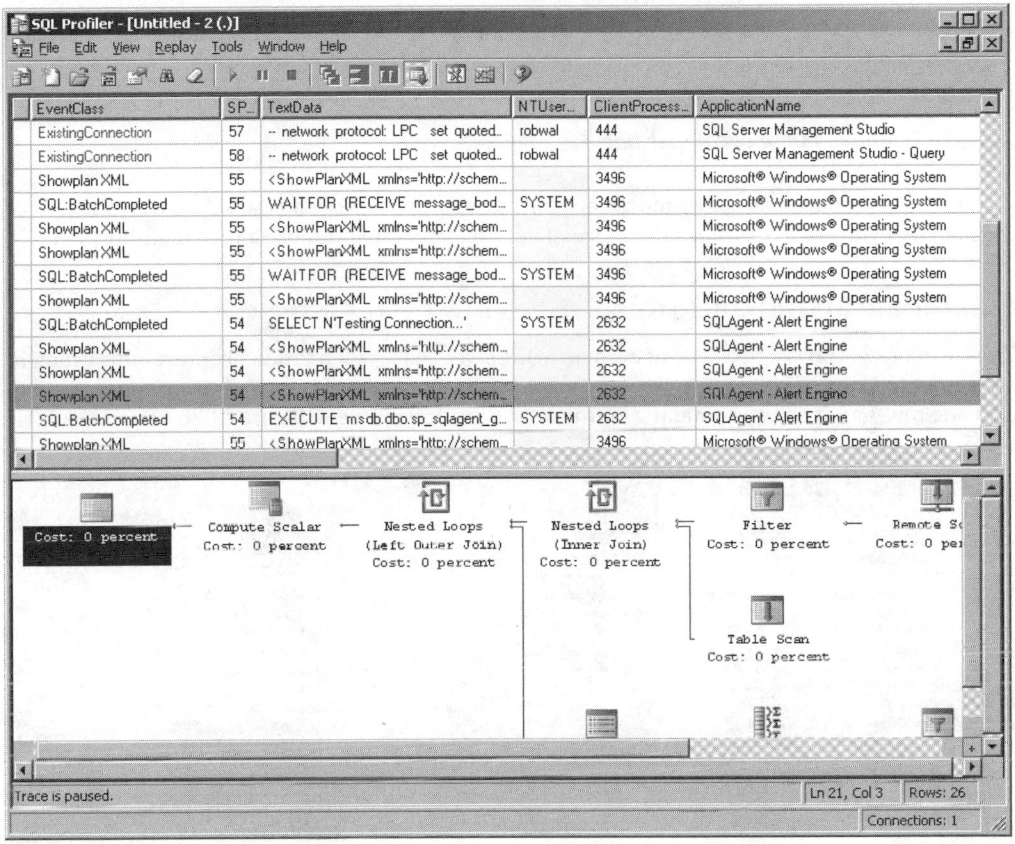

Figure 13-36. *ShowPlan inside Profiler*

To manually save the current trace file for offline access, select File ➤ Save As ➤ Trace XML File. Later, you can load this trace file and view the saved ShowPlan by selecting Trace File from the File ➤ Open menu item.

■**Note** You'll have to change the Files of type setting from SQL Profiler trace files (*.trc) to XML files (*.xml) in order to load trace files saved as XML.

ShowPlans can become quite large and are difficult to view in a single UI. When a ShowPlan exceeds the size of the visible screen, a + button appears toward the bottom-right side of the Show-Plan output. When clicked, a small pop up appears that shows a bird's-eye view of the entire plan. The image was not intended to be completely legible, rather it's designed to show an outline of the complete plan. An example of this is shown in Figure 13-37.

Figure 13-37. *ShowPlan navigational aide*

The smaller rectangle can be moved around by using the mouse and is used to select the part of the plan that you want the UI to show. A small but useful feature for those larger-than-life plans.

Deadlock Visualization

The Deadlock graph is a new type of event in SQL Server 2005. When Profiler captures this event, it shows the `<deadlock-list>` tag in the TextData column. To display a graphical visualization, simply click the row, and it will appear at the bottom of the tool as you see in Figure 13-38.

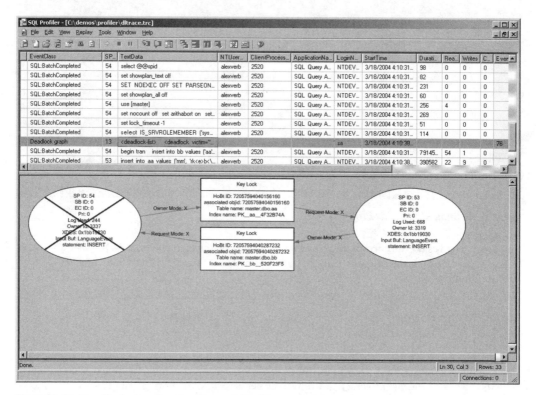

Figure 13-38. *Deadlock visualization through Profiler*

Each ellipse is a process within SQL Server. In this example, we can see that both SPID 54 and 53 are trying to acquire the same lock. In the end, SPID 54 was chosen as the victim, and its actions were rolled back. The rectangles show the resource IDs and some additional information about the object. As with ShowPlan XML, the Deadlock graph can also be saved to a file separately through the same Events Extraction Settings tab on the Trace Properties dialog box. SQL Server Management Studio can also load the graph in its user interface for further analysis by the user.

Summary

SQL Server 2005 provides some additional features and functionality that make it easier for database administrators to manage their servers. SQL Server Agent provides multiple proxy accounts, allowing system administrators the ability to define with more granularity access to SQL Server Agent and its related subsystems. The new Maintenance Plan feature gives a whole new meaning to management in SQL Server. With workflow and easy ability to configure maintenance tasks, database administrators will have an easier and more flexible way of performing scheduled server maintenance. In addition to maintenance plans, scripts are a large part of the everyday life of a database administrator. SQLCMD, the replacement for isql.exe and osql.exe, provides better performance and some added features like variables. Variables allow users to easily reuse scripts and make the overall management experience easier. SQLMail is being deprecated starting this release and is replaced with an asynchronous SMTP-based mail solution called Database Mail. This new mail system has made sending mail from SQL Server incredibly more reliable than previous versions of SQL Server. Profiler has extended its feature set in SQL Server 2005 and brings together a variety of technologies, such as Performance Monitor correlation, to extrapolate a fairly accurate image of actual server resource utilization and bottlenecks. Together these new features mentioned in this chapter scratch the surface of the most recent release of SQL Server 2005. SQL users should be pleased overall with the advancements made in the product.

CHAPTER 14

■ ■ ■

Integration Services

SQL Server Integration Services (SSIS), formerly known as Data Transformation Services (DTS), is Microsoft's extraction, transformation, and loading tool bundled with SQL Server 2005. Truly a Swiss army knife of the ETL world, SSIS enables you to perform many tasks, including

- Importing and exporting data between SQL Server instances and heterogeneous data sources
- Applying sophisticated transformations against data
- Automating SQL Server maintenance tasks and business processes
- Executing scripts
- Sending e-mail notifications
- Using FTP to receive or send files
- Interacting with message queues
- Launching Analysis Services processes
- Submitting data mining queries
- Processing and manipulating XML files
- Querying your computer using Windows Management Instrumentation (WMI) queries and responding to events accordingly

When DTS was first introduced in SQL Server 7.0, DBAs and database developers viewed it with both interest and skepticism. Many who attempted to use more than the Import/Export Wizard experienced bugs and instability.

Microsoft listened to DBA and developer feedback, and with SQL Server 2000 DTS it worked hard to tighten the screws of this high-potential tool, improving stability, fixing bugs, and adding additional DTS tasks.

Now with SQL Server 2005, DTS has changed dramatically, as Microsoft has added several new features, improved existing features, and removed problem areas. The changes are so significant that the name even changed to SQL Server Integration Services (from now on referred to as SSIS). DBAs and developers alike can use SSIS to address a wide variety of business solutions. The following are some example scenarios in which SSIS can be used:

- A real estate company is building a property search website that allows users to search for properties by city and county. It receives several denormalized flat files from third-party multiple listing services. Each of the third-party providers produces flat files differently, so the solution must be flexible. Each of these files must be imported, scrubbed, and put into the same normalized tables in the database. SSIS is used to import the files via FTP, scrub them using transformations, and load them into the production tables.

- A manufacturing company trains new plant managers on how to use a parts-tracking mainte-nance application. During training, trainees are allowed to connect to their own test database, where they can modify the data without doing harm to the production data. Nightly, an SSIS package is scheduled to refresh the data in the training databases, based on real data from a production database.

- A financial services company uses legacy systems to track an individual investor's transac-tions to his or her savings plan. These legacy systems allow simple OLE DB connectivity to the raw transactional data. A reader-friendly reporting database isn't available. Executives want to be able to view aggregated transaction data grouped by investment and time period. SSIS is used to extract data from the legacy systems into a SQL Server database.

- An information technology company wants to automate the extraction and reporting on the condition of its SQL Server environment. The company wants to maintain a central reporting database in SQL Server that will contain various statistics about all SQL Server machines (SQL Server Agent jobs, SQL Error and Agent logs, database file locations, and the last time each database was backed up). SSIS is used to query each server and extract the data to the central-ized reporting database.

- A human resources (HR) department in a small regional office receives daily "new employee" files from corporate headquarters. Each file contains a single record of data for each new employee. Included in this record is a BLOB image containing the photo of the new employee. The HR department uses SSIS to import the character data into one table and output the image BLOB into a separate image file (using the Export Column transformation).

What's New in SSIS?

Although some SQL Server 2000 DTS concepts remain the same in SSIS, be prepared for an entirely new paradigm. Several of the components provided in DTS 2000 have been moved around, renamed, improved, or eliminated entirely in SSIS. Some feature highlights include

- A new integrated development environment (IDE) used for developing SSIS packages called *Business Intelligence Development Studio* (*BIDS*).

- In DTS 2000, connections, tasks, transformations, and workflow precedence constraints all shared the same workspace, sometimes resulting in clutter and confusion. With SSIS, *control flow* elements (containers, tasks, and workflow precedence constraints) and *data flow* elements (data sources and transformations) are now divided into their own separate design surfaces. *Connections* also get their own workspace, resulting in a much cleaner and streamlined IDE. New design surfaces were also added for event handlers and Package Explorer.

- Existing tasks have been enhanced since DTS 2000. For example, the *File Transfer Protocol task* now allows you to FTP files out, instead of just in.

- Several new tasks have been created to help minimize custom ActiveX coding. For example, the *File System task* allows numerous file manipulation activities that would have required copious coding in previous versions of DTS.

- The *Send Mail task* now uses Simple Mail Transfer Protocol (SMTP) instead of relying on the cumbersome MAPI client. If you have a valid SMTP server on your network, you can now send mail through SSIS without installing or configuring MAPI profiles on the SQL Server machine.

- SSIS package files are now saved in XML format, instead of binary format.

- Custom SSIS components (tasks and transformations) can now be created using .NET languages.

- The Visual Basic .NET language is now used within the new *Script task*, providing a full-featured language that removes the language limitations encountered with VBScript and JScript in DTS 2000.

- Digital signatures can now be applied to SSIS packages, to prevent loading of altered packages.

- New "container" objects have been introduced that allow the grouping of related tasks (which can be expanded or collapsed for package readability) and loop containers that allow repeating workflows based on user-defined conditions.

- Using checkpoints, packages can now be restarted after a package failure, without re-running tasks that succeeded prior to the failure.

- The addition of new command-line executables, including DTEXEC (which replaces 2000's DTSRUN), DTSEXECUI (which replaces 2000's DTSRUNUI), and DTUTIL, allows you to move, copy, delete, and check for the existence of DTS packages, and apply a digital signature to an SSIS package.

We'll discuss these new features and improvements in the sections that follow.

SSIS's New IDE

If you've worked with Visual Studio before, you'll be familiar with the layout of this new IDE. BIDS has adopted the Visual Studio concept of projects and solutions:

- A *project* is a container that groups related files and can contain one or more SSIS packages (in this chapter, we'll discuss just Integration Services projects).

- A *solution* is a container that groups and manages projects used to develop business solutions.

The method of accessing the new IDE has also changed. In SQL Server 2000, Enterprise Manager had a Data Transformation Services folder that allowed you to create, modify, and delete DTS packages. You had four options for saving your packages: to SQL Server, to a structured storage file, to a Visual Basic file, or to Meta Data Services.

You created a package by opening Enterprise Manager, starting a new package in DTS Designer, and then saving it in SQL Server. The integration was tight, but informal. DTS packages were treated as additional database objects, rather than self-contained, stand-alone projects.

Beginning with SQL Server 2005 Beta 2, handling of SSIS packages is significantly changed from Enterprise Manager's way of doing things. With SQL Server 2005, the two primary management tools are Business Intelligence Development Studio (BIDS) and SQL Server Management Studio (SSMS).

Management Studio is loosely related in features to SQL Server 2000's Enterprise Manager and Query Analyzer. With regard to SSIS, Management Studio allows you to import packages to and export packages from the MSDB database and file system, as well as schedule SSIS packages to execute from a SQL Server Agent job.

Microsoft has also introduced the *Integration Services* service, a new Windows service installed with SSIS. You can use the Integration Services service to monitor remote and local packages (viewing their execution state), stop packages (locally or remotely), manage package storage, and customize storage folders.

Connecting to SSIS in Management Studio

This exercise assumes that you installed SSIS when you installed SQL Server 2005 and that it was enabled using the SQL Server Configuration Manager or the SQL Server Surface Area Configuration tools. Having done that, here are the steps you need to follow:

1. Open SQL Server Management Studio.

2. In Object Explorer, click the Connect button and select Integration Services.

3. In the Connect to Server dialog box, type in the Server name where the Integration Services service is located (i.e., the machine name).

4. The Integration Services service node will now appear in Object Explorer.

5. Expand the Running Packages folder. Unless SSIS packages are currently running, you won't see any packages.

6. Expand the Stored Packages folder. Notice the File System folder and MSDB folders. By right-clicking either of these folders, you can create subdirectories for storage of your packages, and execute, rename, or perform other package operations. Unlike in SQL Server 2000 DTS, you can't edit the package from this window. We'll review how you create and edit packages in the next section.

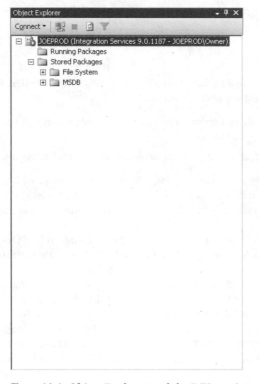

Figure 14-1. *Object Explorer and the DTS service*

Notably missing from SSMS functionality is the ability to actually execute, create, modify, debug, and deploy a DTS package. For this, you must use BIDS, which integrates analytic tools and resources, such as reports, cubes, and DTS packages. It is here that you are able to create, modify, debug, run, and deploy SSIS packages. This is your new SSIS package design environment.

Creating a New SSIS Project in BIDS

Follow these steps to create a new project called MyFirstDTSProject:

1. Open BIDS.

2. From the File menu, select New Project.

3. In the New Project dialog box, under Templates, select Integration Services Project. In the Name field, type **MyFirstSSISProject**. Leave the check box for Create Directory for Solution checked.

4. Click OK.

If you've used previous versions of DTS, you'll notice that there are many more windows and design surfaces in BIDS. In this chapter, we'll review each of these design surfaces and windows, describing what they are and how they are used.

SSIS Fundamentals

Although much has changed in SSIS since DTS 2000, the core of SSIS remains the *package*. A package is a collection/container of tasks, connections, containers, and workflow that can be executed via a command-line utility (DTEXEC), scheduled as a SQL Server Agent job, or designed and debugged from the SSIS Designer (now found in BIDS).

In previous versions of DTS, the DTS Designer had a single design surface for placing all DTS tasks, connections, workflow (precedence constraints), and transformations. For simpler packages, this was acceptable; however, as the packages increased in complexity, it became more difficult to discern what activities the package was actually performing. To address this, the SSIS Designer has divided the workspace into five new areas (see Figure 14-2): the Control Flow design surface, the Data Flow design surface, the Event Handlers design surface, Package Explorer, and Connections. We'll describe each area in the sections that follow. (There are a number of other windows in the IDE that we'll describe shortly as well.)

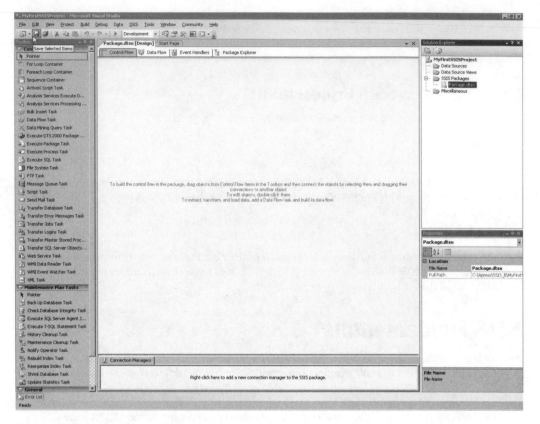

Figure 14-2. *SSIS Designer interface*

Control Flow Design Surface

You use the Control Flow design surface to place tasks, containers, and precedence constraints (which define package workflow).

At a minimum, a functional SSIS package can contain one or more *tasks*. A task is a unit of work performed during the runtime of an SSIS package execution. Tasks perform various activities such as moving data, executing T-SQL commands, using FTP, sending mail notifications, and much more. SSIS provides several out-of-the-box tasks that perform various operations (we'll review some of these tasks later in the chapter).

SSIS also introduces a new type of object and concept, the *task container*, of which there are three kinds: the Sequence container, the Foreach Loop container and the For Loop container (these are described in detail in the "Containers" section later in the chapter).

These containers are used to hold other tasks or containers, providing hierarchical (parent/child container) control to the package. Containers group tasks together into a meaningful unit of work, allowing you to, for example, participate in an SSIS transaction (described later in the chapter). Depending on the type of container task, you can also perform iterative and conditional loop processing against the tasks held within the container (see Figure 14-3).

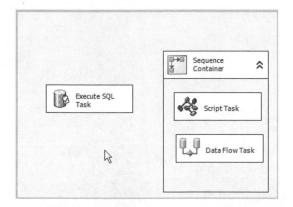

Figure 14-3. *A Sequence container that contains tasks*

Packages and tasks are also considered to be containers in SSIS. A package is a container that can contain other containers or tasks. A TaskHost container encapsulates a single task.

Using the SSIS Designer, you can add a task within your SSIS package by simply dragging the selected task from the toolbox window (by default on the leftmost side of the development environment) onto the Control Flow design surface. After placing a task on the design surface, you can proceed to set the various properties and settings, unique to the type of task you're configuring.

Once you've defined the tasks that should execute within the package, you'll most likely want to define their workflow. For example, you may wish to run a specific task only if the preceding task succeeds. Other workflow possibilities include executing a task only if the preceding task fails, or regardless of failure or success. You can define both the order of operation and workflow by using *precedence constraints*. Precedence constraints are used to connect executables in the package, helping to order the workflow as well as define the conditions under which the tasks run. If no precedence constraints are defined, during package execution (runtime), all tasks will attempt to run simultaneously (or in no particular order).

Figure 14-4 shows the On Success and On Failure precedence constraints between tasks. The left arrow (which is green in the UI) defines the On Success precedence, and the right arrow (which is red in the UI) defines the On Failure precedence constraint. A blue arrow (not shown here) indicates an On Completion precedence constraint.

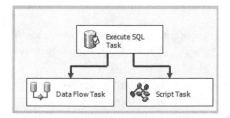

Figure 14-4. *On Success and On Failure precedence constraints between tasks*

Annotations are text labels that can be added to the Control Flow and Data Flow design surfaces, allowing you to self-document the SSIS package (see Figure 14-5). You can add an annotation by right-clicking the package surface and selecting Add Annotation.

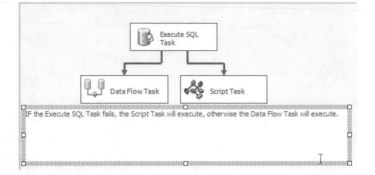

Figure 14-5. *Adding an annotation to the Control Flow design surface*

Data Flow Design Surface

When you add at least one Data Flow task to the Control Flow design surface, you can access the Data Flow design surface tab. The Data Flow task (which replaces the Transform Data task from DTS 2000) has several other control components associated to it. By introducing more granular control for the Data Flow task, the SSIS developer is now able to introduce more flexible processing and handling of data movement, modifications, and extraction.

The Data Flow task consists of source adapters, transformations, and destination adapters. These objects are available from the Toolbox menu on the Data Flow design surface (see Figure 14-6).

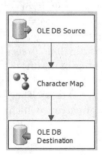

Figure 14-6. *Data Flow design surface*

- *Source adapters* access data from different types of data sources, making the data available to the Data Flow task. Source adapters produce *outputs*, meaning they feed output columns and rows to the receiving destination adapter or transformation.

- *Transformations* are tasks used within the data flow of a package to modify data per your particular business needs. Transformations require *inputs*, meaning they expect an input of columns and rows from either another transformation or from a source adapter. Transformations also provide outputs that contain columns and rows, making them available to other transformations or destination adapters.

- *Destination adapters* write data in a data flow to different types of data sources. Destination adapters use inputs to receive columns and rows from source adapters or transformations.

When working with data flow components, you use *paths* to connect them together. A path connects two components by connecting the output of one component to the input of another. A path allows two workflow options: a "success" (green) path or an "error" (red) path.

Once connected by a path, the resulting set of connected data flow components is called a *graph* (see Figure 14-7). In this case, an OLE DB source is used as a source adapter, connected to a Character Map transformation, which writes data to an OLE DB destination adapter. (The Character Map transformation allows you to apply string functions to character data—for example, to change the source data from lowercase to uppercase.)

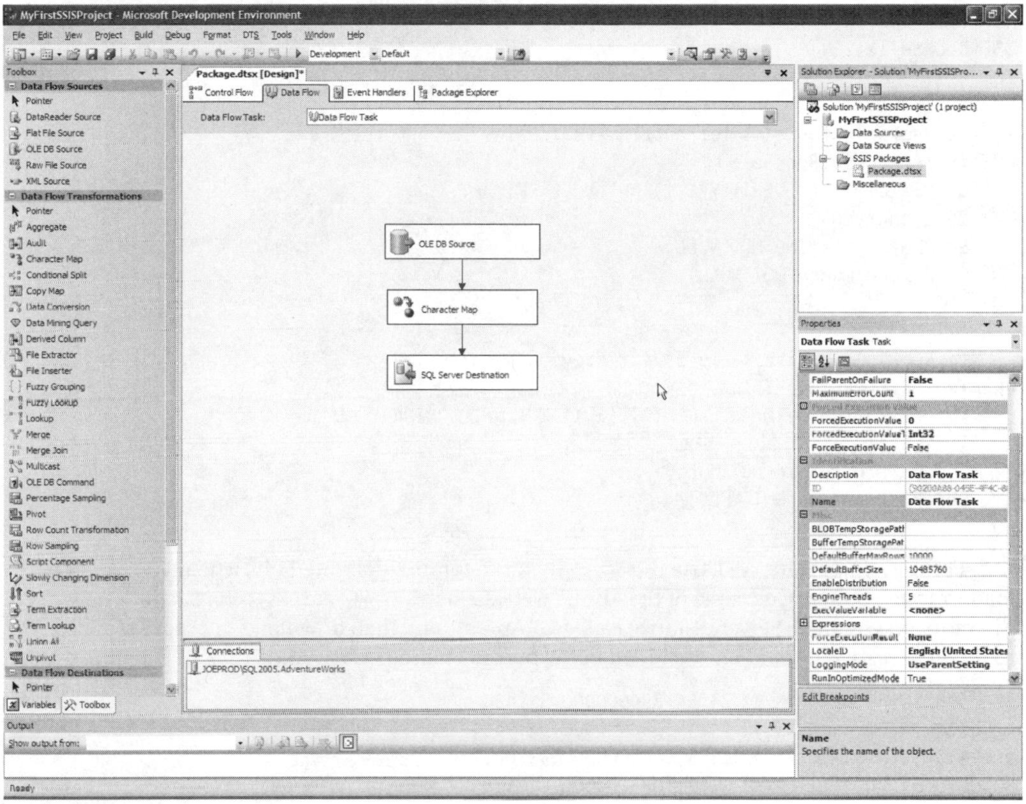

Figure 14-7. *Example data flow graph*

A Data Flow Example

The example in this section will give you a preview of the new SSIS Data Flow functionality. Don't worry if you don't understand all the steps you're performing—the purpose of this exercise is just to familiarize you with the primary concepts before diving into the details later on in the chapter.

One of the more common uses of SQL Server 2000 DTS was importing data from external flat files into SQL Server. Flat file integration is often an easier data exchange solution than attempting to move data directly between different relational database or mainframe systems. A DB2 database administrator, for example, may find it easier to dump out data into flat files for the SQL Server DBA to consume, rather than attempting to connect via native methods.

In this example, we'll use SSIS to import data from a single BookSales.txt file. We'll import this data into two tables in the BookSale database (which we'll create in this exercise). Data from the year 2005 will be imported into BookSale table. Book sales from before 2005 will be put into the BookSaleArchive table. We'll begin by creating the data source and destination.

Creating the Sample Data Source and Destination

In SSMS, open a new query window connected to your SQL Server 2005 instance and execute the following script (to create the BookSeller database and tables):

```
-- Create the BookSeller database with Default settings
CREATE DATABASE BookSeller
GO

USE BookSeller
GO

-- The BookSale table is for current-year sales
CREATE TABLE dbo.BookSale
    (BookSaleID int IDENTITY(1,1) NOT NULL PRIMARY KEY,
     ISBN char(10),
     SoldDate datetime NOT NULL,
     SoldPrice money NOT NULL)
GO

-- The BookSaleArchive table is for previous-year sales
CREATE TABLE dbo.BookSaleArchive
    (BookSaleArchiveID int IDENTITY(1,1) NOT NULL PRIMARY KEY,
     ISBN char(10),
     SoldDate datetime NOT NULL,
     SoldPrice money NOT NULL)
GO
```

For the source data, we'll use the BookSales.txt comma-delimited file, which you can download from the Source Code area of the Apress website (http://www.apress.com). Create a new directory on your SQL Server instance called C:\Apress\ and then download the BookSales.txt file to that directory. The columns included in the file are ISBN, SoldDate, and SoldPrice, in that order:

```
1700670127,2004-10-13 12:23:54.890000000,31.434
2190414452,2004-12-11 12:23:55.080000000,91.5634
9163370433,2004-10-23 12:23:55.080000000,93.8803
8240890662,2004-11-02 12:23:55.080000000,72.5189
9724485384,2004-11-01 12:23:55.080000000,42.3559
3818073842,2004-10-10 12:23:55.080000000,35.5185
4354109840,2004-11-07 12:23:55.080000000,77.4156
3841883691,2004-10-19 12:23:55.090000000,5.2721
8248344093,2004-11-23 12:23:55.090000000,27.8866
7742829934,2004-09-29 12:23:55.090000000,96.8699
3972918159,2004-11-30 12:23:55.090000000,80.8913
3387357000,2004-11-05 12:23:55.090000000,37.0749
3020951299,2004-10-31 12:23:55.090000000,55.7052
5062025755,2004-10-01 12:23:55.090000000,25.1956
7794466091,2004-12-15 12:23:55.090000000,79.8708
```

```
3613708504,2004-11-09 12:23:55.090000000,17.2435
7033565864,2004-10-22 12:23:55.090000000,92.4496
4632544057,2004-10-08 12:23:55.090000000,89.7585
5004909486,2004-09-23 12:23:55.090000000,31.6866
1916341917,2004-12-02 12:23:55.090000000,42.531
9828905102,2005-03-12 12:24:05.837000000,31.4099
4401326876,2005-02-01 12:24:05.837000000,29.9687
4439395032,2005-02-14 12:24:05.837000000,13.013
6062292933,2005-02-12 12:24:05.837000000,5.6384
2497442656,2004-12-29 12:24:05.837000000,92.9495
4405919414,2005-02-19 12:24:05.837000000,39.628
7499038595,2004-12-29 12:24:05.837000000,55.5942
799884766 ,2005-03-02 12:24:05.837000000,32.4062
7137023232,2005-01-04 12:24:05.837000000,64.077
9857116326,2005-03-25 12:24:05.837000000,21.5201
6858375361,2005-02-04 12:24:05.837000000,79.6188
2811816672,2005-02-07 12:24:05.837000000,77.5774
6066791506,2005-02-17 12:24:05.837000000,51.4393
8398729596,2005-02-15 12:24:05.837000000,27.2878
6016191510,2005-03-28 12:24:05.837000000,15.7501
5739941273,2005-01-19 12:24:05.837000000,71.9712
2507570361,2005-03-12 12:24:05.837000000,56.2592
6272684851,2005-03-13 12:24:05.847000000,93.4991
388103114 ,2005-04-03 12:24:05.847000000,76.8347
9602390361,2005-02-15 12:24:05.847000000,2.4937
```

Creating a Connection to SQL Server

This next set of steps shows you how to create a connection manager to SQL Server, which you can then use as a data source and destination.

1. Open BIDS.
2. From the File menu, select New Project.
3. In the New Project dialog box, under Templates, select Integration Services Project. In the Name field, type **BookSalesImport**. Leave the check box for Create Directory for Solution checked.
4. Click OK.
5. From the Toolbox, drag the Data Flow task onto the design surface of Control Flow tab.
6. Double-click the Data Flow task to switch to the Data Flow design space.
7. In the Connections window, beneath the Data Flow design surface, right-click a blank area and select New OLE DB Connection.
8. Click the New button to create a new data connection manager.
9. In the Connection Manager dialog box, in the Server name field, select or enter the name of your SQL Server instance and select the logon method. For the database, select BookSeller (see Figure 14-8).

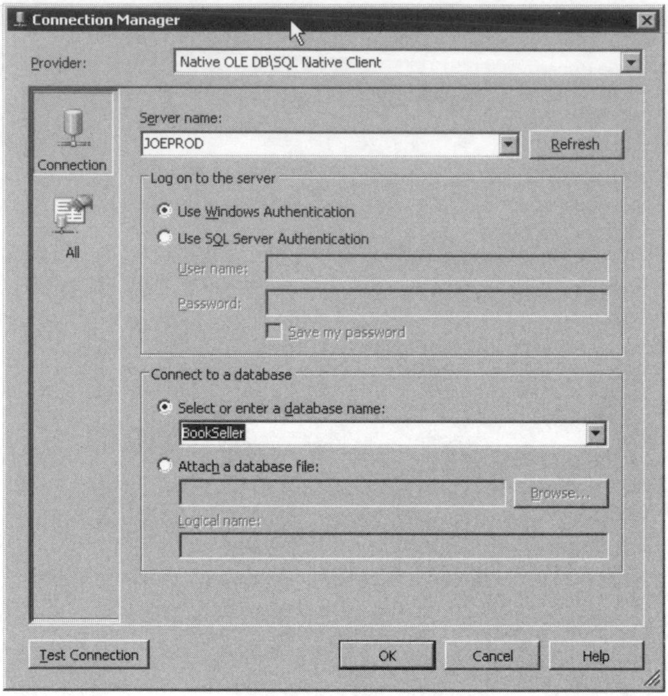

Figure 14-8. *Choosing the SQL Server instance in the Connection Manager dialog box*

10. Click OK, and then click OK again to select the new data connection manager.

Your new connection manager should now appear in the Connections section of the SSIS Designer.

Creating a Data Source

Next, we'll create a connection for the BookSales.txt text file that will be used to pull the data into a transformation.

1. In the connection manager pane, click a blank area and select New Flat File Connection.

2. In the Flat File Connection Manager Editor dialog box, type **BookSales.txt** in the "Connection manager name" field. In the "File names" area, select the location of the BookSales.txt file (see Figure 14-9).

3. Click the Columns selection in the left navigation pane. This will show the default row and column delimiters identified by the application (comma delimited should be selected). You should see that the three columns were identified: ISBN, SoldDate, and SoldPrice (see Figure 14-10).

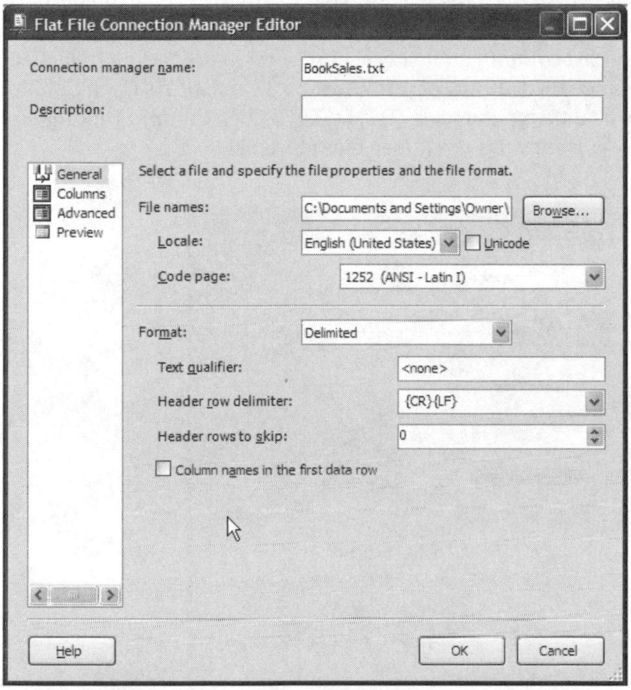

Figure 14-9. *Flat File Connection Manager Editor dialog box*

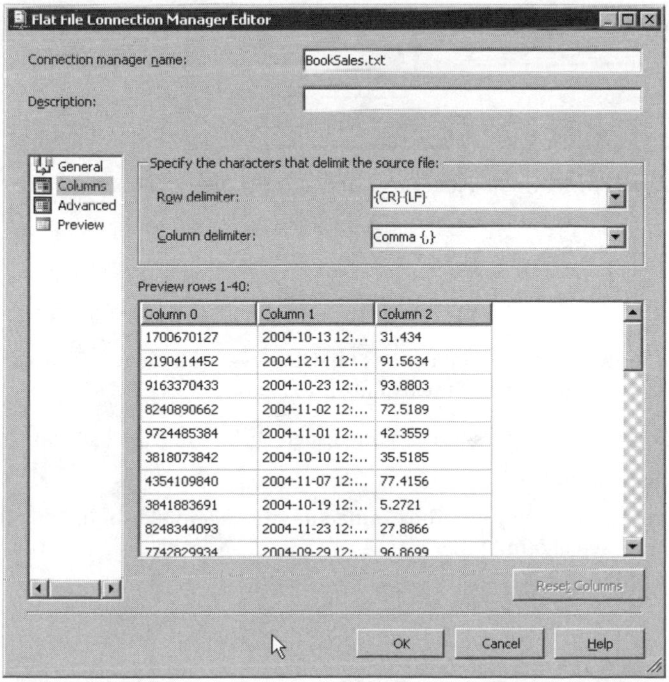

Figure 14-10. *Columns selection in the Flat File Connection Manager Editor*

4. Click the Advanced selection in the left navigation pane. This will show the properties of each column. You need to ensure that each column is interpreted as the proper data type. Column 0, which is the ISBN column, is already set properly to the "string [DT_STR]" data type. For Column 0, change the OutputColumnWidth to a value of 10. Click Column 1 (SoldDate) and change its data type to "date [DT_DATE]". Click Column 2 (SoldPrice) and change its data type to "currency [DT_CY]" (see Figure 14-11).

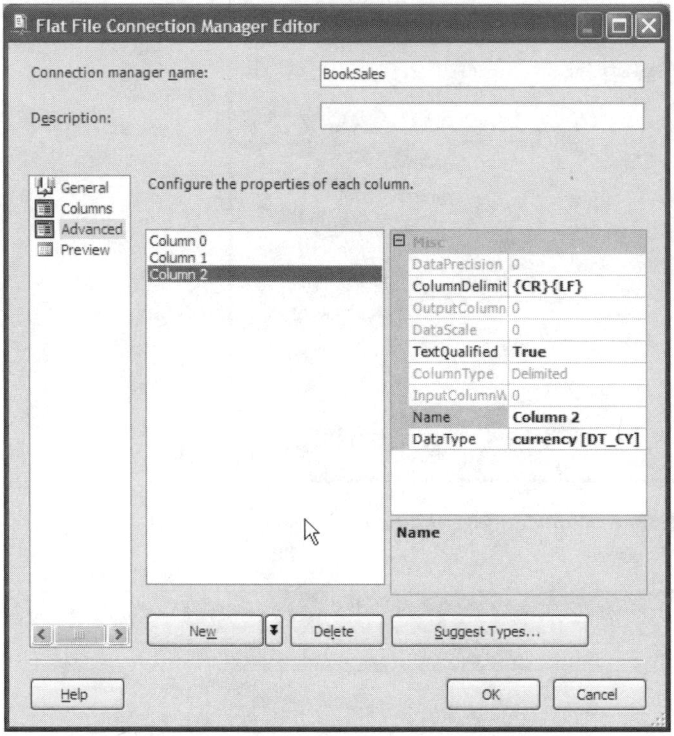

Figure 14-11. *Advanced settings in the Flat File Connection Manager Editor*

5. Click OK to accept the settings.

Creating the Data Flow

The next steps demonstrate how to use the connections to SQL Server and the text file to create a data flow, allowing you to import the values of the text file into a table.

1. From the Toolbox, drag the Flat File source to the design surface of Data Flow tab.

2. Double-click the Flat File source.

3. In the Flat File Source Editor dialog box, the Connection manager field should default to the BookSales connection (see Figure 14-12).

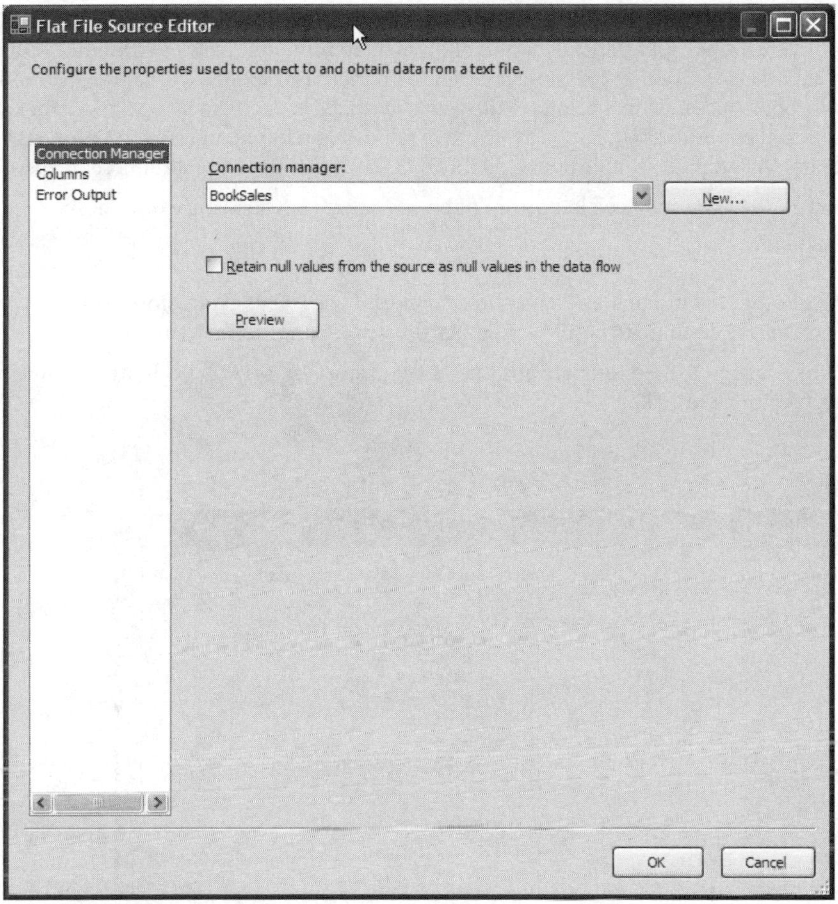

Flat File Source Editor
Configure the properties used to connect to and obtain data from a text file.
Connection Manager
Columns
Error Output
Connection manager:
BookSales
New...
Retain null values from the source as null values in the data flow
Preview
OK
Cancel

Figure 14-12. *Flat File Source Editor dialog box*

4. Click Columns in the left navigation pane. Notice the three checked columns. Click OK to accept the defaults.
5. From the Toolbox, drag the Conditional Split transformation to the design surface of the Data Flow tab.
6. Click the Flat File source so that a green arrow appears. Click and drag the green arrow to the Conditional Split transformation (see Figure 14-13).

Flat File Source
Conditional Split

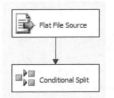

Figure 14-13. *Flat File source and Conditional Split transformation*

7. Double-click the Conditional Split transformation.

8. The Conditional Split transformation allows you to route data rows to different outputs based on a condition/expression you define. In this case, you'll use this transformation to route book sales rows that belong to the year 2005 to the BookSale table, and rows from previous years will be routed to the BookSaleArchive table. Begin by expanding the Columns folder in the upper-left pane. Notice that available columns from the Flat File source are listed.

9. Click in the Condition cell in bottom pane and enter the following expression:

```
YEAR( [Column 1])==2005
```

10. Press Enter. Notice that the default output name is Case 1. This expression evaluates Column 1, the SoldDate column, to confirm whether the row belongs to the year 2005.

11. Write a second expression beneath Case 1 (see Figure 14-14) that evaluates if a row belongs to a year prior to 2005:

```
YEAR( [Column 1])<2005
```

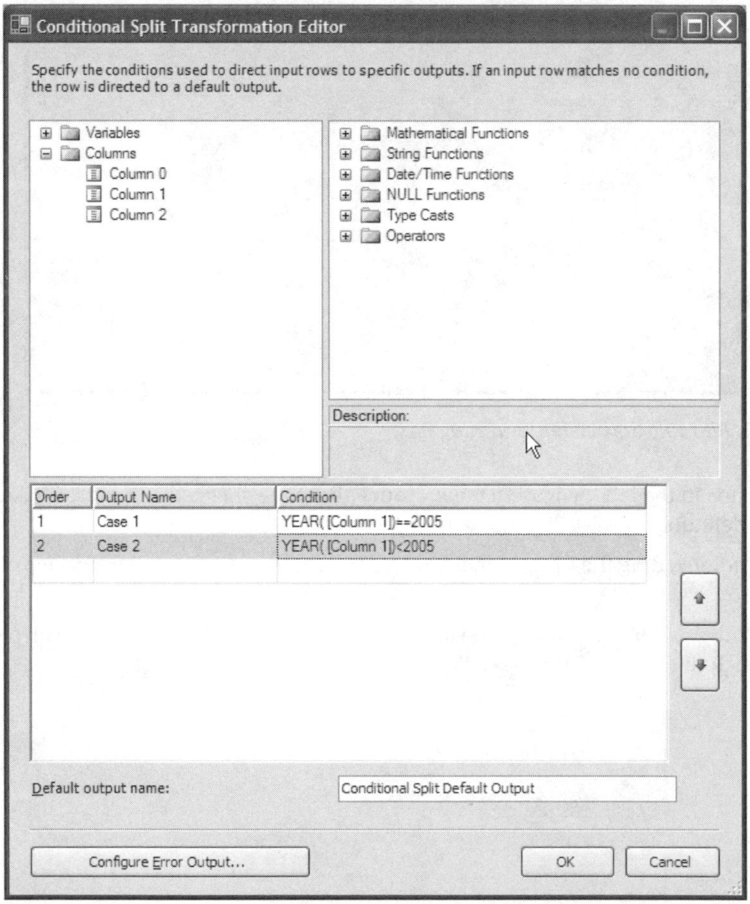

Figure 14-14. *Conditional Split Transformation Editor dialog box*

12. Click OK.

■**Note** YEAR([Column 1])<2005 is an example of an SSIS expression. Expressions are used within the Conditional Split and Derived Column transformations, and within variables, precedence constraints, and loop containers. If you have used T-SQL before, some of the functions and operators in the expressions may be familiar to you; however, there are several differences, too. For more information on SSIS expressions, see the Books Online topics "Using Expressions in Packages" and "SSIS Expression Concepts."

---

13. From the Toolbox, drag the OLE DB Destination to the design surface of Data Flow tab.

14. Connect the Conditional Split transformation to the OLE DB Destination by dragging the green connector (which appears when you click the Conditional Split). You will be prompted in the Input Output Selection dialog box to select an Output (see Figure 14-15). Select Case 1, which evaluates rows belonging to the year 2005.

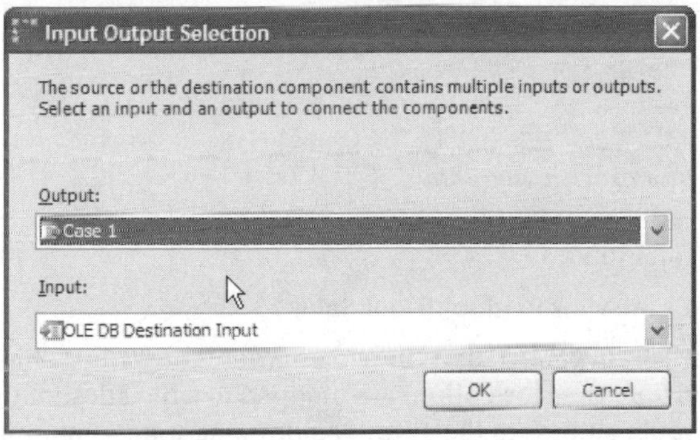

Figure 14-15. *Input Output Selection dialog box*

15. Click OK. Notice that Case 1 now appears by the green path.

16. Click the OLE DB Destination, and in the Properties window (the lower-right window) rename it to **BookSale** (see Figure 14-16).

■**Tip** The Properties window is context sensitive. It will display properties for the currently selected SSIS object (task, transformation, package, etc.).

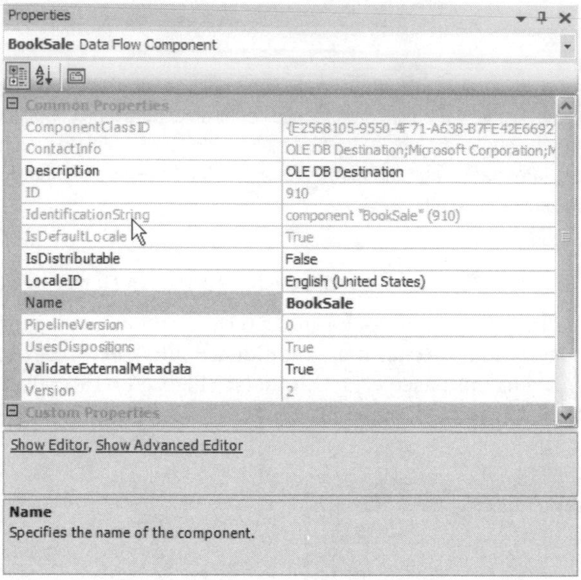

Figure 14-16. *OLE DB Destination Properties window*

17. Double-click the BookSale destination.

18. Change the name of the table or the view to **[dbo].[BookSale]**.

19. Select Mappings on the left navigation pane. This is the screen where you define which input columns (from the Conditional Split transformation) are mapped to which destination columns. Click and drag the input columns to the output column mappings, mapping Column 0 to ISBN, Column 1 to SoldDate, and Column 2 to SoldPrice (see Figure 14-17).

20. Click OK.

21. From the Toolbox, drag the OLE DB Destination to the design surface of the Data Flow tab.

22. Connect the Conditional Split transformation to the OLE DB Destination by dragging the green connector (which appears when you click the Conditional Split). You will be prompted in the Input Output Selection dialog box to select an Output. This time, select Case 2, which evaluates rows belonging to the years less than 2005.

23. Click OK. Notice that Case 2 now appears by the green path.

24. Click the OLE DB Destination, and in the Properties window rename it to **BookSaleArchive**.

25. Double-click the BookSaleArchive destination.

26. Change the name of the table or the view to **[dbo].[BookSaleArchive]**.

27. Select Mappings on the left navigation pane. Click and drag the column mappings, mapping Column 0 to ISBN, Column 1 to SoldDate, and Column 2 to SoldPrice.

28. Click OK when you've finished. Your design surface should look something like Figure 14-18.

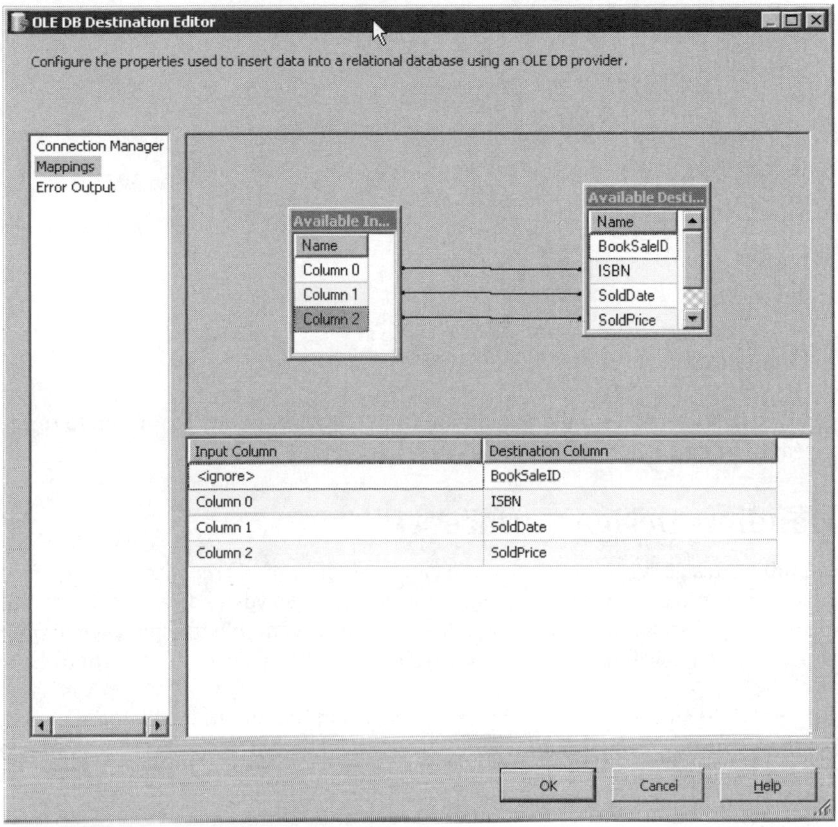

Figure 14-17. *OLE DB Destination Editor Mappings page*

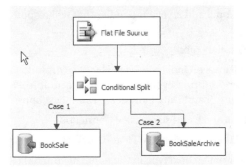

Figure 14-18. *Finished Data Flow design surface*

Running the SSIS Job

From the Debug menu, select Start. Data will flow from the flat file (40 rows), into the Conditional Split transformation, routing 18 rows (belonging to 2005 year sales) to the BookSale table, and 22 rows (belonging to pre-2005 sales) to the BookSaleArchive table (see Figure 14-19).

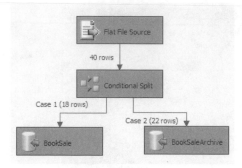

Figure 14-19. *Data Flow design surface after debugging*

Now that we've reviewed a simple implementation of data flow, we'll move on to review other important areas of functionality within SSIS.

Event Handlers Design Surface

The Event Handlers design surface allows you to create programmatic reactions to specific package or task events. For example, if an error occurs within the package, you can use the Send Mail task to issue a warning to a particular user. Events are organized by executable (the package or other tasks/containers). Each executable has its own event handlers, capturing errors, status changes, failures, and more.

Let's take a look at an example whereby we add an event handler that will e-mail us when the package encounters an error. This example requires you to have a valid SMTP server on your network or on your local machine.

■**Caution** In order for this exercise to work, your SMTP server must have relay access.

1. Create a new SSIS project and package. You'll add an event handler that will respond to any errors within the package.

2. In your new package, click the Event Handlers tab.

3. Under the Executable drop-down, select Package. Under the Event Handlers drop-down, select OnError. Click the "Click here to create an 'OnError' event handler for executable 'Package'." A blank design surface (similar to the Control and Data Flow design surfaces) appears.

4. In the Connections area, right-click the surface and select New Connection.

5. In the Add SSIS Connection Manager dialog box, select SMTP and click Add.

6. In the SMTP Connection Manager Editor dialog box, type in the name of your SMTP server and click OK.

7. Drag a Send Mail task onto the Event Handlers design surface.

8. Double-click the Send Mail task.

9. In the General section, change the Name field text to **Error Email** and the Description field text to **Emails on Package Errors** (see Figure 14-20).

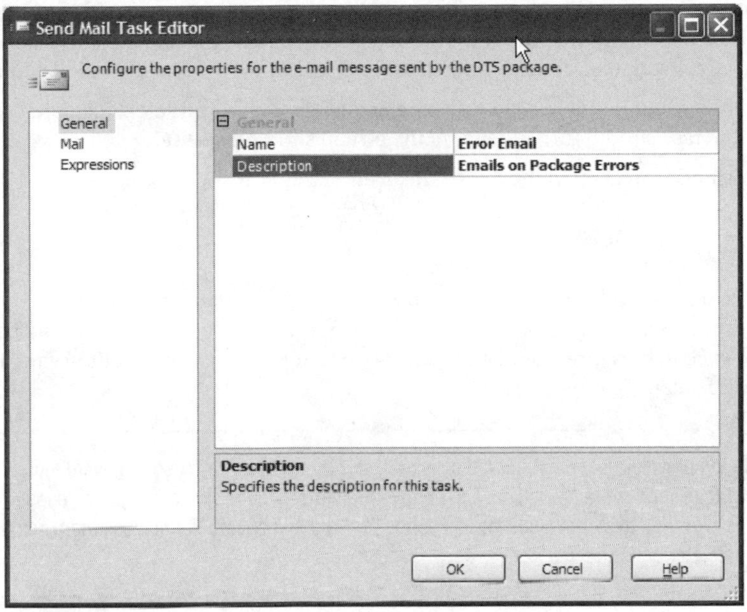

Figure 14-20. *Send Mail Task Editor dialog box*

10. On the left navigation section, select Mail. Select the SmtpConnection created earlier. Type in the e-mail addresses for From and To. In the Subject field, type in **Example Package Error**. In the MessageSource area, type **There has been an error in the package** (see Figure 14-21).

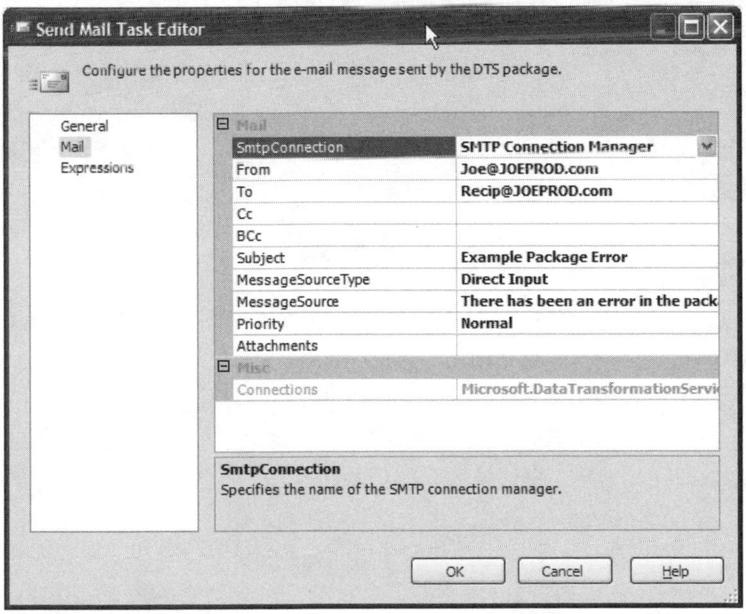

Figure 14-21. *Mail properties of the Send Mail Task Editor*

11. Notice that the MessageSourceType is equal to Direct Input. This means you manually enter the body of the text. Keep in mind that the body of the e-mail can also be derived from a package variable (variables are described later in this chapter) or an external file. Click OK.

12. To test the error event handler, right-click the Error Email task and select Execute Task. If successful, the task should turn green and the e-mail should be sent.

13. Select Debug and Stop Debugging to exit the event handler test.

Package Explorer

Package Explorer is a separate tab that allows you to view the various elements of the SSIS package in a hierarchical fashion. You can use Package Explorer to view many elements of the SSIS package, including variables, executables, precedence constraints, event handlers, connections, and log providers (see Figure 14-22).

■ Note Variables and log providers have not been discussed yet. *Log providers* are used in event logging to text files, SQL profiler, SQL tables, and more. We discuss log providers in more detail in the "Logging" section later on in the chapter. *Variables* allow you to store values for use during package execution. We discuss them in more detail in the "Variables" section later on in the chapter.

Figure 14-22. *Examining an example package in Package Explorer*

Connection Managers

Beneath the Control Flow and Data Flow design surfaces is the Connection Manager area. An SSIS Connection Manager is used to connect to data sources. Some of the available sources include a flat file, OLE DB, Excel, ODBC, and FTP to name a few. By default, on a new package this area is empty. Note that connections are not the end-all, be-all when it comes to transferring data. A connection can be used in conjunction with Data Flow or other Control Flow tasks. For example, if you were to create a connection to a specific SQL Server instance, that connection will be available for use within the Execute SQL task and Data Flow task.

■Tip To create a new connection, right-click anywhere within the empty Connections area.

Solution Explorer

Solution Explorer (see Figure 14-23) allows you to view and manage executables within your SSIS project. By right-clicking the SSIS Packages folder, you can choose to create a new package for the solution, launch the import/export wizard, or migrate DTS packages from SQL Server 2000.

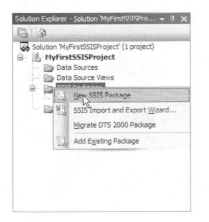

Figure 14-23. *Solution Explorer*

Properties Window

The Properties window (see Figure 14-24) allows you to view and modify the properties of the SSIS package and its objects (tasks, containers, and connections). This window is context sensitive and will display properties based on the selected object.

Properties	▼ ᵖ ×
Package Package	

Forced Execution Value	
ForcedExecutionValue	**0**
ForcedExecutionValueType	**Int32**
ForceExecutionValue	False
Misc	
CertificateContext	0
CertificateObject	
CheckpointFileName	
CheckpointUsage	Never
CheckSignatureOnLoad	True
Configurations	(Collection)
CreationDate	8/4/2004 6:17 PM
CreatorComputerName	
CreatorName	
DelayValidation	False
Description	
Disable	False
DisableEventHandlers	False
EncryptCheckpoints	False
FailPackageOnFailure	False
FailParentOnFailure	False
ForceExecutionResult	**None**
ID	{C7800DB8-C595-41ED-837C-66029
IsDefaultLocaleID	False
IsolationLevel	Serializable
LocaleID	English (United States)
LoggingMode	UseParentSetting
LoggingOptions	Microsoft.SqlServer.Dts.Runtime.Lo
MaxConcurrentExecutables	-1
MaximumErrorCount	1

Misc

Figure 14-24. *Properties window for an SSIS package*

Control Flow Toolbox Tasks

As mentioned earlier, an SSIS package is defined by tasks, connections, containers, and precedence constraints. A package can contain one or more tasks (also called *executables*).

SSIS has added several new tasks and enhanced others (see Figure 14-25), and we will briefly review some of these tasks in this section. Different SSIS tasks will appear in the Toolbox window depending on which design surface you are working in (i.e., Control Flow or Data Flow).

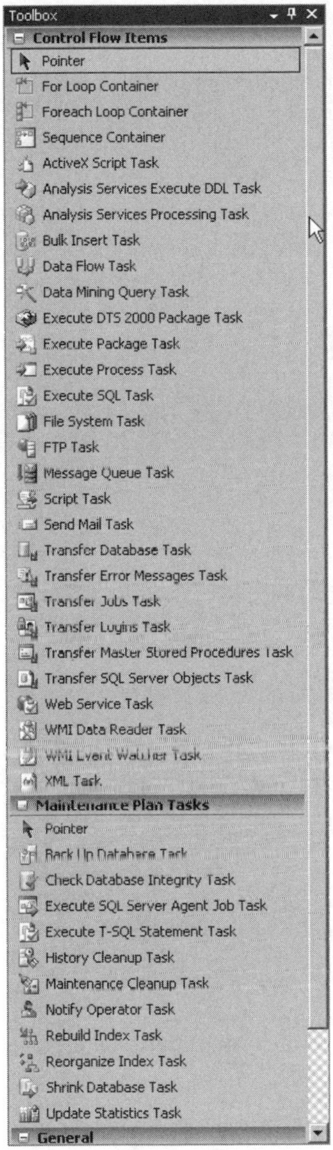

Figure 14-25. *Toolbox for the Control Flow design surface*

Containers

Containers are a new feature/concept in SSIS. DTS 2000 didn't provide a way to logically group tasks together for readability or dependency purposes. To address this, SSIS provides three Control Flow container tasks: the For Loop container, the Foreach Loop container, and the Sequence container. We'll describe each in the sections that follow.

The Sequence Container

The Sequence container can contain one or more tasks, or other containers, allowing you to logically group tasks together. Because these tasks are contained within a Sequence container, they can be managed as a unit. This task provides visual benefits as well—by selecting the upper-right corner of a container, you can expand or collapse the detail of the tasks within, enhancing readability of the package further (see Figures 14-26 and 14-27).

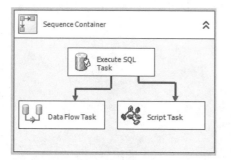

Figure 14-26. *An expanded Sequence container*

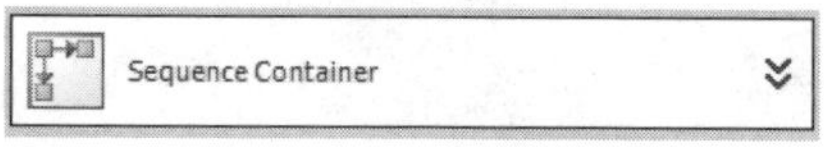

Figure 14-27. *A collapsed Sequence container*

Using a Sequence container also allows you to do the following:

- Enable or disable all tasks within the container (e.g., if you are debugging the package and do not wish to fire off the tasks within this container).

- Isolate workflow by container (e.g., have a container that is executed upon success of the previous task, or a different container that is executed on failure of the previous task).

- Define scope for a transaction, meaning that the rollback of a transaction can apply to all tasks within the Sequence container.

- Connect to other containers or other tasks by precedence constraints. Tasks within a container can also be connected to each other in the same way.

The For Loop Container and Foreach Loop Containers

These are two new tasks that eliminate the excessive coding required in previous versions of DTS.

- The For Loop container, like the Sequence container, allows you to place one or more tasks within it. Unlike the Sequence container, the For Loop container task executes the tasks within it repeatedly, based on an evaluation condition. Once the condition returns false, execution of the tasks within ceases.

- The Foreach Loop container executes the tasks based on an iteration statement. The iteration statement can be based on rows in an external table, files in a folder, objects within a variable, SMO objects, or even an XPath expression. We will demonstrate this task in the next exercise.

Let's take a look at example that uses the Foreach Loop container. We wish to have a nightly process that evaluates error logs generated by SQL Server (under the C:\Program Files\Microsoft SQL Server\MSSQL\LOG directory).

■**Caution** Your directory may be different from the one listed in this section, so change it to match your own path. As with the other exercises, use a safe test environment.

In our hypothetical scenario, an external application will evaluate each error file in that directory. After the external process is finished, it will delete the row from the table. Our process is responsible for letting the application know which files need to be processed. In this exercise, we will explore this directory (in real time), finding each file within and populating the filename in a table of files pending processing.

1. Create the PendingFileProcess table in a test database:

```
CREATE TABLEPendingFileProcess
(FileID int IDENTITY(1,1) NOT NULL PRIMARY KEY,
 FileNM nvarchar(1000) NOT NULL)
```

2. Create a new SSIS project called "Foreach loop example".

3. In the new SSIS package, right-click the Control Flow design surface and select Variables. This will bring focus to the Variables window. (We will review variables in more detail later on in this chapter.)

4. Select the Add Variable button (see Figure 14-28).

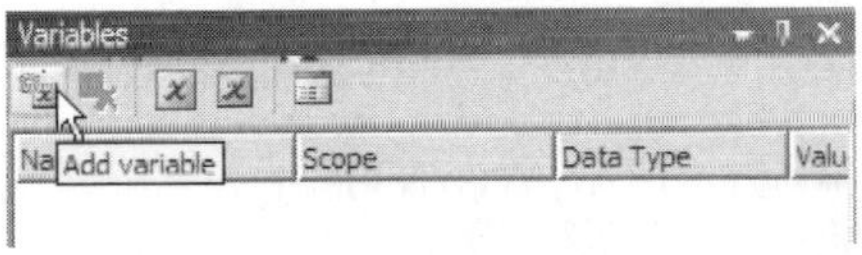

Figure 14-28. *Selecting Add Variable in the Variables window*

5. A new package variable appears. Change the Name field text to **FileName** and the Data Type field text to **String**.

6. Click the Toolbox tab and drag a Foreach Loop container onto the Control Flow design surface.

7. Double-click the Foreach Loop container.

8. In the Foreach Loop Editor dialog box, change the Name field to **Error Files**.

9. In the left navigation pane, select Collection.

10. Leave the default Enumerator of "For Each File Enumerator". This means your task will loop through each file contained within a specified folder. Change the Folder field to the directory where your SQL Server 2005 error logs (or for the purposes of this example, any directory where readable text file logs are located). See Figure 14-29.

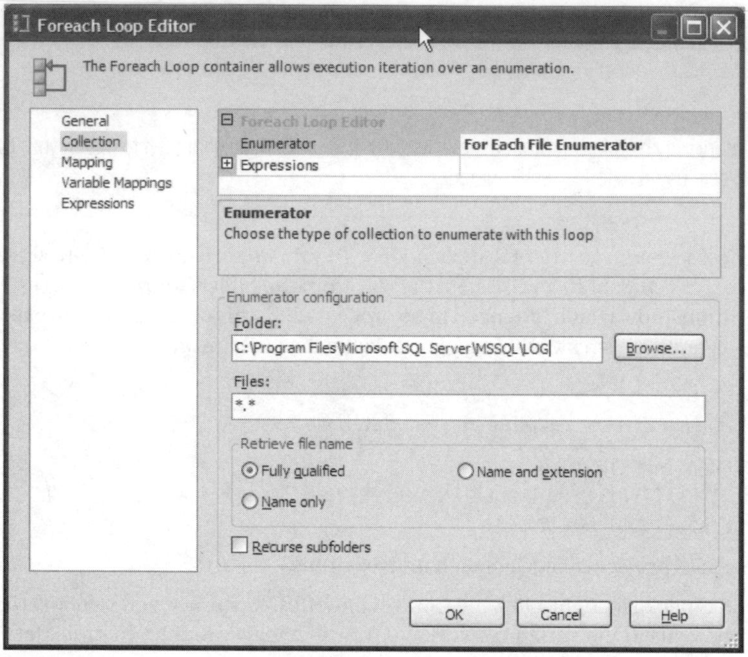

Figure 14-29. *Foreach Loop Editor, Collection Properties*

11. In the left navigation pane, select ***Variable Mappings***.

12. In the Variable section, select the variable User::FileName from the drop-down, which you created earlier. This variable will contain each filename found in the specified folder. The Foreach loop will loop through each file, changing the variable value at each pass.

13. Click OK to exit the Foreach Loop Editor.

14. In the Connections area, create a new connection that points to the test database where you created the PendingFileProcess table in step 1.

15. Drag an Execute SQL task into the Error Files container (see Figure 14-30).

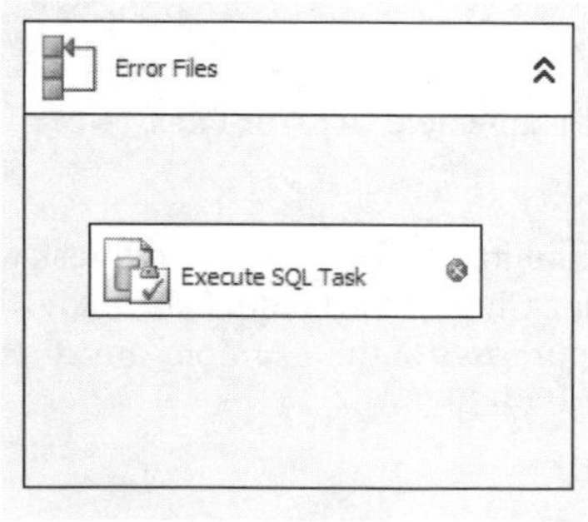

Figure 14-30. *Error Files Sequence container*

16. Double-click the Execute SQL task.

17. In the Execute SQL Task Editor dialog box, change the Name field to **Insert Error Files**. In the Connection drop-down, select the connection you created in step 14. Set the SQLStatement property to the following statement:

```
INSERT dbo.PendingFileProcess
(FileNM)
VALUES (?)
```

The question mark is a placeholder for a parameter mapping. In this case, you will map the FileName variable to this parameter.

18. In the left navigation pane, select Parameter Mapping and click the Add button.

19. Select the User::FileName variable from the drop-down. Change the Data Type value to **nvarchar** (matching the FileNM column in the PendingFileProcess table). Change the ParameterName to a value of **@P1**.

20. Click OK.

21. Select the Debug window and then choose Start. This will execute the SSIS package, looping through each file in the error log directory. For each file, a new row will be inserted into the PendingFileProcess table. Check this table in SSMS to confirm the table was populated:

```
SELECT FileID, FileNM
FROM dbo.PendingFileProcess
```

22. Select File ➤ Save All.

You will use this package in the upcoming Scripting task exercise.

Analysis Services Tasks

If you use Analysis Services, you'll want to be aware of three tasks. First, the SQL Server Analysis Services Execute DDL task allows you to submit Data Definition Language (DDL) statements to the selected Analysis Services connection. Second, the SQL Server Analysis Services Processing task processes Analysis Services objects (such as cubes and dimensions). Third, the Data Mining Query task allows you to submit prediction queries based on Analysis Services data mining models.

Data Flow Task

A Data Flow task represents an instance of the SSIS Data Flow engine executable. This executable is responsible for calling the data sources, data destinations, and any transformations that have been added to the Data Flow.

When you add the Data Flow task to the Control Flow design surface and double-click it, you will be directed to the Data Flow design surface. A Data Flow task can contain one or more Data Flow tasks (which we'll review later on). You can also have more than one Data Flow task on the Control Flow design surface.

Microsoft introduces new terminology centered on Data Flow functionality. In essence, these terms describe how data moves from a data source (*source adapter*), and how the data is modified and mapped (*transformation*) to a destination (*destination adapter*). In other words, we take data from somewhere, change it in some way, and then store the results somewhere else.

This mapping of source to transformation to destination is called a *graph*. A graph is a set of connected data flow components. One graph represents, for example, the data population of one table from another table. Unlike DTS 2000's Transform task, a single Data Flow task can also update multiple tables (which is to say, multiple graphs). All of these components are reviewed later in the chapter, in the "Data Flow Designer Tasks" section.

Execute Package Tasks

SSIS includes two separate tasks for executing SSIS packages: the Execute Package task and the Execute DTS 2000 Package task. Unfortunately, the upgrade path for packages created in SQL Server 2000 is less than perfect. Although best efforts to upgrade are attempted by the upgrade wizard, certain features have changed too significantly in SSIS to provide a smooth upgrade path from prior versions. To address compatibility issues, SSIS includes the Execute DTS 2000 Package task.

The Execute DTS 2000 Package task will allow the execution of a DTS 2000 package from within an SSIS package. This way, you can continue to use your older packages until you have an opportunity to rewrite in the new version. The Execute Package task is used to execute other SSIS packages as part of the workflow. Both tasks allow you to encapsulate and reuse existing packages, rather than creating task or data flow redundancy within your package.

Bulk Insert Task

The Bulk Insert task imports text files into SQL Server tables. Although you cannot validate, scrub, or transform data using this task, it is usually the fastest method for importing data from a text file into SQL Server. We will demonstrate this task in the next exercise.

Execute SQL Task

The Execute SQL task allows you to run SQL statements or call stored procedures against a SQL-compliant connection. For example, you can use this task to create a table, and then populate it with data based on a query. We will demonstrate this task in the next exercise.

In the following example, we'll use both the Execute SQL and Bulk Insert tasks .We'll demonstrate deleting data from a staging table and populating data from a text file into a SQL Server table using the Bulk Insert task. Consider using the Bulk Insert task when data file import performance (to SQL Server) is important.

The following exercise uses the BookSeller database and BookSales.txt file used earlier.

1. Create a new staging table (in Management Studio) in the BookSeller database:

```
USE BookSeller
GO

-- The BookSale table is for current-year sales
CREATE TABLE dbo.Staging_BookSale
    (ISBN char(10) PRIMARY KEY,
    SoldDate datetime NOT NULL,
    SoldPrice money NOT NULL)
GO
```

2. In BIDS, create a new project called Import Book Sales.

3. In the new SSIS package, create two new connections: one for the BookSeller database and the other for the BookSales.txt file.

4. Drag an Execute SQL task onto the Control Flow design surface.

5. Double-click the Execute SQL task.

6. Under Connection, select the connection for the BookSeller database. For the SQLStatement property, type the following:

```
DELETE dbo.Staging_BookSale
```

7. Click OK.

8. Drag a Bulk Insert task onto the Control Flow design surface.

9. Double-click the Bulk Insert task.

10. Change the Name property to **Import BookSales File**.

11. On the left navigation pane, select Connection.

12. Under Connection, select the BookSeller database connection. For the Destination table, select the dbo.Staging_BookSale table. Change the column delimiter to a comma-based delimiter. Under the File property, select the BookSales.txt connection.

13. Click OK.

14. Click the Execute SQL task and drag the green arrow to the Import BookSales file task (see Figure 14-31). The green arrow means that the first task (deleting data from the dbo.Staging_BookSale table) must execute successfully before the BookSales.txt data is imported.

Figure 14-31. *Execute SQL and Import BookSales tasks*

15. From the Debug menu, select Start.

16. Select Debug ➤ Stop Debugging.

17. From Management Studio, within a new query window, execute the following query to confirm the rows were loaded:

```
SELECT ISBN, SoldDate, SoldPrice
FROM BookSeller.dbo.Staging_BookSale
```

Execute Process Task

The Execute Process task, which was carried over from DTS 2000, allows you to execute a Win32 executable or a batch file within an SSIS package. For example, you could use this task to call a third-party application that performs business functions unrelated to SSIS task functionality. Be careful not to call executables that require user feedback; otherwise, your package execution may hang.

File System Task

The File System task allows you to perform several different file-based operations, all without having to create custom code (e.g., in DTS 2000, if you wanted to rename a file you would be required to either use xp_cmdshell or write an ActiveX script). The File System task allows you to copy a folder from one location to another, copy a file from one location to another, create or delete a folder in a specified location, delete all files and folders in a folder, delete a file in a specified location, move a file or directory from one location to another, rename a file in a specified location, and change file or directory attributes.

File Transfer Protocol Task

The File Transfer Protocol task allows you to both send and receive files using FTP. The original File Transfer Protocol task in DTS 2000 was able to use FTP only to receive files. If you wanted to FTP out files, you had to use the Execute Process task to instantiate a BAT file and use an ActiveX script or xp_cmdshell. Now with SSIS, you can send files, receive files, create or remove a local directory, create or remove a remote directory, delete local files, and delete remote files, all without writing a bit of code.

Maintenance Plan Tasks

Microsoft has added several new SSIS tasks designed to assist in the maintenance of your SQL Server database environment. These new tasks (found under the Maintenance Plan Tasks group on the Toolbox) provide a flexible and enhanced set of tools that replace the Database Maintenance Wizard functionality provided in SQL Server 2000.

Maintenance Plan tasks (see Figure 14-32) allow you to back up databases, check database integrity, defragment (using ALTER INDEX, REORGANIZE) or rebuild indexes (using ALTER INDEX, REBUILD), execute SQL Server Agent jobs and T-SQL statements, clean up database history (backup and restore history, SQL Server Agent Job history, and Database Maintenance Plan history), notify operators, shrink databases, and update table statistics.

■**Tip** One particularly helpful new feature in these tasks is that each provides a View T-SQL button, so you can see exactly what each task is doing.

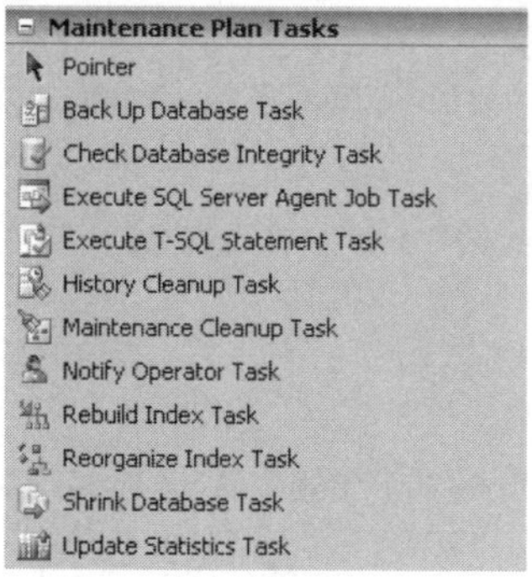

Maintenance Plan Tasks
- ▸ Pointer
- Back Up Database Task
- Check Database Integrity Task
- Execute SQL Server Agent Job Task
- Execute T-SQL Statement Task
- History Cleanup Task
- Maintenance Cleanup Task
- Notify Operator Task
- Rebuild Index Task
- Reorganize Index Task
- Shrink Database Task
- Update Statistics Task

Figure 14-32. *Maintenance Plan Tasks in the Toolbox*

Message Queue Task

The Message Queue task is used to send or receive messages between SSIS packages or custom application queues using MSMQ functionality. These messages allow asynchronous communication between systems and applications, meaning that messages can be delivered to a queue, where they will await pickup and processing from the MSMQ service on the server or workstation. Once the message is received, the receiving SSIS package can process and act upon the received message. Messages can be sent in text, file, or variable format.

Send Mail Task

The Send Mail task has been enhanced significantly in SSIS with the removal of dependence on a MAPI client for e-mail messaging and a reliance instead on a valid SMTP server. If you have a valid SMTP server on your network, you will be able to use this task to send e-mail notifications on package failures or successes, specific task events, or reporting of SQL Server data (e.g., reporting on the status of database file sizes). This task lets you define an e-mail's To line, From line, CC line, BCC line, Subject line, and priority level, as well as include file attachments. The e-mail body (called the *message source*) can be directly entered text, or it can be based on the value of a variable or external file.

Scripting Tasks

SSIS includes two separate scripting tasks: the ActiveX Script task and the Script task.

The ActiveX Script task is a carryover from DTS 2000. It allows you to write scripts using the VBScript or JScript language to define logic within packages, write functions, access data using ActiveX Data Objects, perform computations, and set variables.

■**Note** In SSIS, you are no longer able to manipulate the DTS package object model. This is to prevent behind-the-scenes package manipulation, which often made DTS 2000 packages difficult to troubleshoot (e.g., hidden ActiveX scripts in the workflow disabling or overriding workflow success or failure).

While the ActiveX Script task has been demoted, the Script task should be used in its place. Unlike the ActiveX Script task, the Script task allows you to write your scripts with the full-featured Visual Basic .NET programming language (C# is currently not supported for this task). Scripts are written in the Visual Studio for Applications (VSA) environment, which includes IntelliSense, debugging, and integrated help modules. Making use of the .NET Framework and COM objects exposes obvious performance and functionality benefits.

In the following example, you will use the Script task to combine multiple files in a directory into a single file (so that it can be imported by the hypothetical application). You will reuse part of the project and package you created for the earlier example demonstrating the use of the Foreach Loop container. As you recall, this package looped through each error file in the C:\Program Files\ Microsoft SQL Server\MSSQL\LOG directory. For each file it found, a row was inserted into the PendingFileProcess table.

With the Script task, you can now perform actions previously not available (or not as easily available) to older scripting languages. In this exercise, you have been asked to loop through each error file and merge them into a new, single, separate file. This way, the external (hypothetical) application can instead load all errors from a single file.

■**Tip** While you proceed through this exercise, consider the different uses for this particular script. For example, SQL Server DBAs and developers often use Visual SourceSafe (VSS) to store their stored procedures and other database objects. When asked to migrate changes, the VSS object checkout process creates several separate files. These files must be separately executed within a query window. You could, however, use a script like the one presented in this exercise to combine all SQL files into a single file.

---

1. In the SSIS package from the earlier exercise, delete the Execute SQL task contained within the Foreach Loop container.

2. Drag a Script task into the Foreach Loop container.

3. Double-click the Script task.

4. Change the Name field to **Merge Files** (see Figure 14-33).

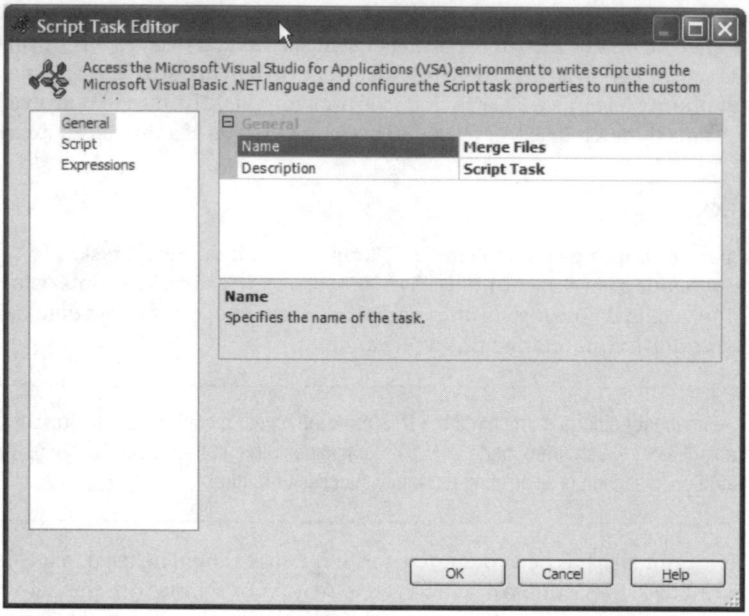

Figure 14-33. *Script Task Editor dialog box*

5. In the left navigation pane, select Script.

6. Click the Design Script button.

7. In the Imports area of the script, add the following line:

```
Imports System.IO
```

This will allow you to access file streaming functionality.

8. Within the `Public Sub Main()`, add the following code:

```
Public Sub Main()

    Dim sw As StreamWriter
    Dim variables As Variables

    'Check for the existence of the FileName variable
    If Dts.VariableDispenser.Contains("FileName") = True Then
        Dts.VariableDispenser.LockOneForRead("FileName", variables)
        Dim FileName As Object = variables("FileName").Value
    End If

    'Populate the source variable with the FileName variable value
    Dim source As String = variables("FileName").Value.ToString
```

```
'The name and location of the merged error log
Dim dest As String = "c:\Apress\MergedErrorLog.txt"

' Creates the MergedErrorLog.txt file if it doesn't already exist
If File.Exists(dest) = False Then
    ' Create a file to write to.
    sw = File.CreateText(dest)
    sw.Flush()
    sw.Close()
End If

' Creates a visual divider within MergedErrorLog.txt between file data
sw = File.AppendText(dest)
sw.WriteLine("----------------------------------------")
sw.Flush()
sw.Close()

' Opens the current file and writes it into MergedErrorLog.txt
Dim sr As StreamReader = File.OpenText(source)
Dim s As String
sw = File.AppendText(dest)
Do While sr.Peek() >= 0
    s = sr.ReadLine()
    sw.WriteLine(s)
Loop
sr.Close()
sw.Flush()
sw.Close()
Dts.TaskResult = Dts.Results.Success
End Sub
```

This code is commented so you can better understand what it does. In a nutshell, the script grabs the value of the FileName variable (which will be populated by the Foreach Loop container task). This is the file that will be combined into the single C:\Apress\MergedErrorLog.txt file.

9. Select File ➤ Save to save the script.

10. Select File ➤ Close and Return.

11. Click OK to exit the Script task.

■**Tip** This example assumes that you are merging log files not currently open in other processes. Since you are merging SQL Server log files, if the SQL Server service is running, one of these log files will, of course, be running. To test this, one option is to copy off the inactive log files to a separate location and then merge them accordingly. For the clarity of this example, however, the script merges all files directly from a single directory of a SQL Server instance that is *not* currently running.

---

12. Select Debug and Start to test the package (see Figure 14-34).

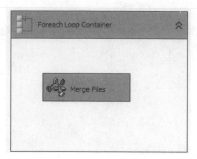

Figure 14-34. *Foreach Loop container and script example after execution*

If the package succeeded, both the Foreach Loop container and the Script task will turn green. You should also find a populated C:\Apress\MergedErrorLog.txt file containing the contents of all error logs from the error log directory.

Web Service Task

The Web Service task executes a web method using an HTTP connection. Within the task, you designate the HTTP connection and the Web Services Description Language (WSDL) file (which specifies the location of the service and the functionality of the web service).

WMI Tasks

Windows Management Instrumentation (WMI) is the programmatic interface provided by Microsoft to allow users to monitor and control Windows 2000 and XP system resources. SSIS includes two new tasks that tie into the WMI interface: the WMI Data Reader task and the WMI Event Watcher task.

The WMI Data Reader task allows you to execute a WMI Query Language (WQL) query against a specific system (e.g., retrieving the application event log file). The WMI Event Watcher task allows you to execute a WQL query that watches for a specific event to happen (e.g., being notified when logical disk space falls beneath a certain threshold).

XML Task

The XML task allows you to perform operations against XML documents. Some of the operations include the ability to compare XML documents (writing the differences to an XML Diffgram document), merge two XML documents into one document, query and evaluate an XML document using the XPath language, and transform an XML document based on an XSLT style sheet.

Data Flow Designer Tasks

Before using the Data Flow design surface, you must first add a Data Flow task to the Control Flow design surface. Once you have added the Data Flow task, you can begin adding items (from the toolbar) to the Data Flow design surface.

Data Flow items fall into three categories: source adapters (where data is extracted from), destination adapters (where data is imported into), and transformations (actions taken against the data before being passed to the next transformation or destination adapter). We'll discuss each category in the sections that follow.

Source Adapters

Source adapters define the source of the data; the specific table, query, or view when applicable; and the specific columns that need to be extracted. In SSIS, you extract data using the data source adapters listed in Table 14-1.

Table 14-1. *SSIS Source Adapters*

Source Adapter	Description
DataReader	The DataReader source adapter works with ADO.NET connections to deliver data to either a transformation or destination adapter.
Excel	The Excel source adapter allows you to read data from a Microsoft Excel spreadsheet.
Flat File	The Flat File source adapter allows you to read from a delimited, fixed-width, or mixed-format text file.
OLE DB	The OLE DB source adapter allows you to extract data using any valid OLE DB provider. This is the adapter you will use to extract SQL Server data. If selecting a SQL Server data source, you'll have the option of reading data based on a table or view, reading based on a variable referencing a table or view, or using a SQL query.
Raw File	The Raw File source adapter is used to read raw data files generated from the Raw File destination adapter. The Raw File destination adapter is used to write intermediary results of partly processed data. The data is stored in a "raw" or native format, which requires little processing from the Raw File source adapter. Raw data can be exported via the Raw Data destination adapter so it can be processed by a different (or the same) SSIS package.
XML	The XML source adapter allows you to extract data from an XML document source.

Destination Adapters

Destination adapters define the endpoint of extracted data, receiving it either directly from a data source adapter or from a transformation. In SSIS, you can extract data using the data destination adapters shown in Table 14-2.

Table 14-2. *SSIS Destination Adapters*

Destination Adapter	Description
DataReader	The DataReader destination adapter works with ADO.NET connections to import data to the selected ADO.NET destination data source.
Dimension Processing	The Dimension Processing destination adapter processes dimensions in data warehouse tables, allowing for incremental, full, or update processing. This adapter is available only in SQL Server 2005 Enterprise and Developer editions.
Excel	The Excel destination adapter allows you to export data into a Microsoft Excel spreadsheet.

Table 14-2. *SSIS Destination Adapters (Continued)*

Destination Adapter	Description
Flat File	The Flat File destination adapter uses a flat file provider to write data to the destination text file. You can designate how the text file is formatted using either a delimited, fixed-width, or mixed format.
OLE DB	The OLE DB destination adapter writes to a destination file using an OLE DB provider.
Partition Processing	The Partition Processing destination adapter processes Analysis Services partitions, and allows for incremental, full, or update processing. This adapter is available only in SQL Server 2005 Enterprise and Developer editions.
Raw File	The Raw File destination adapter writes data to a raw data file, which can then be read by a Raw File source adapter.
Recordset	The Recordset destination adapter creates and uses an in-memory ADODB recordset that is used to receive data from a source adapter or transformation.
SQL Mobile	The SQL Mobile destination adapter allows you to write to a table in Microsoft SQL Server 2005 Mobile Edition.
SQL Server	The SQL Server destination adapter allows you to import into SQL Server using the high-speed Bulk Insert interface.

Transformations

SSIS provides several new and enhanced transformation tasks, shown in Table 14-3, that are used to modify data as it moves from the source data adapter to the destination data adapter.

Table 14-3. *SSIS Transformations*

Transformation	Description
Aggregate	The Aggregate transformation applies aggregate functions (Group By, Sum, Average, Count, Count Distinct, Minimum, and Maximum) against column values provided by the source adapter.
Audit	The Audit transformation allows you to capture and include environmental data within the data flow. With this task, you can designate additional fields to be captured during the data flow (such as the package name, version, and execution start time) and send them to the destination adaptor (or as an input to the next transformation).
Character Map	The Character Map transformation allows you to apply character modifications to existing string data type columns or to a separate copy of an existing column. Modifications include changing text to all uppercase or lowercase, byte reversal, and other language conversions.
Conditional Split	The Conditional Split transformation allows you to route data rows to different outputs based on a condition/expression you define. For example, you can use this task to route all employees who belong to the "East" sales territory to their own table, and those belonging to the "West" sales territory to their own table.

Table 14-3. *SSIS Transformations (Continued)*

Transformation	Description
Copy Column	The Copy Column transformation allows you to create new columns in the output by copying input columns. The new copies are added to the transformation output and can be modified without changing the original column data.
Data Conversion	The Data Conversion transformation modifies the data type of the input column and copies it to an output column.
Data Mining Model Training	The Data Mining Model Training transformation is used to "train" (i.e., estimate a model's parameters based on the dataset) data mining models by sending the input data through the data mining model algorithms. This transformation is available only in SQL Server 2005 Enterprise and Development editions.
Data Mining Query	The Data Mining Query transformation is used to perform prediction queries against data mining models, using Data Mining Expressions (DMX). This transformation is available only in SQL Server 2005 Enterprise and Development editions.
Derived Column	The Derived Column transformation creates a new column by using expressions against input columns and variables. The expression can be built using the original input column, variables, functions, and operators.
Export Column	The Export Column transformation is used to read data from the data adaptor to generate a file for each row. For example, if your Employee table contains a BLOB image column, you could use the Export Column task to extract the BLOB into an individual file for each Employee row. We'll demonstrate this in the next exercise.
Import Column	The Import Column transformation does the reverse of the Export Column; it reads data from separate files and adds the data columns to the existing data flow.
Fuzzy Grouping	The Fuzzy Grouping transformation uses an algorithm to cleanse duplicate data. This transformation requires access to a SQL Server 2005 database, to create the temporary tables and indexes it needs to perform its operations. This transformation is available only in SQL Server 2005 Enterprise and Development editions.
Fuzzy Lookup	The Fuzzy Lookup transformation also performs a lookup against a lookup result set, but rather than using an equi-join, it uses a fuzzy matching algorithm, allowing lookups to return matches on exact or close matches from the reference table. This transformation also outputs a similarity and confidence score (both decimal values between 0 and 1, where 1 is an exact match). The *similarity score* indicates the mathematical difference between the input and a lookup record, whereas the *confidence score* calculates the likelihood that a given looked-up value is the best match compared to other matches found in the lookup table. This transformation is available only in SQL Server 2005 Enterprise and Development editions.
Lookup	A "lookup" operation involves referencing a value from a separate dataset, based on the value of a source column or columns. The Lookup transformation is used to perform a join of the source data against a separate lookup table result set. The lookup uses an equi-join and must match exactly between the two values.

Table 14-3. *SSIS Transformations (Continued)*

Transformation	Description
Merge	The Merge transformation is used to combine two sorted data sets based on values in their key columns, outputting the results into a single result set to the next transformation task or data adapter.
Merge Join	The Merge Join transformation creates a single result set based on the joining of two sorted result sets. Like a T-SQL query, a Merge Join transformation can use varying join types to combine result sets, including INNER, FULL, and LEFT joins.
Multicast	The Multicast transformation takes a single result set and distributes it to multiple destinations (transformations or data adaptors). This task allows you to spread out your data (e.g., across different servers at the same time).
OLE DB Command	The OLE DB Command transformation executes an individual SQL statement for each row in the data flow.
Percentage Sampling	The Percentage sampling transformation generates a sample dataset by selecting a percentage of the transformation input rows.
Pivot	The Pivot transformation is used to transform a normalized data set into a less normalized version by pivoting the input data on a column value.
Row Count	The Row Count transformation is used to capture row counts as they move through the data flow, allowing you to store the results into a variable.
Row Sampling	The Row Sampling transformation creates a sample dataset by selecting a specified number of the transformation input rows.
Script Component	The Script Component transformation allows you to write your own .NET-coded transformation, destination adapter, or source adapter. The script is created in VSA using the Visual Basic .NET language.
Slowly Changing Dimension	The Slowly Changing Dimension transformation allows you to update and insert into data warehouse dimension tables.
Sort	The Sort transformation sorts the input data prior to sending it to the next transformation or data destination adapter. This can potentially improve table load performance if you match the sort of this transformation to the destination table clustered index sort order.
Term Extraction	The Term Extraction transformation provides the ability to extract individual words or phrases from input columns. For example, if you wanted to derive the individual street names from an Address column, the Term Extraction transformation searches the column and extracts the individual address names. This transformation can extract words only, phrases only, or both. Exclusion tables can be referenced to not re-extract existing terms (if you are, for example, populating a search-term table based on common text field values). This transformation is available only in SQL Server 2005 Enterprise and Development editions.

Table 14-3. *SSIS Transformations (Continued)*

Transformation	Description
Term Lookup	The Term Lookup transformation allows you to take an input result set, reference it against a term reference table, and output those rows that associate to each term. For example, if you wanted to see the frequency of search terms within an Address column, the output result set will return the search term from the reference table, the address column where it was identified, and a reference count of 1. The resulting data can then be grouped in later queries, to identify the frequency of search term matches. This transformation is only available in SQL Server 2005 Enterprise and Development editions.
Union All	The Union All transformation (like the T-SQL UNION ALL command) gathers outputs from multiple data sources or transformations and combines them into a single, unsorted dataset. If you need sorted outputs, use the Merge transformation.
Unpivot	The Unpivot transformation does the opposite of the Pivot transformation, taking the pivoted data and reversing it into a more normalized version (moving values from columns into multiple records with the same value in one column).

Using the Export Column Transformation

In this example, imagine you've been asked by a hypothetical third-party catalog provider to generate thumbnail image GIFs for all of the products in the AdventureWorks application, for use in the third party's online sales application.

1. Create a new project and package in BIDS.

2. Create a new connection manager to a SQL Server 2005 instance set to the AdventureWorks database.

3. Drag a Data Flow task onto the Control Flow tab.

4. Double-click the Data Flow task to enter the Data Flow tab.

5. From the Toolbox, drag an OLE DB source item onto the Data Flow design surface. Double-click it.

6. In the OLE DB Source Editor dialog box, under Connection select the SQL Server 2005 instance containing the AdventureWorks database. For the "Data access mode option," select SQL command. For the SQL command text, enter the following query:

```
SELECT ThumbNailPhoto,
        'C:\Apress\' + ThumbnailPhotoFileName AS PhotoFileName
FROM Production.ProductPhoto
```

■Tip Notice that the query designates the actual file directory where you'll be placing the thumbnail images. In a real-life situation, you could designate either a local or a UNC path.

7. Click OK.

8. From the Toolbox, drag an Export Column transformation task onto the Data Flow design surface.

9. Click the OLE DB source and drag the green precedence constraint to the Export Column task.

10. Double-click the Export Column task.

11. In the Export Column Transformation Editor, under the Extract Column, select ThumbnailPhoto. This table column will define the actual name of each file generated. In the File Path Column, select the column PhotoFileName (see Figure 14-35).

Export Column Transformation Editor   _ □ ×

Configure the properties used to export data with the DT_TEXT, DT_NTEXT, or DT_IMAGE data type into files.

| Columns | |
| Error Output | |

Use Extract Column to specify which columns in the data flow contain data to be extracted.
Use File Path Column to specify which columns in the data flow contain the file paths for the extracted data.

Extract Column	File Path Column	Allow Ap...	Force Tr...	Write B...
ThumbNailPhoto	PhotoFileName	☐	☐	☐

| OK | Cancel | Help |

Figure 14-35. *Export Column Transformation Editor dialog box*

12. Leave the other defaults unchecked, and click OK.

13. From the Debug menu, select Start.

You should see that 101 rows were processed by the Export Column task (see Figure 14-36).

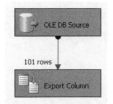

Figure 14-36. *Export Column package after execution*

The files should have been generated to your C:\Apress directory. You can then use the File Transfer Protocol task to send the files to the client.

Export a Row Sampling to a Text File from SQL Server

In this example, you've been asked by your company's HR department to generate a text file containing a random sampling of 20 employees who will be asked to participate in an employee survey. You'll use the AdventureWorks table HumanResources.Employee for the SQL Server source data, and you'll use the Row Sampling transformation to export the sampling to a text file.

1. Create a new project and package in BIDS.

2. Create a new connection manager to a SQL Server 2005 instance set to the AdventureWorks database.

3. Drag a Data Flow task onto the Control Flow tab.

4. Double-click the Data Flow task to enter the Data Flow work area.

5. Drag an OLE DB source to the surface area. Double-click it and for the name of the table or the view, select HumanResources.Employee.

6. Select Columns from the left pane. In the Available External Columns check box list, deselect all fields except EmployeeID, ManagerID, and HireDate.

7. Select OK to exit the OLE DB source.

8. Drag a Row Sampling transformation onto the surface area.

9. Click the OLE DB source and drag the green precedence constraint to the Row Sampling transformation.

10. Double-click the Row Sampling transformation. In the Row Sampling Transformation Editor, change the number of rows to 20 and click OK.

11. Drag a Flat File destination onto the surface area.

12. Click the Row Sampling transformation and drag the green precedence constraint to the Flat File destination. In the Input Output Selection, select the Sampling Selected Output (this feeds the 20 rows selected, rather then the remaining rows *not* selected). Click OK.

13. Double-click the Flat File destination. Click the New button next to the Flat File Connection Manager drop-down.

14. In the Flat File Format dialog box, select Delimited. For the filename, select C:\Apress\ EmployeeSampling.txt (it doesn't need to already exist). Check the "Column names in the first data row" check box. Click OK.

15. Back in the Flat File Destination Editor, in the left pane, select Mappings. Verify that the input columns map to the destination columns appropriately. Click OK.

16. Select Debug and Start Debugging.

After debugging the package, check the contents of the C:\Apress\EmployeeSampling.txt file for the 20 sampled employees. Also, if you redebug the package again, notice that you'll get a different set of employees exported to the file.

Logging

Microsoft has made significant improvements to SSIS logging over previous versions. DTS 2000 was often criticized for providing cryptic logging files that were difficult to normalize and extract into tabular format.

SSIS logging has addressed this shortcoming by providing new logging options (see Figure 14-37):

- Log events to text files
- Log events that can be captured by SQL Profiler
- Log events to a SQL Server table
- Log events to the Windows Event Log
- Log events to an XML file

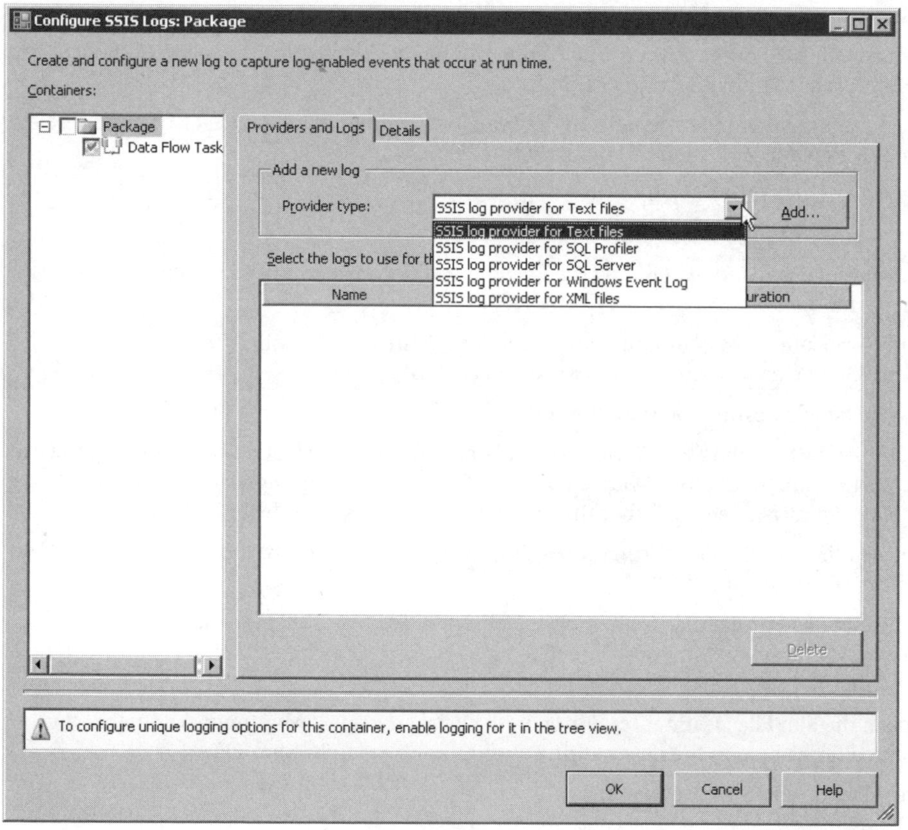

Figure 14-37. *The Configure SSIS Logs dialog box*

In addition to new logging locations, you can now control what events you actually log in the first place. SSIS can log events such as errors, execution status changes, informational events, postexecution events, postvalidation events, pre-execution events, prevalidation events, progress notifications, task failures, variable changes, and warnings.

You can also determine *which columns* are logged, including the date the log event occurred, the computer name where the log event occurred, the user who launched the package, the name of the container or task where the log event occurred, the package's unique identifier, the unique identifier of the package execution, the event message text, the start time of the task/container execution, the end time of the task/container execution, and the elapsed time based on the start and end time.

In this example, you will set up an Execute SQL task that will generate an error. You will enable error logging for the task, execute the package, and then examine the resulting Windows Event Log entries.

1. In a new SSIS package, create an OLE DB connection manager to the SQL Server instance containing the AdventureWorks database.

2. Drag an Execute SQL task onto the Control Flow design surface.

3. Double-click the Execute SQL task.

4. Under the Connection property, select the AdventureWorks connection. In the SQLStatement property, type in the following SELECT statement (the statement will cause a "divide by zero" error):

   SELECT 1/0

5. Click OK.

6. In the Control Flow design surface of a new SSIS package, right-click an empty area. Select Logging.

7. In the Configure SSIS Logs: Package dialog box, enable logging by selecting the check box in the Containers treeview for the SSIS package (based on the name of your package) check box (see Figure 14-38).

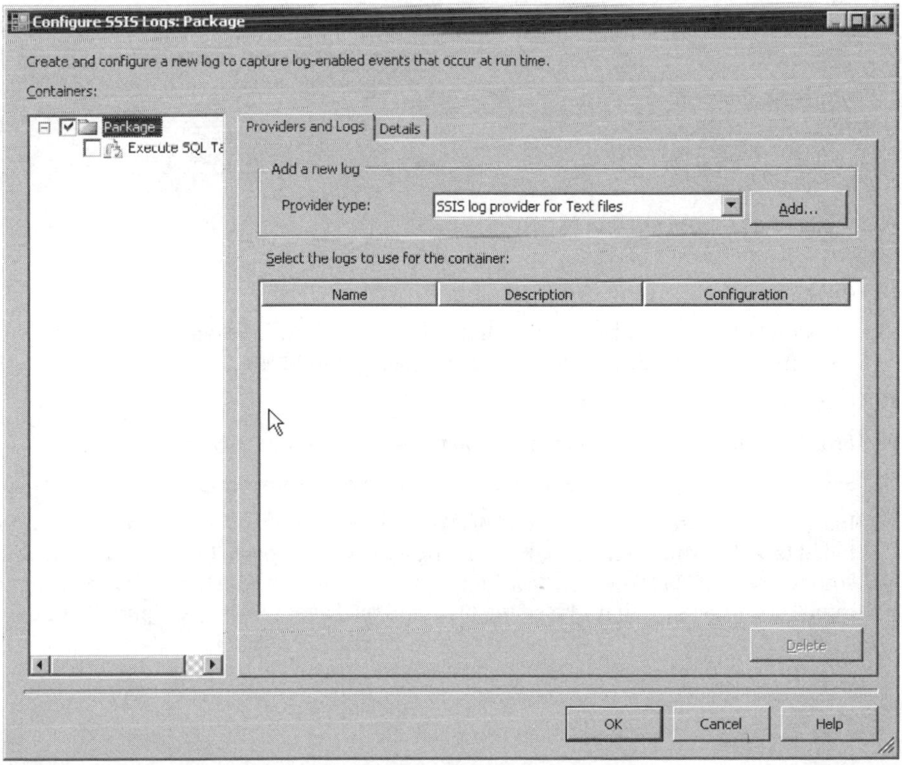

Figure 14-38. *Configure DTS Logs dialog box*

8. In the "Add a new log" section, select SSIS log provider for Windows Event Log from the Provider drop-down and click the Add button.

9. In the "Select the logs to use for the container" section, select the check box of the new logging item (see Figure 14-39).

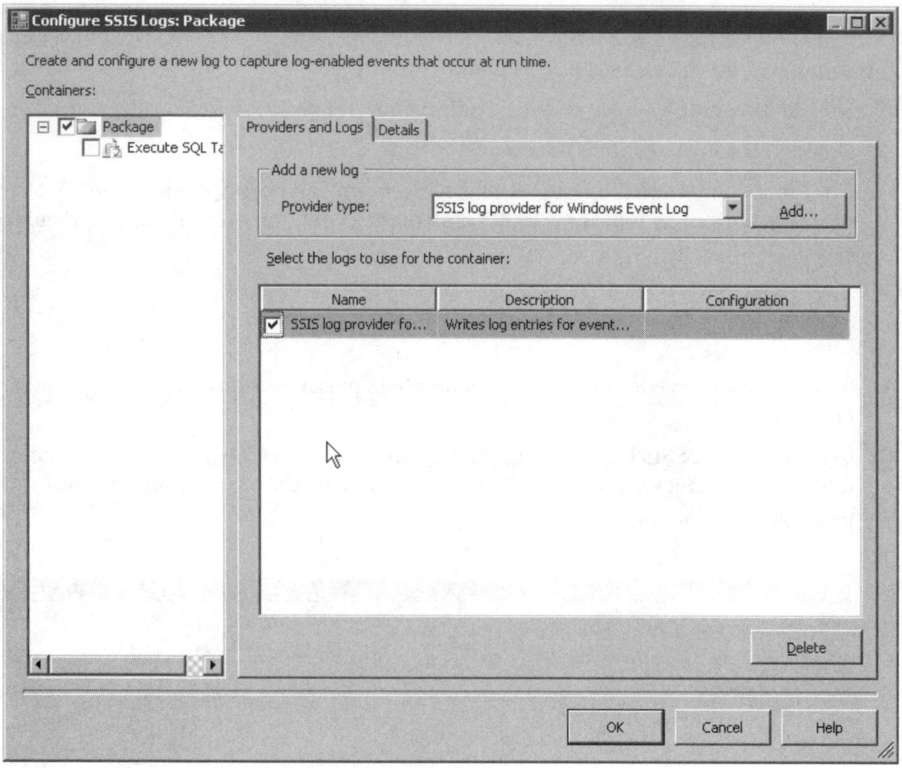

Figure 14-39. *Adding Execute SQL task logging*

10. Click the Details tab and check the OnError event.

11. Click the Advanced button. Notice that the events are preselected, as well as the associated columns that will be logged for each event (see Figure 14-40).

12. Click OK to set the defaults.

13. From the Debug menu, select Start. You will see the Execute SQL task fail.

14. Select the Windows Start menu and select Run. Type **eventvwr** and click OK.

15. In Event Viewer, select Application Log. You will see three errors of varying granularity for the failed task. Click through each. Within the description of each, look for the error with a source name of "Execute SQL Task". It is here you will see the "Divide by zero error encountered" error message that caused the task (and package) to fail (see Figure 14-41).

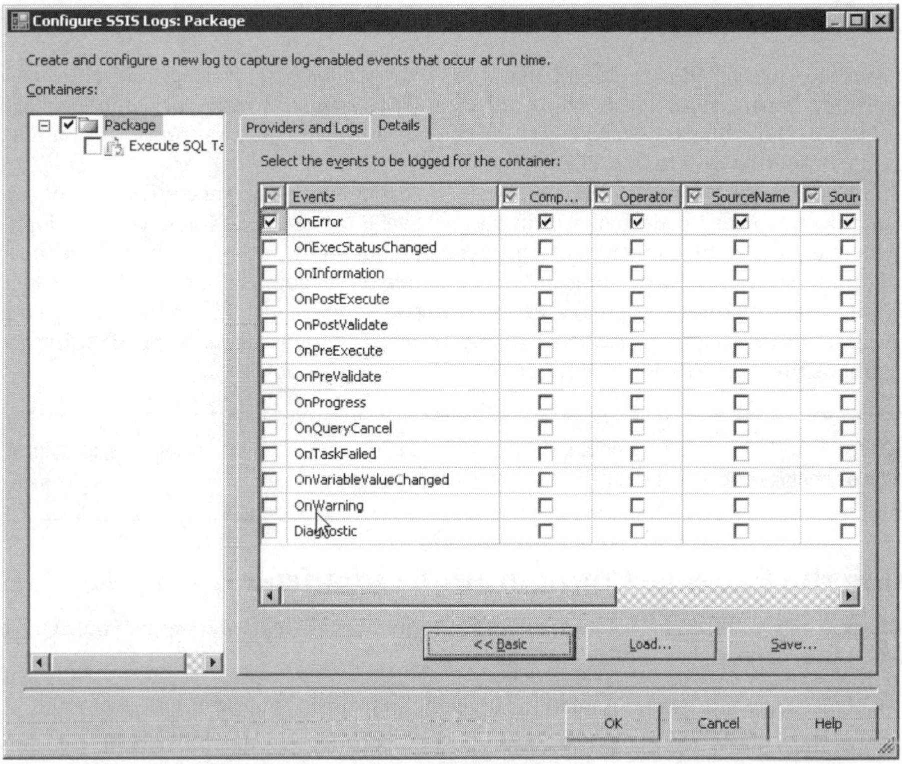

Figure 14-40. *Details screen of Configure DTS Logs dialog box*

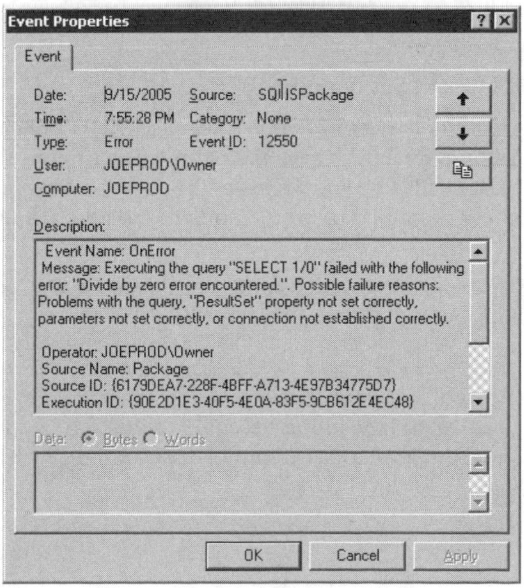

Figure 14-41. *Example of event logging from SSIS in Windows Event Viewer*

Configurations

The Package Configuration Organizer allows you to dynamically set package properties based on machine environment variables, XML configuration files, registry entries, or parent package variables (sent by the calling the Execute Package task). This functionality was previously handled by the Dynamic Properties task in DTS 2000.

Setting configurations dynamically allows you to change important connections or settings without having to hard-code them within the package. For example, if you have a development, staging, and production environment where you port your SSIS packages, you can use the Package Configuration Organizer to dynamically set the source server connections based on the local machine name environment variable. *These settings are applied when your SSIS package is loaded (e.g., if you add an existing package to a different project)*. Settings are *not* applied during execution time, unless the configuration is sent from parent package variables.

■**Tip** You'll most likely use this functionality prior to setting up a package in the Package Deployment Wizard, so that deployments are able to run from different computer contexts.

Using the Package Configuration Organizer

In this example, you'll create a package configuration that can be used to update the SQL Server instance and database based on an XML file.

1. In BIDS, create a new Integration Services project called PackageConfigExample.

2. In the default `Package.dtsx` package, create a new data connection to your SQL Server 2005 instance (to the AdventureWorks database).

3. Right-click the Control Flow design surface and select Package Configurations.

4. In the Package Configurations Organizer dialog box, select "Enable package configurations."

5. Click the Add button to add a new configuration.

6. Click Next at the DTS Configuration Wizard welcome screen.

7. On the Select Configuration Type screen, for the Configuration type select "XML configuration file." Keep "Specify configuration settings directly" selected. This means the configuration will expect the XML file to be in the same file location wherever the package is loaded. Use the other option, "Configuration location is stored in an environment variable," if you expect this location to change.

8. Under Configuration file name, type **C:\Apress\test.dtsConfig** (see Figure 14-42). A new file will be created if one does not already exist.

9. Click Next.

10. On the Select Properties to Export screen, under the \Package\Connections folder, expand your SQL Server instance connection. Expand the Properties folder, check the Connection-String, InitialCatalog, and ServerName properties (see Figure 14-43), and then click Next.

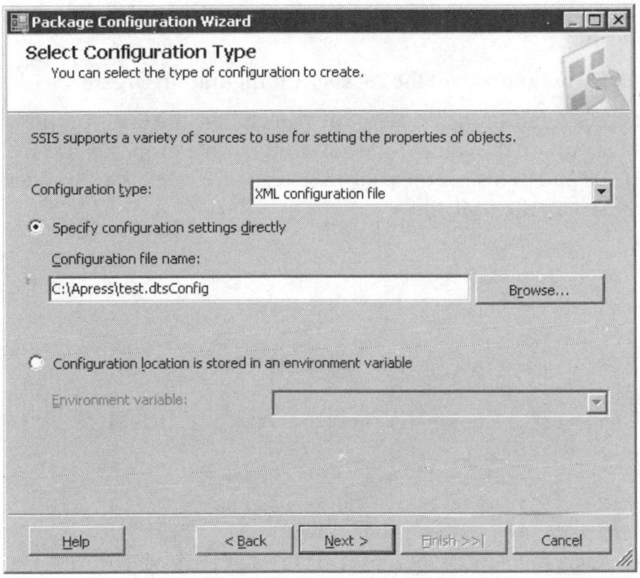

Figure 14-42. *Selecting the configuration type in the DTS Configuration Wizard*

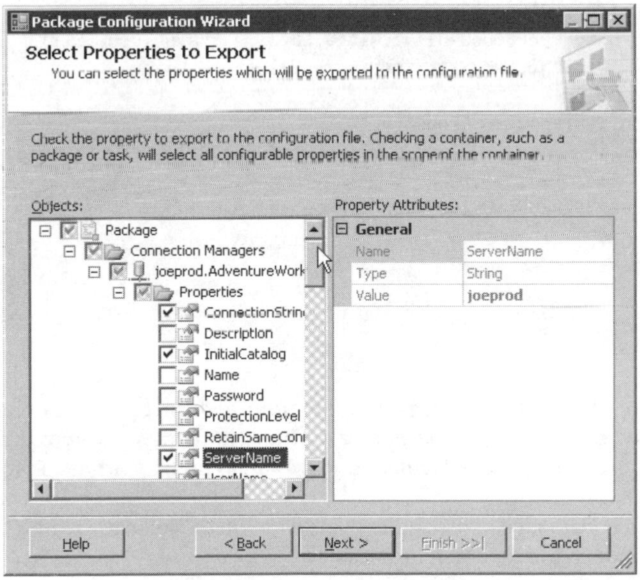

Figure 14-43. *Selecting properties to export in the DTS Configuration Wizard*

11. In the Completing the Wizard screen, type **SQL Server Connection Change** in the Configuration name text box. Click Finish.

12. Your new configuration will now appear in the Package Configuration Organizer. Click Close.

13. Open the new C:\Apress\ test.dtsConfig file. Here you can change the three property values. The ConfiguredValue tags outline the values for each configurable property. If you change the property in the XML file and then load the package to a new project, the SSIS package will inherit the properties based on the XML file.

```xml
<?xml version="1.0"?>
<DTSConfiguration>
  <DTSConfigurationHeading>
    <DTSConfigurationFileInfo
GeneratedBy="JOEPROD\Owner" GeneratedFromPackageName="Package"
GeneratedFromPackageID=
"{FA099B09-C230-4688-AF93-E88C73C8683F}" GeneratedDate="1/1/2005 9:28:29 PM"/>
    </DTSConfigurationHeading>
    <Configuration ConfiguredType="Property"
Path="\Package.Connections[{C2FB43E4-2DD7-44D0-B616-
D9EF80D60901}].ConnectionString" ValueType="String">
<ConfiguredValue>Data Source=JOEPROD\SQL2005;Initial Catalog=AdventureWorks;
Provider=SQLOLEDB.1;Integrated Security=SSPI;
Auto Translate=False;</ConfiguredValue>
    </Configuration>
    <Configuration ConfiguredType="Property" Path="\Package.Connections
[{C2FB43E4-2DD7-44D0-B616-D9EF80D60901}].InitialCatalog" ValueType="String">
      <ConfiguredValue>AdventureWorks</ConfiguredValue>
    </Configuration>
    <Configuration ConfiguredType="Property" Path=
"\Package.Connections[{C2FB43E4-2DD7-44D0-B616-D9EF80D60901}].ServerName"
ValueType="String">
      <ConfiguredValue>JOEPROD\SQL2005</ConfiguredValue>
    </Configuration>
</DTSConfiguration>
```

Variables

SSIS variables (shown in Figure 14-44) allow you to store values for use during package execution. Variables can be used to update package properties during runtime, store integer values used for controlling container looping, provide lookup information, store values for use within a T-SQL statement or Script task, and build expressions.

A variable is defined by its namespace (either *system* or *user defined*). You can create new user-defined variables, but you cannot create new system variables.

A variable is also defined by its scope, variable data type, and value. *Scope* defines where the variable can be seen from within the package. A variable with package-level scope can be viewed by all objects within the package, whereas variables defined within a task's scope can only be viewed by the task. Allowed variable data types include Boolean, byte, char, datetime, DBNull, double, int16, int32, object, sbyte, single, string, and Uint32.

Name	Scope	Data Type	Value
CreatorName	Package	String	
CreatorComputerName	Package	String	
VersionComments	Package	String	
ExecutionInstanceGUID	Package	String	
TaskID	Data Flow Task	String	{3A411B18-6FF5-4EBB-A9D2-5821C9F02544}
VersionGUID	Package	String	{7DCD656D-9805-4922-A3CA-C8E60A7849AC}
PackageID	Package	String	{C7800DB8-C595-41ED-837C-660293AC6E54}
VersionMinor	Package	Int32	0
MyTaskVariable	Data Flow Task	Int32	0
MyVariable	Package	Int32	0
VersionMajor	Package	Int32	1
VersionBuild	Package	Int32	10
CancelEvent	Package	Int32	1320
CreationDate	Package	DateTime	8/4/2004 6:17 PM
StartTime	Package	DateTime	8/8/2004 8:59 PM
TaskName	Data Flow Task	String	Data Flow Task
CreationName	Data Flow Task	String	DTS.Pipeline.1
LocaleID	Package	Int32	English (United States)
LocaleID	Data Flow Task	Int32	English (United States)
OfflineMode	Package	Boolean	False
InteractiveMode	Package	Boolean	False
MachineName	Package	String	JOEPROD
UserName	Package	String	JOEPROD\Owner
PackageName	Package	String	Package

Figure 14-44. *Variables window*

To configure variables within your SSIS package, follow these steps:

1. Within the SSIS Designer of a new SSIS package, right-click the Control Flow design surface and select Variables.

2. The Variables window will appear. To view system variables, click the Show System Variables button (an image of an "X" in a gray square). System variables will now appear.

3. To create a new user-defined variable, click the Add Variable button (a function symbol with an orange star in the upper-left corner). This will create a user variable with the name Variable and a scope of your SSIS package.

4. To create a variable scoped at the task level, click and drag a File System task from the Toolbox to the empty Control Flow design surface.

5. To create a task-scoped variable (in this case, based on a File System task), simply create a new variable while the task is selected in the Control Flow Designer.

Now that you know how to configure variables, let's run through a business scenario. Say that your company's HR department has an application that uses the AdventureWorks table [HumanResources].[JobCandidate] to track job candidates in the queue. Once a week, the HR group wishes to evaluate the number of candidates in the queue, to determine whether or not to pull the job advertising campaign from the local newspaper.

In this example, you will create a variable called JobCandidateCount, populate it from the table, and e-mail an advertising update to HR based on the variable value.

1. In a new package, add a new connection to the AdventureWorks database.

2. Create a new user-defined variable called `JobCandidateCount` with a data type of `Int32`.

3. Drag an Execute SQL task onto the Control Flow design surface.

4. Double-click the Execute SQL task.

5. In the General properties, in the SQL statement section, change the Connection property to use the AdventureWorks connection. Change the SQLStatement to use the following query:

   ```
   SELECT COUNT(*) as 'CandidateCount'
   FROM HumanResources.JobCandidate
   ```

6. Change the ResultSet property to Single row.

7. On the left navigation pane, select Result Set and click the Add button. Change the Result Name to CandidateCount. In the DTS Variable Name, make sure JobCandidateCount is selected. Click OK to exit the Execute SQL Task Editor.

8. Create a new SMTP connection manager (use a valid SMTP server in your network or on your desktop).

9. Drag a Send Mail task on to the Control Flow design surface. Double-click it.

10. In the Send Mail Task Editor in the General properties, change the Name property to **Pull Advertising**. In the Mail properties in the SmtpConnection property, select the SMTP connection manager. Since this is just an exercise, in the From and To properties, select your own e-mail address. In the Subject line, type **Pull Advertising**. This will be the notification to remove advertising if the Job Candidate queue exceeds ten candidates. Click OK.

11. Copy the Pull Advertising task and paste a copy on the design surface. Double-click it. On the General tab, rename the Name property to **Retain or Start Advertising**. In the Mail properties, just change the Subject property to **Retain or Start Advertising**. Click OK.

12. Create a precedence constraint from Execute SQL task to the Retain or Start Advertising task. Double-click the green arrow to configure.

13. In the Precedence Constraint Editor, change the Evaluation operation to **Expression**. In the Expression, type in the following expression:

    ```
    @JobCandidateCount<11
    ```

    This expression evaluates your user variable, testing to `TRUE` if the variable is less than 11. Click OK. Notice that a small function symbol appears by the Retain or Start Advertising task.

14. Create a precedence constraint from Execute SQL Task to the Pull Advertising task. Double-click the green arrow to configure.

15. In the Precedence Constraint Editor, change the Evaluation operation to **Expression**. In the Expression, type in the following expression and then click OK:

    ```
    @JobCandidateCount>10
    ```

16. From the Debug menu, select Start to test the package.

Since the candidate count is more than ten, you'll see the Execute SQL task turn green, and then the Pull Advertising task will turn green afterward. The Retain or Start Advertising task is not run, as the variable value was *not* less than ten.

Precedence Constraints

In the previous example, you saw how to use a precedence constraint that used an expression to determine which e-mail should be sent. As you've likely gathered by now, precedence constraints are used to define package workflow, determining if and when specific tasks are executed and in what order. Tasks (including containers) can be connected to other tasks or to other containers.

The following example reviews how to configure precedent constraints within the Control Flow design surface.

1. In SSIS Designer, using a new package, drag and drop a File System task onto the Control Flow design surface.

2. Next, drag and drop a Send Mail task onto the Control Flow design surface.

3. You will not configure the properties of either task; rather, you will only demonstrate how precedence constraints work. To make sure that the File System task executes first, click the File System task and drag the green arrow onto the Send Email task.

4. Notice that the arrow defaults to a green color, meaning that the Send Email task will only execute if the File System task executes successfully. Double-click the green arrow.

5. This raises the Precedence Constraint Editor. The Evaluation operation drop-down list designates whether or not a constraint is evaluated, an expression, an expression and constraint, or an expression or constraint. When Constraint is selected, the Exception result drop-down lists whether or not the next task executes on success, failure, or completion of the preceding task.

    If Expression is selected as an evaluation operation, the Expression dialog box becomes available for use. Expression evaluation was demonstrated in the previous exercise, when you evaluated the value of the JobCandidateCount user variable.

    The Multiple Constraints section applies to multiple constraints referencing the *same* task. In DTS 2000, if multiple constraints pointed to a single task, the default behavior was that *all* constraints must evaluate to true for the task to execute. In SSIS, you now have two options: logical AND and logical OR. Logical AND is the default behavior of 2005. Logical OR allows *either* one of the constraints pointing to the single task to evaluate to true for the destination task to execute.

6. Keep the Evaluation operation selection of Constraint. Change the Execution result to Failure and click OK. Notice that the green arrow has turned to red. The Send Mail task will now be fired only if the File System task fails.

Checkpoints

In DTS 2000, if a task failed in the middle of a DTS package, rerunning that package would cause *all* tasks to rerun from the beginning. For packages that perform significant data movement and processing, this could mean hours of unnecessary rework.

SSIS has addressed this issue by introducing *checkpoints*. When an SSIS task fails, the new checkpoint functionality allows you to restart the package, beginning from the point of failure.

To enable checkpoints for an SSIS package, follow these steps:

1. In SSIS Designer, click an empty area in the Control Flow tab to focus the Properties window on the SSIS package.

2. In the Properties window, type in a filename for the CheckPointFileName property. This file does *not* need to exist already.

3. Enable checkpoint usage for the package by selecting Always for the CheckpointUsage property.

The checkpoint file will be used to save all completed tasks, package configurations, containers, system variables, and user-defined variable information. When the SSIS package runs successfully, it deletes the checkpoint file it originally created. If you select the Always option, the SSIS package will *not* execute unless the checkpoint file exists. If you select the IfExists option, the package will use the checkpoint file if a previous execution failed, but if the previous execution succeeded, it will execute as normal.

Note During the checkpoint process, a unique package identifier is written to this file, preventing the use of a checkpoint on a modified SSIS package. To restart successfully from the point of failure, the SSIS package design must not be modified between the initial failure and the restart.

Transactions

SSIS packages support *transactions*, which combine a group of tasks into a logical unit of work that is either wholly committed or rolled back. If two tasks are enlisted within a transaction, and the second task fails, the first task will roll back database changes previously made to a consistent state before the package executed.

To enable transactions for your SSIS package, follow these steps:

1. In SSIS Designer, right-click an empty area on the Control Flow surface and select Properties.

2. In the Properties window, change the TransactionOption property to Required. The Required option means that the SSIS will start a transaction. The Supported option does not actually start a transaction; rather, it joins any transaction already started by the package or its parent container.

3. To enlist a specific task or container within the package transaction, click the task in the Control Flow surface. In the Properties window, change the task's TransactionOption property to Required.

Debugging

In DTS 2000, troubleshooting and debugging of your DTS package meant running the package from DTS Designer and waiting for the error message to appear. Once you received the error message, most of the time it was cryptic and unhelpful.

With SSIS, Microsoft has added several new debugging and troubleshooting features, which we cover in detail in the sections that follow.

Control Flow Visual Debugging

While creating your SSIS package, as you add and configure tasks, containers, or data flow objects, you will see real-time warning icons within them (see Figure 14-45). These warning icons contain tooltips that describe what properties are either missing or configured incorrectly.

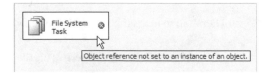

Figure 14-45. *File System task with a warning icon*

During package debugging, the SSIS Designer also displays task color-coded progress reporting. Without waiting for the SSIS package to finish executing, you can watch the task icons change colors, indicating their current status: gray indicates waiting to run, yellow indicates executing, green indicates success, and red indicates failure.

Progress during package execution can also be monitored by viewing the Progress tab (called the Execution tab when the package is *not* debugging) in SSIS Designer (see Figure 14-46). From here, you can monitor the start and finish times of tasks and containers, as well as view any events, errors, and warnings.

■**Tip** The Progress tab is an easy way to identify the cause of errors within your package. You can scroll through the various tasks and search for red "x"s. If there is, for example, a divide by zero error in a SQL task or a missing property in a Send Mail task, the Execution/Progress tab will indicate this.

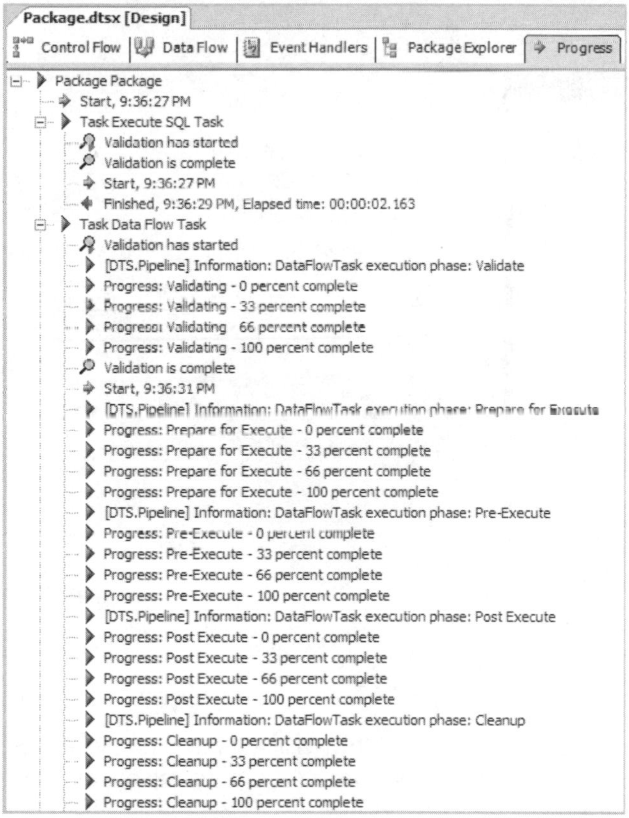

Figure 14-46. *Progress tab*

Data Flow Visual Debugging

In SSIS Designer, during package execution all Data Flow paths display the number of rows that have passed through them on the design surface, saving you from having to validate the actual row counts after the package finishes executing.

Data Viewers

Data viewers allow you to watch data as it moves through a path, enabling you to identify transformation issues or bugs. You can add a data viewer to the Data Flow tab by right-clicking the path between two data flow components and selecting Data Visualizer. In the Data Flow Path Editor dialog box, you can then add one or more viewers, which allow you to view data in a grid, histogram, scatter plot, or column chart format.

During runtime, a Data Viewer window will appear (see Figure 14-47), enabling you to continue moving the data, copy the data to a clipboard, truncate all data from the table, or reconfigure the data viewer.

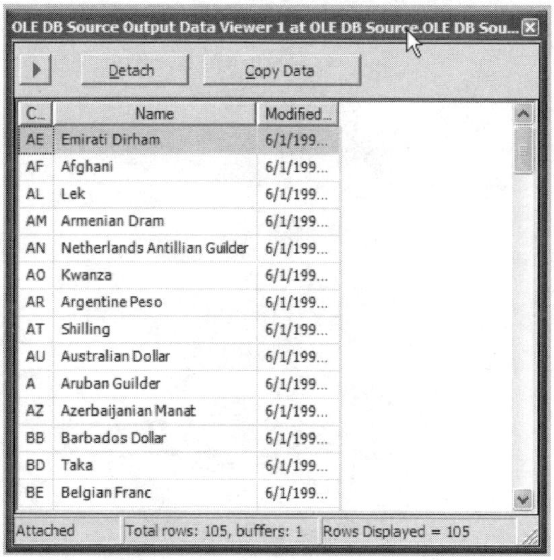

Figure 14-47. *Data Viewer window during runtime*

Breakpoints Window

SSIS Designer allows you to set *breakpoints* (i.e., a point in the SSIS package at which the task can be interrupted for manual intervention) within SSIS tasks, containers, or data flow components. You can configure breakpoints for various events (see Figure 14-48), including OnPreExecute, OnPostExecute, OnError, OnWarning, OnInformation, OnTaskFailed, OnProgress, OnQueryCancel, OnVariableValueChanged, and OnCustomEvent.

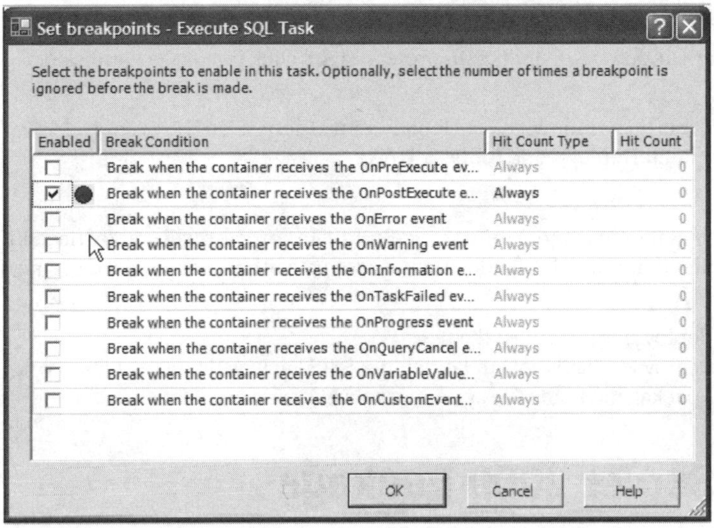

Figure 14-48. *The Set Breakpoints dialog box*

During package runtime, you can view the Breakpoints window, which lists all enabled breakpoints within the SSIS package.

Other Debug Windows

In addition to the Breakpoints window, Microsoft includes other windows useful for debugging runtime of the package:

- The *Call Stack window* shows SSIS objects that are currently running during debug mode.

- The *Command window* can be used for executing commands directly into the BIDS environment (e.g., if you wanted to exit Debug mode during the execution of an SSIS package, you could type **Debug.StopDebugging** and return). The Command window uses IntelliSense and allows you to browse through the various IDE commands.

- The *Immediate window* is used for executing commands in order to debug expressions, statements, and variables.

- The *Watch window* allows you to read, edit, and save variables.

- The *Output window* displays status errors related to project compilation and validation.

The SSIS Package Deployment Utility

The BIDS creates a package deployment utility that you can use to deploy your packages to any computer. After building the Package Deployment Utility, you can use the DTSInstall.EXE executable (created in the folder of your deployed project) to install packages using the SSIS Package Installer Wizard, which guides you through the process of installing files on either the file system or SQL Server.

The following steps will create a simple deployment utility for a completed SSIS package.

1. In the Solution Explorer window of an open SSIS project, right-click the project and select Properties.

2. In the Configuration Properties window, select Deployment Utilities. On the property window, configure the CreateDeploymentUtility to True.

3. Click the OK button.

4. Right-click the project in Solution Explorer and select Build. This process will create the SSIS deployment manifest file under the bin\Deployment directory, with its name based on the deployed project.

5. Double-click the SSIS deployment manifest file (e.g., BookSalesImport.SSISDeploymentManifest) to launch the SSIS Package Installer, where you are able to deploy your package(s) to the file system or to a SQL Server instance.

Migrating SQL Server 2000 Packages

SQL Server 2000 packages can be migrated by using the Data Transformation Services Migration Wizard. The wizard maps tasks within the SQL Server 2000 package to their equivalent DTS tasks in SSIS. For those tasks that do not map to SSIS, the new package structure will encapsulate non-SSIS-compliant functionality within an Execute DTS 2000 task.

Caution DTS object model references within a SQL Server 2000 ActiveX task are no longer allowed in SSIS.

To launch the SSIS Migration Wizard, perform these steps:

1. In the BIDS, within an SSIS project, right-click the SSIS packages folder in the Solution Explorer window.

2. Select Migrate DTS 2000 Package. The wizard will now step you through the migration process.

Scheduling an SSIS Package

As in SQL Server 2000 Enterprise Manager, SSIS packages can be scheduled using SQL Server Agent jobs in SQL Server Management Studio. Jobs can be scheduled to execute SSIS packages stored in SQL Server, on the file system, or the SSIS store.

Note The *SSIS store* is simply the default folder on the file system used to store packages deployed with the Package Deployment Wizard. The SSIS service looks for packages in this folder, rather then searching the entire file system for DTSX files.

This exercise shows you how to schedule an SSIS package that is stored within SQL Server (in the MSDB database).

1. In SQL Server Management Studio, in the Object Explorer window, expand the SQL Server Agent node and Jobs folder.

2. Right-click the Jobs folder and select New Job.

3. Enter the Name and Owner of the job.

4. Select the Steps page from the "Select a page" left window.

5. Click the New button to create a new step.

6. Enter the step name and select the type of SQL Server Integration Services package from the drop-down box.

7. Under Package source area, keep the default of SQL Server. Under the Server area, type in or select from the drop-down the SQL Server instance name.

8. For the Package field, type in the package name or select it by pushing the ellipsis button and selecting it from the "Select an SSIS package" dialog box, and then click OK.

■**Note** If the SSIS package is nested within a folder, use the naming convention of /Foldername/PackageName.

---

9. Select the Schedules page from the "Select a page" window. Click the New button to define your job schedule, and then click OK.

10. Click OK on the Steps dialog box, and click OK again on the main New Job dialog box.

Summary

SSIS has changed significantly since SQL Server 2000. The result of this rearchitecture is a truly enterprise-ready, scalable, and extensible ETL application.

In this chapter, you learned about some of the features introduced in SSIS, as well as the new integrated development environment (IDE). You learned about the new division of labor within the SSIS Designer: Control Flow and Data Flow. You examined all the tasks and features available for use both in the Control Flow and Data Flow toolboxes. You were introduced to the improved logging features, variables, and debugging features. Lastly, you reviewed how you can deploy and schedule SSIS packages as SQL Server Agent jobs.

This chapter just barely scratches the surface of SSIS. Coverage of SSIS could easily fill an entire book of its own (and has certainly done so in previous versions), so be on the lookout for a future Apress title devoted to SSIS.

CHAPTER 15

■ ■ ■

Database Mirroring

In many organizations today, data availability and business continuance is a major concern. Without the data to drive it, the business can't perform its necessary functions. While making the data, and the technology that houses that data, highly available is a primary concern for many IT managers, there are many barriers to achieving this high availability. Having the right technology is one piece of the puzzle, but high availability also is achieved by having consistent processes and well-trained people. In this chapter, we'll focus on the technology aspects, and we'll leave people and process as your issues to resolve.

One of the primary goals of SQL Server 2005 was to take *high availability* (*HA*) to the next level. Many of the HA technologies included in SQL Server 2000, such as failover clustering and log shipping, are valuable but somewhat cumbersome to configure and use. Also, they solve only half of the problem for many applications—namely, failing over the database server. This leaves the application developer in a lurch, since all applications have to be programmed with special code to failover the application to a new database server in the case of a failure in the original database server.

With database mirroring, SQL Server solves both database availability and application availability through the SQL Native Access Client (SNAC) stack, which understands and can work with database mirrors.

In this chapter, we'll investigate this new database mirroring capability and give detailed instructions on how to set up and use it. We'll relate existing technologies, such as failover clustering, replication, and log shipping, to the new SQL Server 2005 capabilities, and provide advice on which technology best solves a particular problem. We'll even look at when to use certain technologies together to achieve the highest level of HA. But, before we dive into the technology, we need to talk about HA at a higher level and define the term.

TURNING ON DATABASE MIRRORING

Please note that in the released version of SQL Server 2005, database mirroring is off by default and provided for evaluation purposes only. Microsoft is doing an extended testing cycle on database mirroring and will announce when the feature is ready for production use. In the meantime, you can develop on and test database mirroring in your environment to see if it meets your needs.

To turn database mirroring on, you need to enable trace flag 1400. There are two ways you can do this. The first is to go into the SQL Server Configuration Manager and find your SQL Server service under the SQL Server 2005 Services section. Under the Properties page, in the Advanced tab, in the Startup Parameters, add **-T1400**. You will need to restart your server for the trace flag to become active and used. Please note this is the preferred way to set the trace flag. The following image shows setting the startup parameters using the new trace flag.

The second way is to use the DBCC TRACEON command, such as DBCC TRACEON (1400, -1). The -1 specifies to set the trace flag globally. If you do not set the trace flags, you will receive errors when you attempt to use database mirroring.

High Availability Defined

Ask ten DBAs how they define HA and you'll probably get ten different answers. We're going to throw our own (informal) definition into the hat as well. In its simplest form, HA is about keeping your servers—and their services—up and running. HA is about making sure that end users do not experience hiccups in the operation of the system, and that the business can perform at an acceptable level. We use the term "acceptable level" because one organization may consider an acceptable level to be one hour of downtime per week while another may consider one second of downtime per week acceptable. It depends on the level of HA that you need.

Downtime comes in one of two forms:

- *Unplanned downtime*: This is what most people are trying to avoid when they implement an HA solution. These are the dreaded crashes, power outages, "Doh!" administrative moments (such as pushing the power button on the server by accident), and so on.

- *Planned downtime*: This includes activities like performing regular maintenance, patching, installing software, upgrading hardware, and other similar tasks that you will know about in advance and can plan for accordingly. Most times, your downtime is planned rather than unplanned. Any HA strategy should try to help you minimize this type of downtime as well.

An effective HA strategy will ensure that the defined acceptable level of downtime is met.

A term that goes hand in hand with HA is *disaster recovery* (*DR*), which is the means by which you protect your system against lost data and restore normal operations in the event of a system failure. DR is a piece of any HA strategy. You need to be able to get your system back up and running even after a disaster to achieve HA.

In essence, your DR strategy is your backup and restore strategy. For the highest level of DR, this involves a secondary site located some distance from the primary site. In the event that a catastrophic failure happens at the primary site, there is a failover to the secondary site. You can combine HA with DR to make servers in both the primary and secondary sites more bulletproof. DR is a key part of any overarching HA solution.

Many SQL Server technologies are available when implementing your HA/DR solutions, so let's first take a high-level look at how database mirroring works, and then we can place it into context with other HA-related technologies such as failover clustering, log shipping, and transactional replication.

Database Mirroring Overview

Figure 15-1 shows the basic architecture of the database mirroring technology.

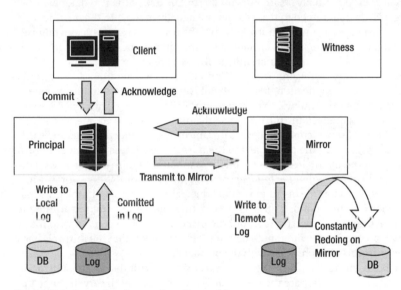

Figure 15-1. *Basic database mirroring architecture*

In the simplest deployment of database mirroring, there are two major server-side components, the *principal server instance* (principal) and the *mirror server instance* (mirror). The principal, as the name implies, contains the principal database. This is the database where you will perform your transactions. The basic idea behind database mirroring is that synchronized versions of the database are maintained on the principal and mirror. If the principal database (or the principal itself!) becomes unavailable, then the client application will smoothly switch over to the mirror database, and operation (from the user's point of view) will continue as normal.

So, a client interacts with the principal and submits a transaction. The principal writes the requested change to the principal transaction log and automatically transfers the information describing the transaction over to the mirror, where it is written to the mirror transaction log. The mirror then sends an acknowledgement to the principal. The mirror continuously uses the remote transaction log to "replicate" changes made to the principal database to the mirror database.

> ■**Note** The way database mirroring works under the covers is that it runs in-process in SQL Server. Unlike repli-
> cation, which is a log reader, database mirroring sends the log buffers stored in memory to the mirror before writing
> them to disk. Sometimes corruption occurs in the log files because of disk errors, failures, or other issues. With
> database mirroring, if the mirror is keeping up with the principal, you can avoid some of these disk-based corruptions.
> One caveat is that if the mirror gets behind for some reason, such as being suspended, or if you have a failover and
> the other server comes back online after a period of time, the principal will have to go to disk to get the older log
> blocks, so hardening your disks and making sure they are reliable is a must with database mirroring.

Database mirroring has a *synchronous* and an *asynchronous* mode of operation. The synchronous mode will force the principal to not consider a transaction committed until the mirror has
entered the transaction into its transaction log and sent back an acknowledgment. In asynchronous
mode, the principal does not wait for the mirror to acknowledge that it has received the transaction
before committing. This mode is potentially faster, but you do run the risk of the two databases
getting out of sync, since it is not guaranteed that a transaction actually made it to the mirror.

What happens, then, in the basic principal/mirror setup if the principal experiences a failure?
Basically, the DBA can manually instigate a failover, so that the mirror becomes the target for the
application. The client is automatically and transparently (to the user) redirected to the mirror. This
transparent client redirection is an interesting innovation. Without this technology, developers would
have to write custom code into their application in order to failover gracefully to the mirror node.

If, instead, the mirror experiences a failure then, in synchronous mode, the principal database
would continue. In asynchronous mode, if the mirror is lost, the principal keeps going as well.

Let's now introduce the third server component into our mirroring architecture—namely, the
witness server instance (witness). Unlike the principal and the mirror, the witness does not perform
any database operations (it doesn't maintain a transaction log or maintain a mirror copy of the database). Its primary function is to allow *automatic failover* (no DBA intervention). When working in
synchronous mode, the witness monitors the operation of the principal and mirror, and if the principal
exhibits no heartbeat response within a defined timeout period, then the witness triggers automatic
failover to the mirror. Furthermore, if the mirror fails, but the principal is still in contact with the
witness, then the principal can continue to operate. When the witness detects that the mirror is back
online, it will instruct the mirror to resynchronize with the principal.

The witness can also break any ties between the principal and the mirror to prevent split-brain
scenarios, where both machines think they are the principal. For example, if both servers come up
at the same time and both think they are the principal, then the witness can break the tie. When a
failure happens, all participants in the mirror get a vote to decide who the principal is. Of course, if
the principal itself is down, then only the mirror and the witness will vote. In this scenario, the
witness and mirror would decide the mirror needs to become the principal and the failover would
occur. When the original principal comes back online, it would assume the role of mirror and the log
buffers would go from the new principal to the new mirror.

When working with a witness, but in asynchronous mode, the principal will send the transaction details over to the mirror to commit, and commit the transaction locally. The principal does not
wait for the acknowledgment from the mirror before committing. Since synchronization cannot be
guaranteed in this mode, you lose the ability to perform automatic failover. Microsoft recommends
that if you are going to run in asynchronous mode you do not use a witness, since quorum would be
required but you are not getting the benefits of quorum because asynchronous mode does not
support automatic failover. Asynchronous mode may be suitable on occasions when you are willing
to sacrifice HA for performance. Since synchronous mode requires committing on both sides, if you
do not have acceptable network bandwidth, or if the mirror gets behind, your overall application
performance could suffer due to delayed transaction commits.

Table 15-1 summarizes the different database mirroring modes, and the pros and cons for each mode.

Table 15-1. *Database Mirroring Modes*

Mode Name	Synchronous or Asynchronous?	Witness Present?	Pro/Con
High Availability	Synchronous	Yes	Supports automatic failover and is the most hardened. If the mirror disappears but the principal and witness are connected, operations continue. The mirror catches up when it comes back online.
High Protection	Synchronous	No	No automatic failover. If the mirror is unavailable, the principal database goes offline.
High Performance (not recommended)	Asynchronous	Yes	Fast performance, but the data is not guaranteed on the other side and there is no automatic failover. This is useful for low-bandwidth connections between the mirror and principal since performance is best. This mode requires quorum before users can connect, so it is not recommended.
High Performance (recommended mode)	Asynchronous	No	Microsoft recommends that if you are going to run asynchronously, you run with this configuration. There is no automatic failover, and the mirror is a hot standby server but not guaranteed to be up to date.

Database Mirroring in Context

Now that you've walked through a high-level overview of what database mirroring is all about, you can look at it in the context of existing HA technologies such as log shipping and failover clustering.

As you may have noted, log shipping is one of the principles by which database mirroring operates. In other words, entries from a transaction log in one database are transferred and applied to another. When the database mirroring feature was originally being developed, it was called *real-time log-shipping*. As development progressed, it made more sense to rename the feature to database mirroring, since, in effect, that is what the feature does. Most administrators understand disk mirroring in a Redundant Array of Inexpensive Disks (RAID) configuration, so the term "database mirroring" for SQL Server made sense.

The main advantages mirroring has over log shipping or transactional replication are that potential data loss is eliminated and automatic failover is enabled. An interesting addition was the transparent client redirection. Without this technology, developers would have to write custom code into their application to failover gracefully.

It's true that failover clustering did provide automatic failover and this client redirection, but mirroring is much easier to set up and use than clustering, which also required specialized hardware. Also, mirroring provides a substantial decrease in potential downtime over clustering.

Table 15-2 lists the technologies that SQL Server 2005 provides to help implement HA/DR solutions and explains the differences between each. We will look at each solution, especially database mirroring, later in this chapter.

Table 15-2. *SQL Server HA/DR Solutions*

Area	Database Mirroring	Failover Clustering	Transactional Replication	Log Shipping
Data loss	No data loss	No data loss	Some data loss possible	Some data loss possible
Automatic failover	Yes, in HA mode	Yes	No	No
Transparent to client	Yes, autoredirect	Yes, connect to same IP	No, but Network Load Balancing (NLB) helps	No, but NLB helps
Downtime	< 3 seconds	20 seconds or more, plus database recovery	Seconds	Seconds plus database recovery
Standby read access	Yes, using database snapshot	No	Yes	Intermittently accessible
Data granularity	Database only	All system and user databases	Table or view	Database only
Masking of disk failure	Yes	No, shared disk solution	Yes	Yes
Special hardware	No, duplicate recommended	Cluster Hardware Compatibility List (HCL) hardware	No, duplicate recommended	No, duplicate recommended
Complexity	Some	More	More	More

Setting Up Database Mirroring

In this chapter, we'll demonstrate how to set up a mirroring architecture consisting of three SQL Server 2005 server instances (principal/mirror/witness). As discussed previously, you can use only two server instances (no witness), but then you lose the ability to do automatic failovers.

MICROSOFT VIRTUAL SERVER

While you evaluate database mirroring, you have a good excuse to look at some other technologies at the same time. For example, you may not have three machines that you can use for the evaluation, and this is where technologies such as Microsoft Virtual Server (MVS) come in handy. With MVS, you can run three virtual machines on a single physical machine.

We recommend the use of MVS to evaluate database mirroring, rather than creating three instances of SQL Server on a single machine, because with the virtual technology you can do a hard shutdown of the virtual machine. In lieu of having three machines, this will provide the most realistic simulation of an "unplanned catastrophe." The database mirroring feature does support the forcing of a manual failover, but simulating a real failure is best for your evaluation.

Prerequisites, Connectivity, and Security

One of the main prerequisites for setting up database mirroring is to ensure that your databases run in full recovery mode, since database mirroring uses the transaction log and requires the more extensive logging and log information created when you use full recovery mode. To do this, you can use the following ALTER DATABASE statement:

```
USE master;
GO
ALTER DATABASE YOURDATABASEHERE
SET RECOVERY FULL;
GO
```

Also, remember that nonlogged operations will not work with database mirroring, so do not use nonlogged Bulk Copy Program (BCP) to load data into the database.

After that, you need to set up your endpoints in the architecture. Database mirroring uses the new endpoint connection model in SQL Server 2005 and requires that you set up endpoints so that the principal and the mirror can talk to each other. You have the option of either using Security Support Provider Interface (SSPI), which uses Windows credentials, or using certificate-based authentication.

Connecting Using Windows-Based Authentication

If you want to use Windows-based authentication, the accounts that you use for your SQL Server service accounts involved in the database mirroring session must be in the same domain or at least in a trusted domain. If the accounts are not in trusted domains, the connection between the principal and the mirror will fail.

You will also have to assign permissions to the accounts to be able to connect to the other server(s), via endpoints, and also to the database, as you will see shortly. The example in this chapter also assumes that you use the same service account for all your instances.

■**Note** If you do not have trusted domains or you do not use Windows-based authentication, you must use certificates for authentication, which is covered in the next section.

To use Windows-based authentication, perform the following steps:

1. Create the endpoints for mirroring. To create an endpoint, you need to use the CREATE ENDPOINT statement. This statement takes the name of the endpoint, the state, the protocol, and the payload. The following example creates a new endpoint that uses a TCP payload on a particular port. This code should be run on the principal server. Make sure to give your endpoint a unique name.

```
CREATE ENDPOINT MirroringEndPoint
    STATE=STARTED
    AS TCP (LISTENER_PORT=10111)
    FOR DATABASE_MIRRORING (ROLE=PARTNER)
GO
```

■**Note** You can have only one endpoint per server instance for database mirroring. If you try to create more than one endpoint, you will receive an error.

---

2. Now that you've created your endpoint, you need to create a login, if one does not already exist, and assign CONNECT permissions to the endpoint for that login. The following code creates a login that maps to the Windows account that the witness will use to log on, and it assigns permissions on the endpoint.

```
USE master;
GO
CREATE LOGIN [YOURDOMAIN\witnessaccount] FROM WINDOWS ;
GO
GRANT CONNECT ON ENDPOINT::MirroringEndPoint TO [YOURDOMAIN\witnessaccount];
GO
```

3. You now need to perform the same operations on the mirror, since the witness needs to be able to connect to and authenticate against both servers. The following code creates an endpoint and a user login, and assigns permissions on the mirror for the witness.

```
CREATE ENDPOINT MirroringEndPoint
    STATE=STARTED
    AS TCP (LISTENER_PORT=10111)
    FOR DATABASE_MIRRORING (ROLE=ALL)
GO
USE master;
GO
CREATE LOGIN [YOURDOMAIN\wintessaccount] FROM WINDOWS;
GO
GRANT CONNECT ON ENDPOINT::MirroringEndPoint TO [YOURDOMAIN\witnessaccount];
GO
```

4. You also need to create an endpoint on the witness to allow the principal and the mirror to connect to the witness. This example assumes that the same Windows account is used to log onto both the principal and the mirror. This step is similar to the preceding steps, so the complete code is listed here for complete clarity:

```
CREATE ENDPOINT MirroringEndPoint
    STATE=STARTED
    AS TCP (LISTENER_PORT=10111)
    FOR DATABASE_MIRRORING (ROLE=ALL)
GO
USE master;
GO
CREATE LOGIN [YOURDOMAIN\dbaccount] FROM WINDOWS;
GO
GRANT CONNECT ON ENDPOINT::MirroringEndPoint TO [YOURDOMAIN\dbaccount];
GO
```

Connecting Using Certificates

As mentioned earlier, you may want to use certificates for authentication rather than Windows-based authentication for your connectivity. Certificates use the encryption technology introduced in SQL Server 2005. Please note that the certificates are used only for authentication and not for encrypting the communication between your principal and mirror. To learn more about encryption in SQL Server 2005, please refer to Chapter 11.

The following steps show you how to create your certificates and assign them for your database mirroring authentication. You should perform these steps on the principal database server.

1. If you have not already set up your database master key for encryption, you must do that now; otherwise, you will get an error when you try to create the certificate in the database. The following T-SQL command creates the database master key, which is secured via a password that you specify.

```
CREATE MASTER KEY ENCRYPTION BY PASSWORD = '!@@@gh!2a*'
Go
```

2. The next step is to create the certificate you want to use inside your database. The following command creates a certificate using the encryption technology in SQL Server 2005.

```
USE master;
CREATE CERTIFICATE HOST_ServerACert
    WITH SUBJECT = 'Server A cert for DBM';
GO
```

3. Next, you need to create your endpoints to use your certificates. Notice that you pass the authentication and the encryption values to the CREATE ENDPOINT function.

```
CREATE ENDPOINT MirroringEndPoint
    STATE = STARTED
    AS TCP (
        LISTENER_PORT=10111
        , LISTENER_IP = ALL
    )
    FOR DATABASE_MIRRORING (
        AUTHENTICATION = CERTIFICATE ServerACert
        , ENCRYPTION = REQUIRED ALGORITHM RC4
        , ROLE = ALL
    );
GO
```

4. Back up the certificate and transfer it securely to your mirror database server. You can back up the certificate using the following command:

```
BACKUP CERTIFICATE ServerACert TO FILE = 'C:\ServerACert.cer';
GO
```

5. Perform steps 1–4 on your mirror database server, except change ServerA to ServerB for the naming. You'll need the certificate from server B copied over to server A.

6. Next, you need to create a login for your mirror database and make that login have permissions to the certificate on your principal. This is for the incoming connection, as opposed to the steps you just performed for the outgoing connection. The following code creates the login and also grants connect permissions on the endpoint for database mirroring.

```
USE master
GO
CREATE LOGIN mirrorlogin WITH PASSWORD = '!@#1579212'
CREATE USER mirroruser FOR LOGIN mirrorlogin
GO
GRANT CONNECT ON ENDPOINT::MirroringEndPoint TO [mirrorlogin]
GO
```

7. You need to assign your user to your newly copied certificate from the mirror server. The following code creates a certificate and uses the mirror's certificate.

```
CREATE CERTIFICATE mirrorservercert
    AUTHORIZATION mirroruser
    FROM FILE = 'c:\ServerBCert.cer'
GO
```

8. You can now reverse the procedure in steps 6–7 on the mirror so that the principal can log onto it. Also, make sure to allow the witness to be able to log onto both the principal and the mirror using the same steps just outlined.

Back Up and Restore the Principal Database

Now that you have security and connectivity set up between your principal, mirror, and witness, you can now get your database ready to go. Again, before performing the steps presented in this section, make sure your database is in full recovery mode. The first step is to back up the database so that you can move it over and restore it on the mirror. The following code will back up your principal database:

```
USE YourDB
BACKUP DATABASE YourDB
    TO DISK = 'C:\YourDB.bak'
    WITH FORMAT
GO
```

Once you copy over the database to your mirror server, you need to restore the database, which will ensure that you have the database in the same state of principal and mirror. You have to make sure that you use the same name for the database on both the principal and the mirror. According to Microsoft's recommendations, the path (including the drive letter) of the mirror database should be identical to the path of the principal database. If these pathnames differ, you cannot add any files to the database. It's not required, but it will make it easier for you since you will not have to change configuration. Also, you must restore your database using the NORECOVERY option with database mirroring. The following code restores the database on the mirror:

```
RESTORE DATABASE YourDB
    FROM DISK = 'C:\YourDB.bak'
    WITH NORECOVERY
GO
```

If you are testing database mirroring on the same server using multiple instances, or your pathnames differ between your principal and mirror for the database, you will have to restore your database with the MOVE keyword when you restore the database. The following code changes the restore path using the MOVE keyword:

```
RESTORE DATABASE YourDB
    FROM DISK='C:\YourDB.bak'
    WITH NORECOVERY,
        MOVE 'YourDB' TO
'C:\Program Files\Microsoft SQL Server\MSSQL.2\MSSQL\Data\YourDB_data.mdf',
        MOVE 'YourDB_log'
TO 'C:\Program Files\Microsoft SQL Server\MSSQL.2\MSSQL\Data\YourDB_Log.ldf';
GO
```

Establish the Principal/Mirror Partnership

You will always want to make sure you configure your mirror server first to be a partner with your principal server before you configure the principal. To do this, you use the ALTER DATABASE statement with the SET PARTNER statement for the database mirroring option. Please note that the ports you set are serverwide, so if you run database mirroring on the same server using multiple instances for testing, you will want to use different ports. The following code sets the partner for the mirror to the principal using the TCP endpoint you created earlier:

```
ALTER DATABASE YourDB
    SET PARTNER =
    'TCP://YourPrincipalServer.YourDomain:10111'
GO
```

On the principal, you need to set its partner to the mirror server using the following code:

```
ALTER DATABASE YourDB
    SET PARTNER =
    'TCP://YourMirrorServer.YourDomain:10111'
GO
```

Finally, you need to set the witness. You can do this from either server. The following code performs this operation:

```
ALTER DATABASE YourDB
    SET WITNESS =
    'TCP://YourWitnessServer.YourDomain:10111'
GO
```

Changing Transaction Safety Levels

By default, database mirroring sets the transaction safety level to FULL. The FULL transaction safety level provides the highest levels of protection and availability, and it is required if you want to run in a synchronous state. If you want automatic failover, you need to have a witness server. If you do not want to run in FULL transaction safety mode, you can modify your transaction safety level using the database mirroring options offered by the ALTER DATABASE statement. The following code shows the different options you have with the ALTER DATABASE statement for database mirroring:

```
ALTER DATABASE dbname SET PARTNER { = 'Partner Server'
                             | FAILOVER
                             | FORCE_SERVICE_ALLOW_DATA_LOSS
                             | OFF
                             | RESUME
                             | SAFETY { FULL | OFF }
                             | SUSPEND
                             | REDO_QUEUE ( integer { KB | MB | GB } | OFF
                             | TIMEOUT integer
                             }

ALTER DATABASE dbname SET WITNESS { = 'Witness Server'
                             | OFF
                             }
```

So, to change your transaction safety level from FULL to OFF, you need to use the following command on the principal:

```
ALTER DATABASE dbname SET PARTNER SAFETY OFF.
```

You may want to run with your transaction safety level OFF if you want to maximize performance. Doing so shifts the session into asynchronous operating mode, which maximizes performance at the cost of safety. If the principal becomes unavailable, the mirror stops but is available as a hot standby. You have to make the failover happen to the mirror.

Database Mirroring States, Heartbeats, and Quorums

In database mirroring, there is a set of database states that your system goes through. These states provide you with the status of your mirror, and you can query for them, as you will see when we look at how to monitor database mirroring using catalog views. Table 15-3 lists the different states for databases that are part of database mirroring.

Table 15-3. *Database Mirroring States*

State Name	Description
SYNCHRONIZING	This is the beginning phase for any mirror, since this is when the principal and the mirror are synchronizing their contents. The mirror is not fully in sync with the principal yet and is lagging behind. Both principal and mirror will normally be in this state, where log records are being sent between the two and being applied on the mirror.
SYNCHRONIZED	This state is when both the principal and the mirror are in sync. The principal is sending any changes to the mirror to be applied, and the mirror is not lagging behind. Both manual and automatic failover can only occur in this state.
SUSPENDED	This is the state where mirroring is no longer occurring, either through administrative intervention or REDO errors on the mirror. The principal is considered to be running exposed, which means that the principal is running without a partner on the other side of the mirror.
PENDING_FAILOVER	This state is only on the principal and occurs when the administrator performs a manual failover but the mirror has not accepted the failover yet.
DISCONNECTED	The partner has lost communications with the other partner and the witness, if the witness is present.

Beyond the database states listed in Table 15-3, database mirroring also implements a heartbeat between the partners in a mirror. By default, this heartbeat is sent every 2.5 seconds between the servers. If the partner does not respond after four pings, a failover is initiated. What will happen depends on whether you're running in synchronous or asynchronous mode, and whether a witness is present. See Table 15-1 for more details.

You can customize the timeout setting to either shorten or lengthen it depending on your situation. For example, you may want to lengthen the timeout setting if you have slow connectivity between your servers and do not want false failovers to occur. To change the timeout setting, you need to use the ALTER DATABASE statement on the principal and set in seconds the timeout period you want as shown in the following code:

```
ALTER DATABASE dbname SET PARTNER TIMEOUT 15
```

The minimum timeout you can set is 10 seconds. If you set the timeout value to any number below 5, SQL will automatically set it to 5 seconds for you. Keep your timeout to 10 seconds or more; otherwise, you may overload your system by having false failovers all the time due to missed ping messages.

Database mirroring uses the idea of a quorum when running in synchronous mode, which requires transaction safety to be set to FULL. A *quorum* is the minimum number of partners that are needed to decide what to do in a mirrored set. In database mirroring, a quorum is at least two partners. The partners could be the principal and the witness, the witness and the mirror, or the principal and the mirror. A full quorum is when all three partners—principal, mirror, and witness—can communicate with one another. If at any point a partner is lost, such as the principal server, the other two partners establish quorum and arbitrate what should happen. Each partner in the quorum gets a vote and, in the end, the witness breaks any ties between the principal and the mirror.

If for some reason all three partners lose communication with each other, automatic failover will not occur. You will want to make sure that your witness can always talk to your mirror over the network, since this link is crucial to making sure that automatic failover will occur.

Initiating a Failover

There may be times, such as when you are testing or after you have upgraded one of the mirror partners, that you want to manually initiate a failover, to make sure failovers will work when you need them to. Rolling upgrades can be supported only if the physical log file format used by SQL Server does not change because of the upgrade. For example, if you want to install a Windows patch on the principal and then on the mirror, and this patch does not affect SQL Server, you can install the patch on the mirror, failover the principal to the mirror, and apply the patch on the old principal. When you're done, you can fail back the mirror back to the principal.

To initiate a failover manually, your mirror must be in the SYNCHRONIZED state. Also, you must connect to the master database before failing over the server, since you cannot be connected to the database that you are about to failover. When you issue the manual failover, the principal will disconnect clients, uncommitted transactions will be rolled back, and the last remnants of the log will be shipped over to the mirror. The mirror then becomes the principal, and the principal becomes the mirror. All your clients will have to reconnect to the new principal. To issue the failover, you use the ALTER DATABASE statement with the FAILOVER option as follows on the principal server:

```
ALTER DATABASE dbname SET PARTNER FAILOVER
```

If you are running without a witness in FULL transaction safety mode, manual failover is the only type of failover you can perform.

If you are not running in FULL transaction safety mode (also called synchronous mode), you can force a failover as well, but there may be some data loss since this mode does not guarantee that the mirror has received all the logs from the principal. To force a manual failover in this mode, you must send a different option using the ALTER DATABASE statement to the principal:

```
ALTER DATABASE dbname SET PARTNER FORCE_SERVICE_ALLOW_DATA_LOSS
```

The reason that database mirroring can failover very fast is that it takes advantage of the new fast recovery technology in SQL Server 2005. The mirror is constantly running REDO when it receives the log files from the principal. When the mirror is failed over to, it moves from REDO to UNDO and opens up the database for clients if you're using Enterprise Edition. For Standard Edition, the database is available after both REDO and UNDO are complete.

Suspending and Resuming Mirroring

There may be times when you want to suspend mirroring and then resume it at a later point—for example, if you find a bottleneck in your system and you want to allow the principal to quickly complete its pending transactions, and at some later point you want to apply the same changes to the mirror. In such cases, you can suspend the session, apply your changes to the principal, and then re-enable the mirror once the bottleneck is removed. When you suspend a mirroring session, client connections are retained. Also, the log is not truncated since the log will need to be sent to the mirror at some point, unless you break the mirror partnership. You will not want to suspend a mirror for a long period of time, since the principal's log file could fill up the available storage on your server.

To suspend the session, you need to use the `ALTER DATABASE` statement on either partner as follows:

```
ALTER DATABASE dbname SET PARTNER SUSPEND
```

To resume the session, just change `SUSPEND` to `RESUME`:

```
ALTER DATABASE dbname SET PARTNER RESUME
```

Terminating Database Mirroring

To terminate a database mirroring partnership, you can use the `ALTER DATABASE` command on either partner. When you terminate a partnership, all information about the session is removed and each server has an independent copy of the database. The mirror database will be in a restoring state until it is manually recovered or deleted. If you want to recover the mirror database, use the `RESTORE` command with the `WITH RECOVERY` clause.

One other thing to remember is to drop all database snapshots, which you will learn about later in this chapter, before breaking your mirror, otherwise, you will get an error stating that the database cannot be restored. The following statement will break a database mirror:

```
ALTER DATABASE dbname SET PARTNER OFF
```

Full-Text Indexing and Mirroring

Since full-text indexing catalogs are now backed up when you back up your databases, when you restore the principal onto the mirror, the full-text catalog is restored as well. As DDL changes are made to the principal's catalog, these changes will be reflected on the mirror. After a failover, a crawl is automatically initiated on the mirror to update the full-text index. If you create a new catalog on the principal and the mirror cannot perform the operation for some reason, your state will become `SUSPENDED` for mirroring.

Service Broker and Database Mirroring

You can use Service Broker and database mirroring together. When combining the two, you must configure Service Broker with two addresses for your route: the principal database server's address and the mirror database server's address. Service Broker will connect to both machines to see who the current principal is, and it will route the message to that principal. If the principal goes down, Service Broker will connect to the mirror, and if the mirror is now the principal, Service Broker will begin delivering messages to the new principal. You can monitor database mirroring when combined with Service Broker by using the database mirroring Transport object, which is under the Service Broker object, which is, in turn, under the SQL Server object in Performance Monitor. One caveat, though, is that to use Service Broker with database mirroring, you must always have your transaction safety level set to `FULL`.

Setting Up Mirroring Using Management Studio

Rather than having to go through the manual steps to set up mirroring, you can perform all the same actions using SQL Server Management Studio.

To get started, launch Management Studio and select the database you want to set up as the mirror. Right-click the database and select Properties. You should see mirroring as a page type in the left navigation, as shown in Figure 15-2.

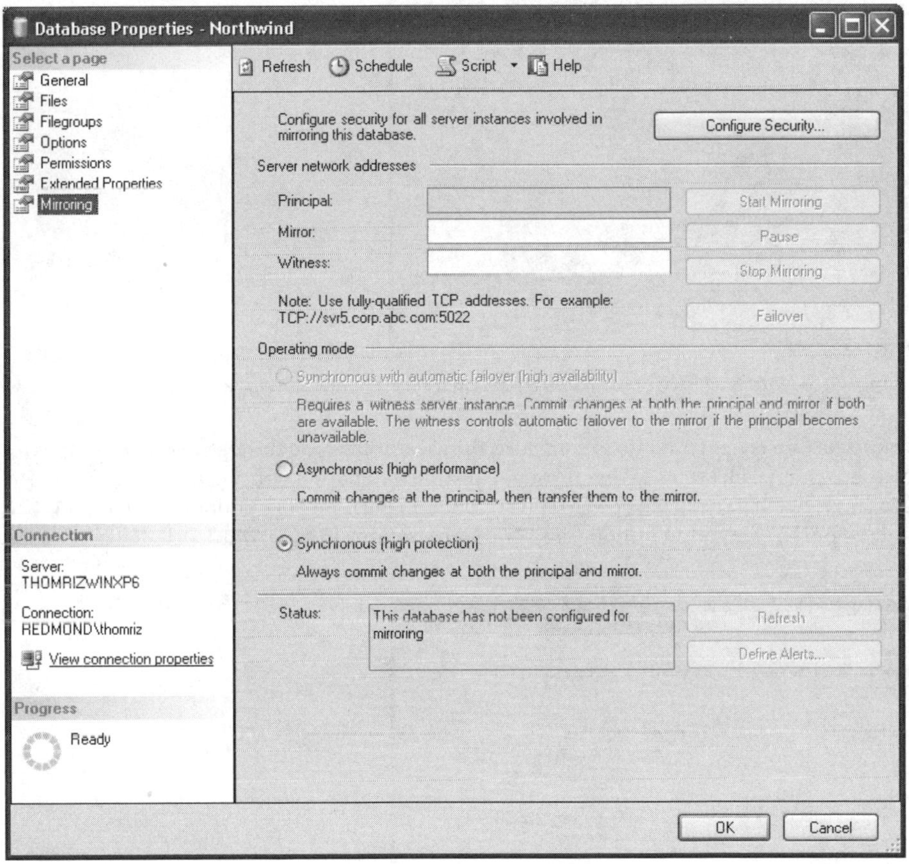

Figure 15-2. *Database mirroring Properties page*

The Configure Database Mirroring Security Wizard will step you through setting up the correct security settings for your principal, mirror, and witness, if used. The wizard will create all the endpoint settings for you automatically. Figure 15-3 shows the security wizard screen where you can select which servers to configure.

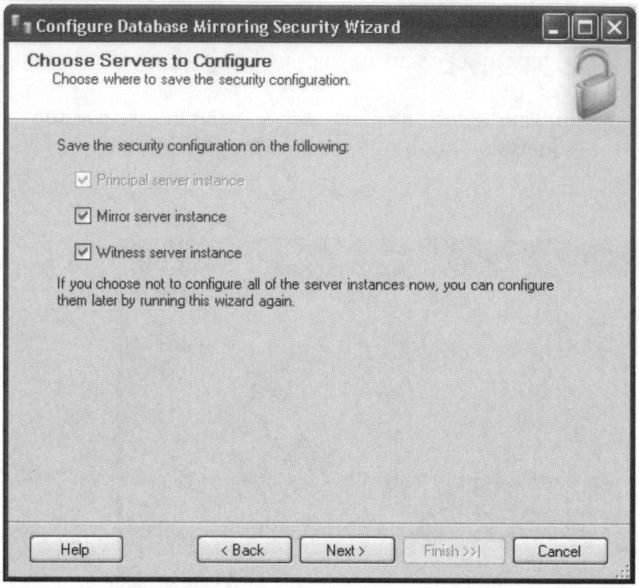

Figure 15-3. *Configure Database Mirroring Security Wizard server selection page*

Once you select the servers you want to configure, the wizard steps you through a set of questions to configure your endpoints. Please note that if you are testing database mirroring using multiple instances on a single machine, you will need to specify different ports for your endpoints. Figure 15-4 shows setting the ports, encryption options, and endpoint options in the wizard.

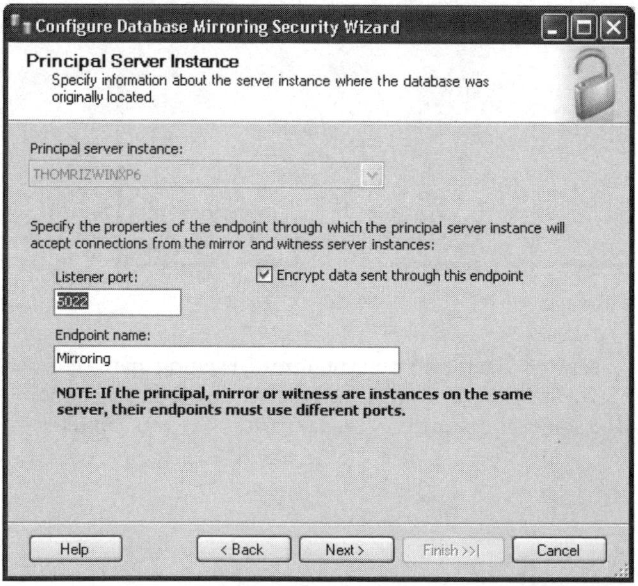

Figure 15-4. *Setting options in the Configure Database Mirroring Security Wizard*

Next, the wizard will step you through setting the exact configuration for the remaining partners in your mirroring set. You will need to fill out the same information as you filled out for the principal, as shown in previously in Figure 15-4.

Finally, you need to specify the SQL service accounts for your servers if they are different. If they are not different, you should leave the text boxes blank, as shown in Figure 15-5.

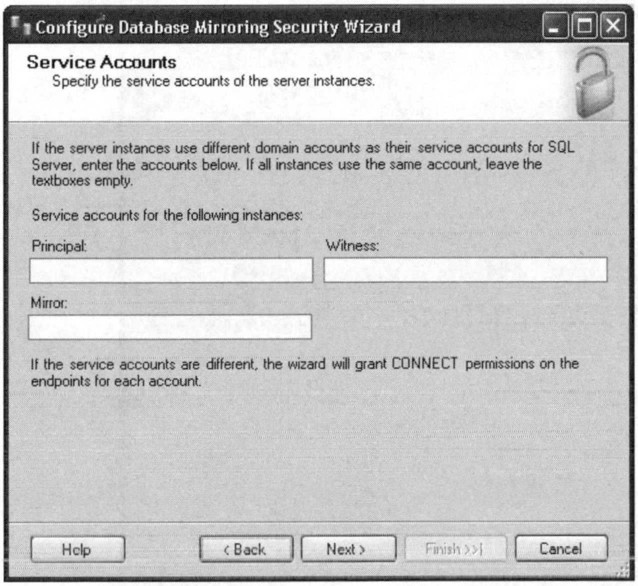

Figure 15-5. *Setting options in the Configure Database Mirroring Security Wizard*

Once you have done this, the wizard will complete and attempt to set up your mirroring configuration. Using the wizard is much easier than writing your own T-SQL code to configure mirroring. However, you will get more control over your configuration using T-SQL.

Figure 15-6 shows the updated database mirroring Properties page once the wizard has completed.

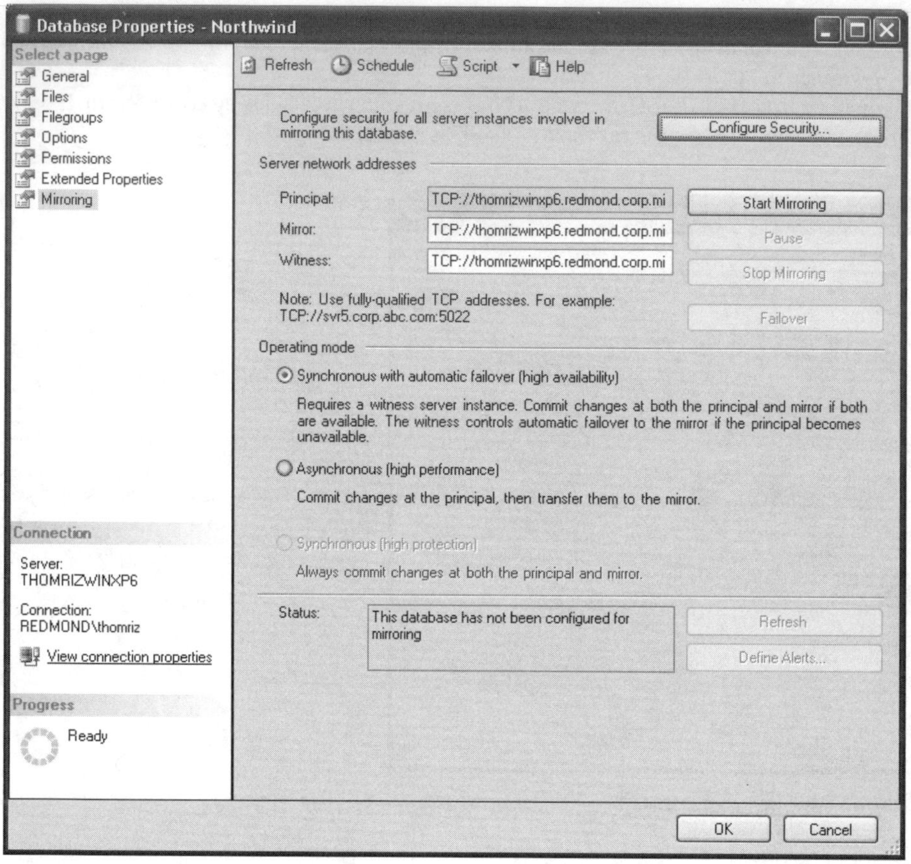

Figure 15-6. *Database mirroring Properties page after running the Configure Database Mirroring Security Wizard*

Once the wizard has completed, you'll need to perform some manual steps before you can click the Start Mirroring button on the Properties page. You'll manually back up and restore your database from the principal to the mirror. Once you've restored the database with the NO RECOVERY option, you can click the Start Mirroring button. Management Studio will attempt to start database mirroring using the same commands you saw earlier to manually set up your mirror pair. Figure 15-7 shows a successfully started database mirroring session in Management Studio.

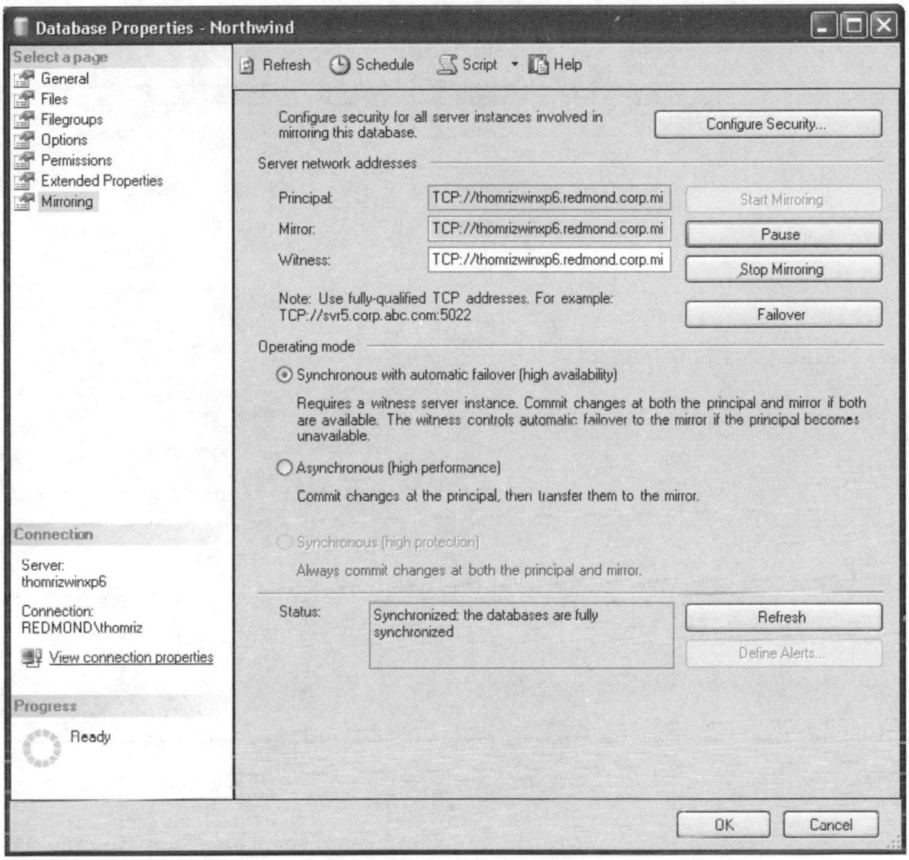

Figure 15-7. *A successfully running mirror being monitored in Management Studio*

One of the nice features of Management Studio is the ability to script out dialog boxes. Unfortunately, this feature does not apply to the mirroring dialog box. So, if you want to see which commands Management Studio is sending to the server to set up and start database mirroring, you will need to run Profiler.

Figure 15-8 shows a running trace that captures the commands that Management Studio sends to the server to set up and start database mirroring. As you will notice in the screenshots that follow, the commands are the same ones you learned about earlier in the chapter.

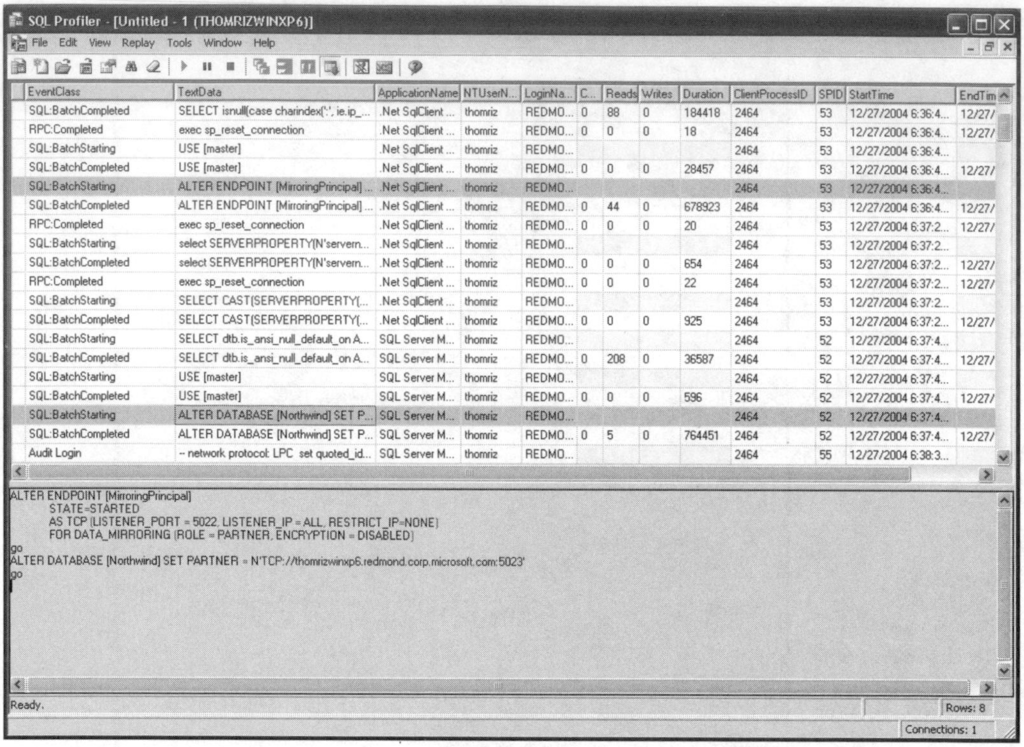

Figure 15-8. *Profiler trace of the Configure Database Security Mirroring Wizard*

For monitoring database mirroring, you can bring up the database mirroring Properties page in Management Studio, which will show the current state of the mirror, or you can get a quick view of the role and status via Object Explorer, as shown in Figure 15-9. It's probably easier to write a little script that you execute that uses the catalog views of database mirroring than to always have to go back to the database mirroring dialog box.

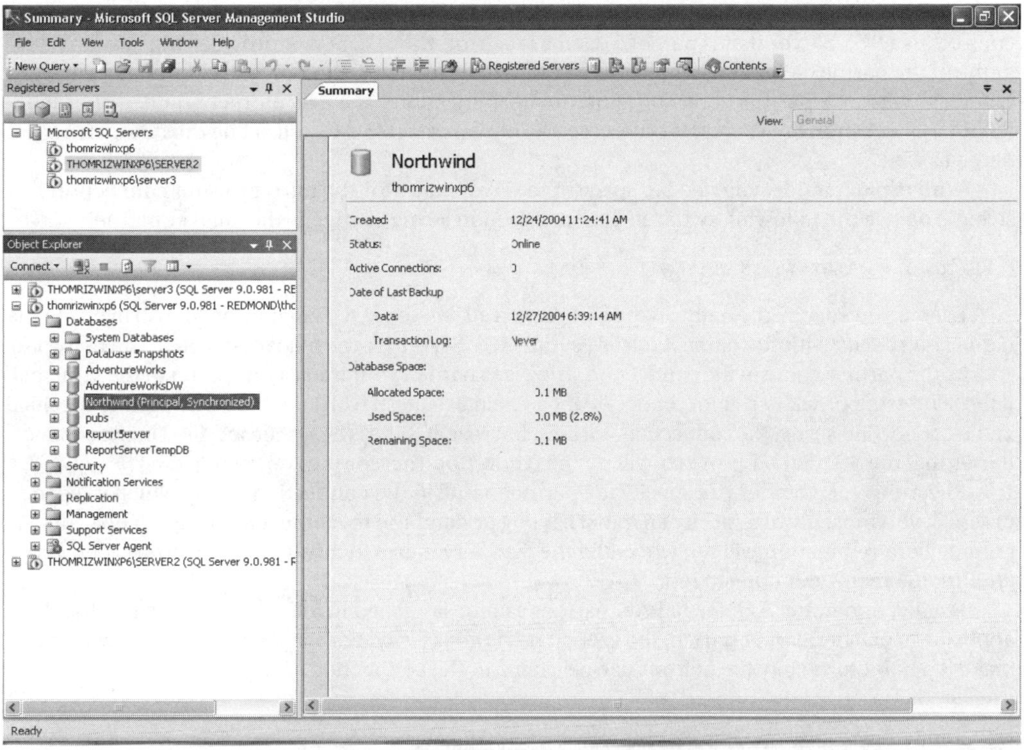

Figure 15-9. *Quick mirroring status in Object Explorer*

Client Applications and Database Mirroring

Normally when programming your client applications for HA, you have to write a lot of special code to handle the failover of your application. With database mirroring and the .NET or SNAC SQL Server providers, transparent client redirection is automatically handled for you.

Before diving into how to change your client application to use database mirroring, we must first emphasize that transparent client redirection is not a panacea. You still will need to write good code that fails when there is an error and retries the operation. If you do not, transparent client redirection will not magically restart your transaction and complete the operation for you.

When working with transparent client redirection, you must be running the version of the SQL Server providers that comes with SQL Server 2005. There are two modes in which you can program database mirroring: implicit and explicit.

In implicit mode, you do nothing special in your connection string code. Instead, when you first connect to a SQL Server that is part of a database mirror, the SQL Server provider will cache the name of the partner server in memory. If the principal goes away, the SQL Server provider will try to connect to the new partner server on subsequent connections. If a new partner is added after the failure as a new mirror, Microsoft Data Access Components (MDAC) will cache the new partner's name as well.

With explicit mode, you need to specify the server name for the mirror in your connection string. You use the following syntax in your connection string to specify the failover partner:

```
";Failover Partner=YourServerName"
```

Even if you specify the name in the connection string, the SQL Server provider will override the name you specify with the name it retrieves from SQL Server for the failover partner. The reason to specify the partner name in the connection string is to harden your initial connection to the principal. If the SQL Server provider cannot connect to the principal to begin with and there is no partner specified in the connection string, the connection will fail. However, if there is a partner specified in the connection string, the SQL Server provider will try the failover partner for the connection.

Regardless of whether you specify the partner name in the connection string, which is a good practice, you must always specify an initial catalog or database to connect to. If you do not, transparent client redirection will not work, and the SQL Server provider will throw an error when you attempt to create your connection.

Finally, remember that the failover partner's name is cached in memory. This means that if the application crashes or is restarted, the cached name goes away. For this reason, you will want to make it a habit to specify the failover partner name in the connection string.

Monitoring Database Mirroring

Beyond what you saw in Management Studio to monitor database mirroring graphically, which was just the text box that showed the status in the database mirroring Properties page, you can also monitor database mirroring using catalog views, Performance Monitor, Profiler, and the Windows event log and the SQL Server error log, as described in the sections that follow.

Catalog Views

Database mirroring has three catalog views: sys.database_mirroring, sys.database_mirroring_endpoints, and sys.database_mirroring_witnesses. All three views can be used, in addition to other views, to monitor your environment. For example, you could use sys.endpoints to view all endpoints in your system, including your database mirroring endpoints. You can retrieve mirroring and other information about the database using sys.databases as well.

Table 15-4 shows the columns for the sys.database_mirroring catalog view.

Table 15-4. *sys.database_mirroring View Columns*

Column Name	Description
database_id	Integer ID of the database that is unique within a SQL Server instance.
mirror_state_desc	Returns back the description of the state as text, such as SYNCHRONIZED, DISCONNECTED, SYNCHRONIZING, PENDING_FAILOVER, or SUSPENDED.

Table 15-4. *sys.database_mirroring View Columns*

Column Name	Description
mirroring_connection_timeout	Timeout in seconds before a failover occurs. The minimum and default setting is 10 seconds.
mirroring_failover_lsn	Log sequence number during the most recent failover.
mirroring_guid	ID of the mirroring partnership. This column, as well as subsequent columns prefixed with mirroring_, will be NULL if there is no mirroring setup.
mirroring_partner_name	Server name of the mirroring partner.
mirroring_partner_instance	Instance, port, and other information about the mirroring partner.
mirroring_redo_queue	Limit of the redo queue in megabytes before the principal waits for the mirror to catch up. By default, this is unlimited, and the column value for unlimited is null.
mirroring_redo_queue_type	String value for the mirroring_redo_queue value, which will be UNLIMITED or the limit in megabytes.
mirroring_role	Returns back the mirroring role for the current server, where 1 is the principal and 2 is the mirror.
mirroring_role_desc	Returns back the description of the mirroring role for the current server, such as PRINCIPAL or MIRROR.
mirroring_role_sequence	Returns back the update sequence number for the changes made by the principal and applied to the mirror.
mirroring_safety_level	Returns back the safety level for the database mirror, where 0 is unknown, 1 is off or asynchronous, and 2 is on or synchronous.
mirroring_safety_level_desc	Returns back the description of the mirroring safety level, such as UNKNOWN, OFF, or FULL.
mirroring_safety_sequence	Sequence number for any changes to the transaction safety level.
mirroring_state	Mirroring status, where 0 is suspended, 1 is disconnected, 2 is synchronizing, 3 is pending failover, and 4 is synchronized.
mirroring_witness_name	Server name of the mirroring witness, if used.
mirroring_witness_state	State of the witness, where 0 is unknown, 1 is connected, and 2 is disconnected.
mirroring_witness_state_desc	Returns back the description of the state of the witness, such as UNKNOWN, CONNECTED, or DISCONNECTED.

When you have to work with endpoints, you will want to use sys.database_mirroring_endpoints. Using this catalog view, you can figure out what ports your servers are listening on and make sure that you have set up your endpoints correctly. Most of the columns in this view are inherited from the sys.endpoints view. Table 15-5 shows the columns in sys.database_mirroring_endpoints.

Table 15-5. *sys.database_mirroring_endpoints View Columns*

Column Name	Description
endpoint_id	Unique ID for the endpoint
is_encryption_enabled	Returns back 1 if encryption is enabled or 0 if it is disabled
name	Friendly name of the endpoint
principal_id	ID of the server principal that created and owns the endpoint
protocol	Protocol used by the endpoint, where 1 is HTTP, 2 is TCP, 3 is named pipes, 4 is shared memory, and 5 is VIA
protocol_description	Friendly name for the protocol, such as HTTP, TCP, NAMED_PIPES, SHARED_MEMORY, or VIA
role	Mirroring role, where 0 is none, 1 is partner, 2 is witness, and 3 is all
role_desc	Description of the mirroring role, such as NONE, PARTNER, WITNESS, or ALL
state	Endpoint state, where 0 is started, 1 is stopped, and 2 is disabled
state_desc	Description of the endpoint state, such as STARTED, STOPPED, or DISABLED
type	Endpoint payload type, where 1 is SOAP, 2 is T-SQL, 3 is service broker, and 4 is database mirroring
type_desc	Description of the payload type, such as SOAP, TSQL, SERVICE_BROKER, or DATABASE_MIRRORING

The final catalog view for database mirroring is sys.database_mirroring_witnesses. This view contains a row for every witness role a server instance plays in a database mirroring partnership. Table 15-6 shows the columns included in this view.

Table 15-6. *sys.database_mirroring_witnesses View Columns*

Column Name	Description
database_name	Name of the database in the mirroring session
family_guid	ID for the backup family in order to match restore states
is_suspended	Indication of whether database mirroring is suspended (1) or not (0)
is_suspended_sequence_number	Sequence number for the last change to the suspended state
mirror_server_name	Name of the server that is the current mirror
mirroring_guid	Unique ID assigned to the mirroring partnership

Table 15-6. *sys.database_mirroring_witnesses View Columns*

Column Name	Description
principal_server_name	Name of the server that is the current principal
role_sequence_number	Sequence number of the last change to the roles for principal and mirror
safety_level	Transaction safety, which can be 0 for unknown, 1 for off or asynchronous, or 2 for full or synchronous
safety_level_desc	Description of the safety level, which can be UNKNOWN, FULL, or OFF
safety_sequence_number	Sequence number of the last change to the safety level

Figure 15-10 shows using the database mirroring views inside of Management Studio.

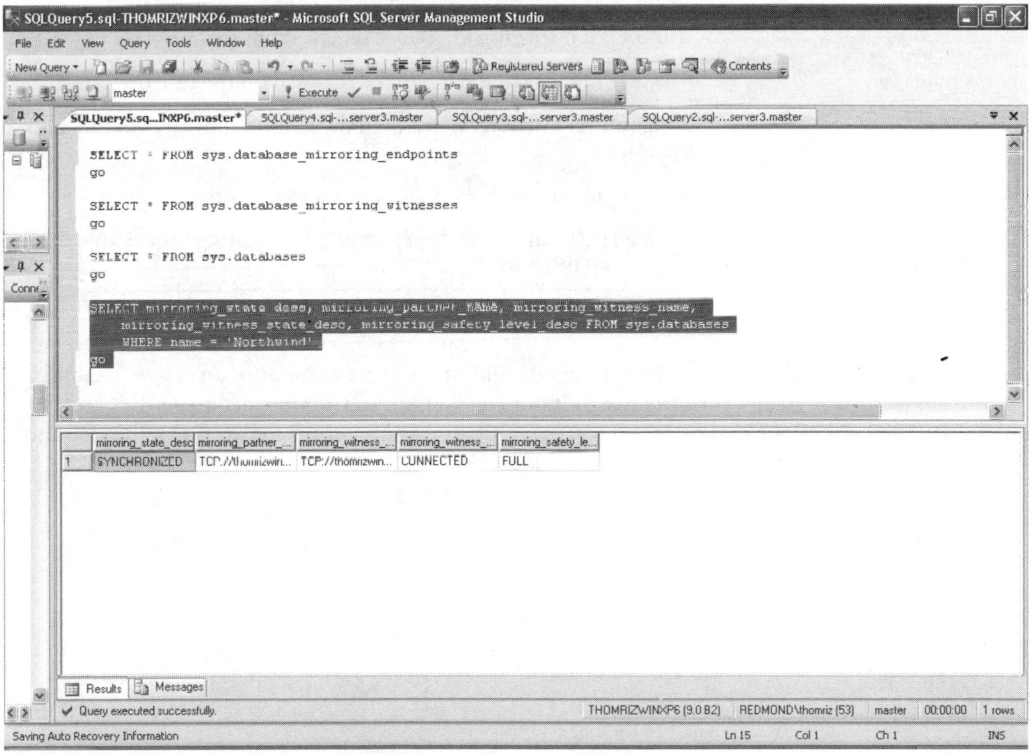

Figure 15-10. *Using the database mirroring views inside Management Studio*

Performance Monitor Counters

You can also monitor database mirroring using Performance Monitor and the database mirroring counters. You can find the Performance Monitor counters under the SQL Server: Database Mirroring object. Table 15-7 lists the Performance Monitor counters that you can use with database mirroring.

Table 15-7. *Database Mirroring Performance Monitor Counters*

Counter Name	Description
Bytes Received/sec	Number of mirroring bytes received per second
Bytes Sent/sec	Number of mirroring bytes sent per second
Log Bytes Received/sec	Number of log bytes received per second
Log Bytes Sent/sec	Number of log bytes sent per second
Log Send Queue	Total number of bytes of log not yet sent to the mirror
Pages Sent/sec	Number of database pages sent per second
Receives/sec	Number of mirroring messages received per second
Redo Bytes/sec	Number in bytes of the log rolled forward on the mirror
Redo Queue	Total number of bytes of hardened log remaining to be applied to the mirror
Sends/sec	Number of mirroring messages sent per second
Transaction Delay	Average delay in transaction termination waiting for acknowledgment from the mirror

Figure 15-11 shows the use of Performance Monitor counters to monitor an active database mirroring session. If you let Performance Monitor run and there is no transaction activity on your principal, you will see the pattern of the database mirroring pings appear in your capture. Monitor the Total Bytes sent/sec or the Mirroring Bytes Sent/sec counter to see the pings.

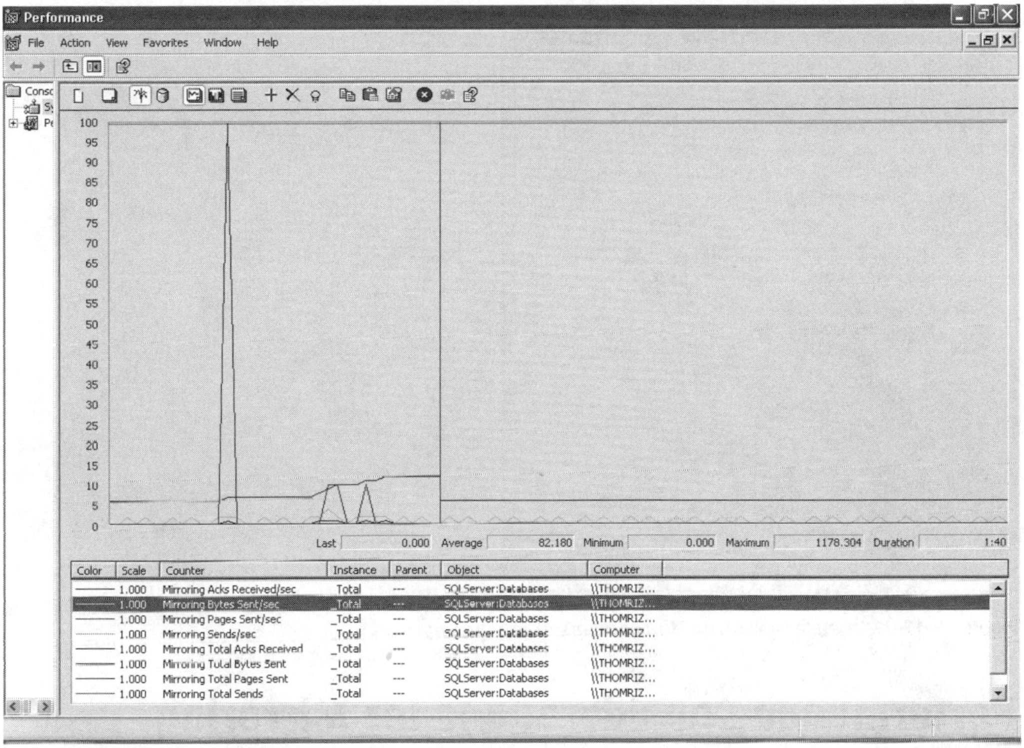

Figure 15-11. *Monitoring database mirroring with Performance Monitor*

Profiler

You can use Profiler to watch the changes that are happening to your databases that are part of a mirror. Profiler will not show the log being shipped from one server to another, but you will see any SQL commands sent to the current principal or any snapshots on the mirror. You can also see the state change events when roles change because of a failover. To find the database mirroring–specific event in Profiler, look under Database and select the Database Mirroring State Change option.

Windows Event Log and SQL Server Error Log

Database mirroring puts out events to the Windows application event log and the SQL Server error log. Some events are information, such as messages telling you that database mirroring has started and what the role of the server is. You can scan the event log to quickly see what's happening with your database mirroring setup or you can use a third-party tool to monitor the log. Database mirroring event IDs are in the 1400 range, so if you want to filter for them, you will want to filter in that range for SQL Server. Figure 15-12 shows a typical message for database mirroring in the event log.

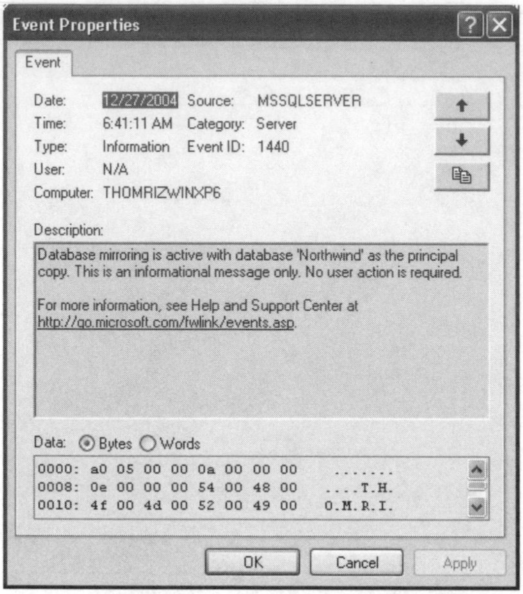

Figure 15-12. *Database mirroring Windows event log message*

Performance Considerations for Mirroring

Depending on how you configure mirroring, you can expect different levels of performance. For example, if you use FULL transaction safety level, your performance on your principal will be affected by two primary things: the mirror's I/O ability on the transaction log and your network connection, since the network packets have to round-trip between the principal and the mirror.

On the mirror, you will want to make sure that you have the same computing and I/O power as the principal. The reason for this is in the case of a failover. You do not want 100 percent load on a larger machine rolling over to a less capable machine. I/O throughout is also very important on the mirror since the mirror is performing sequential log writes and singleton lookups. Make sure to put your data, log, and tempdb files on different drives that use different disk controllers if possible.

The edition of SQL Server that you use also affects database mirroring. Even though the Standard Edition of SQL Server supports database mirroring, it has limited capabilities. Transaction safety level must always be FULL in Standard Edition, and the mirror database server always uses a single thread for the REDO queue processing. In Enterprise Edition, one thread is created per four CPUs for the REDO queue processing.

Finally, make sure to keep your backup and restore procedures in place, even if you use database mirroring. You should back up your databases from the principal server.

Limitations of Database Mirroring

There are a few limitations with database mirroring. First and foremost is that database mirroring supports only two nodes in terms of failover support. Both log shipping and failover clustering support more than two nodes. For scale-out, read-only scenarios, you should consider peer-to-peer replication, not database mirroring.

Please note that you can use both log shipping and replication with database mirroring. You should make the principal database server the primary in your log shipping topology. You can then make one or more other database servers your secondary database servers that get the log shipped to them. Do not make the mirror database server your secondary database server. As for replication, you can use your principal database server as a publisher and secondary servers as subscribers.

You cannot mirror master, msdb, temp, or model system databases. Furthermore, you have to keep all your logins and jobs in sync manually, since database mirroring does not mirror your logins and jobs between servers. Also, make sure to remove all snapshots on the mirror before breaking your mirror. While many customers have requested this feature, you cannot back up your database from the mirror. Instead, you need to back up your databases from the principal server.

Finally, mirroring supports the relational engine only at a database level. If you want instance failover, you will have to configure mirroring for every database in an instance. Also, if you want HA for other components, such as Analysis Services and Reporting Services, you will need to use Windows clustering.

Sample Application Walk-Through

To help you better understand how to set up and use database mirroring, we've included a sample application with this book written using Visual Studio 2005 that sets up and tests database mirroring. The sample application takes some input on the server names, endpoint addresses, and how often to insert data into the principal to put a load on the server. You can also failover the principal to the mirror and the mirror back to the principal using the sample application. Please note that the application works with the Pubs database out of the box, but it can easily be modified to work with any database. Figure 15-13 shows the user interface for the sample application.

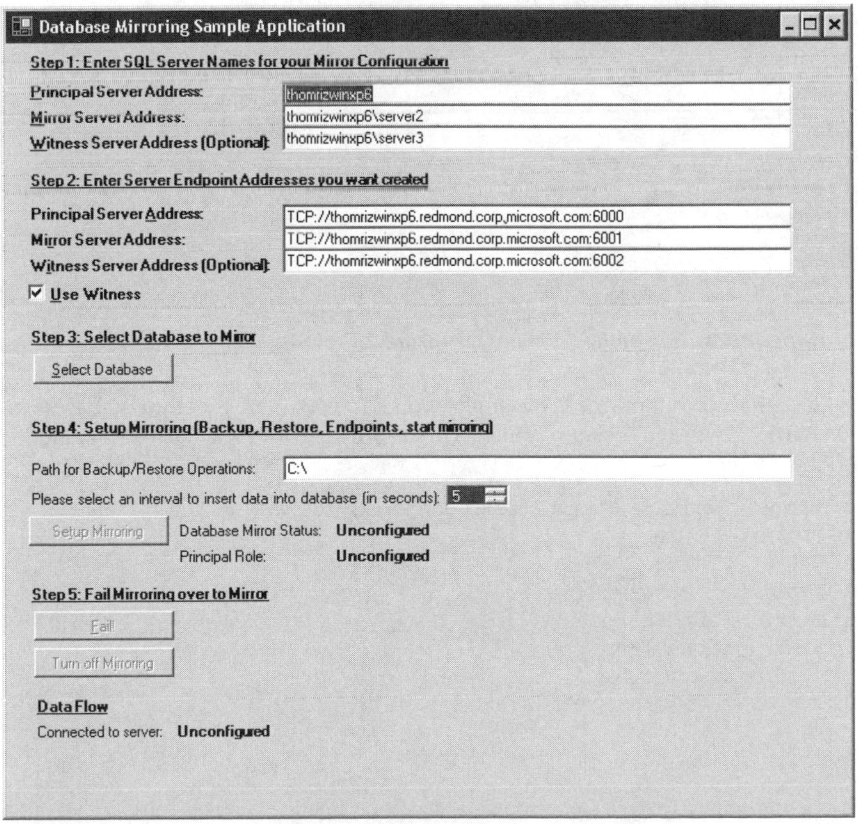

Figure 15-13. *Database mirroring sample application*

Once configured, the application will start up mirroring and show the status of the mirror using the catalog views for database mirroring. Also, the application will show the ID of the publisher inserted into the Publishers table. Figure 15-14 shows a fully configured and running version of the sample application.

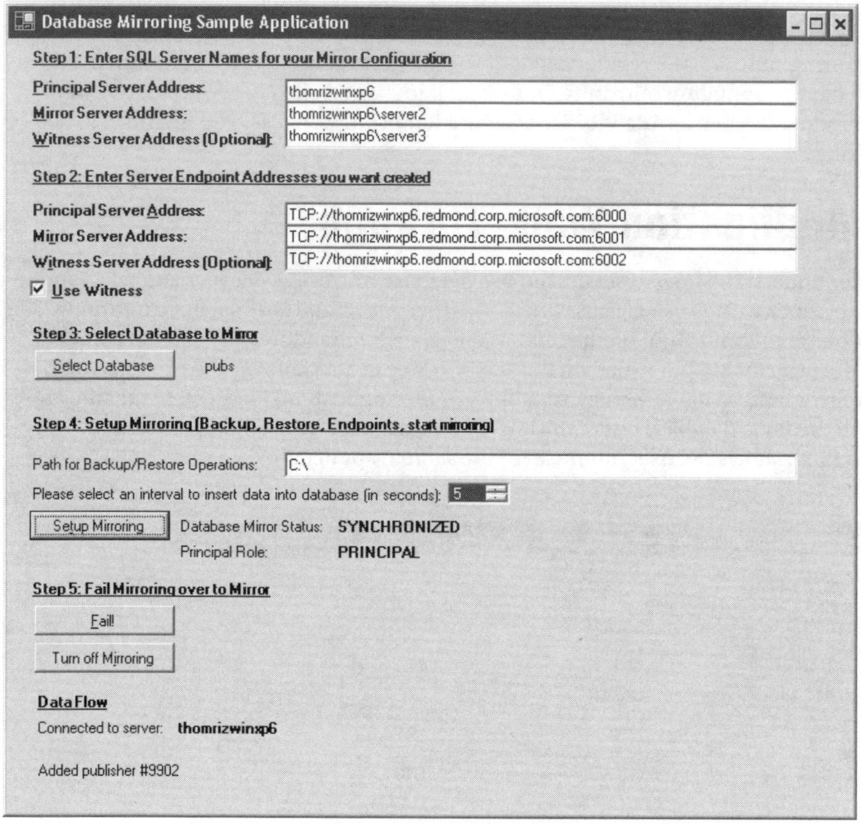

Figure 15-14. *Fully configured version of the database mirroring sample application*

The first step in setting up your mirror in the application is to make sure that the database is in full recovery mode. To do this, the application connects to the principal and sets the recovery mode, as shown in the following code:

```
'First, connect to the Principal and make sure it's in Full Recovery Mode
Dim boolError As Boolean = False
Dim strSQL As String = ""
strDatabaseName = lblDatabaseName.Text()
strPrincipalName = txtPrincipalServer.Text()
strMirrorName = txtMirrorServer.Text()
strWitnessName = txtWitnessServer.Text()
strBackupRestorePath = txtBackupRestorePath.Text()

'Create our connection string
strConnectionStringPrincipal = "Initial Catalog = " & _ strDatabaseName & _
";Data Source = " & strPrincipalName & ";Trusted_Connection=Yes;"
```

```
'Attempt to make it full recovery
strSQL = "ALTER DATABASE [" & strDatabaseName & "] SET RECOVERY FULL;"
boolError = ExecuteNonQuery(strConnectionStringPrincipal, strSQL)
If (boolError) Then
     MsgBox("Error making recovery model full for principal.")
     SetCursorBack()
     Exit Sub
Else
     MsgBox("Success! Recovery model set to full.")
End If
```

Then, the application backs up the database so that it can be restored on the mirror. After backing up the database, the application restores the database to the location specified by the user. Remember that you want to restore your database with the NO RECOVERY keyword for mirroring. The following code performs the backup and the restore:

```
'Back up the database
strSQL = "BACKUP DATABASE " & strDatabaseName & " TO DISK = N'" & _
     strBackupRestorePath & _
     strDatabaseName & ".bak' WITH NOFORMAT, INIT,  NAME = N'" & _
     strDatabaseName & _
     "-Full Database Backup', SKIP, NOREWIND, NOUNLOAD,  STATS = 10"
boolError = ExecuteNonQuery(strConnectionStringPrincipal, strSQL)
If (boolError) Then
     MsgBox("Error backing up principal. Exiting setup.")
     SetCursorBack()
     Exit Sub
Else
     MsgBox("Success! " & strDatabaseName & " backed up.")
End If

'Restore the database to the mirror
strConnectionStringMirror = "Initial Catalog = Master" & _
";Data Source = " & strMirrorName & ";Trusted_Connection=Yes;"

strSQL = "RESTORE DATABASE [" & strDatabaseName & "] FROM  DISK" & _
     & "= N'" & strBackupRestorePath & _
     strDatabaseName & ".bak' WITH  FILE = 1, MOVE N'" & _
     strDatabaseName & "' TO N'" & strBackupRestorePath & _
     strDatabaseName & ".mdf',  MOVE N'" & _
     strDatabaseName & "_log' TO N'C:\" & strDatabaseName & _
     ".ldf',  " & _
     "NORECOVERY,  NOUNLOAD, REPLACE, STATS = 10"
boolError = ExecuteNonQuery(strConnectionStringMirror, strSQL)
If (boolError) Then
     MsgBox("Error restoring to mirror. Exiting setup.")
     SetCursorBack()
     Exit Sub
Else
     MsgBox("Success! " & strDatabaseName & " restored to mirror.")
End If
```

The next step is to create the endpoints on the servers. Since there can be only one mirroring endpoint per server, the code checks to see if the endpoints already exist and drops them. It then creates the endpoints. The code searches for endpoints by name, since the sample application shouldn't drop endpoints that the sample did not create. However, you could also search endpoints on your server using the type of endpoint in the endpoints catalog view. The following code shows how the endpoints are dropped and created for the principal. Since the mirror and witness code is very similar, we do not list it here.

```
'Create the endpoints.  Start on the principal

'See if the endpoint already exists and if so, drop it
'since we can only have one mirroring endpoint per server
strSQL = "SELECT name from sys.endpoints WHERE name = & _
    'MirroringPrincipalSampleEndPoint'"

Dim strReturnValue As String = & _
    CStr(ExecuteScalar(strConnectionStringPrincipal, strSQL))
If strReturnValue = "MirroringPrincipalSampleEndPoint" Then
    'It exists, drop it
    strSQL = "DROP ENDPOINT MirroringPrincipalSampleEndPoint"
    boolError = ExecuteNonQuery(strConnectionStringPrincipal, & _
        strSQL)
    If (boolError) Then
        MsgBox("Error dropping endpoint.  Exiting setup.")
        SetCursorBack()
        Exit Sub
    End If
End If


Dim strPrincipalPort As String = & _
    RetrievePortNumber(txtPrincipalEndPoint.Text)

strSQL = "CREATE ENDPOINT [MirroringPrincipalSampleEndPoint] " & _
    "STATE = STARTED" & _
    " AS TCP (LISTENER_PORT = " & strPrincipalPort & _
    ", LISTENER_IP = ALL, RESTRICT_IP=NONE)" & _
    " FOR DATABASE_MIRRORING (ROLE = PARTNER," & _
    " ENCRYPTION = DISABLED)"

'Create the endpoint
boolError = ExecuteNonQuery(strConnectionStringPrincipal, strSQL)
If (boolError) Then
    MsgBox("Error creating endpoint.  Exiting setup.")
    SetCursorBack()
    Exit Sub
Else
    MsgBox("Success! Created endpoint on Principal.")
End If
```

After creating the necessary endpoints, you next need to set your partners. You need to start with the mirror and tell the mirror who its principal partner is. Then you do the same with the principal. If a witness is used, you must set the witness as well on the principal server. The following code shows these three steps:

```
'Alter the mirror database to set the partner
strSQL = "ALTER DATABASE " & strDatabaseName & _
    " SET PARTNER = '" & txtPrincipalEndPoint.Text & "'"

boolError = ExecuteNonQuery(strConnectionStringMirror, strSQL)
    If (boolError) Then
    MsgBox("Error setting partner on the Mirror.  Exiting setup.")
    SetCursorBack()
    Exit Sub
Else
    MsgBox("Success! Set partner on the mirror.")
End If


'Alter the principal database to set the partner
strSQL = "ALTER DATABASE " & strDatabaseName & _
    " SET PARTNER = '" & txtMirrorEndPoint.Text & "'"

boolError = ExecuteNonQuery(strConnectionStringPrincipal, strSQL)
If (boolError) Then
    MsgBox("Error setting partner.  Exiting setup.")
    SetCursorBack()
    Exit Sub
Else
    MsgBox("Success! Set partner on the principal.")
End If


'Check to see if they want to use a witness.
If checkWitness.Checked = True Then
    'Set Witness
    strSQL = "ALTER DATABASE " & strDatabaseName & _
      " SET WITNESS = '" & txtWitnessEndPoint.Text & "'"

     boolError = ExecuteNonQuery(strConnectionStringPrincipal, & _
       strSQL)
    If (boolError) Then
        MsgBox("Error setting witness.  Exiting setup.")
        SetCursorBack()
        Exit Sub
    Else
        MsgBox("Success! Set witness on the principal.")
    End If


End If
```

Setting the partners turns on mirroring, so the next step in the sample is to start inserting data and displaying the status of the mirror. The code uses a timer control to wake up, insert the data, and check the status of the mirror. To check the status, the code queries the mirror_state_desc column for database mirroring in SQL Server's catalog views. This column will return back SYNCHRONIZED, SUSPENDED, or the other states that database mirroring can be in. The code also queries the principal to ask what role the principal is currently playing, such as PRINCIPAL or MIRROR, just in case the user failed over the application. The code to insert data and retrieve the status is as follows:

```
Dim strSQL As String = ""
Dim boolError As Boolean = False

strConnectionStringPrincipal = "Initial Catalog = " & _
  strDatabaseName & _
  ";Data Source = " & strPrincipalName & ";Trusted_Connection=Yes;"

If UCase(strDatabaseName) = "PUBS" Then
    'Insert data into pubs
    'Increment the counter
    iPubsCounter += 1
    strSQL = "INSERT INTO [publishers] (pub_id, pub_name, city, & _
    state, country) VALUES ('" & CStr(iPubsCounter) & _
    "','Test','Test','WA','Test')"

    boolError = ExecuteNonQueryForMirror(& _
      strConnectionStringPrincipal, strSQL)
    If (boolError) Then
      lblDataFlowText.Text = "Error inserting data."
    Else
      lblDataFlowText.Text = "Added publisher #" & iPubsCounter
    End If

End If


'Try to query the principal to get status of database mirroring
Dim strReturnValue As String = ""
Dim strSQL As String = ""

strConnectionStringPrincipal = "Initial Catalog = Master" & _
  ";Data Source = " & strPrincipalName & ";Trusted_Connection=Yes;"


'First, get the state description
strSQL = "SELECT mirroring_state_desc from sys.databases WHERE " & _
    " name = '" & strDatabaseName & "'"

strReturnValue = ExecuteScalar(strConnectionStringPrincipal, strSQL)
If strReturnValue = "" Then
    strReturnValue = "Unconfigured"
End If
lblDBMirrorStatusText.Text = strReturnValue


'Get the Principal's role
strSQL = "SELECT mirroring_role_desc from sys.databases WHERE " & _
    "name = '" & strDatabaseName & "'"

strReturnValue = ExecuteScalar(strConnectionStringPrincipal, strSQL)
If strReturnValue = "" Then
    strReturnValue = "Unconfigured"
End If

lblPrincipalText.Text = strReturnValue
```

The application supports failover by giving you a button to click to perform a manual failover, or you can just turn off the principal either by turning off the machine or by stopping the SQL Server service. Either way, the application, powered by database mirroring, will failover to the mirror and start inserting data into the mirror. The application uses the transparent client redirection built into the .NET SQL provider. You can bring back up the principal, which will become the new mirror. You can then fail back if you like. The application for manually failover uses the ALTER DATABASE dbname➡ SET PARTNER FAILOVER statement to failover the mirror.

The final piece of the application is the cleanup code when you want to turn off mirroring. The application will attempt to clear out the inserted data so that you can try the sample application again without having to manually clean up the data. Plus, the application will turn off the timer. Finally, the application will stop the databases from mirroring by sending ALTER DATABASE dbname➡ SET PARTNER OFF to the principal.

Some things that you can do beyond what the application does is turn on Performance Monitor on the principal and mirror to track mirroring sends, receives, acknowledgments, and also client connections. In addition, you may want to have the application set up database mirroring for you, so that you can try out database snapshots on the mirror server, which you will learn about next.

Database Snapshots and Mirroring

When you have a mirrored system, you may want to use the mirror as the server that users query to generate reports on their data. There are two reasons for this. First, you do not want users querying your primary OLTP system, since it has to handle the load for all your transactions. Second, you may want to get more usage out of your mirror, since you have already invested in the hardware for the mirror.

Before we dive into a discussion about creating snapshots on your mirrors, though, there are some things you need to think about. First and foremost is that allowing users to query the mirror using snapshots will be a performance hit on the mirror. This could, in turn, slow down your entire database mirroring solution. The second thing you need to consider is that when there is a failover to the mirror, you do not want your clients querying your new principal; rather, you want to failover your snapshots and your clients to the new mirror if it's available.

Database Snapshots Overview

The easiest way to define database snapshots is to use the term "copy-on-write." Snapshots use a copy-on-write technology, so that only changes to the database are written to the snapshot. Therefore, the entire database does not have to be copied when creating a snapshot; only the changes do. Now, if your entire database is changing over the lifetime of a snapshot, then your snapshot will become larger in size as the changes are applied. Let's look at the technology behind database snapshots.

Database snapshots are a read-only, point-in-time, static view of your database. Snapshots work at the data-page level. This means that when a data page changes, the original page is copied over to the snapshot. If the same data page is modified later, the snapshot does not change and is unaware of the new data page. To update the snapshot with the new data, you need to create a new snapshot. The process details of creating a snapshot should make this clearer.

When a snapshot is created, a sync Log Sequence Number (LSN) is created in the source database. SQL then runs recovery on the snapshot, since uncommitted transactions need to be rolled back on the snapshot. This does not affect the transactions on the source database. SQL creates a New Technology File System (NTFS) sparse file to hold the snapshot. NTFS sparse files work as you might guess: when they are initially created, sparse files are in fact *sparse*. They don't contain any data, and they grow as data is added to the file. Allocations to the sparse file are in 64KB blocks. When a copy-on-write happens, all the pages are zeroed out except for the changed data page, if a new 64KB block is allocated. When other pages change, individual pages are copied over to the 64KB block.

Let's look at typical operations and how they affect snapshots. When an application updates a value in the database, before the new value is written, the database makes a copy of that page to the snapshot in its sparse file. SQL Server maintains a bitmap for the related sparse file so that SQL can quickly decide where the I/O should go on a read operation, since the snapshot or the original database may contain the correct information. When a read operation comes in, if the snapshot already contains the correct data, SQL will go to the snapshot for the information. If the data has not changed in the original database and therefore hasn't been copied to the snapshot, SQL will go to the original database to retrieve the information. No locks are taken on the original database when a read happens for a snapshot. Figure 15-15 shows this process for database snapshots.

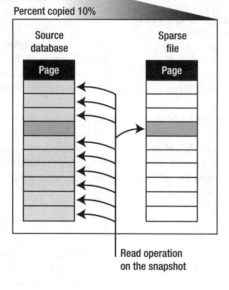

Figure 15-15. *Database snapshots*

You may be wondering how database snapshots can work with database mirroring since the database on the mirror is restoring. Through the magic of code, database snapshots get an exclusive latch on the mirror database, so that snapshots can read the data in a mirrored database.

Finally, you can speed up the population of a snapshot with some routine maintenance on your source database. For example, if you rebuild an index, you may find that your snapshot will start growing very fast as the index is rebuilt. You may not have intended for this to happen, so be aware that if anything changes the source database, the snapshot will grow.

Working with Snapshots in T-SQL

There are some common operations you want to perform with snapshots in T-SQL, such as creating, deleting, and reverting to snapshots. The sections that follow explain how to perform these operations.

Creating a Database Snapshot

To create a database snapshot, you need to use the CREATE DATABASE statement with the new AS SNAPSHOT OF argument. Plus, you must specify every database file of the source database. The following example creates a snapshot of the Northwind database on a mirrored server. One best practice to follow is to use descriptive names for your snapshots so you know when they were created, just in case you have many snapshots on your system. You can have multiple snapshots on your system so that you have different point-in-time views of your databases. Please note, though, that you will have to explicitly connect to the snapshot from your applications, as you will see when we look at programming using snapshots later in this chapter.

```
CREATE DATABASE Northwind_snapshot_12_27_04_7AM ON
    ( NAME=Northwind,
      FILENAME= 'C:\Program Files\Microsoft SQL
    Server\MSSQL.4\MSSQL\
    Data\Northwind_snapshot_12_27_04_7AM.ss')
    AS SNAPSHOT OF Northwind;
Go
```

Deleting a Database Snapshot

To delete a database snapshot, you just need to use the DROP DATABASE statement. All the sparse files associated with your snapshot will be deleted as well. The following code deletes the snapshot without affecting the source database just created.

```
DROP DATABASE Northwind_snapshot_12_27_04_7AM
Go
```

Reverting to a Database Snapshot

We all make mistakes. Thankfully, database snapshots can help us recover from our mistakes. When you revert to a snapshot, the pages stored in the snapshot are rewritten back to the original database. The log is also overwritten and rebuilt in the process. Any updates to the database since the snapshot was taken, from both a data and metadata standpoint, are lost, so you must be completely sure that you want to revert to the snapshot.

There are a number of restrictions when reverting a source database to a snapshot:

- You cannot revert if the source database has read-only or compressed file groups.
- You cannot have filegroups currently offline that were online when the snapshot was taken.
- You cannot have multiple snapshots in existence when you revert. You must remove all other snapshots except the one snapshot that you want to revert to.
- You cannot have a full-text catalog when you revert. You must drop your full-text catalog before reverting to a snapshot.
- You cannot revert on the mirror.

If you want to revert in a database mirroring scenario, you need to be taking snapshots on the principal. Please note that you may lose your metadata about mirroring if you revert to a snapshot. After reverting, you may have to re-set up your database mirroring configuration.

You should back up your log before you revert to a snapshot. You cannot use this backup to roll forward changes after reverting, but the log may be useful in helping to understand what changes were made to the database after the snapshot was taken by using a log explorer tool. In addition, if you are using full recovery mode for your logs, you can restore the database on a separate server and use the point-in-time recovery feature to restore only up to the point that the failure or error was made. You can then bulk export the changes and bulk import the changes into your newly reverted database. Finally, perform a full backup of your database after you revert to the snapshot.

The following code will revert back to the snapshot created earlier:

```
RESTORE DATABASE Northwind from
    DATABASE_SNAPSHOT = 'Northwind_snapshot_12_27_04_7AM'
go
```

Performance Considerations When Using Snapshots on Mirrors

There are some special considerations when using snapshots on your mirrors. Remember that if you are running with FULL transaction safety on, the principal will wait for an acknowledgment from the mirror. If you are running many snapshots that users are querying against on the mirror, that will affect the performance of both the mirror and, in turn, the principal. One of the ways that you can make your snapshots more performant is to place your snapshots on a different drive than your mirror's log. This way, the two technologies do not contend for I/O with one another.

You will also want to move the snapshots from the old mirror to the new mirror when it comes back online. This is not done automatically for you, so you will need to script the creation of the snapshots on a failure. Also, you will need to change your client applications, since the snapshot will now be on a different server.

Using, Monitoring, and Managing Database Snapshots

You will want to use, monitor, and manage your database snapshots. Since they look like real databases, you can easily query them for the data contained in the snapshot. Rather than specifying the source tables, you can use the tables contained in your snapshot. The following query returns back a list of customers from the Customers table in the snapshot:

```
USE Northwind_snapshot_12_27_04_7AM
go

SELECT CompanyName, ContactName, ContactTitle, Country FROM Customers
go
```

Management Studio will display the snapshots you have created. Unfortunately, you cannot graphically create snapshots using Management Studio. Figure 15-16 shows browsing your snapshots in Management Studio.

If you want to view the physical path to the database snapshot, you can use the physical_name column of the sys.master_files catalog view. One thing to note is that if you query the same column in sys.database_files, the view will always return back the source database files, even if you specify the database snapshot.

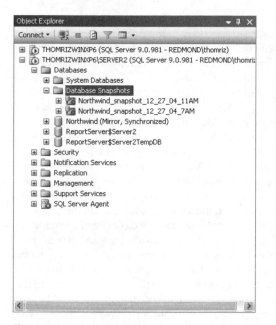

Figure 15-16. *Viewing database snapshots in Management Studio*

To get back the actual size of the sparse files, you can use the `BytesonDisk` column from the `fn_virtualfilestats` function. This function takes a database ID and a file ID as values. The function will then return the file statistics. Also, you could use Windows Explorer to view the size of the file using the Size on Disk value from the Properties page for the file.

The following code returns information about the snapshot file. Notice the use of the `DB_ID` and `FILE_IDEX` functions to get the database ID and the file ID. Please note that the file ID will correspond to the logical name of the file from `sys.master_files`. You could also retrieve both these values from `sys.master_files`.

```
SELECT *
FROM fn_virtualfilestats(DB_ID(N'Northwind_snapshot_12_27_04_7AM'),
    FILE_IDEX(N'Northwind'));
go
```

Programming Database Snapshots

Programming against a database snapshot is very straightforward. Instead of connecting to the original database, you just connect to the snapshot in your connection string. The only caveat is that you will need to manually connect to a different snapshot if you want to change snapshots.

Limitations of Database Snapshots

While there are many benefits to database snapshots, there are also some limitations you should be aware of. The biggest one is that database snapshots are only available in the Enterprise Edition of SQL Server 2005. If you have the Express, Workgroup, or Standard Edition, you do not have access to the database snapshot functionality.

Second, the database and its snapshot must exist in the same instance. You cannot create a snapshot in a separate instance. While snapshots exist on a source database, you cannot drop, detach, or restore the source. You must first delete all snapshots for that database. Backup of the source database is unaffected by snapshots, so you can back up the database while you have active snapshots. Also, you cannot snapshot the master, tempdb, or model databases.

For the snapshot itself, remember it is a read-only copy reflecting the exact state of the source database at the creation time of the snapshot, with any uncommitted transactions rolled back. Files cannot be changed on the snapshot. Permissions are inherited from the source and cannot be changed. This is important, because if you change the permissions on the source database, these changes will not be reflected in existing snapshots. You may have users who you no longer want to have permissions on your data, but if you have snapshots, you have to make sure to re-create your snapshots after changing permissions. Snapshots cannot be backed up or restored, nor can they be attached or detached. Also, you cannot create snapshots on FAT32 or RAW partitions. Finally, snapshots do not support full-text indexing, and any full-text catalogs on the source will not exist in the snapshot.

Please remember that the snapshot is not an entire copy of the source database. The snapshot will go back to the source database for data that has not changed. This means that the state of the source database will affect the snapshot. If the source database goes into recovery mode, some data may not be available in the snapshot. If the source database takes a file offline, some data in the snapshot may not be available as well. If when you created the snapshot a filegroup was offline in the source and you bring it online later, it still will be considered offline in the snapshot. You will want to make sure you understand the state of both the snapshot and the source database, otherwise you may get interesting errors from the snapshot that you may not realize are caused by the state of the source database.

Windows Clustering in SQL Server 2005

Another way to achieve HA with SQL Server is to use Windows clustering. While clustering is mainly the same from 2000 to 2005, there are some notable additions to clustering in the latest release. The biggest change is that Analysis Services, with its multi-instance support, can be clustered, as can full-text indexing.

Also, setup now supports a much easier installation of clustering. There is a new component in setup called the System Configuration Check, which will see if setup is being run on a cluster. If a cluster is found, you have the option to install SQL Server as a virtual server on the cluster. Overall, you will find that setting up a cluster is easier with SQL Server 2005 as compared to 2000.

The main reason for discussing clustering here is to compare it to database mirroring. You can use mirroring with clustering. However, you must mirror between clusters, not within a cluster. Therefore, you could have a principal running on a two-node cluster that communicates with a mirror that runs on a separate two-node cluster. The only thing to watch out for when using mirroring and clustering is the failover times and conflicts. For example, if you set the timeout of mirroring to 1 minute and clusters usually failover after 30 seconds, you may have clusters that failover before your mirror or vice versa. Plus, you could get into some weird situations where the cluster and the mirror failover at about the same time. You definitely will want to test any configuration on which you have mirroring and clustering running together.

The main difference between mirroring and clustering is that clustering is at an instance level while mirroring is at a database level. Mirroring does not failover other services of SQL Server or other services of the operating system. Therefore, if you use mirroring, you will need to make sure that any ancillary services that you expect to be running on the server, such as Agent or others, must be started and running on the mirror server.

One of the benefits of mirroring as compared with clustering is that mirroring does not require special hardware, nor does it require a shared disk subsystem. Your mirrored database servers can exist in separate locations.

Replication in SQL Server 2005

SQL Server 2005 offers many new enhancements in replication. We're going to highlight just a few of the enhancements in this section and then concentrate on comparing replication with database mirroring. The major enhancements for replication are as follows:

- New replication monitor for tracking performance of replication
- Support for Oracle as a publisher, not just as a subscriber
- Replication of schema changes without using special stored procedures
- Peer-to-peer transactional replication
- Synchronization over HTTPS for merge replication
- Scalability and performance improvements, including subscription streams and precomputed partitions
- New object model: Replication Management Objects (RMO)
- Managed code conflict handlers for merge replication

There may be times when replication will make more sense for your data availability needs than database mirroring. For example, if you want a scale-out, read-only reporting solution, peer-to-peer replication is a much better solution than mirroring, since replication can support many peers in its topology. With mirroring, you can have only a single mirror currently. However, replication does not natively support failover transparently, as mirroring does. You must write your applications in such a way to understand failures in a replicated environment. Plus, replication is at the DML level while mirroring is at the log level, so you may find that mirroring has better performance in certain scenarios.

That said, you can combine mirroring and replication. You could replicate the principal using replication or even log shipping. However, this introduces a bunch of complexities that you may not want to deal with. For example, if the principal fails over and then comes back up as the mirror, replication will break since the database will not be readable.

Summary

This chapter walked you through the new database mirroring and snapshot technologies in SQL Server 2005. Understanding how these technologies fit into your overall HA strategy is an important step in planning your SQL Server deployment. Even with database mirroring, you may need to use clustering, tape or disk backup, or replication to fill the needs of your SQL Server solutions. While mirroring is an important technology, there is more to achieving high availability with SQL Server than just implementing database mirroring.

CHAPTER 16

■ ■ ■

Notification Services

When building solutions, many developers look for a way to provide dynamic subscription and publication mechanisms inside of their applications. Over the years, developers have created a number of roll-your-own solutions, and these can range from simple database queries to complex programming exercises. In fact, Microsoft had its own roll-your-own solution as part of MSN Mobile (http://mobile.msn.com).

MSN Mobile provides end users the ability to subscribe to certain events with specific criteria. For example, you could subscribe to stock quotes for your favorite stocks when they reach a certain price or at certain times during the day. You could also subscribe to traffic alerts, news alerts, or even your daily horoscope. When MSN Mobile first developed its website, it built its own subscription and publishing application, the business logic for which was written using procedural logic. When a new event came in, the application would loop through all the subscribers to see if they subscribed to the event and then, if there was a match, the application would generate the notification and deliver it to the user.

As you can guess, scalability in the beginning was hard to achieve due to the ineffectiveness of the algorithm used. When the MSN team looked further at the problem, they realized that their application's business logic looked like a big database join. You want to take some event, some subscribers, join them, and the result is the set of people you need to notify. Well, there was technology that could do that join in an efficient way, which was SQL Server. So, the MSN and the SQL team got together and built out a solution for MSN Mobile. Based on the success of this MSN Mobile application, and also the recognition that a broad set of customers may need this type of solution, the decision was made to productize it. This was Notification Services 1.0, even though it wasn't officially called that.

Roll ahead a year or two, and Notification Services 2.0 was released for SQL Server 2000. Notification Services 2.0 is available as a free download for any SQL Server 2000 customer who has a valid server license on their server. It comes in two versions: Standard and Enterprise. The Standard edition is suited for smaller deployments where scalability isn't a major factor and where you also can run the components all on the same machine. The Enterprise edition allows you to deploy the Notification Services components on different machines and offers more scalability features than the Standard version. The Enterprise edition allows you to also run more threads for the core components of Notification Services, which will allow you to scale better across multiprocessor machines.

With SQL Server 2005, Notification Services ships as a core component of SQL Server. You no longer have to go to the web to download NS but can select it as part of your setup. In addition, Notification Services can now be managed using Management Studio, just like the other components of SQL Server 2005. You can continue to use NSControl if you like, and NSControl is still great for scripting Notification Services.

In this chapter, you'll learn the following:

- The Notification Services architecture
- Creating Notification Services applications
- Programming Notification Services from Visual Studio

Notification Services Architecture

Notification Services—abbreviated to NS from here in—is a multicomponent application that sits on top of SQL Server. NS actually comprises a number of individual components that work together. This architecture consists of four key elements: *subscribers*, *subscriptions*, *events*, and *notifications*. Figure 16-1 shows the NS architecture in more detail.

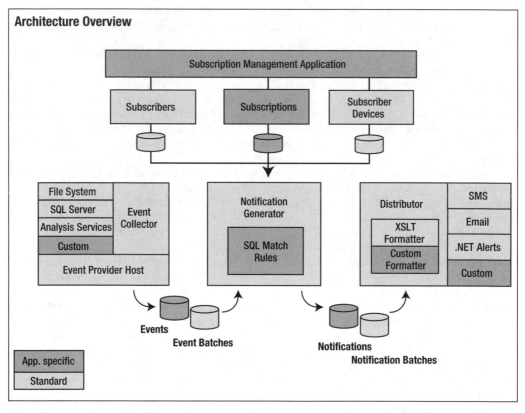

Figure 16-1. *Notification Services Architecture*

As you can see, the NS architecture includes a Notification Generator and a Notification Distributor. The generator does subscription processing, which will match the events coming from the event provider such as the file system, SQL Server, or a custom event provider with the rules you create. Next, the distributor processes and delivers notifications. These notifications can be formatted by the formatters, and the delivery channels can be either the built-in ones such as SMS, e-mail, or .NET alerts or via custom delivery channels you create. In addition, you build a subscription management application that allows your end users to decide what events they are interested in subscribing to, what are the rules of that subscription, and what devices and formats they want those notifications delivered to. It's important to understand these pieces exist in the NS architecture, since you'll have to define them as part of your overall application definition file.

Subscribers

Subscribers are users of the notification application. Subscribers can be either end users or other applications. It doesn't matter to NS whether the end notification is delivered to a human being or another computer. Therefore, you can use NS to batch-feed information to other systems when that information changes in a source system. NS doesn't provide a subscription management application. Instead, you'll have to build this application yourself using the Subscription Management Objects library. The object model is very extensive and easy to use to build your applications.

Normally, the subscription management application would be a web application, but it could also be Windows or even non-Windows based. Its role is to collect subscription information for the clients, which includes information about the subscriber, the data they would like to subscribe to, and the device they would like the information delivered to. A good subscription management application will allow clients to change their subscriptions at any time.

Subscriptions

Subscriptions inform the system of the changes in the data about which a particular subscriber cares. The subscription contains information about the subscriber's device and the fields the subscriber is interested in monitoring. In addition, the subscription will contain the rules that will decide whether a new notification will be sent to the subscriber if that field changes.

There are two basic types of subscriptions:

- *Event-driven subscriptions with optional chronicle support*: This type of subscription notifies the user when a certain threshold is reached or exceeded. Such subscriptions don't constantly notify the user, but instead are on an exception basis when the threshold is exceeded. There could be hundreds of events the system sees, but only ten notifications may be sent.

- *Scheduled subscriptions*: A scheduled subscription batches up the information and only delivers it at the time specified by the subscription. Therefore, if the threshold was exceeded ten times during a 24-hour period, then rather than receive ten notifications, the user would receive just one notification, at the appointed time.

An example of an application that may use both event-driven and scheduled subscriptions is a stock ticker. For example, during the day you may want to notify a user if the price of their stock goes above a certain threshold level. However, you also may want to provide an end-of-day summary of the day's activity for the stock.

Events

In order to notify subscribers of changes to the data in which they are interested, NS must listen for those changes. In order to do that, NS implements an *event provider* interface. Event providers monitor and retrieve information from event sources. NS provides three event providers out of the box, as follows:

- The *File System Watcher* event provider monitors a file system folder for the addition of a particularly formatted XML document. This provider runs constantly, and quickly loads up new events that are placed into the folder.

- The *SQL Server* event provider allows you to query a SQL Server table at defined intervals. You define the T-SQL to be sent to the database to look for new events. Since SQL Server can connect to other SQL Servers or heterogeneous data sources, the SQL Server event provider can actually listen for events from other data sources beyond SQL Server.

- The *Analysis Services* event provider allows you to query an Analysis Services cube at defined intervals. You define the MDX to send to the cube to look for new events. The most common scenario for using the AS event provider is to query KPIs to see whether the KPIs have changed. The Analysis Services event provider is new to NS in SQL Server 2005.

Since the event provider infrastructure is exposed to the public, you can write your own custom event providers using either COM or .NET interfaces. For the best performance, you should write your event providers using .NET, if possible. There are two types of event providers that you can create, hosted and nonhosted, and choosing one or the other depends on whether you want to submit events continuously or defined by the NS application. Nonhosted event providers run on their own schedule separate from the NS application. However, they do run out of process, so performance may be a little slower than a hosted event provider.

- Hosted event providers run in the NS process and start when the NS process starts. Hosted event providers are governed by the configuration parameters you set for all of NS.

- Nonhosted event providers run external to NS and provide their event information via calling different NS interfaces. NS doesn't control these external providers, and you only have to provide the name of the provider for later troubleshooting to NS.

Notifications

The final piece of the NS puzzle is notifications. Notifications are the things your application sends out to your subscribers. Notifications can be formatted using a content formatter such as XSLT and can be delivered through a delivery channel such as HTTP, file , SMTP, or even a custom delivery protocol that you implement using the .NET language of choice. We'll look at notifications in more detail when we look at how to create them using NS later in this chapter.

Building a Notification Services Application

The first step with any application is planning. When planning your NS applications, you should consider the following:

- The data that you want to monitor as part of your application and its schema. That includes where that data lives, how you can recognize new events from the data, and specific information that subscribers may be interested in.

- Your subscription management application. You have to decide whether you want to use COM or .NET to build your application.

- Are you going to offer scheduled notifications, event driven notifications, or both?

- What is the volume of notifications that your application has to deliver and what size are those notifications?

Once you have considered these issues, you then need to create an instance configuration file (ICF).

Defining an NS Instance: The Instance Configuration File

The ICF is an XML file that defines an NS instance. Each NS instance can host one or more NS applications. The configuration file contains critical NS application metadata such as parameter defaults, version information, application information, protocol information, and delivery channels.

You can create your configuration file from scratch. However, it is easier if you take an existing configuration file and just modify it to meet your needs. A configuration file is made up of a number of XML nodes. Notification Services ships with an XML Schema (XSD) file that defines the schema for the configuration file. Following is a skeleton configuration file. Please note that the XML tags will be left out for brevity.

```
<NotificationServicesInstance>
  <ParameterDefaults>
    <Parameter>
      <Name>
      <Value>
  <Version>
    <Major>
    <Minor>
    <Build>
    <Revisions>
  <History>
    <CreationDate>
    <CreationTime>
    <LastModifiedDate>
    <LastModifiedTime>
  <InstanceName>
  <SqlServerSystem>

  <Database>
    <NamedFileGroup>
      <FileGroupName>
      <FileSpec>
        <LogicalName>
        <FileName>
          <Size>
          <MaxSize>
          <GrowthIncrement>
      <LogFile>
        <LogicalName>
        <FileName>
        <Size>
        <MaxSize>
        <GrowthIncrement>
    <DefaultFileGroup>
    <CollationName>
  <Applications>
    <Application>
      <ApplicationName>
      <BaseDirectoryPath>
      <ApplicationDefinitionFilePath>
      <Parameters>
        <Parameter>
```

```
<Protocols>
  <Protocol>
<DeliveryChannels>
  <DeliveryChannel>
    <DeliveryChannelName>
    <ProtocolName>
    <Arguments>
      <Argument>
<EncryptArguments>
```

Let's step through and discuss what each section does in a bit more detail. To begin with, you need to have XML declarations at the top of the file to make sure that you have a valid XML file. Next, you must define a NotificationServicesInstance node. In this node, you declare your XML namespaces. One namespace that you should declare here is the ConfigurationFileSchema namespace, which provides the namespace for your configuration schema and is as follows:

```
xmlns="http://www.microsoft.com/MicrosoftNotificationServices/
ConfigurationFileSchema"
```

You can place your optional ParameterDefaults section after the NotificationServicesInstance node. The default parameter section is where you'll declare the values for any replaceable elements in the file. For example, you may want to create a default parameter for the database server name throughout your file. Using parameters and defaults is a best practice, as it makes it easier to go from development to testing to production. The following code snippet creates such a parameter and then demonstrates the use of the token, %DBName%, in the rest of the file instead of a distinct database server name:

```
<ParameterDefaults>
    <Parameter>
        <Name>DBServerName</Name>
        <Value>MyDatabaseServer</Value>
        <Name>BaseDirectoryPath</Name>
        <Value>C:\NSapps\</Value>

    </Parameter>
</ParameterDefaults>
. . .
<SqlServerSystem>%DBServerName</SqlServerSystem>
```

Next are the Version and History tags where you can store version and history information about your instance. It's a good practice to keep these sections up to date after you deploy your instance so that you can always roll back to a previous version. To do this, you must keep the prior versions of your XML configuration files.

InstanceName and SqlServerSystem come after your history and version information. InstanceName stores the unique instance name for your NS instance. Don't confuse this with the SQL Server instance name. This instance name is an NS instance name.

The SqlServerSystem node contains the name of the SQL Server instance that you want to use for the NS instance. You cannot use IP addresses or FQDN in this name. You can use a named instance of SQL Server. To specify a named instance, use the server name followed by a slash (\) and then the instance name: MyServer\MyInstance. If you are using a port other than port 1433 for your SQL Server, you can specify that port as follows: MyServer,1242\MyInstance.

Once you have specified the NS and SQL Server instance information, you can use the Database section to specify further information about the database. If you leave this section blank, the model database will be used as a template for your NS instance database. As long as the model database meets your needs, this is fine.

In this `Database` section, you can specify the database name, file groups, the initial size, max size, and growth increments for the database. These nodes are pretty self-explanatory, and the following example snippet should help you understand their purpose:

```
<Database>
    <DatabaseName>MyNSInstanceDB</DatabaseName>
    <SchemaName>MySchema</SchemaName>
    <NamedFileGroup>
        <FileGroupName>My1stFG</FileGroupName>
        <FileSpec>
            <LogicalName>My1stFG</LogicalName>
            <FileName>%BaseDirectoryPath%\My1stFG.mdf</FileName>
            <Size>30MB</Size>
            <MaxSize>100MB</MaxSize>
            <GrowthIncrement>30%</GrowthIncrement>
        </FileSpec>
    </NamedFileGroup>
    <NamedFileGroup>
        <FileGroupName>My2ndFG</FileGroupName>
        <FileSpec>
            <LogicalName>My2ndFG</LogicalName>
            <FileName>%BaseDirectoryPath%\My2ndFG.mdf</FileName>
            <Size>20MB</Size>
            <MaxSize>40MB</MaxSize>
            <GrowthIncrement>20%</GrowthIncrement>
        </FileSpec>
    </NamedFileGroup>
    <LogFile>
        <LogicalName>MyLogFile</LogicalName>
        <FileName>%BaseDirectoryPath%\MyLogFile.ldf</FileName>
        <Size>5MB</Size>
        <MaxSize>10MB</MaxSize>
        <GrowthIncrement>20%</GrowthIncrement>
    </LogFile>
    <DefaultFileGroup>My1stFG</DefaultFileGroup>
    <CollationName>SQL_Latin1_General_CP1251_CI_AS</CollationName>
</Database>
```

Applications come next in your configuration file. Since one NS instance can host multiple applications, you can have multiple application nodes in a single configuration file. For every application, you need to specify the name of the application, the base directory path, the path to the application definition file, which you'll learn about in the next section of the chapter, and finally any parameters that you want to pass to the application definition file. The following sample contains two NS applications, `stock` and `traffic`, and defines different parameters to pass to each application.

```
<Applications>
    <Application>
        <ApplicationName>Stock</ApplicationName>
        <BaseDirectoryPath>%BaseDirectoryPath%</BaseDirectoryPath>
        <ApplicationDefinitionFilePath>
        appDefinition\StockappADF.xml
        </ApplicationDefinitionFilePath>
```

```
            <Parameters>
                <Parameter>
                    <Name>DBServerName</Name>
                    <Value>%DBServerName%</Value>
                </Parameter>
                <Parameter>
                    <Name>NSSystem</Name>
                    <Value>NSSystem1</Value>
                </Parameter>
            </Parameters>
        </Application>
        <Application>
            <ApplicationName>Traffic</ApplicationName>
            <BaseDirectoryPath>%BaseDirectoryPath%</BaseDirectoryPath>
            <ApplicationDefinitionFilePath>
            appDefinition\TrafficappADF.xml
            </ApplicationDefinitionFilePath>
            <Parameters>
                <Parameter>
                    <Name>DBServerName</Name>
                    <Value>%DBServerName%</Value>
                </Parameter>
                <Parameter>
                    <Name>DefaultTrafficMonitor</Name>
                    <Value>SR-520</Value>
                </Parameter>
            </Parameters>
        </Application>
    </Applications>
```

The next section is the `Protocols` section, where you define any custom protocol delivery extensions that you want to use in the instance. If you're just using the built-in protocol delivery extensions such as SMTP, you can leave this section out or just use blank elements. Since, if you're like many developers, you won't be creating or buying custom protocol extensions, we'll move on.

Next, you specify the delivery channels that your instance will use in the `DeliveryChannels` section. A delivery channel uses a delivery protocol. You can have multiple delivery channels that use a single delivery protocol. The only difference between the channels may be the configuration you set for the channel. For example, you can create two file delivery channels, one to one fileshare and another to a different fileshare, and only use one delivery protocol, which is the file delivery protocol. You can name these channels and the protocol that they will use for delivery. The following sample shows how to set up two delivery channels. One uses the built-in SMTP delivery protocol, and the other uses the built-in file delivery protocol.

```
<DeliveryChannels>
    <DeliveryChannel>
        <DeliveryChannelName>EmailChannel</DeliveryChannelName>
        <ProtocolName>SMTP</ProtocolName>
        <Arguments>
            <Argument>
                <Name>SmtpServer</Name>
                <Value>MyMailServer</Value>
            </Argument>
        </Arguments>
    </DeliveryChannel>
```

```
<DeliveryChannel>
    <DeliveryChannelName>FileChannel</DeliveryChannelName>
    <ProtocolName>File</ProtocolName>
    <Arguments>
        <Argument>
            <Name>FileName</Name>
            <Value>C:\AppOutput.htm</Value>
        </Argument>
    </Arguments>
</DeliveryChannel>
</DeliveryChannels>
```

Finally, you have the `EncryptArguments` node. This node contains a Boolean value of true or false and specifies whether to encrypt your delivery channel and event provider arguments before storing them in the instance database. You should enable encrypting sensitive information using this node before storing it and secure your XML source files.

Defining the NS Application: The Application Definition File

Once you have your instance configuration file (ICF) created, as shown previously, you need to create your application definition file. The application definition file (ADF) defines your application. This will include your event classes, your subscription classes, your notification classes, event providers, generators, and distributors. The subscription management application and ADF are the two most important pieces of your NS application. The ADF is an XML file just like the ICF.

Let's step through each of the different nodes of the ADF so you can get an understanding of what makes up this file. Just as for the ICF, you can either start your ADF from scratch or copy one of the sample ones included with NS. Either way, you'll want to use Visual Studio or another XML editor to modify your ADF.

As with any XML file, you need to first declare that your file is XML. After that, the first element in any ADF is the Application node, which is where you define your XML namespaces. In this case, you want to use the following namespace:

```
xmlns="http://www.microsoft.com/MicrosoftNotificationServices/
ApplicationDefinitionFileSchema"
```

The next nodes are the `ParameterDefaults`, `Version`, `History`, and `Database` nodes. Since we already discussed these nodes in the ICF, we won't cover them here.

Hosted Event Providers

You specify your event providers using the `Providers` node and its subnodes. Most times you'll use one of the three built-in event providers: SQL Server, File System Watcher, and Analysis Services, as described earlier. The following XML shows the layout for the `Providers` node:

```
<Providers>
    <!--Multiple HostedProvider Nodes Allowed-->
    <HostedProvider>
        <ProviderName></ProviderName>
        <ClassName></ClassName>
        <AssemblyName></AssemblyName>
        <SystemName></SystemName>
        <Schedule>
            <StartTime></StartTime>
            <Interval></Interval>
        </Schedule>
```

```
                <Arguments>
                    <!--Multiple Argument Nodes Allowed-->
                    <Argument>
                        <Name></Name>
                        <Value></Value>
                    </Argument>
                </Arguments>
            </HostedProvider>
        <!--Multiple NonHostedProvider Nodes Allowed-->
        <NonHostedProvider>
            <ProviderName></ProviderName>
        </NonHostedProvider>
    </Providers>
```

Let's walk through the creation of a HostedProvider section for each of the three event providers.

SQL Server Event Provider

This provider allows you to look at a SQL Server database to see if any data has been inserted or updated. The following example uses the SQL Server event provider:

```
<Providers>
    <HostedProvider>
        <ProviderName>MySQLEventProvider</ProviderName>
        <ClassName>SQLProvider</ClassName>
        <SystemName>MySystem</SystemName>
        <Schedule>
            <Interval>P0DT00H30M00S</Interval>
        </Schedule>
        <Arguments>
            <Argument>
                <Name>EventsQuery</Name>
                <Value>SELECT CustomerName FROM Customers</Value>
            </Argument>
            <Argument>
                <Name>EventClassName</Name>
                <Value>CustomerEvent</Value>
            </Argument>
        </Arguments>
    </HostedProvider>
</Providers>
```

To use this provider, you specify a unique provider name in the ProviderName node such as MySQLEventProvider, and in the ClassName node, you specify SQLProvider. You don't need the AssemblyName element since this is a built-in event provider and is implemented in the NS DLL itself.

For the SystemName, specify the name of the system that will run the SQL Server event provider. Since you can run different components of NS on different machines in the Enterprise edition, this name may be different than the database server used to host the NS instance. In the Standard edition, these names may be different if you have a remote database deployment.

Next, you have to enter the schedule information for the provider. Since the SQL provider is a scheduled provider, you must specify this information. For the StartTime, you need to input the start time using UTC notation. So, for a UTC start time of 3 p.m., you would enter 15:00:00. The Interval node is a duration type, so you must specify its value using the duration type format, which is P0DT00H00M00S. In addition, the interval must be evenly divisible into a 24-hour period. This means that you cannot make the duration 28 minutes or 3 minutes 19 seconds. A valid interval would be 5 minutes, 15 minutes, 30 minutes, etc.

The next section is the Arguments section. There are three arguments that you can specify to the SQL provider:

- The EventsQuery argument defines the T-SQL query or stored procedure that you want to call that will return from your database the rowset data containing new or changed information.

- The optional PostQuery argument allows you to run another query after the EventsQuery to do any postprocessing on the database such as flagging items as processed or any cleanup work.

- The required EventClassName argument specifies the event class that this event provider uses. Your queries must return their data according to the schema you specify in the event class.

You'll see how to define an event class later in this chapter, but you should understand that multiple event providers can submit events to the same event.

File System Watcher

This provider continuously monitors the file system for any changes to the folder specified. When a new file is added to the folder, the XML is parsed from the file and validated against an XML schema. The event provider then adds the events to the events table that NS uses to store events from data sources and renames the original file, so that it isn't processed again, by giving the file a unique name using the time and date of processing and a .done file extension. If there is an error, an entry is made into the event log, and an .err extension is added to the file. The following example shows using the File System Watcher event provider in your ADF with both required and optional arguments:

```
<Providers>
    <HostedProvider>
        <ProviderName>MyFSWatcher</ProviderName>
        <ClassName>FileSystemWatcherProvider</ClassName>
        <SystemName>MyServer</SystemName>
        <Arguments>
            <Argument>
                <Name>WatchDirectory</Name>
                <!--Could as be \\server\share\folder-->
                <Value>C:\MyFolder\</Value>
            </Argument>
            <Argument>
                <Name>EventClassName</Name>
                <Value>FileEvents</Value>
            </Argument>
            <Argument>
                <Name>SchemaFile</Name>
                <Value>C:\App\schemas\FSEventSchema.xsd</Value>
            </Argument>
            <Argument>
                <Name>RetryAttempts</Name>
                <Value>5</Value>
            </Argument>
            <Argument>
                <Name>RetryQueueOccupancy</Name>
                <Value>50</Value>
            </Argument>
```

```
        <Argument>
            <Name>RetryPeriod</Name>
            <Value>10000</Value>
        </Argument>
        <Argument>
            <Name>RetryWorkload</Name>
            <Value>50</Value>
        </Argument>
    </Arguments>
  </HostedProvider>
</Providers>
```

The `ClassName` for the File System Watcher event provider is `FileSystemWatcherProvider`. This provider takes seven arguments. The `EventClassName` argument is the same as for the SQL provider except it specifies a file system event class for this provider to use.

The other arguments are the `WatchDirectory`, `SchemaFile`, `RetryAttempts`, `RetryQueueOccupancy`, `RetryPeriod`, and `RetryWorkload` arguments. Only the `WatchDirectory`, `SchemaFile`, and `EventClassName` arguments are required. The other arguments are optional.

The `WatchDirectory` is the path to the folder to be watched. You can use shared drives, UNC paths, or complete local paths if you like for this argument. The `SchemaFile` is the XSD file you want the XML event files to have the provider validate against.

`RetryAttempts`, `RetryQueueOccupancy`, `RetryPeriod`, and `RetryWorkload` specify how often, how many times, and at what level of resource consumption to retry files that may be locked

The `RetryAttempts` argument specifies how many times to retry processing the file. The default value is 10. The `RetryQueueOccupancy` argument specifies how many files can be in the retry queue at once and has a default value of 1024. The `RetryPeriod` specifies how many milliseconds the provider should wait before processing the queue between attempts. The default value is 10000, which is 10 seconds. If you specify a value of 0, the queue will only be processed at provider startup. The final argument, `RetryWorkload`, specifies the maximum number of files that can be retried in a single processing of the queue and has a default value of 1024. For example, you may be using FTP to move the files into the directory, and the FTP process has not completed yet, so the file is locked by the FTP application. By setting these retry arguments, you can raise the default values so that big files will be processed.

Analysis Services Provider

The Analysis Services provider is a scheduled provider like the SQL Server provider. Instead of passing T-SQL to this provider, you pass MDX commands. This provider supports both static and dynamic MDX queries. The following example shows how to use the Analysis Services provider. The first example is using a static query and the second is using a dynamic query.

```
<Providers>
    <HostedProvider>
        <ProviderName>StaticAS</ProviderName>
        <ClassName>AnalysisServicesProvider</ClassName>
        <SystemName>MyASSystem</SystemName>
        <Schedule>
            <Interval>P0DT00H30M00S</Interval>
        </Schedule>
        <Arguments>
            <Argument>
                <Name>EventClassName</Name>
                <Value>MyASEventClass</Value>
            </Argument>
```

```xml
            <Argument>
                <Name>AnalysisServicesInstance</Name>
                <Value>MyASInstance</Value>
            </Argument>
            <Argument>
                <Name>AnalysisServicesDatabase</Name>
                <Value>MyASDB</Value>
            </Argument>
            <Argument>
                <Name>MDXQuery</Name>
                <Value>SELECT
                {
                [Measures].[Total Sales],
                    [Total Product Cost],
                    [Total Commission]
                } ON COLUMNS,
                {
                [Customers].[Customer].[Bill Gates],
                    [Customers].[Customer].[Tom Rizzo]
                } ON ROWS
                FROM [Customers]
                WHERE [Stores].[Store].[Seattle]
            </Argument>
        </Arguments>
    </HostedProvider>

<HostedProvider>
        <ProviderName>DynamicAS</ProviderName>
        <ClassName>AnalysisServicesProvider</ClassName>
        <SystemName>MyASSystem</SystemName>
        <Schedule>
            <Interval>P0DT00H30M00S</Interval>
        </Schedule>
        <Arguments>
            <Argument>
                <Name>EventClassName</Name>
                <Value>MyASEvents</Value>
            </Argument>
            <Argument>
                <Name>AnalysisServicesInstance</Name>
                <Value>MyASInstance</Value>
            </Argument>
            <Argument>
                <Name>AnalysisServicesDatabase</Name>
                <Value>MyASDB</Value>
            </Argument>
            <Argument>
                <Name>RowsQuery</Name>
                <Value>SELECT CustomerName
                        FROM Customers</Value>
            </Argument>
```

```
        <Argument>
            <Name>SlicerQuery</Name>
            <Value>SELECT DATEPART(year, DATEADD(year, -1, GETDATE()))</Value>
        </Argument>
        <Argument>
            <Name>XsltFileName</Name>
            <Value>C:\MDXTrans.xslt</Value>
        </Argument>
    </Arguments>
  </HostedProvider>
</Providers>
```

The provider name is AnalysisServicesProvider, and this provider takes eight arguments.
    The first three arguments are straightforward:

- EventClassName, which specifies the event class for the provider.

- AnalysisServicesInstance, which is the name of the AS instance for the provider to connect to. The AS instance can be on a local or remote machine.

- AnalysisServicesDatabase, which is the name of the AS database for the provider to query.

What you specify for the next set of arguments will depend on whether you want to use *static* or *dynamic* MDX. If you want to use static MDX, you'll set the MDXQuery argument. In this argument, you specify the MDX query that will return back a two-dimensional view of the data that you want to use to generate events.

If you want to use dynamic queries, you'll fill out the RowsQuery, SlicerQuery, and XsltFileName arguments:

- The RowsQuery argument specifies a T-SQL statement whose return value will be used by the XSLT specified in the XsltFileName argument to create the ROWS axis of your dynamic MDX query.

- The SlicerQuery is the same thing except the results will be used to generate the slicer portion of your query, which is your WHERE clause.

- The XsltFileName argument is a path to the XSLT file that you want to use with the other arguments specified here.

The final argument is the MDXQueryTimeout argument. By default, the timeout is 10 minutes. If you want to specify a different timeout, you should use the duration notation that you saw in the schedule arguments to specify how long the timeout should be.

Nonhosted Event Providers

There may be times when you want to use a nonhosted event provider. These providers are external application that submit events to NS programmatically. The interaction with NS can be through the EventCollector class or EventLoader class, or by calling the event collection stored procedures that NS provides. For nonhosted event providers, you only need to specify the name of the event provider in your ADF. An example of a nonhosted event provider could be an existing application such as a CRM application that submits events when sales exceed quotas or new customers are added to the system.

Event Classes

While event providers tell NS what technology to listen for events from, they don't specify what an event actually is. To help NS make sense of the data returned from the providers, you need to specify event classes. Each distinct event in NS requires an *event class definition*, which defines, along with the name of the class, the fields for the event, any indexes to create to make performance faster, and the *chronicle rules* for your event.

Field Events

After giving the class a name, the first thing you need to do is to define the fields in the event class. These fields will contain the event data schema. The event data schema takes three elements:

- FieldName: A unique name for the field
- FieldType: A SQL type for the field such as varchar, int, float, etc.
- FieldTypeMods: A T-SQL statement that describes the nullability and default value for the field

The following example shows creating three fields of different types and different default values:

```
<Schema>
   <Field>
      <FieldName>CustomerName</FieldName>
      <FieldType>char(50)</FieldType>
      <FieldTypeMods>NOT NULL</FieldTypeMods>
   </Field>
   <Field>
      <FieldName>CustomerState</FieldName>
      <FieldType>char(2)</FieldType>
      <FieldTypeMods>NOT NULL</FieldTypeMods>
   </Field>
   <Field>
      <FieldName>CustomerCategory</FieldName>
      <FieldType>int</FieldType>
      <FieldTypeMods>NOT NULL DEFAULT 2</FieldTypeMods>
   </Field>
</Schema>
```

Optionally, you can specify, as part of your event class, the SQL filegroup where you want your event table. This is done by using the FileGroup element. The filegroup must exist as part of the Database node.

Indexing Event tables

If you want to index your event table to speed up performance, you can create the index using a T-SQL statement in the IndexSqlSchema element. The following example indexes on the customer name:

```
<IndexSqlSchema>
   <SqlStatement>
   CREATE INDEX CustomerIndex
   ON Customers (CustomerName)
   </SqlStatement>
</IndexSqlSchema>
```

Chronicle Tables and Rules

There may be times when you want to capture events that have happened, but not immediately send notifications for those events. Instead, you want to queue the notifications so they can be delivered at a later point in time. If you have a need for this, you can specify *chronicle tables and rules* in your event class.

You'll often use chronicle tables and rules if you have scheduled subscriptions in your application. You don't want to miss relevant events in your scheduled subscriptions, so you need to keep a history of all relevant events that happened in the system up to the point that the scheduled subscription fired. Chronicle tables keep this history, and you can use the data stored here to check for duplicates, high and low values, or even to generate reports.

You need to create chronicle tables as part of the `EventClass` itself, using T-SQL code. When an event comes in for your event class, Notification Services will also place it into your chronicle table using the rules that you specify, which you'll learn about in the next paragraph. The following code creates a chronicle table for storing event information. It is a good practice to check for the existence of the chronicle table and drop it so that if you reinstall the application, you won't run into an error. Also, you can often speed up searches by creating an index on your chronicle table as part of your statement. Finally, you can have multiple chronicle tables as part of your definition, depending on your application needs.

```
<Chronicles>
  <Chronicle>
    <ChronicleName>CustomerEventsChron</ChronicleName>
      <SqlSchema>
        <SqlStatement>
          IF EXISTS(SELECT name FROM dbo.sysobjects WHERE name = 'CustEventsChron')
            DROP TABLE dbo.CustEventsChron
            CREATE TABLE CustEventsChron
            (
              [CustomerName] char(50),
              [CustomerCategory] int
            )
            CREATE INDEX ixCusName ON CustEventsChron(CustomerName)

        </SqlStatement>
      </SqlSchema>
  </Chronicle>
</Chronicles>
```

Once you have defined the event chronicle table, you need to define the rules that will populate the chronicle table with event information. You can either define them using inline T-SQL statements or you can call stored procedures. As part of your event rule definition, you should have code that will allow updates of existing items without generating new notifications. For example, if your application does automobile traffic monitoring, you want the most recent data to be delivered as well as recorded in your chronicle table. Since chronicle rules are based on T-SQL statements, you can have multiple statements, one for new events and one for updating existing events, as part of your rule. The following code shows how you can capture new events into your chronicle table and update existing events with the latest information:

```
<ChronicleRule>
  <RuleName>CustomerChronRule</RuleName>
  <Action>
    -- Insert New Customers
    INSERT dbo.CustEventsChron (CustomerName, CustomerCategory)
    SELECT e.CustomerName, e.CustomerCategory
      FROM dbo.CustEvents AS e
      WHERE e.CustomerName
      NOT IN (SELECT CustomerName FROM dbo.CustEventsChron);
    -- Update Existing Customers
    UPDATE dbo.CustEventsChron
```

```
      SET CustomerCategory = e.CustomerCategory
      FROM dbo.CustEvents AS e
   JOIN dbo.CustEventsChron AS c
      ON e.CustomerName = c.CustomerName
      WHERE e.CustomerCategory &gt;&lt; c.CustomerCategory;
  </Action>
  <ActionTimeout>P0DT00H00M60S</ActionTimeout>
</ChronicleRule>
```

> ■**Note** Since the ADF is based on XML, you need to encode some of your special characters such as greater than and less than as shown in the example.

Subscription Classes

As you would expect in a publish-subscribe application, subscriptions are an important part of the equation when building NS applications. As noted earlier, subscriptions describe what events the subscriber cares about and when and how to notify the user. Just like event classes, subscription classes use XML definitions to describe a schema, indexing, and also the subscription logic itself written using T-SQL.

The SubscriptionClass node of your ADF is the base node for your subscription class. You can have multiple subscriptions in a single ADF if you want to have subscribers be able to receive immediate notification for certain changes while having other subscriptions for a scheduled summary notification. For example, you may want to be notified of major changes in a particular value throughout the day, but at the end of the day you want to be notified of the start value and the end value.

The first step in creating a SubscriptionClass node is to define a name for the class. You can also optionally define a SQL filegroup to which the subscription class belongs.

After defining these items, you need to define the schema for your subscription.

Defining a Subscription Schema

You'll want to define custom schema for things you care about in your subscription. For example, a weather application may want to store a zip code for the user for customized weather notification. For a stock application, you'll want to store the stock symbol. NS will automatically create SubscriptionID, SubscriberID, Created, Updated, and Enabled fields, regardless of the schema you specify. SubscriptionID is a column that uniquely identifies the subscription. SubscriberID is a string value that your application must supply to identify the subscriber. Created and Updated just store information about when the subscription was created and the last time it was updated. Finally, Enabled is a Boolean that you can use to suspend notifications to a subscriber.

If you have scheduled subscriptions, you'll also see a ScheduleId field, which is used to join the subscriber with the subscription schedule table. You cannot create schemas with the same names, or else when you try to compile your application, you'll get a failure.

Two fields that you'll want to think about adding are the DeviceName and SubscriberLocale fields:

- The DeviceName is the name of the device the notification should be delivered to such as e-mail, IM, etc.

- The SubscriberLocale allows you to specify the locale for the subscription. If you want to support international clients or change locales dynamically, you'll want to add this field.

The following sample creates the subscription schema and index on the subscription schema:

```
<SubscriptionClasses>
  <SubscriptionClass>
    <SubscriptionClassName>CustomerSubscriptions
      </SubscriptionClassName>
    <FileGroup>Primary</FileGroup>
    <Schema>
      <Field>
        <FieldName>DeviceName</FieldName>
        <FieldType>nvarchar(255)</FieldType>
        <FieldTypeMods>not null</FieldTypeMods>
      </Field>
      <Field>
        <FieldName>SubscriberLocale</FieldName>
        <FieldType>nvarchar(10)</FieldType>
        <FieldTypeMods>not null</FieldTypeMods>
      </Field>
      <Field>
        <FieldName>CustomerName</FieldName>
        <FieldType>char(50)</FieldType>
        <FieldTypeMods>NOT NULL</FieldTypeMods>
      </Field>
      <Field>
        <FieldName>CustomerTriggerValue</FieldName>
        <FieldType>char(2)</FieldType>
        <FieldTypeMods>NOT NULL</FieldTypeMods>
      </Field>
    </Schema>
      <IndexSqlSchema>
        <SqlStatement>CREATE INDEX
          CustomerSubscriptionsIndex ON
          CustomerSubscriptions ( CustomerNameSymbol )
        </SqlStatement>
      </IndexSqlSchema>
```

Matching Events to Subscriptions

The next step is to create the rules that define how to match events to subscriptions. If there is a match, a notification is generated. There are two types of rules when creating subscriptions: **event rules** and **scheduled rules**. Event rules fire almost immediately when an event happens. Scheduled rules fire on a predefined schedule.

Event Rules To create an event rule item, you need to create an EventRule node in the ADF file. The EventRule node consists of a name for the rule, the action, and then the action timeout. The action provides the logic to connect an event to a subscription. All actions are defined as T-SQL statements, and NS runs these statements to get the resulting notifications that need to be sent. You can use chronicles with subscriptions so that you can limit nuisance notifications when a new event comes in. For example, you can include a condition that only notifies users if they have not been notified in the last 24 hours.

The following code snippet shows the structure for an EventRule node. Please note that with SQL Server 2005, the notify function has been replaced with standard T-SQL statements. The reason for this is that the notify function would have to execute on every notification. Plus, the function was limited to its implementation only. By replacing the notify function and using T-SQL, NS can just use standard joins to combine the data. With standard T-SQL statements, you can query data from other tables beyond what the `notify` function supported. The code snippet uses the new formatting and won't work in previous versions of NS.

```
<EventRules>
  <EventRule>
    <RuleName>CustomerSubscriptionEventRule</RuleName>
    <Action>
    INSERT INTO dbo.EventNotificationsNotify(S.SubscriberId,
      S.SubscriberDeviceName, S.SubscriberLocale,
      E.CustomerName, E.CustomerTriggerValue)
      FROM CustomerSubscriptions S JOIN CustomerEvents E
      ON S.CustomerName = E.CustomerName
      JOIN CustomerEventChron C
      ON S.CustomerName = C.CustomerName
      WHERE S.CustomerTriggerValue &lt;&gt; E.CustomerCategory

    INSERT CustomerSubscriptionChron
      (SubscriberId, CustomerName, CustomerCategory)
      SELECT S.SubscriberId, S.CustomerName, E.CustomerCategory
      FROM CustomerSubscriptions S JOIN CustomerEvents E
      ON S.CustomerName = E.CustomerName
    </Action>
    <ActionTimeout>P0DT00H01M00S</ActionTimeout>
    <EventClassName>CustomerEvents</EventClassName>
  </EventRule>
</EventRules>
```

Schedule Rules You'll use scheduled rules with scheduled subscriptions. When the scheduled time arrives, the rule is triggered and used to match the subscription to data contained in your chronicle table. If a match is found, a notification is generated based on your specifications. The one difference you'll notice between a scheduled rule and an event rule is that scheduled rules don't have to be associated with an event class. Scheduled rules aren't triggered by events but by a schedule, hence no association to an event class. Finally, scheduled rules can only access information in the chronicle table, not in the event table, since they aren't triggered by events. The sample that follows shows how to create a scheduled rule. You can have scheduled and event rules together in a single application.

```
<ScheduledRules>
  <ScheduledRule>
    <RuleName>CustomerSubscriptionScheduledRule</RuleName>
    <Action>
      INSERT CustomerSubscriptionChron
      (SubscriberId, CustomerName, CustomerCategory, LastProcessed)

      SELECT S.SubscriberId, S.CustomerName, E.CustomerCategory
      FROM CustomerSubscriptions S JOIN CustomerEvents E
      ON S.CustomerName = E.CustomerName
      WHERE NOT EXISTS (
        SELECT C.SubscriptionID
        FROM CustomerSubscriptionChron C
        WHERE C.SubscriptionID = S.SubscriptionID
      )
```

```
        INSERT INTO dbo.EventNotificationsNotify(S.SubscriberId,
        S.SubscriberDeviceName, S.SubscriberLocale,
        E.CustomerName, E.CustomerTriggerValue)
        FROM CustomerSubscriptions S JOIN CustomerEvents E
        ON S.CustomerName = E.CustomerName
        JOIN CustomerEventChron C
        ON S.CustomerName = C.CustomerName
        WHERE S.CustomerTriggerValue &lt;&gt; E.CustomerCategory

        --Update existing chronicles
        UPDATE CustomerSubscriptionChron
        SET LastProcessed = GETUTCDATE()
        FROM CustomerSubscriptionChron C
        JOIN CustomerSubscriptions S
        ON S.SubscriptionID = C.SubscriptionID
      </Action>
      <ActionTimeout>P0DT00H00M30S00</ActionTimeout>
    </ScheduledRule>
  </ScheduledRules>
```

As with event chronicle tables, you can have subscription chronicle tables. With subscription chronicle tables, you may want to store a history of notifications that were already sent to the subscriber.

Notification Classes

Notifications are the payload of NS applications. Just as you defined a Subscription class, so you need to define a Notification class. As part of your class, you need to tell NS what notification fields you want, along with the formatting and the delivery channel to use.

In order to create a valid NotificationClass, you must define the name, schema, formatter, and delivery protocols. Optionally, you can define whether you want digest or multicast delivery, and the notification batch size, but this capability is only in the Enterprise edition. In all editions, you can optionally define the notification expiration age and the filegroup to use for the NotificationClass. The following sample shows creating a NotificationClass:

```
<NotificationClass>
  <NotificationClassName>CustomerNotification</NotificationClassName>
    <Schema>
      <Fields>
        <Field>
          <FieldName>CustomerName</FieldName>
          <FieldType>char(50)</FieldType>
          <FieldTypeMods>NOT NULL</FieldTypeMods>
        </Field>
        <Field>
          <FieldName>CustomerState</FieldName>
          <FieldType>char(2)</FieldType>
          <FieldTypeMods>NOT NULL</FieldTypeMods>
        </Field>
        <Field>
          <FieldName>CustomerCategory</FieldName>
          <FieldType>int</FieldType>
          <FieldTypeMods>NOT NULL DEFAULT 2</FieldTypeMods>
        </Field>
      </Fields>
```

```xml
        </Schema>
    <FileGroup>MyFG</FileGroup>
    <ContentFormatter>
        <ClassName>XsltFormatter</ClassName>
          <Arguments>
            <Argument>
                <Name>XsltBaseDirectoryPath</Name>
                <Value>%BasePath%\NSConfig</Value>
            </Argument>
            <Argument>
                <Name>XsltFileName</Name>
                <Value>FormatMsg.xslt</Value>
            </Argument>
            <Argument>
                <Name>DisableEscaping</Name>
                <Value>true</Value>
            </Argument>
          </Arguments>
    </ContentFormatter>
    <DigestDelivery>true</DigestDelivery>
    <NotificationBatchSize>100</NotificationBatchSize>
    <Protocols>
        <Protocol>
            <ProtocolName>SMTP</ProtocolName>
            <Fields>
                <Field>
                    <FieldName>Subject</FieldName>
                    <SqlExpression>%SubjectLine%</SqlExpression>
                </Field>
                <Field>
                    <FieldName>From</FieldName>
                    <SqlExpression>%fromAddress%</SqlExpression>
                </Field>
                <Field>
                    <FieldName>To</FieldName>
                    <FieldReference>DeviceAddress</FieldReference>
                </Field>
                <Field>
                    <FieldName>Priority</FieldName>
                    <SqlExpression>%mailPriority%</SqlExpression>
                </Field>
                <Field>
                    <FieldName>BodyFormat</FieldName>
                    <SqlExpression>&quot;html&quot;</SqlExpression>
                </Field>
            </Fields>
            <ProtocolExecutionSettings>
                <RetrySchedule>
                    <RetryDelay>P0DT00H30M00S</RetryDelay>
                    <RetryDelay>P0DT00H45M00S</RetryDelay>
                    <RetryDelay>P0DT01H00M00S</RetryDelay>
                </RetrySchedule>
```

```
                        <FailuresBeforeAbort>10</FailuresBeforeAbort>
                        <MulticastRecipientLimit>10</MulticastRecipientLimit>
                        <WorkItemTimeout>P0DT00H30M00S</WorkItemTimeout>
                    </ProtocolExecutionSettings>
            </Protocol>
        </Protocols>
        <ExpirationAge>P0DT02H30M00S</ExpirationAge>
</NotificationClass>
```

As you can see in the sample code, you define a content formatter node, which will tell NS which formatter will format your notification message. You can only have a single content formatter per notification class. In this sample, you use the built-in XSLT formatter. You can specify different XSLT files based on the user's device or locale. For the XSLT formatter, you need to specify the base directory path, which is the root folder for the search path for the XSLT file. You also need to specify the XSLT filename so that NS can find your XSLT file to use to transform the notification. The following code shows the relevant section:

```
. . .
<ContentFormatter>
        <ClassName>XsltFormatter</ClassName>
          <Arguments>
            <Argument>
                <Name>XsltBaseDirectoryPath</Name>
                <Value>%BasePath%\NSConfig</Value>
            </Argument>
            <Argument>
                <Name>XsltFileName</Name>
                <Value>FormatMsg.xslt</Value>
            </Argument>
            <Argument>
                <Name>DisableEscaping</Name>
                <Value>true</Value>
            </Argument>
        </Arguments>
    </ContentFormatter>
. . .
```

Note If you don't want to use the XSLT formatter, you can create your own custom content formatter. To do this, you must implement the `IContentFormatter` interface. Building a custom content formatter is beyond the scope of this book, but SQL Server Books Online provides some good reference material to show you how to build one rapidly.

You can also see that the sample specifies a value for a `DigestDelivery` node. With NS, you can have NS do either a digest delivery or a multicast delivery:

- Digest takes all notifications to an individual and sends them all at once in a single message.

- Multicast allows you to take a message that would be delivered to multiple subscribers, format that message once, and send it off.

You can have either digest or multicast but not both in a single notification class.

The notification batch size allows you to specify how many notifications to send in a single NS batch. By limiting the batch size, you can force NS to parallelize its work across multiple distributors. Limiting the batch size is a good practice when you aren't using digest or multicast delivery. Digest and multicast delivery works within batches, so if you produce too many batches, you'll affect performance of digest and multicast delivery.

Next in the sample, you see the Protocol section. This section specifies the delivery protocol to use. NS ships two protocols out of the box: SMTP and File. Your delivery protocol must correspond to a delivery channel in your ICF. If you use the File protocol, you specify the name of the file to write the notification to. If you use the SMTP protocol, you need to specify the subject, from address, to address, and optionally the priority of the message and the body format. As part of the field values, you can put in any valid T-SQL expression using the SqlExpression node. Also, you can use the FieldReference node to specify a notification field to use in the protocol header.

The protocol execution settings allow you to specify the retry limits, timeout values, and other protocol-specific settings. You can also limit the distributor's timeout for its worker threads. If this timeout is reached and there are pending notifications, these pending notifications will be thrown back into the overall notification pool, which will execute at the next specified interval.

The final part of the sample is the expiration age. The expiration age defines how long the notification should exist if it can't be delivered. One way you can use the expiration age is to automatically delete notifications that users may not find valuable if they aren't delivered by a certain time. For example, imagine if you are sending notifications to customers to tell them your store is having a 24-hour sale. If you can't deliver that notification within 24 hours to the subscribers, you may want to let the notifications expire, since no customer wants to be notified of a sale after the sale has occurred.

Generator and Distributor

As part of your ADF, you can configure the resources available to the generator and distributor. With the generator, you need to create a generator node. As part of this node, you can specify the name of the system where the generator will run, since NS can support scaling out your NS application to multiple systems. You can also specify the ThreadPoolSize for the generator up to a maximum of 25 threads.

For the distributor, you can specify the same two values, SystemName and ThreadPoolSize. Plus, you can also specify the QuantumDuration, which defines the length of time between calls to the distributor.

The following sample shows setting both the generator and distributor in your ADF file:

```
<Generator>
    <SystemName>Gen1</SystemName>
    <ThreadPoolSize>1</ThreadPoolSize>
</Generator>
<Distributor>
    <SystemName>Dist1</SystemName>
    <ThreadPoolSize>1</ThreadPoolSize>
    <QuantumDuration>P0DT00H00M30S</QuantumDuration>
</Distributor>
```

Application Execution Settings

As part of your ADF, you can also specify application execution settings, via the ApplicationExecutionSettings node. These settings will help you fine-tune your application by allowing you to specify generator quantum durations, quantum limits, logging, and data removal. Take a look at the following sample, and then we'll walk you through each section:

```
<ApplicationExecutionSettings>
  <QuantumDuration>PODT00H30M00S</QuantumDuration>
  <ChronicleQuantumLimit>10</ChronicleQuantumLimit>
  <SubscriptionQuantumLimit>5</SubscriptionQuantumLimit>
  <ProcessEventsInOrder>false</ProcessEventsInOrder>
  <PerformanceQueryInterval>PODT01H00M00S
    </PerformanceQueryInterval>
  <EventThrottle>5000</EventThrottle>
  <SubscriptionThrottle>5000</SubscriptionThrottle>
  <NotificationThrottle>5000</NotificationThrottle>
  <DistributorLogging>
    <LogBeforeDeliveryAttempts>true</LogBeforeDeliveryAttempts>
    <LogStatusInfo>true</LogStatusInfo>
    <LogNotificationText>true</LogNotificationText>
  </DistributorLogging>
  <Vacuum>
    <RetentionAge>P10DT00H00M00S</RetentionAge>
    <VacuumSchedule>
        <Schedule>
            <StartTime>20:00:00</StartTime>
            <Duration>PODT01H00M00S</Duration>
        </Schedule>
        <Schedule>
            <StartTime>01:00:00</StartTime>
            <Duration>PODT01H00M00S</Duration>
        </Schedule>
    </VacuumSchedule>
  </Vacuum>
```

Quantum Clock

The quantum duration that you specify within this node tells NS how often to fire the generator to create notifications. The interesting part here is that NS should really move this setting under the Generator node, rather than placing it here, to be consistent with the way you specify the distributor settings.

NS uses a quantum clock, which you can think of as an application-specific clock. There may be times where this clock falls behind your real-time clock in your system because NS is taking too long to process or the NS service has gone down. You can specify how far behind NS can get for both event chronicle and subscription rules, since the amount of time behind can differ for the two. By limiting the quantum that NS can fall behind, you can push notifications into the next click of the quantum clock so NS can catch up and not consume all system resources. To set these limits, you'll use the ChronicleQuantumLimit and SubscriptionQuantumLimit elements. Both these elements take an integer that is the quantum limit NS can fall behind the real clock before skipping firing of rules to catch up. For example, if you don't want NS to get more than 30 minutes behind the system clock, and your quantum duration is 10 minutes long, you take 30 and divide it by 10, which is 3 for your quantum limit.

Batching

You can also specify whether to have NS process events in the order they come in, via the ProcessEventsInOrder node. This will serialize your processing of events if you enable this. Batching works with quantums. NS can process multiple batches within a single quantum. As a best practice, you should not process events in order for the best performance. If your application does depend on strict order sequences, make sure you do process events in order as they arrive.

Performance Tuning

So as not to overload the host system, NS also allows you to specify how often to update its performance counters by using the PerformanceQueryInterval node. By default, the performance counters are updated every 60 seconds.

In addition to limiting updating performance counters, NS also allows you to throttle the number of events, subscriptions, and notifications it can process in a quanta to save system resources. By providing this level of fine-tuning for all its different components, NS allows you to tweak your NS applications to make the most efficient use of your system and network resources.

Logging

In the world of compliance that we all live in, logging is also an important piece of your NS application. Through the application execution settings, you can configure whether NS should log just failures or all delivery attempts, whether successful or not. The LogBeforeDeliveryAttempts element lets you specify a Boolean that tells NS whether to write to the log before any delivery attempts. The LogStatusInfo is a Boolean that will either log all status information for all notifications when set to true or just for failed notifications if set to false. Finally, the LogNotificationText element is a Boolean that, when true, logs all notification text for all deliveries and, when false, logs information for only failed deliveries.

Vacuumer

The final piece of the application execution settings is the vacuumer. You can think of the vacuumer as the garbage collector of NS. It hunts down and deletes information in your NS databases that is no longer needed. To set up vacuuming, you'll create a vacuum node. The vacuum node has RetentionAge and VacuumSchedule elements. RetentionAge is the XML duration datatype and specifies how long to keep data around. After this duration is reached, when the vacuumer comes through, that data will be deleted except for data in the chronicle tables.

The VacuumSchedule element specifies a start time and a duration for vacuuming. You can have multiple VacuumSchedule elements in order to set multiple schedules for vacuuming. The StartTime element is a UTC string that is the daily start time for the vacuumer. The Duration element is an XML duration datatype that specifies how long the vacuumer should run after it starts.

History and Version Settings

Since the history and version settings are the same as what you can define in your ICF, you should refer to that section of the chapter to understand this section. In a nutshell, you can track version information such as major, minor, build, and revision information, and history information such as creation and modification dates and times.

Compiling and Running Your NS Application

Now that you've completed your ICF and ADF files, you need to compile these files in order to create your NS application. There are two ways you can turn your files into NS applications. The first is using the command-line interface for NS called NSControl. The second is to use Management Studio.

To launch the command line, you should use the menu item called Notification Services Command Prompt. By using this command line, some environment variables are set for you that NS needs, and you are placed into the directory where NS is installed. In order to view the environment variables that are set for you, enter **SET NS**.

The most common operations you'll perform with NSControl is creating new databases from your ICF and ADF, registering your NS applications, enabling the instance or disabling it, updating, unregistering, and deleting the application.

The following script creates databases for NS, registers an application, and enables the application. Documenting all the parameters for the different NSControl commands is beyond the scope of this book, but SQL Server Books Online provides a good reference for this information.

```
nscontrol create -in AppConfig.xml ParameterName=ParameterValue
nscontrol register -name instance_name -service
  -serviceusername "service_username"
  -servicepassword "service_password"
nscontrol enable -name instance_name
net start NS$instance_name
```

While NSControl has some uses, you'll probably use the new graphical administration tools more often than the command-line tools. With the new Management Studio integration for NS, you can easily select your NS configuration file and have Management Studio create all the necessary infrastructure for you. You can create instances, configure subscription management, update existing instances, and delete unwanted instances, all graphically. Figure 16-2 shows creating an NS instance from Management Studio.

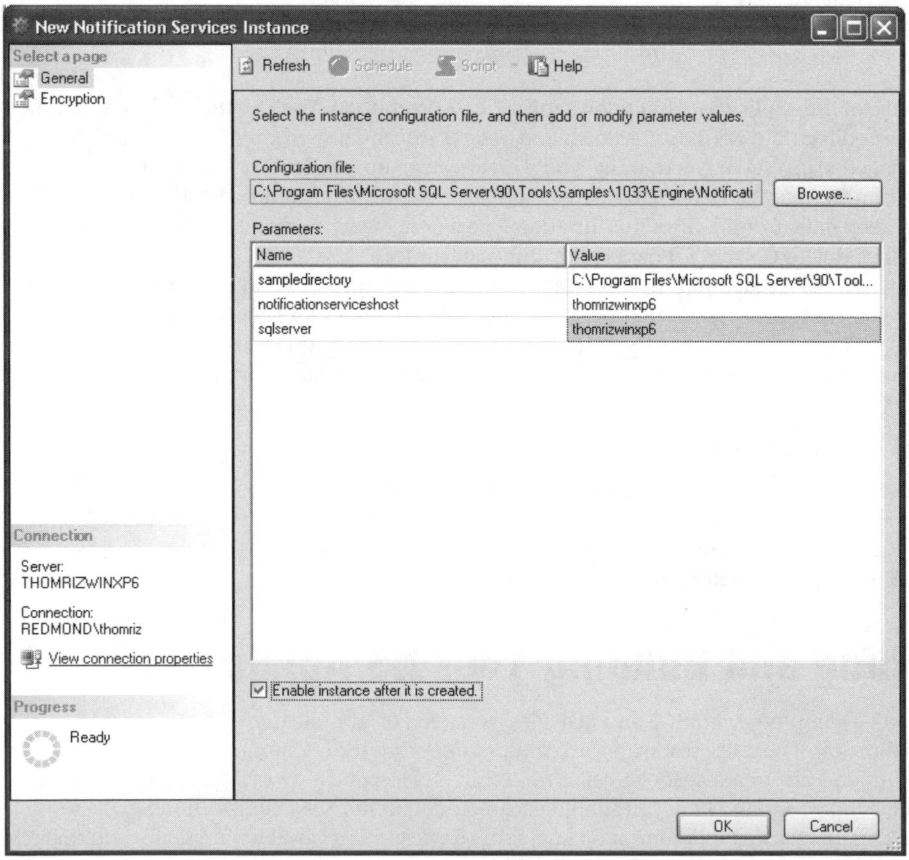

Figure 16-2. *Creating an NS instance from Management Studio*

Once you have created your instance, you can enable that instance or you can automatically have Management Studio enable it when you create it. When you build your instance, at least two databases are created if you specify new databases. NS can also use existing databases. One database holds event information, and the other contains notification information. Once you have created and enabled your instance, you need to register it. Registering an instance creates the Windows service for the NS application, updates the registry, and creates the correct Performance Monitor counters for your instance. Figure 16-3 shows registering an instance through Management Studio.

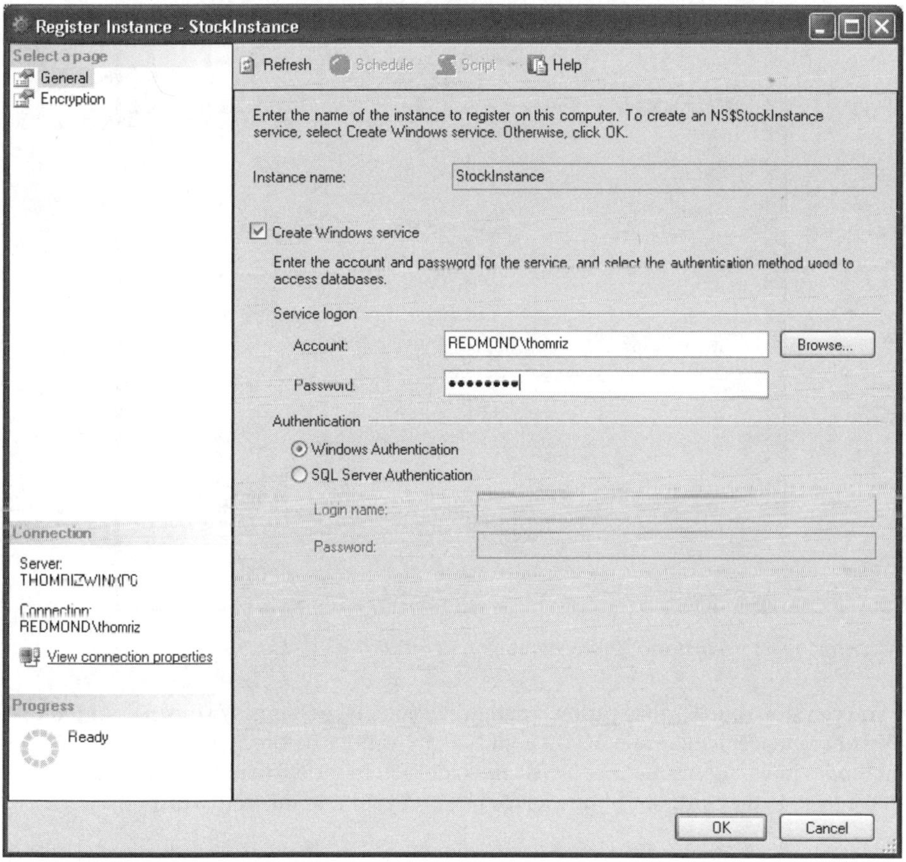

Figure 16-3. *Registering an NS instance from Management Studio*

Please note that if you use a low-privileged account for your NS service, as you should, you must grant permissions to the SQL Server, both the server itself and any data such as the relational or OLAP databases, in order for that account to be able to listen for events. If you don't make sure that the service has the right permissions, you'll get errors when the service attempts to connect to your data sources. NS creates database roles to make assigning permissions easier. These roles are the NSEventProvider, NSGenerator, NSDistributor, NSSubscriberAdmin, and NSRunService.

Once registered, you need to start your instance if it has not started already. Starting the instance turns on the Windows service that you just registered. Once this is complete, you can monitor and maintain your NS application from Management Studio. By right-clicking your instance and selecting Properties, you can see information about your application, subscribers, and Windows services as shown in Figure 16-4.

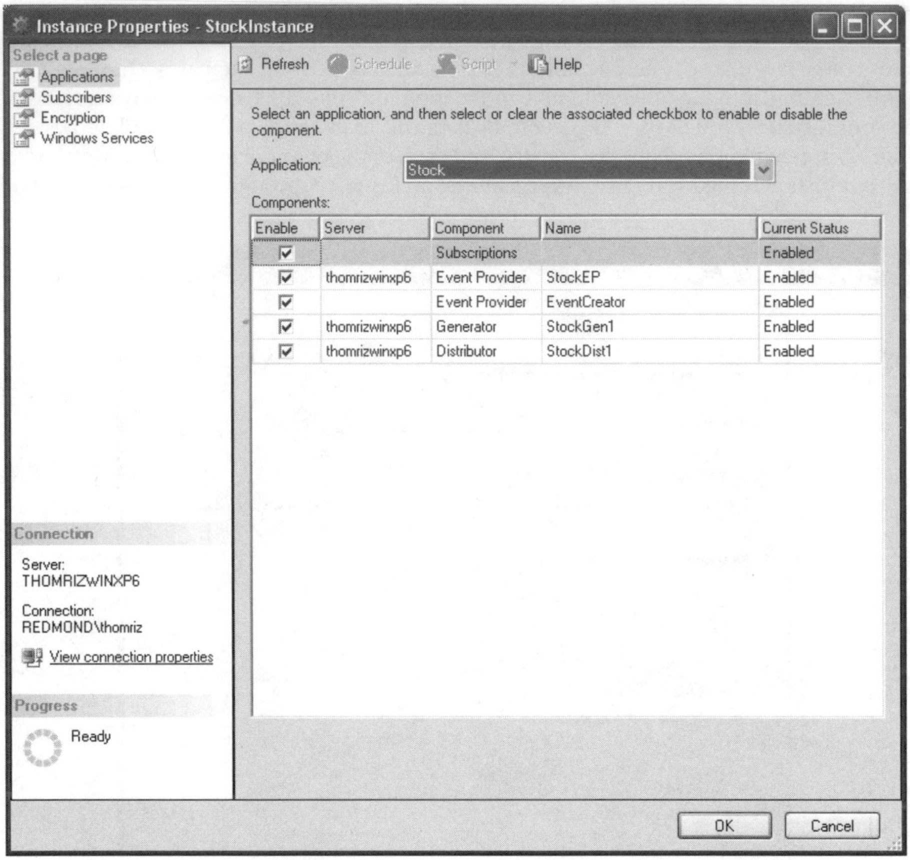

Figure 16-4. *Monitoring an NS instance from Management Studio*

Finally, you can stop your NS application, upgrade it if you make changes to the ADF, or remove it completely from Management Studio. If you built NS applications before SQL Server 2005, Management Studio integration should be a welcome addition to the NS feature set. No longer do you always have to go to the command-line tools to perform your administrative tasks.

Monitoring and Troubleshooting Your NS Application

After you deploy your NS application, you'll want to monitor and troubleshoot the application to make sure that it's performing to the level of scalability and reliability that you want. NS includes a number of different tools to monitor and troubleshoot NS applications including integration with SQL Server Management Studio, the Windows Event Log, integration with Performance Monitor, and NS-specific stored procedures, and using SQL Profiler.

While Management Studio will probably be the primary way you view your NS deployment, you may find that you have to look in the event log for diagnostic information about NS. NS logs both error and information to the event log depending on how you have configured the server. By default,

NS will only log errors and warnings. However, you may want to have NS log information events. By using the NSService.exe.config file, which you can find in the Bin directory for NS, you can configure the logging level for your NS events. You can configure from no logging all the way to verbose logging. This file is an XML file and is easily modifiable to meet your needs, since NS breaks out the logging level per component. One warning is that the verbose setting is very verbose, so you'll want to use this setting sparingly and only when you want to troubleshoot a complex problem in NS. Plus, this setting affects all instances on the machine! A sample config file is shown here:

```xml
<?xml version="1.0" encoding="UTF-8"?>
<!--
    The default logging levels for all components is Warning

    Off = 0 < Error = 1 < Warning = 2 < Info = 3 < Verbose = 4

    Change the values of the value attribute to change the logging
    level.

    Setting the logging level enables all log events which are less
    than or equal to the log level setting
-->
<configuration>
  <system.diagnostics>
    <switches>
      <add name="LogAdministrative" value="2"/>
      <add name="LogService" value="2"/>
      <add name="LogEventProvider" value="2"/>
      <add name="LogEventCollector" value="2"/>
      <add name="LogGenerator" value="2"/>
      <add name="LogDistributor" value="2"/>
      <add name="LogVacuumer" value="2"/>
      <add name="LogOther" value="2"/>
      <add name="LogPerformanceMonitor" value="2"/>
    </switches>
  </system.diagnostics>
</configuration>
```

Beyond the event log, you can also use Performance Monitor to view information about your NS application. When you register a new NS instance, perfmon counters are added so that you can monitor that instance. NS has three different categories of perfmon counters:

- Component group of counters that include statistics for individual components such as your delivery channels, distributors, generator, and event providers

- Application group of counters that include performance objects for the vacuum, events, subscriptions, and notifications

- Instance group of performance objects that includes information about subscribers

Please remember that you can customize how often NS updates its performance counters using the `<PerformanceQueryInterval>` setting in your ADF. By default, these counters will update every minute so the values will stay the same until the update happens. Figure 16-5 shows using Performance Monitor to monitor NS. Since NS is a SQL Server application, many times you'll want to monitor the same counters you monitor for SQL Server such as processor, disk, and memory usage.

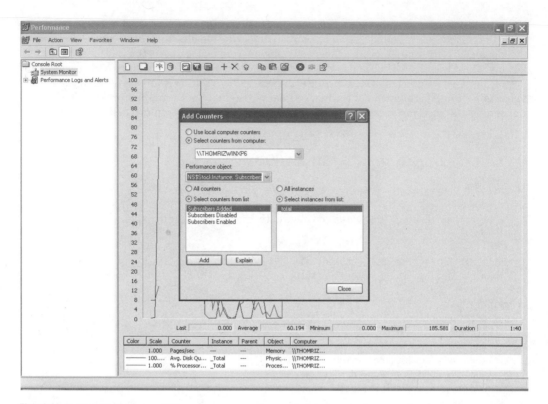

Figure 16-5. *Monitoring your NS performance using perfmon*

NS ships a set of built-in stored procedures to troubleshoot and diagnose your NS applications. These stored procedures can be broken up into a number of different categories such as instance, details, diagnostic, quantum, and snapshot reports. The most common categories of report that you'll use are the instance, details, and snapshot reports. SQL Server Books Online does a good job of explaining the details of these reports, so instead of listing them all, the code that follows shows calling some of the commonly used built-in reports:

```
Use NSInstanceMain
-- Your instance name should go above here
Go

EXEC NSSnapshotEvents
Go

EXEC NSSummaryInstance
Go

EXEC NSQuantumPerformance
Go
```

Since NS is built on core SQL Server relational technology, you can also use Profiler to monitor events that NS is performing against your server. If you find your NS application performing slowly and you can't figure out why through the NS diagnostic tools, Profiler may be able to help you get to the root cause. For example, you may be deadlocking, queries may be taking too long to execute, or there may be fatal errors that are occurring.

Programmatically Working with NS

NS 2.0 includes a namespace called `Microsoft.SqlServer.NotificationServices` that allows you to programmatically work with your instances, creating and modifying your subscribers, devices, and subscriptions, submitting events to NS, and working with custom components. Table 16-1 lists the classes available with the NS object model.

Table 16-1. *NS Namespace Classes*

Class Name	Description
DeliveryChannel	Provides information on delivery channels including protocol information
EventClass	Represents a single event so you programmatically create an event
EventCollector	Lets you take your Event object and pass it to NS
NotificationHeaders	Lets you create headers if necessary for delivery of notifications
NotificationStatus	Used by the delivery protocol to pass back status information to the distributor
NSApplication	Lets you specify and retrieve an NS application
NSInstance	Lets you specify and retrieve an NS instance
NSInstanceDescription	Used to get instance information such as name, db server, and version
RecipientInfo	Used by the distributor to retrieve recipient information such as device address and ID
Subscriber	Provides subscriber management capabilities such as adding, changing, or deleting
SubscriberDevice	Lets you work with subscriber devices such as adding, changing, or deleting
SubscriberLocale	Lets you specify the subscriber locale
Subscription	Lets you manage subscriptions such as adding, deleting, or changing
SubscriptionClass	Lets you access metadata from your subscription classes in your ADF
TimeZone	Lets you create time zones that you can use for subscriptions

Programming NS from Visual Studio

To show you how to use the NS object model, let's step through some examples of the most common programming tasks that you'll do with the object model.

Adding a Reference to the Object Model

The first task would be adding a reference to the object model to your application. The object model is supported both from COM and .NET. For the best performance, you'll want to write your applications using .NET, which avoids the performance penalty of going through the COM interop layer.

To add a reference to the NS object model, you'll want to use the standard Add Reference dialog box in VS. The NS object model is implemented in the DLL called Microsoft.SqlServer. NotificationServices.dll which is located in the Bin directory where you installed NS. Figure 16-6 shows adding a reference to NS in Visual Studio.

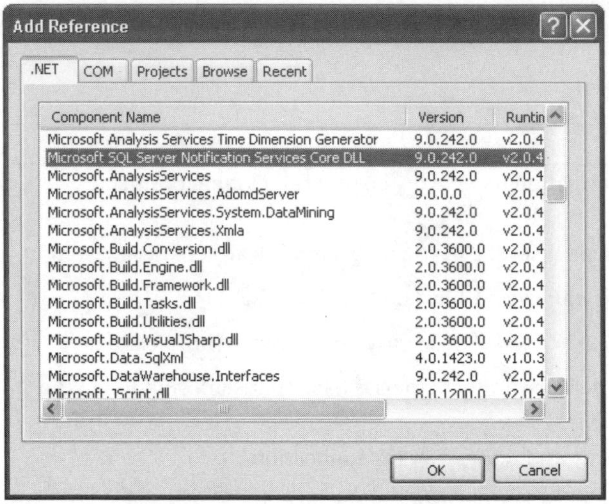

Figure 16-6. *Adding a reference to the NS object model*

Connecting to the NS Instance and Application

Once you have added a reference, you can start coding against the NS namespace. The first thing you'll want to do is connect to your NS instance and application. This is very straightforward and is done using the NSInstance and NSApplication classes. Both take constructor arguments that allow you to connect to each type of NS object. The code that follows connects to an instance and then connects to an application in that instance. Please note that you can use SQL-based authentication, but you'll need to set the SqlUser and SqlPassword properties. It is recommended that you use Windows-based authentication for your SQL applications.

```
    Dim oNSInstance As New
Microsoft.SqlServer.NotificationServices.NSInstance("Stock")
    Dim oNSApp As New
Microsoft.SqlServer.NotificationServices.NSApplication(oNSInstance, "Stock")
```

If there are any errors in your code, NS will throw a special type of an exception called NSException, which inherits most of its methods and properties from the regular Exception object. The main difference is that the Message property returns back an NS-specific message. You can capture the NSException and throw a regular exception if you want.

You can also verify your instance or application before using these objects with other objects in the NS hierarchy. To verify these objects, you can use the Verify method. This method will try to connect to the database. The reason to use the Verify method is to keep all your connection-related code in one location in your application.

Working with Subscriptions

Without subscriptions, notification applications are useless. One of the most common scenarios for using the NS object model is to create, modify, or delete subscriptions and subscribers. To work with subscriptions, you'll work with the Subscriber and SubscriberDevice objects.

To create a new subscriber, you need to create a new Subscriber object. The Subscriber object takes two properties, the subscriberID and a property indicating whether the subscriber is enabled or not. Once you set the subscriberID, you need to call the Add method to add the subscriber to your NS application. The following code adds a new subscriber:

```
Dim oNSSubscriber As New Subscriber(oNSInstance)
oNSSubscriber.SubscriberId = "SubscribeID123"
oNSSubscriber.Enabled = True

oNSSubscriber.Add()
```

To enumerate all subscribers in your application, you can use the SubscriberEnum collection. All you need to do is declare a new object using this class and then loop through using the enumerator all your subscribers. Performing this action is shown in the following code:

```
Dim oSubscriberEnum As New SubscriberEnumeration(oNSInstance)

For Each oNSSubscriber In oSubscriberEnum
    'Change their device info, list them, etc.
Next
```

Once you have created a subscriber, you'll also want to create a subscriber device and subscriptions for the subscriber. To create a subscriber device, you'll use the SubscriberDevice class. To create and manage subscriptions, you'll use the Subscription object.

To create a subscriber device, you need to create a new object, populate the properties, and save the object. The subscriber device object takes the subscriber ID, device address, delivery channel, and device type name. The following code shows creating a new subscriber device:

```
Dim oSubscriberDevice As New SubscriberDevice(oNSInstance)

oSubscriberDevice.SubscriberId = "SubscribeID123"
oSubscriberDevice.DeliveryChannelName = "SMTP"
oSubscriberDevice.DeviceAddress = "myaccount@mydomain.com"
oSubscriberDevice.DeviceTypeName = "Email"

oSubscriberDevice.Add()
```

You may want to enumerate your devices so you can present them in a drop-down list in your application. In order to do that, you'll use the SubscriberDeviceEnumeration object. Once you have this object, you can enumerate over all the subscriber devices in your application.

```
Dim oSubscriberDeviceEnum As SubscriberDeviceEnumeration

For Each oSubscriberDevice In oSubscriberDeviceEnum
    'Your code here
Next
```

To create a subscription, you use the Subscription object. You must set the subscription class name, subscriber ID, any needed data field from your ADF, and if required the schedule for the subscription. The following code creates a new subscription that sets a recurring event for that subscription. As you'll notice in the code, you set recurrence start information using the following formats, either TZID=TimeZoneId: yyyymmdd T hhnnss or yyyymmdd T hhnnss Z. For the recurrence information, NS understands the ICalendar format. The ICalendar format can set the frequency, whether it is daily, weekly, monthly, or yearly. You can also set the days of the week, days of the month, and also which months to have the recurrence fire. The sample that follows creates a recurring notification the 1st and 15th day of the month for every other month.

```
Dim oSubscription As New Subscription(oNSInstance, "MySubscriptionClass")

        oSubscription.SubscriberId = "SubscribeID123"
        oSubscription.Enabled = True

        'Set ADF properties
        oSubscription("CustomerName") = "Rizzo"
        oSubscription("CustomerState") = "WA"

        'Set the recurrence information
        Dim strScheduleStart As String = ""
        Dim strRecurrence As String = ""

        'Start Oct 1st at 10am
        'We could also set the timezone
        'This will use UTC
        strScheduleStart = "20051001T100000Z"

        '1st and 15th of every month, every other month
        strRecurrence = "FREQ=Monthly;BYMONTHDAY=1,15;BYMONTH=1,3,5,7,9,11"

        oSubscription.ScheduleStart = strScheduleStart
        oSubscription.ScheduleRecurrence = strRecurrence

        'Save our changes
        oSubscription.Add()
```

Finally, you can fire events programmatically using the Event and the EventCollector objects. This chapter won't cover this, but Books Online has a good reference for these objects. Since most of your NS applications will use the File System Watcher, SQL, or OLAP event providers, you normally won't have to fire events programmatically to your NS application.

Managing NS Programmatically

One welcome addition to NS in SQL Server 2005 is the ability to programmatically manage your NS environment. You can still use NSControl.exe if you like, but NS now has an object model, built on top of the SQL Server Management objects (SMO), to manage NS. These new capabilities are implemented in the Microsoft.SqlServer.Management.NotificationServices namespace. This is the same namespace that Management Studio calls to implement the management functionality in its GUI.

The first step to programming with the management API is to add a reference to SMO. SMO's namespace is Microsoft.SqlServer.Management. When you add a reference in Visual Studio, you should see this namespace listed. To get the NS information from your server, you'll need to first connect to your server using SMO. Then, you can use the NotificationServices property to get back a NotificationServices object. From the NS object, you can work with your NS applications and instances such as creating, modifying, enumerating, or deleting them. The following code shows you how to get started with the NS management object model by connecting to an NS server and enumerating all instances and then all the applications in those instances.

```
Imports Microsoft.SqlServer.Management.Nmo
Imports Microsoft.SqlServer.Management.Smo

        Dim oServer As New Server("thomrizdb2")
        Dim oNSServer As NotificationServices = Nothing
        Dim oNSInstance As Instance
        Dim oNSApp As Application

        oNSServer = oServer.NotificationServices
        For Each oNSInstance In oNSServer.Instances
            MsgBox("Instance name: " & oNSInstance.Name)
            For Each oNSApp In oNSInstance.Applications
                MsgBox("App name: " & oNSApp.Name)
            Next
        Next
```

Summary

In this chapter, you have seen how you can build subscription and publication applications with NS. The NS infrastructure makes it fast for you to build very complex applications. If you are an existing NS user, you'll see the addition of an OLAP event provider, management object model, and rules as key additions to NS. If you aren't an NS user today, hopefully you have learned about the benefits of NS and will use it in the future in your applications that provide subscription and notification capabilities.

Index